THE GEORGIAN CENTURY
1714–1837

The Georgian Century
1714–1837

By

S. E. AYLING M.A.

GEORGE G. HARRAP & CO. LTD
LONDON TORONTO WELLINGTON SYDNEY

First published in Great Britain 1966
by GEORGE G. HARRAP & Co. LTD
182 High Holborn, London, W.C.1

© *S. E. Ayling* 1966

Composed in Linotype Caledonia and printed by
Western Printing Services Ltd, Bristol
Made in Great Britain

Acknowledgment

Mr C. J. Bawdon read this book in manuscript, and I am heavily indebted to him for his comprehensive and searching criticism. I would like, too, to thank Mr L. M. Wallace for his kindness on reading the proofs and for a multitude of helpful suggestions.

Contents

Maps

Chapter 1

Early Georgian Society

1. England in 1714

England in 1714 was a country on the verge of transformation. Looking back now over a quarter of a millennium to that period, we see plain hints of the social and economic upheaval that was soon to grip her, rumblings of the volcano that was to erupt and to go on erupting as the industrial revolutions based successively upon water-power, steam, electricity, and electronics crowded after one another at a hurtling pace. Already, for instance, by 1714 Englishmen had discovered how to use a coke furnace to smelt iron and how to pump water from flooded mines by means of a steam-engine. These were the preliminary signals of the greatest change to overtake the nation in its history. It was to revolutionize the pattern of men's lives, reshape the old social and political order, permit a sensational rise in the population, and establish Britain as the first and richest among the world's great powers.

Yet the England of 1714 was a small country, not to be compared for population or resources with neighbouring France. For every eight Englishmen now, there was only one then. England and Wales together did not exceed around five and a half millions in population. Ireland added two millions, and Scotland a million more. Moreover, the rapid rise which was to be so sensational and central a feature of our subsequent history did not begin until fairly late in the eighteenth century; for thirty years or so following 1714 the nation's numbers remained fairly static, and over the next thirty years the growth was only gradual and erratic. In London, indeed, and in the rising manufacturing towns of the West Riding, Lancashire, Tyneside, and the West Midlands, there *was* a considerable increase in numbers in the first half of the century; yet the paradoxical fact is that it was exactly in these areas that the death rate was highest, rising even above the (by modern standards) very high birth rate. In the London of 1740, the height of the era of cheap gin, the death rate was approximately *double* the birth rate, and three children out of four died before the age of five. Dysentery, infantile enteritis, small-pox, tuberculosis, typhus, typhoid, influenza, together with the many infectious children's diseases, were among the great killers of the age. The rise in the urban population at this period was due entirely to the magnetic pull that the big cities exerted on rural workers and Irishmen, drawing them with the lure of higher wages and greater opportunities, dazzling them (especially London) with the glamour of the big city. A large majority, however, of the population of the British Isles followed rural occupations. (Not until after 1850 would the typical Englishman be a townsman.)

A bird's-eye view in 1714 would have shown a landscape about half-way between primeval wildness and modern suburbanization. A thousand years earlier England would have projected skyward a rough picture of forest, marsh, moor, mountain, and downland, with here and there at thousands of points the small clearings of the early Anglo-Saxon cultivators and their tiny hamlets. Today, east and south of the Welsh and Pennine heights, the predominant picture is of the irregular chequer-board of innumerable fields and hedges, with great and growing splashes and sprinklings of industrial and residential areas. Early Georgian England lay midway between these extremes. A thousand years and more of labour had extinguished most of the primeval forest and converted its territory into ploughland and pasture. The oaks and other hardwoods that had for centuries supplied the houses, ships, furniture, tools, and furnaces of Englishmen had, indeed, become dangerously thinned, and already the cry had gone up for conservation and reafforestation. In the South, particularly, the shortage of fine oaks had driven the Admiralty to turn to the Baltic and America for battleship timber to supply the dock-yards of Plymouth, Portsmouth, Chatham, and Woolwich. The ironworks of the Weald could move to Shropshire in search of smelting fuel, but the roads of England were so clogged and sluggish that it was cheaper to bring in timber from overseas than pay for land-haulage over such long distances.

2. Farming

The farms of England, wrested from the ancient wilderness, were over much of the country still cultivated as they had been for centuries on the open-field system, with its two, three, or more rarely four great communal fields. And the better the farming land, the more easily could cultivators 'get by' under these antiquated conditions; in particular, most of the richest corn-growing country of the Midlands and East Anglia remained in open fields, though intelligent farmers had long complained of their wastefulness. Steadily, however, the modern pattern of hedge and chequer-board encroached on that of the ancient strip-fields, especially in southern, western, and northern England, as enterprising landlords secured field-enclosure either by private statute or by local agreement under common law. Significantly, too—though still exceptionally— the new crops and methods that were in the long run to revolutionize farming were creeping in: field turnips, clover, sainfoin, and lucerne grass, the fodder-crops that were eventually to transform beef and milk production, were already being grown by enlightened farmers in the South and East long before "Turnip" Townshend lent the most important of these new crops the prestige of his name. Many of the procedures that gave 'Norfolk husbandry' its fame the best part of a century later, when Coke of Norfolk was a national figure, were beginning to be practised as early as 1714: the four-course rotation of wheat, turnips, barley, clover, that did away with the necessity for regular fallow, and the treating of light soils with marl were already raising yields on lands where progressive farmers and enclosed fields made such experimentation possible. (Holland, whose land-shortage of necessity bred invention, had pioneered these practices long before.) Already Jethro Tull had for some years been proving to himself on his Berkshire farm the virtues of the seed drill and the horse hoe that he was many years later to extol in his *Horse-hoeing*

Husbandry of 1731.[1] Many less famous writers, inspired by the newly scientific approach to practical problems that had been so significant a feature of the late seventeenth century—the age of the Royal Society and of the great Newton—began to apply their brains and pens to agrarian improvement. The wind of agricultural change, however, blew, by modern standards, only gently. The improvements of 1700 were *generally* adopted not much before early Victorian times; and the "Agrarian Revolution of the Eighteenth Century" did not reach its climax until the eighteen-fifties. In George I's reign, and long afterwards, the typical English farmer sowed seed broadcast and killed off many of his cattle when the fodder failed in the late autumn. His domestic animals bred promiscuously on the commons and stubbles, and perpetuated lean and diseased stocks: the sheep being "poor, tattered, and poisoned with rot", as one propagandist for enclosure put it, and the cattle "starved, todbellied runts, neither fit for the dairy nor the yoke".

The English farm labourer, poor and backward as he was, lived better, probably, than his counterpart anywhere else in Europe. Defoe was indulging in some patriotic exaggeration when he wrote that "English labouring people eat and drink, especially the latter, three times as much in value as any sort of foreigners of the same dimensions in the world"; the general, if not literal, truth of his picture, however, is broadly borne out by other evidence. There was much variation in different areas of the country; but a labourer might, on average, expect to earn in a week seven or eight shillings, or rather more than £20 (with harvest money) in a year; and to this would probably be added the earnings of his wife[2] and of his children, to add up to an average family wage of about £30 a year. Out of this, between £1 and £2 would be likely to go on rent, and similar amounts (*a*) on wood fuel to supplement what could be picked up and (*b*) on soap, thread, and the innumerable small necessities. (Candles were usually beyond the poor man's reach.) The amount spent on boots and clothing was very

[1] Professor T. S. Ashton, however, a notable authority, considers that Tull was a crank, the importance of whose teaching has been "vastly exaggerated" (*The Industrial Revolution*, p. 27).

[2] Usually from spinning, stocking-knitting, lace-making, glove-making, or straw-plaiting.

variable but necessarily little. Far the greater portion of the wages—on average an amount roughly equal to the whole of the *man's* earnings—was spent on food. This food was mainly cereals: largely wheaten bread in the South, with some rye and barley; rye, oats, and barley bread in about equal quantities in the North. Not much meat was eaten. Occasionally there would be a little bacon; but, even when the labourer killed a pig, he would be likely to sell most of the meat for cash. In most parts of the country a good deal of cheese was eaten, and among the more fortunate families sugar and butter. Milk was not often drunk, though in the North it went into oatmeal. Cheap, smuggled tea eked out the cottager's lot as the century progressed; and poaching offered a risk—a heavy risk in view of the penalties—that many could not resist. Like smuggling, it offered both the spice of dangerous adventure and the lure of a little luxury. Poorest and most numerous of the country folk were the cottagers (with perhaps an acre or less of their own land, subsisting on payment for herding the bigger farmer's cows or making his hay, and on the subsidiary earnings of both wife and children), and, lowest of all, the squatters, living in hovels on the waste and farming a patch of land to which they had no legal title.

All this seems hard to reconcile with Defoe's picture of the most prosperous labouring class in Europe; but it has to be set against the world-wide normality of grinding poverty for the mass of mankind in every era of history. In early Georgian Britain it goes without saying that a large majority of people, especially country people, were very poor. A vast gulf between rich and poor was taken for granted. Sometimes the lower orders went hungry, and it behoved the rich to be charitable, as many were. In theory, nobody starved in England, because the law required every parish to raise a poor rate to avoid such straits. But a family had to be pretty desperate before it repaired to the poor house, and starvation was not unknown in years of shortage and high prices, like 1728 or 1740. The desperation of hunger not infrequently drove men to loot and riot, despite the attendant penalties of death or transportation; and many a hungry countryman preferred to take his chance in the maelstrom of London or the growing industrial towns, rather than face the miseries of rural pauperism. Even so, Defoe was right: in a world where the lives of the poor were "nasty, brutish, and short" a smaller proportion of Englishmen than of foreigners sank beneath destitution and famine.

Above the squatters, cottagers, and labourers came that loosely defined farming class known as yeomen—those who were their own masters. At its lower boundary this class was little better off than the labourers. A yeoman might well have to feed his family on as little as five or ten acres, and was by no means necessarily a freeholder; in the old acceptance of 'yeoman', he might equally be leaseholder, copyholder, or tenant. At the upper boundary of the class, the yeomen freeholders farming their hundred acres or more merged imperceptibly with the squires; as freeholders of land worth more than forty shillings a year they possessed a parliamentary vote; traditionally, they had been the backbone of Tudor and Stuart England. In George I's reign the yeomen farmers were still enjoying a period of fair prosperity. The Government bounty on corn stimulated its cultivation, and the demand for wool was great and growing. Given harvests neither too good nor too bad, they did well—better than they were to do for many a decade subsequently. Bumper harvests, however, could well be a calamity for the farmer, for prices were very sensitive to surpluses, and if (as in the first half of George II's reign) crops were too good for several years running, many smaller yeomen were ruined. In any case, in the longer term, the independent yeomen faced a poor future, lacking as they usually did the capital to expand or experiment. While the squires and rich landowners marled and manured, introduced new crops and rotations, bred fine new fat stock, and thrived on the new enclosures, the independent yeomen were destined to be squeezed out of existence.

3. Gentry and Aristocracy

Above the yeomen were the squires, the country gentlemen. Again, their status and prosperity ranged widely. At one end was the small country squire of a few hundred acres, little educated, rough of speech, disposing of perhaps £300 a year or a little more, distinguishable from the yeoman only by the coat of arms on his carriage and his right to shoot game—a privilege limited by law to those with over £100 a year. (For a yeoman freeholder below that figure it was illegal to shoot game even on his own land.) At the other end of the scale were the upper gentry whose thousands of acres and numerous tenantry put them on the fringes of the aristocracy. In 1714 the gulf between the humbler and the wealthier squires was widening fast, and the consequent resentment of the lesser gentry was bitter. The wars of Marlborough had done nothing to sweeten their tempers, for whoever else had made money out of the wars the squires certainly had not. Many of the new rich of early Georgian times were merchants, speculative builders, war profiteers, or financiers, who could afford to buy out the older gentlefolk many times over. The weight of war taxation, predominantly on land, pressed heavily on the smaller squire. He tended to look back to the good old days of his father and grandfather, when his family had been, he thought, relatively richer and more respected. When, in 1719, Sir Thomas Cave dropped dead, leaving four children and heavy debts, his wife dismissed most of the servants, turned the deer park back to farming, sold jewellery, silver, horses and hounds, and thereby just enabled the estate to scrape by. Sir William Chaytor, baronet, was taken in his own manor house by the sheriff's bailiffs, and died in the debtors' prison in 1721. His wife pawned her belongings. Others, less desperate than this, contented themselves with grumbling at the corrupt government of Walpole, himself a supreme example of the squire-turned-grandee, the type that focused their deepest envy and anger. These men tended towards an independent-minded Toryism in politics, at least during the first half of the century. A few became resentful Jacobites. Some of them were boorish enough to merit the many caricatures of them preserved in our literature, from Fielding's Squire Western to Goldsmith's Tony Lumpkin. Port, hounds, and horses played a big part in the lives of most of them. But many of them were sober, educated men, responsible landlords and magistrates, paternally directing the affairs of their locality. Frequently they were unable to afford tutors for their children, who were therefore sent to the local grammar school to hobnob with shopkeepers' sons. The eldest son of the squire would expect to succeed to his father's estate; but younger children had to fend for themselves. The Law, the Church, the Army, the Navy, provided natural destinations for them; many were apprenticed to a merchant and entered business. Only if they succeeded in these professions and enterprises and made enough money to buy themselves in their turn a landed property would these children of the gentry re-enter the heritage and reclaim the prestige of a full-fledged country gentleman.

While the grand aristocracy were building mansions like palaces upon their estates, the lesser gentry would confine themselves to a more modest expansion or modernization of their manor houses: putting in sash windows instead of the unfashionable casements, coating maybe the old stone façade with a shell of modish red brick, adding a classical portico or a new wing to the old Tudor house, introducing into their gardens the many new trees, shrubs, and flowers that were being propagated or naturalized in English soil at this time, among them the weeping willow from China, the spruce, the cedar, the larch, the acacia, the magnolia, the rhododendron.

Every man now, be his fortune what it will, is to be doing something at his place, as the fashionable phrase is, and you hardly meet with anybody who, after the first compliments, does not inform you that he is in mortar and heaving of earth, the modest terms for building and gardening. One large room, a serpentine river, and a wood are become the absolute necessities of life, without which a gentleman of the smallest fortune thinks he makes no figure in his country.

In habits and sympathies these country gentlemen were much nearer to the tenant farmers and prosperous yeomen than to the nobility. Their eldest sons would marry daughters of neighbouring squires, until a close-knit network of inter-marriage spread over a county; younger sons and daughters in many cases married among local merchants or professional men. The presence of money could compensate for lack of birth. Both together represented a family triumph; alliance with a powerful aristocratic name offered at the same time status and power.

The clergy of 1714 had not yet reached that position of social and financial respectability that was theirs a century later. Addison was still, at this time, able to censure those lordly squires "who dismissed their chaplains from table before dessert, and forbade them to touch the jelly"—unlike Sir Roger de Coverley, who played backgammon with his. Many country vicars received stipends of no more than £50 a year; the average for a curate would be not much over £30. "It has not been customary", wrote a bishop in 1730, "for persons of either birth or culture to breed up their children to the church." Village parsons tended to be the sons of village parsons; if not, of farmers. Things, however, were changing. Queen Anne's Bounty had been established in 1703 to supplement inadequate stipends; good investment and rising national prosperity enhanced the Church's resources; and well before the end of the century the village rector was likely to be building himself a neat red-brick Georgian residence second only in local dignity to the manor house, and taking part with the squire on terms almost of equality.[3]

With the high aristocracy nobody sat on terms of equality. They towered over their neighbours like elms over hawthorns. Closely interbred, this charmed circle of Britain's hundred or two magnates was a society itself; yet it was preserved from becoming a rigid caste, partly by the law which relegated all sons but the eldest to the rank of commoner, and partly by its readiness to compete with the commonalty in trade and industry. For although land was the basis of their power and a nobleman like the Duke of Newcastle might own estates in thirteen counties, the nobility had not been averse to supplementing their wealth by marrying their daughters to bankers; by dabbling in stocks and shares (like the Earl of Sunderland, who fell down dead in 1722 with £75,000 invested); by promoting town-building (like Robert Harley, Earl of Oxford, who 'developed' the Harley Street–Wimpole Street area); by building their own docks and running their own merchant fleet to the Indies (like the Dukes of Bedford); or perhaps by engaging in such large waterworks projects as those undertaken by the Earl of Nottingham and the Dukes of Devonshire,

[3] For the clergy see also Chapter 11.

Somerset, and Chandos. Chandos, in particular, was a tycoon among dukes. Oyster fisheries, coal-mines, copper-mines, alum-mines, glass-works, and soap-making were among his many projects; and his stock investment was usually undertaken in units of £50,000. He lost £700,000 in the South Sea Bubble, to set against his numerous and diverse profits.

Commercial and industrial enterprise and financial specula-tion—both these played a part in building up the wealth of the magnates. So too did office and the profits of office, either within the Government or at Court. 'Place' was sought after by high as hungrily as by low, and the rewards of the greatest offices or certain key posts such as Paymaster-General were immense. As an extreme example, the Duke of Marlborough received £60,000 a year from his various offices, plus an un-specified amount from Army contracts and perquisites of many kinds. The capital for Chandos's big enterprises was built up while he was Paymaster-General during the period of Marl-borough's wars. But basically the power of the aristocracy—economic, social, and political—was founded on land and the rents from land. Many of them lorded it over domains more extensive than those of continental princelings.

The nobility's wealth was matched by its prestige. In a Britain acutely conscious, and quite unashamed, of class differences, the high aristocracy's eminence was supreme and almost unquestioned. When Sir Robert Walpole—earlier a mere squire, but now using his power and fortune to vie with the greatest in the land—wished to build himself at Houghton in Norfolk a palace to match Marlborough's Blenheim (itself designed to compare with Versailles) it did not seem improper that he should demolish the village and rebuild it where it would not detract from the view. Neither did it appear wrong that it should cost half a labourer's annual wage for one night's candles to illuminate the great house. Status was a serious matter, and it took serious money to uphold it. It had not yet seemed self-evident even to the most enlightened of philoso-phers that all men were created equal.

The style of most of these rural mansions was Palladian[4]—

[4] According to the principles of Andreas Palladio (1518–80), based on Roman originals.

a variety of the Renaissance style that was at once ponderous, solid, and elegant, though lacking the exuberance of Baroque. The principal English mansions in Baroque are Sir John Vanbrugh's Blenheim Palace and Castle Howard. Against them the Earl of Burlington championed the purer Palladian style; and among its leading masters at this time were Colin Campbell, who rebuilt Houghton House for Walpole, and William Kent, the architect of that other splendid Norfolk house, Holkham, later given national fame by the great agriculturist Coke. Kent was also responsible for the Horse Guards building in Whitehall, and planned many famous gardens. The great stone porticoes and façades of Campbell, Kent, and the rest served admirably to proclaim the princely pretensions, as well as the fashionable classicism, of their employers and patrons. Pediments, cupolas, ornamental staircases at the entrance front, terraces, heavy cornices surmounted by statuary, urns, pilasters, Ionic and Corinthian columns in the high Roman fashion —all conspired to give the exteriors of these noble houses a symmetrical solidity, a weighty magnificence. They were meant to impress, and they did. They still do, even if their vastness and the circumstances of our time make it impossible for them to subsist as residences and force their conversion to show-places, like the Duke of Bedford's Woburn, or perhaps to boarding-schools, like Lord Cobham's Stowe. There was watchful competition between rival owners. "'Twill be a stupendous fabric", wrote a visitor to the partly finished Wentworth Woodhouse. "As Lord Tilney's [Wanstead House] has been thought so fine a house, as some people imagined would never have been excelled, I am very glad for the honour of Yorkshire to see a pile going forward that will in every respect infinitely exceed it." The finished edifice indeed exceeded everything, whether for the honour of Yorkshire or of Lord Strafford, its owner. Wentworth Woodhouse became the largest private house in Britain, bigger even than Vanbrugh's Castle Howard.

The Wanstead House referred to above reminds us of the imposing wealth built up by the mercantile aristocracy. Wanstead was built by the son of Sir Josiah Child, who was one of the most famous merchant princes of his generation. In 1691

Child held over £50,000 in India stock alone, merely one of his numerous interests. Sir James Bateman, Governor of the Bank of England and Deputy Governor of the South Sea Company, bequeathed handsome estates to all of his three sons, gave his daughters marriage portions of £10,000 each, and had plenty left to scatter among grandchildren and the deserving poor. Every port in England had its great families, some of whom (as the Swiss de Saussure wrote in 1727) were "certainly far wealthier than many sovereign princes of Germany and Italy". Thomas Pitt was one of these fortune-hunters, the great Chatham's tough, pushing grandfather. There were Colston, the Bristol slave and sugar trader, and the other Bristol princes of the sugar and tobacco trades; the Hull merchants of the Baltic and Holland trade; the great coal-masters of Newcastle, the Blacketts, Liddells, and Ridleys; Walpole's kinsmen, the Turners of King's Lynn, whose business was widely based on wine, wool, corn, hay, coal, and a good deal else. Men like this, richer than all but the greatest territorial magnates, dominated their local politics, sometimes bought their way into Parliament, and not infrequently married their daughters into the old aristocracy. There was a good deal of common ground, after all, between dukes who aspired to make a fortune in coal-mines and coal-masters who disposed of a fortune large enough to buy out a duke.

The settings and décor of these great Georgian houses had to be as imposing as their exteriors. Gardens and parks were laid out on a vast scale, at first in as severely symmetrical and geometrical a pattern as the buildings. Later, fashion dictated a studied carelessness, an artificial naturalness. To move with the times, thousands of tons of earth were moved, streams diverted, rustic bridges artfully sited, woods planted here and cleared there, obelisks, mausoleums, temples of Venus, artificial ruins constructed, all kinds of flora and fauna, both domestic and exotic, disposed picturesquely over the estate.

Again, competition was keen. Archibald Hamilton even advertised for a *hermit* to add a unique touch of character to his grounds; while agents the world over were commissioned to supply the Duke of Chandos at Canons with every conceivable rarity, from acorns of the evergreen oak to Muscovy ducks

and flamingos. Supremely confident of themselves and the
stability of their world, they planted their infant lime avenues,
oak plantations, and beech groves—trees that in many cases
would not mature before the days of their great-grandchildren.

Inside, these stately homes proclaimed their owners' taste,
or their pretensions to it, by a rich display of antique statues,
paintings of the old masters, and objects of art; these had
frequently been brought back from the Continent—a Grand
Tour that was the culmination of every young nobleman's
education. The collections and studios of Italy, in particular,
were ransacked to fill the packing-cases of the young English
milords; and though not all the trophies they brought back
were genuine, and among them was a good deal of forgery and
grandiose trash, many at least of their treasures were true gold.
The greatest painters of the day, such as Thornhill and
Cipriani, were employed to decorate ceilings; the finest craftsmen worked on the furniture, the decorative plasterwork, the
wood-carvings, the furnishings. The Duke of Chandos maintained a full-time orchestra of twenty-seven players, which
cost him £1000 a year in wages alone. Pepusch conducted
it, and Handel was commissioned to write a set of anthems for
the Duke's concerts.

It may well be imagined what an important part this liberal
and competitive spending played in promoting business and
employment. Armies of servants were maintained, indoors and
outdoors. All kinds of luxury trades—wig-making, lace-making,
millinery, jewellery, cabinet-making, and many more—were
stimulated. Every kind of artist and craftsman depended on
the aristocratic patron's commands. All the basic industries
and all the building trades to some extent benefited from this
"conspicuous consumption" of goods and services. The quar-
ries of Portland and Purbeck, for example, thrived on the great
houses' pressing demand for fine-quality stone. When the
company at Houghton in 1731 sat down, a "snug little party",
as Lord Hervey reported, "of about thirty odd, up to the chin
in beef, venison, geese, turkeys, etc., and generally over the
chin in claret, strong beer and punch", a considerable number
of suppliers had benefited in providing the feast. It might
indeed be argued that it would have been still better to divide

the geese and turkeys among the cottagers on the estate, and that the purchasing power of the nation would have risen more steeply still if the strong beer were more generally available; but that would be to obtrude the ideas of the twentieth century among the circumstances of the eighteenth. (And it should not be forgotten that the nobility's hospitality to the poor could on occasions be as extravagant as its other ostentation: on one occasion later in the century Lord Fitzwilliam, who inherited Wentworth Woodhouse and an additional fortune from the coal discovered underneath and around it, entertained 20,000 there.) As it was, over much of England then, wherever the gentry were richest or most numerous, trade tended to be briskest. As Defoe wrote of Bury St Edmunds: "Here is no manufacturing in this town or but very little, except spinning, the chief trade of the place depending on the gentry who live there or near it."

4. Industry

Easily the most important of English industries, next to agriculture, was the manufacture of woollen cloth. As well as supplying internal needs, this accounted for two-fifths of all British exports; and it was largely the location of the woollen industry that determined the relative density of the national population. The manufacture of cloth was widely dispersed, but it was specially important in the West Country (from Exeter to the Cotswolds), in East Anglia, Kent, and the West Riding of Yorkshire. Of all cottage industries, spinning was the most widespread and important; and, as we have seen, it provided a vital supplementation of the small farmer's family earnings. Weaving, however, even as early as 1714 was an urban occupation; and 'urban' can imply anything from a town like Norwich, the third biggest in Britain, to an industrial village of no more than five hundred people. In the West Country, where the finest-quality cloth was made in textile towns such as Stroud or Exeter or Taunton, and in many other parts, the weavers worked in their own homes (two men to a loom were vital before Kay's invention of the flying shuttle in 1733), but they were virtually in the employment of the capitalist clothiers, who supplied them with their materials, paid them for their finished cloth, collected it, and marketed it. Some of these men employed a thousand weavers, and their wealth was impressive. In districts such as these the factory system was still in the future.

In Yorkshire, however, the pattern of the woollen industry was different. Here were large numbers of semi-rural manufacturing communities, with many independent weavers of small or medium standing, often possessing two or three acres and a cow as well as their looms. The West Riding did not yet know large towns: Leeds was the biggest with a population of about 10,000; Halifax was much smaller, and Bradford a village. But here an embryonic factory system was already in existence. At every "considerable" manufacturer's house, wrote Defoe of the valleys around Halifax, was "a manufactory or workhouse", each with its stream of water vital to its working. Round this workshop clustered the cottages of its employees, and inside the cottages the womenfolk and children were busy with combing, spinning, and carding; but most of the men's work of weaving, dyeing, bleaching, and finishing was already being done in the "manufactory".

In Defoe's day Lancashire cotton was only just beginning to challenge the ancient primacy of wool; most of the cotton spun there was at this stage combined with other linen or woollen fabrics. The wool manufacturers, however, were certainly alive to the threat of competition; already they had persuaded Parliament to prohibit the wearing of imported East Indian printed cottons. But what if Lancashire cottons and calicoes should move with the times and catch the coming fashions? In 1714 it was a cloud no bigger than a man's hand—and, as it turned out, the future was big enough for Yorkshire wool and Lancashire cotton to grow each to giant size, side by side.

Next in importance to woollens came mining and metals. Coal was already being mined in all those centres that were later to be dominated by it—on Tyneside in particular; but often in very small and shallow workings, and sometimes by single proprietors. Altogether perhaps two or three million tons were being raised, against the 1913 figure of 270 million tons, or the modern figure of rather under 200 millions. Deep mining had always run into the problem of flooding—the necessity that had mothered the invention of the steam-engine, Newcomen's among others; and the risks from fire-damp explosion run by the miners of those days were desperate indeed. Conditions underground (where women and children were already being employed) were primitive in the extreme; small wonder that miners, working naked in the black bowels of the earth, were reputed to be as dark and mysterious as the coal they hewed.

Of the other principal metals, copper was mined in Cornwall, Wales, and Lancashire; tin in Cornwall; lead in Wales, Derbyshire, Yorkshire, and Scotland. Wherever oak was readily available, shipbuilding flourished. The royal dockyards were among the biggest manufacturing establishments in the whole country.

As well as its traditional coal, Newcastle was producing increasingly the heavy metal goods that were coming into demand. Sheffield had long been famous for its fine steel and cutting tools; and Birmingham was growing fast, with its machinery, nails, and hardware of all kinds. (By the reign of George II these three towns, with Manchester, Hull, Liverpool, Norwich, and Bristol, comprised the most populous English towns next to London. Bristol, with a population approaching 100,000, was double the size of the next biggest, Norwich. Fewer than a dozen towns in the whole country exceeded 15,000, even by the mid-century.)

The five ancient centres of iron-smelting were Sheffield; North Lancashire; the West Midlands from Birmingham to the Shropshire borders; the Forest of Dean; and the Weald of Sussex, Kent, and Surrey. Iron was smelted in charcoal furnaces, which over the centuries had consumed (together with building and shipbuilding) such a quantity of forest that, in the Weald particularly, there was, by the beginning of the eighteenth century, a grave shortage of oak. Defoe, in the twenties, impressed with the wealth of timber all round him, considered that concern at the shortage was exaggerated. He was wrong. By 1740 there were only ten furnaces working there, where once had been 140. But another necessity had mothered another invention. As early as 1709 Abraham Darby of Coalbrookdale in Shropshire had discovered a means of

POPULATION AND MANUFACTURES
Circa 1750

POPULATION DENSITY OVER
128 PER SQUARE MILE
■ TOWNS OVER 20,000
⊙ TOWNS 10,000 – 20,000

EDINBURGH
WOOLLENS, LINENS
SHIPS

NEWCASTLE
COAL
CARLISLE
LEAD
DURHAM

COAL
COPPER
IRON

KENDAL
WOOLLENS

YORK

PRESTON
FUSTIANS
& COTTONS
WIGAN
MANCHESTER
LEEDS
COARSE
WOOLLENS
HULL
SHIPS

LIVERPOOL
SHIPS
SHEFFIELD
STEEL
SALT
CHESTER
SILK
LINCOLN

LACE
DERBY
SILK
NOTTINGHAM
STOCKINGS

SHREWSBURY
LEICESTER
KING'S LYNN
PETERBOROUGH
WORSTEDS
NORWICH
SHIPS

IRON
BIRMINGHAM
HARDWARE
WORCESTER
GLOVES
COVENTRY
CAMBRIDGE
BURY ST EDMUNDS

NORTHAMPTON
BEDFORD
IPSWICH
SHIPS
COLCHESTER

LEAD
GLOUCESTER
IRON
OXFORD
WOOLLENS

COPPER
IRON
COAL
CARDIFF
BRISTOL
BATH
MANUFACTURES
OF LONDON ALL
KINDS
MAIDSTONE
CANTERBURY
DOVER

PEMBROKE

BARNSTAPLE
BRIDGWATER
TAUNTON
SALISBURY
WINCHESTER
TUNBRIDGE WELLS
IRON
SOUTHAMPTON
CHICHESTER

EXETER
SERGES
LACE
DORCHESTER
SHIPS
PORTSMOUTH

LYME REGIS

TIN
PLYMOUTH
SHIPS
DARTMOUTH

FALMOUTH

NEN
ELFAST

smelting iron in a coke furnace, coal itself being notoriously
unusable on account of the brittleness of the iron it smelted.
New techniques in those days travelled slowly (Coke once said
that Norfolk farming moved at a mile a year); and it was many
decades before improved versions of Darby's process pointed
the way ahead. When they did, and were succeeded by the
'puddling' and 'rolling' inventions of Cort, the new coal-based
iron industry made the old oak-based one look small indeed.
But the Iron Age proper, when iron, coal, and steam conquered
all, was some way ahead of our present chapter.

The Industrial Revolution, as popularly understood, still,
then, lay in the future. There were no really large manufacturing towns. Phenomena such as Thomas Lombe's silk factory,
already water-driven and employing hundreds of workers by
the time Defoe was writing, were very rare. But many of the
features generally associated with the Industrial Revolution
were already present in early Georgian England. Already
pauper apprentices were sold off to masters in need of labour
and were often treated quite as badly as Oliver Twist a century later. Child labour was general, and generally approved.
Defoe praises the fact that, both in the Colchester and Taunton
clothing areas, "there was not a child in the town or in the
villages round it of above five years old, but, if it was not
neglected by its parents and untaught, could earn its bread".
And in the West Riding, "hardly anything above four years
old but its hands were sufficient for its support". Women and
children were exploited as harshly then as in the days of Lord
Shaftesbury, whether in the mines or in the fields, whether
spinning in the poor man's cottage or sweeping the rich man's
chimney. The fact that in 1740 towns and coal-mines were
smaller than in 1840 does not mean that the mines and slums of
1740 were more pleasant. The great cotton-master of the nineteenth century was no more ruthless a capitalist, waxing fat on
the underpaid labour of his mill-hands, than the merchant
clothier of the eighteenth on the equally underpaid labour of
his weavers and spinners, or than the master-hosier of Derby,
with his poor stockingers similarly employed, or than the master
nail-maker whose employees walked perhaps ten miles into
Birmingham each week, returning the finished nails for meagre

reward and collecting their coming week's supply of iron. It is indeed true that, except in London, the squalor and exploitation of the earlier period took place in a Britain where the "green and pleasant land" was only up the lane, a little walk away; but it is important, all the same, not to romanticize that earlier time before factories and steam-engines took charge.

Probably the greatest difference, apart from sheer volume, between the industries of pre-industrial and fully industrial Britain lay in this: in the earlier phase (with those important exceptions such as mining, textiles, the metal trades, etc., dealt with above) British industry was, in the main, local, thinly spread, and unspecialized. Houses, for example, except the lordliest, were still built, not as they were later of cheap railway-borne Bedford brick or Welsh slate, but of locally quarried stone, local timber, brick, flint, thatch, slates, and tile. The typical English town was not Newcastle or Sheffield or Leeds, with their specialities, but the small market town whose industry consisted in small manufacturers and craftsmen supplying the needs of the town and its surrounding villages: stonemasons, thatchers, carpenters, building workers of all kinds; farriers, wheelwrights, blacksmiths, shoemakers, maltsters, upholsterers, "butchers, bakers, candlestick-makers".

5. Communications

Industries remained local, and localities remained largely self-supplying, primarily because communications were bad. So bad, indeed, were the roads of Britain that, wherever possible, goods were transported by sea or river, usually in boats small enough to penetrate well inland up the thousand miles and more of the country's navigable rivers. Canals, common in Holland, were little developed here; but local groups of businessmen had here and there formed companies to improve the natural waterways. Even on navigable rivers, snags and blockages abounded—particularly water-mills with their associated weirs and dams.

The normal means of cross-country goods transport was by pack-horses, thirty or forty to a string, carrying every type of merchandise, even to coal. Such pack-horse trains were usually a faster and more economical proposition than the lumbering, eight-horsed wagons whose progress, even on the 'improved' roads, was desperately slow and expensive.

In theory, the duty of road maintenance, by a statute of Mary Tudor's reign, rested on every parish in the kingdom; and every parish was empowered thereby to make its inhabitants labour for a few days every year and to raise a local rate for the maintenance of highways. Practice, however, lagged far behind theory. 'Repairs' carried out under the direction of a local way-warden by villagers anxious only to get back to their own affairs often consisted of shovelling a load or two of gravel or a few lumps of rock into some of the worst potholes; and in clay-soil districts especially, many ways were entirely impassable to wheeled traffic after heavy rain. Surfaces were further pounded and fouled by the many thousands of cattle, pigs, and sheep that shepherds and drovers took along the highways, often for great distances. Every year, for instance, 70,000 cattle and 150,000 turkeys trod the roads from East Anglia to the London markets.

The effect of all this was to retard the nation's economic growth. Light goods presented serious enough transport problems; for heavy goods, water transport was absolutely imperative. Like coke-smelting or 'Norfolk farming', turnpikes were another new idea that spread from district to district at the universal snail's pace. There had, indeed, been one or two turnpike roads as early as Charles II's reign, but they did not begin to become general until the mid-eighteenth century.[5] By 1748 there were only 160 of them, and even then many of them were wretchedly bad: as late as the 1760's the author-farmer-traveller Arthur Young wrote that it was "a prostitution of language" to describe many of them as turnpikes at all.

The root of the trouble was that not for 1500 years or so, since the heyday of the Roman occupation, had anyone in Britain *constructed* a road; even the best of them, even most of the turnpikes, were only glorified and overworked farm lanes and cross-country tracks.

[5] The principle of a turnpike road was that local gentlemen and men of enterprise should form themselves into a company, or trust, and be enabled by Act of Parliament to maintain a section of highway in return for the right to charge graduated tolls.

As for passenger travel, it was always tedious, usually expensive, and frequently dangerous. In town the gentry could hire a sedan-chair; but long-distance journeys by stage-coach were at best an ordeal. In 1714 it took two days to travel from Oxford to London and about a week from York or Cornwall. A lifetime later it was still taking a week to go from London to Edinburgh. Defoe tells of one road in Sussex along which "an ancient lady . . . of very good quality was drawn to church in her coach with six oxen; nor was it done in frolic or in humour, but mere necessity, the way being so stiff and deep, that no horses could go in it". Bruises and broken ribs from spills were not at all unusual, and there was substantial danger to property, if rarely to life, from attacks by highwaymen. These tended to infest the more frequented main roads, and especially places near London, like Hounslow Heath, Epping Forest, or the Wimbledon–Kingston area, where the natural cover was good.

6. London

Easily the greatest of towns in Britain was London, with its population of approximately 650,000, and growing fast. It was the sheer diversity of London that gave it its overwhelming supremacy and attracted into its maw ever more money, ever more of the ambitious in every walk of life, ever more victims. London beckoned alike the gentleman's younger son (bound perhaps to be prenticed to a merchant) and the desperate rural poor; the craftsman in search of higher wages; girls in search of domestic employment (large numbers of these were lured into prostitution); all those anxious to cut a dash in society or rise in their profession.

First and foremost, London was the largest port in the kingdom, with almost all the East Indian trade and a great deal of the European. The masts of hundreds of sea-going ships crowded its river below London Bridge; Defoe, who was not above a little exaggeration, said he once counted two thousand. It was a city of sailors, merchants, brokers, dealers, tradesmen, foremen, clerks.

Then, too, it was the most important manufacturing town in

Britain, with a great diversity of industry, and a high concentration of the highly skilled and luxury trades. (The Spitalfields silk industry of the refugee Huguenot immigrants was one of them.) Clerkenwell and Shoreditch were full of miscellaneous metal trades, and all sorts of consumer goods were manufactured in and around London, including cloth. Eighteenth-century maps of the city show clearly the numerous 'tenter grounds' breaking up the concentration of the built-up areas— open land where the cloth was stretched and dried upon its 'tenter-hooks'. Many of London's occupations were closely connected with her maritime importance: the riverside districts of Shadwell, Wapping, Rotherhithe, and Limehouse were full of rope- and chain-makers, anchor-smiths, shipwrights, sail-makers, boat- and barge-builders, and chandlers. A further group of trades—chief among them printing—drew their vitality from the fact that London was a centre of culture, law, and government. London, then, was a city also of manufacturers, apprentices, journeymen, casual labourers—and unemployed.

Much of the industry well before this time had overflowed from the old City of London into the northern, southern, and eastern suburbs, but the City itself still housed nearly a third of Londoners. It was not, as it is now, a place abandoned overnight to charwomen and caretakers; shopkeepers, merchants, and their families still lived over their shops and counting-houses, with servants and apprentices occupying the upper floors and attics. London sites were too valuable to waste, and the whole square mile and beyond, where the Great Fire had left a trail of ruin, had been closely rebuilt, only slightly less insanitary than before, even if a little less combustible because of the new preponderance of brick. London in 1714 was an intensely overcrowded and noisy place. The narrow pebbled streets clattered with all kinds of traffic; overhead still swung the huge, creaking signs on their ornamental brackets. Inside its ancient gates and bars the City existed as a world on its own, between fashionable, residential London to the west and industrial London to the east.

The City of London, a mile or two from the national seat of government at Westminster, was, by virtue of that proximity, and its own traditions and wealth, a political force in itself, almost an estate of the realm. The combined force of its Lord Mayor, its 200 Common Councillors, its 89 ancient Livery Companies, and, on occasions, its easily roused rabble, could not be lightly disregarded by any king or government. It was the hub of financial power; without its bankers' support, wars could not be waged or Ministries maintained in power.

London was the wealthiest and most wretched of cities. The rich in their splendid town houses, with their Ranelagh and Vauxhall amusements, their clubs and theatres, rubbed shoul ders, a world away, with a swarming population of casual workers, unemployed, thieves, prostitutes, and beggars, inhabiting such 'rookeries' as St Giles's, Drury Lane, Alsatia, or Shoreditch—dismal and dangerous networks of courtyards and alleys, unpoliced and stinking, breeding-grounds of disease, vice, and crime. Anyone with a room to let in St Giles's found no difficulty in filling it with fifteen to twenty people at twopence a night. Damp cellars and draughty garrets were alike tight-packed. Even in the somewhat less evil neighbourhoods the streets were narrow, dirty, and ill-paved, where the passerby was liable to receive upon his person the slops pitched from upper windows or to breathe the stench from the 'kennels' that ran down the middle of the road. Hogarth, a keen-eyed and sensitive recorder of this early Georgian London, painted such a kennel choked with dead cats. This was the racy, vicious town that Gay prettified in *The Beggar's Opera*. This was the London of Hogarth's *Four Stages of Cruelty*, *Gin Lane*, and *The Cock Pit*, a city of squalor, neglect, crime, and cruelty that tax the imagination. The town was smoky from the innumerable coal fires and industrial fumes, full of the reek of slaughter-houses, domestic refuse-dumps, and offensive rubbish. The Fleet Ditch became so repulsive, with its dead dogs and discarded offal, that it was at last enclosed in George II's reign. In many churchyards paupers were buried in a common grave, which was not earthed over until the last space had been occupied. This was the London where, in the heyday of cheap gin ("drunk for a penny, dead drunk for twopence, clean straw provided"), the death rate rose to the figure of 50 per 1000 of population per annum; where deserted and homeless children slept at night in the streets under what shelter they could find, and were pretty sure, if they survived at all, to find their future as beggars, thieves, or prostitutes. (Dr Johnson, who arrived in London in 1737, records how, as a young man, he sometimes used to slip a penny into their hands to buy them a breakfast.) This was the London where the kindly sea-captain Thomas Coram was so shocked at the plight of the many unwanted babies deposited in the dockside gutters that he started the Foundling Hospital in Lamb's Conduit Fields, where it became the pride of London.

7. Manners, Customs, and Amusements

A populace living amid such severe conditions was wellnigh impossible to police, and the authorities relied mainly on savage penalties to deter from crime. In George II's reign alone thirty-three new offences qualified for the death penalty. As late as 1719 a young man was hanged, drawn, and quartered for a quite minor treasonable offence; in 1738 a girl of sixteen was burned at the stake in Winchester for poisoning her mistress. Many London workmen expected to take a day off every six weeks to enjoy the Tyburn hangings. The condemned men and women would be taken in a cart slowly from Newgate Prison along Tyburn Road (Oxford Street) to the gallows by what is now Marble Arch. It might occupy in all two hours. The cart halted under the crossbar of the gallows, and, when the nooses had been fixed, drew away. The victims were left dangling to their often slow death. When a really notorious criminal was to meet his end, like Jack Sheppard the highwayman, in 1724, or, the next year, Jonathan Wild (who organized thefts on an impressive scale and then opened an agency in London to help citizens recover the very property he had earlier enabled them to lose), the crowds were nearly as big as those at a modern Cup Final, reaching a hundred thousand, maybe. (Many reporters said more.) Not only the poor attended; the better-off citizens paid good money for a seat in the grandstands. Attendance, indeed, was quite respectable: "Sir," said Dr Johnson, "executions are intended to draw spectators. If they do not draw spectators they don't answer their purpose."

His logic was good, but his psychology perhaps was not. Picking pockets was punishable by death; yet never were the pickpockets busier than among the crowds at a Tyburn hanging day.

It was not, of course, just at Tyburn that executions took place; nor was the delight in violence and cruelty confined to the metropolis. It was in many places a sight to see some poor devil in the pillory, his face muddy and perhaps bloody with what the mob had thrown at him; or a condemned man flogged at the cart's tail, or a woman whipped at the house of correction. Even the poor lunatics of Bedlam (Bethlehem Hospital in Moorfields) provided one of London's most popular entertainments. A contemporary guide-book to London's *Amusements, Serious and Comical* rates it "a pleasant place . . . one entire amusement. Some were preaching, and others in full cry a-hunting; some were praying, others cursing and swearing; some were dancing, others groaning; some singing, others crying; and all in perfect confusion." Hogarth, again, has left a tragic vision of this place, in the last scene of his *Rake's Progress*; and William Cowper, the poet, records visiting Bedlam as a youngster and, even then, being angry with himself for being entertained. Visitors, having paid their penny or two, were free to walk the wards, tease the wretched inmates, and stimulate their ravings. To complete the picture, Bedlam was a notorious haunt of prostitutes.

When human violence and misery were not available to provide popular entertainment there was always the brute creation to provide an opportunity for gambling and excitement. Cock-fighting was such a sport, popular in town and country, among rich as well as poor—in fact, *the* sport of the day. The comb and wattles of the young bird having been cut away, and the neck feathers clipped, its legs were reinforced with metal spurs. Its owner would then *pit* it against another, and the bets, as well as the feathers, would fly, until one or the other of the birds was dead. Real matches, or 'mains', sometimes lasted four days: "At Epsom, on the 14th of May 1751 and following Days (being the time of the Races) Mr. *Bennet Senr.* fought Mr. *Howell*, shewing forty-one cocks on each side, for six Guineas a Battle and an Hundred the Main." A rich fancier might back his prize bird for as much as 1000 guineas. 'Cockings' could take place anywhere, indoors or out; the village churchyard was a favourite place. Bull-baiting required a little more organization. The bull was chained to a tough iron ring sunk deep into the ground, and anyone willing to pay a shilling might set his dog upon it. Bull-'hankers' carried long poles with which to break the fall of the dog when he was tossed— as he often was—high into the air. The much baited bull, though he had taken his toll of plenty of bull-terriers, was a sorry sight, with bitten muzzle, and head and neck covered with wounds. Badgers could be baited similarly, in the yard of any public house; with them, the securing chain was passed *through* the tail. A badger might get the better of half a dozen dogs before a good one killed him.

Here is an advertisement posted in London at this time:

AT THE BEAR-GARDEN IN HOCKLEY IN THE HOLE, NEAR CLARKEN-WELL-GREEN

These are to give notice to all Gentlemen and Gamesters that this present Monday, there will be a Match fought out by four Dogs, two of Westminster against two of Eastcheap, at the Bull, for a Guinea.

And a Mad Bull let loose to be baited, with fireworks all over him, and Dogs after him.

With other Variety of Bull Baiting and Bear Baiting. Being a general day of Sport by all the Old Gamesters.

Beginning at Three a clock The Gentlemen are desired to come betimes because the Sport will be long.

'Hunting' at this time implied chasing the hare, at least in the South. Up North fox-hunting was already the fashion; its slowness to develop in the South was partly due to a shortage of foxes; and some were already being imported. Stag-hunting had long been in decline. As for shooting, it was essentially an upper-class pursuit; severe penalties threatened anyone "outside the Game Act" (that is, lacking property worth £100 per year) who took deer, hare, pheasant, partridge, or rabbit. With the improvement in firearms that came with the flintlock and the shorter-barrelled gun, gentlemen now began to take pride in shooting pheasant and partridge on the wing, with spaniels to put up the pheasants, and setters the partridges.

Throughout this period horse-racing was everywhere increasing in popularity. Race-meetings were informal occasions by modern standards; everybody arrived on horseback, and it was not always easy to sort out competitors from onlookers. Indeed, this is a prime point of contrast between Georgian amusements and ours: their horse-racing, their cricket on the village green, their rough football that was more like an inter-village riot than a modern football match, their prize-fighting, all their sports and games, had a quality of spontaneity that modern sport has lost. Their athletic pastimes were not, certainly, lacking in toughness or sometimes in brutality; but on the other hand they were still uncorrupted by over-organization and the bright lights of professionalism and journalism. It is true that men gambled their money on every kind of sport; but not yet had either gambling or sport itself become national industries.

In London the *beau monde* had already escaped westward from the overcrowded central and eastern districts. Already the West End had extended to Hyde Park, and, as Fielding remarked, only the Park walls had prevented the town from linking up with Kensington. Bloomsbury, Soho, Mayfair, and St James's were full of the town houses of the wealthy, terraced, dignified, and orderly. Some of them were grouped in squares, which still proclaim in their names, if not always in their condition, their aristocratic past: Hanover Square, St James's Square, Cavendish Square, Berkeley Square, and Grosvenor Square are among them. The complete north side of Bloomsbury Square was taken up by Bedford House, which the Duke and his establishment occupied for the London season. These elegant purlieus constituted at this time the outer fringes of London proper. Beyond were Lamb's Conduit Fields, and the villages of Marylebone, Paddington, and Kensington to the west; Islington to the north (with its Sadler's Wells, where one might drink the waters for threepence, and, in the summer, watch "tight-rope walking, rope-dancing, tumbling, and pantomime"). To the south lay St James's, one of the two royal palaces in the London area (the other was Kensington). South again of St James's Palace lay its park, still laid out in those days with severely straight lines of trees, along the Mall and elsewhere, and an austerely rectangular lake. At the head of the lake presided the still new Buckingham House; it remained in private hands till George III bought it in 1761. To the south of this again lay Tothill Fields, stretching towards the horse ferry south of Westminster Abbey.

Just over the river were the pleasure gardens of Vauxhall—with their alcoves and supper-boxes, their Grove and Cascade, their "green retreats" and "wildernesses"—though to approach these sylvan pleasures from the West End the reveller would have either to hire a boat from Whitehall Stairs or the Temple or make the long detour by London Bridge. On the north side of the river, set among the still green fields and market gardens of the village of Chelsea, lay Vauxhall's younger rival, the gardens of Ranelagh, where, said Horace Walpole, "you can't set your foot without treading on a Prince of Wales or Duke of Cumberland". Ranelagh, with its canal, Chinese Building, and impressive 150-foot-diameter Rotunda, had "totally beat" Vauxhall, said Walpole. In these two pleasances the quality paraded in their flowered waistcoats and powdered perukes, listened to the music, admired the illuminations, ate and drank and flirted, talked scandal and quizzed the rest of the company. Walpole complained that such was the congestion on the road to Ranelagh that "in a string of coaches, we had a stop of 36 minutes"; while one evening in 1749, if the *Gentleman's Magazine* is to be credited, a Vauxhall concert had an audience of 12,000, and there was "such a stoppage at London Bridge, that no carriage could pass for three hours".

Evenings at Ranelagh or Vauxhall implied mixed company; coffee houses were essentially for men only. London had nearly five hundred of them at the beginning of the eighteenth century, and they were used by many men of middling station and above as political, business, and social clubs. They consisted mostly of one large common-room, with a good fire in winter. Their business was as much to provide news as to serve coffee and chocolate—for, in these days before newspapers were plentiful or cheap, a coffee house was the likeliest place to be up with events. The Windsor, at Charing Cross, guaranteed "the best chocolate at twelve pence the quart and the translation of the *Harlem Courant* soon after the post is come in". Gossip, scandal, and politics provided the staples of discussion. Some coffee houses, however, specialized: Jonathan's and Garraway's, for example, in stockjobbing; the fashionable clubs of St James's—Boodle's, Almack's, and White's—in cards and gambling; Lloyd's of Lombard Street, the most "historic" of them all, in the sale and insurance of ships; Button's, the Bedford, and George's, in the Strand, in literary discussion. At the Bedford "every branch of literature is critically examined, and the merit of every production of the theatres weighed and determined". Fielding and Hogarth frequented there, as Addison and Steele had in an earlier generation patronized Button's.

In due course the clubs like White's, that went in for 'high play', became, almost exclusively, fashionable gambling centres. (A single member's blackball was enough to exclude an applicant.) Gambling, indeed, was one of the great national preoccupations. Everybody with a penny or a thousand guineas to spare gambled in Georgian England—on the Stock Exchange, on the prowess of cocks and bull-terriers, in lotteries, on prize-fighters or horses, on the result of cricket matches, on the fertility of duchesses, in card games of every kind. At the high-class clubs gambling, often for very high stakes, became crazed and obsessive. When cards palled some other triviality had to be found to occupy the members' idleness. Here is a selection of entries from White's betting book:

Feb. 3, 1714 Lord Montford betts Mr. Wardour twenty guineas on each, that Mr. Shepherd outlives Sir Hans Sloan, the Dowager Duchess of Marlborough, and the Duke of Somerset.—Voide.

Mr. Jno Jeffreys betts Mr. Stephen Jansen fifty guineas that thirteen members of Parliament don't die from the first of Jany 1745 to the first of Jany 1746 exclusive of what may be killed in battle.

16 July, 1746 Mr. Heath wagers Mr. Fanshawe five guineas that the eldest son of the Pretender is dead, on, or before this day. To be returned if the Pretender was dead.—pd. Nov. 28.

Nov. 14 1746. Lord Montford wagers Sir Wm. Stanhope twenty guineas that Lady Mary Coke has a child before

Ly Kildare, and twenty guineas more that Ly Mary Coke before Ly Fawkner.

January the 14, 1748. Mr. Fanshawe wagers Lord Dalkeith one guinea, that his peruke is better than his Lordship's, to be judged by the majority of members the next time they both shall meet.

On one occasion, Horace Walpole wrote, "a man dropped down dead at the door [of White's], was carried in; the club immediately made bets whether he was dead or not, and when they were going to bleed him, the wagerers for his death interposed, and said it would affect the fairness of the bet". Not only the men gambled. "The ladies", complained Horace Walpole, "game too deep for me. The last time I was in town I lost fifty-six guineas before I could say an Ave Maria."

At six in the evening or thereabouts (that is to say, after dinner, which in fashionable circles was taken in mid-afternoon) the theatres opened. It was not a great period in the history of English drama; a reaction had set in against the licentious wit of the Restoration dramatists, and the age associated with the great names of Garrick and Sheridan still lay some way ahead. Stiffly conventional classical dramas, sentimental comedies, and showy spectacles held the stage. If old plays were put on, their indecencies had to be expunged; Shakespeare could be presented only when thoroughly bowdlerized. The squeamishness and gentility thus evinced seem at first out of tune with an age which in many respects was gross and coarse. But "hypocrisy is a homage that vice pays to virtue"; the Georgian audience, it was once remarked by a critic of the day, "lauded abstract morality in inverse ratio to their observance of it". Theatre-going was never more popular or more socially *comme il faut*; and it was certainly a period of ingenuity and invention in the art of theatrical production. Rich, the director of Covent Garden, specialized in ingenious spectacular effects, such as those reported by the Swiss visitor de Saussure. Rich, he says, spent £4000 on a production of *Orpheus*, where

the serpent that kills Eurydice is of enormous size, and is covered all over with gold and green scales and with red spots; his eyes shine like fire, and he wriggles about the theatre with head upraised, making an awful but very natural hissing noise.... When Orpheus learns that his beloved is dead, he retires into the depth of the stage and plays on his lyre; presently out of the rocks appear little bushes; they gradually grow up into trees, so that the stage resembles a forest. On these trees flowers blossom, then fall off, and are replaced by different fruits, which you see grow and ripen. Wild beasts, lions, bears, tigers creep out of the forest attracted by Orpheus and his lyre. It is altogether the most surprising and charming spectacle you can imagine.

In opera it was the era of the Italians, who first took London by storm at the close of Queen Anne's reign. With the notable exceptions of Gay's native ballad-operas, *The Beggar's Opera* and *Polly*, the Italian style was *de rigueur*, and Purcell was regarded as old-fashioned. The great Handel, a German living in England, inevitably composed his thirty-seven operas in the Italian style, and to Italian librettos.

Outside London the greatest social magnet in early Georgian times was Bath; and here, too, much of the early attraction of the place arose from the opportunities it gave for gambling. Beau Nash established the town's fortunes, and his own, on public gaming-tables, until these were suppressed by a law of 1745. (He took 2½ per cent of the bank's receipts at each table.) Nash, however, was a disciplinarian, and his dictatorial regime at Bath was orderly and civilized. Its aim was to maintain the twin dignities of Richard Nash (hence his immense white hat, his chariot drawn by six greys, his laced lackeys and French horns) and of the town of Bath, his child. The visitor to Bath drank the allegedly health-giving waters in the Pump Room, and (optionally) bathed in them; breakfasted in the Assembly Rooms; after further sociable pursuits, and dinner, attended the 'parades' in the Pump Room and elsewhere; and finally, in the evening, went to a ball or a theatre or a concert. Polite society gravitated to Bath in order to gamble, to be frivolous, to see and be seen by other polite society. It became the Mecca of match-making mothers, marriageable daughters, hopeful widows, and young men bent on social or matrimonial adventure. Wesley, among others, railed against its immorality, which he may very well have exaggerated. Bath survived the law against public gaming. It flourished into Jane Austen's day and beyond, and, indeed, its parades, squares, terraces, and Royal Crescent—the creation of the Woods, father and son— still present the finest extant urban monument to Georgian civilization.

Bath had many imitators and rivals. Scarborough was the oldest of English 'spaws' (the word was thus spelt and pronounced), senior even to Bath; but Cheltenham, Harrogate, and Tunbridge Wells all modelled themselves on Bath. Epsom was another place to discover therapeutic properties in its waters, and the neighbouring downs proved ideal for horse-racing. Soon the new craze for sea-bathing—taken in conjunction with the *drinking* of sea-water—transformed villages like Margate, Brighton, and Eastbourne, and older seaports like Dover, Deal, and Portsmouth, into seaside watering-places, well before the close of George II's reign. Many fashionable folk moved on to the seaside in the late summer after passing the earlier months at an inland spa.

Polite society was not, of course, confined to London and the spas, though it was heavily concentrated there. The gentlefolk, professional classes, and "middling sort" of the provinces often found getting to London an exhausting business, and staying there an expensive one. Those of them who cared for such things could find their own urban enjoyments in at least the bigger provincial centres. It is a mistake to think of the provinces as cut off in bucolic dullness. Of Maidstone, for instance, Defoe wrote: "A man of letters, and of manners, will always find suitable society"; while at Ipswich there was to be found "very good company" of "persons well-informed of the world, and who have something very solid and entertaining in their society". As prosperity and the century progressed, more and more provincial towns established their own assembly rooms and public halls, where they held periodic 'routs' and concerts. Few achieved theatres of their own before George III's reign; but in some places there were repertory companies using what building they could find, and, much more commonly, companies of strolling players, using tents and booths.

One of Nash's achievements as master of ceremonies at Bath

was to discourage duelling, which he pronounced to be barbarous and old-fashioned. Gentlemen might carry swords in London, but in Bath they should learn to leave them behind with their luggage. However, it took more than Beau Nash to put an end to duelling, for, as Trevelyan says,

> it was the privilege of all gentlemen, from a Duke downwards, to wear swords and murder one another by rule. As soon as men were well drunk of an evening they were apt to quarrel, and as soon as they quarrelled they were apt to draw their swords in the room, and, if manslaughter was not committed on the spot, to adjourn to the garden behind the house, and fight it out that night with hot blood and unsteady hand.

Generalizations about early Georgian life always run up against the contradictions that underlay it. On the one side, mercantile and industrial expansion, settled government, political freedom, classical elegance in the arts; on the other, brutality, violence, corruption, squalor. Certainly it was not what it has sometimes been represented to be—a static time of dull prosperity between seventeenth-century turmoil and the dynamic progress of the industrial age. Seldom has a time been more alive with variety and vigour.

Chapter 2

The Government of Britain

1. Powers of the Crown

George I came to an England that had already severely limited the royal power and had set down, a quarter of a century earlier in the Bill of Rights, what a king could and could not do. The Revolution Settlement had made it impossible for a British monarch to be a Catholic or to rule without Parliament; but it by no means established the total domination of Parliament. The powers of the King were still large. First, his consent was vital to all legislation—and, although it is true that since Queen Anne's death that consent had never been *formally* withheld, royal opposition to a measure could effectively kill it, as, for instance, Fox found in 1783 with his India Bill, or the younger Pitt with his proposals for Catholic Emancipation. Secondly, the appointment and dismissal of Ministers was entirely in the King's hands, and public pressure for or against a certain Minister in no way guaranteed his acceptance or removal.[1] George I appointed the Ministers who suited him and whom his German advisers recommended. His first Ministry in 1714 almost totally excluded Tories, although they held a majority in both houses of Parliament. Only extreme public, parliamentary, and ministerial pressure at last persuaded George II to appoint Pitt to office; and eventually, under George III, Bute and North as chief Ministers were little more than the royal mouthpiece and executive. Thirdly, although Parliament controlled the main area of Government expenditure, a considerable financial province was left to the monarch by virtue of his annual personal allocation, the Civil List, voted not annually but for life, and large enough to permit a wide dispensation of pensions and offices to men within his approval. Sinecures and appointments

[1] See also Chapter 8, *passim*, and Chapter 13, Section 6.

of many kinds, both civil and ecclesiastical, were ultimately in the King's hands; he could directly nominate the Members of Parliament for over thirty Treasury boroughs; he held in his possession the coveted gift of honours, a powerful incentive to loyal service; even Ministers were paid in part by their royal master; and for the greater part of the eighteenth century most Members of Parliament regarded themselves as normally under an obligation to support the King and his Ministers, though they reserved the right of free criticism in a last resort or under the pressure of powerful convictions. Fourthly, in foreign and military (and even naval) matters, the early Georges expected to retain an ultimate supremacy of direction that was by no means nominal. George II even carried military command to the point of active presence on the field of battle at Dettingen in 1743, and for half a century British foreign policy had always to take into account that the constitutional King of England was also the absolute Elector of Hanover, a circumstance which led him and his Ministers into severe trouble with 'patriotic' Englishmen, chief among them the elder Pitt.

2. "The Free-born Englishman"

All these powers of the Crown were important and undoubted; but the same William Pitt, Earl of Chatham, emphasized the other and more important side of the coin in famous and memorable words. The King was so far from being an autocrat, so subject to the laws of his realm, so circumscribed by the liberties of his people, that "the poorest man in his cottage may bid defiance to all the forces of the Crown. It may be frail—its roof may shake—the winds may blow through it— the storm may enter—but the King of England cannot enter. All his force dare not cross the threshold of the ruined tenant." It is easy to show that the eighteenth-century labouring classes were dominated by their landlords, and that the Glorious Revolution of 1688 was glorious above all for landowner, merchant, and Anglican; yet there remained truth behind Chatham's oratorical flourishes. And this truth is underlined by the observations of such visiting foreigners as the German Carl Philipp Moritz, who wrote home to a friend in 1782:

When you see . . . how high and low, rich and poor, all concur in declaring their feelings and their convictions that a carter, a common tar, or a scavenger is still a man, nay, an Englishman: and as such has his rights and privileges defined and known as well as his king, or his king's minister—take my word for it, you will feel yourself very differently affected from what you are when staring at our soldiers at their exercises in Berlin.

There was certainly no equality of treatment between rich and poor; but the poor man, equally with the rich, enjoyed the rights of habeas corpus and trial by jury; and, equally with the peer's mansion, the labourer's cottage was immune (except in one single respect) from entry by any official of the King's Government. The Englishman's home, even his crumbling shack, was to that extent his castle. The one exception underlines the preciousness of the general freedom. Of all the Georgian occupations that of exciseman was the most reviled, for only the exciseman had this right of entry into people's houses, to search for smuggled goods.

Liberty was the sacred word of the eighteenth century. Britain, said its most famous legal writer, Blackstone, was "a land, perhaps the only one in the universe, in which political and civil liberty is the very aim and scope of the constitution". "Britons", shouted its most celebrated patriotic song, "never shall be slaves." "Liberty!" roared the London mob; "Wilkes and liberty!" And that same rogue, Wilkes, who was the century's foremost champion of the legal liberties of the subject against authority, and above all royal authority, began the first number of his extremely libellous paper, the *North Briton*, with the same clarion call: "The liberty of the press is the birthright of a Briton, and is justly esteemed the firmest bulwark of the liberties of the country." Frenchmen, Spaniards—indeed, foreigners in general—might languish under the tyranny of kings, papists, feudal lords, and tax-collectors. Spain had its Inquisition, France its Bastille; in France a man might still be broken on the wheel, as Calas[2] was, for a murder he had not

[2] Calas, a French Protestant merchant wrongly accused of the murder of his own son; tortured and broken on the wheel (1762). Voltaire succeeded, after a three years' campaign, in clearing the dead man's name.

committed, having been denied every elementary legal justice.
To set against such iniquities, perhaps the most flagrant invasion of "the liberty of the subject" suffered by the Englishman came from the activities of the press gangs. This, indeed,
provided a glaring exception to the general rule of law; but, on
the whole, the free-born Englishman of the eighteenth century
considered himself happily emancipated from the medieval
tyrannies that foreigners endured; and a remarkable number
of visiting notabilities agreed with him. Montesquieu, French
grandee and political philosopher, although he misunderstood
the British constitution, praised it, and the British way of life,
almost equally with that of the ancient Romans; the great
Voltaire himself, a temporary exile here, fell in love with
English freedom and justice, and with English science and
philosophy—above all with Newton and Locke. It is characteristic of the eighteenth-century contrast between Britain and
France that Voltaire's book praising the intellectual and civil
liberty of the English (*Lettres Philosophiques sur les Anglais*)
was publicly burned in France as "a scandalous work, contrary to religion and morals and to the respect due to the
established powers". It is true that Rousseau wrote that the
English were free only at the moment of a general election;
but even he was happy enough to avail himself of a stay in the
land of liberty when he had been expelled successively from
France and Switzerland. (He did not remain long: his persecution mania persuaded him that every man's hand was against
him.)

This pride of the British in their freedom from tyranny
sprang very largely from the events of the seventeenth century
and, above all, the Revolution of 1688. The Tudor and Stuart
monarchs and their Privy Councils had been paternal and
authoritarian in religious, social, and political matters alike.
Everything had been directed from Whitehall: the local
justices of the peace received endless directives from the Privy
Council, relating to the administration of the Poor Law, and to
the regulation of labour, of wages, and of prices. Similarly, the
Church of England had attempted to enforce its ideas of
uniformity and correctness of worship through both bishops
and local justices. But the time came, in 1688, when the policies

of the Crown, by that time Catholic as well as authoritarian, no longer commanded the support either of the bishops and clergy, or of the unpaid lay magistrates—the local squires— who had been the principal wheels upon which the whole Elizabethan–Stuart machine of government turned. Still less were they liked by that other most important element in the nation, merchants and men of business. So the Revolution of 1688 swept away the Stuarts, with the all-commanding authority of their Privy Council. Judges were freed from the risk of royal dismissal; the Law was confirmed in its majesty and independence, and above all in its supremacy over the King; and the business of the Law was to protect the freedom of the Englishman. As the authority of the Privy Council shrank, that of Parliament (at the centre) and the local justices (at the circumference) grew. A Church of discipline was succeeded by one of latitude—one, indeed, that allowed latitude to drift into laxity. The strict regulation of trade lapsed in the direction of *laissez-faire* and free enterprise. The censorship of printed matter ended, so that the British Press became the freest in the world, and even the laws of libel and obscenity were not sufficient to prevent it from becoming among the most scurrilous: to instance Wilkes again, it was quite possible for him unmistakably to insinuate, in the *North Briton*, that the King's mother was the Prime Minister's mistress.

With the Revolution of 1688 had come the Toleration Act of 1689. True, it was an imperfect toleration that it brought, a grudging and partial measure. Unitarians and Catholics were excluded; and Nonconformists were prevented, at least in law, from having positions of importance in the state. It is true, too, that religious bitterness continued to play an important part in British politics for many decades. It remains a fact, however, that, just as Britain was the freest of eighteenth-century states, so also it was the most tolerant. Even Catholics and Unitarians were not actively persecuted; neither were free-thinkers until the panic days of the French Revolution, in the closing decade of the century. As Trevelyan wrote: "[after 1689] like dogs that have been flogged off each other, Anglican and Puritan lay down and snarled"—but at least they were no longer allowed to tear one another to pieces. The smell of faggots receded into the memories of Englishmen. The greatest of the theoretical apologists for the 1688 Revolution, John Locke, the most influential political philosopher of his day, considered that toleration was due to all those citizens whose beliefs did not tend to the overthrow of the state—in theory, even to atheists and Roman Catholics if they qualified under the last proviso, which in practice he considered they did not. "The whole jurisdiction of the magistrate", declared Locke, in a memorable passage, "reaches only to civil concernments . . . it neither can or ought in any manner to be extended to the salvation of souls."

If a belief in civil and religious liberty is one pillar of eighteenth-century conviction the rights of property provide another. The most notable victors in the Revolution of 1688 were the property-owners, and above all the owners of land. And once again it is John Locke, the don of Christ Church, Oxford, who gives to the practices and assumptions of half a dozen generations of aristocrats, squires, lawyers, merchants, manufacturers, parsons, investors, stockbrokers, propertied persons of all sorts, a theoretical and philosophical expression. The revolutionary who had provided arguments for deposing a king who had "dethroned himself" by his actions, and had championed the ultimately supreme rights of "the People", showed in his remarks on property how far he was from thinking of the rights of the great propertyless masses. In this he mirrored his age.

The chief end of civil society, wrote Locke, is the preservation of property, "the great end of men's entering into society being enjoyment of their properties in peace and safety". The citizen should "not be subject to the inconstant, uncertain, arbitrary rule of another man"; every man should, under the protection of the state, be able to sit, as it were, "under his vine and under his fig tree, with none to make them afraid". Only in a very theoretical sense were all men equal. A man's importance was generally felt to correspond to his "stake in the country"; and although Locke and other writers of the time make frequent use of phrases like "the People", it is plain that they are thinking, in practice, of "the people who matter", the aristocracy and gentry, the mercantile and educated classes.

Somehow the rude and unlettered masses had delegated their power and entrusted their interests to those classes in the country, and particularly in Parliament, who should naturally speak for them. It was another hundred years before the French Revolution was to enthrone (in theory) the sovereign people, and a century and a half before Marx was to idealize the revolutionary working class. Locke, although a revolutionary, was a conservative revolutionary writing for an aristocratic world; he is at the opposite pole from the socialist revolutionary Proudhon, who, a century and a half later, was to describe property simply as theft: "Qu'est-ce que la propriété? La propriété—c'est le vol."

It may be said that in the Revolution of 1688 'the masses' were irrelevant. They had no hand in making it, and they were considered neither by those who made it nor by those who benefited by it. That, however, is not to say that the masses were dumb and unimportant. The Mob was a persistent and vital element in the Georgian scene; and in an age whose characteristic freedom was underlined by its almost total absence of police a riot was never far below the political surface. There were pro-Jacobite riots in 1715, anti-Jewish riots in 1753, anti-Catholic riots in 1780, anti-Methodist riots on numerous occasions, riots against Walpole and his Excise Bill in 1733, riots in Edinburgh in 1736 against the hanging of convicted smugglers, riots in London against the attempt to regulate gin-drinking in 1736, riots arising out of the imposition of turnpike tolls or import duties, or from taxes on Scottish beer, or the introduction of labour-saving machinery, or industrial strikes, or unpopular wage-fixing, or parliamentary elections, or a hundred and one matters, great and small. "It may seem strange", wrote Fielding, "that not one of our political writers in their learned treatises on the English Constitution should have taken notice of any more than three Estates— King, Lords, and Commons; all entirely passing by in silence that very large and powerful body, which forms the Fourth Estate in this community and has long been dignified and distinguished by the name of 'Mob'." Horace Walpole, the statesman's youngest son, wrote ironically in 1743 of "our supreme governor the mob"; and the retreat of the Government from its 1753 proposal to allow the Jews to become naturalized citizens provides one example, from many, of the sensitiveness of Governments to the pressure of popular violence. As Lord Hardwicke said over this Jewish question: "In a free country I do not think an unpopular measure should be proceeded with." Thus the Fourth Estate, although in the main it lacked a vote in parliamentary elections, was by no means without influence. Even when it was not itself powerful or vociferous enough to decide issues, it could add an important weight in delicately balanced scales, as in 1739, when it shouted loudly, with Pitt and the merchants, against Walpole and in favour of a war with Spain. Walpole despised the mob's judgment—but he made war on Spain.

The insistence, both in the writings of Locke and in the convictions of the ruling classes who consciously or unconsciously echoed him, upon men's natural rights and liberties and upon the dangers of arbitrary power had other noteworthy effects. Georgian politicians, and especially Whig politicians, were so convinced that wrong had been for ever righted by the Revolution of 1688 that they took their principal task to be the *safeguarding* of that glorious event and the *preservation* of the matchless British constitution reinforced by it. To improve it was all but impossible; and therefore to legislate, which the nineteenth and twentieth centuries took to be a prime—perhaps *the* prime—function of Parliament, was considered of much less importance by the eighteenth. The reigns of George I and George II, in particular (1714–60), form an outstandingly sterile period in this respect, a legislative Age of Stagnation to put beside the Age of Reform that, beginning in the eighteen-twenties, has continued ever since. To the early Hanoverian Whigs it would have seemed an act of folly to tinker with a form of government that safeguarded so admirably their own primacy, the nation's freedom, and the general prosperity. Even a later Whig such as Burke favoured only those reforms (such as cutting back the royal influence) that aimed to get back to the spirit of 1688, or, as he characteristically put it, to "those rules of Prudence which are formed upon the known march of the ordinary Providence of God". "It is for fear of losing the inestimable treasure that we have", said Burke in reply to a modest proposal of the younger Pitt to secure a fairer system of representation, "that I do not venture to game it out of my hands for the vain hope of improving it. I look with filial reverence on the constitution of my country, and never will cut it in pieces. . . ." To lawyers like Blackstone the British constitution was unimprovable: it was in complete harmony with the laws of nature. Even to a Tory like the Duke of Wellington, at the end of the Hanoverian era, when the Whigs had come round to favouring a modest extension of the franchise, it was inconceivable that tinkering with the sacrosanct British constitution could do anything but harm. A few years later the last Whig Prime Minister, Lord Palmerston, having given unenthusiastic support to the Great Reform Act of 1832 and the other Whig reforms that followed in its wake, made a remark that illuminates the whole Whig approach to politics, dominated by the once-for-all Revolution of 1688, as modified by the once-for-all Reform Act of 1832. After all, as Palmerston said, "we cannot go on legislating for ever". Lord John Russell, the chief architect (with Grey) of the Great Reform Bill, shared this once-for-all mentality to such an extent that he became known as "Finality Jack". The Whigs saw the venerable and everlasting Tables of the Law as having been righteously reaffirmed in 1688. The wisdom of God (so satisfactory and profitable to his chosen people the Whig landowners) hardly needed reforming; at most an occasional editing.

Thus there is a great dearth of legislation in the years following 1714. Such matters as social improvement or the betterment of the poor were regarded as outside the province of government; they were more properly looked after by charity, philanthropy, and the natural processes of a flourishing economy. Yet the phrase 'the Age of Stagnation', taken generally, is in almost every important respect misleading. Free of governmental interference, the Englishman was free also to make his money and spend it as he pleased. It was a period of tremendous commercial activity, of financial development (rising to a fever in 1720), of scientific discovery, of agricultural improvement, of industrial movement, of colonial expansion: an age of great literary, artistic, and architectural

distinction, of adventurous movement and individual enterprise—full alike of racy eccentricity and gritty vigour; as far
removed from the humdrum as any age in our far from humdrum history. It is only in the strictly legislative field that we
can talk of stagnation; and here the striking paradox is that
this above all was the great age of Parliament. Never in the
whole history of Britain has the prestige of Parliament been
higher. Never were men so anxious to gain a seat there. Never
were the deliberations and decisions of this unique assembly
more central to the whole life of the nation.

3. The House of Commons

The House of Commons before 1800 consisted of 513 members from England and Wales and 45 from Scotland. Each
English county returned two members, regardless of size or
population; the Welsh counties one each; and the Scottish
rather less than one each on average. This left over three-
quarters of the seats to represent the parliamentary boroughs,
each of which also sent two members to Westminster. In the
counties every freeholder, or leaseholder for life, of property
whose annual value exceeded 40 shillings possessed a vote. In
the boroughs, on the other hand, the most bewildering
medieval variations everywhere persisted; so that it might be
every local ratepayer that could vote, or it might be owners of
certain specified local properties (burgages), or members of
the local municipal corporation, or (as in the City of London)
members of Livery Companies, or 'freemen' of a town, or all
those who had a hearth upon which a pot could be boiled (this
was the relatively democratic 'potwalloper franchise'). The
voters in some boroughs were absurdly few: at Gatton in
Surrey and Bosinney in Cornwall there was one only. In others,
such as Preston, every adult male could vote; but only about
two or three dozen boroughs in the country numbered more
than a thousand on the voting roll,[3] and only about a dozen

[3] In 1792 there were 32: Newcastle, Durham, Lancaster, York, Beverley,
Hull, Liverpool, Flint, Chester, Lincoln, Nottingham, Leicester, Cardigan,
Cardiff, New Radnor, Hereford, Worcester, Gloucester, Coventry, Bedford, Norwich, Colchester, Oxford, Cricklade, Bristol, Westminster, City
of London, Southwark, Canterbury, Dover, New Shoreham, and Exeter.

had anything approaching universal male suffrage. Even these varied, ludicrously from a modern standpoint, from the large and important city of Westminster with 12,000 voters, to little Gatton in Surrey with its universal suffrage and one voter. Dunwich, an ancient borough on the Suffolk coast, had largely disappeared from the map of England, having been eroded by the sea; yet it continued, as did Old Sarum, the deserted hill-site of ancient Salisbury, to return members. Cornwall returned practically as many members (44) as all Scotland (45), and three times as many as Lancashire (14). Wiltshire and Devonshire returned 60 members between them, while Birmingham, Manchester, Leeds, Bradford, Sheffield, Wolverhampton, Stoke, Sunderland, and dozens of other large and growing towns did not return one between them. One-quarter of the members of the Commons came from the five south-western counties. Everything was determined by long-standing local tradition, nothing by principles of logic or equality.

Tradition, then, gives us one key to grasp the unreformed Parliament; wealth and influence provide another. In the first place it was assumed that only persons of substance would seek to enter Parliament. Indeed, it was enacted so: no candidate in the counties was eligible to sit unless he owned land producing an annual income of £600, or in the boroughs £300. We have already noticed how no-one without a stake in the country was considered fit to judge national issues responsibly. The Member of Parliament's wealth might have been inherited or acquired by enterprise at home or abroad. Either way it put a man among the 'quality' from whom the ruling class was drawn. As for distinctions of birth, nearly everyone, rich or poor, accepted them as inevitable and natural; as Burke said, "some decent regulated pre-eminence, some preference given to birth is neither unnatural nor unjust". Yet a man might buy his way into the 'quality', perhaps by virtue of a big fortune amassed in India, or in the West Indian trade; his first move would then be to acquire a country estate, build himself a fine new mansion, surround himself with servants—and seek a seat in the Commons, "the best club in England". For, as Lord Chesterfield said, "You must make a figure there if you would make one in the country"; or, as Admiral Rodney wrote:

"To be out of Parliament is to be out of the world, and my heart is set on being in."

There were many avenues of approach. One of the most promising was for the aspiring candidate to recommend himself to the notice of some great lord, for a large number of borough seats were entirely in the hands of the magnate who owned the property. He might, indeed, own several, as did Lord Lonsdale, or the Dukes of Beaufort, of Newcastle, or of Rutland. The delicate relationship thus created between the member and his patron involved some give and take; although not precisely in his patron's pocket, a member was plainly expected, in a general way, to support the policies and Ministers that his patron supported, in much the same way, though not so rigidly, as a modern party member is expected to support his party's policies. The greatest patron of all was the Crown; and increasingly as the Hanoverian age proceeded, this came to mean the Government itself.

The supreme specialist in the management of this patronage was Thomas Pelham-Holles, Duke of Newcastle. This timid, querulous man, put out by trifles, nervous of his health, rambling in his conversation, incoherent in his public speeches, contrived for forty years to be the most indispensable of the Whigs.[4] Hardly a Ministry between 1724 and 1765 could do without him. Blessed with the initial advantage of an income of £40,000 a year—something approaching half a million in modern money—and with the control of a score of seats, he assiduously built up, through his family connections and the constituencies that his busy governmental colleagues were happy to leave under his control, a great parliamentary empire: Crown boroughs, Treasury boroughs, Admiralty boroughs,

[4] He was supposed to be in chronic fear of catching cold, and Horace Walpole gossips about him with his customary alert malice. At the funeral of George II in Westminster Abbey, "he fell into a fit of crying at the moment he came into the chapel, and flung himself back in a stall, the Archbishop hovering over him with a smelling-bottle; but in two minutes his curiosity got the better of his hypocrisy, and he ran about the chapel, with his glass to spy who was or was not there, spying with one hand and mopping his eyes with the other. Then returned the fear of catching cold: and the Duke of Cumberland, who was sinking with heat, felt himself weighed down, and turning round, found it was the Duke of Newcastle standing on his train, to avoid the chill of the marble."

private boroughs, the original boroughs of the Pelham family itself. The most meticulous care was bestowed upon the appointments in the Customs and Excise, the Post Office, the Treasury, or the Admiralty; for these were likely to qualify their holders to vote in one or another of the various boroughs associated with these departments of state. Newcastle became a sort of permanent Government agent, a seat-broker responsible for the maintenance of the Whig dominance; and, in the course of time, a kind of market price developed for a parliamentary seat—something between £1500 and £2000. By 1809, in which year an Act prohibited the sale of seats, the price had risen to £5000. Owners of seats were content to take the market price (advanced by Newcastle out of the Secret Service fund) and leave the choice of a suitable candidate in his experienced hands. Other parliamentary constituencies were in the patronage of great enterprises such as the East India or South Sea Company; and members sitting under the protection of these giants, it was assumed, would naturally press inside Parliament policies favourable to their patrons' commercial interests.

It has been estimated that, by 1760, 224 seats were under patronage, and that roughly equal numbers of the patrons were peers and commoners—rather over a hundred of them in all. Very few, however, of these 224 seats were in one man's outright possession, as Old Sarum was. The great majority of them had to be worked for and 'kept sweet' in the dominant landlord's interest. Other landlords might challenge, possibly by such methods as buying up vote-carrying burgage properties, often at inflated prices, as they came into the market. Thus Sir Richard Worsley bought up two tumbledown cottages at Newtown, in the Isle of Wight, for a thousand guineas; and when the Walpoles were challenging the Howards for control of Castle Rising in Norfolk the price of burgage cottages rose suddenly from £30 to £300 each. In other places there was much entertaining to be done of voters, much visiting and being affable with them, much promising of favours and kissing of babies. Not only babies, indeed. The poet William Cowper, although voteless, found himself one day approached by a candidate, one of the Grenville clan, who, rebuffed by the maid at the front door (since Cowper's tame hare was out of her box and liable to escape), penetrated to the parlour via the back door,

> and advancing towards me, shook me by the hand with a degree of cordiality that was extremely seducing.... I assured him that I had no vote, for which he readily gave me credit. I assured him I had no influence, which he was not equally inclined to believe.

On Cowper's reiteration of his total lack of influence,

> Mr. Grenville squeezed me by the hand again, kissed the ladies, and withdrew. He kissed likewise the maid in the kitchen, and seemed upon the whole a most loving, kissing, kind-hearted gentleman. He is very young, genteel and handsome. He has a pair of very good eyes in his head, which not being sufficient, as it should seem, for the many nice and difficult purposes of a senator, he had a third also, which he wore suspended by a ribbon from his buttonhole.
> The boys hallooed, the dogs barked, Puss [the tame hare] scampered; the hero, with his long train of obsequious followers, withdrew.

This was the kind of thing that happened, whether or not the issue came at the end to a contested election. Sometimes a local Member of Parliament drew from the Duke of Newcastle a yearly allowance for in this manner maintaining favourable public relations in a constituency or group of constituencies. Thus Thomas Holmes, M.P. for Yarmouth, Isle of Wight, for long years managed the three Isle of Wight boroughs in the Whig interest, in return for an annual payment. Indeed, he felt he had done his work with such success that some reward —for instance, an Irish peerage—was overdue to him. "The annual thing I asked," he wrote in remonstrance to the Duke, "as I have no employment, was only to repay me the money I am out of pocket in the several services we support. I never meant it should tie me down from receiving some honourable mark of distinction for having brought a factious part of the country over to His Majesty's interest; everyone knows I have a greater weight in the Island of Wight than any Governor or any other person ever had." And he ended his letter with a rebuke to Newcastle for the tardiness of his favours. In due course the Irish peerage arrived.

The heavy expense of nursing constituencies and wooing voters often meant that it was convenient and prudent for a deal to be done between contesting groups and families. Since both borough and county constituencies carried two seats each, it was plainly cheaper, in places where the balance was nice, that the Whigs should take one and the Tory the other. When, however, an uncompromising ambition or a personal quarrel brought a fight to the death for both seats, there was hardly a limit to the expenses that a wealthy candidate and his backers would run to. There were posts, pensions, livings, sinecures—an attractive variety of favours—to be dangled before the bigger fish, either for personal enjoyment or for disposal among friends and relatives. There were kind words to be spoken to landlords, or perhaps to bishops, or to those having the right to present to a benefice. There was the hint of a profitable contract, or even of a dinner for the corporation voters, like that promised by the Earl of Bristol at Bury St Edmunds—twenty-nine dishes with toasts to match. For humbler voters there was a prodigious largesse in meat, cheese, ale, and other comestibles. Negatively, there might be the threat of an employee's dismissal, the boycott of a shopkeeper, a raised rent, or even eviction for a tenant. Moreover, since all voting was public, with the poll-books freely available to the scrutiny both of presiding officers and of candidates, it was easy enough to check on a man's loyalty, or lack of it. Even in the county elections, which were slightly less liable to the extremes of corruption than those of the boroughs, the forty-shilling freeholder often held some of his land or buildings *as a tenant*, and was in that case only slightly less bound to vote at the landlord's bidding; and even an out-and-out freeholder was not above receiving a favour. In fact, the elections in thirty-nine of the forty English counties developed into battles between rival groups of aspiring landlords, the great aristocracy (in general) supplying the Whig candidates and the somewhat lesser country gentlemen the Tories. In the election of 1761 only forty-eight constituencies finally went to the polls on election day: in all the others the affair had been settled previously. Even, however, in elections arranged or conceded before polling day the Georgian populace found matter for excitement. The German Moritz, reporting such an affair at Westminster in 1782, tells how Sir Cecil Wray was elected to share the representation with Charles James Fox:

> At length when it was nearly over the people took it into their heads to hear him speak, and everyone called out *Fox! Fox!* I know not why; but I seemed to catch some of the spirit of the place and time; and so I also bawled *Fox! Fox!* and he was obliged to come forward and speak: for no other reason that I could find, but that the people wished to hear him speak. . . . When the whole was over, the rampant spirit of liberty, and the wild impatience of a genuine English mob were exhibited in perfection. In a very few minutes the whole scaffolding, benches, and chairs, and everything else, was completely destroyed; and the mat with which it had been covered torn into ten thousand strips or pieces, or strings; with which they *encircled* or enclosed multitudes of people of all ranks. These they hurried along with them and everything else that came in their way, as trophies of joy: and thus, in the midst of exultation and triumph, they paraded through many of the most populous streets of London.

It must again be emphasized that this noisy and corrupt electoral scene must not be looked at through the virtuous wrong end of the twentieth-century telescope. The great property owners who controlled the electoral system regarded themselves, and were regarded by envious foreigners, as defenders of the nation's liberties. The fact that they spent fortunes, or like the Duke of Newcastle a lifetime of patient industry, in securing their parliamentary interests does not mean that they were merely self-seeking or unscrupulous adventurers. The fact that they aspired to office and to power does not mean that their patriotism was less than a modern politician's. The fact that they bought and schemed their entry into the Commons does not mean that they lacked integrity when they arrived there. Politics was a game, indeed, in which they played to win, and it was a game in which the rules were not twentieth-century rules. But the House of Commons, for all its short hours and leisurely ways—it met only for a few months in the year—was at least as deeply concerned for the national prosperity, safety, and power as the modern House of Commons. Its intellectual calibre was probably as high or higher. Its eloquence was unquestionably greater, though in a style that modern taste might find over-studied and over-full of classical references. Its very abuses enabled young men to reach office at an age when their vigour was at its summit. Wealth and influence could purchase the younger Pitt a seat at twenty-one, and his name and ability could then make him Prime Minister at an age (twenty-four) only half of that considered a practicable minimum for a modern Prime Minister. It is, however, in the days of his father, the elder Pitt, and the days before that, of Walpole—that is to say, during the reigns of the first two Georges—that the House of Commons rode upon its highest crest of prestige, responsibility, and seriousness that belie the apparent irresponsibility of its electoral methods and the seeming caprice of the franchise.

4. The House of Lords

"Nobody cares a damn about the House of Lords; the House of Commons is everything in England and the House of Lords is nothing." So said Wellington at the beginning of the nineteenth century. It was not true even then, and it was much farther from the truth during the preceding century. Yet the element of truth in the exclamation is important. Politically, the relative influence and prestige of the Lower House was increasing throughout the Georgian period, while that of the Upper House somewhat declined. During the reigns of William III and Anne the Lords were at the peak of their political power—an Upper House in every respect. In the following decades, too, peers continued numerically to dominate the Ministries, but it is noteworthy that Walpole and both Pitts, the three leading statesmen of the century, as well as such parliamentary giants as Burke and Charles Fox, were all commoners, at least at the period of their greatest importance.

However, in a world that instinctively paid homage to birth and wealth, the Lords continued to carry great weight. Their territorial power itself, their outright ownership of some boroughs, and their great influence in others, as well as in all the counties, allowed them a considerable control over elections to the Commons. Then again, inside the Commons, since many members owed their seats to a peer, there was inevitably a certain reluctance to clash with a House of Lords that was also a House of Patrons—though there were occasions, as during the Peerage Bill debates of 1719, when the Commons asserted their opposition to the Lords very powerfully. The Commons forced Stanhope to drop his proposal to freeze the total number of peers; but in fact very few new creations were made until towards the end of the century. The peers remained a small assembly—under 200, plus 26 bishops; a select and dignified band, conscious of their majesty, jealous of their power. As a purely legislative and debating chamber, they were certainly not the equal of the Commons; even so, they had no compunction about throwing out measures they thought undesirable. Their real authority, however, lay elsewhere. They were very conscious of their centuries-old position as "the king's great hereditary council". They provided the nation's supreme court of appeal, and, when sitting in this capacity, by no means limited attendance to the Law Lords, as is now the practice. They still maintained, and fairly frequently exercised, their right to try their fellow peers (the rebel Jacobite lords, for instance), and their solemn prerogative to sit in judgment over accused Ministers or officers of the Crown, in the impressive ceremonies of impeachment, when Westminster Hall, presided over by the Lord High Steward, was brilliant with scarlet-robed peers, hearing the prosecution mounted by the Commons. The most famous of all such trials was that of Warren Hastings, at the end of the century, for misconduct in India; it spread itself out over a period of seven years. Above all, the House of Lords was the chamber wherein the richest and most powerful men in the country sat. Its position and authority came from the wealth and prestige of its individual members; and at the heart of that wealth and prestige lay the possession of land. There were indeed a few poor peers—relatively poor by the standards of an eighteenth-century peer. There were mad peers, religious peers, scholarly peers, dissolute peers, scientific peers, eccentric peers, literary peers, sporting peers—every variety of peer in a century brimming over with variety. All, or almost all, of them owned extensive estates, often in half a dozen different counties[5] (up to the Duke of Sutherland's 2000 square miles of Scotland); and they commanded the uncritical esteem of a century that valued landed property above everything. Great and growing as was the authority of the House of Commons, many a squire or merchant, ambitious for a seat there, dreamed beyond it of the ultimate glamour of a coronet. The "flaxen-headed cow-boy" of the old Norfolk folk-song day-dreams of the ever-ascending pinnacles of his ambition; plough-boy, footman, butler, steward, masterman, member of the Commons, peer. It was a natural ascent; not many made it—and none, probably, in the one generation of the ploughboy's fancies. But the ultimate Everest of those daydreams was the House of Lords.

> When lolling in my chariot
> So great a man I'll be
> You'll forget the little ploughboy
> Who whistled o'er the lea.

5. Cabinet and Prime Minister

The central direction of executive power in Britain lay in Stuart days with the monarch and his Privy Council. In modern Britain it lies with the Prime Minister and his Cabinet. There is no precise point in British history where we can say that here the modern Cabinet was born, or here is the first Prime Minister. All the processes were gradual; all the distinctions are blurred. But it was in the early years of the Georgian era that some decisive moves were made and some vital lapses allowed to occur.

In Queen Anne's reign the great policies of state, domestic and military, had been hammered out by the 'Lords of Committee', or Inner Cabinet. Admirals, generals, junior Ministers, and ambassadors were summoned before this comparatively

[5] Thus the principal seat of the Dukes of Norfolk and Newcastle lay in Sussex, of the Duke of Devonshire in Derbyshire, of the Earls of Derby in Lancashire, et cetera, et cetera.

small body, which then framed proposals to be put before the full Cabinet Council. This larger body, sitting, with the Queen presiding—often after Sunday dinner—was more formal and altogether more authoritative than the Lords of Committee. It was to the smaller body, however, which thrashed out the main business, that we must look for the true ancestor of the modern Cabinet. George I inherited both committees; and at first he continued Anne's practice of presiding at the meetings of the full formal Cabinet. The business here was conducted in English for the most part, but to some extent in French. All state papers were duplicated in French, the only tongue common to the King, the Prince of Wales (also normally present), and the Cabinet Ministers. When, early in the reign, George I was away in Hanover it was customary for the Prince of Wales to preside in his stead. Then, in 1717, when George quarrelled violently and publicly with the Prince, he refused for a time to see him or speak to him, still more to sit with him in Cabinet meetings. Yet without the Prince present to interpret the major part of the discussion carried on in English, the King was at a loss. The proceedings therefore became tiresome and often meaningless to him, and he began the practice of absenting himself from all but purely formal meetings. Thus what had begun as the Lords of the Committee, or small Inner Cabinet, became in practice the effective Cabinet, with the King normally (though not invariably) absent from it and a leading Minister presiding. A Cabinet of 1720 or 1750 or even 1780, however, was very different from the modern Cabinet: it was an informal affair still, meeting wherever convenient, frequently at dinner, and maintaining no formal records; and, after its sessions, the principal Ministers or the Minister specifically involved in a decision always had to consult the King and obtain his approval before acting on Cabinet recommendations.

Walpole had a smaller influence on the development of the Cabinet than has been imagined. He did, indeed, use his influence with the King to secure the dismissal of his rivals, so that the Cabinets of his day appeared to be 'his' Cabinets and he himself the 'Prime' Minister over a harmonious Cabinet that spoke with one public voice, like a modern Cabinet. Even

Walpole, however, did not choose his own Cabinet, as a modern Prime Minister does; neither did his colleagues resign when he did. His twenty-year dominance was built upon his own personal prestige and love of power, and upon his usefulness to the King in being able to command a consistent Commons majority. His successors enjoyed no such primacy, and it was sometimes difficult to determine who in fact was the 'Prime' Minister at any given moment, though normally the First Lord of the Treasury was so described. Frequently, however, the chief of his duties was rather to act as liaison between Cabinet and King than to direct and dominate Cabinet policy. In this manner the nominal head of the famous Fox–North Coalition of 1783 was neither Fox nor North, but the First Lord of the Treasury, the Duke of Portland. Certainly it was normal, especially in time of war, for the Cabinet to be consulted by the King before a policy was adopted; but both George II and George III acted on occasions without consulting it at all; they merely saw the individual Minister concerned. As for the older, full Cabinet, a body attended by the Archbishop of Canterbury, the Lord Chief Justice, and the great officers of the Royal Household, such as the Master of the Horse and the Lord Chamberlain, it rapidly went the way of the Privy Council, and lapsed into insignificance.

6. Political Parties

Parties in the modern sense did not exist in the eighteenth century. It is true that politicians were described as Whigs or Tories; but the terms were descriptive rather of an attitude, an approach to political problems, than of official political organizations. One might talk of the 'Whig interest' or of 'Tory principles'; but if by 'party' one means the modern conception of a disciplined political body of kindred convictions, with an agreed programme, a more or less rigid solidarity, a leader, a nation-wide political army organized for electoral battle and either parliamentary government or parliamentary opposition, as the fortunes of the polls dispose, then such a conception was entirely alien to Georgian Britain.

The terms 'Whig' and 'Tory' had originated under the restored Stuarts; and they shared with the later term 'Prime Minister' a hostile flavour: they were commonly used as terms of abuse. The party of the Whigs, as their enemies called them, grew up round the attempt by strong Protestants to exclude James, Duke of York, the Catholic heir to the throne of Charles II. In the course of time the Whigs came to stand for a limitation of royal power; for the privileges of Parliament; for a Protestantism on the whole unfanatical, with a degree of toleration for Nonconformists, though less for Catholics; and for the interests of the rich merchants and bankers. In the days of Marlborough the Whigs had formed, broadly speaking, the war party. The Tories, originating as true-blue champions of the royal prerogative and divine right, stood also, and more rigidly than the Whigs, for the Church of England, in particular for the High Church party therein; they were hostile to Nonconformists; taking their support largely from the country squires, they distrusted both the great money-lending merchants and the grand estate-owning Whig magnates. Since taxes were principally land-taxes, and since wars meant high taxation, the Tories in Marlborough's day and after stood on the whole for peace. War was most likely to benefit not tax-paying squires but 'tax-eating' Whig money-lenders and contractors. The division between the two great opposing interests and philosophies was sufficiently clear to justify a broad and imprecise division of political Englishmen into Whigs and Tories. Both were, of course, parties of the propertied classes; the unpropertied and non-voting masses watched the battle (if, indeed, they had time or interest to watch it at all) from afar, ready on occasion to shout in a good cause or riot against an unpopular one. The time was still far off when the great political parties could survive only by appealing to the interests and votes of the masses.

It is to some extent misleading to think of eighteenth-century politics in terms of *policies* at all, whether Whig or Tory. Men went into Parliament primarily to pursue not policies but their own advancement and influence, whether professional, social, or commercial; they went into the Government for office and the fruits of office, and for power. Walpole pocketed enough from his tenure of office to rebuild Houghton in Norfolk in the grandest style, furnish it like a millionaire, and adorn its walls with pictures worth tens of thousands of pounds. Nobody thought this in any way odd. A William Pitt who refused to accept the perquisites of his post, or an Edmund Burke who lived above the snow-line of principle, was an exception to the rule. Inside Westminster members naturally gravitated towards certain groups. There were, first, the 'placemen', those who owed their position there solely to the influence of the Crown, and who were, therefore, bound to support the King and his Ministers in almost any circumstances. These (known for a time under George III as "the King's friends") and others who either were in office or stood in reasonable prospect of profiting by Government influence, together composed what was often known as the Court Party: the stability of the regime owed them a good deal. Even under the Whig administrations of 1714–60 this Court Party might well consist of a broad mixture of self-styled Whigs and self-styled Tories. The House of Commons by no means divided itself neatly into Whigs on one side and Tories on the other. There was an Opposition, indeed, and its nucleus came most frequently from another general group of members, whom the twentieth century would think of as Independents, but the seventeenth and the eighteenth often described as the Country Party. Most of these were country gentlemen who would normally support the King's Government as a matter of principle, but were in no way bound to do so, and were a permanent potential Opposition when they felt their interests challenged. A majority of these, but by no means all, would probably have described themselves as Tory by inclination. They were liable to be joined, in times of governmental trouble, by professional trouble-stirrers in Parliament, thwarted place-seekers, or ambitious individualists; but the erring loyalty of these last was often to be purchased by a timely bribe. All these groups may, in a sense, be equally reasonably thought of as 'parties' as may the Whigs and the Tories.

To this matter of party there is yet another approach which affords another aspect of the complicated truth. Each great magnate in the Georgian Parliament was the centre of a little political kingdom of his own, with 'subjects' numbering perhaps as few as half a dozen or as many as a score or so. The great aristocratic families of England were few in number, and the junior branches of each of them ramified broadly. A grandee like the Duke of Portland, the Duke of Devonshire, or the Duke of Bedford was the head of a compact political clan whose several loyalties produced the nearest thing in Georgian days to party sentiment in a modern sense; and, at different times in the eighteenth century, the families of Stanhope, Pelham, Yorke, Courtenay, Edgcumbe, Lowther, Townshend, Manners, Grenville, and many another commanded their own considerable forces in the Lower House. An alliance of several of these clans and 'connections' could produce a formidable and perhaps decisive voting power.

7. Local Government

The English are the least systematizing of peoples. They take over whatever is already there. They adapt; they reform; they improvise; they borrow; they invent. They rarely abolish. So it is with our school 'system' today, or our legal 'system', or our traffic 'system'. So it was in the eighteenth century with the 'system' of local government. Nothing could have been less systematic. It is rather as if a dozen different pictures had been painted over the same canvas without any one of them ever being fully erased.

If the resulting picture is complicated it is certainly a vital one to understand, for in many ways local government was of much greater importance than central government. For instance, the Civil Service of Georgian England was a tiny affair, employing altogether only a few hundred officials, of whom a large proportion were excisemen. 'Whitehall', in a modern sense, hardly existed. The whole burden of conducting the internal affairs of the nation fell upon local organizations and dignitaries; and neither Westminster nor Whitehall—that is, neither Parliament nor its executive arm—interfered at all with local administration except in times of high crisis, when serious riot or rebellion threatened.

Oldest of all the organizations lingering into Georgian times were the ancient Saxon units of the shire (or Norman 'county') and the hundred. Of these the hundred was very nearly dead; but the shire, as we have seen, was still the basis for the election of a proportion of the Members of Parliament, and for the royal appointments of sheriff and lord lieutenant. Of these last two offices, that of lord lieutenant was the more important. By the eighteenth century the lord lieutenancy of a county was likely to be in the hands of its greatest landowner—a Pelham in Sussex, Nottingham, or Middlesex; a Lowther in Westmorland, a Herbert in Shropshire, a Courtenay or Carteret in Devonshire. This grandee would, in the first place, be of importance as a link between the locality and Westminster; he would be the likely patron of many parliamentary seats; and, in time of stress, it would be through him that measures would be taken against riot or rebellion, and through him that the militia, or the 'volunteers' at a time of threatened invasion, would operate. It was his recommendation that determined appointments to the bench of local magistrates, as, indeed, it still is.

Other Anglo-Norman manorial relics persisting into Georgian times were the court baron and the court leet: feudal vestiges that, although still widely in existence and preserving the formalities of former days, had almost everywhere fallen under the effective control of local landowners, prosperous farmers, or burgesses. In many small towns the meeting of the manor court, the borough court, and the parish vestry had in effect been amalgamated into a single meeting, normally controlled by a handful of the richer inhabitants. The small decayed borough of Brading, in the Isle of Wight, may be taken as typical of many places. It had for centuries enjoyed a court leet and a market court (or court of piepowder); it simultaneously employed many of the ancient usages and institutions of manor, parish, and borough. Yet by 1753 its courts, sharing a single 'law day', had become indistinguishable, and the Town Steward for that year, writing up in the Town Book his annual records of the one-day meeting, entitled them with a grandiose comprehensiveness, "A View of Frankpledge, Court Leet, Borough, and Law Day"; he might well have added, as other town stewards did, Court of Piepowder; and the parish vestry meeting would probably consist of the same people, with the parson present, meeting under a different formal guise. The forms were fossilized; the people—the local people of standing—were the almost identical oligarchy in all the forms.

The parish was both an ecclesiastical and a civil unit, and its vestry meeting naturally regulated the many small affairs of church and 'parish-pump'. The vestry was in law responsible also for raising a rate to maintain paupers and highways; but in fact it was the local magistrate who often determined the amount of the rates that the parish paid (in any case his approval was necessary), and who appointed the surveyors of highways, the overseers of the poor, and often the parish constables too. 'Parish' is a word covering an extraordinary variety of places in the eighteenth century. Equally with Little Mudcombe, Manchester was a parish; Birmingham was a parish; so were Halifax, Leeds, Sunderland, Wolverhampton, and many other quickly growing urban areas. Lacking an ancient charter and a corporation, they all possessed, in theory, the government of a medieval village; and were, like most country districts, under the effective (or ineffective) control of local magistrates—at least until the exasperated leading citizens in the later eighteenth or early nineteenth centuries took steps to get matters altered by applying to Parliament for permission to set up Improvement Commissioners.

The Improvement Commissioners did more to improve urban conditions—or at least to prevent the deterioration of urban conditions getting out of hand—than all the old municipal corporations put together. These older, 'close', corporations, self-electing, corrupt, lethargic, sunk in conservative complacency and religious orthodoxy, had become local companies of prosperous men cosily running their town as a business proposition in their own interests, rather than genuine town governments promoting the general welfare. Civic feasts were normally regarded as more pressing than reformed water-supplies; the privilege of electing a Member of Parliament (often vested solely in corporation members) more worth considering—often in a simple cash sense—than the duty of providing lighting, paving, sewerage, or police. The Improvement Commissioners, on the other hand, were active and impatient men, often Radical in politics and Nonconformist in religion, who took keen pride in promoting civic benefits; and the most eloquent testimonial to their vigour is supplied by the surprising fact that leading citizens of many ancient corporate towns took steps themselves to set up improvement committees independent of their inert, tradition-bound corporations. The Improvement Commissions look ahead to the bustling, bourgeois, reforming, utilitarian world of the Industrial Revolution and Victorian Britain: indeed, to the 'Age of Improvement'. The old corporations looked back to a world which, though it was not static, found it profitable to behave as if it were so. They "had what they held"—rights and privileges secured on ancient parchment; and they believed, as Trevelyan wrote, that, "Whatever is, is right—if it can show a charter." This world of the little ruling oligarchies of the market boroughs was the very core of conservatism. To the prosperous citizens who formed it Heaven had ordained society so, and reformers who called for change were of the Devil's party.

8. Justices of the Peace

To the ordinary countryman, who was unlikely to have travelled twenty miles from his home more than once or twice in a lifetime, 'government' did not mean the Government in London at all. Westminster was distant and unreal, London as misty (and probably to him as wicked) as Babylon. He had, very possibly, never even heard of Walpole or of Pitt. A great warrior like the Duke of Marlborough—or even a minor one like that Marquis of Granby whose likeness swings on so many inn signs—was far more likely to provide a name and an image in popular circulation. The world, to the average 'man in the field' of 1700 or 1750, was primarily the world of his parish and its immediate neighbours; and it was governed by the squire. The Parliament House at Westminster played no part in his consciousness; the 'big house' in the valley or over the fields was another matter. Its owner was lord of this little world, despot, benevolent or tyrannical, over its politics. He was squire, lord of the manor, justice of the peace. He employed the gamekeepers, and enforced the severe laws against poaching. He and his fellow magistrates, at the Quarter Sessions, fixed the wages of farm labourers, tried all serious cases except those (a growing band) that carried the death penalty, and authorized a county rate. Three magistrates sitting together could sentence a man to seven years' transportation for such an offence as burning ricks. At Petty Sessions two justices were normally present; but very often a single justice, sitting in his own parlour, at any time of day or night, administered the law in a wide variety of less serious matters. Here he committed a man to the stocks for drunkenness or fined him for swearing and disorderly behaviour. Here too he administered the laws of settlement and vagrancy in the manner least likely to cause expense. A beggar from a near-by parish would be removed to the parish where he was legally 'settled'; one from more distant parts, too expensive to repatriate, would be more likely to be first whipped and subsequently 'passed' to the next parish, which would probably repeat the process, until, in theory at least, home was at last reached.[6] The local justice also licensed the public houses; he appointed the overseers of the poor; he supervised the maintenance of bridewells and lock-ups. In his other capacity as principal landowner he fixed many local rents; again, as principal employer in a rural area, he could provide work or withhold it. Directly controlling the destinies of perhaps a quarter of the village, he indirectly presided over the fortunes of all. On Sundays he sat in his big box-pew in church and was not above interrupting the parson's sermon. In some parishes, indeed, the over-long service was punctuated by the arrival of servants bearing refreshments to the squire's pew. For five Englishmen out of six he *was* the Government. "I have sometimes thought", wrote Horace Walpole, "that a 'squire and a vestry were a king and a republic in miniature." The almost despotic powers of the justices of the peace were not confined to rural districts. Towns equally with villages were at the mercy of bad magistrates and under

[6] For some professional beggars this provided a way of life: transport, if painful, was at least free. In fact (especially in towns and especially for men), these Laws of Settlement could not be effectively enforced; but a young woman of child-bearing age apprehended in her 'wrong' parish would be liable to summary 'passing-on', for fear of her presenting the locality with the expense of maintaining an illegitimate child.

a debt to good ones—and the plays and novels of the time attest that there were plenty of both. In some towns a type of 'trading justice' grew up: the unscrupulous climber who used his influence to get himself nominated to the Bench in order to pursue his own profit. In relation to the total, they were few; a much greater curse was the ignorant and unfeeling justice who vented his class prejudice upon those of the lower orders who came before him. The pages of Fielding and Smollett are eloquent of such men's practices; and Fielding at least had a good claim to know what he was writing about, for he was much more than a novelist: he and his blind half-brother, Sir John Fielding, were among the most enlightened and hard-working magistrates of their day. Indeed, Westminster, where they presided, was, together with neighbouring Middlesex (*i.e.*, greater London), the very heart and centre of turbulence, crime, and vice; and the public service rendered by the Fieldings at Bow Street provided the beginnings of a less amateur magistracy, that developed eventually into the institution of stipendiary (or professional) justices. Eighteenth-century justices, of course, like most of their successors today, were unpaid. Usually wealthy, they regarded their work as an aspect of their natural supremacy; and so long as the social philosophy of the nation was summed up in

> God bless the squire and his relations,
> And keep us in our proper stations,

this ruling-class mentality could be tolerated. When, however, the Industrial and French Revolutions had sharpened the teeth of class consciousness and radical opinion it led to a powerful and explosive feeling in the days after Waterloo, when it seemed to many of the poor that the ruling class was referee as well as contestant in the battle of the Two Nations, the rich and the poor. The fierceness of their resentment against this 'Establishment' was heightened by the large number of Tory parsons who by that time constituted a sizeable proportion of the judicial Bench.

Chapter 3

George I and the Whigs

1. The Hanoverian Succession

In 1700 the Princess Anne's only surviving child, the eleven-year-old Duke of Gloucester, ended his brief life. It was the final domestic bereavement in a long, mournful chapter of Anne's miscarriages and infant burials—every one of her numerous children was now dead—and it brought to a full-stop the Protestant line of direct descent from the Stuart monarchs. Before Anne succeeded two years later to the throne of her brother-in-law William III, the English Parliament had already looked ahead to her eventual death and made legal provision to ensure the continued exclusion from the throne of James II and his Catholic descendants. By the Act of Settlement of 1701, Parliament endeavoured to secure the Glorious Revolution and its achievements: the supremacy of the Church of England, toleration for Dissenters, parliamentary control of expenditure and of the Army, the freedom of judges from dismissal at the royal displeasure, an end to Divine Right and to the royal power to dispense with inconvenient laws. It was a settlement that had been underwritten by the money with which Whig merchants and bankers had backed (at a well-secured 8 per cent) Protestant William's cause in the wars against Louis XIV. Anglicans, Dissenters, bankers, merchants, lawyers, Members of Parliament—both Whig and, less emphatically, Tory—those, in short, who had rejoiced to see the defeat of James II and the Catholics, could not now afford to let their great victory slip from their grasp by the unhappy accidents of Anne's unsuccessful motherhood. James II and his Catholic heirs must be disinherited for ever, even if this meant settling the Crown upon the remote and foreign heads of Charles I's niece, Sophia of Hanover, and her lawful heirs.

Anne had lived another thirteen years, a sick woman, latterly dropsical and enormous, but regularly presiding every week, after Sunday dinner, at the meetings of her Ministers. By the spring of 1714, however, it seemed unlikely that the Queen could live much longer. Her leading Ministers, since the downfall of Marlborough and the winding up of the long war, had been principally Tories, and, outstandingly, two men bitter in mutual hatred—Robert Harley (Earl of Oxford), the Lord High Treasurer, and Henry St John (Viscount Bolingbroke), the Secretary of State. Of these men, quarrelling at last openly before the Queen, Oxford was a personally ambitious but politically moderate man; Bolingbroke, however, a figure of much greater brilliance, was playing with fire. He had conceived a plan for obtaining the support of the extremer Tory squires, persuading James III, the Old Pretender, to abandon his Romish faith, thwarting the purposes of the Act of Settlement, and bringing back to the throne of England the 'legitimate' Stuart line. When Oxford was dismissed by the dying Queen in July 1714 it looked to some that Bolingbroke's hour might have struck; but an alliance of Whigs and moderate Tories within the Privy Council prevailed. Had Anne lived a little longer, Bolingbroke's schemes might have matured somewhat, but they could hardly have borne fruit. Bolingbroke himself thought that in six weeks, if the Queen lived, he might be able to put sufficient posts in Army and Government into the hands of men strong enough to secure the Stuart succession. There was not, however, the slightest prospect of James relinquishing his religion; and there was equally not the faintest hope of a restoration of Catholicism in England. Too many people stood to lose too much by such an event. Bolingbroke's hoped-for six weeks did not even amount to six days. "The Earl of Oxford was removed on Tuesday", he wrote to Swift; "the Queen died on Sunday. What a world is this! And how does fortune banter us!" The emissary was dispatched to the Hanoverian Court, when the Queen's death was seen to be imminent, with letters requesting George of Hanover to make haste to England. (Sophia, like James II, was by now dead.)

George, however, who was already fifty-four and punctilious in preliminaries, preferred to take his time. He made his leisurely way through Holland and over the Channel, and the royal barge did not arrive at Greenwich till the autumn. The Whigs and moderates had full command of the situation. George knew his backers. Oxford's letter protesting loyalty and indirectly suggesting his own re-appointment was ignored; apart from a few minor appointments, all the posts in the new Ministry were offered to Whigs. Atterbury, Bishop of Roches-ter, did indeed threaten to go to the Royal Exchange "in his lawn sleeves", and there proclaim James III; but Bolingbroke saw that the cause was lost so long as James retained his faith. "England would as soon have a Turk as a Roman Catholic for a king," he said. Everything for George went as smoothly as could be; the Hanoverian succession was quietly established with hardly a serious hitch.

2. George I

George Louis, Elector of Hanover and now George I of Great Britain, had been unable to resist the prize of the English Crown, but nevertheless had taken it reluctantly, almost grudgingly, much as a middle-aged man, set and com-fortable in his ways, might be expected to accept a business promotion that involved him in a vexatious change of house, added burdens of work, new and difficult staff.[1] The English had a reputation abroad for unruliness and faction. They criticized, hampered, exiled, and even executed their kings. Power was uneasily divided between monarch, Ministers, and what George II later flatly described as "that damned House of Commons". In Hanover, on the other hand, George's sub-jects were amenable, uncritical, and unparliamentary. His pleasant little Court provided trusted servants, a variety of

[1] Lady Mary Wortley Montagu, whose husband was one of George's Commissioners of the Treasury, went so far as to write that "he would have been so well contented to have remained in his little town of Han-over, that if the ambition of those about him had not been greater than his own, we should never have seen him in England. . . . Our customs and laws were all mysteries to him, which he neither tried to understand, nor was capable of understanding if he had endeavoured it."

simple if sometimes coarse amusements, and a quiet life of
well-loved routine. His regime was one of simple autocracy:
when, for instance, his wife, Sophia Dorothea, had fallen in
love with the handsome Swede, Count von Königsmark, George
had summarily divorced her and immured her in a castle, away
from her children, where she stayed for the remaining thirty-
two years of her life. (Her lover was unaccountably murdered.)
Above all, in Hanover people spoke German, and the more
polite ones a little French; and when George gave orders they
were understood. When he came, half reluctantly, to England,
not very surprisingly he brought with him as much of the
Hanoverian environment as would travel: his personal man-
servants, the Turks Mustapha and Mohammed, whom he had
captured in a youthful campaign; his refugee Huguenot private secretary; his old and trusted Hanoverian advisers, and
his equally old and trusted Hanoverian mistresses. Of these
ladies, one, the Baroness von Schulenburg (later to be Duchess
of Kendal) was emaciated and approaching sixty; the other,
the Baroness Kielmannsegge (Lady Darlington), was fierce of
eye and wonderfully fat. The two ladies were received with
incredulity; they became known respectively as the "Hop-
pole" and the "Elephant." "No wonder", wrote Horace Walpole, "that the mob of London were highly diverted at the
importation of so uncommon a seraglio!" George I was no
monster; he was intellectually simple, physically brave (he was
an experienced soldier), stubborn, reserved, and sensual. His
habits, good and bad, could not be altered by a passage of the
English Channel. He resented the good fortune, the ill fortune,
that had brought him to the Court of St James's and to the
estate of monarchy over these contentious foreigners. He
longed for home; and 'home' was always Hanover, with its
comfortable Court, and the little summer residence near the
capital, with its shooting, its park and gardens, its uncompli-
cated relaxations.

3. The Whigs in Power

The Hanoverian succession was established, but it had to be
secured. Since the existing Parliament had a Tory majority in

both Houses, George and his Whig Ministers wasted no time before holding the general election which was in any case necessitated by the change of monarchy, and in which they romped home with a majority of 150, largely, but not entirely, owing to their powerful use of the royal patronage. Once in, the Whigs were determined to take steps which would keep them in for a very long time and close the door against any possible Jacobite counter-revolution. They succeeded so completely that their party remained supreme in British politics for half a century—throughout the reigns of George I and George II. The Revolution of 1688 had secured the dominance of the Protestant aristocracy. In these early days after 1714 many of them had motives of revenge, too, against those leading Tories who had handled the Whigs far from gently between 1710 and 1714; Robert Walpole, for instance, had spent some time in the Tower on a charge of bribery; and now they moved ominously against their late oppressors. Throughout the early months of 1715 things looked blacker and blacker for the Tory leaders Ormonde, Oxford, and Bolingbroke; the Whig-dominated Commons set up a secret committee to investigate their past conduct, especially their share in the Treaty of Utrecht, that infamous humiliation (in Whig eyes) by which the fruits of Marlborough's glorious victories had been treacherously cast away. Proceedings of impeachment were begun but never concluded. One night in April Bolingbroke went to the theatre, slipped quietly out during the performance, and crossed the Channel to Saint-Germain, where the Pretender's mother, Mary of Modena, held court. Ormonde hung on until August, encouraged by a succession of anti-Hanoverian riots, and making little attempt to conceal his plans for a Jacobite rising in the Tory west of England; but in August he too fled to Saint-Germain. Only Oxford remained, awaiting trial in the Tower of London for two years; but, the Jacobites having by that time lost the day, the prosecution lapsed, and he was released. As a politician he was finished. The flight of Ormonde and Bolingbroke had for the Whigs the satisfactory effect of making it much easier for them to smear every Tory with the name of Jacobite. Meanwhile, throughout the country, Tory landowners found their commissions as justices of the peace withdrawn, their Deputy-Lieutenancies transferred to Whig hands. The foundations of the long Whig rule to come were being broadly laid.

4. The 'Fifteen'

Bolingbroke, arriving at Saint-Germain, found an atmosphere of rare confusion. The Pretender's mother, Mary of Modena, single-minded, unpractical, and intolerant, was against all compromise: England must be attacked and Catholicism re-imposed. Her son James Edward, "James III" to the Jacobites, the "Old Pretender" to the Whigs, a somewhat trivial but honest young man of twenty-seven, was not allowed by the terms of the Utrecht Treaty to live in France; neither could he obtain direct help from Louis XIV; but in his exile at Bar-le-Duc, just over the Lorraine border, he was the ineffectual recipient of much contrary advice. The Earl of Mar counselled a more moderate policy than that of the diehard papists; and Bolingbroke, upon his arrival, urgently argued in favour of an assurance to the Churches of England and of Scotland, to the moneyed interests in the City of London, and to the universities, that their interests would be respected. He begged James not to rely on the Scots and the Irish: it was only by persuading the *English* that Jacobitism could succeed. "Frequent and popular appeals" to the largely Tory-minded countryside and town artisan were the only way to defeat the Whigs—and, indeed, the continuing riots (especially in the Midlands), the burning of Dissenters' chapels, the coolness of the reception given to George and his Hanoverian entourage, all confirmed, to Bolingbroke's thinking, the strength of the innate loyalty to the old monarchy. But the Pretender, eventually, would have none of Bolingbroke's advice. He gave secret assurances to the Pope of his intentions fully to restore Catholicism. He allowed the Scotsman the Earl of Mar to 'jump the gun' with a premature rising in Scotland in September 1715. Furthermore, this luckless enterprise was undertaken at the very moment of Louis XIV's death. Louis, precluded by the Treaty from overt help, had nevertheless contrived support for the Jacobites in a dozen ways; but the new Government of

his little grandson Louis XV was under the control of the
Regent, the Duke of Orleans, whose personal ambitions as
well as his judgment of French economic interests steered him
towards a reconciliation with the Hanoverians. "My hopes,"
said Bolingbroke later, "sank as Louis XIV declined and died
when he expired." James Edward, with events out of his control, lived increasingly in a dream world of confusion and
futility. His correspondence and messengers, moreover, were
constantly under the watchful eyes of the agents of the British
ambassador in Paris; the Jacobite secret code was well understood by them.

The cause of the old religion had always been stronger in
the Scottish Highlands and in the North and West of England
than in the South and East. It was not surprising, therefore,
that the Earl of Mar gained enough support north of Perth to
muster an army eventually of 10,000 men, or that the Jacobite
leaders in the North, Forster and Derwentwater, were strong
enough to take an army into Preston. But the unco-ordinated
nature of the risings gave the Whig Government, under the
direction of Earl Stanhope (himself a soldier of distinction),
plenty of time to make its dispositions. Likely Royalist strong-
holds in the West Country and Midlands, such as Oxford,
Bristol, and Bath, were secured; Southampton and Plymouth
were garrisoned with reliable troops; and Stanhope was at one
with Bolingbroke in thinking that the real test, if there was to
be one, would be in the South of England; so that when
Ormonde made successive attempts to gain a Jacobite foothold
in Devonshire, first in October and later in December, he
found the support negligible and was on each occasion forced
to sail ingloriously back to France. It was one thing to grumble
about the new King and his foreigners, or to toast the true King
over the water; but it was quite another thing to leave the
autumn ploughing and risk one's neck in a Catholic cause
more certain to be lost even than Monmouth's Protestant cause
thirty years before. The future lay with the Whigs, and nine
Englishmen out of ten knew it, even if the proportion of those
happy about it was a good deal lower.

In the north the Jacobite armies stumbled upon twin failures
on the same day in November. At Preston, Forster s army was

scattered, with the loss of 1600 prisoners; and at Sheriffmuir, to the south-east of Edinburgh, the Earl of Mar, with forces three times as numerous as the veterans of Oudenarde and Malplaquet that faced them, could only succeed in fighting an indecisive action, as a result of which he fell back again to Perth, where Jacobite spirits ebbed and the weeks of opportunity passed. Argyll, in command of the Hanoverian troops, had won time to reinforce his strength with Dutch regiments and Swiss mercenaries.

Things were thus looking bleakly unpromising by the time that the Pretender himself, who "had talked [said Bolingbroke] like a man who expected every moment to set out for England or Scotland, but who did not very well know for which"—yet who was not at all deficient in courage—at last landed at Peterhead in Scotland to join the Earl of Mar. He joined an already dispirited and dispersing army, whose leader, Mar, was himself about to abandon the struggle. While the disorganized remnants of his supporters were mercilessly mopped up by the mixed Hanoverian forces, James Edward, hoping by his retirement from the scene to give his followers a better chance of avoiding the rebel's noose, returned to France. The Regent, Orleans, would not allow him to go back to Lorraine, still less to Saint-Germain, but insisted on his distancing himself farther from English shores. Thus the Old Pretender, after a sojourn in the papal city of Avignon, retired eventually to Rome, having first dismissed Bolingbroke. The 'Fifteen' was all over by April 1716. Although the ruthless harrying of the Highlanders was bitterly and long remembered, the captured rebels were, by the standards of the times, leniently dealt with. Only thirty-three Jacobite leaders and officers were sentenced to death, and, of these, four had their sentences commuted to imprisonment, and a further one, Lord Nithsdale, escaped from the Tower in his wife's clothing the day before his execution was due, having exchanged his own for hers while she was visiting him. Of the 14,000 or so Jacobite prisoners of private or non-commissioned rank, only about 700 were sentenced to seven years' transportation in the West Indies. As the triumph of the Whigs became ever plainer and more complete, further clemency was extended to other

rebels in prison. The Whigs could afford this almost contemptuous mercy. They had seized the opportunity of the Rebellion
to persuade George I to rid the Ministry of its few remaining
Tories. Walpole had been promoted to the Treasury as First
Lord and Chancellor of the Exchequer. The Tories were in
confusion and disarray, so much so that the Whigs could afford
the luxury of a struggle for power within their own ranks: the
most important political quarrels of the next six or seven years
were not between Tory and Whig, but between the rival Whig
factions themselves.

5. The Whigs secure their Power

Before these came to open hostility, however, the united and
victorious Whig Ministry (whose leading figures were Stanhope, Sunderland, Townshend, and Walpole) put through an
important Act intended to perpetuate their own power. The
Jacobites, though rebuffed and even humiliated, were by no
means destroyed. The Tories, though defeated, might contrive
to use some future popular discontent to win a victory at the
polls despite the Whigs' management of their advantages. A
new election was due in 1718. Hence in 1716 the Septennial
Act was passed, extending the legal life of an elected Parliament to seven years instead of the three that the Whigs had
themselves insisted on at the time of the 1688 Revolution; and
thus a general election was to be avoided until at least 1722.
At one stage, a little later, Stanhope and Sunderland even
proposed a further prolongation, but were persuaded at last
against its wisdom. This Whig Septennial Act of 1716 remained
law until the Parliament Act of 1911, when the seven-year
duration was reduced to five, where it now stands.

The principal causes of dissension within the Whig ranks
arose partly from foreign policy[2] and partly from personal
quarrels. The death or infirmity of almost all the older generation of Whig leaders—Godolphin, Wharton, Halifax, Somers,
Marlborough—had left the field of leadership clear for a new
generation of thrusting, ambitious, younger men. One of these
was Argyll, whose influence was powerful in Scotland; another

[2] See Chapter 5.

was Sunderland, Marlborough's son-in-law and the son of that devious Sunderland who had been a leading Minister in the Governments of Charles II, James II, and William III. This younger Sunderland was well placed to succeed with George I; speaking excellent French, he was one of the few leading politicians who could make himself easily understood to the King. He was an intellectual, and an outspoken one (he had often in the past proclaimed himself a republican); yet now he managed to retain George's confidence. Restless, intriguing, bitter, ambitious, intolerant of rivals, he did not make an easy colleague. Then there was Townshend, who ran in political harness with his brother-in-law Robert Walpole. These two had been prominent among those who demanded full retribution against the captured Jacobite Scottish leaders: like George I, they had wanted to see the rebel heads on Temple Bar. Townshend was a tough, impetuous, transparently power-loving politician; it is a matter for irony that his countrymen finally came to remember him, even to immortalize him, for his promotion of turnip cultivation. Walpole was a carthorse of a man, of immense ability, shrewdness, toughness, and industry, who of all the contenders for power was eventually to emerge on top, and to stay there for an unprecedented stretch of time. Finally, in this group of jockeying politicians was the man in some ways the most distinguished and certainly the most likeable of them all—Stanhope, who was the dominating figure during the period 1714–21: a soldier, a scholar (like Sunderland, speaking excellent French, and therefore accessible to the King), a man of subtle intelligence and moral courage, whose foreign policy had a drive and consistency that put him, in this respect at least, in the front rank of Georgian statesmen.

These Whig factions soon clarified themselves into two main groups: the alliance of Stanhope and Sunderland, who had the ear of the King and his German mistresses, and who followed the Court in 1716 when George at last felt England secure enough to return, belatedly and impatiently, to his well-loved Hanover; and the family alliance of Townshend and Walpole, who on the King's departure were left behind to languish at Hampton Court with the Prince of Wales (between whom and the King there was hearty mutual hatred). Argyll, having been himself dismissed, persuaded the Prince that Townshend and Walpole were spying for the King, while Sunderland persuaded the King in Hanover that they were intriguing against the Crown on behalf of the Prince. George, returning in anger, authorized Stanhope to dismiss Townshend; and Walpole, taking his courage in both hands, resigned in sympathy. Behind all this mischief-making and intrigue there lay also more respectable causes of difference. Walpole in particular was alarmed at the possible consequences of Stanhope's aggressive policies abroad; he was convinced that his own financial policies[3] would succeed only if the country were kept at peace.

Thus from 1717 the Whigs were split into two groups; and Townshend and Walpole found themselves in rancorous opposition to Stanhope's Government and in noisy and unnatural alliance with the Tories. This opposition soon found its natural headquarters at Leicester House, where the Prince of Wales and his fascinating wife, Caroline of Ansbach, had set up their establishment—practically a rival Court—when George I, on his return from Hanover, expelled his son from St James's. Throughout the Georgian period it remained true that the monarch hated his heir and *vice versa*; and for a century, over four generations, the 'Court' of the Prince of Wales was the magnet for all ambitious politicians of the Opposition. Under the first two Georges these were Tories and dissident Whigs; under George III they were mainly Whigs. It was a matter for further irritation to the monarch that normally the Royal Court's dullness was in contrast with the gaiety and smartness of the rival establishment. Thus to Leicester House in 1717 came the ambitious, the disgruntled, and the younger men who were looking forward to a perhaps not distant day when there would be a new king, and who were prepared to gamble on the future. In any case, even in the shorter term, the Prince of Wales had many favours, even parliamentary seats, to bestow. He was worth cultivating. And his wife, Caroline, sharp-witted and floridly handsome, was worth cultivating too. Walpole, who with Townshend soon came to frequent Leicester House, rapidly saw in her the dominant partner in the

[3] See Chapter 4, Section 5.

marriage (despite the Prince's habitual infidelities and his un-
pleasant habit of snubbing his wife in public), and established
a friendship with her that was in future days to stand him in
constant stead. He was already, in his own downright words,
taking "the right sow by the ear". She too, a woman of intellectual pretensions (George I called her "Cette diablesse
Madame la Princesse"), was quick to see, among the gossips
and wits that frequented Leicester House, something of more
consequence in the shrewd, solid, but subtle Walpole.

For three years (1717–20) the Stanhope–Sunderland Ministry,
in which Stanhope was the leading force, conducted a domestic
policy of mingled far-sightedness and opportunism. Among the
most punitive measures that Bolingbroke and the High Church
Tories had forced through between 1711 and 1714 were the
Occasional Conformity and Schism Acts. 'Occasional Conformity' was the means by which Nonconformists had qualified
for office in local or central government by *occasionally* taking
the sacraments of the Church of England; and the Occasional
Conformity Act had robbed them of this right to qualify. The
Schism Act, which was hurried through Parliament by Bolingbroke a month or two before Anne's death, had gone even
farther and deprived Nonconformists of the right to educate
their own children, the avowed object of the measure being to
extirpate Dissent in a generation. Now Stanhope proposed to
repeal these two Acts and thus both to honour the promises
made to the Nonconformists by George I on his accession and
to reward them for the support they had given to the new
regime. Political calculation and a genuine desire for toleration both pointed Stanhope in the same direction. When these
measures were safely removed from the statute book (1718),
against the opposition of Tories and Walpole–Townshend
Whigs, Stanhope then turned to a design which was much
more revolutionary and, by modern standards, statesmanlike:
nothing less than to repeal the Test and Corporation Acts, and
thus to give full civic equality to Nonconformists as well as
some measure of it to Roman Catholics. Perhaps it was inevitable that he should fail. Popular opinion was strong against
him, especially on the matter of 'softness' towards Catholics;
continental Catholic persecution of Protestants was blatant

and in England well publicized; and the Catholics themselves, in Stanhope's negotiations with them, obstinately refused to concede any points towards a compromise.

Stanhope's last major domestic Bill was also a failure, but less regrettably. It, too, sprang from an intention to make it impossible for Tories ever to repeat their policies and strata- gems of 1711–14—to double-lock and treble-lock the door against them. In 1712 they had forced their peace policy through the Lords by encouraging Anne, that good Tory, to create twelve new Tory peers. Now Stanhope and Sunderland proposed in their Peerage Bill (1719) to limit the number of new English creations, as distinct from replacements, to six. In 1719 there were 178 English peers (without the bishops); thus 184 would have been the new maximum. The 16 Scottish peers, elected anew for each Parliament, were to be replaced by 25 new hereditary members. The plain purpose of the Bill was to ensure the existing Whig majority in perpetuity, a pros- pect so pleasant to the Whig lords that they twice emphatically passed different versions of the Bill. The Commons, however —even its Whig members—were very far from happy about a measure that would almost certainly remove from the grasp of knights and baronets the glittering prize that so many of them saw at the end of the road—a peerage. For this was an age in which the political and social prestige of nobility was very great; Ministries were in general composed overwhelmingly of peers (21 out of 25 in Stanhope's 1714 Ministry); and the House of Commons was composed largely of aspirants to the senior chamber, or of men whose feelings were voiced by Sir John Packington, the original of Addison's Sir Roger de Coverley, when he said: "For my own part, I never desire to be a lord, but I have a son who may one day have that ambition." Walpole now found something worth getting his teeth into; and he did not let go until he and his fellow commoners had forced Stanhope to abandon his Bill. Only eighteen of the eighty county members voted for the Government, only twenty- four of the House's ninety-five baronets. Stanhope's defeat caused him to reconsider the wisdom of provoking such power- ful enemies as Townshend and Walpole; and they were accordingly invited to join the Ministry once more, though in minor posts. It was not only the Ministers who were reconciled; urged on by both Stanhope and Sunderland, and by Walpole and his ally Caroline, the Prince of Wales was persuaded to kneel red-faced before a spluttering George I, and thus a superficial, embarrassing, and graceless reconciliation was patched up there too. Hating him no less than before, but fortified by his son's submission, the King gladly escaped back with his mistresses to Hanover for the summer of 1720.

6. The South Sea Bubble

George was not allowed to relax there long, for within a few months this reconstructed Stanhope Ministry was faced with the crisis that brought it down and opened the door for the great Walpole administration that was to dominate the next two decades. The famous South Sea Bubble had various causes; prominent among them was the general desire of thoughtful men of the day to reduce, or even if possible to wipe out, the National Debt. It was a novelty to them—before the wars of William III it had been negligible—and its size, £54,000,000 in 1714, was highly alarming to them. In a little over a decade of war in Anne's reign it had more than trebled, and, of course, it carried a high rate of interest, which had to be met by unpopular taxation. Herein lay the attractiveness of the offer made by the South Sea Company. On its incorporation eight years previously it had proposed to take over £9,000,000 of the National Debt in return for a monopoly of the South American trade ('South Seas' at this period denoted 'South American' rather than 'Southern Pacific'); and although its privileges and opportunities had been reduced by the Treaty of Utrecht, it was riding the financial boom of these years, despite disappointing slave-trade receipts, with growing profits and growing public reputation. In fact, however, its profits arose far less from South American trade than from financing the capital expansion of other companies of all kinds. It had always been more a banking house than a commercial enterprise, a Tory rival, in fact, to the Whig Bank of England. And when in 1718 Stanhope's foreign policy led Britain into a war with Spain, and the South Sea Company's assets in South

America were seized by the Spaniards, the purely commercial aspect of its activities patently ceased; it became a finance corporation pure and simple.

The skilful and self-confident professionals in charge of it now proposed a truly regal gesture of public benevolence and self-enrichment: no less than, in the fullness of time, to relieve the Government altogether of the National Debt, which by this time Walpole and Stanhope between them had whittled down to £51,000,000. The South Sea Company would, if Parliament agreed, take over the bulk of this sum, paying £7,500,000 for the privilege, and proceed to invite owners of Government stock to exchange their holdings for South Sea stock. When this process had been completed the Company would still receive from the Government an annual sum of about £1,500,000. The Ministry and Parliament did agree to this grandiose scheme, though not before the palms of many of them had been greased by gifts of stock or by sales of stock at prices *guaranteed* below their realizable value. The King's mistresses, too, were not neglected: the Company's directors, ambitious financial manipulators and wizards in the new and fascinating magic of credit promotion, saw to it that influential people of all kinds were on their side. The arch-manipulator was John Blunt, a dominating and quite unscrupulous tycoon.

Suddenly, the Bill once passed, the Company's stock began to rocket. Five-eighths of the owners of Government securities within a week transferred to South Sea stock as planned. It seemed foolish not to, for stock dangled before their eyes at 375 had already, thanks to energetic manoeuvring by the directors, been worked up to 450. The public—much of it with money to gamble, and it was a gambling age—began to join in the scramble. The King himself bought a substantial holding. Indeed, as Governor of the Company, he symbolized its prestige, respectability, and official standing. At the beginning of 1720 South Sea stock stood at 128½; by June it was 890; in July it touched 1000. There never had been so simple a recipe for rapid riches. As William Windham, one of Walpole's neighbours in Norfolk, wrote, "I am glad you have disposed of my horses, for I have business enough on my hands. I grow rich so fast that I like Stock Jobbing of all things." Another of his family wrote: "The ladies sell their jewels to buy, and happy are they that are in. Never was such a time to get money as now."

It certainly seemed to be so, and not only in England. In France the brief reign of the Scottish economist John Law was in full flower. His grandiose Mississippi Company and its allied projects provided a beacon to lure onward the English South Sea Company. All Paris was stock-crazy, and in addition 30,000 foreigners had flocked thither to join the joyful scramble. "Never was such a time to get money as now." From the French capital the British Ambassador was writing home to his Government: "By the success of Mr. Law's project the public debts are paid off at a stroke." So sensational, indeed, was Law's apparent success, before inflation overwhelmed him, that the ambassador advised the British Government to expedite its own scheme, lest Law "raise the trade of France on the ruins of our trade". Thus boom called to boom, bubble to rival bubble, across the English Channel. In Amsterdam, as in London and Paris, stock prices soared confidently to the skies. In London other companies, spawned by some of the least scrupulous of the South Sea Company's directors, floated along in the current of wild financial optimism brought about by the parent company's success. The price of these satellite companies' stock, too, rose rapidly to an inflated price many times greater than their ability to pay dividends; and, as might be expected, not a few rogues were willing to float bogus companies to soak up any spare capital that might be available from simple optimists ready to invest in schemes to get gold from sea-water, to import broomsticks from Germany, or to drain the Irish bogs. The nominal value of the stock of all the companies reached £224,000,000 by July 1720.

The more responsible of the South Sea Company directors were by now alarmed, and applied for a writ against four shaky companies. It came at the critical moment when the whole monstrously inflated bubble of swollen credit was trembling in the wind of popular doubt, and it played a part in the pricking and bursting that ensued. People who lost money in the bogus companies were now forced to realize their South Sea holdings to meet their losses, and South Sea stock itself immediately suffered a sympathetic weakness. In a few weeks the price had dropped from 1000 to 180. The same Norfolk squire, admitting himself "a very silly fool", was now writing: "Allmost all one knows or sees are now on ye very Brink of Destruction. . . . Those devills of Directors have ruin'd more men's fortunes in this world, than I hope old Beelzebub will do souls for ye next." Many indeed had gone beyond the brink of destruction; as Windham wrote, there were "100,000 men not worth a groat and it grieves me to think of some of them". Thousands stood in the same position as the grandfather of the historian, Gibbon: "his fortune was overwhelmed in the shipwreck of the Year Twenty, and the labours of thirty years were blasted in a single day".

Some had been lucky and netted big capital gains, among them the old Duchess of Marlborough. Sir Isaac Newton, who claimed to be able to calculate the motion of the stars and planets but not the madness of the people, sold his £7000 stock at 100 per cent profit; however, he was subsequently persuaded to re-enter the market and lost £20,000. Thomas Guy, the shrewd old stationer, former M.P., and philanthropist, did much better. Selling his large holding in thousand-pound parcels over six weeks, he reaped over a quarter of a million pounds profit—say, £2,500,000 in modern money. The hospital that he founded with his gains was the best and most surprising outcome of the Bubble. But with the great majority of the investors, greedy expectation now gave way to righteous rage. George I came hurrying back from Hanover, as the cry for vengeance again threatened the future of his dynasty. Stanhope travelled with him, and a deeply involved and alarmed Sunderland posted on ahead of them. The King had more than his political future to worry about; like nearly everybody else, he had financial cause for anxiety: his £66,000 outlay had now shrunk below £10,000.

As for Stanhope's Ministry, which had sponsored the South Sea scheme in Parliament, it blew away in the storm. One Minister, James Craggs the younger, died of smallpox; the elder James Craggs died a month later, possibly from suicide; Aislabie, the Chancellor of the Exchequer, being found guilty by the House of Commons of "the most notorious, dangerous, and infamous corruption", was expelled from the House and imprisoned. Charles Stanhope, Secretary to the Treasury and the cousin of Earl Stanhope, escaped a similar condemnation by only three votes; and Earl Stanhope himself, in the course of a vigorous rebuttal of charges against him in the Lords, was seized with a brain haemorrhage and died three days later. The estates of the South Sea directors, fourteen of whom were at one time in prison, were confiscated, and the proceeds put to the relief of sufferers from the Bubble. They were perhaps lucky to get off so lightly; many, like "Cato" in the *London Journal*, demanded their necks as well as their money.

Walpole's part in the South Sea Bubble and its aftermath has been much misunderstood. Although it is true that in 1711 he had attacked the South Sea scheme when it was first put forward, preferring the Bank of England's scheme, he did not later oppose the South Sea Company's moves, and himself invested heavily in its stock. Neither was his buying and selling any shrewder than most people's—and a great deal less successful than, say, Thomas Guy's or the Duchess of Marlborough's. He did sell, early on, at a modest profit; but, bemused like everybody else by the apparent prospect of easy gains, he was anxious to re-invest later, at a time when South Sea stock stood dangerously high. He lost quite heavily at this stage, and would have lost much more if it had not been for the cautious wisdom of his financial agent, a certain Jacombe. The oft-told tale, therefore, that Walpole "saw through" the Bubble from the start appears to be legendary—the repetition, probably, of his supporters' successful propaganda. Certainly, however, Walpole appeared to many in 1720 to be less desperately involved than other members of the Government in South Sea bribery and governmental confusion. At the height of the panic he had quietly removed to his home in Norfolk, to tend his estates (lately much enlarged) and perhaps deliberately to dissociate himself from the muddle and scandal. Thither in the autumn of 1720 his adviser Jacombe wrote: "Everybody longs for you in Town. . . . They all cry out for you to help them. . . ." Walpole accordingly returned, and proceeded to supervise the complicated tasks of salvaging what remained from the financial wreck, and at the same time of screening the Government and the Court from an excess of public vengeance. He performed this thankless rôle with uncommon skill and toughness. The prime danger he saw to be the violence of popular rage, which could lead to riot and even to revolution. It was Walpole, speaking for the Government, who stood his ground against the pack of outraged squires howling for the blood of South Sea directors, King's Ministers, and King's mistresses. Even the King himself stood in some danger. But, here again, Walpole has been unjustly praised for his financial sagacity at this juncture, and for far-sighted schemes to restore the national economy. 'His' scheme was, in reality, Jacombe's, and it was in fact never put into operation. What Walpole did was rather to restore the political equilibrium and to maintain authority while the natural strength of the economy righted the financial ship with surprising speed. He fended off all the attacks upon the surviving Ministers and upon the Court, thereby, incidentally, building up a store of that valuable commodity, royal gratitude. Even Sunderland was stubbornly shielded by his old rival, though the exercise did nothing to increase their mutual love and brought Walpole (the "Screen-Master General") much abuse from opposition ranks. Inside the Government, the Walpole–Townshend group had by now achieved parity of influence with the Sunderland–Carteret group. By April 1721 Walpole had been invested with the offices of Chancellor of the Exchequer and First Lord of the Treasury, but ascendancy was not yet his. He fought to get control of the Secret Service money, that most potent instrument of patronage, but unsuccessfully. Even when Sunderland, bitter and intriguing to the last, followed Stanhope to sudden death in 1722, and thus yet another of Walpole's main rivals was eliminated, still there was Carteret, who challenged Walpole's primacy for another two years. But his political stature by 1722 was very high. The Bubble and the disgrace or death of most of his principal rivals had given him his opportunity. He had shown an immense capacity for work, a shrewd moderation, and a firm parliamentary hand. He had had rare luck and shown still rarer skill. By 1722 his position was very powerful. For another two decades he was to dominate his country's affairs.

Chapter 4

Walpole and Domestic Affairs (1721–42)

1. Walpole's Character and Career

Sir Robert Walpole was the Crown's principal servant between 1721 and 1742, a longer period of continuous ascendancy than that of any other chief Minister of the past three centuries. Even if it is argued that in the initial years of this period he was forced to share primacy, first with Sunderland and then with Carteret, still no other British national leader of recent times, except the younger Pitt, has so continuously dominated his generation.

In some respects his character repels. He pursued self-advancement and personal power with single-minded ruthlessness, brushing aside one political rival after another; he feathered his own financial nest to a degree that aroused the indignation, as well as the hatred and envy, even of his own far from squeamish age; he was relentless, cynical, and materialistic, as coarse in language as he was gross in bulk. (Queen Caroline, no prude, had to ask him to restrain his anecdotes in the presence of the young princesses.) Moreover, he is not now considered to hold the unique place in the nation's constitutional history that he was once thought to have held: he was *not* "the first Prime Minister"; he did *not* create the modern Cabinet; he did *not* invent Cabinet solidarity—*i.e.*, the principle that the Cabinet must speak with a united voice and that dissidents must resign. He did not even diagnose the shakiness of the South Sea Company, as was once generally said, or prophesy the ruinous Bubble; in 1720, as we have seen, he dabbled as recklessly as most, lost heavily, and was saved from worse disaster by luck and the shrewd initiative of his financial agent. All this, and much more, may be said about, or against, Walpole. Yet he remains the outstanding political giant of his day, a man of supreme common sense, of monumental industry, of tireless thoroughness, and astonishing mastery of petty detail; one of the greatest of administrators; the staff on which each of the first two Georges came in turn to lean; the master for two decades, though not without bitter struggles, of both the Commons and the Lords; a statesman who, next to his own power and interest, pursued for his country the ideals of efficiency, stability, prosperity, and peace.

Born in 1676, the third son of an old Norfolk county family, squires of Houghton, whose relations were to be found in a dozen or more surrounding manors, his future pointed to the Army or the Church until his elder brother's death steered him into politics. It is a pleasant fancy: the Archbishop Walpole that might have been, with his hounds, his vast drinking and his vaster eating, and his fund of coarse stories to entertain the ears of anxious archdeacons or aspiring deans. Doubtless, the eighteenth-century Church was broadminded enough and casual enough to have found room even for him; but, instead, his elder brother's death meant, first, that he returned home from Cambridge to help run the family estates, and then entered Parliament as member successively for Castle Rising and King's Lynn. He always remained a Norfolk man, speaking in a Norfolk accent, assiduous to maintain his family's and the county's interests—it was convenient to take the two as synonymous; always spending some fraction of each year at his Houghton home, first in the modest manor house where he was born, and then amid the ever-growing magnificence of the mansion that he built to supplant it. Even when all London was screaming abuse at him, at the height of the Excise riots of 1733, the gentry of Norfolk and the citizens of Norwich came out to greet him on his customary summer visit, "midst the loud acclamations of all sorts of people"; the Corporation of Norwich presented him with a gold box; his brother and mouthpiece, Horatio, promised every possible assistance to the city's woollen manufacturers; a feast was consumed of appropriate Walpolian dimensions; and a cavalcade escorted him home to Houghton. In Norfolk at least he never wanted for friends. True, those friends were often dependants, relatives, and beneficiaries of his power and patronage; but Walpole would have been the first to understand that the most lasting bonds are often based on mutual self-interest.

One such friendship, which lasted for thirty years, was with Charles Townshend, who in 1713 married Walpole's sister Dorothy, lived in near-by Raynham, and, being a viscount, was long regarded as the senior of the pair. The time was to come when Walpole was to overtop his brother-in-law, just as Houghton came to outshine Raynham; and at last personal and political quarrels caused Walpole to force Townshend's retirement to his estates. In the early years, however, their fortunes were linked, and each derived strength from the other. It was Townshend who introduced Walpole to London society—for instance, to the most select and dashing of the Whig clubs, the Kit Cat.

Walpole's first important office was the Secretaryship of War, which he held from 1708 to 1710, during the years of declining fortunes for Marlborough and the Whigs. Dismissed by the Queen after Harley had risen to the top, he was accused by the Tories of corruption and spent some time in the Tower of London, not too uncomfortably: he had his own servants and a stream of distinguished visitors. King's Lynn even returned him again, unopposed, to Parliament, but Bolingbroke and the Tories would have none of it. Even on Walpole's release from the Tower his expulsion from the Commons remained effective until November 1713. "I heartily despise", he had written to his sister from prison, "what I shall one day revenge"; and, indeed, he never forgave or ceased to detest Bolingbroke. Both their futures lay in the lap of Queen Anne's failing health; and when rapid decline and her death in the summer of 1714 caught Bolingbroke with his plans for a Jacobite succession unripe, Walpole knew that the prospects of revenge, of office, and of the fortune that in those days accompanied office were rosy.

The next years (1714–22) were occupied with the struggle for power, the story of which has been largely recounted in the preceding chapter. As Paymaster-General, Walpole achieved at least one of his ambitions: he made a large fortune by ruthless exploitation of his position, at the same time securing his relations and supporters in a variety of comfortable and influential posts.[1] Further, he used his office to expel the Tory Treasurer of Chelsea Hospital from his official residence (Orford House) and set himself up there on Thames-side in a handsomely enlarged mansion, where he could play the grand gentleman, entertain his powerful friends, intrigue with his political allies, and plan his enemies' discomfiture. Even when, later, he lavished another and a greater fortune on the aggrandizement of Houghton, Orford House, together with a later acquisition, the Old Lodge of Richmond Park, remained in his possession. Both Houghton and Orford he decorated with pictures worth many tens of thousands; and at Richmond he came to keep two packs of hounds, as well as the mistress who became his second wife; his annual bill for wine rose to about £1000; and one of his victories at the King's Lynn election was washed down with fifty gallons of port. At Orford in 1729 he entertained Queen Caroline with the pomp of fireworks and of music from barges moored in the Thames; from Orford, too, many years later, he was to take the title of his earldom. But in addition to these various suburban and country houses, he needed, of course, a town house proper; and this he found in Arlington Street, whither, as the years progressed, an ever larger and ever more distinguished company of those seeking his favours sat hopefully in the waiting-room. Few men have enjoyed power more transparently than Walpole; and it is hardly surprising that the hatred of his enemies grew as rapidly as the prosperity of his investments, the magnificence of his properties, or the girth of his waist.

2. Continued Fear of Jacobitism

So dominating and lasting does Walpole's position seem to have been as we look back on it through the distances of history that it must be stressed how, at the time, there was

[1] A little later a hostile writer listed the positions held in 1722 by him and his close relatives alone: "First Lord of the Treasury, Mr. Walpole. Chancellor of the Exchequer, Mr. Walpole. Clerk of the Pells, Mr. Walpole's son. Customs of London, second son of Mr. Walpole, in Reversion. Secretary of the Treasury, Mr. Walpole's brother. Postmaster-General, Mr. Walpole's brother. Secretary to Ireland, Mr. Walpole's brother. Secretary to the Postmaster-General, Mr. Walpole's brother-in-law."

always struggle and uncertainty, constant necessity to manipulate and purchase support, constant danger of being outlobbied by the Opposition or deserted by the Court. Then, too, there was the fear of Jacobitism that was never long out of his thoughts. Hindsight shows us that Jacobitism was doomed after the failure of 1714–15; it did not seem so to contemporaries; and, to Walpole, fear of a Stuart restoration was an everpresent preoccupation. Of his principal political enemies from early days, Oxford soon ceased to be of much account after 1715; but Bolingbroke was a different proposition, and Walpole never ceased to fear a revival of his power. Walpole had been one of those agitating most loudly against showing mercy to the defeated rebel leaders after the 'Fifteen'; and afterwards he came to see Jacobite spies round every corner, and built up a great network of counter-spies throughout Scotland, France, Spain, Austria, and the Austrian Netherlands. Money for this information service was never lacking; he would personally spend long hours cross-examining witnesses, and was ready to tolerate, if not encourage, the harshest treatment of suspects.

When, therefore, the agents sniffed out a Jacobite plot in 1722, Walpole was enthusiastic to make the most of it. The Jacobites had been too weak to strike during what should have been to them the advantageous confusion of the Bubble; but they hoped to plan an insurrection while the King was spending the summer of 1722 in Hanover. At the centre of the conspiracy was the Bishop of Rochester, Atterbury, the truculent High Churchman who had been prepared, on Anne's death, to proclaim James III from the steps of the Royal Exchange. Atterbury had a following not only among Tory Jacobites, but also among the discontented poor of London, who pressed sympathetically round his carriage on its way to the Tower. Walpole would have dearly liked to nail a charge of treason upon him, but Atterbury, reckless though he was, had covered his tracks well enough to make a conviction on such a charge improbable. Walpole had to content himself with the sanguinary punishment of a lesser conspirator against whom the evidence was more certain—an unimportant Norfolk lawyer named Christopher Layer. This unfortunate was duly sentenced to be drawn on a hurdle to the place of execution, and there to be hanged, disembowelled, beheaded, and quartered. He claimed, with reason, that Walpole had promised him mercy and tricked him into admission of guilt. The mercy, however, extended only as far as allowing him to be, simply, beheaded: with Walpole, no holds were barred in dealing with Jacobites, and the end of securing the dynasty (and with it his own position) justified some pretty tough means. For a time habeas corpus was suspended, and the Catholic community expelled from London. They had, moreover, to suffer a collective fine of £100,000 to pay the Government's 'expenses' in quelling the conspiracy. Even so, by the standards of the day, the plotters were not unjustly punished. Atterbury was, after all, an unabashed and extreme Jacobite, even if the evidence against him was defective. He was proceeded against in Parliament under a bill of pains and penalties and banished for life. Two other Jacobites were imprisoned, including Atterbury's secretary, who, however, later escaped, and survived to become one of Bonnie Prince Charlie's tiny band of invaders in 1745, the "Seven Men of Moidart". For the remainder of his Ministry Walpole never ceased to spend money liberally in picking up crumbs of Jacobite gossip all over Catholic Europe. No hint of invasion was too nebulous, no whisper of plot was too slight, for him to seize upon it and delve into it. Many times he used these sub-plots and vague rumours to bolster up his ever-reiterated arguments against getting involved in a European war that would be the conspirators' opportunity. And it was not, in fact, until Britain was at war—against Walpole's judgment—in the forties that the Jacobites did strike, with the 'Forty-five' rebellion.

One development after the Atterbury plot Walpole was unable to prevent. On the day that the exiled Bishop of Rochester landed at Calais a pardoned Bolingbroke arrived there on his way back to England, a penitent convert to Hanoverianism. He and his charming French wife had managed to bribe the Duchess of Kendal to persuade the King to permit at last what many had been discussing for a long time. And if the King and his mistress, as well as many public voices, said yes, Walpole was unable to say no. All that he managed to do was to insist that Bolingbroke should not be allowed to resume his seat in the Lords. Open, formal political activity was closed to him; but that did not prevent him from gathering round him a band as brilliant as himself of Tory wits, poets, satirists, and pamphleteers, among them a certain Nicholas Amhurst, who in 1726 began to edit the *Craftsman*, a vehicle for a brilliant ten years' attack on Walpole and all his works—the "Robin-ocracy".

3. Relations with the Court

The relations between Walpole, on the one hand, and George I, George II, and his wife Caroline on the other are of basic importance in a study of the great Minister's career. Royal support, was, as it turned out, forthcoming steadily for twenty years; but nothing seemed more precarious than Walpole's hold on George I in 1721–24, or on his son at his accession in 1727. During the period of recovery from the South Sea Bubble, Walpole, as what his enemies called "Screen-master General", had been invaluable in protecting George I and his German mistresses from the over-zealous probings of the Bubble's angry victims. George, however, had no liking for either Walpole or his ally Townshend; indeed, his dislike of Walpole at one stage was near to loathing. Even during the years 1722–24, Walpole, although we think of him by then as 'Prime' Minister, had no confidence that the King would in the long run prefer him to Carteret, the Secretary of State.

Carteret was young, clever, and ambitious, with strong opinions on foreign policy; he spoke French and German, and the King liked him. Often George would have Carteret and Townshend in his room together arguing contrary foreign policies; when he went to Hanover both men had to accompany him. For months Carteret on one side and Townshend on the other were pursuing rival machinations in Paris, each side with its own independent ambassador; characteristically, the Townshend–Walpole man in Paris was Walpole's own brother Horatio. Most fortunately for Townshend and Walpole, Carteret's schemes overshot themselves. He mixed his policies in Paris with an intrigue on behalf of Lady Darlington,

George's fatter mistress, and thus offended the thinner one, the Duchess of Kendal, as well as George himself. The brothers-in-law were accordingly able to overcome the royal reluctance to dismiss Carteret. From this point (1724) Walpole could feel relatively safe in George I's favour, and he secured powerful and diligent allies in the newly promoted Ministers, the Duke of Newcastle and his brother Henry Pelham.

The fact was, Walpole had made himself indispensable to the King. Nobody else could manage the Commons as he could. By unending attention to detail, by constant lobbying of influential men, by a ruthless manipulation of the patronage resting in his hands, by merciless rooting out of his opponents from positions of authority, he managed continuously to control Parliament even when his policies and personality were unpopular. He was a great House of Commons man, and the first leading Minister to abjure a peerage and stay in the Commons. This again was useful to the Crown; for in the House of Lords, thanks to the subservience of courtiers and bishops, the Government could normally command a majority. The Commons was a less predictable body that needed the sort of skilful handling at which Walpole excelled. A squire himself, he knew what squires would stand and what they would jib at. He knew how to withdraw and bend to a defeat, rather than to hold on towards collision and disaster. He seldom threatened; he frequently persuaded; he knew better than any man how to dangle promises that would catch votes and sway the doubtful. Certainly, his hold upon Parliament was sometimes precarious, but by and large he remained its master until 1742. He knew, however, as well as anyone, that to maintain control of Parliament he must continue the servant of the King. For this, one obvious recipe was to ensure that the Civil List provision for the royal income was maintained at a generous level; here again Walpole was the indispensable intermediary between Crown and Commons. Then again Walpole was a passionate, some might say an obsessed, anti-Jacobite, which further recommended him to George I. Slowly, the King's original dislike of Walpole turned to grudging acknowledgment of his value. By 1726 the King was accepting an invitation to dinner at Richmond Old Lodge, and even called casually there on a later occasion without being invited. The often repeated legend, erected upon a misleading observation of Walpole's youngest son Horace, that George, being unable to converse with Walpole in his own language, was therefore reduced to passing notes in dog-Latin, is manifestly absurd. Walpole's French, though never fluent, came to be adequate. The mutual trust built up between King and Minister by 1727 was such that George's sudden death that year from apoplexy, while summering in Hanover, was a serious shock to Walpole.

The new King, George II (1727–60), was brave, restless, talkative, obstinate, and quick-tempered; incapable of thought on large issues, but uncannily knowledgeable on such unimportant matters of detail as regimental dress and historical dates. He loved parades, and in later days both envied and detested his brother-in-law Frederick of Prussia, who had such a splendid army. He loved music: everyone remembers how he reverently stood up for Handel's Hallelujah Chorus, and thus started a long-lived fashion. He had hated his father, who had bullied and resented him, and worshipped the memory of the mother who had been locked away from him. In public he frequently abused his wife Caroline, but always returned to her from his mistresses. In a passage whose "dreadful humour" and "grotesque horror" (said Thackeray) "surpasses all satire" the courtier and gossip Hervey tells how, at her last illness in 1737, George was overcome with simultaneous exasperation at her being ill and remorse at her steadfast tenderness towards him. The dying Queen tried to get him to promise to marry again. Moved, tearful, and tactless as ever, George II stammered out, "Non, j'aurai des maîtresses." "Ah," murmured the philosophical Queen, "Mon Dieu! cela n'empêche pas." For years George had relied on her absolutely; and luckily for Walpole he had become used to taking her advice.

Most men assumed in 1727 that with the old King's death Walpole was finished. George, as Prince of Wales, had already described Walpole in public as an "impertinent fool" and his brother Horatio as a "dirty buffoon". In any case, it was hardly to be considered that George would employ the Minister of so hated a parent, and George II added to this impression by a first, and typically peremptory, instruction to Walpole to take his orders from a certain Sir Spencer Compton, the Speaker of the House. Walpole, however, had a friend in the new Queen, who had always relished his salty company and perceived his abilities. Many thought that Mrs Howard, the new King's mistress, was the lady through whom to seek his favour. Walpole was fond of congratulating himself that he made no such mistake. His old investment in Caroline's friendship now paid off: in his own words, he had "taken the right sow by the ear." As usual, Caroline's advice conquered: George was soon closeted with Walpole, who proceeded to play his trump card. He proposed that the King's provision in the Civil List should be raised to the record sum of £800,000 (with various further perquisites) and the Queen's to £100,000; and George and Caroline may well have judged that only a Walpole would be likely to succeed in persuading the Commons to agree to such a sum. Sir Spencer Compton was soon forgotten (Walpole prudently bestowed on him the lucrative post of Paymaster-General); Bolingbroke, Pulteney, and the other leaders of the anti-Walpole opposition were, for the time being, brushed aside. Suitable pensions and places were found for those who had been the cronies and henchmen of the new King in his old Leicester House days; and Walpole remained at the centre of the web of power. As the years passed, George came to rely on him, to trust him, and to give him steady support, at least as long as Caroline lived. After her death (1737) George's whims and ambitions grew less easy to weather, the occasions upon which Walpole had to submit more numerous. For he was never likely to forget that the whole increasingly unpopular structure of his power rested on royal support, and on the ability it gave him to control the royal patronage.

4. Dispensation of Patronage

This power of patronage extended over the whole field of public life. In Chapter 2 we have seen how it affected parliamentary elections, and how the King's Government had scores of seats under its direct or indirect control. Walpole immersed himself in the minutest details of this parliamentary manipulation, and after 1724 had the co-operation of Newcastle, who became its arch-specialist. Their agents were everywhere. Hard money was spent in bribes and pensions; the loyalty of great local families was expertly assessed and continuously buttressed at sensitive points. The enemies' bribes were warily explored and then economically outbid. "Every town," wrote Walpole's agent in Devon and Cornwall before the election of 1727, "has been tampered with ... and this I believe, if you don't send money here beforehand, you may miss your views in more towns than one." In particular, many of the Scottish Members of Parliament, both lords and commoners, were simply his hirelings, receiving a salary from Walpole out of the Secret Service funds that he controlled. In 1721, for instance, the following Scots members, among others, had their Whig loyalties reinforced by direct bribes: the Earl of Hopetoun (£3000), the Earl of Leven (£2000), the Earl of Orkney (£2000), the Earl of Loudon (£1000), the Hon. Mr Ross (£2000), the Earl of Marchmont (£1000), Lord Polwarth (£1000), Robert Sinclair, John Scot, John Hay, John Kerr (£1000 each).

Another extensive domain over which Walpole could exert authority was that of Church appointments. Seldom was the Church of England so unprotestingly subject to political control as in the early eighteenth century. "All these men have their price", Walpole is supposed to have said of his fellow members in the House of Commons; but the price did not lie necessarily in direct payment. Often a deanery for a younger brother, an archdeaconry for a cousin, a prebend for a nephew, might be the member's reward for steady attendance in the Government lobby at Westminster. The bait of a snug canonry for a dependant might well keep warm a tepid vote. As for bishops, never were they so obediently Whig. Here, it must be said, luck was again with Walpole. No sooner had his principal political rivals died off (by 1722) than the mortality of bishops too began to show a steep and providential rise. Within six months in 1723, five bishops died and a sixth, Atterbury, was banished; they were all replaced by safe Walpole nominees. Since, however, both Archbishops were Tory and stubbornly retentive of life, Walpole and Townshend proceeded to promote Gibson, the Bishop of Lincoln, to the diocese of London, where he became the Ministry's official adviser on Church patronage. He attempted, it is true, to use Walpole's backing to advance his own and the Church's interests to a degree that Walpole later found awkward; but for a long time not only bishops (with their vital votes in the House of Lords) but candidates for preferment through the whole hierarchy of clergy, often down to mere parsons, were 'vetted' in political terms.

Then there was a rich sprinkling of ornamental and ceremonial posts, sinecures and near-sinecures carrying salary and prestige, that lay within the gift of the Crown—that is very largely to say, of Walpole and his fellow-Whigs. From the start Walpole packed his friends and supporters into these as fast as he could, and altogether shamelessly. In 1721, on his promotion to First Lord of the Treasury, his cousins, allies, and dependants suddenly and happily found themselves occupying such positions as Clerk of the Cofferer of the Household, Inspector of the Treasure and Teller Vouchers, Collector of the Port of London, Chamber Keeper of the Treasury, Treasurer of Greenwich Hospital, and Usher of the Receipt. When, in 1727, George II, succeeding to the throne, maintained Walpole in power against the general expectation, George's friends and hangers-on of his Prince of Wales days—the Leicester House set—had to be rewarded and, if possible, sweetened. There were always obscure offices in the royal household to be dispensed, but always with shrewd conservatism and calculation. All men had their price, but there must never be overpayment or squandering of prizes. At that moment in 1727 even the Twickenham set, the poets, intellectuals, and scribblers who had lampooned Walpole and his "Robinocracy" so bitterly, and were soon to redouble their attacks, came in for some crumbs—of bait rather than reward. Even the great and bitter Swift himself visited him, perhaps in hope of preferment to an *English* deanery; and the poet Gay was glad to accept, amid some amusement, the post of Gentleman Usher to the Princess Louisa, aged two.

Commissions in the Army and business contracts provided two further areas where rewards could be related to services rendered to the King's Government. There were honours, too, to be dispensed to the deserving. New creations within the peerage were rare at this time, though Walpole managed, characteristically, to secure a barony for his eldest son, Robert. Knowing, too, the political value of a fund of high and glamorous decorations, he persuaded George I to revive the Order of the Bath. (Indeed, he himself received it and revelled in it; and a little later his own naïve pleasure in ostentation and display gained greater scope still in the award of the Garter, a rare and signal honour for a commoner.) There were, again, a number of official posts to be considered in the Civil Service. The Government's civilian servants were few in those days compared with today's hundreds of thousands; these posts were eagerly sought and carefully assigned with the fullest consideration of political services and loyalties. In an age when the total number employed in the offices of George I's two Secretaries of State totalled only about two dozen, not only could every official be known to his chief, but the allocation of every post could be made to count. Even the Treasury, a much bigger office, was not so big that its staff could not be known individually to the man at its head.

In all this management of patronage Walpole brooked no rival. Newcastle, it is true, did a great deal of its administration and became a master of its detail; his letters, largely occupied with it, eventually filled 800 folio volumes. Over the dinner-table at Orford House Walpole would discuss with Newcastle and his brother Henry Pelham, and (until 1730) with Townshend, the intricacies of the game; they would balance Commons votes against available places, men against the price to be paid for them; but it was Walpole who carried the final decision. One after another the Whigs who challenged him were outmanœuvred and ousted—Carteret, Pulteney, Townshend, Chesterfield, Cobham; more and more, the men around him became complaisant figures, minor administrators, or fellow beneficiaries of the "Robinocracy". And in order to maintain his ascendancy he was almost as assiduous in matters of detail as Newcastle himself. Nothing was too trivial. An under-clerkship in the Treasury was, however humble, a counter, perhaps, in the political game. The appointment of a collector of customs was not too inconsiderable for his attention even in the midst of grave issues of European policy. There are many stories of Walpole's love of hunting, of how he always opened first the letters from his gamekeeper, of his vast eating and drinking, his reckless extravagance in making Houghton into a palace, his freedom with women, his coarse ostentation. It is all less than half the truth. The secret of his strength lay in his tireless industry and attention to detail. He was often up by six o'clock attending to correspondence; normally he was at the Treasury by eight; he attended parliamentary sessions far more punctiliously than a modern Prime Minister (though, of course, the sessions themselves were shorter). The scope, as well as the bulk, of his correspondence was enormous: the expenses of an election in Cornwall, the fortunes of the woollen trade in Norwich, the promotion of a captain in the Guards, the gossip of the diplomatists in Paris— a thousand varying matters, great and small, and some of them apparently tiny, filled his days. Sometimes his great frame groaned under a combined load of worry, self-indulgence, and work. His mastery of petty facts was as great as his passion for power. Indeed, it was the former that made possible for so long the gratification of the latter.

One effect of Walpole's devotion to the techniques of place management was that, during his time and long after it, never a useless post, never an archaic survival, was abolished. The more places there were to fill, the more practicable became the prolongation of his power even amidst unpopularity. Efficiency, indeed, he sought; but not reforms that would undermine the foundation of his stable edifice. Besides, as J. H. Plumb (the greatest of modern authorities on this subject) writes:

> Deeply rooted in Walpole was the belief that men had a prescriptive right to rewards from the institution they served. It was as natural for him to establish generations of Popples in the Board of Trade, and Cardonnels in the Salt Office as to give places for life to his own children. Loyalty, the prescriptive right of birth, weighed more with him in the end than efficiency.

5. Economic and Financial Policy

Walpole, as he himself remarked, was "no reformer". In general, he both accepted the moral standards of his day, public and private, and also followed its political and economic assumptions. His trade and colonial policies were in no sense revolutionary. Without being in any way a free-trade theorist, he reduced export duties over a wide range of goods, and import duties on those raw materials necessary for British manufacturers; his aims were to increase the total volume of business and to promote a favourable balance of trade. He gave bounties to home industries requiring support against foreign competition, such as sugar-refining and silk manufacture. He provided bounties, too, for grain exporters, to satisfy the special claims of the farmers and landowners. He maintained the Navigation Acts to safeguard and increase British shipping, although he did not always manage to enforce them strictly. Like all his contemporaries, he saw colonies as a source of raw materials for British manufacturers, as well as of naval supplies and such semi-tropical commodities as sugar and tobacco. Colonial or Irish manufactures were heavily discouraged or banned altogether. Thus, from 1732, Americans were encouraged to send beaver *skins* to Britain, but forbidden to send beaver hats: the English hat trade must be protected. The powerful interests of the East India and South Sea Companies, and of the West Indian, Baltic, and Levant merchants, were respected, if not from conviction, then from the necessity of considering their parliamentary voting power—normally from a combination of both these motives. Although Walpole fell foul of the shopkeepers, artisans, and smaller merchants, it may be said in general that he held the balance between the mercantile, manufacturing, and landed interests.

Certainly during his years of office the country grew richer. Both the standard of living and the level of real wages (*i.e.*, wages in relation to prices) showed a rise. Fresh meat began to be eaten by the peasantry to supplement their salt beef, and wheaten loaf supplied, for the first time, perhaps one-third of their bread-stuff. Under the stimulus of the export bounty

England became one of the granaries of Europe. General exports rose by 43 per cent in value, imports by 20 per cent; the balance of trade (excess of exports over imports) by 244 per cent. All this does not necessarily mean that the prosperity was brought about by Walpole; much of the expansion might well have proceeded in any case from the innate buoyancy of the British economy. But at least Walpole provided a realistic combination of current practice, sensible adaptation, efficient administration, and expedient concession.

In only one sphere, that of taxation policy, did he attempt large changes; and here, either he was diverted from his original aims or he very largely failed. He tried to reduce the National Debt by means of a Sinking Fund, but was persuaded more and more frequently to raid his own fund and see his original goal recede; and in his excise measures he attempted a large-scale attack on tax evasion, but was forced to withdraw in face of the howl of popular fury provoked by his Excise Bill of 1733.

The general alarm shown by Georgian public opinion at the rapid rise of the National Debt has already been noticed.[2] Walpole had been, in Stanhope's day, an enthusiastic supporter of debt redemption, and was, with Stanhope, a main architect of the original Sinking Fund scheme of 1717: a scheme by which "monies arising from time to time" (that is, sundry receipts from taxation) were to be put aside to build up a fund for eventually extinguishing the National Debt. In 1721, after the disasters of the Bubble, Walpole returned to the Sinking Fund. In general it was found to have a reassuring effect on the investing public's psychology: men felt that eventually the National Debt would be paid off, and that national bankruptcy was improbable. Yet this confidence had a paradoxical result: it encouraged investment in Government loans; in other words, it *increased* the National Debt. And however much one paid lip-service to the basic idea of a Sinking Fund, receipt of a comfortable income from Government securities was very heart-warming. Thus one came to hope

[2] See Chapter 3, Section 6.

that the National Debt would be abolished, but not just yet. Walpole, therefore, concentrated rather on reducing the rate of interest on the securities (and on reducing too the burden of taxation) than upon extinguishing the securities themselves. With trade good and financial credit restored during the twenties, foreign financiers invested heavily in London stock. The Dutch alone held ten million pounds-worth, and Walpole's Government had no inclination to discourage such foreign funds; indeed, one is not surprised to learn that the daughter of one of the leading Dutch bankers, van Neck, married into Walpole's family. The Sinking Fund continued and indeed flourished with the greater tax yields resulting from prospering trade; but Walpole, instead of gratefully pouncing on this money to redeem the Debt according to his original intention, raided it for ordinary revenue purposes, in order to keep down the land tax. He did this in 1727 and in 1733, and it grew to be a habit. Many times his enemies, and especially Pulteney, attacked him for "the Sinking Fund fraud". In a sense it *was* a fraud; but it was rather a case of the nation deceiving itself than of Walpole deceiving it. In any case, a fully applied Sinking Fund could have eaten into the Debt only by a flea-bite. Every new national war for the past two and a half centuries has sent it rocketing skyward, until it now stands hundreds of times as high as it stood in Walpole's day. If indeed a high Debt was a bad thing Walpole's greatest contribution to keeping it within bounds lay, not so much in his erratically pursued Sinking Fund, as in his consistently pursued policy of peace.

One aim that Walpole did pursue with a faithful consistency was low taxation, and in particular a low land tax. Of the major forms of wealth in the eighteenth century, land was the most easily taxable; concealment of ownership was all but impossible; collection was relatively easy. Similar considerations recommended the two shilling house tax to Governments, with its additional levy according to the number of windows. Income tax, the core of the modern system, lay far in the future ahead of Walpole's England. It was land tax and national loans that had borne the brunt of the wars against Louis XIV; they had caused the intense unpopularity among landowners of "King William's war" and the wars of Marlborough in their later phase, when it seemed to the English squires that they were being asked to subsidize the inordinate personal ambitions of Marlborough himself and the greed of moneylenders and war contractors. Sir Robert Walpole was always and essentially an English squire. In his early days, before the loot of office rolled in and Houghton was expanded into a miniature Versailles, he had known what it was to be saddled with debt and burdened with taxation. The policy of keeping the land taxes down, therefore, was instinctive with him, and it was part of the secret of his continued hold over the Commons; for the Commons was full of squires like himself, whether they called themselves Whig, Tory, or independent. The mere contrivance of patronage, important as it was, could not have held loyal for ever the votes of men whose pockets were pillaged by governmental policy. The squires grumbled about the land tax; Walpole himself argued that it fell harshly on a small section of the community, and particularly upon the smaller gentry: "The Land Tax falls on 400,000 out of 8 millions", he wrote in 1732. "Since 1688, they have paid £65,000,000. Great towns and moneyed men pay little or nothing." He preferred other taxes, such as that upon salt, that hit all classes alike, poor as well as rich. Walpole would not have been impressed by the modern argument that the poor should be sheltered from the full blast of taxation. He believed that the poor ought to be taxed. For one thing, there were *more* poor than rich; for another, the necessity to find money to pay taxes discouraged idlers. But his greatest desire was to find means of exacting their full share of the load from the rich merchants, and it was this desire (as we shall see) that was a powerful factor in drawing him eventually towards the extension of the excise.

Since in general the trading and manufacturing classes did well in early Hanoverian times, and since Walpole and prosperity are thought of as almost synonymous, it is sometimes assumed that the merchants, as a class, favoured Walpole. After all, it is assumed, Walpole was a Whig, and the merchants were Whig in sympathy. But 'Whig' is an expression of considerable elasticity. Some of the most savage attacks on

Walpole came from Whigs; and among his enemies he always counted many of the mercantile interests and, above all, the City of London.

Conscious of their independence, their riches, their traditions, and their power, the City Fathers of London bitterly opposed Walpole in the years of 1722 and 1724, and again a decade later. The City sheriffs and aldermen were elected on far too democratic a franchise for Walpole's liking; many of the common artisans, traditionally Tory in sentiment, had a vote, and it was all too easy to have the City controlled by men who were either Tories, or Whigs violently hostile to Walpole. So unfriendly, indeed, was London that Walpole and Townshend promoted an Act in 1724 for securing "the government of that important place entirely in the hands of those who are zealous for your Majesty's interest"; but the next decade showed how slight was their success. It was London merchants and mobs that were loudest in the attacks on the corrupt "Robinocracy". It was they who shouted most violently for a war of colonial aggression, for revenge on the Spanish coastguards who maltreated honest English merchant captains. They eventually had their way with the wars too; and in Pitt they eventually found their hero. Walpole's relations with the great moneyed companies, such as the East India and South Sea Companies, and with the Bank of England, were, by contrast, remarkably good. These great financiers and wealthiest merchants were indeed props of the Walpole regime, as he was of theirs. It was the lesser merchants, and in particular the Common Councillors of London, who constantly opposed him. In particular it was they who won the great battle of 1733 against his proposed excise on wine and tobacco.

If the rate of taxation was to be kept low the taxes themselves must be efficiently gathered and evasion made difficult. The trouble in Georgian Britain was that evasion was practically a national industry. The whole country was to some extent dependent on the smuggler. Every stretch of coast, every stretch of river near the sea, had its adventurous and profitable traffic, in tea, in brandy, in wine, in tobacco, in silks, in every import that was subject to heavy customs duty. Tens of thousands were engaged in the trade, which brought profit, adventure, and danger to the smugglers themselves, and softened the harshness of life for many of their customers among the common people, few of whom could have afforded tea, spirits, or tobacco legally purchased. Rich and poor alike bought smuggled goods without any sense of guilt. In earlier days, when he was Secretary-at-War in Anne's reign, Walpole himself smuggled his own linen and brandy over the Norfolk coast and ran his own wines up the Thames. Later, when he was at the Treasury, he used to receive letters from his old mother explaining with the most open pleasure how she had managed to get her little cargoes past the Norfolk coastguards and customs officials, and even himself received contraband lace from Holland. This, however, did not prevent him from passing ever more severe measures against smugglers, including one in 1726 imposing the death penalty for those caught with blackened faces. The severity of the penalties against the relatively few offenders who were caught and punished for an activity with which public opinion sympathized roused popular anger and resentment. Every man's hand was against the revenue men; any story was believed against them. They were accused of physical violence, false witness against law-abiding shopkeepers, and rapacity in demanding bribes for turning a blind eye.

However Walpole the private individual thought or acted, Walpole as First Lord of the Treasury was determined to tighten the net by every practicable means, and win back for the nation's balances the millions of pounds of revenue escaping in the general fraud. Petty smuggling was best dealt with by the fear of harsh punishments; but the large tax evasions of the shopkeepers and merchants could be best dealt with, he calculated, by a major reform of the practices of the ports and a gradual extension of the excise. He had begun this reform in 1723. In that year he exempted tea, coffee, chocolate, and cocoa from import duties; these commodities were to be taxed only when they were taken out of store for domestic sale.[3] If a merchant imported tea for re-export elsewhere, no tax was payable; when a shopkeeper offered tea for sale in Britain,

[3] A customs duty is levied on goods arriving at the ports, an excise on their being taken for sale inside the country.

however, he could be made to produce a document certifying tax paid. Thus the attractiveness of smuggling and the chance of openly selling smuggled goods were alike diminished. Tax administration was simplified; tax yields on these four excised commodities had increased within seven years—and despite Walpole's lowering of the duties—by £120,000 a year. The innovation was a conspicuous success, and, therefore, conspicuously unpopular.

Smuggling, of course, still continued on a vast scale, often under the skilful organization of 'big fish' in London and elsewhere. With it went crime and violence on a large scale—beating-up of customs men, bribery, fraud, perjury, manslaughter, murder. A parliamentary committee of 1732 found a mountain of evidence too enormous fully to proceed with. But they reckoned the Port of London alone to be losing £100,000 a year. The 28,000 pounds of tea seized annually throughout the country, or the 70,000 gallons of brandy, represented only a small fraction of the volume successfully dodging the law. And the emphasis that the report laid on the huge losses of duty on tobacco and wine gave a strong hint of what Walpole planned to do. He would extend his excise device to those commodities too, and thus turn the tables on those merchants who had been crying fraud and corruption against him for over a decade. He would at the same time enrich the revenue, defeat the smuggler, and lighten the load on the hard-pressed squire. It might well be that he could abolish the land tax altogether.

Throughout the winter of 1732–33 the opposition developed their attack on the proposal. The tobacco excise that Walpole was about to introduce, they declared, was only the preliminary to a general excise. The Englishman's freedom was in danger. Honest citizens would be in perpetual danger from brutal excisemen, swollen in numbers by the new measure. No shopkeeper's wife would ever be safe from the monsters. No fair trial could ever be expected from the summary courts of the commissioners. Before it had finished, the Government would destroy the jury system and introduce a despotism as severe as that suffered by the wretched French. The wealth that would roll in to the Crown would be used in the fullness of time to destroy Parliament itself. Indeed, excise, declared all the opposition newspapers, pamphlets, ballads, and broadsheets, was essentially tyrannical and un-British; Pulteney referred in Parliament to "that monster, the Excise, that plan of arbitrary power". The honest Englishman, it was widely put about, would end up wearing wooden clogs like a benighted Frenchman. Hence the famous warning slogan of the anti-excise crowds: "Excise, Wooden Shoes, and No Jury." It was not difficult for the London merchants to whip up a frenzy among mobs always ready for a beery fracas, but also genuinely hating the vile reputation, real as well as imagined, of the excise officials. Every wall sprouted its anti-Walpole handbill. The most famous of them shows the hated Minister in his coach being drawn by a dragon with its long neck bent back to spew a rain of golden guineas into his lap. The song below the illustration was the top 'hit' of 1733:

> See this Dragon, EXCISE,
> Has Ten Thousand Eyes,
> And Five Thousand Mouths to devour us,
> A Sting and sharp Claws,
> With wide-gaping Jaws,
> And a Belly as big as a Store-house.

Anti-Catholic and anti-French prejudices came readily to hand:

> This Monster, Plague rot him,
> The Pope first begot him,
> From Rome to King *Lewis* he went;
> From a Papist so true,
> What good can ensue?
> No wonder he'll make you keep *Lent*.

And the Monster would not stop at tobacco. Sugar and wine would follow:

> Grant these, and the Glutton
> Will roar out for Mutton,
> Your Beef, Bread and Bacon to boot;
> Your Goose, Pig and Pullet
> He'll thrust down his Gullet,
> Whilst the Labourer munches a Root.

These and seventeen further verses all ended with the chorus that painted the gaunt prospect in rollicking rhyme:

> *Horse, Foot and Dragons*
> *Battalions, Platoons,*
> *Excise, Wooden Shoes and No Jury,*
> *Then Taxes increasing*
> *While Traffic is ceasing*
> *Would put all the Land in a Fury.*

Walpole had brazened out many previous storms, and was confident that his resources were equal to this one too. The Court was solid behind him: "He is a brave fellow," said George II; "he had more spirit than any man I ever knew." His henchmen in the Commons were well lobbied. His mastery of detailed evidence and cogent arguments was never finer. The Duke of Newcastle was as confident as Walpole himself: "Excise will be the grand affair", he wrote, ". . . and will certainly be carried by a great majority in both houses." But Newcastle was wrong. Gradually it came to be understood by Walpole, as his majority in the Commons sank first to 56, then to 16, that both there and, worse still, in the Lords, where even his faithful bishops wavered, he might be defeated. Former supporters of his, men close to the King, defected, and he saw the chasm beginning to open before him. Howling mobs, a popular campaign of hatred, the scurrility of Opposition journalists—these things he was accustomed to and could brush off; but a possible parliamentary defeat and the withdrawal of George's support—these would be final disasters. He forced home a last nominal victory over the City of London by insisting that the Commons reject its petition against excise; but then, in Downing Street, "after supper [as Hervey reports] when the servants had gone, Sir Robert opened his intentions with a sort of unpleased smile". He said, "This dance it will no further go, and tomorrow I intend to sound a retreat." The next day he withdrew the Excise Bill, and afterwards was manhandled by an angry mob. The news spreading, London celebrated its victory with liquor, bonfires, and fireworks; effigies of Walpole and Queen Caroline were burned in the streets; and riots were such that Walpole was able to save a little from the political wreck by forcing even the leaders of the parliamentary Opposition, Pulteney, Barnard, and Wyndham, to join him in reducing tension and promoting good order again.

6. Walpole and his Critics

Walpole had made a tactical withdrawal; but he was all the more determined to assert his supremacy within the Cabinet and in the King's Closet. He must strike hard or have his position undermined; and soon he had the satisfaction of persuading George II to dismiss some of his most powerful critics: the Earl of Chesterfield, the Earl of Burlington, Lord Clinton, the Duke of Montrose, the Earl of Stair, Lord Marchmont, Lord Cobham, and the Duke of Bolton. Of these, though Chesterfield—wit, man of fashion, dilettante, and cynic—is the most famous, Cobham was probably the most important. His family—that of the Temples—was allied in marriage to the Grenvilles, the Lytteltons, and the Pitts; and his great house at Stowe became a notable political centre for dissident Whigs, especially of the younger generation—"Cobham's Cubs", ridiculed by Walpole as the "Boy Patriots". Yet Walpole and Newcastle rode out the storms of 1733 and managed, by hard playing of the game of patronage, to come through the election of 1734 with a loyal majority of fifty or so. Their electoral success at last persuaded Bolingbroke to take no further direct part in British politics. He retired to France again, to devote himself to history and to the writing of his *Idea of a Patriot King* (1749).

For eight years Bolingbroke had been at the heart of one of the angriest and most gifted oppositions in English political history. It had numbered among its ranks Jonathan Swift, whose mordant genius, in 1726, had given the world *Gulliver's Travels*, that fiercest of satires upon the political world of his day, and, indeed, upon mankind in general. Others of Bolingbroke's circle carried lighter armament than Swift, but maintained for years a rapid fire of witty and wounding ridicule of this 'Prime' Minister, with his paunch and his pocket-lining, his family hangers-on, his great mansion at Houghton swelling on swindled gains. Sometimes the attacks were agile and witty (Pope, Gay, and Arbuthnot were among the Tory satirists and pamphleteers); sometimes they were coarse and bludgeoning. The journal that was at the heart of this opposition was Bolingbroke's *Craftsman*, founded in 1726, and its theme, unendingly repeated over the next ten years, was that an unprincipled politician was ramming home an unpopular and unpatriotic policy by means of crude corruption. "Corruption", moralized the *Craftsman* during the election of 1727, "is a poison, which will soon spread itself thro' all ranks and orders of men; especially when it begins at the fountain head." The *Craftsman* was not always so measured; on another occasion, for instance, it portrayed Walpole, in the scarcely veiled language of fiction, as a bluff ruffian, "with a smile, or rather a snear" sitting on his face and "an arch malignity" leering in his eye:

> They no sooner saw him, but they all turned their faces from the canopy and fell prostrate before him. He trod on their backs, without any ceremony, and marched directly up to the Throne. He opened his Purse of Gold which he took out in handfuls and scattered among the assembly. While the greater part were engaged in scrambling for these pieces, he seized, to my inexpressible surprise, without the least fear, upon the sacred *Parchment* itself. He rumpled it unduly up and crammed it into his pocket. Some of the people began to murmur. He threw more gold, and they were pacified.

Thus Bolingbroke pictured Walpole pocketing the very Constitution itself and trampling on the rights of the people. (That particular attack of 1727 succeeded in so infuriating Walpole that he caused the editor, Amhurst, and the printer to be arrested, although the case against them proved too flimsy to proceed with.) Part at least of the brilliant success of John Gay's *Beggar's Opera* (1728) sprang from its scarcely veiled allusions to Walpole. The highwayman, "Robin of Bagshot, *alias* Gorgon, *alias* Bluff Bob, *alias* Carbuncle, *alias* Bob Booty" could hardly be intended for anyone else; and when he sang

> How happy could I be with either
> Were t'other dear charmer away,

nobody failed to catch the allusion to Walpole, his wife, and his mistress Molly Skerrett. When Gay followed up *The Beggar's Opera* with *Polly*, in which a character called Ducat (again plainly intended for Walpole) buys the heroine for his amusement, the Lord Chamberlain, acting for Walpole, stepped in and banned the show. Following the incident, Gay's friend, the Duchess of Queensberry, violently insulted the King himself and was banished from the Court, amid general sensation. As the years proceeded the clangour grew: insinuations about his relations with Queen Caroline; attacks on his corruption; his megalomania (at Houghton his own bust was ranged beside those of the Roman emperors); his broken first marriage; the rich favours procured for the large army of his own family; his personal coarseness; his corpulence. As J. H. Plumb writes:

> Nothing was too gross for the public; the French ambassador sent the cartoons and caricatures back to amuse Versailles. . . . There he is down on his knees licking the Royal backside or stuffing his breeches full of guineas or brutally treading on the necks of his supplicants.

This was the sort of vilification that reached its deafening climax in the anti-excise campaign of 1733.

Henry St John, Viscount Bolingbroke, is among English history's more brilliant failures. A self-advertised drunkard, lecher, and atheist, he had a quickness of mind and keenness of ambition that early marked him out. As Minister to Queen Anne, he had tried to build up a supreme Tory party as ruthlessly in control of every organ of central or local power as the Whig party was later under Walpole. Disgracing Marlborough, he had concluded peace with France at Utrecht, and was aiming at a complete understanding with her—a policy, incidentally, which the Whigs in general, and Walpole in particular, continued for thirty years. By his action, however, Bolingbroke had convinced George of Hanover that he was a Jacobite and a traitor to his allies. He was thus faced with the certainty that a Hanoverian monarch would dismiss him, and was consequently led, first, to a desperate bid to defeat George's accession and, eventually, to the panicky flight to France des-

cribed in the third chapter of this book. It was a fatal move that
no amount of subsequent contrition could ever quite undo.
Pardoned by George I, but never by Walpole, Bolingbroke
returned from exile in 1723, founded the *Craftsman* in 1726,
and contributed to it tirelessly for a decade under a variety of
pseudonyms. Having been denied his seat in the Lords by
George and Walpole, he was obliged to work principally
behind the scenes as journalist and intriguer. In later years,
and largely under the nineteenth-century influence of Disraeli,
the Tories built up a quite mythical Bolingbroke. The intricate
intriguer and scintillating boon companion was submerged;
the far-sighted philosopher was raised aloft on what proves to
be a cardboard pedestal. Bolingbroke was descried aloft with
his head swathed in visions; he was seen in Disraeli's interpretation principally as the creator of the *Idea of a Patriot
King* (the title of his most famous book): a king wedded to the
welfare of his people, one who would be above parties; who
would destroy the corrupt and antiquated Whig-and-Tory set-
up of his time; who would choose his Ministers from wherever
he wished; who would patriotically and wisely rule in person.
In view of Bolingbroke's own record of corruption and ruthlessness on the Tory behalf in the years before 1714, it is
difficult to believe in the lofty motivation of this philosophy,
which was, in fact, little more than the rationalization of his
one overriding and ever-present aim: to destroy Walpole. All
his venomous wit, his mordant newspaper articles, his lucid
and elegant prose, his dinner-table intrigues, his secret communications with the French, his spurious philosophical
idealism, boiled down to the one thing he longed for and
could not achieve—the overthrow of his hated opponent.
Walpole returned his hatred.

William Pulteney, later first Earl of Bath, was the second
most important member of the opposition to Walpole, and its
chief spokesman in the Commons. Unlike Bolingbroke, he had
once been Walpole's ally and colleague; but his appetite for
money and power was as great as Walpole's own, and no
Government was big enough to contain the two of them. For a
time Walpole tried to buy his support with the Lord Lieutenancy of the East Riding and the highly profitable position of

Cofferer of the Household. It did not work. When Pulteney joined with the Tories in attacking Walpole's financial trickery and personal greed, Walpole secured his dismissal from the Household. He made doubly certain of Pulteney's lifelong hatred: for many years this man was at the heart of the parliamentary onslaught upon Walpole's policies: his pacific foreign policy and what Pulteney alleged to be its weakness, its confusion, and its subordination to the interests of Hanover; the "Sinking Fund fraud"; the salt tax and the excise; the everlasting government-by-bribery. Pulteney was a brilliant and eloquent speaker, a master of financial detail, an implacable opponent. There is a story that, when Walpole fell at last in 1742 and, going to the Lords as Earl of Orford, was followed a few months later by Pulteney, now Earl of Bath, he greeted his ancient rival with the remark: "You and I are now two as insignificant men as any in England." Certainly for twenty years and more their enmity had dominated the Commons, as, later, did that of Fox and the younger Pitt, or that of Gladstone and Disraeli.

Pulteney was a disgruntled Whig: indeed, he claimed to represent true Whiggery, Walpole being a traitor to Whig ideas. Of the Tories in the Commons in the twenties and thirties, Sir William Wyndham was Bolingbroke's principal follower, a man of dignity and an able orator; William Shippen was the leader of the swashbuckling extremists. The Opposition's chief difficulty lay in establishing cohesion; the only basis of their coalition lay in their common hatred of the hated chief Minister. Outside the Commons it was the same story: brilliant and colourful opponents of Walpole abounded, but they rarely became anything more than a miscellany of groups and individuals. In addition to the writers already mentioned, there was the novelist and magistrate Henry Fielding; there was the poet James Thomson; there was the aged and virulent Sarah, Duchess of Marlborough; there was Lord Carteret, whom Walpole had removed to a safe distance (as Lord Lieutenant of Ireland) after the struggle for Whig leadership had gone in Walpole's favour in 1724, but who returned in 1730 to plague his own constitution with a mighty consumption of liquor, and Walpole's Government with a flow of bitter criticism. "It is difficult", wrote Horace Walpole of him, "to say whether he was oftener intoxicated by wine or ambition." There was Frederick, Prince of Wales, who proved a focus for opposition to his father's Ministry, as inevitably as George II himself had proved when Prince of Wales. If George II patronized the great Handel and his operas in the Haymarket or Covent Garden, then perforce Frederick had to take under his wing Bononcini, Handel's now half-forgotten rival, and patronize *his* operas at Lincoln's Inn Fields. Frederick, destined to predecease his father in 1751, tenanted Leicester House, as his father had done in his own days as Prince of Wales, and held there a sort of rival Court to which wits, men of fashion, and ambitious politicians with an eye to the future found it natural to gravitate; among them, significantly, was the twenty-seven-year-old new member for Old Sarum, a cornet of the Horseguards named William Pitt. Horace Walpole judged Frederick to be childish, affected, pretentious, and insincere; his own mother, Caroline of Ansbach, hated him with an unnatural hatred. "If I was to see him in Hell," she said, "I should feel no more for him than for any other rogue that ever went there." His father, George II, loathed him as "a monster and the greatest villain that was ever born". Such were the normal domestic felicities of the Hanoverians.

Walpole in a sense throve on opposition. In the game of politics all men were potential opponents; and although he was not quite so insensitive to criticism as might be imagined of so seasoned an in-fighter (Pulteney, in particular, was capable of goading him to a measured fury), Walpole *was* undoubtedly tough. He hit back. He coaxed and bribed. He dismissed rivals. He clung to the Court. If in the last resort "the dance it would no longer go", he bent before the storm. The last thing he contemplated was resigning for a principle. In 1725 he had bowed before the Irish storm that had been blowing for three years over the patent granted to an ironmaster named Wood to mint copper coins in Ireland. As so often, bribes to the Duchess of Kendal had been involved, and Swift, in his *Drapier's Letters* (1724), had played upon Irish suspicions of a debasement of the coinage to provoke such massive resentment that Walpole had prudently withdrawn the patent and granted Wood a pension to console him. The greatest storm of all had been over the Excise Bill, and Walpole had bowed again. Then in 1736 he again yielded, this time to popular indignation in Edinburgh at the Government's cancellation of the city charter. A certain Captain Porteous had been condemned to death for firing on a rioting crowd at the execution of a popular smuggler. The Government intervened on Porteous's behalf, whereupon the mob again took a hand and lynched him. The charge of weakness was less considerable to Walpole than the chance of disaffected Scotland; Edinburgh's charter was restored. (In 1736 there were riots in London, too, against Walpole's attempt to control gin-drinking. It cannot be said, however, that Walpole retreated in the face of this particular violence; the truth was that his Gin Act, with its punitive raising of the duty, was submerged by the determination of the people, and particularly Londoners, to drink themselves to ruin.) In Walpole's colonial as well as his purely domestic policies there is the same strong vein of bowing to the inevitable: if the colonists of Georgia and Carolina wished to send their rice, and the West Indian merchants their sugar, direct to the ports of Europe without first calling at British ports—well, then, since it was very difficult to enforce the full rigours of the regulations and very easy to incur the colonists' hostility, let them continue to evade the navigation laws. He would be satisfied so long as they used British ships. *Quieta non movere*: let sleeping dogs lie. It may be that he was building up trouble for future, stricter, British Governments; but meanwhile the colonists prospered, and Walpole kept out of trouble.

There were limits to the amount of domestic criticism he was prepared to tolerate. Journalists and pamphleteers, versifiers and ballad-mongers, were allowed a degree of licence which would have astonished an earlier generation, and which strongly impressed continental visitors. "No government", Walpole claimed, "ever punished so few libels, and no government ever had provocation to punish so many." Ever since 1695, when the censorship lapsed, the Press had remained remarkably (many would say dangerously) free. The stage fared differently. When the ex-Quaker merchant Sir John

Barnard introduced a Playhouse Bill whose main object was to limit the number of theatres in London, and thus to defend public morality from the bawdiness that he deplored, Walpole stepped in to support it and extend its scope so that all public stage performances would have to be first licensed by the Lord Chamberlain (1737). In view of Walpole's own tastes, it may be reasonably inferred that his main preoccupation was to stop not so much the licentious plays as the savage political attacks upon himself. We have already seen how he intervened in 1728 to suppress stage performances of Gay's *Polly*. Now he set about transforming Barnard's Bill: all new plays were to be submitted to the Lord Chamberlain a fortnight before the first performance. Failure to comply would mean, first, the loss of the theatre's licence and, second, a fine of £50. Cunning managers sometimes got round the law by charging for a concert and throwing in the play for nothing as an extra; but it is of interest to ponder that this one piece of Walpole's legislation which has lingered on to the present day arose out of his passionate, and by 1737, ever-increasing, need to smother hostile criticism.

That year the Queen died. His principal prop was removed. In the Commons Pulteney, the "Patriot Boys", and the rest stepped up their attacks. Popular indignation at Walpole's apparent meekness in the face of foreign 'provocation', and in particular of the injuries suffered by English sea-captains at the hands of the Spanish coastguards in Latin America, rose to an ever louder and eventually to a deafening pitch. It was this that brought him to his last attempt to weather the storm by bending before it. Since the only way to maintain office in 1739 was to declare war on Spain, he declared war, against his better judgment. War was what he had striven for twenty years to avoid; and now its onset heralded the period of his decline and fall. This, however, takes us into the realm of foreign and colonial affairs, which it will be convenient to consider in a separate chapter.

Chapter 5

Britain, Europe, and the Colonies (1714–50)

1. Early Eighteenth-century Europe

Unquestionably in 1714 France was the greatest of European powers—greatest in military strength, the equal of the Dutch in the arts and sciences, and approaching them in the prosperity of industry and commerce. It had taken the combined power of Britain, the Netherlands, and the Habsburg Empire to challenge the vaulting ambition of Louis XIV, yet France was far from defeated. Nor was she left quite so impoverished by the long wars as has often been suggested. What *was* true about France was that her great wealth was divided among her people with grosser inequality than that of Britain, and many more of her numerous peasantry lived on the verge of starvation. Her political system was more bureaucratic, her finances less adaptable, her society more rigid, her laws more confused, than Britain's. Her monarchy was more extravagant, her aristocracy less useful; privilege and ostentation were more unchecked, the liberty of the individual less jealously preserved, intolerance in religion more fanatically pursued. All these weaknesses, and others, would one day combine to produce the explosion of the French Revolution. But in 1714 France, despite everything, was the hub of Europe. Every Court in Europe looked to Versailles as its great archetype. French styles queened it in painting, in furniture-making, architecture, sculpture, gold and silver ware, fine porcelain, cookery, dancing, tapestry-making—everything that pertained to fashion, to polish, and to style. Every educated European spoke French, often as his first language.

The Treaty of Utrecht had, moreover, left the grandson of Louis XIV on the throne of Spain, to the disgust of many Whigs; and although there were clauses forbidding his

succession to the French throne, the fact of the Bourbon connection on both sides of the Pyrenees was ever present in the
eighteenth century. In 1721 the Infanta of Spain was betrothed
to the young Louis XV, and though this marriage never took
place, later decades brought France and Spain together in a
Family Compact. France's position after 1713 was still immensely strong.

The United Netherlands, Britain's ally in the long wars
against Louis XIV, was also, like France, approaching the close
of its 'grand siècle'. In the seventeenth century Dutchmen had
traded over the world's oceans and in all the European markets. Her fleets had been the carriers of other nations' merchandise. Her ports had waxed prosperous as the depots of
overseas produce destined for trans-shipment throughout
Europe. They teemed with shipping. Her merchants and
bankers prospered as those of no other nation. Her painters,
scientists, and philosophers were second to none in the whole
world. Such a people, commercial, maritime, and Protestant,
was an inevitable ally and an equally inevitable rival of the
English. Resentment was mutual. William III had been constantly criticized in England for sacrificing English interests to
those of Holland; Marlborough was jealously watched by the
Dutch for every sign of a betrayal of Dutch interests. As the long
struggle went on, the sea-protected English had profited by war
while the Netherlands were exhausted and to some extent actually devastated. At Utrecht in 1713 the Dutch, like the Austrians,
considered that the British had deserted them. Increasingly
conservative and defensive in their outlook, they more and more
resented the growing prosperity of their dynamic and faithless
English allies; and certainly the early policies of George I and
his Ministers did a good deal to confirm their feelings.

Spain for her part, by the settlement of Utrecht and by
Rastadt, though she kept the great Spanish American territories, lost the Southern Netherlands (Belgium), Milan, Sardinia, and Southern Italy (Naples) to Austria, and Gibraltar
and Minorca to Britain. She could not accept these humiliations, and her policies over the next few decades would be
directed towards nullifying them. But Spain was declining
rapidly in political power: her Bourbon King Philip V lived on

the edge, and sometimes over the edge, of insanity; her Army, Navy, and finances were alike unequal to the tasks of reconquest. Her relations with Britain during this period would be bedevilled partly by her resentment at the loss of Gibraltar and Minorca, and still more by her resolve to give at least no more away to the British merchants and sailors than they had acquired by treaty in 1713–14—*i.e.*, the right to the monopoly of the West Indies slave trade (the *Asiento des Negros*) up to a maximum of 4800 slaves a year, and to send one ship a year to trade through Porto Bello with Spanish America. On their side, the British traders would consider that they had been swindled by the Utrecht agreement of the just fruits of Marlborough's victories, and would angrily resent the attempts of the Spanish authorities to limit the British in Spanish-American waters to the strict terms of 1713.

Spain's losses in 1713–14 had mostly been Austria's gains—gains, that is, of the Habsburg Emperor, Charles VI, head of an already heterogeneous collection of lands acquired by shrewd marriages and by ancient victories over Hungarians and Turks. Charles was variously described in the eighteenth century as the "German Emperor" (Walpole's appellation), "Emperor of the Romans" (he is so described in the English version of the Barrier Treaty of 1715), or "Holy Roman Emperor". In other words, he was the heir of Charlemagne and liege lord of the various electoral princes of Germany, among them George of Hanover. In 1714 the interests of the Austrian Habsburgs lay in maintaining and extending their hold on Italy, an arena where they were directly challenged by the Spanish Bourbons; in promoting trade from such outposts in the Netherlands as Ostend, where the establishment of an Austrian East India Company infuriated Dutch and English alike; but, above all, in maintaining the integrity of the Habsburg dominions themselves, by gaining the approval of all the European powers to the rightful claim of the Emperor's daughter and heir, the Archduchess Maria Theresa, to the entire Habsburg lands on Charles's own death. For twenty years this determination haunted Austrian diplomacy: the so-called Pragmatic Sanction (*i.e.*, 'Official Decree') sought to gain acceptance by all the European powers of the full legal rights of female inheritance, which was denied by some legal codes. (In a twinkling, on Charles's eventual death in 1740, the whole laborious diplomatic edifice was destined to be blown away by the aggression of Frederick of Prussia.)

In Northern Europe, as our period opens, great changes were being accomplished. The power of Sweden was declining while that of Peter the Great's Russia was growing fast, and in 1714 the Great Northern War, in which they were the principal protagonists, had still another seven years to run. Neither Britain nor Holland was prepared to cede mastery of the Baltic to either the Swedish or the Russian Navy, and for both the Western powers the Baltic trade was vital to supply their naval needs. It must be remembered, too, that George I was also Elector of Hanover, a North German power with ambitions to acquire Sweden's territories round Bremen and Verden at the mouth of the Elbe. As for Prussia (Brandenburg), that small state with so big a future, it was polishing its weapons. The obsessed soldier-king, Frederick William I, was combing Europe for his giant Pomeranian Grenadiers, turning his Court into a barracks, and tyrannizing over his artistic young son, Frederick, who was to inherit his father's Army and turn all Europe upside down.

Poland in 1714 was a very large but basically very weak state, dominated by its unruly aristocracy, who elected their king, oppressed their feudal peasantry, and enjoyed a Constitution which allowed a single hostile vote to block all legislation and permitted a built-in right to inaugurate civil war. Unprotected by any natural barriers such as sea, river, or mountain, it was virtually indefensible, and this combination of political and geographical weakness was later in the century to offer a standing invitation to its powerful neighbours to engulf it.

Russia (the hungriest and largest of these neighbours) was in 1714 a new phenomenon in Europe. Until the reign of Peter the Great (1689–1725) she was to the West a distant and barbaric land, of which next to nothing was known; and when embassies from Moscow visited Paris, The Hague, or London, they were objects of legitimate curiosity. As Pepys wrote, "Not a man that speaks Latin, unless the Secretary of State by chance." Peter had altered all that. He had tried to pitchfork

Russia into Europe. His armies had destroyed the Swedes and threatened the Turks. He had rifled western Europe for ideas and for craftsmen to build a more "contemporary" Russia. His new capital St Petersburg, built on the Neva and a not inconsiderable number of his subjects' corpses, symbolized his work and its challenge to the lands of the West and North. The days of independent Poland and conquering Sweden were numbered. The northern Europe of the new giants, Russia and Prussia, was about to be built over their ruins.

2. Foreign Policy of George I and Stanhope

The Whigs, when they returned to power in 1714, naturally turned again to the old policy of alliance with Holland and Austria which had been the core of the coalition against Louis XIV. The Barrier Treaty of November 1715, signed by Britain, Holland, and Austria, guaranteed the cession of the Southern Netherlands to Austria and maintenance of existing Anglo-Dutch commercial and shipping rights, and agreed that an Austro-Dutch army of 30,000 to 35,000 should provide a garrison there against any future French incursion. The whole temper and intention of the treaty was anti-French. That same year, however, Louis XIV died, and the picture of Western Europe was suddenly changed. The great Louis was dead; his great-grandson, Louis XV, was a sickly lad for whom many predicted an early death; and the affairs of France were effectively in the hands of a Regent, the Duke of Orleans. The fact that the French Regent had an interest in the maintenance of the Utrecht settlement[1] put him in the same boat as the British

---

[1] Summary of the principal terms of the *Treaties* of *Utrecht, Rastadt,* and *Baden* (1713–14) and the *Barrier Treaty* (1715):

Spain and Spanish America to be ruled by Philip V, grandson of Louis XIV.

French and Spanish thrones not to be united.

Southern Netherlands (Belgium) to pass from Spain to Austria.

Seven Barrier fortresses near Franco-Belgian frontier to be manned by the Dutch against possible future French aggression.

Joint Austro-Dutch troops to guard the rest of the Southern Netherlands.

Sicily to the Duke of Savoy: a reward for services to the Grand Alliance. (Sicily was later exchanged for Sardinia.)

Gibraltar and Minorca to be retained by Britain.

and Dutch Governments; for, if the young King of France were
to die the Regent's only possible rival for the succession would
be Philip V of Spain (Louis XIV's grandson), whose right to the
Spanish throne had been confirmed by the Utrecht treaty, but
who had been barred for ever from succeeding to the throne
of France. Thus suddenly came about an *entente* between
Britain and France, which incidentally proved disastrous for
the Old Pretender. Britain, France, and Holland signed the
Triple Alliance of 1717; and for twenty years or so, until the
decline of Walpole, a close understanding with France became
an essential part of Britain's foreign policy. These are twenty
years of exception to the general rule of the eighteenth century:
at any other time between 1688 and 1815 a cardinal principle
of European politics is that Britain and France are on opposite
sides of the fence.

Of George I's Whig Ministers, it was Stanhope who (under
the King) carried the main responsibility for foreign policy.
George and Stanhope were the more ready to come to an
understanding with France (Austria's ancient enemy) since
George was particularly angry at the treatment he was receiving from the Emperor. In general, the Emperor was unwilling
to guarantee the Hanoverian succession; more particularly, he
was stalling on the question nearest to George's heart, the
recognition of his title to the bishoprics of Bremen and Verden.
This would help to destroy the Swedish hold on North German
territory. But in these ambitions George received no encouragement from the Emperor, and his relations with Prussia, Holland,
and Denmark (all hostile to Sweden) were full of mutual suspicion. In theory it was only the Elector of Hanover who from
1715 was at war with Sweden, not the King of England; and
it was fortunate for George that the interests of British merchants and shipbuilders, to whom the Baltic supplies of naval
stores and timber were vital, happened to be in harmony with
his own dynastic aims. If it had not been so, George and his
Ministers would certainly not have been able to extract sup-

British traders to have monopoly of West Indian slave trade, and the
right to send one ship a year to trade with Spanish America.
    France acknowledged British ownership of Nova Scotia (Acadia)
and Newfoundland.

plies from the Commons—who would have been on firm
ground, too, for the Act of Settlement of 1701 specifically forbade British resources to be used for purely Hanoverian ends.
But orders were now given to the British Navy under Sir
George Byng "to attack the Swedish ships wherever he meets
with them" and also "to seize all vessels which come out of any
of the ports of Sweden". The Dutch, to whom the Baltic trade
was equally important, did not make up their minds to co-
operate in time. They felt further affronted, and their trade
suffered again in comparison with that of the English.

The Swedes retaliated by intensifying the support they were
already offering secretly to the Jacobites. In 1718, however,
the "Swedish meteor", Charles XII, died, and the Swedes,
their power shrunken and their resources dwindling, began to
look towards a settlement with their many enemies—Russia,
Poland, Prussia, Denmark, and Hanover–Britain. The aims of
George I and Stanhope now became more complicated: first,
to secure a joint front with Prussia to negotiate with a more
friendly Sweden than before, with the end of securing the
Elbe estuary (Bremen and Verden) for Hanover, and Stettin
and Pomerania for Prussia; second, to prevent a victorious
Russia from gaining too complete a mastery of the Baltic, both
on land and at sea. When Carteret arrived in Stockholm to
present the joint Prusso-Hanoverian demands he found
Russian forces raiding deep into Swedish territory, and the
Swedes ready to give almost anything away to the Tsar.
Agreement was therefore reached all the sooner to satisfy the
claims of those two uneasy and jealous partners, the rulers of
Prussia and Hanover. Sweden retired from Northern Germany;
George and Frederick William acquired the coastal territories
that they sought; Carteret and Stanhope had secured a notable
success; and even France, England's new associate, was in-
duced to underwrite the treaty, despite her long-standing
support for Swedish intervention in the affairs of Germany and
the Empire. Peter the Great of Russia, however, continued to
be a thorn in the side of George I. The weighty British warships were not speedy enough to intercept the lighter Russian
ships, and, even though in the long run the British Baltic trade
was not damaged, George and Stanhope were not able to

achieve their immediate undertaking to the Swedes to assist them in rescuing something from the wreck of the long war with Russia. At the eventual Treaty of Nystadt in 1721 that ended this Great Northern War, Peter was able to retain all his Baltic conquests. Russia had in fact succeeded in dominating the Baltic Sea.

In the south of Europe the acutest quarrels centred on Italy. Here, at the end of the War of Spanish Succession, the Kingdom of the 'Two Sicilies' (Naples and Sicily), which had long been Spanish, had been divided. Sicily had been awarded to Savoy, for services rendered in the war, and Austria had taken the province of Naples—*i.e.*, the southern mainland. Nobody was satisfied with this: Charles VI wanted to reunite the provinces under Imperial rule, and Spain aimed at reconquering Sicily. It is, of course, characteristic of the age that nobody yet contemplated the Italians themselves ruling these territories, least of all the Italians. Dynastic considerations, here as elsewhere throughout Europe, were still dominant.

Philip V's second wife was an Italian from Parma, Elizabeth Farnese, a redoubtable woman who was the real ruler of Spain for thirty years. Frederick the Great said of her that she combined "the pride of a Spartan and the stubbornness of an Englishman with Italian finesse and French vivacity"—high praise from a generally severe critic. She humoured her husband's insane whims and nursed him through his sessions of craziness. (He would stand as a target for dishes hurled by the Court dwarfs, or refuse to be shaved for months at a time, or go to bed all day and get up at night, or at one period refuse to go to bed at all for three years.) Elizabeth acted as his secretary and adviser, and dominated his foreign policies. Loathing the Austrian intruders in Italy, she was determined to see her sons (excluded by treaty from the French throne) established as rightful rulers of her native Parma and of neighbouring Tuscany. Until 1719 her chief Minister, too, was from Parma—Alberoni—and, under these two, Spain's Italian policies became strongly aggressive.

Stanhope was anxious for a general pacification of Europe, and attempted, with the co-operation of the Regent Orleans and his Minister Dubois, to secure a compromise by which one of the Farnese princes, Don Carlos, would be granted the succession to Parma and Tuscany, while Austria took Sicily. The Duke of Savoy, who would thus lose Sicily, would be compensated with Sardinia. The Emperor agreed to this arrangement, joined the powers of the Triple Alliance (Britain, France, Holland), and thus converted it to the Quadruple Alliance (1718).

All Stanhope now needed to do was to bring Spain into the general settlement and produce a quintuple alliance of the principal powers; and to this end he himself set out for Spain, old campaigning country to this experienced soldier-diplomat. The Spaniards, however, would have none of the Sicilian settlement. Further, they pressed Stanhope hard for the return of Gibraltar and Minorca, and in fact Stanhope would have been willing to cede these bases in return for general amity. But the jubilant Spanish were not in the mood for reasonableness—their fleet had seized Sardinia from Austria, and by July 1718 had struck at Sicily and landed a garrison there. Stanhope departed unsuccessful from Madrid. Perhaps it was just as well that he did: news did not arrive till just after he had left that a fleet under Sir George Byng, which the British Government had earlier dispatched in the hope of restraining the activities of the powerful Spanish flotilla, had in fact destroyed it off Cape Passaro in Sicily (August 1718). This in turn meant Spanish assistance for Ormonde's Jacobite project of 1719. When Jacobite plans again miscarried, however, Philip and Elizabeth dismissed Alberoni, accepted the Italian settlement proposed earlier, and hoped by their show of reasonableness to hold Stanhope to his promises concerning the return of Gibraltar. The offer, however, was no longer open; even if George and Stanhope had still intended to honour it, the House of Commons would never have permitted such a concession, especially to a power whose 'aggressions' against English merchants abroad were a source of growing complaint. Stanhope died in 1721; George I sought refuge in vague promises that Britain would consider abandoning Gibraltar "at the first favourable opportunity"; and Philip V was left complaining that English ownership of the Rock was "a thorn in his foot".

3. Walpole's European Policies

In the years 1721–24 responsibility for the prosecution of
George I's foreign policy was collectively shared between
Carteret, Townshend, and Walpole. After the disgrace and
relegation of Carteret in 1724, Walpole's general leadership
was recognized, but he was content for some years to leave the
conduct of foreign affairs to Townshend. In the main, Stanhope's policies were not questioned; the alliance with France
was still the king-pin; and the main task was to make effective
the arrangements agreed to in principle by the Quadruple
Alliance, and, after 1720, by Spain as well. The situation, however, was changing all the time. The Emperor Charles VI,
feeling his position to be stronger, especially after he had concluded peace with the Turks (1718), contrived endless delays
in permitting the Farnese prince, Don Carlos, to take over
Parma and Tuscany, and affronted both his Dutch and English
allies by promoting his own overseas trading company at
Ostend with a charter to trade in the Indies, China, and Africa.
Then in 1725 signals of acute alarm were raised both by the
House of Commons and by Townshend himself, when the two
previous arch-enemies, the Spanish Bourbon and the Austrian
Habsburg, negotiated an *entente*, under which Spain accepted
the Pragmatic Sanction (the succession of Maria Theresa on
Charles VI's death) and promised support for the claims of the
Ostend Company, while the Emperor promised a like support
for Spanish claims on Gibraltar and Minorca. Townshend in
particular became belligerently anti-Austrian and busied himself in the attempt to build up an anti-Imperial alliance of
Britain, France, Hanover, Prussia, Holland, Sweden, and, if
possible, Russia. In this diplomatic game he was beaten by the
Emperor, who detached both Prussia and Russia from the
proposed *bloc*. It was at this point that differences between
Walpole and Townshend first grew serious; for Walpole, intent
above all else on keeping the peace, feared that Townshend
was taking a dangerously bellicose anti-Imperial line. As
J. H. Plumb writes:

The credit of England had never been so flourishing. Money was ready and cheap; stocks firm; harvests bumper; taxation low; commerce flourishing.... It was grievous to him that this should be jeopardized by war or threats of war, and his letters to Townshend harp constantly on the need for caution....

The rumblings of these differences grew louder over the next few years, until in 1730 Walpole finally broke with his old ally and brother-in-law and secured his exclusion from the Cabinet. From that year onward it was Walpole alone who was the director of British policy, Harrington and Newcastle, the two Secretaries of State, being carried along in his powerful wake.

In broad outline, Walpole aimed at preserving European peace by negotiating terms with the Emperor, by maintaining the French alliance, and by preventing the commercial rivalries with Spain from assuming warlike postures. In the end he failed in all but the first. From 1726, when the already aged Cardinal Fleury became Louis XV's chief Minister, the French attitude to Britain grew steadily more hostile and her attitude to Spain steadily more friendly. Anglo-French quarrels multiplied: there were disputes over English interlopers in French West Indian trade, over the ownership of West Indian islands, and of forts in French Canada that menaced the security of New England. By 1733 Fleury not only had signed a treaty of neutrality with Britain's old ally Holland, but had secured the Family Compact between the two Bourbon royal houses of France and Spain. It was true that Walpole had kept Britain out of continental wars (apart from a second brush with Spain in 1727, when the Spaniards besieged Gibraltar and a British fleet Porto Bello); but it was also true that British influence on the Continent was smaller in 1733 than it had been in Stanhope's day. As for the Emperor, Walpole soft-pedalled the warlike preparations that preceded Townshend's dismissal, and in 1731 agreed both to the Pragmatic Sanction and to a guarantee of Imperial lands, in return for a similar Imperial guarantee of British possessions and the abolition of the Ostend Company. The 1720 settlement of Parma and Tuscany was finally put into effect; and Don Carlos, escorted by vessels of both Britain and Spain, sailed at last to take up his Italian duchies.

Europe, however, was far from any general settlement: the dynastic chessboard was busy with moves and counter-moves. Poland, in particular, with its elective monarchy, provided plentiful scope for manœuvre; and when in 1733 Augustus II, King of Poland, died, all the great continental dynasties and many of the minor ones busied themselves in intrigues and calculations of advantage attaching to their support for one or other of the main contestants—Stanislas Leszczynski, Louis XV's father-in-law, and Augustus of Saxony, the candidate backed by Russia and Austria. Russia, Austria, and France all mobilized and deployed their armies; and when French bribes prevailed and Stanislas was elected King of Poland, Russian armies chased him out of Warsaw and set up Augustus in his place. Russia was difficult for French armies to attack, but they could present great danger to the Austrian camp in Lorraine, Lombardy, and Sardinia. With Spain inside the Family Compact of the Bourbons, and Holland neutral, the Emperor felt himself dangerously isolated and called on Britain to honour her promises under the 1731 agreement and to come to his aid. George II detested the French—the foxy old Cardinal Fleury, all smooth words and reassurance; his Keeper of the Seals, Chauvelin, who, unlike his master, was at least at no pains to conceal his hostility; and, most of all, the French ambassador in London, Chavigny, a patriotic braggart—and he feared a Franco-Spanish triumph, for this must mean an Anglo-Hanoverian humiliation. Hence, thought the King—and the Queen and many Englishmen thought so too—Britain must fight, for her own honour and in her own interest. But Walpole obstinately persuaded himself to believe what he wanted to believe—that the French were loyal allies. Who cared, thought Walpole, who the new King of Poland was? For Englishmen it was a remote and irrelevant quarrel, and the Opposition's 'patriotism' was compounded of false heroics and miscalculation of the national interest. "I think the circumstances and true interest of England should have such a share in our consideration", he once wrote, "as not to be quite carried away by heroism, unless it was as easy really to conquer and reduce kingdoms as 'tis to magnify our own power in writing and to talk big to one another, to which I wish our swaggering was entirely confined."

Walpole patiently talked the King and Queen out of their conviction that war was wise, arguing the increased Jacobite danger that war would bring, the inevitably unpopular rise in taxation, the risk of losing the 1734 election, after the excise crisis of the previous year; and for another five years he had his way, against the Opposition, sometimes against the King, and increasingly against the judgment of some of his own colleagues, such as Harrington and Newcastle. "Fifty thousand men killed this year in Europe," he said after the outbreak of the War of the Polish Succession, "and not one of them an Englishman." The argument carried force, and must be set against the contrary argument of the war party: that Britain had backed dishonourably out of her treaty obligations and permitted Fleury to weaken Britain's 'natural' European ally, the Emperor, and to consolidate France's alliance with Spain.

4. Anglo-Spanish Trade

It was colonial and commercial issues, rather than continental and dynastic, that at last brought Walpole reluctantly to war. This should not be surprising, for it was always trade that touched "the nation of shopkeepers" in its most sensitive nerve.

The English had long conducted profitable commerce with both Spain itself and the Spanish dominions in the Caribbean. In particular, Spanish America, like the French and British plantations in the West Indies, had an insatiable appetite for slaves; but the Spaniards differed from the French and British in lacking a source of supply of their own. Hence for many decades English merchants of the South Sea Company had been legally transporting Negroes and selling them to Spanish dealers, though sometimes with disappointing profits or actual loss. It had further been officially conceded in the Utrecht treaty that one British ship a year, of up to 500 tons, should be allowed into Porto Bello to trade British goods for sale at the regular Spanish fairs held at Vera Cruz and Cartagena. From the British Government's point of view, the sale of slaves and other commodities to the Spanish colonies was most useful. Payment was in gold and silver, which in turn served to pay for the import of naval stores from the Baltic. The Spaniards both desired the trade and resented it: like all eighteenth-century colonial masters, they clung jealously to the principle of a trade monopoly in their own overseas possessions.

As it happened, the so-called 'annual' British ship licensed to infringe this monopoly was so far from annual that only eight ships reached the fairs over the years between 1717 and 1739. Twice hostilities caused delays of several years, and frequently those vessels that did reach Porto Bello encountered such obstructiveness from ingenious Spanish port officials that, by the time the last regulations were fulfilled, the goods were too late for the fairs. On their side the English captains and merchants resented the dues they had to pay and the rules that harassed them at every turn, and they contrived their own ruses and retaliations. More than once the 'annual' British ship arrived with an accompanying fleet of tenders, so that as fast as the official cargo was dispatched ashore, fresh supplies were taken on board to await unloading. The most serious source of trouble, however, lay not in this official trade but in the scope that the Spanish Caribbean colonies offered for un-official British traders. To the Spaniards these were simply smugglers, for, to the Spaniards, this was indeed the Spanish Main, and the English captains were as much intruders and pirates as Drake and Hawkins in an earlier era. But the English sailors and merchants claimed a general freedom to sail the seas and make money where they could. They recognized no forbidden zones, least of all those maintained by the old papist enemy.

To control the British 'contraband' the Spaniards maintained a fleet of armed 'coastguards', not all of whom were discreet law-abiding officials. Some were themselves little better than pirates, and between them and the English adventurers from Jamaica, Bermuda, and New England a state of permanent small-scale war developed, in which not a few throats were slit on dark nights. As Rear-Admiral Charles Stuart wrote from Jamaican waters, "The sloops that sail from this island on that illicit trade have more than once bragged to me of having murdered seven or eight Spaniards on their own shore." This kind of guerrilla naval war continued for many years, and there was nothing particularly out-of-the-way in the misfortunes of Captain Robert Jenkins, of the *Rebecca*, in 1731. This subsequently notorious martyr was caught by the Spaniards, who removed from the *Rebecca* all its instruments and a good deal of its equipment, including one of the captain's ears. It was his left ear, which, said the *Daily Advertiser*, was slit down by the cutlass of a Spanish officer, "and then another of the Spaniards took hold of it and tore it off, but gave him the Piece of his Ear again, bidding him carry it to his Majesty, King George". They then left him, as he told an outraged House of Commons seven years later, drifting and helpless, but nevertheless remembering to commit his soul to God and his cause to his country. The authentic ear, prudently preserved and bottled, served on that later occasion to concentrate so powerful a brew of patriotic fury, humane sentiment, religious prejudice (for it was said that the Spanish had delivered some of their prisoners to the Inquisition), historic resentment, and thwarted commercial enterprise, that all Walpole's patient attempts to improve the Anglo-Spanish atmosphere by negotiation came to nothing. Appeasement had been tried and had failed, declared the parliamentary Opposition and the popular Press. This was not altogether true, for between 1732 and 1737 (that is, after Walpole's 'appeasement' of France and Spain and his refusal to make war by Austria's side) the Spaniards had been somewhat slacker in their check of smuggling; and it was only when in 1737 the reinforced coastguard patrols seized five British ships that boiling-point was reached. It was the age of *Rule, Britannia!*[2] Were Britons indeed to be slaves? "Seventy of our brave sailors," declared Alderman Wilmot—they were from the crews of the five ships—"are now in chains in Spain. Our countrymen in chains, and slaves to Spaniards! Is not this enough to fire the coldest?" It was more than enough. The whole country began to shout for war.

Walpole did what he could. He gave Jenkins the captaincy

[2] *Rule, Britannia!* was part of a masque (words by James Thomson, music by Thomas Arne), first performed before the Prince of Wales in 1740.

of an East Indiaman. He instructed the British ambassador in Madrid to present a stiff list of demands for redress. He asked the Spanish ambassador in London to discount the fevered language of Pitt and the Opposition. He personally intervened to tone down the effect of a tough note dispatched to the Spanish Government by Newcastle. The Spaniards were not unwilling to negotiate, but an English demand for £200,000 compensation (subsequently whittled down to £140,000 by a Spanish counter-claim for the cost of ships sunk at Cape Passaro in 1718) had been reduced to £95,000 before the Spanish Government agreed to pay—and against even this was to be offset back payment of £68,000 claimed by Spain from the South Sea Company. A paper agreement was reached (Convention of El Pardo, January 1739), but, although Walpole struggled hard for it in the Commons, the feeling of the House was with Pitt as he attacked the Convention for its failure to end the Spaniards' right of search, for its inadequate terms of compensation, and for its neglect of any settlement of the boundary dispute between Georgia and Florida. "A war with Spain," Walpole had declared, "after the concessions she had made . . . would be unjust, and if it is unjust, it is impolitic and dishonourable." For Pitt, however, it was the *settlement* that was dishonourable, condemned "by your despairing merchants—by the voice of England". It was "a stipulation for national ignominy . . . a surrender of the right and trade of England . . . directly repugnant to the resolutions of Parliament and the gracious promise from the Throne".

By now Pitt had really 'arrived'. Rhetorical as always, he demanded, "*Is this any longer a nation?*" We had a navy stronger than the combined navies of Europe, and were we afraid to use it? His friend Lyttelton declared that "peace at the expense of rights, of essential justice, peace exposed to insults, peace exposed to injuries, is the most abject, is the most deplorable, is the most calamitous circumstance of human affairs". Inside the Cabinet, Newcastle, Harrington, and Hardwicke were strong for war. The King was for war, and the Prince of Wales likewise, so fervidly that he kissed Pitt after his Commons speech. The City merchants were sure that Spain was weak, and good markets were to be had. The British West

Indian sugar-planters were anxious to destroy their Spanish counterparts. The South Sea Company had no wish to pay up its £68,000. The Navy itself was spoiling for a fight, and Vice-Admiral Vernon could hardly wait to be sent out with instructions to destroy all the Spanish West Indian ships he could find. Most men, even if they lacked Pitt's moral fervour, shared his conviction that a war against Spain would be a war of plunder: "Sir, Spain knows the consequences of a war in America. Whoever gains, it must prove fatal to her." Only one man's will stood in the way of a declaration of war that the whole nation would welcome; and within six months he capitulated perforce to the clamour. The heralds proclaimed the war; the mob roared their patriotic approval; the Prince of Wales drank a toast with them in a London tavern; and a Walpole, unconvinced, bitter, and contemptuous, but still clinging to power, said to his old colleague the Duke of Newcastle, "It is your war and I wish you joy of it."

5. War with Spain, 1739

The war flattered to deceive. At first there was general rejoicing when Vernon, with only six ships, fulfilling and exceeding his instructions, not only burned all the Spanish shipping he could find, but captured Porto Bello itself in a swift two-day assault. However, little else went right for a long time. The fleet, for all Pitt's glorification of its strength, had not been prepared for war—Walpole had kept it on a tight budget for many years; equipment was low, and ships were undermanned; and there were dangerously divided counsels over what to do with the ships and men there were. Certainly Vernon's own advice was to dominate West Indian waters with a powerful fleet and not to attempt land conquests, especially in view of the dangers of fever. Newcastle, however, old-womanish as ever, but strangely dominant in this reorganized Walpole War Cabinet, took the lead in promoting a large combined force of thirty ships under Admiral Vernon and 10,000 soldiers under General Wentworth, to follow up the good work begun at Porto Bello. It failed to take Cartagena, failed again to take Santiago de Cuba, and failed a third time in an attack on the town of Panama. Vernon himself was one of the more vigorous commanders in the Navy at this undistinguished period in its annals; but his ships were insanitary, his bearing truculent, and his relations with the incompetent Wentworth deplorable.[3] About half of the original military force were lost in the brief campaign, mainly from fever. As for the conditions in Vernon's pestilential ships, Smollett has given them an unsavoury immortality in *Roderick Random*. He knew what he was writing about, being surgeon's mate on the expedition. Its remnants were ingloriously withdrawn in 1742.

A diminished and querulous Walpole, not enthusiastic for the war in any case, had been even less so for the West Indies expedition. He had pleaded with Newcastle in the Cabinet not to leave home waters unguarded. "What, may not one poor ship be left at home?" he asked; and then—a man plainly defeated and unfit to conduct a war—"I give in to everything. . . . I dare not do what I think right. . . . Let them go, let them go." The Cabinet had good reason to fear any weakening of the home fleet. A large French squadron in Brest was a constant menace from 1740, and there was reasonable fear of a junction of the French Brest and the Spanish Ferrol fleets, especially as much vocal opinion both in France and England was advocating war. Even if it was not the French who attempted to invade, there were always the Jacobites. Ormonde, their now veteran commander, was understood to be himself near Ferrol. So Walpole had good reason to be worried, and worried he was. His son Horace reports him in October 1741 to be sleeping badly, whereas in the old days he was asleep as soon as his head touched the pillow. Now, too, he would sit "without speaking and with his eyes fixed for an hour together".

The situation was that Walpole had geared all his policies

[3] Smollett's judgment on Vernon was harsh: "of weak understanding, strong prejudices, boundless arrogance, and overboiling passions". As for the famous "grog", named after Vernon (of the grogram cloak), Smollett had little good to say either. This "unpalatable drench", as he described it, consisted of a quart of water mixed with a half-pint of spirits; but, writes Smollett, "the water was corrupted and stunk so abominably, that a man was fain to stop his nose with one hand, while with the other he conveyed the can to his head".

to the maintenance of peace, and now war had come to throw him and everything he had worked for out of gear. He had gambled everything on peace, and now it looked as if he had gambled dangerously. By keeping aloof from the Polish Succession War, and allowing France to govern the terms of peace in 1738, he had presented her with a dangerous pre-eminence. Spain was now her close associate in the Family Compact. Lorraine was hers. Her trade and influence were expanding in Turkey and the Near East, in India, in North America. Her army mustered 130,000 regular troops, her navy 60,000 sailors and eighty men-of-war. Her merchants were taking advantage of the Anglo-Spanish war to supply Spain with manufactures that the English had previously supplied. Her West Indian sugar trade and her northern trade in fur and fish were expanding. Not only was she, as Frederick the Great said, "the arbiter of Europe"; she was reviving memories of glory and looking ahead to future ascendancy. In short, the situation between Britain and France was rapidly reassuming its normal shape. The alliance which had been at the heart of Walpole's policies, and which had been languishing ever since Fleury took over the direction of affairs in 1726, was now patently dead, and the untypical interlude of Anglo-French co-operation over.

6. The War of the Austrian Succession, 1740–48

Since 1740 the European situation had been transformed by the death, in the same year, of Frederick William I of Prussia and the Habsburg Emperor Charles VI. For twenty-seven years the Emperor had laboured to gain general adherence to his Pragmatic Sanction securing the succession of all his Habsburg lands to his daughter Maria Theresa, despite the fact that she would, as a woman, be unable to succeed to the Holy Roman Empire. But now within a few months of his death the whole rickety system tumbled at one blow from the new King of Prussia, Frederick II. Silesia was successfully invaded by the Prussian Army, and Bohemia threatened. A new force had arrived in Europe, and one, moreover, that was allied with France. This time Britain could not stand aside and watch her Austrian ally be dismembered. Many welcomed war with France; everyone saw that it was inevitable; and hardly anyone thought that Walpole was the man to wage it. He lingered on in office until 1742, when at last he was forced to resign. He went to the Lords as the Earl of Orford, spent a good deal of his last years in retirement at Houghton, continued to be an influential background figure whose advice was sought by both Ministers and the King, and at least lived long enough to enjoy the downfall of his successor and old rival, Lord Carteret.

Carteret, whose advent in 1742 was received with enthusiasm by George II, was a Minister in the tradition of Stanhope and Townshend: under him Britain resumed full and vigorous participation in the military and diplomatic activities of continental Europe. Now, however, nobody doubted that it was France that was the principal enemy. Carteret, a man who combined brilliance with industry and subtlety with vigour, was a soldier, a linguist, and an expert in continental affairs. He refused, however, to demean himself with the sort of detail whose manipulation helped to give Walpole and the Pelhams their mastery of affairs. "What is it to me," he was reported as saying, "who is a judge or a bishop? It is my business to make kings and emperors, and to maintain the balance of Europe." Certainly Carteret was at home amid the dynastic complications of Europe, threading his way through the diplomatic maze in a continent where sovereign powers were far more numerous than today. The dovetailing and reconciliation of intricate plans and bargains was Carteret's forte, and soon he was involved in manifold negotiations with Austria, Russia, Bavaria, Savoy, and half a dozen other powers—the broad aim being to build up a sufficiently strong complex of strength to force Frederick of Prussia to negotiate peace with Austria, and thus to leave Britain free to concentrate on her own main enemy, France. With this end in view he succeeded in persuading George II, who had previously remained nervously neutral, to enter the war as Elector of Hanover; British money was to pay for the Hanoverian Army. Agreement was reached with Maria Theresa for the Austrian subsidy to be raised from £300,000 to £500,000, and a big allied army (sometimes known as the Pragmatic Army) was mustered along the river Main—a combined force of English, Dutch, Hanoverians, Hessians, and Austrians, under Lord Stair, aged seventy. Meanwhile intricate negotiations proceeded to gain Charles Emmanuel of Savoy, the ruler of Sardinia, for the Anglo-Austrian alliance; here Carteret aimed to outbid the French, partly with good British gold and partly with concessions that he would persuade the Austrians to make to Savoy in North Italy.

Early in 1743 all seemed to be going well for Carteret, who was behaving towards both his Cabinet colleagues and his continental allies with the aloof arrogance of a man who senses success ahead and sees himself destined for great things. (Frederick the Great had earlier observed that this English milord treated the princes of Europe "en petits garçons".) By 1743 Frederick had made peace with Austria; Russia and Britain had promised to render one another assistance in their respective wars with Sweden and Spain; the Italian negotiations promised favourably. And then in the summer a French army, 50,000 strong, under Noailles, was defeated by the combined allied force on the Main at Dettingen. This provided the last occasion upon which an English king personally led his forces on the field of battle: George II, at the head of English and Hanoverian infantry, but wearing *Hanoverian* colours (which was later remembered against him), first withstood the attacking French cavalry and later led a successful attack, sword in hand, on the enemy's infantry, who fled in some disorder across the river. The effects of Dettingen, apart from giving George II a fleeting popularity in England, were to force the French on the defensive and to hasten the successful culmination of the negotiations with Savoy.

These successes, however, boomeranged against Carteret and his allies, who, intent on diplomatic niceties, seemed quite unable to follow up their military advantages. Frederick of Prussia was frightened by the Anglo-Austrian diplomatic successes into renewing the war against Maria Theresa; the French Government was alarmed into converting the vague Family Compact with Spain into a firm military alliance; and Carteret himself found that his own Cabinet refused to accept his lavish employment of British gold in foreign bribes and subsidies.

By the autumn of 1743 criticism and opposition were mounting from every quarter. Even George's victory at Dettingen, only a few months old, was forgotten in charges that he had shown favouritism to Hanoverian troops. Pitt and his supporters found as little to praise in Carteret as in Walpole; for them the spendthrift interventionism of the one was as bad as the parsimonious pacifism of the other. Newcastle both resented Carteret's *hauteur* and disapproved of his excessive sensitivity to German interests. Walpole at Houghton, the oracle behind the scenes, missed no opportunity of criticizing the Foreign Minister's "infatuation" and ridiculing his "labyrinth of expectations". And these expectations were proving ever more expensive. British money not only went in subsidies to German princes to pay for their mercenaries; in particular it went to pay the King of England for the upkeep of a Hanoverian army of 16,000—and this, as Pitt pointed out, without the consent of Parliament. Of all Carteret's many critics, Pitt was the most virulent. Suffering at this time from one of his recurring attacks of insomnia and nervous prostration (made worse by gout), and arriving in the Commons with bandaged leg and crutches and the tragic airs of a man near to death—which many thought he was—he lambasted Carteret and the King:

> Neither justice or policy required us to be engaged in the quarrels of the Continent. ... The confidence of the people is abused by making unnecessary alliances; they are then pillaged to provide the subsidies. It is now apparent that this great, this powerful, this formidable Kingdom is considered only as a province of a despicable electorate.

Carteret, thundered Pitt, was an "infamous minister ... who seems to have renounced the name of Englishman". His policies would ruin the country's credit and prosperity, and make people in the end glad to welcome the Jacobite Pretender.

Feeling inside the Cabinet against Carteret had been reinforced since mid-1743 by the appointment of Newcastle's brother, Henry Pelham, to the Treasury, instead of Pulteney

(Lord Bath), whom Carteret had favoured for the post.[4] By the beginning of 1744, Carteret, though still enjoying the friendship and support of the King, was badly in need of a victory or two. However, at this very moment (February 1744) the worst of news greeted him and the nation: the English fleet watching Toulon not only failed to prevent a less numerous French fleet from emerging, but failed miserably to inflict serious loss on it. The two principal British admirals, Mathews and Lestock, both subsequently court-martialled but exonerated, were hardly on speaking terms; and Lestock in fact took no part in the fight, ignoring—or probably pretending not to understand—orders. Only a few days later another French fleet, from Brest, whose task was to cover a Jacobite invasion from Dunkirk, appeared off Dungeness, to the general alarm. When this time another numerically superior British fleet, under Admiral Norris (aged eighty-four) barred their passage, it was perhaps fortunate that the issue was not left in Norris's hands. Once more, as in 1588, "God blew with his winds and they were scattered."

Setbacks ensued on the Continent. In the Austrian Netherlands, Menin, Courtrai, and Ypres were lost to an army led by Louis XV and directed by Marshal de Saxe. Frederick the Great attacked Bohemia again, and Austrian troops had to be rushed back for its defence. Even so, Prague fell. In Italy the Anglo-Austrian-Savoy alliance fared no better: Milan fell and eastern Piedmont was overrun.

For these and other defeats each side in the British Government could, and did, blame the other; and by mid-1744 relations grew impossibly embittered. Carteret's *grand seigneur* manners were too much to bear; and Henry Pelham, whom he contemptuously referred to as "Sir Robert Walpole's chief

[4] It is a commentary on the inchoate condition of the office of Prime Minister that although, after this appointment, Carteret still *behaved* as though he were Prime Minister, and Pitt was in fact *attacking* him for being "sole minister", Newcastle frequently referred to his brother as "the premier". Pelham was officially First Lord of the Treasury, whereas Newcastle and Carteret were the two Secretaries of State. More and more the 'premiership' came to reside with the First Lordship of the Treasury; yet Pelham's predecessor in that office had been Lord Wilmington (Spencer Compton), whom no one would readily think of as 'premier'.

clerk", began, with Walpole and Pitt, to engineer his over-throw. As for Newcastle, Carteret ignored him when he could and humiliated him on all other possible occasions. "No man can bear what I put up with every day", wrote Newcastle; and Newcastle, though he was fussy and sometimes nerveless, a figure to laugh at, was not one to be either despised or ignored. Abetted by Pelham, Hardwicke, and Harrington, "the inner ring", he conspired with friends and enemies alike to force George II's hand. Walpole's advice was sought by the King, and given in clear terms: Carteret must go. "For God's sake, Sir, give the proper support and authority [to the Pelhams]." The King returned Walpole's letter unanswered, but he took its advice. Grumbling and resentful, George had no option. "I was forced, I was threatened," he complained to Hardwicke. Again, as in 1742, it had been demonstrated to the King that his confidence in a Minister was not enough. To retain office a Minister must have the confidence of Cabinet and Parliament, and especially of "that Damned House of Commons". Carteret (Lord Granville now) went; and George was forced to accept a new coalition Ministry of Pelham Whigs and Opposition leaders—in the language of the day, a 'Broad-Bottomed' administration. Even Pitt's friends, Grenville, Chesterfield, Cobham, and Lyttelton were included. But at one name George II drew the line, and the Pelhams hardly yet had the audacity to press for it. William Pitt, who had sneered at George's military prowess and time after time attacked his policies, his Ministers, and his "despicable electorate", was not to be considered—not yet. Even so, with his friends in the Cabinet, Pitt's hostile fires were damped; there was for the time being no more of that inspired oratory that had sometimes reached beyond obsession almost to frenzy.

In one respect Pitt's men had their way: the Hanoverian army was no longer to be paid for out of British funds. As Maria Theresa's subsidy, however, was increased, and she continued to hire Hanoverians to support the allied army, the difference was more apparent than real. In the war itself—that "unintelligible, huge English-and-Foreign Delirium", as Car-lyle described the War of Austrian Succession—the new administration had no more success than its predecessor. Less, indeed, for whereas Dettingen had been a fruitless victory, the battle of Fontenoy in 1745 was an undoubted defeat; a glorious defeat, with the outnumbered English foot-guards distinguishing themselves valiantly, but still a defeat. After it Marshal de Saxe was able to make himself master of the whole of Belgium. Soon all English troops were withdrawn from continental operations, for Prince Charles Edward Stuart had landed in the Highlands, and Britain was in the panicky throes of the Forty-five rebellion.[5]

An important effect on the political scene of the Jacobite alarms was the enforced acceptance by George II of Pitt. In December 1745 when the Young Pretender's army had reached Derby, and an advance towards London was still a strong possibility, Pelham finally came to terms with Pitt and offered him the post of Secretary at War. At this George II jibbed. He also deplored the Pelhams' conduct of the war— they had just succeeded in persuading Maria Theresa for the second time to make peace with Frederick, still leaving Prussia in possession of Silesia—and still hankered after a Ministry led by Carteret. The Pelham Ministry resigned on February 10th, 1746—the first instance of a Government resigning *en bloc* on a matter of policy; two days were sufficient to convince the King that his attempt to construct a new administration round Carteret (Granville) and Pulteney (Bath) was futile; by February 13th the Pelhams were back, on their own terms, and the chief of these was a major office for Pitt. George II still revolted against having him as War Minister, but grudgingly consented to appointing him Paymaster-General. The cynics smiled; for the Paymastership was the most notorious of all offices for providing opportunities for personal enrichment. It was to the Paymastership, for instance, that an impoverished Walpole had thankfully gone in 1714 "to get some fat on his bones" before going to the Treasury. The censoriously upright Pitt was doubtless about to follow along the well-trodden primrose path. However, fortified by the not inconsiderable £4000 a year that was the post's official emolument, and by the recent windfall of a £10,000 legacy from the Duchess of Marlborough, Pitt ostentatiously spurned the huge perquisites

[5] See Chapter 7, Section 3.

open to him, confounded the cynics, and enhanced his reputation for both honesty and oddity. By this calculated and well-publicized self-denial he silenced the criticism of those of his supporters who had considered his acceptance of office under the Pelhams as a betrayal.

The arrival of Pitt among the administration did not change its policy. Once more, from 1746, an English army—under the King's third son, Cumberland—played its part (no more successfully than before) in allied military operations in the Low Countries; the payment of subsidies to Dutch, Austrians, Russians, Saxons, Hanoverians, and Hessians continued as before, and, indeed, mounted by 1748 to £1,750,000; the confusion of the multiple European wars and their interlinked dynastic and territorial rivalries grew worse confounded; and the British Government grew no better fitted to conduct the struggle, some being in favour of a 'strong' war policy, like Newcastle, some in favour of negotiating peace, like Pelham and Chesterfield, and some in favour of ending the European war in order to concentrate on colonial plunder, like Pitt. Only at sea did British fortunes revive, when in 1747 Anson captured six French battleships in the Bay of Biscay, together with four East Indiamen and other prizes for which the total prize money was nearly £300,000. A few weeks later a British squadron captured forty-eight ships from a French West Indian convoy; and later in the same year Hawke and Pocock between them, in two separate engagements, defeated a French battle squadron and captured forty more merchant prizes.

Thus by 1747 all the combatants—even the French, so victorious on land in Europe—had good cause to desire peace; and in the following year, at Aix-la-Chapelle (Aachen), a treaty of peace was signed. In Italy the Spanish Don Philip obtained Parma and Piacenza, which Britain had been fighting (and paying out) to prevent; Savoy secured North Italian territory from Austria; Frederick of Prussia kept Silesia; Britain and France mutually restored their colonial conquests. Yet there was no real settlement; everybody regarded the arrangements as a mere truce. In Paris the phrase *"bête comme la paix"* became a catchword. In London Handel composed his *Music for the Royal Fireworks* to celebrate the peace (1748); but discerning observers of the political scene knew there was no peace to celebrate: neither in the dynastic European struggle nor, more emphatically still, in the global conflicts for markets and colonies. As for the quarrel over the Spanish coastguards (for Britain the original cause of the war), it was hardly remembered, and the treaty failed to mention it.

7. The Anglo-French Colonial Struggle to 1750

This naval and colonial war, which Pitt and his merchant friends understood to be the only war that really mattered, had nothing whatever to do with the Austrian succession, or the ownership of Silesia, or the special interests of Hanover, or the protection of the Low Countries against the French, or the struggle for power in Italy between Habsburgs, Bourbons, and the House of Savoy, or any of the other diverse issues that kept the continental dynasties fighting and the opposing groups of allied diplomats haggling amongst themselves.

Ever since Columbus had discovered the New World the 'frontier' of Europe had been expanding to contain more and more of the globe. A Europe which in 1492 contained an estimated 100 million persons, living at an average density of 27 to the square mile, suddenly found itself potential master of three new continents, islands without number, gold, silver, timber, furs, all the boundless wealth of an area five times the size of Europe. Almost at a blow the population density of this combined Old and New World had changed from 27 to 5 per square mile; there were potentially 148 acres available per person, instead of 24. The wealth of the world lay open to the exploitation of the West Europeans, supreme as they were in navigation and in firearms. For this reason some historians have seen the discoveries of Columbus and of his contemporaries as constituting the most influential event in modern history. This it was that made possible the white conquest of the world (only so recently challenged); this permitted the vast accumulations of wealth in commercial and colonial ventures that in its turn provided the capital for the Industrial Revolution. Already, in 1776, Adam Smith, inquiring into *The Nature*

and Causes of the Wealth of Nations, was writing: "The discovery of America, and that of a passage to the East Indies by
the Cape of Good Hope, are the two greatest and most
important events recorded in the history of mankind." The
history of the world between 1492 and a few decades ago can
be written in terms of the expanding 'frontier' of Europe.

Throughout the Hanoverian era this expansion was proceeding fast. The original pacemakers in the race, the Spanish and
Portuguese, were still masters of vast and only partially exploited territories, but the running had been taken up by the
three maritime powers of North-western Europe, the Dutch,
the French, and the British. It was not territory that they
sought, but trade; with the exception of the French colony of
Louisiana (New Orleans, 1717) and the English colony of
Georgia (1733)—the latter basically a philanthropic enterprise
undertaken by General Oglethorpe for convicted debtors—no
new settlements were founded by the nations of Europe at
this time. But men's notions of the profits to be derived from
tropical trade seemed limitless. Indeed, great as the realities
were, the dreams wildly exceeded them; and hence the readiness with which Frenchmen, Dutchmen, and Englishmen alike
rushed into bubble schemes about the year 1720.

In the Far East, beyond the Malacca Strait, at this time the
Dutch were still supreme. In the Indian trade all the colonial
countries had some share; but the English East India Company
and the French Compagnie des Indes were both expanding
rapidly. In particular the British, with their fortified headquarters at Bombay, Madras, and Calcutta, were pushing
ahead fast; and a very favourable trade agreement with the
Nawab of Bengal, by which East India Company goods were
exempted from all customs duties in Bengal, had enabled
Calcutta to grow from a village to a city of 100,000. The
French at Pondicherry and Chandernagore had, like the
British, fortified their trading stations and entered into profitable arrangements with local princes. Both French and
English trained Indian troops (sepoys) to fight for them under
European officers with European weapons; and these small
armies frequently defeated the much larger military rabbles
that fought for the Indian princes.

The Indian trade, however, though it brought to England valuable cargoes of silks, cotton yarn, calico, tea, dyewoods, porcelain, pepper, ginger, nutmeg, and drugs, had one great drawback. The Indians could not yet take much in the way of British manufactures, and hence practically all the Indian imports into Britain at this time had to be paid for in bullion. Consequently, in an age when the level of gold stocks was watched very seriously, the East India Company's activities were treated with a certain mistrust.

It was above all the Atlantic trade that fired the ambitions and excited the dreams of the English traders, and, indeed, those of all Western Europe. There were great fortunes to be made in sugar, one of the relatively new tropical luxuries (like tobacco) for which the European demand was leaping. Sugar was still dear; labour costs were cheap; profits were soaring. It was not only Europe that spent its money on West Indian sugar: the New England colonies, too, were anxious to trade their fish and timber for it; and one worry of both the English West Indian planters and of the British Government was that Martinique, Guadeloupe, and Dominica, the principal French sugar islands, managed to produce and market their supplies more efficiently than their rivals. Hence in 1733 Walpole's administration introduced a Molasses Act to impose prohibitive duties on French sugar, and thus to stifle its legal importation into New England.

The value to Britain of the West Indian trade was well appreciated. A pamphlet of 1731, for instance, dedicated to Walpole, calculated that the sugar island of Barbados alone was worth £95,000 a year,

> a prodigious Sum to be gained annually from an Island but very little bigger than the Isle of Wight. . . . And the vast Advantage it is to this Kingdom will farther appear, when we consider the numbers of People which are constantly employed for the supplying of that Island with almost all sorts of our own Manufactures: And if it be farther considered and allowed that not less than 1000 of our Seamen are constantly employed, on account of that Island only . . . which Shipping, or at least three-fourths of the whole, if not built in England are always repaired, refitted, victualled

and constantly paid here; and it never yet was suggested that one Penny of Money or Bullion was ever carried there from England.[6]

Besides sugar and tobacco, the fortunes of the West India trade were swollen by raw cotton, rum, coffee, ginger, pepper, lime-juice, coconuts, logwood, and tortoiseshell; and the spectacular advance in the importation of these articles into Britain may be measured by the parallel rise of the great ports of Bristol and Liverpool and of the mercantile families that dominated them. The financial beauty of it was that all these tropical products depended on a steadily expanding supply of cheap labour fitted to work in a tropical climate; and that meant slaves and more slaves. In one decade at the beginning of the eighteenth century Jamaica alone swallowed 44,000 of them. Spanish America, as we have already seen, had an inexhaustible appetite for them. And the trade in African Negroes, which flourished for more than a century, fitted perfectly into the pattern of Europe's Atlantic trade. In 1700 London was the greatest of the slaving ports; by 1720 Bristol had become pre-eminent; but from about 1730 Liverpool increasingly outdistanced its rivals in England and abroad. By the year 1751 this port, whose population fifty years earlier had been under 5000, was sending fifty-three slavers a year on the triangular run to Africa and the Indies.[7] Specially built fast vessels sailed south with gin, rum, muskets, beads, trinkets, and brightly coloured cottons to pay for the main west-bound cargo of Negro slaves. These had already been captured by some local chief in inter-tribal raids and held in anticipation. Branded like cattle with hot irons and manacled, the wretched victims were scientifically packed aboard on slave-decks normally two feet high, and were eventually sold in the markets of Spanish America, the West Indies, Virginia, and the Carolinas.[8] After this 'Middle Voyage' the 'Triangle of Trade'

---

[6] This extract has in it the basic assumptions of those trade theories which are now described as 'mercantilist'. See also Chapter 9, Section 2.

[7] French, Dutch, Portuguese, Danes, Germans, and New Englanders all took part in the African-Atlantic slave trade; but England's was the lion's share.

[8] Slaves were at first forbidden in Georgia, together with strong drink.

was completed by an eastward run that fetched home to an avid European market the luxuries and raw materials of the Caribbean and the American South. It is impossible to estimate just how great a factor in Lancashire's dynamic industrial growth was this booming commerce based on Liverpool's trade in slaves and in the fruits of slave labour. It certainly played a giant part, providing both the cheap raw material, cotton, and much of the investment capital, derived from commercial profits.

Europe, taken as a whole, conducted a greater volume of trade with Africa and the West Indies than with the mainland of North America; but it was in the mainland trade that the British enjoyed the maximum advantages. By 1748 a million and a half British settlers were rapidly developing the thirteen colonies of the eastern American seaboard. There were French to the north and west of them in Canada, and both French and Spaniards to the south in Louisiana and Florida; but the populations of these areas were tiny compared with those of the British colonies—only about 30,000 in Canada and 5000 in Louisiana. Both as sources of raw material and as markets for French manufactures, these territories, with their numerous small forts and trading stations, mere specks among the vast emptiness, could not compare with the flourishing British settlements. Moreover, by the terms of the Navigation Acts and the accepted existing notions of colonial status and function, the whole of the raw materials and all the surplus food and luxuries of the British colonies flowed over the Atlantic to the motherland: furs, tobacco, rice, timber, tar, naval stores. In return, a big and profitable market awaited British manufactures throughout America, since the colonists' own industries were negligible, and it was the policy of the British Government that they should remain so.

If, however, the trade advantages lay with the British, the strategic initiative did not; for the French were in possession of, or expanding up, the two great river systems that reached out behind the Thirteen Colonies, and offered to a power in total control of them the opportunity to confine the British in the relatively narrow space between the Allegheny Mountains and the Atlantic. From New Orleans the forts of Louisiana

reached northward up the enormous Mississippi. From Louisbourg those of New France curved in an ever-extending arc
westward and southward up the St Lawrence and the Great
Lakes. It was as though two slender arms were reaching ever
farther round the body of the British colonies, straining and
stretching until their long fingers should one day meet and
interlock. If ever that union were achieved it must be in the
valley of the Ohio, the vital link between the Great Lakes and
the Mississippi. Thus, however much in Europe Walpole might
seek the friendship of France, across the Atlantic the story was
bound to be different: the British Americans, fast reaching and
even bursting beyond the temporary geographical barrier of
the Alleghenies, saw past it the possibility of a permanent
political barrier—a New France stretching from the Great
Lakes to the Gulf of Mexico—unless the means were grasped
of nipping the French plans in the bud. Many of the British
colonists were indeed too busy tending their farms and busi-
nesses, or furthering their own state's interests against those
of the other twelve, to see the bigger issue clearly; but, to the
growing number of those who did, a military clash appeared
to be as inevitable as the trade struggle already in being. And
the French, outnumbered by the British in North America by
something like twenty to one, looked naturally to those other
trade rivals of the British—the Spaniards—as their destined
allies.

Thus in the three most important areas of commercial and
colonial struggle, India, the Caribbean, and North America,
the British and the French were jealous rivals. To men like
Pitt the stubbornly pacific policies of Walpole appeared blind
and petty because they ignored the basic political realities of
the day—the global struggle for trade supremacy, which carried with it wealth, glory, and the chance of world mastery.
Also when, after Walpole's fall, Carteret and George II pursued Hanoverian policies and played the sophisticated intricate
games of European dynastic diplomacy, to Pitt and his City
friends it was largely an extravagant anachronism: we poured
guineas down the European drain, and neglected the real
battle and the vital prizes—the rich, vulnerable world of the
French and Spanish colonies.

The colonial wars, being things apart and distinct, followed their own logic and ignored European declarations of war and signatures of peace. The 'War of the Austrian Succession' ended in 1748 with the Treaty of Aix-la-Chapelle; the Seven Years War did not begin until 1756. But in the colonial wars these dates and these appellations are alike meaningless: the actual fighting was indeed spasmodic, but the wars were continuous, at least until 1763.

In India and the Indian Ocean two Frenchmen, La Bourdonnais, the Governor of Mauritius, and Dupleix, the Governor of Pondicherry, launched a combined naval and military attack on the British station of Madras, and easily captured it (1746). Then, two years later, when the British Navy attempted to take Pondicherry and the French successfully held them off, it began to appear that French influence in that part of India (the Carnatic) would prevail. It was, therefore, a great blow to Dupleix and to the French in India when, by the terms of the Treaty of Aix-la-Chapelle, Madras had to be restored to the British. Even so, Dupleix continued the struggle by other means, expanding French influence over Southern India by backing, with French-trained and French-officered sepoys, his *protégés* for the disputed thrones of Hyderabad and the Carnatic. By 1750 both his candidates were successful; the French were in the ascendant; and the British in Madras had good cause to be despondent.

The reason why Madras had had to be given back to the East India Company in 1748 was that a bigger prize was at stake in an even more vital area of conflict: Louisbourg, at the mouth of the St Lawrence. Madras (together with the withdrawal of French troops from the Low Countries) was the price that the French negotiators were prepared to pay for the restoration of Louisbourg.

In North America the one strategic flaw in the grand plan to envelop the English colonies by linking Canada and Louisiana had been that the Treaty of Utrecht had awarded Newfoundland and Nova Scotia to Britain. Thus, in a war, the English were likely to be in a position to close the mouth of the St Lawrence to French shipping, unless the French could find an answer of their own. Louisbourg had been that answer. Built

on Cape Breton Island, just off Nova Scotia, to the plans of the
great military engineer Vauban, it was the most up-to-date
fortress in the world, garrisoned by 2500 regular soldiers and
an equal number of settlers. When, however, colonial hostilities began in America in 1745 the Governor of Massachusetts,
William Shirley, acting on his own initiative, but assisted by
four ships from the West Indian squadron, laid siege to this
Gibraltar of the St Lawrence with 500 militiamen (*i.e.*, civilian
soldiers) and forced its capitulation. The treaty-makers of
Aix-la-Chapelle later returned it to the French, and there
followed as bitter protestations from the New Englanders as
came from Dupleix's men in India at the surrender of Madras.
As in India, however, the treaty, though it could re-assign a
fort, could not stem the flow of the struggle, whoever held
Louisbourg; and, during 1749, a French expedition penetrated
southward into the Ohio Valley, nailing an occasional shield
to a tree or burying a leaden plate in the ground to assert
French ownership, entering into friendly relations with the
Indians, and expelling the British pioneers. The arms were
rapidly, if as yet feebly, closing round the British settlements.
The decisive struggle was soon to come.

Chapter 6

The Elder Pitt and the Seven Years War

1. The Continuing State of War (1750–56)

The British colonists in America were slow to recognize the challenge of the French. Enjoying a good measure of prosperity and freedom, and outnumbering their rivals overwhelmingly, they seemed at liberty to ignore foreign encroachment, and to concentrate on their own domestic and inter-colonial quarrels, for each of the thirteen colonies was a separate and largely independent unit, with its own governor and popular assembly. The French, on the other hand, though few in number, had important advantages of the sort that autocracies normally have over democracies. The French were co-ordinated and directed by a single Government in Versailles; where British governors had to persuade, French could command; the French had systematically courted the friendship of the Indians; their relatively few settlers and traders were nearly all trained in backwoods fighting; and the whole web was held together at nodal points by forts and strongpoints. Only in Nova Scotia and in Virginia did the British seem to be taking resolute measures. The new President of the Board of Trade in London, the Earl of Halifax, caused the fortress named after him to be built in Nova Scotia against the French; and, feeling desperately insecure in an island where the settler population was still predominantly alien, the British at last took the decisive and ruthless step of deporting 8000 French off the island. In Virginia an energetic governor, Dinwiddie, faced with the vigorous expansion of the French under Governor Duquesne, who was destroying British trading posts on the Ohio and constructing forts along the river-bank, organized his own Volunteers and dispatched them, in 1754, under a twenty-two-year-old lieutenant-colonel of the militia, a certain George Washington, to construct a rival strongpoint, Fort Necessity, and to attack the latest of the French forts, named after Duquesne himself. It was a rash move: Washington, his men, and his fort were captured; but these events did have the effect of forcing Newcastle's Government[1] to take vital political and military decisions. The English Ohio Company must be supported, and regular troops dispatched, despite the reluctance of George II, to reinforce the local militia. Major-General Braddock was the leader chosen; it was his misfortune to run into the resentment of the colonial volunteers (who saw him as a high-handed and routine-bound martinet) and into eventual defeat and death at the hands of a French ambushing force a few miles from Fort Duquesne (July 1755).

The war was still undeclared, though it was actively proceeding by land and sea. In India, Thomas Saunders, Governor of Madras, gave the young Robert Clive his first great opportunity to snatch an improbable glory. Leaving Madras and Fort St David dangerously bare of troops, the English moved against the local French-supported Nawab, Chanda Sahib, and stormed his capital, Arcot (1751). Clive, recently a clerk in the East India Company and still only twenty-six, having taken Arcot with 500 men, held its crumbling citadel for fifty days against an army of 10,000 Indians stiffened with French troops. This brilliant young daredevil, who a little earlier had twice attempted suicide, thus sensationally inaugurated his legendary career of conquest. Ill-health brought him back to England by 1753; but by then the mountain stronghold of Trichinopoly had been relieved of the long French siege, Chanda Sahib murdered, and a British nominee installed in his place as Nawab of the Carnatic. Big steps had thus been taken out of the gloom that had beset the British as recently as 1750. Then the directors of the Compagnie des Indes, finding Dupleix's ambitious schemes too expensive, recalled him; and it looked for a time as if a peaceful Anglo-French compromise would work itself out in Southern India, with France supreme in the

[1] Henry Pelham died in 1754 and was succeeded as principal Minister by his brother the Duke of Newcastle.

Deccan and Britain in the Carnatic. However, later events in Bengal upset such prospects.

At sea the war was already active by 1754, when the French learned of the British decision to send regular troops to America. At this, naturally, the French too decided to send further reinforcements of their own. Admiral Boscawen, under orders to intercept them, failed to catch more than two of their transports; but Admirals Hawke and Byng between them captured 300 French merchantmen in a few months (1755). Only fear of the consequences to Hanover held up a full-scale declaration of war; for George II was, reasonably, afraid that his electorate would be an early victim of a Franco-Prussian invasion.

It was not only Hanover that stood in danger of invasion. The French Marshal Belleisle was known to be preparing an elaborate scheme for an assault upon England itself, with diversionary attacks upon Scotland, Ireland, and Minorca, which caused a more than usually worried Newcastle to propose the engagement of Hessian and Hanoverian mercenaries to defend this country. Pitt, for attacking the policies of Newcastle's Government in which he himself was Paymaster, had, together with two other Ministers, just been dismissed by George II (1755). He was, moreover, in the midst of one of his painful bouts of illness, down in the country "with a swelled face, which it was thought he would gladly avail himself of to avoid the debate; but Lord Temple[2] went down and hauled him to the House with blisters behind his ears and flannel over his cheeks"; and he proceeded again to attack Newcastle and oppose the introduction of foreign troops with something like the violence he had once expended upon Walpole and Carteret: a child, he called Newcastle, "driving a go-cart on a precipice". (The King was in the go-cart.) Surely he, Pitt, "was bound to take the reins out of his hands".

[2] Richard Grenville, eldest of the five nephews of Lord Cobham of Stowe; in his early days one of the famous "Cousinhood", or "Cobham's Cubs"; succeeded to the ownership of Stowe and the title of Earl Temple; entertained at Stowe on a vast scale and spent royally in beautifying the estate; a Rabelaisian practical joker; as head of one of the greatest of the Whig clans, saw himself as an important political leader; in early days a generous friend of Pitt, giving him political and financial support; later, became jealous of him and attacked him.

Pitt did not think Marshal Belleisle could successfully invade England: the Royal Navy's Western Squadron was too strong. As for Hanover, "the present war, I say, has not been undertaken to defend Hanover, but for the long-injured, long-neglected, long-forgotten people of America". That was where our main attack should be. But danger threatened, if not directly in England, at least in the Mediterranean, where the French were known to be planning an assault upon Minorca. The question was: where was the main attack to come—in the Channel or the Mediterranean? So blatantly did the French advertise their Minorca plans that the British Government long thought that their true intention must lie elsewhere, and fatally delayed the dispatch of Mediterranean reinforcements. When Admiral Byng at last arrived 15,000 French troops had already landed and were pressing the small British garrison hard. Byng, having been engaged indecisively with the French Toulon fleet, elected to draw back to Gibraltar and await further reinforcement; and soon, trickling into London from enemy sources, came the sad and disgraceful news: Minorca, one of the two great naval prizes of Marlborough's wars, had fallen. A distracted Newcastle cried woe, and damned the unfortunate Byng before he had even received the Admiral's own dispatches. The mob booed Newcastle and pelted him in his coach. Aware of their own shortcomings and the likely verdict of public opinion upon their conduct of operations, the leading Ministers sought rather despicably to focus responsibility upon Byng. Writing to his fellow Minister, Hardwicke, Newcastle asked him to "talk seriously to my Lord Anson to prepare materials . . . for the immediate trial and condemnation of Admiral Byng if, as I think, there can be no doubt that he deserves it. . . . Could any object of attack, either in the Mediterranean, the West Indies or North America be agreed upon, that would keep up people's spirits and divert their resentment?" The last three words seem especially eloquent of Newcastle's state of mind. And this was not improved by the torrent of bad news that now struck the nation and the Ministry. Fort Oswego on Lake Ontario was lost, with its artillery and ships. Maria Theresa, our old ally, signed the fateful alliance with France that was sealed with the betrothal of the infant Marie Antoinette and the little Dauphin. Frederick of Prussia, our new but obstreperous ally, invaded Saxony, and so, to the consternation of George II and his Minister, made a resumption of the continental war certain. Murray, a leading Minister, resigned his office; and finally, to fill Newcastle's cup of woe to the brim, Henry Fox (father of Charles) ostentatiously followed Murray's lead, and campaigned for Pitt to become Secretary of State. Meanwhile the tragedy of Admiral Byng slowly proceeded to its last act. Despite a recommendation to mercy from the court martial and the efforts of friends and sympathizers (Pitt among them) to secure a reprieve, this uninspiring and unimpressive, but not cowardly, sailor was at last shot upon his own quarterdeck (March 1757). A scapegoat, he suffered for the sins of the Ministry; and Newcastle, Hardwicke, and George II all come badly out of the business. The most devastating comment was left to Voltaire, in *Candide:* "Dans ce pays-ci [England] il est bon de tuer de temps en temps un amiral pour encourager les autres."

2. The Diplomatic Revolution

By the time the war became official in 1756 a diplomatic revolution had transformed the European situation. Ever since 1713 there had been those in France who thought the ancient antagonism with Austria out of date: habit rather than policy, reflexes rather than intelligence, now dictated the old Habsburg–Bourbon hostility. This was still sufficient to take the two powers into the wars of 1733 and 1740 on opposing sides; but, with France's future secure in Lorraine, she seemed to have no further grounds for inveterate enmity. In Austria, too, opinion was slowly shifting; and Kaunitz, her ambassador in Paris, worked hard from about 1750 to foster the idea of a treaty of friendship, gaining the influential support of Louis XV's current mistress, Madame de Pompadour. But the decisive factor was the aggressive ambition of Frederick the Great: if Austria was to regain Silesia from Prussia, or even to resist further Prussian attacks, she must have the most powerful of possible allies on her side. Thus plans for a treaty proceeded.

They were perhaps somewhat spurred forward by the whip-lash of Frederick's tongue, which gave both the Pompadour and Maria Theresa cause to share a common sense of outrage. The Pompadour was "Mlle Poisson", her maiden name, but also a reference to the rumour that her mother was a fishwife; Maria Theresa was "the Apostolic Hag"; and for the Tsarina Elizabeth, another powerful and capricious factor in the European political situation, Frederick had a nickname which must remain unprinted.

The major preoccupation of George II and his Ministers was with Hanover. It was easy for Pitt in opposition to scoff at the "despicable electorate", but the time was soon coming when, as responsible Minister, he too would have to come to terms with the inescapable fact that the King of England was the Elector of Hanover. Even Pitt could not absent himself from the dynastic jungle of his times, and in that jungle Hanover was an inviting victim to the predatory French, and desperately vulnerable if France and Prussia were leagued together. It was prudent, therefore, for Britain (since France was now recognized as an inevitable enemy) to come to terms with Prussia. In the continental war whose resumption grew imminent Prussia could both protect Hanover and draw off troops from France that might otherwise be used against the British colonies or even Britain herself. Frederick, on his side, could obtain English gold to maintain his large army against Maria Theresa. Even so, Frederick of Prussia was a second-choice, last-minute ally for Britain in this approaching Seven Years War. Britain's first overtures had been to Elizabeth of Russia, and, indeed, an agreement had been made with her which so displeased Frederick (who had no wish to see Russian troops in Hanover) that he bargained his own services with the British. Thus the Treaty of Westminster was signed in 1755. Kaunitz, by now chief Minister in Vienna, used this Anglo-Prussian bargain to clinch his own Austro-French treaty. When Russia, in her turn having taken umbrage at the Anglo-Prussian alliance (coming on top of the royal Prussian remarks), also joined the Austrian camp, the diplomatic revolution was complete, and the partners were lined up for what some have called the "first world war".

3. Pitt and the King (1755–57)

The disasters of 1755–56 that culminated in the loss of Minorca signalled the end of Newcastle's Ministry; but still the King would not have Pitt. "Mr. Pitt will not do my German business." But, argued Newcastle, "If he comes into your service, Sir, he must be told he must do your Majesty's business." "But I don't like Pitt," replied George; "he won't do my business." In any case, Pitt refused at this juncture to serve under Newcastle, though he was the following year to see the value of an accommodation with him. It was through the royal mistress, Lady Yarmouth, that Pitt eventually got in touch with the King, though even she jibbed at presenting what practically amounted to an ultimatum from Pitt concerning the membership of the new administration. Even when, grudging and growling, George at last brought himself to invite Pitt to accept one of the two Secretaryships of State, it was that of the Southern (and usually less important) Department, not the Northern, which included German affairs. It is difficult to blame George II, for Pitt had frequently gone out of his way to be offensive about Hanover; yet the strange fact is that Pitt was overwhelmingly attached to the sacredness of the royal person. He revered monarchy. Later, unable to stand in the royal presence because of the pain from his gout, and having therefore been graciously invited to sit down, he would refuse and kneel respectfully on a cushion; and the King, although he disliked having to listen to Pitt's long speeches and found his letters "affected, formal, and pedantic", learned at last to respect him, and treated him with a gruff correctness.

Pitt's position, however, in this first tenure of the Secretaryship, was essentially weak. It was not so much that he had to spend most of the time in bed (Pitt, like Darwin and Florence Nightingale, could get through more work as an invalid than the great majority of the healthy); but he was beset by powerful political enemies—Newcastle in particular—with whom he had not come to terms, and the King, of course, fundamentally distrusted him. "I know that I can save this country and that no one else can," Pitt told Devonshire, the First Lord of the Treasury; and he vigorously set about his task in a hundred different ways that were to pay high dividends in two or three years' time. But when the Duke of Cumberland insisted as a condition of his accepting command of the new Hanoverian–Hessian–Prussian army of the Rhine that Pitt should be dismissed, dismissed he was. The King, however, soon discovered that he could not make a new Ministry without Pitt, as popular a figure as Cumberland was unpopular. London and eighteen other cities hastened to present Pitt with their freedom. The whole merchant fraternity "rained gold boxes" upon him, and Lord Waldegrave, asked by George to form a Ministry, was forced to reply, "The popular cry without doors was violent in favour of Mr. Pitt." For nearly three months the country was led by ramshackle Governments lacking both authority and popularity; and then—since the King could see no alternative and Pitt came to see the value of a political understanding with Newcastle and the vote-managers—in June 1757, for the second time in six months, George was forced to submit to the inevitable. Public opinion at all levels demanded it. As Dr Johnson put it: "Walpole was a minister given by the King to the people; Pitt was a minister given by the people to the King."

The new arrangement worked out remarkably well, considering the incompatibility of the three principals. The King accepted Pitt, who accepted in return Hanover and its implications. No longer did the King need to grumble that "Pitt will distress my affairs abroad". Newcastle, the First Lord, although he protested excitedly to Hardwicke, "He shall not be my *superior!*" was also ready to accept Pitt and content to leave the direction of the war to him. For his part, Pitt was only too happy to leave the details of patronage and parliamentary manipulation to Newcastle, the old hand.

4. Pitt's Background and Character

Pitt's policies are much easier to understand than his character. He came from a family notable for its energy and violence. His grandfather was a thrusting "interloper" in the Indies trade, penniless at nineteen, who gatecrashed his way to great wealth in the following ten years. The East India Company began by putting out a warning to its members against this "desperate fellow" who would "stick at nothing", and finished up by making him Governor of Madras. He bought up many properties in England, including Boconnoc in Cornwall, that cost him £53,000, and the rotten borough of Old Sarum that was to provide his grandson with a parliamentary seat at the age of twenty-six. He speculated in diamonds, buying for £25,000 the mighty 410-carat stone that gave him his nickname of "Diamond" Pitt; and after thirteen years of hawking it round Europe to get the top price he sold it to Orleans, the Regent of France, for £133,000. Although his volcanic rages erupted as dramatically as his financial fortunes, and always denied him the affection of friends and the love of family, this testy go-getter, taking a fancy in his old age to his young grandson William, would send over to Eton for the lad to come down to Berkshire with his "comrogues", and there they would listen to the old villain embellishing tales of his stormy youth in India, as the young Raleigh, perhaps, listened to the veterans on the Devon shore. Pitt's own political philosophy grew to be essentially the same as that of his formidable grandfather. Clothed in the crimson robes of patriotism, bright with the jewels of eloquence, the bare body underneath was identical. Pitt's policy like his grandfather's was a policy of colonial plunder.

Governor Pitt's three sons all married the daughters of peers and one of his daughters an earl. Thus the family, previously provincial and obscure, came to have money, social connection, and political influence; yet they were an ill-starred brood. Of William Pitt's own immediate family, one brother was wild and cruel almost to the point of madness, and four of his five sisters were in some degree mentally unstable. Violent family quarrels were chronic, though Pitt himself, haughty and difficult as he was, never lacked tenderness and natural affections. His love in later years for his wife and his children (the "dear Tribe" or the "Infantry", as he liked to call them) was constant and true. But he too was smutched with the family stain: he walked through life on the razor-edge of sanity, with the abyss always at his side.

His childhood was chequered. A delicate boy, he was packed

off to Eton at the age of ten, largely to be company for his elder brother, and hated it: he later told Shelburne "that he scarcely observed a boy who was not cowed for life at Eton", a place he considered suitable only for those "of turbulent disposition". The most important friendships he made there were with the Grenville brothers, Richard and George, whose sister Hester it was that he eventually married.[3] Together with the numerous Grenvilles and his brother-in-law Lyttelton, he became a member of the anti-Walpole Stowe House group— Cobham's Cubs; it was Lord Cobham who secured him a cornetcy of the King's Own Regiment of Horse; and it was Walpole, stung by the young officer's waspish attacks, who robbed him of his commission. He hated Walpole with the full Pitt intensity; and hatred, as J. H. Plumb writes, "was an exultation, releasing the violence that tortured his lonely heart".

Pitt's psycho-physical troubles were in his day diagnosed either simply as gout, or, more strangely, as "gout in the bowels" (George Grenville's phrase), or, most curiously of all, when his reason seemed threatened, as in 1744 or 1751–53, by the euphemism of "gout in the head". He was, indeed, frequently bedridden from painfully swollen limbs; but he also, and much more alarmingly, suffered periodic attacks of acute nervous prostration, with digestive troubles, insomnia, and black moods of extreme depression. Between these disorders, or sometimes in the middle of them, he would be swept by a tornado of energy; this was the Pitt of whom it was once said that no-one ever went into his closet without coming out a

[3] When Hester Grenville married William Pitt he was already forty-seven, a middle-aged cripple. She had known him for twenty years. Her entire life was devoted to him and to making possible his career. She admired him with passionate devotion, and, as well as bringing up his five children, she became on many occasions his nurse, secretary, bailiff, and public relations officer. The stilted nature of some of his letters to her should not blind the modern reader to the depth and sincerity of his love. "My Fame, my Pride, my Glory is centred in you", he wrote to her. Imprisoned up in London by pressure of work, he longed to hear from her, down at his home at Hayes in Kent, "of all those *little-great* things ... which so far surpass in excellence ... all the *great-little* things of the restless world". Both Pitt and his wife lavished infinite care and love on the upbringing of their five children, whose abilities and characters generously repaid them.

braver man. Sometimes, haggard and emaciated, he would
emerge from his sick-bed to make a parliamentary speech of
passionate eloquence. Suddenly, after seeming to many near
death, he would get up, ride fifteen miles a day, eat like a
horse (in the words of his brother-in-law, Lyttelton), and enjoy
"as much wit as ever in his life". Some could not believe that
his illnesses were genuine, and there may well have been
present, on occasions, an element of hypochondria and a
willingness to exact the maximum drama from his condition.
Horace Walpole, needle-eyed as usual, ridicules thus one of
his rare appearances in the Commons in 1756:

> The weather was unseasonably warm, yet he was dressed
> in an old coat and waistcoat of beaver laced with gold: over
> that a red surtout, the right arm lined with fur, and appen-
> dent with many black ribands, to indicate his inability of
> drawing it over his right arm, which hung in a crape sling,
> but which, in the warmth of speaking, he drew out with
> unlucky activity and brandished as usual. On his legs were
> riding stockings. In short, no aspiring Cardinal ever coughed
> for the Tiara [the papal crown] with more specious debility.

Yet Pitt's sufferings, if nervous in origin, were real enough.
Modern medical theories suggest that gout, like many of the
rheumatic afflictions, though its victim may well inherit a pre-
disposition to it, is liable to be triggered off by psychological
strain; and the alternation of violent mental and physical
activity with troughs of helpless dejection is a well-known
feature of that kind of mental disease which is now described
as 'manic-depressive'. When the crests get less and less frequent, and the troughs coalesce into one gulf of level despair,
a stage which Pitt mercifully never reached, a man's reason
has come to its end.

Pitt, then, possessed great gifts and desperate weaknesses.
All recognized his greatness, his singleness of mind, energy,
decision, grasp of complicated affairs. In every sense, physical,
psychological, intellectual, he was a dominating figure. Yet his
egoism, his disdainful airs of superiority, the severity of his
rectitude, his obsessive sense of mission, meant that he could
have no colleagues, but only subordinates. He could command
infinite respect, even awe; but never, outside his family circle,

love or friendship. He was a great patriot, a towering personality, a "man of destiny". For modern taste his rhetoric and
his posturing are a little 'ham'; sometimes the sublimity of his
language and sentiments seems only one perilous step from
the ridiculous; while the naked imperialism of his policies no
longer brings forth the old instinctive patriotic reaction. Yet he
remains the most extraordinary of Georgian statesmen, and
no-one—not Lloyd George, not Winston Churchill, his nearest
rivals—can challenge his primacy among British War Ministers.

5. Pitt's Strategy

By 1756 Pitt was a responsible Cabinet Minister. It is not
surprising, therefore, that he had abandoned some of the
extremism of his previous carefree anti-Hanoverian line.
Although his main objectives remained maritime and colonial,
he was now ready to send British troops to the Continent to
assist Prussia and other allied German states,[4] and he was
willing to allocate large annual sums to subsidize Frederick
the Great. Thus he would, in his own words, "conquer America
in Germany". He planned, too, a series of sudden, small-scale
attacks on the French coast at such sensitive points as Rochefort, Saint-Malo, Cherbourg, and Belle Isle, to destroy shipping, keep the enemy permanently on tenterhooks, and draw
away troops which would otherwise be available to fight
against the German armies or in the overseas theatres of war.
Essential to these operations, and to Pitt's whole global scheme
of attack, was a powerful Navy—to protect British expeditions,
to prevent essential supplies getting into France, and, most
important of all, to sever the threads that bound France to her
colonies. Canada and the West Indies could be conquered in
the Bay of Biscay and the Mediterranean, if French reinforcements and supplies could be prevented from sailing or be sunk
en route. Britain disposed of less than half the manpower of
France; but if 150,000 French troops had to remain at home or
in Germany the smaller power—so long as her Navy ruled the

[4] But still not as many as George II would have wished. "Your
America," complained George to Pitt, "your Lakes, your Mr. Amherst."

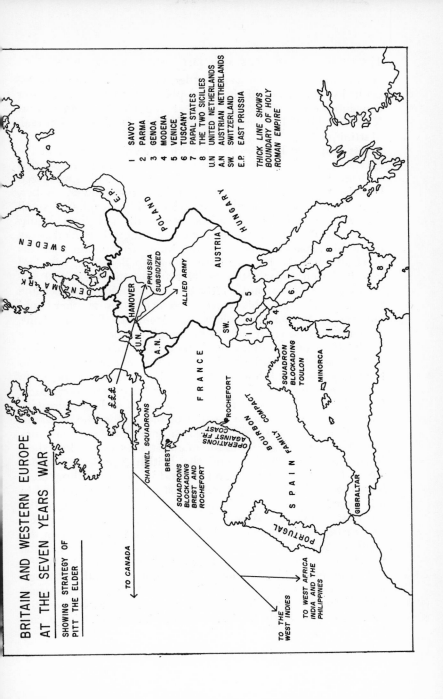

BRITAIN AND WESTERN EUROPE
AT THE SEVEN YEARS WAR

SHOWING STRATEGY OF
PITT THE ELDER

1 SAVOY
2 PARMA
3 GENOA
4 MODENA
5 VENICE
6 TUSCANY
7 PAPAL STATES
8 THE TWO SICILIES
U.N UNITED NETHERLANDS
A.N AUSTRIAN NETHERLANDS
SW. SWITZERLAND
E.P. EAST PRUSSIA

THICK LINE SHOWS
BOUNDARY OF HOLY
ROMAN EMPIRE

SWEDEN
DENMARK
E.P.
POLAND
HUNGARY
AUSTRIA
PRUSSIA
SUBSIDIZED
ALLIED ARMY
HANOVER
U.N.
A.N.
SW.
FRANCE
£££
CHANNEL SQUADRONS
BREST
ROCHEFORT
SQUADRONS
BLOCKADING
BREST AND
ROCHEFORT
OPERATIONS
AGAINST FR.
COAST
BOURBON FAMILY COMPACT
SQUADRON
BLOCKADING
TOULON
MINORCA
SPAIN
PORTUGAL
GIBRALTAR
TO CANADA
TO THE
WEST INDIES
TO WEST AFRICA
INDIA AND THE
PHILLIPPINES

oceans and the French were bottled up in Toulon and Brest—could be the master of time and place, and bring the greater concentration of force to bear at the chosen points, Fort Niagara, Fort Duquesne, Louisbourg, Quebec, Montreal, Martinique.

Pitt had long been in touch with powerful interests in the City of London, and had both interviewed and corresponded with many merchants at home and overseas, with specialized knowledge of the trades in sugar, fish, furs, slaves, timber, gum, ivory, and so forth. Smugglers, ship's captains, small traders, colonial factors, missionaries—all had their brains picked by Pitt and their schemes and suggestions filed away inside his capacious and voracious mind. In London itself his chief ally was the Jamaica-born Alderman Beckford, who had inherited rich sugar interests. Not for nothing was Pitt the grandson of "Diamond" Pitt: ten years before he became Secretary of State, his correspondence with another bold buccaneer, William Vaughan, an American fish merchant, demonstrates how, already in his mind, the demands and the implications of the attack on Canada were maturing. Quebec was the key to Canada; and Canada was not only the key to the entire trade in fish and furs, but also a significant factor in the struggle for the West Indian sugar trade (for shortage of Canadian lumber would force up the price of French sugar), and in the competition for naval armaments (for France would be unable to build ships in America or import Canadian timber). Further, French domestic manufactures would lose their North American market, and the British American colonies would be able to develop and expand in peace, unthreatened from the north and west. Britain must capture Quebec; and to this overriding necessity the affairs of India, of Africa, of the Far East, even of the West Indies, must take subordinate place. The cartographer James Cook, later to win immortality in the Southern Seas, was sent (1759) to make a detailed survey of the St Lawrence river, soon to be of the greatest value to Wolfe. Pitt worked with immense thoroughness, and although America came first in his calculations he took care to instruct himself in the local information relevant to each potential theatre of war. Early in 1757 we find him interviewing a certain Thomas Cumming, a Quaker merchant knowledgeable in the affairs of the West African coast, and discussing the strategy of attacks on the French trade there in slaves, gum,[5] ivory, and gold-dust. Eventually Cumming was sent off with a letter to "the High and Glorious Monarch, the Mighty and Right Noble Amir Sultan, King of Legibbilli" from "Your most affectionate Friend, George R."; and the Admiralty and Ordnance were instructed to prepare and hold ready a secret plan of attack. This was the way Pitt worked. But even when news arrived of Clive's great victory at Plassey, where, in 1757, 1000 white troops and 2000 sepoys defeated an ill-organized host of 60,000 Indians, and secured Bengal, Bihar, and Orissa for the East India Company, Pitt insisted that India must remain a subordinate theatre of war. He built up the British naval forces in the Indian Ocean to a force *equal* to the French (no more), but on land the Company must make do with its own armies. Canada must come first.

In the first year of his Secretaryship (1757), apart from the capture of Beauséjour in Canada and Clive's dramatic victory in India, Pitt had no success to report. Neither did British continental forces or the troops of her allies. Frederick of Prussia had been severely mauled at Kolin, while the Duke of Cumberland, crushed at Hastenbeck, had been forced to sign the Convention of Klosterzeven, which left Hanover for the time being at the mercy of the French, but gave Pitt the opportunity to replace Cumberland by Ferdinand of Brunswick as leader of the allied force. However, all these months Pitt had been sowing the seed that was soon to yield so spectacular a harvest. Older and less enterprising commanders, and seconds-in-command, were replaced by younger men of mettle more like his own—Wolfe, Forbes, Barrington, Howe, Ligonier, Ferdinand of Brunswick, Keppel, Saunders; and even when royal opposition prevented him having his way entirely, compromise choices like Amherst proved successful enough.[6] He strained every resource to raise sufficient men, both at home

[5] Gum arabic was used in the manufacture of silk fabrics, and therefore was of great importance to the French.

[6] Some controversy exists here. Pitt's judgment of men was not infallible, and he picked a few losers like Lord George Sackville as well as some famous winners.

and in America, to strengthen forces by land and sea. He raised two Highland regiments from the very areas so recently disaffected and Jacobite. By building up a county militia for home defence he freed the regular Army for overseas campaigns. In America he managed to remove much of the resentment previously felt by the colonists against the airs of superiority and automatic seniority assumed by the redcoats. He devised minutely detailed plans of attack in Canada, and prepared to take the initiative in half a dozen other places when the propitious moment should arrive. His attacks on the French coast, though they appeared to achieve little positive, served to keep the French from concentrating upon the defeat of Frederick.

6. The Years of Triumph

At last, in November 1757, the good news began to come through—at first a trickle and mainly foreign, but gathering volume and pace until the flood of triumph in 1759, by which time, Horace Walpole said, the bells were worn threadbare with ringing for victories. The first triumphs were Frederick's: in swift succession his Prussian armies defeated the French at Rossbach and the Austrians at Leuthen, and, having yet no heroes of their own to worship, the English were quick to take him to their hearts as "the Protestant hero"—a strange title for so convinced an unbeliever as Frederick. "It is incredible how popular he is here . . .", wrote Horace Walpole. "As I was walking by the river the other night, a bargeman asked me for something to drink the King of Prussia's health." A few months later the Thames bargemen, and Englishmen everywhere, were cheering another, and a British, victory: Louisbourg had been retaken by the 'new men'—Amherst, Wolfe, and Admiral Boscawen; no event in the whole war was received with greater popular enthusiasm, not even the capture of Quebec the following year, for the paramount strategic significance of Louisbourg was well recognized. Lord Temple wrote to his brother-in-law Pitt: "Nothing but congratulations to you my dear Brother Louisbourg; I shall never call you by any other name except that of Quebeck in due time." And away to the south, Forbes (like Wolfe, a dying man) was soon marching over the Alleghenies to the successful assault upon Fort Duquesne. He renamed it Fort Pitt, whence it has proceeded, through Pittsburgh, to the modern Pittsburg. The year 1758 had its setbacks, certainly: Abercromby, one of the older generals Pitt had not uprooted, failed to take Quebec, though his troops outnumbered the French by three to one. But in Germany Ferdinand of Brunswick managed twice to defeat the French, who retired over the Rhine, so that Hanover and George II could breathe again. By the close of 1758 Commodore Keppel and Colonel Worge had appeared off the French fortress of Goree (Dakar) in West Africa, one of their principal depôts for the trade in slaves and gum, bluffed the garrison into surrendering without a fight, and proceeded to take over the French posts in Senegal. A fortnight later, as more plans began to bear fruit, another combined sea-and-land force under Commodore Moore and General Hopson, though it found Martinique's artillery too strong for it, captured the neighbouring sugar island of Guadeloupe (whose capital value was put at nine and a half million pounds), together with some of the smaller islands near by. Hopson, a cautious veteran, died during these operations, and much of their success was due to the initiative of his second-in-command, another of Pitt's young nominees, the Hon. John Barrington. Within a few months handsome plunder was on its way home to England—cotton, rum, cocoa, spices, ginger, coffee, and, most profitable of all, molasses and sugar. (The value of Guadeloupe to Britain may be appreciated by studying the public argument that took place in 1762, over which of the two, Guadeloupe or Canada, should be returned to France. Many thought it was Guadeloupe we should keep.)

In the summer of 1759 resounding news came in, too, from Germany. Ferdinand of Brunswick's allied force had beaten the French decisively at Minden on the Weser; and although the leader of the British cavalry, Sackville—Pitt's man—had disgraced himself by five times flatly disobeying Ferdinand's orders to charge, the British infantry and artillery had performed prodigies of valour. (Pitt, though he had secured Sackville's appointment, did not hesitate to support his being court-martialled and dismissed with ignominy.[7] Minden was the first really substantial triumph for Pitt's continental schemes and served to offset disappointing news from the Prussian armies.

There were dangers as well as triumphs. As in 1756, again in 1759 there were complicated and ambitious French plans for an invasion. This time French strategy, directed by Choiseul and Marshal Belleisle, envisaged troops from Brest being landed in the Clyde, while the main French fleet sailed round the north of Scotland and, thereafter, made southward to secure the passage of the principal invading armies from Flanders to the Essex coast. Simultaneously, Ireland was to be raided. However, the only chance of French success in these operations lay in the junction of the Toulon and Brest squadrons, and Pitt had sufficient faith in the Royal Navy's vigilance to refuse to credit that this could be achieved. Admiral Boscawen, based on Gibraltar (now that Minorca had fallen), kept the tightest watch on both Toulon and Marseilles, while Admiral Hawke, with the Western Squadron, maintained a stranglehold over Brest and France's Biscay approaches. A third squadron, under Rodney, watched the Channel. Pitt, therefore, believing in the Navy's power and the spirit and skill of its leaders, and refusing to be put on the defensive, would not withdraw a single regiment from his far-flung overseas enterprises. Instead, the militia was put on a war footing in the summer of 1759, which made a fine patriotic noise, enabled many young bloods to cut a dash on parade in their scarlet uniforms, gave a general impression of defiant preparedness that deceived neither Pitt nor the French (but succeeded in maintaining morale), and cost half a million pounds. Edward Gibbon, greatest of English historians, did his stint with the South Hampshires, while, at the head of a Norfolk battalion, young Lord Orford, Walpole's grandson, was reported by his uncle Horace as "looking gloriously martial and genteel" on the occasion of a review by the King in Hyde Park. The amateur army served its purpose, but Pitt

[7] Lord George Sackville was by no means done for. As Lord George Germain, he was, twenty years later, the Minister chiefly responsible for the handling, or mishandling, of the War of American Independence.

also took the precaution of stationing 5000 professional troops in the Isle of Wight, ready to be rushed to any invaders' beach-head. This had the additional advantage of appearing to the French like a preparation for further *offensive* action.

Pitt's confidence in the Navy, now out of its earlier doldrums and approaching the peak of achievement that it was soon to reach under Nelson, was to be brilliantly vindicated. First it was the turn of Boscawen's Mediterranean squadron. When he had temporarily to relax his grip on Toulon in order to revictual at Gibraltar, the French seized their chance and came out, trying to slip through the Straits by night. Spotted by a frigate, they were chased and overhauled; and a day-long running fight ended with their seeking the neutral haven of Lagos Bay. Boscawen, ignoring Portuguese neutrality, went in after the four remaining French battleships, burned the two which had run aground, and captured the two at anchor. The opportunity of Hawke and his Western Squadron came a few months later, when the big Brest fleet of twenty-six ships under Conflans ventured forth to make contact with troop-carrying invasion transports in Quiberon Bay. Hawke's forces, already seriously needing a relief after their arduous vigil, had been forced off station by foul weather and were sheltering in Tor-bay; but fortunately British intelligence was apprised of the French intentions, and when Hawke sailed again for Brest and found the birds flown he straightway made for Quiberon. Arriving immediately after the French and lacking their advantage of pilots among these treacherous rocks and shoals, he boldly, in a full gale, followed home and destroyed four French ships by nightfall. Next day Conflans' flagship went aground and was set afire by his orders; another ship sank; seven made off up-river; and the rest escaped to Rochefort. The transports in the bay were left at the mercy of the English. Hawke's was the boldest defiance of the laws of naval prudence until Nelson's at the Nile; and any serious threat of invasion was, for the time being, over. He had erased the memory of Byng. In company with Clive and Wolfe, he had given a fore-taste of 'the Nelson touch'. Like them, and like Pitt himself, he had achieved the impossible; but then, as Pitt himself once said, pointing out his crutches to an ordnance officer who protested the impossibility of providing certain equipment in time, "Sir, I walk upon impossibilities."

The Battle of Quiberon Bay was in November 1759, and was duly celebrated on New Year's Eve at Drury Lane by David Garrick and his company in their brand-new number:

> Come cheer up my lads, 'tis to glory we steer
> To add something new to this wonderful year. . . .
> > Hearts of oak are our ships,
> > Hearts of oak are our men,
> > We always are ready,
> > Steady, boys, steady,
> We'll fight and we'll conquer again and again.

Thus Quiberon bravely rounded off the year of victories; but the greatest victory of all had preceded it by two months. After his failure to take Quebec in 1758, Abercromby had been replaced by Amherst, whose orders in 1759 were to make a two-pronged attack on Canada from the south, one from Ticonderoga to Montreal, the other by way of the Mohawk river to the Great Lakes and Fort Niagara. The new attack on Quebec was entrusted to General Wolfe and Admiral Saunders, both protégés of Pitt and men after his own heart. Wolfe in particular, desperately ill with tuberculosis, despised and openly insulted by his aristocratic subordinates, was a man hungry for glory in the short time left to him. They make a strange trio, the three great imperial conquerors of this Seven Years War: the invalid Pitt, with his alternating fits of demonic energy and mental collapse; Clive, neurotic and suicidal, but with a will of steel and reckless daring; and the chronically delicate Wolfe, with his unsoldierly appearance yet self-confident ambition, fortunate only in the hour of his death.

Wolfe had a dying man's impatience and a patriot's disappointment at being baulked, as seemed likely, of his great prize. Only four days before his death he wrote apologizing to Pitt: "My constitution is entirely ruined, without the consolation of having done any considerable service to the State; or without any prospect of it." The French under Montcalm were well fortified on the northern bank of the St Lawrence and had managed to gain, through their intelligence, full details of

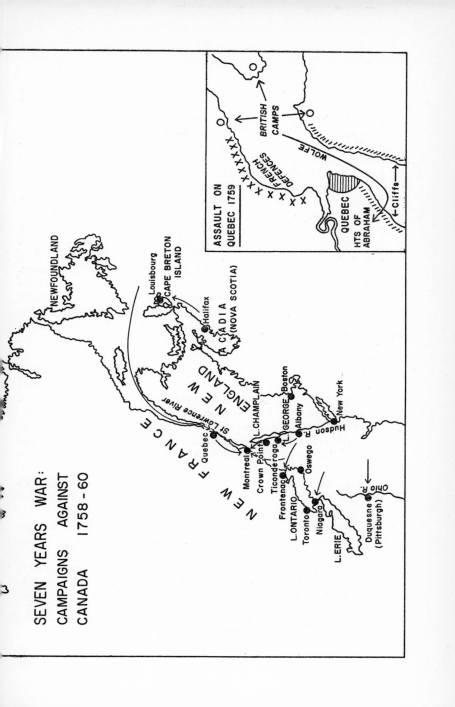

SEVEN YEARS WAR:
CAMPAIGNS AGAINST
CANADA 1758-60

NEWFOUNDLAND

Louisbourg
CAPE BRETON
ISLAND

Halifax

ACADIA
(NOVA SCOTIA)

St. Lawrence River

Quebec

Montreal

NEW FRANCE

Crown Point
L. CHAMPLAIN
Ticonderoga

L. GEORGE

Frontenac

Oswego

L. ONTARIO

Toronto

Niagara

L. ERIE

Duquesne
(Pittsburgh)

Ohio R.

Albany

Hudson R.

Boston

NEW ENGLAND

New York

ASSAULT ON
QUEBEC 1759

FRENCH DEFENCES

BRITISH CAMPS

WOLFE

QUEBEC

HTS OF
ABRAHAM

Cliffs

Pitt's broad plans. Worse, a naval convoy of three frigates and seventeen supply vessels under Bougainville had earlier in the year contrived to slip through the blockade, so there was little chance of starving out the garrison. Wolfe and Saunders, with a full-scale fleet, were able to worry the French with a succession of probing attacks on the north bank over a fifty-mile front, but Montcalm, entrenched high in Quebec and flanked by a tributary of the St Lawrence, had only to fend off the British until the autumn, and the ice would drive their ships back to the open sea. The months wore on; September arrived with no decisive battle. When Wolfe's brigadiers[8] advised a landing far upstream he concurred, and began the operation. The French moved to counter it, and in so doing denuded of troops the high ground near Quebec. Wolfe saw his chance. Textbook tactics were suddenly abandoned, to his subordinates' horror; "If I am mistaken, I am sorry for it," he said, "and must be answerable to his Majesty and the public for the consequences." Everything was now to be risked in a direct assault upon the city. So, under cover of a feint naval bombardment to distract the enemy, 5000 men were rowed by night to land in a little cove under the Heights of Abraham, a few miles upstream from Quebec. By dawn the British had climbed the cliffs and stood with every man that could be mustered waiting for Montcalm's men, who, somewhat outnumbered, were hastening from their defences to meet them. (Bougainville's forces were stranded far upstream in anticipation of the orthodox, but abandoned, attack.) The British allowed Montcalm's troops to approach within forty paces; fired a second and a third volley; charged; and one of history's decisive battles was over. Montcalm was dead, Wolfe lay dying. The unlikely triumph was his after all.

It was another year yet, however, before Canada was Britain's, and at one moment in April 1760 Quebec was all but recaptured by the French. The city's garrison had suffered terribly from cold and scurvy, and its stores were desperately depleted; only the melting of the river ice and the timely arrival of a British frigate, soon followed by a larger fleet,

[8] One of them was a Townshend, who amused himself by drawing obscene caricatures of his commander.

prevented the French from re-entering. Once again sea power proved decisive. To ram the lesson home, a convoy of supplies from Bordeaux which had slipped through Boscawen was captured at the mouth of the St Lawrence. "Happy, happy day", wrote Pitt to his wife. "My joy and hurry are inexpressible." In the months that followed, Amherst set the seal on Wolfe's achievement. His own progress in 1759 towards Montreal had been slow but steady. Now his army moved methodically down-river again from Lake Ontario, while two more British columns, Murray's from Quebec and Haviland's from Lake Champlain, converged with Amherst's on the city. When the well co-ordinated British columns met outside Montreal, the outnumbered French accepted the inevitable and capitulated. Pitt's major project was fulfilled, and French power in Canada ended.

7. Pitt, Cabinet, and King (1757–61)

During these years of imperial conquest the Pitt–Newcastle–George II arrangement had worked tolerably well. "The Duke of Newcastle and Pitt", wrote Chesterfield, "jog on like man and wife, seldom agreeing, often quarrelling, but by a mutual interest on the whole, not parting." Newcastle was chronically in a state of alarm at Pitt's rashness in denuding these islands of troops in order to squeeze more reinforcements for the American campaigns. He had been brought up in the old school that considered European affairs of primary importance and colonial affairs secondary; but, although he nagged and grumbled, he stopped short of obduracy, swallowed his humiliations, and gave Pitt his head. As for Newcastle's management of finance, Pitt, on his side, was by no means inclined simply to sit back and let Newcastle do as he pleased. For example: "The demand of forage for the Hessians last year is preposterous", he wrote to the Duke in 1758, and requested him "to reduce things to a reasonable bulk", so that the House of Commons could be dealt with "openly and fairly". A few months later, when Pitt saw the estimate for nearly two million pounds for maintaining the King's German troops for the coming year, he sent Newcastle another of his peremptory notes: "I must confess I have never seen anything in my life that astonished or grieved me so much, in a word, the burden is impossible to be borne.... Your humble servant despairs on such a foot to be of any use. This is peculiarly your Grace's province." The very same day he protested vehemently to Newcastle against having to persuade the Commons to budget for yet another 38,000 Germans. "In the name of God, my Lord, how comes such an idea upon paper?" (Newcastle duly managed to get half a million knocked off the estimate.[9]) When Pitt actually dealt with the Commons on financial matters they ate out of his hand, and coolly voted sums which to that age seemed colossal. "You would as soon hear 'No' from an old maid as from the House of Commons", wrote Horace Walpole in 1758, and Chesterfield: "Mr. Pitt declares only what he would have them do, and they do it *nemine contra-dicente*."

Pitt's position in the Commons was supreme, as Robert Walpole's had once been; he was the "Great Commoner". His position with the general public was also very strong: he had always been an honest man, above corruption and scandal, and now he was the organizer of victory as well. His standing with the King, which had been the weak leg of the tripod, was now, inevitably, much strengthened. "Give me your confidence, Sir," he had said to George when he came to power, "and I will deserve it." "Deserve my confidence," George replied, "and you shall have it." In fact that was exactly what happened. This is not to say that George accepted Pitt's plans tamely: he too, like Newcastle, Hardwicke, and the others, protested frequently; and almost his last action was to veto Pitt's plans for a raid on the island of Belle Isle, off Brittany.

---

[9] Each Minister had his difficulties in dealing with the other: the fussy, old-maidish Newcastle (who could not bear the cold) and the invalid, Olympian Pitt (whose irritable skin was sensitive to the heat). Newcastle once visited Pitt to discuss Hawke's instruction before Quiberon Bay. Pitt was working in his unheated bedroom though it was November. Newcastle "grew more and more uncomfortable with cold till he could bear it no longer and plunged fully dressed into another bed which he saw made up in the room. From here he continued the conversation, which eventually became so argumentative that an astonished under-secretary came in to find the two ministers shouting at each other from bed to bed." (B. Tunstall: *William Pitt Earl of Chatham*, p. 248.)

In general, however, Pitt's successes were so signal that George could hardly fail to approve of them, especially as Hanover's integrity was preserved; and, indeed, George contributed £2,500,000 of his own Hanoverian money towards the war.

When, therefore, the King died suddenly in 1760, Pitt was bereft of an important prop. The new King, George III, the late King's grandson, strongly disapproved of him, and once said he had "the blackest of hearts". Pitt had not furthered his own position by having treated both George, when Prince of Wales, and his friend and tutor, Bute, "as a parcel of school children". Within the Cabinet, too, there was an understandable feeling that they had long enough been ridden over roughshod. Pitt began to pay the price for his grandiose tantrums, his massive lack of personal tact. In particular the Dukes of Devonshire and Bedford were furious with him.

Plans were being hatched in his fertile mind for an extension of the war, now that forces had been liberated by the fall of Montreal. Still there was Martinique, the richest remaining French possession, and the lesser prizes of St Lucia and Dominica. There was Mauritius, the naval base for all French operations in India. There was the Belle Isle project already mentioned, which was in due course actually sanctioned by George III, and in 1761 the island was captured. Pitt's aims, however, stretched out beyond the conquest of the French empire towards the vast, vulnerable lands of overseas Spain— Florida, Cuba, Mexico, South America, the far Philippines. It seemed probable that Choiseul, the French Foreign Minister, would manage to persuade the Spaniards in any case that their only hope of self-preservation lay in an alliance with the French. Would it not then be best, Pitt argued, to seize the initiative and attack Spain first? The neutrality of Spain was no longer important now that the power of the French fleet was shattered. The Spanish colonies were legitimate prey.

All this alarmed Cabinet and King alike. They were for taking seriously the peace negotiations with France which had already begun; to Pitt these were little more than a prevarication. Further good news was coming in: following the defeat of the French at Wandewash, Pondicherry in India had fallen, and Dominica in the West Indies; preparations for the assault on Martinique were well advanced. Why should Britain make the severe concessions that Choiseul insisted on before peace could be concluded—chief among them the restoration of French fishing rights off Newfoundland and the St Lawrence estuary? Pitt saw no need to compromise. But he could no longer count on carrying all before him in the Cabinet. Newcastle, Hardwicke, Devonshire, Bedford, and others were all perturbed at the likelihood of a big European coalition being built up by Choiseul against Britain, consisting of France, Spain, and perhaps other neutral powers embittered by the majestic ways of the British Navy in searching ships for contraband. Sweden, Russia, Denmark, Holland, and the Italian maritime states all had strong and legitimate complaints against Britain for seizure of their ships and cargoes. By July 1761 France and Spain had already signed the secret Bourbon Family Compact; and Pitt (seeing that at least a Spanish war seemed inevitable) was for bold measures immediately, which he insisted on recommending personally in writing to a very displeased George III: the British ambassador in Madrid ought to be recalled, and the Spanish treasure fleet from the Caribbean pounced upon. For months there had been plans waiting to be taken out of the drawer for an assault on Havana and Manila; let them now be put in hand.

Inside the Cabinet, Pitt now faced the outright opposition of Bedford and Devonshire, and the worried criticism of Newcastle, Hardwicke, Anson, and others. It was no light matter to take on Spain in addition to France, with half Europe, perhaps, to follow. Even some of Pitt's City supporters, like Beckford, had doubts about a colonial grand slam: might there not, for instance, be a glut of sugar, a fall in price, and a slump in profits? George III and his new Secretary of State, Bute, were in a quandary. By supporting Pitt they would run a great risk. By provoking his resignation they would stand in parlous danger through flouting a public hero. Pitt remained as imperious and intransigent as ever: "Being responsible I *will* direct, and will be responsible for nothing I do not direct." The Cabinet decided against him in the matter of giving way on the St Lawrence fishing rights; and in October 1761 Pitt resigned on the issue of the war with Spain. Surrendering his seals to a George III who was trying very hard to do the right thing, and who invited him to name his own reward, he withdrew, "sensibly touched with the grandeur and condescension of the proceedings". Refusing a sinecure office for himself, he suggested that his wife should receive any marks of royal approbation that were to be offered. So the barony of Chatham was bestowed on Hester Pitt, and a modest annuity of £3000 (out of the 4½ per cent sugar plantation funds) on Pitt himself. This odd arrangement, modest as its financial rewards were for him, occasioned a good deal of criticism, some against the King and Bute for an apparent humiliation of Pitt, some against Pitt and his wife for accepting anything at all. "Oh! that foolishest of great men", wrote the poet Gray, "that sold his inestimable diamond for a paltry peerage and a pension." But by the time of the Lord Mayor's Banquet, a month after his resignation, Pitt was back on his popular pedestal, the object of a demonstration of affection alike from the City fathers and the mob, some of whom clung to his coach, hugged the footmen, and kissed the horses.

The war with Spain had indeed been almost certain to come, as even Bute and Newcastle knew, and in January 1762 hostilities officially began. Although the Spanish treasure fleets were by then safely in port, the British soon netted very substantial plunder. All Pitt's military and naval investments continued to pour their dividends into London. One of his last official acts had been to send Admiral Rodney with reinforcements to the West Indies, and soon Martinique (at last), St Lucia, St Vincent, and Grenada were all captured, with great quantities of ammunition and stores. The French West Indies had ceased to exist, and the British could now concentrate their power upon the vital Spanish fortress of Havana, in Cuba. It fell in August 1762, with fourteen warships (a fifth of the Spanish Navy), thirty merchantmen loaded for Europe, three million dollars belonging to the royal treasury, and many more choice pickings. The military and naval leaders of the expedition, Admiral Pocock and the Earl of Albemarle (Keppel), each received a cool £122,697 as their share of the prize money— sums which even in that age raised some outraged eyebrows. All three Keppel brothers were in the action and managed to net £200,000 between them, a quarter of the total. By contrast, each private soldier received £4 1s. 8d., and an ordinary seaman £3 14s. 9¾d. Two months later Manila, too, the clearing-house for the trade between Mexico and Canton in China, was captured in a surprise attack—a surprise, that is, to the Spaniards there, who had not yet learned that their country was at war. Manila was to the Spaniards what Singapore later became to the British. Through it from Mexico came wines, manufactures, and great quantities of silver; from the Far East came spices, silks, and calicoes for the New World and Spain. It surrendered to a British combined force, who nevertheless pillaged it scandalously. Not the least ironical feature of the story is that at the very moment that the town was captured (and, indeed, in theory, all the Philippines, according to the surrender terms), peace negotiations were being successfully concluded in Paris, and in fact news of the fall of Manila did not reach London for another eight months, by which time the Peace of Paris was signed, and British proprietorship automatically a dead letter.

Once Pitt had resigned, the chief complication in bringing the Seven Years War to a conclusion lay in Germany. Frederick the Great was our ally. His fortunes were low, and his defeat would jeopardize both Hanover and Britain's position in the peace negotiations. It would therefore be a serious matter simply to cut him off without a penny. George III, however, was anxious to bring the German war to an end and spoke of Frederick as "that proud, overbearing Prince" who must be made to see that "he has no safety but in peace". Eventually Bute informed Newcastle in April 1762 that he proposed to end the subsidy to Prussia. Newcastle had advised the King and the Cabinet that this was the wrong policy, and when he was outvoted (and had clearly lost royal support) he resigned, hoping to outmanœuvre Bute by pulling in good time the appropriate strings. He miscalculated. It was, at last, the end of Newcastle, the arch-manipulator, the eternal go-between, the indispensable Minister for nearly forty years—and the end, too, of his friend Hardwicke and others of the "Newcastle Whigs". George was pleased to see them go: he had now rid his administration of Pitt the tyrant and Newcastle the fount of corruption. It was left in the anxious hands of Bute, the King's friend.

8. The Peace of Paris

The 1763 Peace of Paris, whose preliminaries were signed in November 1762, was hotly attacked, as the Peace of Utrecht had been half a century earlier, because it appeared to cheat a victorious Britain of its just and attainable rewards. A pallid, emaciated Pitt, carried by his servants into the Commons, wrapped in flannel from the middle down, his hands thickly gloved, his voice low and quavering, made a three-and-a-half-hour onslaught upon it: the desertion of Prussia was base, the cession of conquered territory was craven and inept. "We retain nothing, although we have conquered everything." The House, however, though it was impressed, even awestruck, was against him by 319 votes to 65. (One of the 65 was Clive.) England had had its bellyful of victories, and surely the Peace was not as bad as Pitt, or the journalist agitator Wilkes, made out.

The most serious of Pitt's criticisms arose from the assumption that France was Britain's permanent enemy. Granted that, then we had missed a perfect opportunity to destroy her commercial and naval capability. We had let her off the hook and allowed her to return to the world's oceans. We had left her with both the need for revenge and the power to obtain it. France's ability to rebuild her maritime commerce and naval manpower had not been crushed, as it could have been, by depriving her of her sugar trade and the Atlantic fisheries—the breeding-ground of sailors as well as cod. A 'soft' peace would not prevent France leading a new European coalition against England; it would merely leave in her hands the strength to make it dangerous.

The principal provisions of the Peace of Paris were as follows:

Minorca was restored to Britain, Belle Isle to France.
Martinique, Guadeloupe, St Lucia, and two smaller islands were restored to France, but Britain retained Grenada, Dominica, St Vincent, and Tobago.

France ceded to Britain Canada, Cape Breton Island, freedom of navigation in the Mississippi, and all Louisiana east of the Mississippi.

Britain restored to France her fishing rights off Newfoundland and in the St Lawrence estuary.

Spain ceded Florida to Britain and the logwood rights in Honduras, but received back Havana and Manila.

In Africa, Goree (Dakar) was restored to France, but Britain took Senegal.

In India the *status quo* of 1749 (before Dupleix's great successes) was officially restored, but Britain also kept all Clive's conquests in Bengal, and France recognized the paramountcy of the East India Company.

Some of all this was indeed very temporary: Minorca, Florida, and Senegal were not destined to remain British. A vast victory had been won, nevertheless. Canada and a paramount position in India were hardly trifles; Britain, from the edge of defeat in 1756, had emerged the dominant colonial, commercial, and maritime power; and certainly the French were under no illusions concerning the magnitude of their defeat. London, Liverpool, and those who had done well out of the war shared Pitt's bitterness; and, as usual, arrival of peace soon produced unemployment and a falling-off in prosperity. However, most of England's taxpayers were glad that the war was over. There was some prospect again that the land-tax might fall from its ceiling of 4s. in the pound, and, Pitt or no Pitt, the country gentlemen were emphatic for peace.

Chapter 7

Scotland and Ireland

1. The Lowlands in 1714

When the Hanoverian period opened, the Union with Scotland was seven years old. The benefits to the Scots of that change, which were eventually to be great, had had little time to show themselves. Scotland was still a land of the harshest poverty, backward in agriculture, industry, and commerce, feudal in social organization, narrow in religion.

Nine-tenths of the Lowlands was still unenclosed. Marsh still clogged much of the potentially best land, while the peasants drove their medieval eight-ox ploughs over the stony hills. Cultivation was on the 'run-rig' system, by which one holding was worked by about half a dozen peasants, each taking the harvest of a different 'rig' or ridge each year—an ancient combination of communalism and individualism that was precariously dependent on the co-operation of the team; and the level of farming always tended to degenerate to that of the laziest or stupidest member. The lairds in their comfortless stone mansions that rose like fortresses out of the poorly timbered countryside still took their meagre rents partly in produce or service; and the peasant's lot included a share in manuring, sowing, and reaping the laird's 'infield'—that quarter or so of the acreage that was permanent arable, the remainder being too poor for cultivation more than one year in every four or five. The peasants themselves inhabited dwellings that were often little more than turf-walled cabins with a hole in their thatched or turfed roof to vent the smoke from the peat fire. Windows were glassless and floors of earth. Meat was a luxury normally reserved for the lairds and the grand folk of the towns. Country folk lived on oats, with barley for scones; their drink was ale—whisky was for Highlanders.

Never far distant was the threat of hunger; and wet, cold summers like those of 1696 to 1702 filled the graveyards and flooded the land with vagabonds. With its wildness, its mists and moorlands, its pervading poverty and unsophistication, Scotland could hardly fail to be a country where superstition lingered. Every stream, every hillside, every peasant's imagination was peopled by ghosts and fairies. Travel in such a country was arduous and communication wretched. Only a handful of Englishmen ever penetrated what they regarded as these uncouth wastes; and the idea of visiting Scotland for the grandeur of its scenery was far in the future; the taste for the rugged and romantic was not acquired until much later in the century. The paucity of trade may be gauged from the size of Glasgow, Scotland's chief port at the time of the Union: it numbered no more than 12,500, and its merchants between them owned only fifteen small merchant vessels. Edinburgh in the time of Defoe was a densely populated, dirty town of 36,000 inhabitants, with a scarcity of water, and primitive sanitary habits that became notorious.[1] In many respects it was still a medieval city, its inhabitants huddled tightly together for shelter and safety.

In learning, Scotland was potentially rich, with four universities (to England's two) and every village under a statutory obligation to provide a primary school. In fact, many villages failed to observe the law, and where a school did exist it was often as wretchedly poor as its half-starved dominie; yet it remains true that a humble but intelligent Scottish student possessed a far better chance of proceeding to the university than his English counterpart. His life there would be as severe as his background or as the religion to whose ministry he was very probably destined. His sack of oatmeal would lean against his lodging wall, to be consumed gradually during the term and replenished from the store at home during the vacation.

[1] G. M. Trevelyan writes of "rough Highland porters swearing in Gaelic as they forced a passage for their sedan-chairs, while far overhead the windows opened, five, six, or ten storeys in the air, and the close stools of Edinburgh discharged the collected filth of the last twenty-four hours into the street. It was good manners for those above to cry 'Gardyloo' (gardez l'eau) before throwing. The returning roysterer cried back 'Haud yer han'', and ran with humped shoulders, lucky if his vast and expensive wig was not put out of action by a cataract of filth."

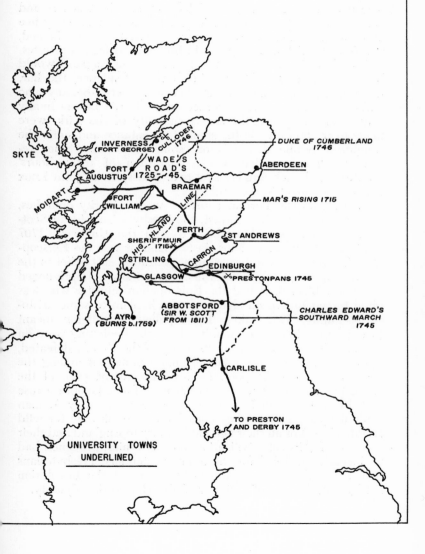

SCOTLAND

SKYE

MOIDART

INVERNESS (FORT GEORGE)
CULLODEN 1746

WADE'S ROAD'S 1725-45

FORT AUGUSTUS

FORT WILLIAM

BRAEMAR

ABERDEEN

DUKE OF CUMBERLAND 1746

MAR'S RISING 1715

HIGHLAND LINE

PERTH

SHERIFFMUIR 1715

ST ANDREWS

STIRLING

CARRON

GLASGOW

EDINBURGH

PRESTONPANS 1745

ABBOTSFORD (SIR W. SCOTT FROM 1811)

CHARLES EDWARD'S SOUTHWARD MARCH 1745

AYR (BURNS b.1759)

CARLISLE

TO PRESTON AND DERBY 1745

UNIVERSITY TOWNS UNDERLINED

At the heart of Scottish life was the Kirk, from St Giles's in Edinburgh to the turf-roofed village church that was little more than a glorified barn. The characters of the Bible were as familiar to the Scotsman as the goblins of his native stream. The ministers were the natural leaders and the teachers and censors of morals for the whole parish, and four in every five of them were Presbyterian. They exercised powers, indeed, which south of the Border would be reserved for magistrates, and some which in comparatively easy-going England would be unthinkable. The laggard in church attendance, the liar, the slanderer, the unmarried mother or mother-to-be, any who had used profane oaths or worked on the Lord's Day or in any way offended against the severe morality of the Kirk, were made to sit, literally, on the stool of repentance and suffer the weight of public denunciation, sometimes many times repeated. Divine service was a marathon of three hours' duration, and each Sunday saw two. The spirit of John Knox was still powerful in the land.

In England the Puritan churches were minority churches, and unestablished; by contrast, the Presbyterian Kirk of Scotland was official and established, and the Union of 1707 confirmed its primacy. Thus, in Scotland, it was the Episcopalian Church (the counterpart in organization and belief to the Church of England) that formed the minority, unprivileged and unestablished. It was the Episcopalian minister who was often forced to live on charity or as chaplain to some aristocratic family. Thus, since Episcopalian in religion meant Jacobite in politics, the Jacobites from the beginning were on the minority side. They were the party of the already defeated, even though they were relatively more numerous among the rich than among the poor. In any case, many, even of the Episcopalians, could feel no enthusiasm for a Jacobite cause that by 1715 seemed to have become irrevocably Roman Catholic; such a cause they considered to be fit only for wild Highlanders. For all their age-old hostility to England and their contempt for its soft civilization and lax ethics, Scotsmen had no incentive to rebel for the Stuart pretenders. Presbyterians had a vested interest in the maintenance of the Revolution Settlement, the Act of Union, and the Hanoverian dynasty.

2. The Highlands before 1745

The Jacobite rebellion of 1715,[2] therefore, roused but small enthusiasm in Scotland. Such support as it did gain came principally from the Highlands, which, though forming half the area of Scotland, were of small importance against the Lowlands.

The 'Highland Line', running north-eastward from the Firth of Clyde, marked the limits of civilization. The north-western half of Scotland was a tribal wilderness, and few from the Lowlands, fewer still from England, had ever penetrated its forlorn moorlands and barren mountain-sides. In 1714 it had not a single road. Such of its soil as had been scratched by the ancient ploughs of the crofters and their labouring womenfolk was poor, stony, and unmanured. Its produce being insufficient to sustain even the Highlanders' sparse diet, once or twice a year forays were made south and east to get oats and barley from the Lowlanders, partly by cattle-trading, partly by plunder. To the Lowlander, in most respects the Highlander was a foreigner, speaking the Gaelic tongue, dressed in the plaid and tartan kilt of his clan, worshipping in his semi-pagan version of the ancient Catholic faith, obeying the customs of his clan, a liege servant of his feudal chief, and respecting no laws, or kings, or parliaments, or churches, that were respected southward of Dumbarton, or Perth, or Aberdeen. Only a very few of the north-eastern clans, Mackays, Rosses, and Munros, and the one great clan of the Campbells in Argyllshire, had become attached to Presbyterianism. Of the few that were not Catholic, most were Episcopalian.

Each Highland chief was an absolute ruler. He commanded the fiercest loyalty from his clansmen; not infrequently he exercised his supreme right of capital punishment. He was the ultimate landowner, leasing it out to a 'tacksman' who in turn sublet the miserably small patches to the crofters of the glen. Rents were high in relation to the soil's poverty, high enough to permit the chieftain to sustain himself and a circle of military

[2] See Chapter 3.

retainers in proud isolation from menial tasks. No-one could explain the beginning of the bitter inter-clan feuds, just as no-one ever expected them to end; they were as closely interwoven into the existence of the Highlander as the moorland heather and the mountain mists, the cattle-raiding and the peat smoke of his scant hovel.

When the Jacobite rising of 1715 was suppressed the rebels' estates were forfeited and it was enacted that the Highland clans should be disarmed. But not for another ten years was a serious attempt made to tackle the problems of the Highlands. Then General Wade was empowered to form six companies of Highlanders (the germ of the Black Watch regiment), who were permitted to wear the kilts and tartans of their clan, but subordinated throughout to officers from loyal Whig clans. Wade, not the least of English empire-builders, rightly judged that nothing would be so likely to tame the lawlessness of the north as a road system opening up the country; and Wade set his Highland companies to work. They built, in just over a decade, about 250 miles of road and some forty bridges, including the five-arched bridge over the Tay. The Lowland towns of Stirling and Perth were linked over the Grampians with Inverness, and with the new garrison stations of Fort Augustus at the head of Loch Ness, and Fort William under Ben Nevis. These were the chief of about thirty forts intended by Wade to safeguard his road system, in the manner of Roman 'chesters'; but the 'Forty-five' rebellion caught his work uncompleted and his stations undermanned, and the Highlanders overran them with fair ease. Wade's 'disarming' of the clans in pursuance of the post-1715 policy was also uncompleted; only the loyal Whig clans (chief among them the Campbells) surrendered their weapons. Yet in the long run Wade's roads did play their important part in the pacification of the Highlands. And they not only permitted redcoats (and, later, even tourists) to travel north; they showed the overpopulated Highlands the road south. Their significance was two-way.

3. The 'Forty-five'

To the Gaels of the north and west King James was the rightful King of the Scots. The fact that the Lowlanders had accepted King George only made him the more unacceptable to them, for, as Wade himself expressed it in one of his reports:

> [Despite their barbarous inter-clan quarrels] they have still a more extensive adherence one to another as High-landers in opposition to the people who inhabit the Low Countries, whom they hold in the utmost contempt. . . . They have also a tradition amongst them that the Lowlands were in ancient times the inheritance of their ancestors, and therefore believe they have a right to commit depredations whenever it is in their power to put them into execution.

In 1745 'James the Third and Eighth' had still a long time to live; but ever since the birth of his son, Charles Edward, in 1720 the Gaelic poets had been proclaiming the child as the saviour-hero who would deliver Scotland from the foreign Protestant usurper. When, therefore, in July 1745, in the middle of the Wars of the Austrian Succession, Charles, in his own words, stole off, "without letting the King of France so much as suspect it," and landed at Moidart, opposite Eriskay in the Hebrides, he was well received by the local clans, despite the misgivings of some of their chiefs. The Duke of Atholl unfurled the crimson and white Stuart banner and read the proclamation from James, appointing "Charles, Prince of Wales, to be sole Regent of his Kingdom of Scotland, England, and Ireland". "Let what will happen", Charles had written to his father, "the stroke is struck, and *I have taken a firm resolution to conquer or to die.*" By all sober reckoning his enterprise must be considered rash, and most of the older heads among his supporters thought, reasonably, that a spontaneous rising, unco-ordinated with any French invasion, had small chance of success. But within little more than six weeks of landing he had forced his way into Edinburgh and proclaimed James VIII at the Market Cross. Two days later he defeated the English forces under Cope at Prestonpans, where in a surprise dawn attack over misty marshes the Highlanders' claymores, axes, and scythes cut down many of the veterans of

Dettingen and Fontenoy—500 dead, 900 wounded. From Prestonpans Charles returned to Edinburgh, still hopeful of French assistance, for which he was negotiating. It was promised, but did not come; and in November, at the head of some 5000 men, he started southward to invade England. Presbyterian Lowlanders had received him coolly, but he hoped for better luck among the numerous English Catholics of the northern counties and North Wales. Carlisle and Preston were taken; Manchester even afforded him 150 recruits; but the spontaneous rallying of a mass of Englishmen discontented with Hanoverian rule was mere wishful Jacobite dreaming. Even though Derby was reached (on December 4th, 1745), the trickle of new recruits was only about sufficient to replace those Highlanders who had deserted north of the border, when they discovered that their leader intended something more than a raid on the Lowlands. But the Jacobite advance was alarming enough to cause a severe flurry in London. December 6th was Black Friday on the London Stock Exchange. The run on the banks was such that they began paying customers in sixpences to gain time. The Government was offering £6 bonuses to men who would enlist. The train-bands were being mustered at Finchley to defend the capital. However, Charles's Scottish advisers, the chief of whom, Lord George Murray, had always been hostile to a headstrong dash into England, now refused to go any farther. Wade's army, bypassed at Newcastle when the Jacobites took the Carlisle invasion route, was still undefeated in their rear, and the young Duke of Cumberland, with another army, was breathing down their necks. Charles's projected assault on London was vetoed; the Highlanders turned about, and were skilfully extricated from England by Murray, who managed to evade both Wade and Cumberland. But the discipline of the clansmen, good on the southward march, now deteriorated, and they left ugly memories behind them in the northern counties.

Once back in the relative safety of Scotland, Jacobite fortunes revived. Stirling and Inverness were captured and a battle won at Falkirk. Recruits from the clans still came in, and Fort Augustus fell in March 1746. Even so, the sands were running out. The British Navy effectively prevented the arrival of men, material, and treasure that were on their way from France. Cumberland's army recaptured Stirling and marched northward to occupy Aberdeen, through which fresh men and supplies could be brought by sea. In April, Prince Charlie's brave but essentially desperate gamble was finally lost, on the bleak and blood-soaked moors of Culloden, near Inverness. His army, still at 5000, but famished, and worn out by a ten-mile night march over boggy ground to deliver what proved to be an unsuccessful surprise attack, faced nearly double their number of well-fed, well-rested, well-equipped redcoats under Cumberland. Macleans and Camerons, Maclachlans and Frasers and Mackenzies, and all the loyal Jacobite clans suffered heavily in the defeat; and after that slaughter began another, when the wounded were massacred where they lay and the prisoners and refugees butchered. Even that was not the end of it: Culloden was followed by a brutal terrorization of the Highlands, with callous atrocities on men, women, and infants, and a systematic laying waste of Jacobite areas by Cumberland's army and anti-Jacobite Scots. Charles, with £30,000 on his head, but unbetrayed by the poverty-stricken crofters and fisherfolk, among whom he was hunted for five desperate months, at last escaped "over the sea to Skye" and into the mists of heroic legend. Sailing at last to France, he was expelled thence by the terms of the Treaty of Aix-la-Chapelle. He travelled Europe in disguise, seeking to keep alive his expiring cause, even daring to come to London; but the defeat of 1745 had killed Jacobitism for ever. A handful of romantic Tories and Catholics might continue to toast "the King over the water" (still James III until his death in 1766), but it was no more than a sentimental gesture. Charles, that glamorous and courageous young prince, grew middle-aged, quarrelsome, and drunken. His childless wife fled from him to a convent in Florence; only his illegitimate daughter was left to solace him in his lonely and undignified exile. Long before his death in Rome in 1788 the principal Catholic powers had withdrawn their support for his claim to the British throne.

4. The Highlands after the 'Forty-five'

The suppression of the 'Forty-five' was followed by measures which destroyed the old Highlands. Rebel estates were forfeited and their owners exiled (a few were executed). The clans were at last effectively disarmed. The wearing of the kilt and tartan was forbidden, and the old patriarchal tribalism disappeared for ever. The chief's right to act as a judge outside the ordinary courts of law was abolished; so was his right to claim military service, which had enabled Argylls and Atholls, Breadalbanes and Sutherlands, to put into battle private armies of from a thousand to three thousand apiece. Besides these measures ending Highland feudalism, important social innovations were introduced. The Scottish Society for the Propagation of Christian Knowledge which had been struggling to convert the half-pagan, half-Catholic Highlanders for forty years now began to achieve some success. Schools were set up. Another 800 miles of road were constructed. The English language began to penetrate, though Gaelic long predominated. After some years the chieftains returned, chieftains no more, but landlords still. The kilt and tartan were allowed back with them. The Highlands had been so well pacified that Pitt was able, as we have seen, to recruit Highland regiments in the Seven Years War without serious fear of disaffection.

There is a darker side to the picture. The old Highlands were primitive and savage, but there was in them a fierce tribal loyalty between chief and clansmen. The breaking of this old relationship destroyed much that was bloody and barbaric, something that was poetic and impressive. From the 1770's onward many lairds became more interested in sheep than men, and over the next eight decades the Highlands were progressively depopulated as the landlords evicted their crofter tenants to make way for the profitable sheep-runs. Later on came the deer and the rich sportsman. It is true that in the old days the Highlands had been over-populated in relation to the yield of the land and the fishing, and it is also true that many a Highlander travelling southward by the new roads found work among the shipyards and slums of Glasgow, or made a new life for himself in Canada, Australia, or the USA. Many, however, were forcibly evicted amid scenes of anguish: women were dragged shrieking from their homes, which were fired after their few sticks of furniture had been thrown out. Whole communities were driven forth; one laird, a Gordon, evicted 2000 in one season from his estates in the Hebrides. Not till the 1840's did Parliament intervene, and then only to assist and humanize overseas emigration. Slowly the Highlands emptied, until the modern tourist began seasonally to fill them up again.

5. Scotland's Georgian Renaissance

In the Lowlands it was a very different story: modern Scotland was born in the eighteenth century, and particularly during its second half. While the population rose from about 1,100,000 in 1700 to 1,600,000 in 1800, the revenue of Scotland multiplied fifty-fold. Two causes among many may be emphasized for this transformation: first, after the Union the Scots enjoyed all the economic advantages open to the English; second, Scottish agriculture underwent a modernization more spectacular even than England's, for it started its rise from a much lower base. In overseas trade Scottish merchants took their highly profitable share of the booming markets in tobacco, cotton, and slaves. Glasgow in particular leaped ahead; within the century its population multiplied over six-fold. At one time it accounted for over a half of Britain's total imports of tobacco. By 1800, cotton-mills were numerous in the villages of Lanark, Renfrew, and Ayr, and in 1792 the new steam-engine of James Watt, a Greenock-born man, first went to work in Glasgow. Soon Irish immigrants were coming to swell the labour ranks— and the slums—of Glasgow almost as fast as those of Liverpool. In many towns of the Lowlands trade was prospering, new industries being established, and old ones expanded. At Carron, in Stirlingshire, Dr John Roebuck, an Englishman, had set up an ironworks as early as 1760. Fifty years later it was linked by canal with the Clyde, employed over a thousand workers, and was accounted the greatest foundry in all Europe; the naval guns manufactured there for service against

Napoleon's fleet were known as carronades. Thomas Telford, of Eskdale, alone was responsible for building in Scotland nearly a thousand miles of good new roads, many splendid bridges, and the Caledonian Canal. John McAdam, of Ayr, revolutionized road-building methods throughout the United Kingdom.

Everywhere there was movement, increasing production, and (except in the Clydeside slums) rising standards of comfort. The outstanding advance in farming took many forms. The antiquated 'run-rigs' disappeared as more and more landlords split their estates into compact farms, and enclosed their fields with hedges or dry-stone walls. Many thousands of acres of new land were reclaimed, especially from the valleys when drainage had made them fit for cultivation, and then they frequently proved better land than the drier hillsides. The horse supplanted the draught ox. Wheat came to supplement oats. Turnips, potatoes, the new fodder crops, liming and manuring, new rotations, new machinery, all helped to banish the threat of starvation that had so recently been so constant, and to bring a new variety into the countryman's basic diet of oatmeal, milk, and ale. By 1800, Scotland, which fifty or a hundred years earlier had been a notoriously treeless land, had been planted with copse and forest on a fine scale. So up-to-date by that time had the farming methods of some parts of the Lowlands become—the Lothians in particular—that their experts travelled south to demonstrate their practice to English agriculturists.

Intellectually, too, Scotland saw a golden age in the later Georgian era. Moderating influences mitigated the severity of her Calvinist church. Edinburgh blossomed as a centre of wide-ranging cultural activity. Robert Adam, himself an Edinburgh-educated Scot, designed many new buildings there, and the city broke through its medieval bounds in both an intellectual and a physical sense; the new Georgian Edinburgh was a city of space and dignity. David Hume, at the heart of this lively Edinburgh culture, was the greatest of Scots philosophers and a notable historian. Among his circle were that other historian and philosopher, Robertson, and the Glasgow professor of moral philosophy, Adam Smith, whose *Wealth of*

Nations, with its criticism of current 'mercantilist' theories, placed him in the forefront of European political economists and among the great precursors of the free-trade movement. In literary criticism, the early nineteenth-century position of the *Edinburgh Review* was commanding, even if its power was not quite sufficient to snuff out the life of Keats (as Byron suggested it did) by a single hostile review. In the science of chemistry the Scots achievement at this period quite outshines the English, both in pure research and in technology. In fact, the British chemical industry was largely the creation of Scotsmen; Professor Joseph Black of Glasgow, Professor Francis Home of Edinburgh, James Watt (who was Black's close associate and first introduced French techniques of bleaching by chlorine into Britain), the Earl of Dundonald, James Keir, and Charles Tennant are a few of them.[3] Scottish engineers, too, in the middle and later Georgian period—Watt and Telford supreme among them—were as daring and inventive as any in the world. The Hunter brothers, the greatest teachers of surgery in eighteenth-century Britain, were Scots, though their school was in London. "John Hunter converted surgery from a trade into a science." Raeburn the portrait painter, Smollett the novelist, and Boswell the biographer were Scotsmen; and in Robert Burns the Scots renaissance found its supreme expression—Burns, the Ayrshire ploughboy whose lyrics, humane, satirical, moralizing, or poignant, became, and remained, a sizeable part of the world image of Scotland itself, and to Scotsmen a sort of national institution. Hard on the heels of Robert Burns came Walter Scott, the very master of romance in an age that revived and made fashionable every variety of the romantic, medieval, Gothic, scenic—or Scottish. Scott romanticized Scots history and legend for an English public that no longer regarded Scotsmen (as they had in Bute's and Dr Johnson's day) as undesirable aliens and parasites upon English prosperity. Scotland had become a part of Britain, and a historic and colourful part. The Union had done its work at last, on both sides of the Border.

[3] See also p. 312.

6. The Condition of Georgian Ireland

In contrast to Scotland's story of steady improvement, the tale of Georgian Ireland is melancholy. Ireland was a conquered country and made to feel like one: a nation five-sixths Catholic and, for the rest, mainly Presbyterian was subjected to the political domination of a tiny minority of Anglicans. The bulk of the Irish multiplied in squalor, or starved, or emigrated, while the country's wealth was constricted by bad laws or sucked away to England.

The English fear of Catholicism was at the root of her misgovernment of Ireland. Every Irish revolt since Tudor times had dug deeper the pit between Catholic and Protestant. The Penal Laws that followed the Catholic rising of 1689–91—most of them passed between 1702 and 1715—were severe indeed. By the time of the Jacobite revolts of 1715 and 1745 the Catholic Irish were so dulled by oppression that not a mouse stirred for the Stuarts, though rebels of adventurous spirit had in their thousands left Ireland to enlist in the service of France, Spain, Austria, and even Russia. An Irish Catholic was debarred from buying freehold land; and a Catholic eldest son could inherit his father's estate entire only if he turned Anglican; otherwise it would be broken up between the family. Thus the Catholic squires loyal to their religion were chopped into poverty and insignificance; and by 1780 about 4000 of them had been coerced by this economic blackmail into conforming to the Church of England. Catholics were barred from trades and professions, from all public office, and from juries. No Catholic could sit in Parliament or (after 1727) vote for it; neither could he carry arms or own a horse worth more than £5. So harsh, in fact, was the anti-Catholic code that it was impossible to enforce it fully. Thus, though a Catholic was forbidden to attend school, keep a school, or send his children to be educated abroad, it was officially estimated in 1732 by the Anglican Primate of all Ireland that there were 594 Catholic schools in existence. Somehow money was found for their upkeep and for that of about 3000 priests, as well as for the compulsory and detested tithes that went towards the upkeep of the Anglican Church (whose membership amounted to only about one in twenty of the population).

Politically, Ireland was under the heel of the English. There was a Protestant Parliament in Dublin; but its legislation was subject to the prior consent of the Privy Council. Presbyterians as well as Catholics were excluded from it, though they were allowed to worship freely and hold petty offices. The Westminster Parliament could make any law it liked for Ireland. General elections were rare: there were none at all between 1727 and 1760. The boroughs were rotten; and the English authorities had no difficulty in manipulating the Irish pension list for their own political purposes.

The trade and industry of Ireland were regulated to suit English interests. No wool might be exported except to England. The manufacture of woollen cloth was forbidden, as was any industrial activity that could offer any competition with English manufacturers. However, a linen industry was tolerated, since England had little of her own. Up to 1758, cattle, sheep, butter, and cheese might not be exported to England, for fear of harming the interests of English farmers, although after that year, as England's demands began to outrun her production, Irish cattle were allowed in. Irish ships were forbidden to trade with America, and in George I's reign there had actually been an attempt, unsuccessful, to prevent the Irish fishing off their own coasts. It is hardly surprising that, in face of all the restrictions, there was a great deal of smuggling, with both England and the Continent: in 1732 Walpole's Government was employing three men-of-war and eight cruising vessels on anti-smuggling patrol in the Irish Channel.

Denied outlets in industry and commerce, the Irish were bound to exist almost wholly by farming; and the mass of the rural population lived in the utmost squalor. Their 'house' was normally a windowless one-roomed mud cabin. Their holdings were small, and grew smaller as the century wore on and the population rocketed. Their rents, on the other hand, were high; and the 'middleman' system adopted by many landlords made these bad conditions worse. By this the landlord would let his estate for a fixed rent to a middleman, who would then sublet to as many tenants as he could accommodate, until sometimes whole families were trying to exist on patches of an acre or two. (A much bigger total rent could be extracted from twenty families with two acres each than from a single tenant with forty acres. Slum landlords inside towns have often adopted similar principles with one-roomed tenements.) By 1837 about four-fifths of Irish farms were of fifteen acres or less, and nearly half of three acres or less. Only the potato, on such minute holdings, could provide a yield to sustain life; but it left its cultivators pitifully vulnerable to a failure in the crop; and as time progressed their increasing reliance on the potato meant an ever wilder gamble for survival. Famines were common in Ireland long before the potato blight of 1846: in 1728 the crop failed, and there were serious food riots in Cork; and the failures of 1739 and 1740 brought such woeful dearth that one in five of the population (according to some estimates) perished—an even bigger proportion than in the "great hunger" of 1845–49. In 1770, 1800, 1807, and several times in the 1820's and 1830's famine took heavy toll. But still the numbers of the Irish rose, as new generations, marrying young (they did not have to wait to save up for a house and home), reared large families of half-naked, barefoot children, surviving and even thriving on potatoes and milk (or buttermilk), which provided a diet not lacking in bulk, or food value, or vitamins. Arthur Young, in his *Tour in Ireland* (1780), after condemning Ireland's unenlightened crop rotations and poor corn-growing practices, praises the "bellyful" of the Irishman's milk and potatoes against the "half a bellyful" of the Englishman's bread and cheese:

> The sparingness with which our labourer eats his bread and cheese is well known; mark the Irishman's potatoe bowl placed on the floor, the whole family on their hams around it, devouring a quantity almost incredible, the beggar seating himself to it with a hearty welcome, the pig taking his share as readily as the wife, the cocks, hens, turkies, geese, the cur, the cat, and perhaps the cow—and all partaking of the same dish. No man can often have been a witness of it without being convinced of the plenty, and I will add the cheerfulness, that attends it.

The cheerfulness is attested by many authorities: among
them Sir Walter Scott, who wrote of the people's "gaiety and
happiness". Indeed, though they were abysmally poor, the
Irish enjoyed plentiful leisure, for the potato requires little
labour except at sowing-time and harvest. "If there be a market
to attend, a fair or a funeral, a horse race, a fight or a wedding,"
wrote another English visitor, "all else is neglected or forgotten." Swift had once said that if the Irish did flourish, it
"must be against every law of Nature and Reason, like the
Thorn at Glastonbury, that blossoms in the midst of winter".

Everything in Ireland stood in the way of agricultural
improvement. In England and Scotland resident landlords saw
before their own eyes the blossoming of their endeavour, and
improvement was bred from incentive. In Ireland good landlords and incentive were alike lacking. The Catholic owner
had no future to look forward to in any case; and the Protestant
English who owned much of Ireland rarely visited their estates,
leaving the management to agents who found it easy enough,
among a land-hungry people, to extract a satisfactory sum.
This absentee rent was not the only wealth that was channelled
away to England: a considerable army had to be maintained
by the Irish exchequer, which was also responsible for paying
a long list of handsome 'political' pensions to Englishmen and
Hanoverians. It was normally Englishmen, too, who were
awarded the well-lined bishoprics and deaneries of the Irish
Church.[4] Altogether, Swift maintained that in his day two-
thirds of the total rents of Ireland were spent in England.

Those rents were paid largely from the sale of everything
except the potatoes on which the Irish lived. Increasingly as
the years progressed, the peasants regarded their small fields

[4] The newly arrived Bishop of Clogher, for instance, Dr John Hotman,
wrote thus to his patron, Lord Sackville, in warm appreciation of his
comfortable new see, which comprised a palace, "a neat and respectable
parish church", a beautiful "demesne" of 560 acres, with servants to
support it. "My beef, mutton, veal, and lamb are all as good in their
kind as can be, the farm is to produce pigs, poultry, cream, and butter,
hay, oats, and straw. The decoy gives me teal and wild ducks. The warren supplies me with as excellent rabbits as ever I tasted; the pidgeon-
house with pidgeons; the water furnishes carp, tench, trout, eels, perch,
and pike; the venison in the park is remarkably good; and a most extensive range of mountains, of which I have absolute dominion, yields in the

of oats, barley, and wheat as earmarked for cash sale. Their pig that shared and contributed to their cabin's homely stench was a valued guest, for he was "the gentleman who paid the rent". And one of the bitterest ironies of all Ireland's bitter history was the uninterrupted export of cereals to England throughout the famines of the eighteen-twenties and -thirties, and even at the height of the great famine of 1845–49. Moreover, the attractive market in the sale of wool to England and of beef-cattle to Europe (and later to England too) had encouraged the larger owners to convert their estates to pasture, which had further diminished the available arable land and brought about (as in the Highlands of Scotland) wholesale and ruthless eviction. Almost all the smaller farmers were tenants-at-will: the landlord's rights were absolute, and when tenants resisted eviction, their cottages were 'toppled' with the authority of the law and the backing of the military. If the evicted tenants subsequently attempted to survive on the old territory by sheltering in 'scalpeens', or holes in the ground, they were driven out of the neighbourhood. It is not surprising, amid such circumstances, to find that many thousands of the more enterprising peasants seized any opportunity that offered to emigrate—to England, to America, to any land where the dice were not loaded so heavily against them.

Only in Dublin did the flower of civilization bloom in Ireland. In numbers it was the second city of the British Isles. It was, for all its subordination to Westminster, a capital city, with an aristocracy, a culture, an air of its own. Its fine Georgian buildings, including its new Parliament House, provided a setting of dignity and grace, however numerous the beggars in the streets. Bookshops were plentiful; theatres flourished, and a host of fine actors trod their boards, among them the father of Sheridan, who was born in Dublin in 1751; Trinity College had 700 students, one of the finest libraries in

---

proper seasons, an astonishing profusion of partridge, hares, and grouse. The city of Clogher stands on my ground, and the citizens are all of course my tenants. The borough is at present secure, and likely to remain so. . . . Finally, the income of the see is not less, as I am informed, than 4000l. per annum. . . ." Well might Dr Hotman render thanks to the "Supreme Disposer of all events, and those steady and active friends with whose assistance He has blessed me in my pursuits. . . ."

the kingdom, and some eminent scholars among its Fellows. It was in Dublin that Handel gave *The Messiah* its first performance.

7. The Irish National Revolt (1779–98)

Ireland was a defeated and oppressed country. But in Dublin at least, and to some extent elsewhere, there was growing a sense of national consciousness that was to become vociferous from the last quarter of the eighteenth century. Some indications of its potential strength were given when Walpole's attempt to introduce "Wood's Halfpence" in 1722 had roused such intense fires of indignation (which Swift had fanned in his *Drapier's Letters*) that the scheme had to be dropped.

The Irish national revolt was begun by Protestants, and in particular by that very minority of Anglicans whose relatively privileged position, it might be thought, would make them servile to the regime. But they proved to be servile only as long as their faithfulness was well rewarded. After 1763 England's need to extract a greater financial contribution from Ireland (as from America) and the resultant quarrels between the lords lieutenant and the corrupt Irish parliamentary managers had produced a tense situation in Dublin and a sense of grievance among the parliamentarians there which they were quick to exploit. On top of this situation came the American revolution, which had a triple effect. First, by curtailing Irish trade with America and Europe, it produced economic depression. Second, it gave the ruling class the opportunity to raise regiments of volunteers to defend the country against French invasion, and this put into Irish hands a powerful weapon in the argument with Westminster. Third, the crisis in which the English found themselves by 1779, facing potential disaster in America and Europe, immeasurably strengthened the bargaining position of the Irish politicians. Non-importation agreements were made against English goods, in imitation of those of the Americans. "Free Trade or else—" cried a big rally of volunteers in 1779, and the Irish Parliament, led by the lawyer Henry Grattan and Henry Flood, passed a vote of thanks to them. "England's difficulty was Ireland's opportunity", and

North's Government was obliged to make concessions. Catholics were allowed to inherit and bequeath property, and some of the Nonconformists' political disabilities were removed. Restrictions were relaxed on trade between Ireland and the colonies. Finally, in 1782, after a great convention of volunteers, the Rockingham Government abolished the ancient dependence of the Irish Parliament upon the English Privy Council, which had been affirmed in Poyning's Law of early Tudor days, and subsequently reaffirmed by an Act of 1719. Henceforth the Irish Parliament was free, in theory, to legislate for itself.

The revolution, however, was more apparent than real. "I am now," said Grattan proudly, "to address a free people"; but the Westminster Government continued to appoint the Lord Lieutenant, the Chief Secretary, and all important officers of the executive. The Dublin Parliament continued to represent nobody but the small Anglican minority, and remained as corrupt as ever; carefully distributed peerages and sinecures continued to secure English influence. Awareness of this led Grattan to demand parliamentary reform, as his friend Charles Fox was demanding it in England; yet at the same time, anxious to gain a genuinely national support for his campaign for Irish freedom, he also urged Catholic Emancipation. He did not envisage, and would never have supported, any weakening of the Protestant ascendancy, but, as he said, "the Irish Protestant can never be free until the Irish Catholic has ceased to be a slave". A true moderate and an eloquent one, he believed that the two religions could come together in a common patriotism.

Such idealism was soon to be denied. At first the younger Pitt seemed to be very close to Grattan. In 1793 still more of the penal laws were repealed, and Irish Catholics were allowed from that year to vote, though not to sit in Parliament. The Pitt Government, it seemed, might soon go the whole hog, and hope thereby to secure not only some belated justice, but the loyal support of Ireland in the war with revolutionary France. In 1795 a new and liberal Lord Lieutenant, Earl Fitzwilliam (Rockingham's nephew), arrived in Dublin and made no secret of his intention to favour full Catholic Emancipation. Alarm among conservative Anglicans both in Ireland and at Westminster was immediate and acute, and it was soon obvious that Pitt was not prepared to force the issue. The hopes that the impetuous Fitzwilliam had aroused among Catholics were dashed, and he was summarily recalled. Nonconformists, too, were quick to quote the Fitzwilliam episode as evidence of the continuing subjection of Ireland to the Church of England, to the British Government, and to propertied conservatism in general.

The quarrel now was not simply between English and Irish, or between Anglicans and Catholics. A new dimension had been added: it had now become a social quarrel between 'haves' and 'have-nots', between conservatives and radicals; and the consciousness of this cleavage had been greatly strengthened by the recent revolution in France. Nothing was more likely to nip Pitt's liberalism in the bud: his fear of France and of revolution, and his powerful sense of political self-preservation, proved much stronger than his hatred of bigotry. He had reason to be afraid. It was not only the Catholics of the south and west that might have welcomed a French invasion; the Ulster Nonconformist radicals had formed a revolutionary "United Irishmen" society, which might well have greeted the French with equal fervour from a different motive. As these United Irishmen grew more extreme, and began to adopt a military organization, they tended to lose support from respectable Ulster Presbyterians, but they gained correspondingly among the Catholic peasantry. The political beliefs of Grattan were strongly akin to those of Burke; those of such United Irishmen as Wolfe Tone were very close to the French Revolution and Tom Paine. By 1797, with French armies triumphant in Europe and the British fleet in mutiny, the dangers in Ireland appeared impossible for the British to ignore; and authority was given to the Yeomanry, representing the social and religious 'establishment', to search out and disarm the United Irishmen.

This meant civil war. It was the end of Grattan and reconciliation. The Yeomanry did not wait for legal proofs before they flogged and murdered; and the United Irishmen did not merely sit waiting to be hunted out. Hopeful of help from

France, they rebelled. As the revolt spread, the cleavage between Presbyterians and Catholics split wide open again, with horrible mutual atrocities performed both by the Catholic 'Defenders' and by the 'Orange Lodges' of the Presbyterians. Lacking sufficient regular troops, the Government was glad to use the Protestant volunteers to quell the serious insurrection which now broke out in the south, where wild, untrained peasant forces were led by their priests. At Vinegar Hill, in Wexford County, in June 1798, the rebel camp was stormed and the organized rebellion, such as it was, was over. What might have happened if the French fleet that had earlier appeared in Bantry Bay had succeeded in landing the 16,000 men it carried, nobody can say. They might well have set the whole island ablaze. The mere 900 French that did succeed in landing twenty months later in County Mayo were too few and too late.[5] The rebellion was by then broken. What remained was a profound bitterness, a legacy of local terrorism and outrage, and a rift between the religions too broad for any statesman to mend.

8. The Act of Union

Pitt, together with his Irish Secretary, Castlereagh, and his Lord Lieutenant, Cornwallis, made a last effort, nevertheless. Their plan was to offer the Irish a complete union with Britain, together with the necessary balm of Catholic Emancipation. The Protestants would be better persuaded to accept full rights for Catholics, Pitt hoped, if these were accompanied by a political union which would leave Catholics still in a voting minority *in respect of the whole British Isles.* The industrial and trading community would enjoy full freedom of trade throughout the British Empire, a strong inducement to the linen manufacturers of Belfast. And the English would all breathe more freely if the troublesome Dublin Parliament were

[5] Wolfe Tone, after a period of exile in America, had gone to France to urge the maximum French assistance for an Irish rising. In 1798 he was on board a French warship that was captured by the British in Lough Swilly. Tried by court martial, he maintained to the death his belief in Irish independence, and claimed the right to die by musket as a French officer. Condemned to be hanged, he slit his own throat in prison.

out of the way and Westminster made directly and entirely responsible for Irish affairs. The obstacle of persuading the Irish Parliament to enact its own decease was surmounted by the employment of lavish bribery. Office-holders and borough-owners were simply bought out with peerages and heavy cash.

So the Act of Union was passed in 1800, and the cross of St Patrick was incorporated in the Union Jack. The Irish obtained 100 seats in the Commons and 32 in the Lords. But George III's stubbornness in resisting Catholic Emancipation, and Pitt's inability to unite his own Cabinet or to win over the King on this issue, meant that a vital ingredient was missing from the final mixture. Pitt's responsibility in this matter is discussed below,[6] but whatever the verdict upon that, the result remains the same: the Irish Catholic community felt that they had been the victims of a swindle. Pitt should at least be exonerated from the charge of conscious trickery. Undoubtedly he had genuinely intended to emancipate the Catholics. He misjudged the situation; he failed; he resigned.

The Union, unlike that with Scotland a century earlier, brought few blessings. The annihilation of trade barriers had brought prosperity to Scotland; but it subjected the backward agriculture of Ireland to much strain, and it failed to attract English industrial capital. At the same time it removed what protection there had been for the few existing Irish industries. Dublin, without its Parliament on College Green, no longer a capital city, dwindled to a ghost of its mid-Georgian self. An Irish writer of the time likened his country to an heiress whose chambermaid and guardians have been bribed, and who is dragged protesting to the altar.

Among the United Irishmen who escaped after the 1798 rebellion was Robert Emmet, the younger son of a distinguished Irish physician, and, like Wolfe Tone, a graduate of Trinity College, Dublin. The poet Tom Moore, his fellow-student there, tells how one day when Moore had been playing an Irish tune on the piano Emmet had jumped up and exclaimed, "Oh, that I were at the head of 20,000 men and marching to that air!" Restless, poetic, and passionate, he was one of the many who refused to treat the defeat of 1798 as

[6] See p. 247.

final. After a stay in France he returned to Ireland and planned a rising which was to include a direct attack on Dublin Castle. But he was over-sanguine and over-trustful; his movement was riddled with spies; and the insurrection degenerated into a brief confused brawl in the streets. He was hunted down and hanged in 1803.

9. Catholic Emancipation and After

The man who was destined to lead Ireland in the next, and successful, phase of its struggle was very different from either Emmet or Grattan. Grattan had stood for what was by 1800 a lost cause, though he continued active in politics, as a member at Westminster and campaigner for Emancipation, until his death in 1820. Wolfe Tone and Emmet had stood for a French-assisted, radical-patriotic, violent overthrow of the English and all they stood for. The new leader, Daniel O'Connell, success-ful barrister, silver-tongued orator, flamboyant descendant of Celtic chieftains, was not a man of violence: he had opposed the methods of Tone and Emmet, and remembered with horror the hangings and atrocities that had followed "the '98". His strength was to lie in the mass organization of the Catholic peasantry in a great national movement for emancipation. The machinery lay ready to hand in the priesthood; the finance came from the 'Catholic Rent', which demanded a penny a month from the poor and soon brought in £1000 a week. O'Connell's Catholic Association of 1823 had within a few years become a nation-wide league against the existing religious and social order. Violence had not, indeed, been altogether removed, but the futility of the old spasmodic outrages had given place to a concerted mass pressure. As Trevelyan wrote, "the unanimity of the people was terrible".

In 1828 (after Catholic Emancipation had been blocked year after year by the cry of "No Popery", the rise of Protestant Evangelicalism, and the veto of the Crown) O'Connell decided to make a direct challenge. In the election of that year Vesey-Fitzgerald, one of the best and most popular of the Protestant landlords, who had himself voted for Catholic Emancipation, was standing for re-election in County Clare. O'Connell decided to stand against him, though the law would prevent him from sitting at Westminster if he won. Until this time, with the system of open voting, fear of the consequences of voting against the landlord had been a powerful deterrent; but now not only was there mighty and genuine enthusiasm for O'Connell, but fear of the priest and of the Catholic Association might well outweigh fear of the landlord. In County Clare, often with the priests at their head, those Irishmen who had a vote marched to the hustings to return O'Connell with a triumphant majority.

For a few months Ireland, that was never without violence, looked as though it might face another uprising. The Government in London was directed by men who were convinced anti-Catholics—Wellington, the Prime Minister, who was himself an Irishman, and Peel, the Home Secretary, who had been Chief Secretary for Ireland and was known to be an extreme Protestant who had frequently drunk the Orange toast ("Orange Peel", O'Connell called him). These men, however, to the horror of George IV and many of their Anglican supporters, swallowed their convictions in the face of civil war and emancipated the Catholics. All offices of state were now to be open to them but four: monarch, regent, Lord Chancellor, and Lord Lieutenant of Ireland. Driven by fear and prudence to this act of belated statesmanship, the Tory leaders failed to combine it with any gesture of conciliation: O'Connell was obliged to get himself re-elected on petty legalistic grounds, and was studiously snubbed by Peel and Wellington. His own comment on Peel—an immensely impressive man without the gift of friendship—has a terse, contemptuous eloquence: "His smile was like the silver plate on a coffin."

Catholic Emancipation brought no peace to Ireland; its griefs and grievances were still too heavy to be borne with patience. O'Connell and his followers entered Parliament, gave general support to the Whig reforms of the thirties, and for payment pressed hard for a relaxation of economic evils and for the appointment of Catholics to positions of authority. But events in Ireland were too powerful for O'Connell's restraining hand. While British troops supported the 'clearances' of evicting landlords, desperate peasants throughout the south-east turned to terrorism and brigandage. At the same time a violent campaign grew against the payment of tithes to the 'alien' and savagely resented Church of England, which annually was claiming £750,000 under this score, the great bulk of it from an agrarian population wretchedly poor and chronically threatened with starvation. O'Connell, increasingly conservative and strongly hostile to violence, was as strongly opposed to the coercive measures which Grey's Whig Government proposed. Fortunately for the O'Connellites, the Government of Grey's successor, Melbourne, was dependent on their votes, and by 1838 they had managed to extract, as the price of their support, a Bill which allowed the replacement of tithe payments by a fixed rent charge. But even this, and other minor reforms passed by the Melbourne Government against the grudging opposition of the House of Lords, did little more than scratch the surface of the Irish problem. A few years later, Gladstone was to describe this as "the upas tree" (the poison tree of Indonesian fable that destroys all life for miles around). It was growing fast in Ireland as our period closes. In the following decade, the era of the Great Hunger and the Great Emigration, it was to drench the whole island with its foul emanation and contaminate the Irish climate for a century to come.

Chapter 8

George III, Wilkes, and the Whigs

1. George III

There has been more dispute over George III and the nature of his constitutional intentions and actions than over any other historical issue in the English history of this period. The orthodox account, accepted until thirty or forty years ago, was that he was brought up by his mother to "be a king"; that he was nourished upon Bolingbroke's *Idea of a Patriot King*; that upon his accession he systematically attempted to destroy the old political parties and get back into the royal hands all the influence and patronage that under his grandfather and great-grandfather had fallen into the hands of the Whigs; that he corruptly forced through his reactionary policies with the aid of the "King's Friends", but that the disastrous outcome of those policies in America and elsewhere and the tenacity of the Whig party combined eventually to defeat his designs and erode his influence, until at last the rise of the younger Pitt and the decline in the King's mental vigour ensured the supremacy of Parliament and party. Popular American history books went farther, and portrayed George as the obstinate tyrant who was triumphantly resisted by virtuous American patriots and lovers of liberty—a sort of dragon slain by St George Washington.

On both sides of the Atlantic the cruder versions of these myths had been long discredited; but between the mid-nineteen-twenties and the mid-fifties the entire foundations of the old orthodoxy about George III and the Whigs seemed to have been dynamited by the researches of Sir Lewis Namier and his followers, and by Professor Richard Pares. Vast documentation was built up for the view that George III had not attempted any constitutional revolution; that he never read Bolingbroke's book; that it was Fox, Burke, and the Whigs who were revolutionaries, attempting to undermine well-established royal prerogative; that George III could not have wished to abolish 'parties', in any meaningful modern sense of the word, because in that period they simply did not exist; that the "King's Friends" were little more than the ordinary, loyal, independent gentlemen who had always constituted a large proportion of M.P.'s; in short, that George III, though obstinate, was an altogether more reasonable, traditional, correct, even idealistic figure than most older books suggested.

There has recently been some criticism of the extremer versions of this view: Professor Butterfield has had some hard things to say about those followers of Namier who pour scorn too liberally on earlier historians, and who sneer too readily at Burke and the other Whig critics of George. Certainly, if George did not intend a "constitutional revolution", putting the clock back to Stuart absolutism and paternalism, he did at least intend to halt and even to reverse the trends that had been, for half a century and more, nibbling away at the historic power of the monarch. Among the booby-traps and barbed wire of this now famous and long-lived controversy it is necessary to pick one's way carefully.

If high intentions were all, George III would be accounted the greatest of English monarchs. Never was a king more firmly encased in high principles. An honest man and a simple one, he made great demands on both himself and his Ministers. Slow to develop, and in his early years very conscious of his own inadequacy, he turned hopefully to others, seeking for a prop. Bute served for a time until his nerve went, Chatham until his mind broke down, North for twelve years until disaster submerged him. It was not until the arrival of the younger Pitt in 1783—by which time the mature George had acquired considerable political toughness of his own—that a Minister of high stature and mettle arrived who would stand by him to defeat his enemies at home and abroad. It seemed to George III that he was beset by wickedness and treason, vice and ingratitude. His Ministers, in the main, he judged to be men of bad character. His eldest son, another bad character, turned against him, and his other children pursued a miscellany of follies and vices. His American subjects made war upon him.

At home the crowds in the streets cheered the infamous Wilkes, and virulent attacks were made everywhere on the King's reputation. In the House of Commons the politicians actually passed, in 1780, the famous resolution declaring that the King's power had increased, was increasing, and ought to be diminished. Only in his latter days, when he was declining towards total insanity and, in the pitiable end, towards deafness and blindness as well, could men come to think of him as the "good old king", and transfer their animosity and contempt to his dissolute son.

George III's father, that Frederick Prince of Wales who had provoked such malignant distaste in his parents, George II and Queen Caroline, died in 1751, following a chill caught playing tennis. His widow continued, as he had done and his father had done before him, to provide at Leicester House a headquarters for opposition to the King and the King's Ministers. The "governors" of the adolescent prince were successively Earl Waldegrave and the Marquis of Bute, a handsome Scotsman who was the confidential adviser of George's mother. For this assured charmer, who was everything the young George was not and would have liked to be, the lonely prince, deprived as he was of the corrupting company of boys of his own age, developed a romantic infatuation. Everything Bute said was gospel, whether it concerned good breeding, wicked politicians, or the duties of a king. When Bute told him that he must not think of proposing marriage to the Duke of Richmond's fifteen-year-old daughter (who held George's heart captive), he docilely resolved "to grieve in silence, and never trouble you more with this unhappy tale; for if I must either lose my friend or my love, I will give up the latter, for I esteme your friendship above all earthly joy".[1]

[1] He married in 1761 Charlotte of Mecklenburg-Strelitz, a plain, unintelligent girl with whom he lived soberly and faithfully, and by whom he eventually fathered a formidable army of children, whose honesty, as they grew up, was matched only by their immoderation. Between them the royal dukes contrived to run the gamut of eccentricity and notoriety, and scandal grew round them as readily as moss on a damp stone. Cumberland (not to be confused with his great-uncle, "Butcher" Cumberland) was a crude reactionary, so unpopular that legend found it easy to credit him with the crimes of incest and murder. Kent, the father of Queen Victoria, was a martinet who caused a mutiny at Gibraltar, and became a sort of socialist, largely to annoy his brother George IV. York,

Earl Waldegrave had found the young prince "strictly honest", obstinate, "uncommonly indolent", and wanting in application. "He has great command of his passions, and will seldom do wrong, except when he mistakes wrong for right." As for religion, "he has rather too much attention to the sins of his neighbour". This last was a shrewd observation; for George, though very ready to confess his own shortcomings, was readier still to blame others. His grandfather, the King, was "shuffling". The elder Pitt was "the most dishonourable of men", Temple "arrogant and ungrateful", Henry Fox "a man of bad character" and "void of principles", Lord Mansfield "but half a man", Bedford "full of passion and absurdity", and so forth. Only Bute was a paragon; Bute his mainstay. "I will exactly follow your advice, without which I shall inevitably sink." His coming kingship he regarded as at once a burden, a challenge, and a mission. The country in general was depraved ("probity and every other virtue absorbed into vice and dissipation"), and politics particularly so. It should, then, be his sacred duty, with the aid of Bute, to purify the one and purge the other, "to restore religion and virtue" so that "this great country" might "regain her antient state of lustre". To this extent the picture of George as the Patriot King is a fair and true one. But never was there a Hercules less well fitted to cleanse the Augean stables.

George III was a man of no vision but much integrity; idealistic, naïve, obstinate, irritable, uncharitable, conventional, prudish, unimaginative: a man not as stupid as some have made him out, but of average or below-average intelligence, harassed by men and events, dogged by failure, and constantly threatened by mental breakdown. He had no tyrannical ambitions. He preserved, on the contrary, great

---

the soldier, allowed his mistress to deal in the sale of Army commissions. Clarence, the sailor, lived in domestic bliss with an actress who presented him with a steady stream of ten little Fitzclarences, until he threw her over to marry Princess Adelaide and become William IV. Cambridge was perhaps the most amiable of the brothers, but as eccentric and unaccountable as the rest—eccentric too by Hanoverian standards in that he lived quietly with his wife. As for the Prince of Wales, his ostentatious high living, his extravagant gambling, and the scandal of his marital affairs, with a bigamy thrown in, brought the reputation of British royalty to a level lower than it had reached for centuries, or has reached since.

respect for the Revolution of 1688. His greatest ambition was to be a successful constitutional monarch. That his reign proved to be one of prolonged crisis was due to many causes: the character of the King himself, his desire to purify the administration, and the swift onset of processes and events that few men at the time understood, least of all the stubborn-witted George—the growing nationalism of the Americans, the mounting call for reforms at home, the hastening of industrial and social change, the political dynamite of the French Revolution, the culmination of the long struggle with France in the great war that ended at Waterloo. All this George III, obstinate in clinging to life as in everything else, presided over in helpless inadequacy, anger, and embarrassment, until at last, his long-threatened mind collapsing, he escaped from the merciless pressure of change and the malice of politicians to sit all day dressing-gowned in his room, his sight and hearing gone, and his white hair and beard as wild and wandering as his words.

One immediate effect of a young King coming to the throne in 1760 was that, for the first time since 1714, there was, for over twenty years, no heir to provide a nucleus for opposition politicians to adhere to. And since it was in the nature of politicians to scheme for power and influence, there was nothing for them to do but to make themselves a nuisance directly to the King and his Government, hoping that it would become worth his while, or the Government's while, to silence their criticism by offering them office; in short, to buy them off. When, therefore, George III found himself at loggerheads with the various Whig groups, and bitterly complained of the "hydra faction" that he was up against, it was a sober and reasonable complaint. These political cliques usually centring round some great territorial magnate, a Bedford, a Temple, a Rockingham, a Devonshire, had come to treat the affairs of the nation pretty well as their collective private monopoly. The ancestors of many of them had played a big part in the 1688 Revolution, and not a few of them made the unconscious assumption that the King was king by their permission. Only a few of them were openly anti-monarchical, but the majority, while professing a patriotic loyalty to the Crown, had come to assume that on vital points of conflict the King could usually be circumvented. George II on several occasions (notably in 1744, 1746, and 1757) had been forced to accept Ministers that he disapproved of, or even (in Pitt's case) detested; and he had been constantly obliged to knuckle under on matters of policy. During his latter years, in particular, the peppery old King's chief prerogative had been that of grumbling. His bark was loud and his growl noisy, but he had lost many of his teeth to bite with. Being king, he was very far from powerless; but the effective makers of Ministries after the fall of Carteret had been Henry Pelham and his brother Newcastle, with Pitt in the wings or, briefly, at the centre of the stage. By 1762, however, not only was there a new King with a strong sense of mission, but Pelham was dead, and Newcastle and Pitt were both out. At the centre of the play now was the King himself, and it was this that somehow seemed to politicians of the day to be dangerous. This made for all the talk (later crystallized by Charles Fox and Burke) of a "tyrannical" King and the dangers of "arbitrary" rule. This was what led to Dunning's motion (1780) that the power of the Crown ought to be diminished. In fact, George III, though he did develop a taste for political manipulation, had an almost exaggerated respect for what he took to be the British constitution.

We read sometimes of the struggle between George III and the Whigs; but the very word 'Whigs' conveys several false impressions to a nineteenth- or twentieth-century reader. In the first place, who were the Whigs? They certainly were not a political party in any accepted modern sense. By 1760 they consisted of a number of the cliques, or factions, or "connexions" already described, plus a large number of semi-independent members. Apart from a vague attachment to the Glorious Revolution of 1688, they shared no common purpose other than that of gaining office or influence for themselves. In fact, by 1760 the terms 'Whig' and 'politician' had become practically synonymous, for there were no Tories of any importance left. Half a century of Hanoverian rule had nearly extinguished them. "In truth," said Horace Walpole, "all the sensible Tories I ever knew were either Jacobites or became Whigs; those that remained Tories remained fools." The alternative to a Whig Government was not, then, a Tory Government, but another Whig Government, with the groups reshuffled and the everlasting coalition reshaped; and this had been true ever since 1717, when Walpole quarrelled with Stanhope. The terms 'Whig' and 'Tory', as party labels, had become practically meaningless by 1760.

2. Ministries Come and Go (1760-70)

The Bute administration on which George had pinned such hopes did not last long. For one thing Bute himself did not have any relish for the tough game of politics; he had no head for political heights. As he himself once said, he could not everlastingly "tread on the brink of a precipice, and this without even the hope of doing good". A cultivated Scottish gentleman, a fair amateur botanist, interested in agricultural science, John Stuart, third Earl of Bute, had jogged along in the background until a combination of accidents thrust greatness upon him. His marriage to Mary Wortley Montagu (daughter of the authoress of the same name) brought him vast wealth. Then one day when heavy rain prevented the departure of Frederick Prince of Wales from Egham races, Bute was on hand to make a fourth at cards, and from that moment never looked back. With the sudden death of the Prince in 1751, the socially acceptable and morally respectable Bute was the obvious choice for a personal adviser to the bereaved princess, and thus indirectly for a mentor to the young prince. Eventually, the death in 1761 of Bute's kinsman, the Duke of Argyll, left him the leader of the 45 Scottish M.P.'s and 16 Scottish peers. He was, as we have seen, the new King's idol. Everything seemed to have gone his way by 1762. Yet already Bute was worried by quarrels inside the Cabinet (especially with George Grenville, who was pressing for economies); by libellous attacks in the Press, where his close relationship with the Dowager Princess of Wales was scurrilously twisted and the strong popular prejudice against Scotsmen was given a great run; and by the violent unpopularity of the proposed new cider excise, whose reception roused memories of Walpole, thirty years earlier. The mob had been signifying its feelings by burning a *boot* (meaning Bute) and a petticoat (meaning the princess); and at times he had been unable to move in the streets unless protected by 'bruisers'. His coach was attacked and the windows of his house smashed. By the spring of 1763, his health not good, he felt that he could stand it all no longer. He resigned without making a fight, and was succeeded as First Lord of the Treasury by George Grenville (April 1763).

At the same time the elder Fox came to the end of his lucrative tenure of the Paymastership. Netting his gains, he exacted what he claimed was part of an agreed bargain—in return for quitting his office, promotion to the Lords. In the spirit of the times, he intimated that if he did not get his peerage he would concentrate upon the Ministry his very considerable talent for making trouble. So this able, dissipated, money-loving politician became Lord Holland. (He needed all his money: a few years later he had to find £140,000 to pay the gambling debts of his sons.[2])

Thus, by 1763, Pitt, Newcastle, Bute, and Fox had all resigned. For three of them George would shed no tears, but at Bute's desertion he was bitterly disappointed. He corresponded with him for a year or two longer; but, intensely disliking George Grenville, his new Prime Minister, George soon continued elsewhere his unrewarding search for a Minister he could trust.

The King mistrusted Grenville, and Grenville certainly mistrusted the King. He always suspected that Bute, behind the scenes, "the minister behind the curtain", enjoyed more influence with George than he did, and that George was engaged in constant manœuvres to eject him. He accordingly bargained toughly, insisting among other things on having the power of patronage in his own hands. Inside the Cabinet, too, there were perpetual jealousies and jockeyings between Grenville, Halifax, Sandwich, and Bedford. The surprising thing is that any policy at all emerged from this chaotic bickering and suspicion. But Grenville's Government was united and con-

---

[2] It was his own fault. From the beginning, he had made them his companions in pleasure, giving them—and Charles in particular—a thorough grounding in sexual dissipation, high play at cards, heavy drinking, and classical literature.

sistent in at least one particular, the need for economy—a popular theme after an expensive war. In harmony with this close examination of pounds, shillings, and pence was, as it turned out, the most far-reaching of Grenville's moves, the famous Stamp Act—what seemed in 1765 a quiet, harmless little measure to ensure that the American colonists played their part in the general scheme of taxation. The explosion that followed will be dealt with subsequently.[3] So too will that other explosion that the Grenville Government provoked —the Wilkes affair.[4] In these respects there was no quarrel between King and Ministers; in these respects alone they walked forward hand in hand into the morass.

In 1765 the King suffered the first of his attacks of insanity: a brief one, but sufficient to give rise to further squabbles over the provision of a regent. (If it were to be the Dowager Princess of Wales, would this be another way of dragging Bute in by the back door?) The state of affairs between George and his Ministers is vividly shown by one of his letters to Bute at this time:

> Every day I meet with some insult from these people; I have been for near a week as it were in a feaver my very sleep is not free from thinking of the men I daily see; ... a mind ulcer'd by the treatment it meets with from all around is the true cause of it.

And when these men were not insulting him they were boring him intolerably; Grenville in particular: "When he had wearied me for two hours, he looks at his watch to see if he may not tire me for an hour more." George tried everything to rid himself of his detested servants. His uncle Cumberland was approached for his advice and good offices. Cumberland advised that Pitt was indispensable, together with "Newcastle's friends"—that is, the "old Whigs" now led by the Marquis of Rockingham. Pitt was approached, but, as usual, proved difficult. He insisted on his own terms: a foreign policy based on Prussian friendship, conciliation with America, a repeal of the cider tax, and (most difficult of all) office for his brother-in-law Lord Temple, who was the senior representative of the

[3] See below, p. 259.   [4] See below, p. 226.

Grenville "cousinhood" and no friend of his brother George, the Prime Minister.

Since Pitt would not yet oblige, George turned to the young Lord Rockingham, who he hoped had "principles and therefore cannot approve of the Crown being dictated to by low men". But Rockingham's principles were as vague as his amiable gentlemanly idealism, and his Government was such a thing of shreds and patches that nobody inside it or out expected it to last: a Ministry "fit only for summer wear", Charles Townshend said. Its one achievement was to repeal the Stamp Act, though here it spoiled any chance of reconciliation with the Americans by insisting on the Declaratory Act, that reiterated Britain's *right* to tax her colonies. Rockingham's principal claim to fame lies in his appointing as private secretary a young Irish lawyer named Edmund Burke. A few years later Burke was arguing that "a great empire and little minds go ill together"; but in 1766 he was voting with his fellow-Whigs (and against Pitt) in favour of the Declaratory Act.

Rockingham's was little more than a caretaker Government while Pitt was waiting to make up his mind to assist the King. At last the great man condescended to form a sort of superior coalition, a "national" Government, a combination of men of goodwill. This, at least, was the theory, and George III was mightily relieved. He knew, he wrote, that Pitt would "zealously give his aid towards destroying all party distinctions". In other words, Pitt would split the factions by detaching some from one, some from another, and thus build a new Ministry which would be above party. But others had doubts whether the new administration was any less patchy than Rockingham's. Burke amused himself at its expense:

> ... such a diversified piece of mosaic; such a tessellated pavement without cement; here a bit of black stone, and there a bit of white; patriots and courtiers, king's friends and republicans; Whigs and Tories; treacherous friends and open enemies; that it was, indeed, a very curious show; the colleagues whom he had assorted at the same boards, stared at each other, and were obliged to ask, "Sir, your name?— Sir, you have the advantage of me—Mr. Such-a-one—I beg a thousand pardons—"

Pitt now became the Earl of Chatham (his wife having already been Lady Chatham in her own right for nearly five years); and although this move was greeted with cries of abuse similar to those of five years earlier, the principal motive behind it may well have been that his health was too insecure for the hurly-burly of the Commons. His colleagues, however, were not made to feel that he was a weakling. Within a few days he was again behaving like the saviour of his country, planning a reconciliation with America, replanning the East India Company's status, and making moves in foreign policy that seemed to indicate he was already dreaming of winning another war. Emissaries were dispatched post-haste to Berlin and St Petersburg; but Frederick the Great's reactions were cool, and those of the French Minister, Choiseul, both shrewd and a little contemptuous: perhaps, he commented, Pitt would discover that he was "a Samson shorn of his locks". French plans for a war of revenge proceeded methodically.

Power excited Pitt. The old exultation returned. The old dictatorial temper reasserted itself. "Lord Chatham," said Charles Townshend on emerging from a Cabinet meeting, "has just shown us what inferior animals we were." He made tremendous exertions and rapidly exhausted his physical and nervous reserves. After only one month he was assailed again by gout. Recovering somewhat, he attacked business and colleagues with equal energy until the old reaction set in. By the summer of 1767 he was sunk deep in melancholia, shut away in a tiny top-floor room at Hampstead. "He sits most part of the day leaning his head down upon his hands, which are rested on the table," reported a visitor. ". . . If he wants anything he knocks with a stick; he says little even to Lady Chatham if she comes in. . . ." His meals were passed to him through a double-doored hatch, so that the servants would not see him, or he them. Deprived of appetite for long spells, he kept a succession of chickens cooking, ready to satisfy sudden bursts of hunger: a Samson shorn of his locks indeed.

To George III this collapse of Chatham's was a disaster. The Ministry of patriotic renewal, centring round the great name, no longer had a centre. George requested Chatham—he summoned Chatham—to attend to business. At last, in October

1768, he lost his great figurehead altogether. Chatham resigned. To George it was desertion.

During his illness Chatham's colleagues had already reversed his policies, especially in the matter of the American colonies, where Charles Townshend had introduced fresh duties payable by the colonists. Ill as he was, Chatham knew that Townshend was "betraying him every hour". Only Shelburne and Camden[5] remained faithful inside the Cabinet to its sick leader's policies; and, when he resigned, only Shelburne followed him.

The sudden death of the wayward, witty Townshend left the Duke of Grafton at the head of affairs, and George III back in his old position of frustration. Grafton was soon engulfed in further trouble with the colonists, following the Townshend duties, and then with Wilkes, who returned from France to serve his triumphant prison sentence and four times to be elected M.P. for Middlesex. At the beginning of 1770, Grafton, beset by multiple tumults, savaged by the brilliant *Letters* of the anonymous Junius, and attacked by a now-recovered Chatham, resigned in his turn. It was the end of the first decade of George III's reign—a decade of unparalleled political chaos.

3. "That Devil Wilkes"

An important characteristic of the eighteenth century is the steady growth in the newspaper-reading public. Ever broader acres of gossip, weightier tons of social chatter, higher mountains of political controversy, were committed to print as the century progressed. As population, prosperity, and literacy simultaneously advanced, "public opinion" (which in earlier centuries must have been minute) grew in both volume and importance. The political journalist hence became an ever more influential and significant figure, until, by the time of Waterloo, Cobbett could command a weekly readership of hundreds of thousands.

In the early sixties Bute had the services of a fellow-Scot, Tobias Smollett, to edit a paper called the *Briton*. In June 1762 there first appeared a counterblast to this pro-governmental

---

[5] Earlier, Chief Justice Pratt, the judge who declared General Warrants illegal.

publication, the *North Briton*, a paper whose very title implied a sneer at Bute and the Scots, and whose early numbers were enlivened by attacks on Bute and his fellow-countrymen, scandalous smears upon the Dowager Princess of Wales, abuse of Hogarth and others known to be friendly to the administration, and a sarcastic description of the Lord High Steward at George III's coronation, upon a horse which, having been taught to go backward in the King's presence, insisted on going no way but backward. The anonymous editor of this sharp-edged journal was John Wilkes.

Born in 1727, he was the son of a new-rich London distiller, who found enough money to send his son on the Grand Tour that was the making (and often the ruin) of the cultured English gentleman. Wilkes married a rich heiress "to please an indulgent father", became a Buckinghamshire landowner, and spent £11,000 of his own and his wife's money in getting himself into Parliament. One of his early Buckinghamshire friends was his predecessor as member for Aylesbury, a certain Thomas Potter, son of an Archbishop of Canterbury and as gay, dissolute, and irresponsible as Wilkes himself. Potter introduced him to Sir Francis Dashwood (later Chancellor of the Exchequer) and to the Hell Fire Club, which used to enjoy some wild goings-on among the Gothic ruins of Medmenham Abbey and in the caverns under West Wycombe Park. These men, the "Mad Monks of Medmenham", brought dissipation, blasphemy, and indecency to a fine art. Lord Sandwich was one of them, another future Cabinet Minister, whose contemporaries knew him for his unscrupulous licentiousness (in an age when aristocratic depravity set tall standards); posterity and the English language have remembered him for a harmless dietetic innovation. Among these men—wits, poets, politicians, rakes—Wilkes was in the company of his peers. Despite his squint and his leer, his wit and charm could carry him anywhere; it took him, he said, only half an hour to talk away his face. It did not take him much longer to gamble away his fortune, with drink and women and electioneering thrown in. (Early on, he parted from his wife.) So, failing to get himself appointed as ambassador to Turkey or Governor of Canada, he took to the trade for which his wits qualified him—quick-fire, hard-hitting journalism. The squib about the Lord High Steward's horse involved him in a duel, which was settled with that show of courage and absence of accuracy (at eight yards) customary among gentlemen. The *North Briton*, meanwhile, ran successfully through forty-four numbers.

Among Wilkes's neighbours was Lord Temple of Stowe, another to whom the well-connected Potter introduced him, and Wilkes was soon an established member of the Temple Whigs and dependent on Temple's funds. One day in 1763, soon after the fall of Bute and rise of George Grenville, Wilkes listened to Temple and Pitt discussing with rage the advance copy of the King's Speech which Grenville (their respective brother and brother-in-law) had been good enough to send them. Wilkes went away and wrote Number 45 of the *North Briton*, paraphrasing and spicing their condemnation. After protestations of loyalty to the Throne, he proceeded to lament "that a prince of so many great and amiable qualities ... can be brought to give the sanction of his sacred name to the most odious measures, and to the most unjustified public declarations, from a throne ever renowned for truth, honour, and unsullied virtue". Bute himself was simply referred to as "the favourite", and the Ministers in general were described as "a weak, disjointed, incapable set", "tools of despotism and corruption". Worst of all, Wilkes wrote that it was a "falsehood" for the King to describe the Treaty of Paris as "honourable to my Crown and beneficial to my people". Was the King, then, a liar?

Grenville and his two secretaries, Halifax and Egremont (as well as the outraged King himself), deemed that Temple and Wilkes had this time gone too far, and they issued a *general* warrant for the arrest of "the authors, printers, and publishers" of the *North Briton*, on a charge of seditious libel. No specific names were on the warrant. Thus began the battle, a scuffle between rival Whig factions; it was to spread until it involved the much larger questions of the liberty of the subject, the tyranny of Government and King, the freedom of the Press, and the need for parliamentary reform. Contest and danger were the breath of life to Wilkes; and he proceeded to behave with the utmost effrontery. He published the correspondence between himself and the Secretaries; he sued them for damages; he insisted on being carried, as befitted his dignity, in a sedan-chair. When he was committed, briefly, to the Tower he specially requested that he should not be put in a room that housed a Scotsman, as he was afraid of contracting the itch. Might he not have the one previously occupied by Lord Egremont's father? (Egremont, the Secretary of State, was son of a Jacobite.) When asked to play a hand at cards he protested he could not tell a king from a knave. And either by luck or by acute political judgment he at once broadened the issue of his own arrest. It affected, so he claimed, "the liberty of all peers and gentlemen *and . . . that of all the middling and inferior sort of people who stand most in need of protection*". So Wilkes the dissolute gambler became overnight Wilkes the champion of liberty and of the rights of the common man; the fashionable good-for-nothing became at one bound a popular hero and the victim of arbitrary power.

He took his first stand on the issue of General Warrants, claiming them to be illegal; warrants for arrest must specify the names of the persons to be apprehended. On this he scored a popular triumph. Pratt, the justice of the Court of Common Pleas, found for him, with £1000 damages for Wilkes and £400 for the printer. (Hogarth, one of the *North Briton*'s victims, took his opportunity to caricature him in court, all sideways grin and squinting cocksureness, holding aloft the staff of Liberty.) Cock-a-hoop now, against Temple's orders he reprinted the "seditious libels", at his own risk and expense. This was sticking his neck out rather far, and Parliament attempted to chop it off: they voted Number 45 a seditious libel by 237 to 111, ordered it to be burned, and expelled its author; and Pitt, who had hitherto shown him friendship, now called him "a blasphemer of his God and libeller of his King". He "did not deserve to be ranked among the human species". Wilkes now fought a second duel with another of his literary victims, and, when he was wounded in the groin, it was thought by many (including Horace Walpole) that there had been an attempt to murder him. Closely watched by Government spies, and with his wound still not fully healed, at the close of 1763 he slipped over to Paris, whither his beloved and only legitimate daughter Polly had preceded him. Two months later he was prosecuted *in absentia* in the King's Bench for publishing pornography, convicted, and, when he did not present himself, outlawed.[6]

For the next five years, while the Governments of Grenville, Rockingham, and Chatham rose and fell, Wilkes lived in Paris or travelled through Europe, attending to his daughter's convent education; living the life of a man of pleasure; visiting Voltaire and being visited by Boswell; attending the fashionable Paris *salons*; but, more and more, longing for a return from his exile. After three brief reconnoitring visits he decided at last to take advantage of the 1768 general election, present himself as a candidate for the City of London, and hope either for a free pardon or for immunity from prison by virtue of membership of the Commons. His letter to the King requesting pardon remained unanswered; and the City rejected him. He decided, therefore, to stand for Middlesex, a constituency where small tradesmen and artisans predominated, and where tumultuous support was likely from the London workmen. ("Middlesex", in fact, meant, very largely, North London.)

Wilkes's candidature was a match among dry tinder. The London mob caught fire and crackled alarmingly. Everywhere "45" was scribbled on walls. The Austrian ambassador was removed from his coach and held upside-down while the Wilkites inscribed "45" on the soles of his shoes; other coaches were denied right of way unless they carried the magic number; unlit windows were smashed; "Wilkes and Liberty" and his blue cockade were everywhere. All this was not purely for disinterested love of Wilkes, or even of liberty. The year 1767 had brought a bad harvest; unemployment was high and dis-

---

[6] Wilkes was in process of publishing privately a poem by the now dead Potter, revised and largely rewritten by Wilkes himself, entitled *Essay on Woman*. This was an indecent parody of Pope's *Essay on Man*, with notes purporting to be by Bishop Warburton, who had edited Pope's original poem. The House of Lords got some amusement out of Warburton himself reading some of the offending passages, and still more from Lord Sandwich, a notorious rake and ex-crony of Wilkes, working up a righteous indignation over this "scandalous, impious and obscene libel". The foreman of Wilkes's printing establishment who had allowed the Government's agents in to extract the evidence was so unpopular among "the middling and inferior sort" that no-one would subsequently employ him, and he committed suicide.

tress general; Wilkes was thus the focus of multiple discontents. In March 1768 he headed the poll by over 400 votes. He was, however, still an outlaw, and was shortly committed to the King's Bench Prison. On his way thither he was disconcertingly rescued by his supporters, who unharnessed the horses and wheeled him off with joy to a Spitalfields tavern. Only with difficulty did he escape from their hectic enthusiasm to the comforts of prison life. A little later, when the crowds threw stones at the Scottish troops detailed to guard the prison, their answering fire killed six rioters, and this became popularly known as the St George's Massacre. Gratuitously, Barrington, the War Minister, wrote to congratulate the regiment, quoting the King's approval; and Wilkes, by his customary pertinacity and good luck, managed to get hold of a letter from Lord Weymouth, Secretary of State, counselling the Lambeth magistrates not to hesitate in calling in military assistance if disorder threatened. Belligerent as ever, Wilkes published Weymouth's letter, with his own characteristic commentary, and when summoned to the Bar of the Commons to apologize for his action justified it instead, describing Weymouth's letter as a "bloody scroll". On top of this, Lord Mansfield at last arrived at pronouncing sentence in respect of the original 1763 verdict of "Guilty of seditious libel"—twenty-two months' imprisonment and a heavy fine. The Commons, too, pronounced its own sentence—expulsion.

Never did prisoner enjoy a more luxurious or exciting twenty-two months. City gentlemen subscribed £20,000 to settle his debts, and the City of London elected him an alderman. The rich merchants of Liverpool and Bristol tumbled over one another to rush to his support and comfort. Hams, pheasants, salmon, turtles, cases of wines, butts of ale, *forty-five* hogsheads of American tobacco, and a great deal more, flowed in to his apartment in the King's Bench Prison from admirers on both sides of the Atlantic. (Wilkes's fame had spread, and his prestige as principal troublemaker for George III and his Ministers was high in the Thirteen Colonies.) No sooner did the Commons expel him than the ecstatic electorate of Middlesex re-elected him; then came a second expulsion; a third election; a third expulsion; a fourth election, with a great four-to-one vote in his favour. And throughout these hectic spring months of 1769 the cry was loud for Wilkes and Liberty. It was, said Burke, "a tragicomedy acted by his Majesty's servants . . . for the benefit of Mr. Wilkes and at the expense of the constitution". The fifth act of the "tragicomedy" was more like farce: a certain Colonel Luttrell, Wilkes's leading opponent in the last election, was declared successful. An egregious motion of the House of Commons declared that he "ought to have been returned". It was at this stage that Chatham, recovered from his mental illness, and overcoming his extreme dislike of Wilkes's morals, lambasted the Grafton Government for its actions both in the matter of Wilkes and of America—though it is likely that enthusiasm for political liberty weighed less at that juncture with Chatham than a desire for revenge on ex-colleagues who had betrayed his policies. Whatever his motives, Chatham was in tremendous form again. Grafton did in fact resign, but, although everyone expected to see George send for Chatham, the King stuck to his guns and Lord North.

The first great issue in the Wilkes affair had been General Warrants. His quite accidental demonstration of their illegality had been a notable victory in the struggle of the individual citizen against arbitrary and indiscriminate arrest, and against the old argument, specifically repudiated by the judge in the General Warrants case, that State necessity overrode the liberty of the individual citizen. The second issue had been the old one of the liberty of the Press. The third was now joined: the right of free citizens of England to elect to Parliament whom they pleased, not merely those the Commons were prepared to tolerate. Lord Conway warned the Opposition not to "set up the liberty of the people against the liberty of Parliament". There were yet other issues beginning to crystallize round the name of Wilkes, and there was even at this time the beginnings of a Wilkite (or Wilkesite) party. A Society for the Defence of the Bill of Rights was founded in 1769, and that same year Wilkite "missionaries" toured the provinces. By the time that Wilkes came out of prison in 1770 there was a Wilkite 'programme', but of so ephemeral a nature and so personal to Wilkes and his status that it is of no serious importance in the history of radicalism or reform. Soon the Wilkites themselves were sundered by quarrels between rival factions. Wilkes, in fact, was not of the stuff of which genuine reformers are made. His principal interests after 1770 lay in carrying on his personal vendetta against the Commons (as City alderman he caused the House's messenger to be arrested), and in securing his own election as Lord Mayor of London, in which, at the third attempt, he was successful. When he was again elected to Parliament in 1774, North's Government wisely made no challenge. He took his seat, but played little part in parliamentary affairs beyond championing the right of London newspapers to print reports of parliamentary proceedings; one parliamentary Reform Bill he submitted in 1776 was withdrawn without a division. Such opinions as he ventured were mildly liberal, supporting such causes as prison reform and religious toleration. To George III, who was at last reduced to meeting him face to face at Court, he said he "never was a Wilkite"; the King was astonished at the gentlemanliness of the man he had once called "that devil". And during the anti-Catholic Gordon riots of 1780 he played a notable part on the side of law, order, and religious toleration, and against his old allies the London mob. The violence of the French Revolution pained him. A back number by now, but a sprightly and kindly one, he divided his last years between his "beloved and excellent" daughter Polly, an affectionate mistress, and various illegitimate children. When he died in 1797 they engraved his coffin with the single inscription he had requested: *The Remains of John Wilkes, a Friend to Liberty.*

In the short term, perhaps the most important effect of the Wilkes incidents was to distract attention from more vital problems, in particular those of the American colonies. In the long term, what Wilkes did above all, even more than the elder Pitt, was to bring that new character, the People, on to the political stage: the "middling and inferior sort", indeed. Some of them were ignorant, noisy, and ready to shout away their grievances in any cause, good or bad; but others were prosperous and intelligent men who read the papers, lacked (very likely) a parliamentary vote, were critical of the corrupt oligarchies who ruled their local towns, and were quite ready to believe that Parliament itself was not much better. The provincial Press was as full of Wilkes and his fight for freedom as London. It was not so much that Wilkes 'stood for' the People, or Liberty, or for that matter anything except a good fight with the Establishment. George III might resent the politicians, and they him; but, as 'top people', they could at least agree on ostracizing the infamous Wilkes, the rebellious outsider, the element of anarchy. "Such is the levelling principle that has gone forth," protested one M.P. in the debate over Wilkes's exclusion, "that the people imagine that they themselves should be judges over us."

The Wilkes affair was far from being a simple quarrel between George III and John Wilkes; there were innumerable cross-currents. In one respect, however, it is reasonable that by many it should have been seen so; for the two men represented exactly the two great opposing principles of Authority and Liberty. One of George's favourite words was Subordination. How could good government be maintained without a proper deference? Wilkes, the impudent immoralist, whose old Hell Fire Club had had as its motto *Fay ce que vouldras*, personified insubordination. His part resembles that of the bumble-bee in Rimsky-Korsakov's opera. The king jumps up on the table, upsetting the dishes, swotting wildly and ineffectually. The courtiers and assembled guests are thrown into confusion and disarray.

4. George III and Lord North

With the Wilkes turmoil, the return of Chatham to the fray, the *Letters of Junius* (the most destructive political invective of the century), the rising tide of trouble in America, and the chronic insecurities of Ministries, the first decade of George III's reign closed in a clamour. At that point, 1770, a book appeared which reflects that situation, and which became one of the great political classics, yet whose author has been perhaps flattered unduly. Burke's *Thoughts on the Cause of the Present Discontents* was written primarily as an apologia for the activities of the Whig gangs, and in particular of the Rockinghams, whose members passed the book round in its preparatory stages and suggested points to the author. Burke was at pains to show how patriotic and politically valuable the Whigs were, and how the King was trying to subvert the constitution, dish the Whigs, and substitute a personal rule; the King was the innovator, the parties were the true conservatives. Deprived of its old naked prerogative, the Crown had built up a substitute, "with much more strength, and far less odium, under the name of influence"; and this influence was under "the sole direction of its private favour". In the nineteenth century, when parties in a modern sense had really arrived, and the Whig view of seventeenth- and eighteenth-century history in general, and George III in particular, had been generally accepted, Burke's *Present Discontents* came to be regarded as one of the canonical books of political freedom and the British way of life. Not only Burke's justification, but the very definition of party, came to be accepted as classical: "a body of men united for promoting by their joint endeavours the national interest upon some particular principle in which they are all agreed". Recent historians have looked somewhat critically at all this high-sounding resonance. First, 'party' to Burke meant what George called 'faction', in particular, Burke's own faction of the Rockinghams—a very different thing from what Lord Macaulay meant, or Gladstone, or the modern Labour and Conservative parties. Second, his view of George III and "the King's Friends", whom royal influence built up in Parliament, is not supported by the facts. Third, the parties of Burke's day were *not* built upon 'principle', but upon the hope of office. Fourth, if any were bringing in political innovations in 1770, it was much more Burke, Charles Fox, and their supporters than George III. In short, Burke's political philosophy, majestically propounded as it is, can no more escape from the circumstances of its own time than any other piece of propaganda. Burke and the Rockinghams wanted office, just as Bolingbroke had earlier, when he wrote his *Idea of a Patriot King* (as much admired by Disraeli and some Conservatives as Burke by Macaulay and the Liberals). Behind Bolingbroke's book stands the hated figure of the one stumbling-block, Walpole; behind Burke's, that of the other, George III.

George had by 1770 weathered the storms of Wilkes, Junius,

and Chatham. When the Duke of Grafton resigned in 1770 most men thought that the King would be obliged to send once more for Chatham; but he had not forgiven him. George saw no need for a change of administration; he simply promoted Lord North from within the old Ministry.

North has had a bad Press among historians on both sides of the Atlantic. How could it be otherwise? He was "the man who lost the American colonies". Failure makes bad propaganda. But if North had disappeared from the scene in 1775 he would have been accounted a considerable success. Within a year or two of the "discontents" of 1768–70 the political temperature at home had dropped; the Rockingham faction had been defeated, while the Grenvillites and the Duke of Grafton had been persuaded to join the Ministry; Chatham had once again retired, unfit any longer for prolonged campaigning; Wilkes gave little trouble; North's handling of the Treasury was generally allowed to be first-class. All in all, the country seemed to have sailed into quiet water after storms.

North was a man of common sense and solid efficiency in financial matters: as far removed from Chatham (in whose allegiance he had first appeared on the political scene) as a man could be, driven by no demon, a stranger to ideas, fired by no great ideals, easy-going to the point of indolence, humorous,[7] affable. He did not regard it as the principal duty of a Government to legislate; a Government's duty was to govern, to run the country's finances in an orderly way, to preserve law and order, and to maintain the national interest abroad. The only legislation of note during this period concerned the powers and constitution of the East India Company.[8] North would not even have regarded himself as Prime Minister; it was a term much disliked; and in any case George was, in a sense, his own Prime Minister at this period. North was, rather, the King's representative in Parliament, as, to

[7] A ragged and tired North, towards the end of his term of office, was being attacked in a Commons debate for disastrous incompetence in America and at sea; and while calamities piled up (the speaker continued), the country's leader was asleep on the Treasury Bench. North stirred, opened an eye, and murmured, "I wish to God I were."
[8] See Chapter 9.

some extent, Walpole had been for George I and George II: an outstandingly successful leader of the House. For his easy relations with the Commons there is no need to seek an explanation in any more-than-ordinary corruption or in Burke's loaded phrase "King's Friends".

Undoubtedly this famous expression was employed; similarly, in 1765 or so, a group in the Commons had been known as "Bute's Friends", and Rockingham's men had been first of all known as "the Duke of Newcastle's Friends". Certainly, too, the King did make use of his patronage, as his predecessors had done, either personally or through their Ministers. (Dundas once said, "Is it not as honourable to be the King's pensioner as Lord Shelburne's?") But the men who supported North in the Commons were not the King's tools. They were members independent of the party cliques who saw no reason to vote against the King's Government while things were going reasonably well. When the American disasters struck in 1777 and after, these same men voted against it often enough, to poor North's pain. He, by then a worried and tired man, constantly besought George to let him go. The King, however, though he might be stupid, was not a coward, as he himself was constantly and generously pointing out; and he did not expect others to be cowards either. North must stay, even if he was feeling ill and tired; stay and help George get the better of the Whigs, and the Americans, and by 1779 half Europe as well. "I know I am doing my duty and therefore can never wish to retract." "I always act from conviction." "I will rather risk my Crown than do what I think personally disgraceful. . . . It is impossible that the nation shall not stand by me; if they will not, they shall have another King."

During this period, of the late seventies and early eighties, it is true that George III, through North, and ignoring defeats in the Commons, was governing personally and pursuing policies the nation disapproved of. We shall later see how he failed, and was forced to let the wretched North go (1782) and to govern through the old detested enemies, the Whigs. The point to be made at the moment is that he did fail; no "King's Friends" could help him because, as such, they hardly existed. Corruption could no more secure George's majority than it could Walpole's earlier. When Walpole lost the support of the independent country gentlemen he could be maintained in office only by George II's personal favour (as he was in his last years as chief Minister). When North similarly lost the support of these independents a like situation existed—but over a longer period, in a more calamitous situation, and with a more obstinately determined monarch.

5. The Demand for Reform

After 1777, when Burgoyne's army surrendered to the Americans at Saratoga, things went from bad to worse for George and North; and as for the two Ministers in charge of the war, Sandwich as First Lord of the Admiralty and Germain (formerly Lord George Sackville) as Secretary of State for the Colonies, they shared the two most disastrous qualities imaginable—incompetence and complacency. By 1779 naval morale was very low, a French invasion was again imminent, Spain was joining the war against Britain, Ireland was threatening rebellion (see Chapter 7), and at home there were once more strong rumblings of unrest.

This domestic discontent took several forms. There was, first, and inevitably, a crescendo of Whig criticism of the King and his harassed but loyal Minister, North. And as calamities and dangers multiplied, there was an ever increasing tendency for the various factions, in particular those of Rockingham, Shelburne, and Charles Fox, to draw together. Even so, their policies were not identical, and there was still nothing that could be called a united Whig party. Fox, the most republican in language, was more and more stressing the need for a major reform of Parliament itself. Burke and Rockingham's group concentrated principally upon the evils of royal patronage and the necessity for cutting back the King's financial resources— in the language of the day, "economical" reform.

Many other currents of reforming thought were beginning to flow, altogether outside the parliamentary groups. In 1776, for instance, Major John Cartwright published a pamphlet attacking the evils of seven-year Parliaments. *TAKE YOUR CHOICE*, it began:

Annual Parliaments	Long Parliaments
and	and
Liberty	Slavery

And what followed was much more than a plea for annual general elections:

> Our representatives, who are in fact our deputed servants, are taught to assume the carriage and haughtiness of despotic masters; to think themselves unaccountable for their conduct; and to neglect their duty.
>
> Whether, indeed, the house of commons be in great measure filled with idle school-boys, insignificant coxcombs, led-captains, and toad-eaters, profligates, gamblers, bankrupts, beggars, contractors, commissaries, public plunderers, ministerial dependants, hirelings, and wretches, that would sell their country, or deny their God for a guinea, let everyone judge for himself.... The revolution which expelled James from the throne, glorious as it was ..., was yet a very defective proceeding.... Trust not, I say, in princes nor in ministers; but trust in YOURSELVES, and in representatives chosen by YOURSELVES alone!

Cartwright, who was the brother of the inventor of the steam-power loom, lived to be the doyen of British radicals in the days following Waterloo, almost long enough to hear his cry for annual Parliaments, universal male suffrage, and the ballot taken up by the Chartists.

In that same year 1776 (the year of the Declaration of American Independence, of Adam Smith's *Wealth of Nations*, of the first volume of Gibbon's *Decline and Fall of the Roman Empire*, and of Jeremy Bentham's *Fragment on Government*), the Rev. Richard Price published *Observations On Civil Liberty*, a sternly moralizing, and best-selling, assault on contemporary corruption:

> In this hour of danger [he wrote] it would become us to turn our thoughts to Heaven. This is what our brethren in the Colonies are doing. From one end of North America to the other they are fasting and praying. But what are we doing?—shocking thought—We are running wild after pleasure and forgetting everything serious and decent in Masquerades.—We are gambling in gaming houses: trafficking in boroughs: perjuring ourselves at elections; and

selling ourselves for places—which side is Providence likely to favour?

Price, Philip Doddridge, and Joseph Priestley (one of the discoverers of oxygen) were the three most distinguished products of the Nonconformist school of political and moral philosophy. Politically radical, morally puritanical, they were as severe on the idle poor as the idle rich, as much the enemies of the poor law as of the sale of rotten boroughs, hating the alehouses of the common people equally with the masquerades of the wealthy and fashionable. This combination of attitudes made them favourite authors of the professional and trading classes, but, notwithstanding their radicalism, objects of working-class hatred. The effigy of Priestley (like Price a Nonconformist minister) had been burned many times by hostile mobs before the Birmingham rabble finally destroyed his chapel, his house, and all his scientific valuables, when he publicly supported the French Revolution.

The defeats in America and the dangers nearer home inevitably quickened the demand for reform, and by 1780 the Marquis of Rockingham was rejoicing "in the spirit which now seems rising in all parts of the country". Certainly by 1779–80, for the first time in the eighteenth century, there was a sense of a national reform movement, critical of the King, critical of his Ministers, critical of Parliament itself. This was the year that was remarkable for the Petitioning Movement.

Once again it was a Middlesex election (just ten years after Wilkes) that raised the political temperature in the autumn of 1779. Following it, meetings were held "to maintain and support the freedom of elections"; and soon not only the London but the provincial newspapers were full of notices advertising meetings of freeholders (that is, of county voters) to petition against wasteful expenditure and corrupt government. There was such a meeting of the "Gentlemen, Clergy and Freeholders" of the County of York, called by the Rev. Christopher Wyvill, in December 1779, and out of it came the Yorkshire Association, which petitioned "the Honourable the Commons of Great-Britain in Parliament assembled" for three reforms: triennial Parliaments instead of septennial; "economical" reform; and, in particular, the creation of a hundred extra county members, it being then considered that members for the counties were less liable to corrupt pressures than those for the boroughs.[9] Rockingham was present at this meeting of the Yorkshire gentlemen, but does not seem to have had any particular notice paid to him. Naturally, however, many among the Whigs, hearing the chorus of national criticism singing their tunes, were not slow to join in. Fox was active in the Wiltshire Association, which was soon flourishing with many more throughout the counties of England. There was even a move to create a national confederation of these county committees, and, among the more radical, revolutionary talk of an alternative "parliament" to be formed from their representatives: a sort of anti-parliament, as one Rockingham Whig described it. This was not new: one of Price's followers, James Burgh, had put it forward, together with universal suffrage, in 1772; but it was dangerous stuff; and even the suggestion of holding a delegate conference of the county associations in London was too much for most of the parliamentary Whigs. Burke said later that it would have been "nosing Parliament in the very seat of its authority". (It is noteworthy that when the Chartists met in their great London convention of nearly sixty years later, this is precisely what they were aiming to do.)

One of the reasons for the sudden decline of the petitioning movement and the county committees lay in the activities of one particularly noisy association, the Protestant Association of the young Lord George Gordon, formed in 1779 to resist any further removal of disabilities from Roman Catholics. (A Bill of 1778 had granted military recruits the right on enlistment simply to take an oath of allegiance; the attempt to extend it to Scotland had brought out the Presbyterian diehards and other Protestant true-blues.) On the day appointed for Gordon to present his anti-Catholic petition to Parliament 60,000 people thronged St George's Fields and swarmed thence over the river to Westminster. For the ensuing week London was in an uproar: Catholic chapels were fired, private houses

[9] This theory was of doubtful validity, but important contemporary opinion supported it. Lord Chatham, for instance, in a speech of 1770, spoke of the representation of the counties as "pure and uncorrupted", while the boroughs had "properly enough been called the rotten part of the constitution".

ransacked; all Newgate's prisoners were freed, and all the other London prisons attacked. The Holborn distilleries were exploded and vast quantities of liquor looted; then the drunken mobs rampaged uncontrollably through London and Southwark, no longer attacking Catholic property only, but property in general. A week went by before the military restored order, and by that time about 450 people had been killed. Certainly, riots were nothing new in Georgian Britain, but this was something bigger and uglier than had been seen previously; and the propertied classes rightly read, and feared, in it something other than Protestant fanaticism. Behind the drunken fury of the mob lay social resentment: "a groping desire to settle accounts with the rich, if only for a day". Prosperous reformers, all but the most deeply convinced, had seen enough of 'associations'; and the taste of Gordon's fiery brew was still strong in the Englishman's mouth when the Paris mob began to run riot a few years later. (Gordon himself, committed to the Tower, was acquitted on a charge of treason; continued his cranky follies through the eighties; was excommunicated; was eventually sentenced on a charge of libel against Marie Antoinette; and died in Newgate, a convert to Judaism.)

Inside Parliament, Burke and the Rockinghamites followed up the petitioning movement with a succession of Bills to abolish sinecure places, bar Government contractors from the House, and cut back the Civil List; but North's Government, even when defeated, as it was from time to time, appeared immovable. Debate after debate during 1780 revolved round the subjects of corruption and royal influence, and at last an Opposition spokesman, the lawyer Dunning, brought forward the most downright of them all: *That the influence of the Crown has increased, is increasing, and ought to be diminished.* True or not, the motion was carried by a narrow majority, but when Dunning passed on to more specific and revolutionary motions (for example, that the House should not be dissolved or prorogued until the balance of the Constitution was restored), he found the independent members turn against him. They had no liking for extreme measures, and some of Dunning's phrases sounded altogether too much like those of Charles I's early Parliaments. As for Fox, they disapproved of his apparent republicanism, and had already written him down as a brilliant man without judgment; they would prefer to put up with the mildly inefficient Lord North, the "safe" man.

However, with defeat in America confirmed at Yorktown (1781), with Gibraltar threatened and Minorca lost again, with Ireland seething, with Holland and the Baltic powers joining the European camp against Britain, even the "safe" man could not go on for ever, backed though he was by the inexorable King. North had never wished to be a war Minister; he well knew, as everybody else did, that he was unfitted to be an organizer of victory; and worry was driving him nearly to nervous breakdown. At last, with Parliament convinced that extrication from the disastrous war was the only policy left to the country, George, still talking of firmness and betrayal, was obliged to let North go (1782).

6. George III, Fox, and the Younger Pitt

In place of North, George was forced to accept a new Rockingham Ministry, pledged to make peace with America; Fox and Shelburne were its Secretaries of State, and Burke its Paymaster. Only Thurlow, the Lord Chancellor, survived from North's Ministry, and he alone was in the King's confidence. Shelburne was just tolerable to George, but Fox he regarded as both a political and a personal enemy. Not only had he made repeated and insolent attacks on the monarchy, but he had of late become the intimate friend of George, Prince of Wales, who, the King rightly thought, needed no encouragement from the experienced Fox in his journey down the road of dissipation. So once again the old Hanoverian pattern was re-establishing itself: an heir hostile to his father and allied to the political opposition.

The only important domestic legislation of 1782–84 concerned the King's patronage and "economical" reform. Frustrated in 1780, Burke was now able to get several Bills passed, pruning the royal household of some sinecures, excluding customs and excise officers from parliamentary elections, and forcing the Paymaster to distinguish between his public and private accounts. Much was made of these reforms by Burke and his friends; but many loopholes were left, and on the whole the Acts were failures.[10] To the abolition of 'rotten' boroughs and the reform of Parliament itself Burke and his friends remained hostile.

Rockingham died within a few months of taking office, which left Fox and Shelburne (who detested each other) jockeying for supremacy. Fox even suggested that the Cabinet had the right to elect a new leader, confident that its choice would fall on himself; but George would have none of it, and appointed Shelburne as the lesser evil. Fox consequently resigned, and proceeded to intrigue with North against his late colleagues. To George's horror, North was ready to play Fox's game. The friend through whom George had governed for twelve years had now, it seemed, turned traitor and allied himself with the basest of his enemies. It was unforgivable. Fox's group (about 90 strong) and North's group (about 120) were together too strong for Shelburne's group (about 140), unless Shelburne could command the votes of the hundred-or-so independents. Since he could not, he was obliged to resign, and the King, after six weeks' contemplation of the infamy of his servants, during which time there was no Ministry at all, was forced to accept the bitter pill of a Fox–North Coalition, under the nominal leadership of the Duke of Portland.

Portland and Fox then faced George III with a new and revolutionary demand: they, and not the King, were to have the right to appoint junior Ministers. George seemed to have come to the end of his road, and again (as he had two years previously) contemplated abdication. To the Prince of Wales he wrote that he could not continue as king without abandoning every principle that he held right; he had "always attempted to act agreeable" to his duty, but from his cruel dilemma only one escape presented itself: "the resigning my Crown, my dear Son to you, quitting this my native country for ever and returning to the dominions of my forefathers". However, second thoughts, and the tougher George, prevailed,

[10] Some historians have regarded them as little more than psychological warfare against the King, "threats to the King of what he might expect unless he gave his confidence to the Rockinghams, and allowed them to settle comfortably on the well-paid royal preserves which they had conveniently overlooked in their purge" (J. H. Plumb).

the obdurate fighter who had learned much in tactical manœuvre from twenty-three years of battle with the politicians. Instead of abdicating, he proceeded to show his political muscle, and embarked on a systematic policy of non-co-operation. He refused to ennoble or appoint to royal 'places' those whom Portland and Fox recommended, and at last let it be known through Lord Thurlow and Lord Temple (an unprecedented thing) that any peer who voted for Mr Fox's East India Bill was the King's enemy. The Bill, which had proposed transferring the management of the East India Company's affairs to sixteen permanent commissioners to be appointed by Parliament, had altogether too much the appearance of an attempt by Fox to secure the vast influence of the Company for himself and his supporters—'jobs for the boys' in perpetuity —since the commissioners were to be practically irremovable. The Whigs, who so recently had displayed themselves bathed in virtue as the confounders of royal corruption, now stood revealed as creators of new corruption themselves. It was George now who could, by implication, accuse Fox of abuse of power—a neat turning of the tables. Heeding the King's message, the Lords rejected the India Bill by 87 votes to 79; and the following day the Fox–North Coalition was dismissed, unceremoniously and without audience. For all his great qualities, Fox never recovered from this defeat. He never again tasted office until the last year of his life.

The man whom the King now invited to head his Government was the young William Pitt, only twenty-four years old, gifted, reserved, self-confident to the point of arrogance, eloquent, ambitious, high-principled—the son of his father. Like his father in 1756, he was not surprised that his king had sent for him; it was in the nature of things that Pitts should be sent for. From both the national and the King's own point of view he had splendid qualifications. Like his father, he was above party and independent of the bickering groups. He was known to be a reformer, yet his loyalty to the King (unlike Fox's) was beyond question. The problem was, how was he to acquire a majority in the Commons or the Lords?

For a time, at least, he could afford to ignore parliamentary defeats (which were, to begin with, numerous, for Fox still commanded a majority). His tasks were to command respect, to win supporters from among the independents, the Rocking-hams and the Northites, and then to win the general election of 1784. All this he did. That he should have won the election is not, indeed, surprising, for Governments did not lose elections in the eighteenth century, and Pitt's men made as sure as any Newcastle or Walpole that local bargains were securely made and that Government supporters were backed by any necessary amount of treasury money or East India money. What was surprising was the decisiveness of the victory that went to Pitt and the King. One hundred and sixty of the sitting Foxites were defeated; and Pitt came back with a majority which no amount of corruption could have procured. Public opinion had declared for him and against both parties to the Fox–North Coalition.

The King, for his part, had every reason to be delighted; he had won a great and lasting victory; and his devoted servant, Pitt, was to remain First Lord of the Treasury for a further unbroken period of seventeen years. George even allowed his Ministers' speeches in favour of reform to go by without pro-test, so long as there was no danger of their recommendations being put into practice. He and Pitt remedied their weakness in the House of Lords by creating, eventually, 87 new peers, thus enlarging the upper house by 50 per cent and swamping the old Whig oligarchs. For Pitt and George many of the new creations killed two birds with one stone: thus the nine new peers created between 1784 and 1792 controlled between them 24 seats in the Commons. Only once, in 1788, did Pitt's position look at all insecure, when George had a second attack of in-sanity, and for a time it seemed likely that the Regency of the Prince of Wales must inevitably bring with it a Fox Ministry. For a brief space political characters stood on their heads; it was Pitt who argued for a Regency of limited powers, and Fox who demanded full royal prerogatives for his friend the regent presumptive. When the Prince was sent for, the King tried to throttle him, and was perforce consigned to a straitjacket. Two nights running the Prince of Wales sat up in his decorations waiting for his father's death. But then, suddenly, George recovered his lucidity, and everybody stood on his feet again.

Twice more, in the long twilight of his reign, before his wits finally departed from him, George III was to put down that high-principled and immovable royal foot. The first occasion was in 1801, when his "sense of religious as well as political duty", as he expressed it, made him veto Pitt's proposed grant of Catholic Emancipation. Six years earlier George had indicated with brutal firmness, in a letter to Pitt, that this was a matter "beyond the decision of any Cabinet of ministers", but Pitt had doubtless hoped to be able to steer his measure safely past George's known opposition. However, the King, whose ancestors had, after all, been brought over from Hanover to exclude Catholicism from Britain, took the line that to accept the admission of Catholics to Parliament would violate his solemn coronation oath to defend the Protestant religion. "My opinions", he wrote to Pitt, "are not those formed on the moment, but such as I have imbibed for forty years, and from which I can never depart." If this meant Pitt's resignation he would be sorry—"I shall still hope his sense of duty will prevent his retiring"—but conscience was more important to George III than even Pitt was. Besides, what nonsense it was, said George, to put political power into the hands of a hostile Irish populace in the middle of a desperate war with France: "The most Jacobinical thing I ever heard of," he exclaimed to Dundas. "I shall reckon any man my personal enemy who proposes any such measure." George's position was strengthened by his knowledge that the Cabinet was far from united behind Pitt's Catholic proposals; by Pitt's own refusal to make a great political issue out of Emancipation, especially in view of the fact that the nation was at war; and by the readiness of Addington, Speaker of the House of Commons, to form a Ministry in Pitt's place. Further, the King had been ill, and the last thing Pitt desired was to drive his royal master over the brink of madness again. So Pitt resigned, without heat or recrimination on either side, and was absent from the King's councils for three years.

On the occasion of his return to the Premiership in 1804 the King put his foot down for the second time. Pitt had expressed a desire to form an all-party coalition, including Fox and William Grenville, to which George replied by imposing two conditions for a new Pitt Ministry: first, Pitt must give a guarantee never to bring up again the "indelicate" matter of Catholic Emancipation; and, second, in no circumstances would the King employ Fox. The King, indeed, was obliged "to express his astonishment that Mr. Pitt should for one moment harbour the thought of bringing such a man before his royal notice". Pitt found it convenient not to challenge his master's obstinacy; and Fox had to wait once again.

It is true that on Pitt's death (January 1806) William Grenville imposed Fox on the King as a condition of forming the so-called 'Talents' Ministry. Once again, however, on the Roman Catholic issue, George's firmness succeeded: in 1807, when Grenville's Government sought to allow Catholics to hold staff appointments in the Army, George used the occasion to rid himself of a crew so dangerously deficient in loyal Protestantism.

When the King's reason finally gave way, in 1811, Fox had been dead five years, and the Prince of Wales, Regent from 1811, was no longer the crony of the Whigs. For all George III's successful insistence on the preservation of his royal prerogative, he died leaving the King's powers smaller than at his accession. Lord Liverpool, the Tory Prime Minister in that year of the King's death (1820), was in no doubt about the relative strength of the political cards held by himself and the King. "Where I feel I am right," he said, "I can press and insist." And, as the Duke of Wellington once said, George IV "liked to talk grandly to make people imagine that his prime minister was a sort of maître d'hôtel which he might dismiss any moment that it happened to suit him"; but Wellington knew that, like so much else in George IV's life, it was mainly a façade. During Victoria's reign, though she was almost as insistent on her prerogatives as her grandfather, the same historical processes continued. The more Victoria fought, against Peel, against Palmerston, against Gladstone, the more she lost. As the two-party system began to take control of British politics, the monarch's power progressively declined, until he finally came, on ordinary occasions, simply to register and dignify the results of general elections.

Chapter 9

America and India

1. "The American, This New Man"

"What, then, is the American, this new man?" asked the French immigrant, Jean de Crèvecœur, in his *Letters from an American Farmer* (1782).

He is either an European, or the descendant of an European; hence that strange mixture of blood, which you find in no other country. . . . I could point out to you a family whose grandfather was an Englishman, whose wife was Dutch, whose son married a French woman, and whose present four sons have now four wives of different nations. *He* is an American, who, leaving behind him all his ancient prejudices and manners, receives new ones from the new mode of life he has embraced, the new government he obeys, and the new rank he holds.

In 1600 there were no English colonies on the American mainland. By 1700 their population had grown to about 225,000, by 1763 to about two millions. There were thirteen of them, which may be separated into three broad groups. New England in the north (Massachusetts, Connecticut, Rhode Island, New Hampshire) was predominantly a community of merchants, shipbuilders, and farmers, strongly English and Puritan by origin and tradition. In the south (Virginia, North and South Carolina, and Georgia) was a plantation economy, with great landowners and large labour forces of poor whites and Negro slaves—a cultural and geographical climate more remote from Boston's than Boston's was from London. The middle colonies (Pennsylvania, New Jersey, New York, Maryland, Delaware) were the least English—in fact, in many parts overwhelmingly un-English. As early as 1650 over a dozen languages were spoken along the Hudson river, where there were already settlements of Dutch, Flemings, Walloons, French, Danes, Norwegians, Swedes, English, Scots, Irish, Germans, Poles, Czechs, Portuguese, and Italians. They had come to seek religious freedom and economic opportunity; and, in the second half of the seventeenth and early eighteenth century, their numbers were rapidly swollen by the misfits of Europe and the victims of her wars and persecutions. Germans, for instance, came into Quaker Pennsylvania in large numbers. So did Scottish crofters and Irish peasants driven by the harshness of their domestic circumstances. To all her American colonies England sent convicts, prostitutes, and bankrupts.

In one respect at least, the colonies were emphatically English. All of them took for granted the basic English tradition of free institutions and the common law. Even in the authoritarian Massachusetts of the early days, where there had been a severe "rule of the saints", there were town meetings from the beginning, and a measure of self-government. And if Massachusetts puritanism proved too bitter for one's taste, there were always unlimited lands and opportunities beyond the horizons. Thus Rhode Island had been founded; thus had been settled the fertile valleys of Connecticut and New Hampshire to the north. By the mid-eighteenth century all these colonies, and most of those farther south, had grasped, through their elective assemblies, the exclusive right to levy taxation, and authorize expenditure. Governors did indeed exist, but, where they were not pliable to the settlers' will, there were plentiful means, even if necessary by withholding payment of salary, of making them so.

Many colonists had, as we have seen, never known Britain; and everything conspired to induce those who had, or whose ancestors had, to forget it. Each of the thirteen states was a commonwealth of its own, with its own politics, its own vested interests, its own rebels. Pennsylvania, for instance, was deeply divided between its old-established and respectable Quaker families and the newly arrived Germans, Irish, and Scots, raw and rough, who made up a majority of the pioneers and frontiersmen and in 1764 actually marched on Philadelphia. New York, New Jersey, and Massachusetts were all beset by similar quarrels between their fourth- and fifth-generation settlers and their newcomers. To the great army of the pioneers, who followed the trails of the traders, and risked the attacks of the Indians, up the Shenandoah and the other river valleys westward towards the Alleghenies, or northward up the rivers Hudson and Connecticut, it was Philadelphia, or Charleston, or New York, or Boston, that was the remote centre of government—too remote, frequently, to pay any attention to. As for London, the question did not arise. How should men wrestling with the wilderness appreciate the niceties of British and European politics or understand the difficulties of George Grenville or Lord North? The statutes and debates of Westminster were as irrelevant to their world as a cheque-book would be to a mariner on a desert island. London was on another planet.

The converse was almost equally true. Among the Government in London, at least until the time of Pitt, there was much ignorance and apathy concerning the colonists. Walpole, for instance, knew very well that American politics were too complicated for him. Even where the colonists flouted certain well-accepted British principles, he was content to turn a blind eye. So long as British merchants were prospering, so long as the colonies were sending to Britain an adequate supply of such materials and foods as could not be produced in this country, so long as they were good customers of British manufactured products, so long as they sustained British shipping and helped to maintain our gold reserve and the balance of trade, the colonies were serving their purpose. This 'mercantilist' reasoning was common ground among all colonizing nations, and it was not overtly challenged even in the colonies. The Governor of Massachusetts, William Shirley, put the position succinctly in 1750:

> The principal articles, in which the value of these colonies consists, are
>
> 1. The addition of subjects which their inhabitants make to the Crown of Great Britain.
> 2. The consumption of British manufactures, and all other European commodities within them.
> 3. The fisheries carried on in the adjacent seas.

4. The several naval stores, with which they supply England.

5. The furs, tobacco, and rice, which are of the natural growth there.

6. The lumber and stores, with which they supply the English sugar islands.

7. The dominion and sovereignty of the Atlantic Ocean, which the possession of them must give the Crown that holds them.

It was only when the French threat quickened in the forties and fifties that Englishmen and Americans began to develop a consciousness of their mutual relations, and then only spasmodically and sporadically; on the whole, too, unsatisfactorily. Pitt was a hero, it is true, to some of the more politically conscious Americans, but there was very far from being a general all-American public opinion; each state was still immersed in its own problems, and the affairs of the Pennsylvania frontier made little sense to the plantation owner of South Carolina or the Boston tradesman. We have already seen how little love was lost between Braddock's redcoats in the Ohio Valley and the Virginian militia; and not much mutual sympathy can have been engendered between Wolfe and his American fellow-citizens of King George's empire:

> The Americans [Wolfe considered] are in general the dirtiest, and most contemptible, cowardly dogs you can conceive. There is no depending on 'em in action. They fall down dead in their own dirt and desert by battalions, officers and all.

Wolfe's subordinate at Quebec, General Murray, considered the Americans "effeminate"; Lord Sandwich wrote them off as "raw, undisciplined, and cowardly". But these English opinions came from soldiers and politicians whose careers had forced them into unwilling contact with these remote compatriots; most Englishmen had been content totally to ignore them until the big crisis blew up.

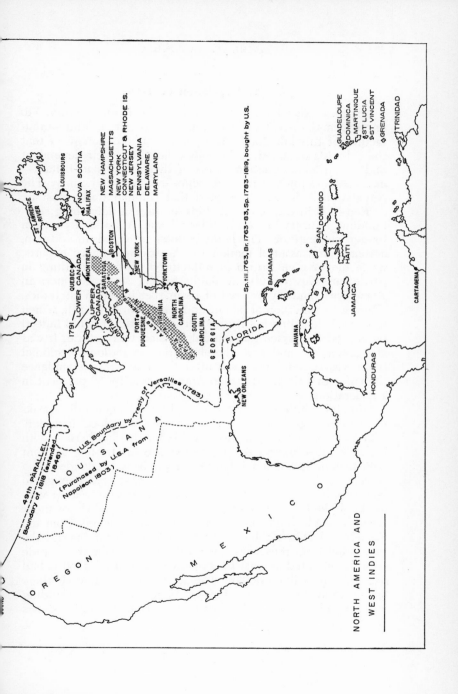

NORTH AMERICA AND
WEST INDIES

ST LAWRENCE RIVER

LOUISBOURG

NOVA SCOTIA
HALIFAX

NEW HAMPSHIRE
MASSACHUSETTS
NEW YORK
CONNECTICUT & RHODE IS.
NEW JERSEY
PENNSYLVANIA
DELAWARE
MARYLAND

1791

QUEBEC
LOWER CANADA
MONTREAL
UPPER CANADA
SARATOGA
ONTARIO
BOSTON
NEW YORK
FORT DUQUESNE
YORKTOWN
VIRGINIA
NORTH CAROLINA
SOUTH CAROLINA
GEORGIA

FLORIDA   Sp. till 1763, Br. 1763-83, Sp. 1783-1819, bought by U.S.

BAHAMAS

SAN DOMINGO

HAITI

GUADELOUPE
DOMINICA
MARTINIQUE
ST LUCIA
ST VINCENT
GRENADA
TRINIDAD

CUBA

HAVANA

JAMAICA

NEW ORLEANS

49th PARALLEL
Boundary of 1818 (extended 1846)

U.S. Boundary by Treaty of Versailles (1783)

LOUISIANA
(Purchased by U.S.A from Napoleon 1803)

OREGON

M   E   X   I   C   O

HONDURAS

CARTAGENA

2. The Regulation of Trade

Colonies existed for the benefit of the home country, "to improve and extend the Commerce, Navigation, and Manufacture of this kingdom". That, however, did not mean that the colonists obtained no benefits at all from their dependent and subordinate situation. Some of their exports to Britain— naval stores, pitch, silk, and wine—received a bounty. The Navigation Acts, which insisted that colonial trade must be carried in British or colonial ships, ensured a flourishing ship-building industry on both sides of the Atlantic, free from foreign competition. The home country provided, in addition, a steady and assured market for American primary exports, while inexpensive British manufactured produce, clothing in particular, was readily available to the settlers. American wheat was similarly assured of its market in the West Indies. There was a division of labour and a division of wealth, which on the whole suited both sides of the Atlantic. It could indeed be argued that since this mutual division was natural, it was also inevitable, and that, therefore, the regulation of colonial trade was superfluous. Even after the War of Independence the value of British exports to America rose by 50 per cent in a generation.

Mid-eighteenth-century America, then, was, generally speaking, prospering; there were, however, points of local irritation. Whereas, for instance, it was possible for the Southerner, with his rice, tobacco, and cotton, to balance his trading account with Britain, it was much harder for the New Englander, who lacked the benefit of such produce. He was glad enough to take supplies of cloth from England, but saw no reason why he should be forced to import dear British-colonial tea or sugar when he could buy such commodities more cheaply from the French and Dutch colonies. Even so, notwithstanding all the smuggling from these foreign territories, the balance of trade steadily mounted against the Americans, until by 1760 it had reached nine million dollars. The accompanying gold shortage led to rapid depreciation of paper money, and it was adding insult to injury when the British Government in the sixties insisted on payment of its newly imposed duties in coin. Even the Southern tobacco planters, suffering from a shortage of liquid sterling, were £4,500,000 in debt to the London and Bristol merchants who marketed the leaf in England and extracted heavy interest on their loans. If only the planters could have exported direct to Europe their situation would have improved; but all such trade had (at least in theory) to be re-exported through London, with the London factors taking their cut. This was because tobaccos, together with cottons, indigo, and many other goods, were classed as "enumerated". "Non-enumerated" goods could flow freely into southern Europe, but they too had to pass through London if destined for northern Europe. (Fish, lumber, grain, and furs might be freely exported wherever the colonists could find buyers for them.)

So long as the practice in trade regulation was not made to conform too closely to the theory, the complaints of the American traders and planters were muted. And for long decades the practice was notably slack. Smuggling was so universal that Americans hardly thought of it as smuggling. Many of the revenue officers were absentees in England, enjoying the salary (often as a political reward) and employing an American deputy to do the work. Prosecutions were infrequent, and convictions still more so, for Americans accused of smuggling offences still, at this time, enjoyed trial by sympathetic jury. Some large fortunes had been made, even during the Seven Years War, by trading with the French. In short, the so-called mercantilist, "old colonial" system was accepted in theory by British and American alike; but, where it was inconvenient, it was ignored; where the shoe pinched a slit was cut in the leather.

By 1763, the year of the Peace of Paris, much of the shoe had become holes, and English politicians felt, not without justice, that the time had come to end all the evasion and slipshod administration and to put the whole relationship between Britain and her North American colonists on a new and firmer basis. Even during the Seven Years War, with Pitt in control, the Americans had agreed to assist the war effort only if they were subsequently paid back their expenses (which amounted to about a million pounds by 1763). In general, the whole financial brunt had been borne by Britain, and it had been, by eighteenth-century standards, enormous. The National Debt had risen from £72,500,000 to £132,700,000, in a war which had saved America from the French threat, while all the time the Americans had seemed most concerned to pursue small inter-state quarrels and argue whether Anglican priests should be paid in free tobacco. There was a general feeling at Westminster, even among reasonable men who did not share Wolfe's extreme opinions of the Americans as "contemptible, cowardly dogs", that these quarrelsome, lawless, and feckless colonists must at least be made to pay a reasonable share of the cost of defending their country and to obey the existing laws of trade regulation.

Accordingly the Government of George Grenville, in which the young Shelburne was President of the Board of Trade, proceeded to tighten up the anti-smuggling machinery. Customs men were required to go to America themselves instead of hiring deputies. They were armed with general search warrants, instead of having to seek a separate warrant for every building they entered. Alleged smugglers were to be tried in Admiralty courts, which did not offer trial by jury. British men-of-war were given orders to assist the revenue men. Suddenly, therefore, from the merchants who had made good money from ignoring the law came a yelp of indignant anguish. The 'right' to smuggle was being denied them.

3. The Western Territories

This grievance was rapidly followed by another. The annexation to the Crown of Canada had solved one problem— the threat of French encirclement—but created another: what was to happen to the vast territory between the western Great Lakes and Tennessee, including Illinois and the Ohio Valley? Here there was a conflict between the interests of French Catholics, partly Christianized Redskins, fur-traders, and Protestant British pioneers and land speculators. The decision of Grenville and Shelburne was altogether to prohibit any further migration into this great area, "for the present"; the limits of westward movement were to be the headwaters of the Appalachians. The motives of the British Government were typical of a mercantilist age: colonies should contribute to commerce and, above all, to navigation. The more deeply settlers penetrated into the interior, the more vulnerable they became (for instance, to Indian attack; British troops, with no assistance from the Americans, had great trouble suppressing Pontiac's Indian rising[1] in 1763), and the greater the military and administrative costs. Backwoodsmen made poor sailors, and, compared with seaboard colonists, they were inaccessible to manufactures. In short, the Government were anxious to have economically concentrated and commercially profitable colonies, preferably coastal or tropical; territory for territory's sake did not interest them.

The American reaction to the Proclamation of 1763 was one of anger. Did not the very charters of some states grant ownership of land "from sea to sea"? And although the wildest dreamer in 1763 did not foresee an independent, homogeneous America stretching from the Atlantic to the Pacific, the possibility and legality of indefinite westward movement had never before been challenged, except by the French. Now it seemed to Americans that a distant, ignorant, and busybody Government was trying to take the bread and butter out of American mouths, probably for the sake of the fur-traders who wished to see the Indians undisturbed. In any case Grenville's proclamation was impossible to enforce; and the pioneers ignored it.

4. Taxation and Defence

Not only revenue men were sent to America by Grenville: ten thousand regular troops also were dispatched there. The question the Americans asked themselves was, in whose

---

[1] Pontiac, a great Indian chief, had correctly foreseen that the defeat of the French, who had traded peacefully with his people and inter-married with them, boded no good for the Redskin. The British pioneer threatened him at best with loss of land, at worst with annihilation. A few years later, during the War of American Independence, the home Government had little difficulty in rousing the Indians to fight against the settlers, and some savage work was done on both sides.

interests and to what end? The French had been defeated; the Indians were being mastered. Was it not likely that these troops were being sent to overawe, not Indians, but colonial assemblies, and to provide backing for those tools of King George, the state governors? Already we can see the essential hopelessness of the situation that was developing. Every action of the British Government after 1763 was construed by the colonists in its least favourable terms. Every criticism from America was seen by the majority of British politicians, and by the King himself, as further evidence of an unreasonable spirit. The gulf was psychological, and it was unbridgeable. Men of liberal views in England, such as Burke or Chatham, begged eloquently for an understanding of American complaints, and concessions to what even they thought to be headstrong American views and actions; but there is no evidence that these men would have had any greater success than Grenville, George III, or Lord North, for even Chatham and the liberals considered that Britain must regulate her colonies' trade and retain her imperial mastery, whereas in America more and more were questioning the very bases of empire itself. In whose interests should America be governed, if not those of the Americans themselves? The whole European conception of colonies was being questioned. The conflict which was developing was too basic to be avoided by friendly hands outstretched across the ocean, the gulf too wide to be bridged by any statesmanship practicable in that age. Geography, economic advantage, political interest, the spirit of the age, all pulled America inexorably away from Britain.

The first of Britain's moves to raise revenue for the costs of imperial defence was the Sugar Act of 1764. The rum trade played a big part in the economy of the northern colonies, rum being distilled from molasses, which is a by-product of sugar manufacture. The molasses from which the Northerners made their rum was imported (under Walpole's Molasses Act of 1733) either duty-free from the British West Indies or at a duty of sixpence a gallon from the foreign-owned West Indies. This, at least, was the theory; in practice, smuggling rendered the regulations farcical. Now, therefore, Grenville proposed to lower the duty to threepence and to see that the threepence was in fact collected. It was an intelligent, sober measure which nicely held the balance between the various parties' interests; but the prospect of enforcement raised bitter protests in Massachusetts.

The rum trade's complaints of 1764, however, were but a whisper compared with the hullabaloo which greeted Grenville's next measure, the Stamp Act of 1765, an attempt to devise a modest revenue (to go towards colonial defence) by requiring certain articles and documents to carry a stamp of varying denominations, mostly of a few pence. Wills, mortgages, licences, pamphlets, newspapers, almanacs, playing-cards, dice, and college diplomas were among the articles listed; and the money for the stamps was to be paid in coin. Grenville hoped that this mild measure of taxation would raise £60,000 a year. In the event it raised nothing but indignation, fury, civil commotion, and a wonderful new all-American solidarity. Where the French wars had failed to unite the colonies, the Stamp Act now succeeded in no time. Every considerable town sprouted its Sons of Liberty; there were concerted moves to boycott British imports; bonfires were made of the stamps in the town squares; stamp agents were forced to resign their posts; on the day the Act was intended to take effect, bells tolled, shops closed, flags hung at half-mast, newspapers printed death's-heads where the stamps should have been, and a screaming mob in New York wrecked the house of the British military commander. More significant than mob violence, however, was the fact that everywhere, from New Hampshire in the north to Georgia in the south, the lead in resistance was taken by the moneyed and professional classes—lawyers, journalists, clergy, businessmen. Partly, no doubt, this was because these were the men who would be most affected by the stamp duty; but, much more, it was because this stamp tax had roused the political consciousness of middle-class Americans as nothing had ever done before, and posed the crucial question of principle: had the British Government any right to tax the colonies at all? In the Virginian House of Burgesses the young Patrick Henry gave the most violent of negatives to this question. This unsuccessful farmer and storekeeper, now turned lawyer, had recently taken to studying history, and aired some sensational historical parallels: "Caesar," he declaimed in thrilling tones, "had his Brutus, Charles I his Cromwell, and George the Third" (here he was interrupted with cries of "*Treason!*") "—and George the Third may profit by their example. If this be treason, make the most of it." For the first time a slogan that the Irish had known for years was heard all over the Thirteen Colonies: *No taxation without representation.* Only the American state assemblies, that is to say, had the right to tax the Americans (for the idea of direct American representation at Westminster was rejected by all thinking people as impracticable). Thus every new move in England, and the Stamp Act most of all, forced Americans to re-think their position, to rationalize their emotions of rebellion against orders from the other side of the Atlantic, to challenge the hitherto accepted notions of colonial status. From the solidarity of revolt emerged the sense of nationhood.

There was genuine astonishment in England at the violence of the outburst against the Stamp Act; and Rockingham's Government, succeeding Grenville's in July 1765, hastened to repeal a measure which had not only occasioned such bitterness, but also caused big losses to British exporters hit by the partial American boycott. Even George III agreed that the tax would have to be at least modified; Rockingham, however, preferred to erase it altogether, but at the same time to re-assert, in his Declaratory Act (1766), the *principle* of Britain's right to tax her colonies; for the English, no less than the Americans, were being forced to clarify their minds on the general subject of the status of the colonies. Pitt, for instance, was clarifying his: the colonists, he maintained, could not rightfully be taxed without their own consent, for they were free citizens, "the sons, not the bastards, of England". He therefore "rejoiced" that America had resisted; but, as to the basic right of the British Government to regulate colonial trade, like almost every man of his time he explicitly and emphatically supported it:

> . . . We may bind their trade, confine their manufactures, and exercise every power whatsoever—except that of taking money out of their pockets without their consent.

Even so, he opposed the Declaratory Act as unnecessarily provocative. The Americans, he thought, had been already provoked too much, "driven to madness by injustice". Conciliation must now be England's policy:

There are two lines of Prior's, of a man's behaviour to his wife, so applicable to you and your colonies, that I cannot help repeating them:

Be to her faults a little blind
Be to her virtues very kind.

Chatham's abilities to measure his statesmanship against the American problem were never fully tested; for, as we have seen, no sooner did he take over the premiership in 1766 than he was struck down by physical and mental disorder, and the direction of American affairs fell principally into the hands of Charles Townshend. The Americans had admitted the British right to regulate trade, but not to impose direct taxation; Townshend therefore devised a new set of import duties (on glass, lead, painters' colours, paper, and tea), ostensibly as a form of trade regulation (1767). The £40,000 a year that these taxes would yield, Townshend considered, would provide a fund from which colonial governors and other royal officials could be made financially independent of their local assemblies. Thus the colonists' hand would be weakened and that of the home Government correspondingly strengthened.

Once more the fat was in the fire. The Massachusetts Assembly sent a circular letter to its twelve sister assemblies denouncing the Townshend Duties as taxation without representation, and in consequence Governor Bernard of Massachusetts ordered the Assembly's dissolution. By 1768 the customs authorities in Boston had pretty well lost the battle: every attempt to collect the new duties was resisted, customs men were tarred and feathered in the streets, and so, too, were some of the merchants who persisted in importing British manufactures. (It was becoming 'patriotic' to wear homespun— a severe test for the womenfolk, even for daughters of the Puritan Fathers.) By October General Gage and his men had landed at Boston, marching, as Paul Revere wrote, "with insolent Parade, Drums beating, Fifes playing, and Colours flying, up King Street". Again, and inevitably, the most sinister interpretation was applied by the Americans: these were the redcoats come to impose tyranny. At least they succeeded in protecting the officials and imposing some order, though it was an uneasy sort of order, liable to be broken by a trivial incident. Thus in March 1770 some Bostonians thought it amusing to start snowballing (and then stoning) a squad of redcoats, and the incident itself snowballed, with, at the end, five citizens lying dead in the snow, the "brutality" of the British further demonstrated, and a "Boston Massacre" to be entered up in the accounts. The incident was worked on for all it was worth by Samuel Adams and the Boston radicals, to keep alive an agitation that had shown some signs of subsiding. Actually the "massacre" had ended with British troops marching off, under stoning, to avoid further bloodshed.

Even before this violence the British Government had decided again to draw back, as anxious as most Americans were to avoid a head-on collision, and hoping to mollify merchants at home adversely affected by the continuing boycott of British cloth. Hence in 1770 all the duties except that on tea were removed, the tea tax being retained more as a token of principle than for its production of revenue. Many Americans thought that the wild men in Boston had gone too far (by a coincidence North proposed the removal of the Townshend Duties on the very day of the Boston Massacre); and on both sides of the ocean most men were relieved to see things quietening down during the early 1770's. By now, however, the radicals (or 'Whigs') of these various colonies were in process of developing a common organization. Committees of Correspondence began to exchange ideas and discuss common tactics. The Sons of Liberty (and some Daughters too) organized parades and social functions, and promoted a vague revolutionary patriotism. Journalist-politicians like Samuel Adams of Massachusetts and political orators like Patrick Henry of Virginia were not afraid of words like independence; men such as these, or such as John Hancock, the rich Boston merchant and radical who had five hundred indictments for smuggling outstanding against him, laboured to keep alive the smouldering fires of revolutionary ardour.

5. Boston Tea Party and Declaration of Independence

In 1773 these burst into flame with the Boston Tea Party. Americans of those days drank a good deal of tea; their consumption of it, wrote Governor Hutchinson of Massachusetts in 1771, "exceeds what anybody in England imagines". But, said Hutchinson, "five-sixths of it was smuggled, and in New York and Philadelphia, nine-tenths. The traders make such an extravagant profit that it will require more frequent seizures to discourage them than there is any reason to hope for." North's Government, however, hit upon an ingenious scheme for circumventing the smugglers and at the same time coming to the rescue of the East India Company, whose affairs by 1773 were in a complicated state of disarray. East India tea was to be excused the shilling English customs duty (though still to pay the threepenny Townshend tax), and the Company were to be given the privilege of shipping direct to America instead of having to go through London. It was hoped thus to relieve the Company of its tea surplus, reduce its startling deficit, and torpedo the smugglers, all in one move. Who would want to buy smuggled tea if it was in fact dearer than lawful tea?

However, North had underestimated the length to which the American tea importers would go to defend their vested interests in smuggling. These men, the John Hancocks and company, were not going to stand by and be quietly undersold by smart Englishmen; and throughout the colonies, except in Boston, the headquarters of Gage's troops, the East India Company's agents were "persuaded" to resign, and the entry of its tea blocked. By December 1773, three tea ships lay in Boston harbour waiting to be unloaded:

> On the evening of 16th Dec., between 6 and 7 o'clock, a large mob assembled with axes, etc. encouraged by Mr. John Hancock, Samuel Adams, and others, and marched in a body to where the ships lay, and there destroyed the whole by starting it into the sea.

Some of the rioters, merry in the spirit of carnival or prudent in pursuit of disguise, had blacked their faces and dressed up as Mohawk Indians for their evening's work. No Government that wished to continue governing could possibly ignore so flagrant a defiance. (North had already allowed the incident of the *Gaspée* (June 1772), when a British revenue cutter had been burned off Rhode Island, to die down quietly; he could hardly be accused of being headstrong.) Accordingly, Boston was punished for its violent insubordination: the port was to be closed till the tea was paid for; the upper house of the legislature was to be nominated by the Crown; barracks were to be put at the disposal of further troops; and the governor was to be allowed to transfer trials to England at discretion.

Almost at the same time North's Government brought in the Quebec Act (1774), which more than confirmed Americans' worst fears aroused by Grenville's Proclamation of 1763. The Canadian boundary was extended southward to the Ohio river and a great measure of legislative, religious, and judicial liberty was given to the French Catholic population. The British Americans saw the Act as the slamming of the door against their westward expansion: an attempt to set up a disciplined autocracy to the north-west of them (the old French threat, with George III taking the place of Louis XV); and a sop to the Roman Catholic religion, which most New England Puritans still regarded as a tyrannical and corrupt idolatry. The Boston Acts and the Quebec Act were lumped together by Americans as the Five Intolerable Acts, and are still so described in American history-books. They, following the Boston Tea Party, really mark the beginning of the War of American Independence. After each side had bared its weapons in this manner and taken its stand, there was no going back till the battle was won or lost.

It is (by definition) not given to the average man and the average Government to be a century or two ahead of their time; and we cannot blame those average men, George III and Lord North, for failing to see the vision of a British Commonwealth of equal and independent partners. Not even Chatham's great imagination had compassed that. It is worth noting, however, that one politician, Burke, in these years when the two sides were drifting towards war, did have glimpses of that vision, or something like it:

But to clear up my ideas on this subject—a revenue from America transmitted hither—do not delude yourselves—you can never receive it—no, not a shilling. We have experience that from remote countries it is not to be expected. [He instanced Bengal.] . . . My trust is in her interest in the British constitution. My hold of the colonies is in the close affection which grows from common names, from kindred blood, from similar privileges and equal protection. These are ties which, though light as air, are as strong as links of iron. Let the colonies always keep the idea of their civil rights associated with your government; they will cling and grapple to you; and no force under heaven would be of power to tear them from their allegiance. . . . Deny them this participation of freedom, and you break that sole bond, which originally made, and must still preserve, the unity of the empire. . . .

Chatham, too, in his interludes of sanity, pleaded eloquently for conciliation, though he supported North's measures for the punishment of Boston, and never for one moment considered American independence as a solution. The Crown must, he thought, always retain its sovereign rights to move troops at will and to regulate trade and navigation. It by no means follows, therefore, that conciliatory measures that he advocated would have furnished any lasting peace; indeed, almost certainly they would not; but his words are worth remembering, all the same:

[Gage's troops, he argued, should be removed from Boston.] They are an army of impotence. You may call them an army of safety and guard; but they are in truth an army of impotence and contempt; and, to make the folly equal to the disgrace, they are an army of irritation and vexation. . . . What, though you march from town to town and from province to province; though you should be able to enforce a temporary and local submission—which I only suppose, not admit—how shall you be able to secure the obedience of the country you leave behind you in your progress? . . . The spirit which now resists your taxation in America is the same which formerly opposed loans, benevolences, and ship-money in England: the same spirit which called all England on its legs. . . . We shall be forced ultimately to retract; let us retract while we can, not when we must. I say we must necessarily undo these violent oppressive acts; they must be repealed; you will repeal them; I pledge myself for it that you will in the end repeal them; I stake my reputation on it; I will consent to be taken for an idiot, if they are not finally repealed. Avoid, then, this humiliating, disgraceful necessity. With a dignity becoming your exalted situation, make the first advances to concord, to peace, and happiness; for that is your true dignity, to act with prudence and justice. . . .

Only a handful of voices—Burke, Chatham, Shelburne, Camden—spoke in this vein. The weight of public opinion was undoubtedly with George III, who wrote to North in September 1774: "The die is now cast, the Colonies must either submit or triumph. I do not wish to come to severer measures, but we must not retreat." Most Englishmen had lost patience with the colonists, as Dr Johnson had: "They are a race of convicts," said that exasperated Tory, "and ought to be content with anything we may allow them short of hanging."

During 1774 and 1775 volunteer armies throughout America prepared themselves for the struggle. On the village greens of New England minute-men[2] gathered to drill; everywhere stores of muskets and ammunition were laid by; even some of the Philadelphia Quakers defied their meetings' condemnation and organized the regiment of the "Quaker Blues". Most important, in Philadelphia in September 1774 there came together the first all-American Congress, "to consult upon the present unhappy state of the Colonies". Fifty-five delegates, from all the states except Georgia, a fair cross-section of American opinion, both radical and moderate, after issuing a Declaration of Rights and Grievances and petitioning the King, proceeded to form "The Association" whose task was to revive the trade boycott and publish the names of the "traitors" who broke it, to encourage patriotic self-sacrifice, and to discourage "every species of extravagance and dissipation, especially all horse-racing, and all kinds of gambling, cock-fighting, exhibitions of shows, plays, and other extensive diversions and entertainments". The heroic age was on the way. Nor was this all words and high resolve: as a result of the

[2] *I.e.*, volunteers who could be ready at a minute's notice.

Association's activities, the value of British imports into New York fell in 1775 to below one-third of the 1774 value. In Virginia Patrick Henry (who, together with his fellow-Virginian George Washington and other land speculators, had just had the value of his shares in the pioneering Vandalia Company reduced to zero by the Quebec Act) found a situation ideal for his flamboyant oratory: "Give me liberty," he proclaimed, "or give me death."

More influential still was a pamphlet published in January 1776 by an Englishman who had been in America only two years. It was the work of a man who jumped clean over the clutter of difficulties, old loyalties, and indecisions to the bold, uncompromising, revolutionary statement: Tom Paine's *Common Sense.* By the time that it was published (and it became an immediate best-seller) the first shots in the war had been fired. Gage had lost nearly three hundred of his men at Lexington in an attempt to destroy rebel stores; Howe had suffered over a thousand killed and wounded in repelling the Boston rebels at Bunker Hill; and rebel forces under Benedict Arnold and Richard Montgomery had invaded Canada and taken Montreal. Paine said in incisive terms what most Americans were beginning to dare to think—the only policy was total independence:

> The sun never shone on a cause of greater worth. ... Now is the seed-time of continental union, faith, and honour. ... But Britain is the parent country, say some. ... Not one-third of the inhabitants, even of this province, are of English descent. ... I challenge the warmest advocate of reconciliation, to show a single advantage that this continent can reap, by being connected with Great Britain. I repeat the challenge, not a single advantage is derived. Our corn will fetch its price in any market in Europe, and our imported goods must be paid for, buy them where we will. ... But the injuries and disadvantages we sustain by that connection, are without number; and our duty to mankind at large, as well as to ourselves, instructs us to renounce the alliance: because, any submission to, or dependence on, Great Britain, tends directly to involve this continent in European wars and quarrels; and sets us at variance with nations, who would otherwise seek our friendship. ...

On July 4th, 1776, six months after Paine published *Common Sense*, the Continental Congress declared the independence of the American states. It was another Virginian who drafted the famous document: the lawyer and future President, Thomas Jefferson, a hitherto inconspicuous member of Congress, a poor public speaker, but an able pamphleteer who had already composed a "declaration of grievances". This he now polished up, adding a preamble that echoed the fashionable sentiments of Locke and the French *philosophes*. The grievances were routine repetition; it is the preamble that is remembered, and has gone on echoing round the world, every phrase a battle-cry:

We hold these truths to be self-evident, that all men are created equal; that they are endowed by their creator with certain inalienable rights; that among these are life, liberty, and the pursuit of happiness; that to secure these rights, governments are instituted among men, deriving their just powers from the consent of the governed; that whenever any form of government becomes destructive of these ends, it is the right of the people to alter or abolish it, and to institute a new government, laying its foundation on such principles, and organizing its powers in such form, as to them shall seem most likely to affect their safety and happiness. . . .

6. The War of the American Revolution (1775–83)

The war that won the Americans their independence, after six years of fighting and two more of waiting for peace, was by no means a war of united people against a hostile tyranny. John Adams, later President of the USA, estimated that about one-third of the colonists were opposed to the Revolution. Many more were neutral or indifferent. Between 30,000 and 50,000 fought for King George as regulars, while others were militiamen or guerrilla fighters. This was not only a war of independence, but a civil war (and an Indian war) as well. During it, or immediately after it, about 100,000 loyalists emigrated from the Thirteen Colonies, mostly to Canada; and not all of these came within Tom Paine's description of them as "interested men, who are not to be trusted; weak men who *cannot* see; prejudiced men who *will not* see; and a certain set of moderate men who think better of the European world than it deserves".

The initial advantages in the fighting seemed to lie with the British forces (many of them, in fact, not British, but German mercenaries, Hessians in particular). The Americans were disunited, and their leaders quarrelsome; their armies were amateur and generally poor in discipline; few only of their leaders were professionals, as Washington was; their finances were feeble, and the Continental Congress lacked the power to raise taxes (its paper money soon became worthless); most of the principal ports were under British control.

Against all this were the inherent weaknesses of the British situation: 3000-mile-long lines of communication, with delays, and sometimes breakdown, in liaison between Government and commanders; the constant danger of attack from European powers thirsting to settle old scores; and always the difficulty that Chatham had prophesied: "Though you should be able to march from town to town and province to province ... how shall you be able to secure the obedience of the country you leave behind in your progress?" On top of these inevitable, and perhaps insuperable, obstacles, the British had other handicaps of their own creation: a Government whose leader, North, disclaimed supreme responsibility and lacked both the ambition and the ability to be a great war leader; politicians directing the war—Sandwich and Germain—who showed gross lack of judgment; generals, like Howe, Clinton, Burgoyne, and Cornwallis, who, though far from incompetent, played the game of war on strictly professional lines, inviting no last-ditch heroism from their troops and displaying none of their own, retiring into winter quarters (as Howe did at the end of 1776) at the prescribed season. Washington, on the other hand, though he often talked as if all were lost, never behaved as if it was. He clung on with iron tenacity, most notably of all at Valley Forge, during the grim winter of 1777–78; only once, for an hour or so, during the whole war, could he spare time to visit his home at Mount Vernon.

The course of the war may be briefly told. By the end of 1776 Howe and Clinton were in control of the coast from

Rhode Island to the Delaware; they had much reduced, but failed to destroy, Washington's army, which had successfully eluded big pitched battles. But with Philadelphia threatened, the Congress was forced to flee to Baltimore; Washington's army was further depleted by desertions, and things looked bad for the rebels. At this point, Washington saved the situation with two victories, one over the Hessians at Trenton and the second over another British force at Princeton (January 1777)—minor battles, but great in psychological importance. For the campaigning season of 1777 the British planned a triple drive to split New England apart from the rest of the rebel colonies. Burgoyne from Canada was to press down the upper Hudson valley, while Howe was to move northward from New York up the lower Hudson. They were to meet near Albany, where a third army would join them, having come down the Mohawk river. Howe's participation in the plan was, however, frustrated by his feeling an obligation first to deal with Washington's army, which had overrun New Jersey. He managed to defeat Washington at Brandywine and take Philadelphia, but suffered many delays and could not fulfil his part of the timetable. Meanwhile Burgoyne with 7200 men was stranded at Saratoga, surrounded by nearly double the number of rebel troops under Gates. Howe had no hope of making the rendezvous at Albany in time; the third force had also run into trouble on the Mohawk river, and in any case Burgoyne was in the dark about the situation of the other British armies. He decided that he had no alternative but surrender.

This was undoubtedly the turning point of the war, for the rebels had demonstrated to themselves and to the world that their cause was hopeful. The French, who had long been watching events and biding their time, now judged the moment to be propitious. Already for two years they had provided ammunition and unofficial help; now (February 1778) they signed a treaty of alliance and declared war on Britain.

One effect of this was to make the British Government anxious to limit the American War to a naval and coastal affair (Philadelphia was evacuated) and to dispose its main forces against France. Peace terms were tried out, too, upon the Americans, but without much prospect of success, for the rebels' spirits were rising. In Britain the Rockingham Whigs now adopted the line that full independence should be granted, so that Britain's hands should be freed for the struggle with France, and a pacified America be persuaded to co-operate in it. It was in challenging this "surrender", this breaking-up of the British Empire, that Chatham made his last journey to the House of Lords to speak on a motion put down by the Rockinghamite Duke of Richmond: a confused, disturb-ing figure, already more than half a ghost, but capable of a flourish still: "My Lords, any state is better than despair. Let us at least make one effort, and if we must fall, let us fall like men." He had forgotten much of what he wanted to say, and sat down. An embarrassed Duke of Richmond replied. Chat-ham made as if to rise again, and collapsed into the arms of his friends. They carried him insensible from the House and took him home to Kent, where he lived a few more weeks. Towards the end, conscious of the fitness of things, he had his son William read to him from the *Iliad* of the death of Hector. Thus this most impressive of eighteenth-century statesmen passed from the scene. All his life he had been obsessed by the necessity of greatness, both for himself and for his country. He had overcome the desperate maladies that beset him, to lead his country to its most triumphant conquests. But he had continued to preach that these were insecure so long as the Bourbon powers were left strong enough to plan their revenge; and he died at the moment when their success began to look alarmingly probable.

In 1779 Spain entered the war and besieged Gibraltar. Once more, as in 1756 and 1759, England faced invasion from the French; in the Channel it was touch and go, with recrimina-tions flying to and fro between rival English admirals and between the commander of the Home Fleet (Keppel) and the First Lord of the Admiralty (Sandwich). (Keppel was court-martialled but acquitted, in itself a blow to the Government.) Then General Howe, returning from America, advised the Government that America was no longer tenable, and General Clinton's forces there deliberately soft-pedalled the war, hop-ing for divisions among the Americans, which were plentiful and vociferous, to enable the British to divide and conquer. In the south, where the loyalists were more numerous, Clinton and Cornwallis were able to establish fair authority; and having soundly defeated the rebel armies in Carolina, they proceeded to invade Virginia, aided by the deserter Benedict Arnold.

By 1781 Clinton himself was in command of the British forces based on New York; Cornwallis had prudently consolidated the scattered southern forces inside the peninsula of Yorktown, in the Chesapeake estuary. This was the situation that Washington exploited. A feint attack on New York kept Clinton guessing. A big French fleet under de Grasse held Hood's British fleet helpless in New York, and prevented reinforcements from Clinton reaching Cornwallis at Yorktown. There Cornwallis's forces maintained resistance until October 1781; but they were hemmed in by combined armies of French and Americans, and were eventually obliged to capitulate. Saratoga had made victory for the rebels possible; Yorktown ensured its completeness.

The situation of Britain in 1781 certainly looked parlous. America was lost, at least partly because, at a crucial juncture, local sea supremacy had been won by the French. The Dutch had entered the war on the side of the Americans, French, and Spanish, anxious to share the spoils from a likely-looking British collapse. The Baltic powers had joined in an "armed neutrality" to protect their shipping interests against the British fleet, and it appeared very probable that they would go a stage further into active war. Both in the West Indies and in India the French were making big efforts to destroy the British position. Florida had been lost. Ireland looked likely to follow America's rebellious example. The tale of woe was long and bitter, and there was little to do but to get out of trouble with as little loss as possible.

One thing was certain: American independence was assured, and the way opened, in the flush of victory, to a federal union of the Thirteen Colonies. The significance of this event—the creation of the USA—can hardly be overstressed.

The Treaty of Versailles that formally concluded the war in 1783 was negotiated on the British side principally by Shelburne; a necessary preliminary had been the resignation of Lord North, released at last from his purgatory by George III. As well as independence, America was granted all the land from the Atlantic to the Mississippi—the trans-Appalachian West. (The West beyond the Mississippi was still too remote even to consider.) The terms exacted by France were somewhat less severe than they might have been, because, in 1782, a reinforced British fleet under Rodney and Hood destroyed nine French sail of the line (out of twenty-four engaged), restored British naval supremacy, and saved the West Indies, in the battle of "the Saints" (fought off Les Saintes Islands, near Guadeloupe). Even so, France received, by the treaty, Tobago, Saint-Pierre and Miquelon, the fishing rights off Newfoundland, Dakar (Goree) and Senegal in West Africa, and the right to fortify Dunkirk, while Spain regained Florida and Minorca. The Dutch came empty away.

For the France of the Bourbons there was irony in her victory. The expenses of the war drove her finally into national bankruptcy, a prime cause of the French Revolution; and the championship by aristocratic France of the sort of revolutionary ideas propounded in the Declaration of Independence was to rebound powerfully upon her in a few years' time. La Fayette helped to make the American Revolution; he returned to assist in the French. Truths which were self-evident to Americans were self-evident in Europe too; what was sauce for the goose proved sauce for the gander.

7. India in the Age of Clive

The first three-quarters of George III's reign (1760–1805) saw the emergence of the East India Company from a merely trading organization to a powerful political force sharing governmental powers with the state itself, and dominating the entire sub-continent of India. This process was largely involuntary, troubled throughout, and productive of much political bitterness at home.

In the first century and a half of their activity in India, Englishmen had been essentially trading adventurers, intent on large and speedy profits. Based on their four 'factories', or fortress stations, at Madras, Surat, Bombay, and Calcutta, tiny communities living closely together (the unmarried dining in hall under the eye of their governor), closing their gates nightly at ten o'clock, taking their wives sometimes from the Indian population, influential among local rulers but not assuming any of their authority, they made good money for their Company by shipping Indian goods to England (most of which was paid for in gold and silver) and by undertaking loans, at high interest, to local princes. In addition, however, there was wide scope for the Company's servants to exploit private trade, sometimes on terms of special privilege from a complaisant ruler, himself hopeful of benefits to come. Some Company servants developed, for instance, a profitable coastal trade between Bombay and Persia, and others worked the eastward routes towards China. In this sort of atmosphere, business morality was easy-going, opportunity was immense, and it paid Englishman and Indian alike to cultivate mutual good relations. In these early days, therefore, there was little colour prejudice or sense of moral superiority, and none of the missionary arrogance that later characterized British rule in India. Englishmen like "Diamond" Pitt were not in India for the good of the Indian.

Knowledge of the opportunities open to a resourceful Englishman in India meant that competition to procure a position with the Company was quite out of proportion to the almost negligible salary offered. Large premiums were often paid by 'good' families to secure a writership for some adventurous (or perhaps, like Clive, 'difficult') son, ambitious to try his luck in the great Eastern lottery. Clive was the heir to a Shropshire squire's estate, but his father was glad to pack him off to what, in theory, was humble pen-pushing in Madras. It did, too, really begin as pen-pushing of the weariest kind, that helped to drive the depressed young man to attempt suicide; but Clive's later history suggests the sensational potentialities before the humblest clerk. When they had made their fortune in India, Englishmen often returned to spend it in England, buying up estates, and perhaps a rotten borough, as "Diamond" Pitt did, parading their wealth, enjoying their new social station, and often exercising important political influence.

INDIA 1714-1837

BRITISH TERRITORIES
IN 1837

EAST INDIA CO. FACTORIES UNDERLINED

KASHMIR

PUNJAB

DELHI

RAJPUTANA
(Protectorate 1818)

NORTH-
WEST
PROV-
INCES

OUDH

BIHAR ✗ BUXAR

BENGAL ✗ PLASSEY

ASSAM 1826

CALCUTTA

ARAKAN 1826

TENASSERIM
1826

M
A
R
A
T
H
A

1818

ASSAYE

HYDERABAD
(Subsidiary state,
bound by treaties,
1766, 1799, with
East India Co.)

SURAT

BOMBAY

GOA
(Port.)

C
A
R
N
A
T
I
C

ARCOT

MYSORE

SERINGAPATAM

TRICHINOPOLY

MADRAS (Ft St George)

PONDICHERRY (Fr.)

FORT ST DAVID

CEYLON

TEA FROM CHINA

OPIUM TO CHINA

SINGAPORE 1819

These were the 'nabobs', the Englishman's pronunciation of 'nawabs', or Indian princes. The nabobs' ostentation gave the stay-at-home Englishman a sometimes exaggerated notion of the real profits of the East India Company; the time came in the 1760's and 1770's when, although many of the Company's servants had made manifest fortunes, the Company itself, near bankruptcy, was seeking parliamentary sympathy and aid, a dangerous situation openly inviting suggestions of fraud and corruption. Yet the Company was well equipped to mount its case in the Commons; its 'interest' was always powerful, and its patronage second only to that of the Crown.

The India in which the Company was trading was wide open to adventurers, both native and European. It was an India where the Moghul Empire, though still magnificent, was on the threshold of collapse. The descendants of Aurangzeb (who died in 1707, the last great emperor of an impressive line) still sat on the throne at Delhi, but precariously: a generation of civil war had enfeebled their hold, enabled the nizams and nawabs of distant territories to proclaim their independence, and invited the rebel Marathas to plunder the north and centre of India. By 1770 the big majority of Indian princes were new-comers, who had seized, or whose father or grandfather had seized, the power and wealth that was going begging all over the sub-continent. In this gamblers' paradise the East India Company found itself with strong cards. The manner in which it intrigued in India's infinitely complicated quarrels, and defeated the French at their own game, has already been touched on in Chapter 6. This was where Clive the despondent clerk was suddenly transformed into Clive the warrior and conspirator and gambler of genius, who touched nothing at this time that did not turn to gold, both for himself and for his employers. His bargain with his protégé, Mir Jafir, before the victory of Plassey, involved payment by Mir Jafir of a million pounds for the Company, half a million for the European inhabitants of Calcutta, various military expenses, £50,000 apiece to members of the Council, and, for Clive himself, £234,000 and an assignment of land revenue (or *jagir*) worth £25,000 a year. In addition, European merchants were exempted from all internal tolls and duties throughout Bengal.

For his part, Clive undertook to sustain Mir Jafir as Nawab of Bengal, and triumphantly did so, defeating all comers, including the Dutch (1757–60).

This incredible good fortune went to the heads of the English merchants in India. No dreams of avarice now seemed unreasonable, either in Bengal, or, to a somewhat lesser extent, in Madras or Bombay. If political and military dabbling paid dividends of this nature, then hurrah for politics and war; and during Clive's five-year absence from India (1760–65) the intrigue and greed of the British merchants became outrageous and intolerable. Indian merchants were outwitted and intimidated; Mir Jafir was deposed, and his successor, Mir Kasim, mulcted of heavy accession bribes; then, when he attempted to impose a small trading tax on Europeans, he was in turn deposed and Mir Jafir restored, after he had paid up all over again, and, this time, promised the Company the Bengal revenue receipts, or *diwani*, previously paid to the Moghul Emperor. War against Mir Kasim involved war with the Emperor too; but by now the Company was equal to such involvement; its victory at Buxar in 1764 signalled complete control of Bengal, Bihar, and Orissa, a threat to Oudh, and the virtual end of the Delhi Emperor's paramount position.

Clive returned to India in 1765 to find, in his own words, "a scene of anarchy, confusion, bribery, corruption, and extortion". Armed with dictatorial powers, he showed military restraint and reforming zeal. He made peace with the Moghul; enforced such standards of rectitude as were practicable among the Company's servants; dismissed some of the worst offenders; attempted unsuccessfully to put down private trading; and suppressed a white mutiny. His financial policy was unrealistic, for he failed to grasp that by its sensational successes the Company had become, in fact, a Government, and must consequently govern. Clive shrank from taking over political administration; he thought that the British could operate through the medium of the Nawab's Government, while pocketing the *diwani*, which he wrongly estimated to be worth £2,000,000 a year. The optimism following his politico-financial settlement (the "Dual Control") was ill-founded: shareholders successfully pushed the dividend up to a totally unrealistic 12½ per cent; long financial shadows began to creep over the Company's affairs; and eventually the British Government had to step in to save the Company from itself and to take a share in the political responsibilities of ruling its vast dominions.

Clive's own career now ran to its tragic close. In 1767, leaving India seething with disgruntled Company servants, and returning to England, to which some of his dismissed victims had preceded him, he obtained a seat in the Commons, and a ten-year prolongation of his *jagir*, which was worth about another quarter of a million to him; but soon he faced hostile inquiries, cross-examination by a select parliamentary committee, and eventually, in 1772, a full-scale Commons attack, led by Burgoyne (later of Saratoga). The motion was that:

> The said Robert Clive abused the power with which he was entrusted to the evil example of the servants of the public and to the dishonour and detriment of the state.

But it was defeated, after Clive had made a most able and hard-hitting speech in his own defence. On the matter of bribery, his words are worth remembering:

> ... Indostan was always an absolute despotic government. The inhabitants, especially of Bengal, in inferior stations, are servile, mean, submissive, and humble. In superior stations, they are luxurious, effeminate, tyrannical, treacherous, venal, cruel. . . . From time immemorial it has been the custom of that country, for an inferior never to come in to the presence of a superior without a present. It begins at the nabob, and ends at the lowest man that has an inferior. The nabob has told me, that the small presents he received amounted to £300,000 a year; and I can believe him; because I know that I might have received as much during my last government. The Company's servants have ever been accustomed to receive presents. Even before we took part in the country troubles, when our possessions were very confined and limited, the governor and others used to receive presents; and I will take upon me to assert, that there has not been an officer commanding his Majesty's fleet; nor an officer commanding his Majesty's army; not a governor, not a member of council, not any other person,

civil or military, in such a station as to have connection with the country government, who has not received presents.

His defence, then, was a longer and more detailed repetition of his earlier outburst to the committee of inquiry: "By God, Mr Chairman, at this moment I stand amazed at my own moderation."

Two years after his parliamentary vindication, the old depression returning, he took his own life. As a soldier he had been the most brilliant of amateurs; as an administrator he had been vigorous, ruthless, and impatient; as a man, ambitious, thwarted, melancholic. "His tragedy was that the instruments of his ambition ... broke in his hand, and what had appeared dazzling to others became for him darkness."[3]

8. North's Regulating Act and the Rule of Warren Hastings

In the twenty or so years that followed the Seven Years War successive English statesmen, from the elder Pitt to the younger, grappled with the problems of the East India Company. We have already seen how Charles Fox's attempted solution provided the occasion for George III to overthrow the Fox–North coalition in 1783. North's earlier Regulating Act of 1773 was of much greater importance, though it was operative for only a little over a decade, being then superseded by the Younger Pitt's Act of 1784.

Discussions of North's proposals came just after the attacks on Clive had reached their height; the affairs of India seemed then to be crying out for remedy more pressingly even than those of America, where a lull was preceding the storm. Indeed, it was a minor feature of North's Indian settlement (that affecting the Company's tea exports) which shattered the lull. From 1766 to 1769 there had been a boom in East India stock, based on the rising dividend and a confident expectation of expanding profits from the new conquests; but when the Company continued to engage in expensive wars, and saw its revenues decline further because of the Bengal famine of

[3] Percival Spear: "Robert, Lord Clive" in *History Today* (January 1954).

1770–72, the price of its stock fell heavily, and it came to the Government for a loan, while still raising its dividend beyond the limits either of honesty or of sanity. The paradox of this situation, dramatized by big stock losses among leading politicians (Shelburne, for instance), and by envious attacks on the patently wealthy 'nabobs' (Clive in particular), forced North, however unwillingly, to reform the whole status of the Company. A trading company intent only on profits and dividends could not be entrusted with unfettered rule of so vast an empire. The British Government accordingly, for the first time, accepted a small but important share in the responsibility of governing the Company's dominions; at the same time it forced its own financial and administrative reforms on the Company's directors. Of these the most important were the unification of Bengal, Bombay, and Madras under a single Bengal presidency, and the nomination by the Government of a Governor-General, who was to be assisted by a supreme Bengal council of four. The Company was still to rule its own Indian affairs, and care was taken to appoint as first Governor-General one of its trusted servants, Warren Hastings; but a vital first step had been taken towards governmental and national involvement in the affairs of India—a first step along the road which led eventually to the supersession of the Company by the Government, and, a century after North, to Victoria's assumption of the imperial crown of India.

North's Act was a compromise; and it could have worked better if only personal animosities on its newly created Council had not been so bitter. Even so, Warren Hastings, whose misfortune it was to govern India during the period of the North settlement, had an almost impossible task. He was Governor-General, representing George III, and he was expected to uphold the King's majesty and the nation's authority; and at the same time he was responsible to the Company's Court of Directors and was expected to produce handsome profits for the shareholders. This was like sitting on two stools at once, one higher than the other. When it is further remembered that Hastings wielded power at a time when the effects of famine sharpened India's endemic troubles; that he inherited all the misgovernment and corruption that Clive's reforms had failed to cure; and that, on top of everything else, he was confronted by war successively from the powerful Marathas in the northwest and the French-supported Hyder Ali in the south, it is hardly remarkable that his methods were far from gentle, and it is surprising that his success was so considerable.

Hastings was an autocrat by nature and conviction, and he chafed constantly at the restraints imposed on him by his colleagues on the Council. One of these in particular, Philip Francis (an intellectual—he well may have been the anonymous "Junius"), arrived at Calcutta as self-constituted guardian of public morality and reformer of corrupt practices. He had preconceived notions about Hastings and was set upon standing up to him as the arch-nabob; and he did this to such good purpose that by 1775 he, with two others of the four-man Council, were accusing Hastings of financial fraud and judicial murder, and frustrating all his actions. Hastings was delivered from a situation of impotence by the timely deaths of both Francis's allies on the Council, and for a time a sort of truce between these unreconciled enemies permitted the policies of the Company to proceed; but when quarrels resumed and Hastings recorded in an official minute that he had found the conduct of Francis "void of truth and honour", the two men met in a duel. Francis was wounded, returned to England, and there continued his vendetta against Warren Hastings.

Hastings had been in India since 1750 (like Clive, he had gone out as a young writer); he had a good knowledge of Indian history, and respect for its culture; he patronized the new Asiatic Society for studying Oriental religion and law; and he despised those plundering barbarians among his compatriots who disgraced the Company's record. Even so, he had, like most Englishmen in India, done well in private trading, accepted rich presents, and made a personal fortune, some of which he made over to the Company. The British were not in India for the good of their health. Every Englishman there expected to make money (not excepting Philip Francis), and Hastings knew well that if he insisted upon a total ban on perquisites and commissions he would not have a loyal Company servant left. Politics is the art of the possible, and Hastings was, inevitably, a politician.

He was more: he was the greatest Anglo-Indian statesman of his century. He reformed the administration, finances, and judiciary of Bengal. He laboured to construct around Bengal a chain of allied Indian states, Oudh being the vital link. Defeating the Rohillas (Afghan warriors of northern India), he gave himself a defensible Ganges frontier against the Marathas. With the Marathas themselves he had hoped to avoid hostilities; but when the headstrong Bombay British became involved against them he energetically gave support, and conquered Gujerat and Gwalior. Then, with the French at war (1778) following Saratoga, he survived the greatest crisis of all when Hyder Ali (Haidar Ali) of Mysore, with French backing, attacked the Carnatic and threatened Madras. Hastings sent the tough old veteran Eyre Coote south, and supported him with all the ships and treasure that he could lay hands on. Hyder Ali, a capable and ambitious Muslim warrior-adventurer, was given a demonstration of the value of sea-power. By 1784, after his defeat and death, the Company was at peace with both the Marathas and Mysore. While America was being lost British India had been saved and even strengthened.

To pay for all this, Hastings embarked on some of his severest, and most questionable, practices. He mulcted the Rajah of Benares of £230,000 (failing to squeeze out of him the half-million that he intended); and he stripped the two dowager princesses of Oudh (the *begums*) of their treasures. Hastings was, indeed, as his enemies complained, ruthless when he chose; subordinate Englishmen and unco-operative Indians alike felt the lash of his displeasure. But, first, wars and empires had to be paid for; and, second, Calcutta was not Westminster. As he wrote himself after his return, "It is necessary that the Governor ... should possess a power absolute and complete within himself and independent of actual controul"; independent also of the "interests, passions, and caprices" of colleagues "united in common interest against their ostensible leader". It was Clive's old argument, and a fair one; you could not, as the Whigs seemed to think you could, govern India as you would England: "Indostan was always an absolute despotic government." Two qualifications, wrote Hastings, were essential to a Governor of Bengal, "an inflexible integrity, and a judgment unsusceptible of the bias of foreign suggestion". He did possess those qualities, and could justly claim on his return: "I have at least had the happiness to see one portion of the British dominion in India [Bengal] rise from the lowest state of degradation; another [Madras] rescued from imminent subjection; and that which gives life to the whole, enjoying the blessings of peace and internal security, while every other part of the general empire was oppressed by war, or the calamities of intestine discord."

The Whigs saw his record differently. To Fox, Burke, Sheridan, and the rest—and of course to Francis—he was the power-hungry, money-loving despot, overbearing and corrupt, riding roughshod over the rights of Indians, an extortioner and tyrant. "English youth in India", said Burke, "drink the intoxicating draught of authority and dominion before their heads are able to bear it, and . . . are full grown in fortune long before they are ripe in principle." Hastings, the nabob of nabobs, was the greatest of a class that had "torn the cloth from the loom, or wrested the scanty portion of rice and salt from the peasant of Bengal, or wrung from him the very opium in which he forgot his oppressions. . . ." These sentiments may have been mistaken, and the facts behind them twisted; yet Burke at least—and to a degree many of his friends—had motives that are to be respected. These men thought they were protecting the rights of natives against the greed of English exploiters. In a way they were, and it was good that Englishmen should think such things important. But they mistook their man and arraigned the wrong victim. For seven years (1788–95) Hastings' impeachment proceeded, while Burke, Fox, and Sheridan eloquently painted every detail of his record in the darkest colours. What had begun as a sensation, with fashionable London flocking to see the accused kneeling in Westminster Hall before his accusers, ended as a bore. The Whigs over-prepared their speeches, overplayed their melo-dramatic revelations, and in the end stooped to fabricating evidence. At last the Lords acquitted Hastings, but the ex-penses of the trial had ruined him, and he was dependent for the rest of his life on an annuity from the Company, which remained faithful to him.

9. British India from 1784 to 1820

One of the younger Pitt's first actions on coming to power was to establish a new relationship between the East India Company and Parliament. His India Act of 1784, as subsequently amended in 1786 and 1793, carried North's settlement a stage further. The Company still retained the monopoly of trade, the administration of its Indian territories, and the right to make its own appointments, but its actions were now subject to the overriding authority of a Board of Control appointed by the Crown. The Governor-General in Calcutta was given absolute power in formulating political policy, with the right to override his council if necessary. Returned nabobs were to declare their fortunes, and wrongs done by British subjects in India were to be answerable in British courts. Thus an attempt was made at once to limit corruption, to profit by Hastings' experiences with his Council, and to strengthen the controlling authority of the home Government. It was a long-lived settlement, lasting broadly till just after the Indian Mutiny of 1857; but the Company's mounting trading difficulties during the Napoleonic Wars put them in no position to argue when their Charter was renewed in 1813, and in that year they lost their trade monopoly. Twenty years later their last commercial privileges disappeared. More and more, as the years went by, India became the political concern of the Government and Parliament of Britain, less and less of the trading Company.

With this process went another. The old easy-going relationship between Christian and Hindu, white man and brown, gave way to something more self-conscious and less happy, a growing sense of imperial responsibility and religious mission. Evangelical clergymen, pursuing the often sparsely rewarded task of spiritual persuasion, frequently came to regard Hindu and Muslim alike as heathens sunk deep in the mire of filthy superstitions. The old vice of the Englishman in India had been commercial rapacity; the new one was the racial and moral arrogance that went with the new sense of vocation and responsibility. Cornwallis, Governor-General from 1786 to 1793, excluded Indians from all senior posts in Government service on the grounds that "every native of Hindustan is corrupt". His successor, Wellesley, went further and excluded them from the social functions held by the ruling whites. Army officers and their wives began to make little exclusive societies of their own. Together with this general feeling of superiority went a sense of "manifest destiny" which is at the same time both ludicrous and impressive. On the one hand, Lord Hastings,[4] Governor-General from 1813, solemnly observed that "the Hindoo appears a being . . . with no higher intellect than a dog, an elephant, or a monkey . . ."; and at Fort William College a subject set about this time for a university prize essay ran as follows: "The probable design of the Divine Providence in subjecting so large a portion of Asia to the British Dominion." On the other hand, it could not be denied that the lordly English governed well. It is certainly amusing to read that Lord Wellesley, the Governor-General succeeding Cornwallis, loved status and magnificence so much that he wore his orders and decorations even on his night attire; but the new Englishman in India, ripe material though he may be for satire, was more than just a *pukka sahib*. At his best, he was sober, vigilant, and incorruptible; his task was to extend the rule of law, to guard against malpractices, to protect the peasant against moneylenders, and generally to spread the blessings of English civilization among the ignorant, superstitious, and corrupt Indians. For some, such as the historian and Whig politician Macaulay, Britain was exporting an ideology, a way of life: "By good government we may educate our subjects into a capacity for better government. . . . Having become instructed in European knowledge, they may, in some future age, demand European institutions."

Cornwallis, although a professional soldier, did not embark on an expansionist policy in India; and when he defeated the forces of Mysore he was careful not to incur the further responsibility of large territorial gains. He regarded it as his principal business to make Pitt's Act work; reform, not conquest, was the main thing. When, however, Lord Wellesley arrived in India in 1798 the French under Bonaparte were in full cry; that very year Bonaparte invaded Egypt, and Egypt

[4] He had no connection with the family of Warren Hastings.

was seen by him as the key to India. Wellesley, therefore, would have been inevitably drawn into campaigns of conquest, as Clive had been, if only to thwart French plans; but in any case the glories of military conquest suited his notions of imperial splendour, and, as he put it himself, "no greater blessing can be conferred on the native inhabitants of India than the extension of British authority, influence, and power". Wellesley, like his contemporary Nelson, found it happily simple to discover a congruency between the majesty of George III and the designs of a benevolent Deity.

Hyder Ali had been succeeded in Mysore by Tipu Sahib, who obtained a treaty of alliance with the French and aimed ambitiously to expel the British from India; but Wellesley, with his young brother Arthur, the future Duke of Wellington, besieged Tipu in his capital, Seringapatam, and successfully stormed it (1799). Tipu was killed fighting in the streets. The territories of Mysore were then partitioned, some becoming British, some going to Hyderabad, some being restored to the earlier Hindu dynasty ruling Mysore; but all these territories, and Hyderabad too, became effectively dominated by the British, who also took over total control of the Carnatic. Having thus become the paramount power of southern India, the Wellesleys turned their attention to the Maratha Confederacy, whose forces were defeated by Arthur Wellesley on the bloody field of Assaye in 1803. By 1805 the Moghul Emperor, who had long existed under the domination of the Marathas, accepted British 'protection'. By that year, the year of Trafalgar, it could be said that Britain was supreme in India. But the Company, alarmed at its falling profits and rising responsibilities, took no joy in Lord Wellesley's triumphs: instead, they forced his resignation, and saw to it that his successor, Minto, understood that he was expected to forgo the luxuries of empire-building and concentrate on avoiding bankruptcy.

The finances of the Company were perplexingly bad. The more powerful it became, the less money it made. Although Englishmen in its service still contrived to do well, the Company itself was obliged to exist with the aid of repeated loans from the Government; and if it had not been for the Chinese trade, in tea and above all in opium, bankruptcy would have supervened. It was in these circumstances that the Company inevitably lost more and more ground to the State.

Wellesley's conquests, like the administrative reforms of North and Pitt, could do no more than mark a semicolon in the history of British India; neither could be a full-stop. Lord Hastings, when he arrived there in 1813, faced Marathas still not finally defeated, a ragged and not easily defensible frontier, and native states beyond it that had Governments too bad for description. The invitation to complete Wellesley's work was irresistible. The Marathas were now crushed. So were the Pindaris. The Gurkhas of Nepal put up the stiffest resistance, but even so their Maharajah was obliged to accept a British Resident. By 1819 all India except the Punjab and Sind lay, directly or indirectly, under the British Raj.

Chapter 10

Economic Progress and Social Change

1. The Growth of Population

English population in the latter years of the eighteenth century began the steep climb that was to continue unchecked until the early decades of the twentieth century. In 1760 the population of England, Scotland, and Wales stood at fewer than 8,000,000; by 1801, the year of the first census, it was about 10,500,000, and in the succeeding century it was to multiply again by almost three and a half. Although not all the causes of this explosion in the national numbers are fully understood, the central fact is basically simple: fewer children (and, especially, fewer young babies) died, and an ever greater fraction of the population survived to become themselves parents. The factors promoting a slight rise in the birth rate during the first half of George III's reign are relatively obscure and debatable; but they are unimportant compared with the cardinal fact of the steady decline in the death rate that set in from about 1750. And this was due chiefly to three things: a rise in the standard of living, and particularly of diet; an advance in medical knowledge; and a groping towards better standards of public hygiene.

In 1765, it was calculated, a labourer could earn the equivalent of a peck of corn a day, whereas in 1714 he could earn only two-thirds of a peck. One sign of the increasing 'real' value of wages—*i.e.*, their buying power rather than their nominal value—was the trend towards the consumption of white bread. But nutritionally more important was the much greater bulk and variety of vegetables, for both men and animals. It was the potato that permitted a sensational increase in the Irish peasant population at this time; in the North of England, too, and in Scotland potato cultivation was spreading rapidly. So, everywhere, was that of other roots and green crops; and turnips for winter-feed allowed more meat and dairy produce (though still little enough) for the labourer's table.[1] A further cause of the fall in the death rate may well have been the decline in gin-drinking after the Act of 1751. (As the consumption of spirits fell, that of tea rose.) It is probable, too, that improved sanitation, street-sweeping, and paving in many of the big towns played a part in lessening the mortality from filth-borne infection, though, by modern standards, conditions remained foul enough.

Medical and surgical enlightenment was spreading, albeit slowly, from the London hospitals, now feeling the influence of such great Scottish teachers as Sir John Pringle, who attacked the causes of dysentery, typhus, and malaria; the brothers Hunter, "the fathers of modern surgery"; William Smellie, a pioneer in the training of midwives; and James Lind, who showed the way to prevent deaths at sea by introducing oranges and lemons into the diet of sailors, previously very vulnerable to scurvy. Scores of new hospitals and dispensaries were founded at this time, in London and in the provinces; and although conditions there were rough by twentieth-century standards, and inmates were regarded rather as objects of charity than as patients by right, these

---

[1] G. D. H. Cole and Raymond Postgate, in *The Common People, 1746–1946*, give the following as a typical southern-counties budget for a labourer, his wife, and four or five children in about 1795:

	Per year	
	£	s
Cereals	23	8
Potatoes	1	19
Cheese	0	13
Meat	2	12
Sugar, Tea and Butter	2	12
Milk	0	13
Beer	0	13
Thread	0	13
Clothes and Boots	2	0
Fuel	2	0
Rent	1	10
Sickness and contingencies	1	0

These figures are for a period when prices, but not wages, had risen sharply with the onset of war. The probable income of the man, his wife, and children would not exceed £35 in a year—which would leave a deficit of several pounds to be made up from poor relief.

institutions saved lives that would have been lost in an earlier age.[2] The regular nurses who ministered in them were not the heartless and drunken harridans that they have often been painted, though the extra women recruited in times of stress at a shilling a night often were.

Smallpox continued throughout the century to take a terrible toll, still in mid-Georgian times accounting for one death in thirteen; and it was not till 1796 that Edward Jenner first vaccinated (*i.e.*, immunized by injecting with cowpox) a child thought to be incubating smallpox. His success was to inaugurate a new era and lead eventually to the near-extinction of this justly dreaded disease. But already by 1760 inoculation (*i.e.*, the injection of a mild dose of smallpox itself, to provide immunity against a severer attack) was becoming well known. Two of the royal princesses, sisters of the future George III, had been inoculated; but the practice was confined mainly to the wealthy, even after Dr Lettsom started a society for inoculating the children of the poor and opened an inoculation dispensary in London (1779). (Similar institutions opened in Newcastle, Chester, and Liverpool.)

At the close of the eighteenth century there was great argument whether the population was, in fact, increasing at all, or whether, as Richard Price, Cobbett, and many others considered, it was declining. Never before had so many books and pamphlets considered this question, still an open one in those days before the first census in 1801 and its successor of 1811 proved who was right and who was wrong. Easily the most important and influential of these publications was *An Essay on the Principle of Population* (1798), by the Rev. Thomas Malthus, whose argument was that population, increasing by geometric progression, always tends to outrun the means of subsistence, which progresses arithmetically. Thus population is kept at a tolerable level only by famine, war, pestilence, and vice. Improvement was self-correcting: any betterment of the labouring class must bring its own eventual cancellation. Malthus concentrated mainly on the rising birth rate (as we

[2] Professor Asa Briggs disagrees: "In fact, hospitals were places of danger rather than of protection, and it was safer to stay outside" (*Age of Improvement*, p. 33).

now know, not the main factor); what concerned him were the proliferating children of the poor, artificially protected from the rigours of life, and of death, by a misguided poor law. In a later edition (1803) he conceded that improvement could indeed come, but only if the poor employed "moral restraint", by which he meant sexual self-discipline and late marriage. Even as amended, his book seemed to prove to many willing readers that progress was difficult and the perfectibility of man (preached by such as William Godwin) an idle dream.

Malthus's fallacies and miscalculations were made much of when it was seen, in Victorian times, that the growing wealth of Britain permitted her to raise her population *and* her standard of living simultaneously, and when later it was realized that improving standards of living, in modern conditions, tend to bring smaller, not larger families. But Malthus's gloomy diagnosis, if based on some errors, was still important. His influence, allied to that of *laissez-faire* economists, tended to provide a ready-made 'scientific' excuse for continuing harsh treatment of the poor, and was thus harmful. But the twentieth century, occupied as it is with its own acute population problems, can see all too easily some uncomfortable truths among the Malthusian fallacies. And it was Malthus's phrase "the struggle for existence" that was one of the stimuli setting Charles Darwin on the road to his epoch-making theory of natural selection in the evolution of the species.

2. Enclosure, the New Farming, and the Rural Poor

The progress that farming had made by 1760 was patchy. Some districts, like East Anglia, had made great strides, but in others, such as the South and East Midlands, and much of the North Country, old habits died hard and modern improvements were slow to spread. Even in progressive Norfolk, and as late as 1796, one-quarter of the arable area was still tilled on the medieval open-field system.

An essential precondition of the general improvement of farming was enclosure—*i.e.*, a reorganization of the medieval strip-and-furrow into compact hedged holdings. Much of the best arable land in England, including most of the Midland

Plain, was still being cultivated in open fields, with their ancient divisions into strips or 'lands'. Villagers held their scattered lands in each of the three great fields of the manor, one spring-sown, one autumn-sown, and one fallow. Ancient custom and communal agreement determined the time of sowing and harvest; ploughs and their oxen were often jointly owned; the whole village pastured their beasts on the common pastureland and waste-land, on the fallow, and on the arable fields after harvest; and the whole village shared rights of gathering wood and turf for fuel. The system had grown to meet the needs of feudal England, and even in 1760 it was not without advantages; but in an age of innovation and experiment it heavily blocked the path of progress. Scientific breeding was impossible where all the animals, healthy and diseased, grazed together. The ancient rotation of (1) Wheat (or Rye), (2) Barley (or Oats), (3) Fallow (or alternatively (1) Wheat or Barley, (2) Beans, (3) Fallow) applied rigidly to the whole community, and prevented the more progressive farmers from trying new crops and rotations. Energy, time, and money were constantly wasted as men trudged and carted their loads between the widely scattered 'lands'. "They reap bushels", wrote one critic, "where they should reap quarters."

Enclosures had been proceeding steadily during the first half of the century, sometimes simply by local agreement or as a consequence of pressure from the biggest local landlords, sometimes by locally promoted Act of Parliament; but from about 1760 the number of enclosure Acts increased rapidly, as more and more farmers and estate-owners saw the profitability of the new farming.

An enclosure award would re-allot the holdings in compact farms roughly proportionate to the previously held strips, with some extra land to go a little way towards compensation for the loss of rights on the common. For the more considerable farmers, and for the productivity[3] of the nation as a whole, the change was entirely for the better. Fallow could be much

---

[3] Wheat may be taken as a key crop. Between 1700 and 1800 the area of land under wheat increased by about one-third. The yield per acre improved by about 10 per cent. Thus the total production of wheat went up by over 45 per cent.

reduced, drainage could be improved, and machinery introduced; clover and turnips, as well as the new grasses, could be
grown; stock could be bred discriminatingly. Among enlightened landlords there was great enthusiasm for the new
farming, with the Duke of Bedford at Woburn, Lord Rockingham at Wentworth Woodhouse, Lord Egremont at Petworth,
and Thomas Coke at Holkham among the leaders of progress.

Of stock-improvers, the best-known was Robert Bakewell.
Until his day stock-breeding had been "the haphazard union
of nobody's son with everybody's daughter". But by intensive
inbreeding from carefully chosen beasts, and by breeding
specifically for desired qualities (flesh quality and fat, for
instance, in beef and mutton) he produced animals vastly
superior to those of previous generations. His 'New Leicester'
sheep, bred unlike most earlier sheep for mutton and not wool,
were, like his cart-horses, the finest in England. From the whole
country, and from abroad, visitors travelled to his Dishley
estate to see his famous black stallion, his bull Twopenny, his
ram Two-pounder, his irrigated meadows, his water-canals.
By 1789, after forty years of increasing success and fame, he
received 3000 guineas for one year's hiring of his rams alone;
yet he spent and entertained so lavishly that he died poor.
With cattle, Charles Colling of Durham was even more
successful than Bakewell, and Durham Shorthorns took pride
of place, both for milk and beef, over the Leicester Longhorns.
A great number of gentleman farmers, not least George III
himself—"Farmer George"—vied to emulate among their
beasts the achievements of these distinguished improvers.

Most eminent and universal of all the Georgian farmers was
the great Coke of Norfolk, who won nation-wide fame for the
transformation he effected in his Holkham estates. When he
inherited them in 1776 they grew only a wretched crop of rye;
but Coke used bones as fertilizers, enriched his dry, thin land
with marl, grew wheat in those parts for the first time, introduced roots and oil-cake for his cattle, and led the way to
breeding the finest sheep that Norfolk had ever seen. He
crusaded among his tenants, demonstrated the superiority of
drill over broadcast, campaigned for "muck, the mother of
money", and in general so improved yields among his tenantry

that he could raise their rents ninefold while still leaving them enough to double their own prosperity. His annual "Holkham Sheep-shearings" began in 1778 as a small conference of local farmers, and thirty years later provided something like a Royal Agricultural Show, with hundreds of visitors inspecting the latest improvements and the finest animals in the country, and Coke himself presiding at the festival, a benevolent patriarch.

If Coke was a king among farmers, the greatest propagandist for the new agriculture was himself a failed farmer, Arthur Young, who in his many farming manuals and travel books, and as Secretary of the new Board of Agriculture, preached ceaselessly the gospel of improvement. Farms must be enclosed; they must be big; they must have capital available; they must be let on long leases, so that the improving tenant could see prospects ahead for himself and his son; the introduction of every proved new crop, new rotation, new machine, new breed of animal must be encouraged. If this meant the extinction of the small man, the yeoman, then that must be faced:

> Where is the little farmer to be found who will cover his whole farm with marl at the rate of 100 or 150 tons per acre? Who will drain all his land at the expense of £2 or £3 an acre? Who will pay a heavy price for the manure of towns, and convey it thirty miles by land carriage? ... Who, to improve the breed of his sheep, will give 1000 guineas for the use of a single ram for a single season?

Not the yeoman, certainly; and there is no doubt that enclosures and the new trends in farming worked against him. Out of the enclosure redistribution he might receive about 30 acres; but these had to be hedged and ditched, which together with legal fees might well cost £100 or more. Worse still, after the enclosure and its accompanying loss of rights on the common, he would be faced with the need to buy fodder and rent grazing land, unless he made inroads on his own arable for the purpose. He battled on, perhaps to the end of the century, perhaps to the end of the Napoleonic Wars, which, by stimulating prices, offered many a temporary reprieve. The bad days after 1815 put him at an increasing disadvantage against his bigger neighbour.

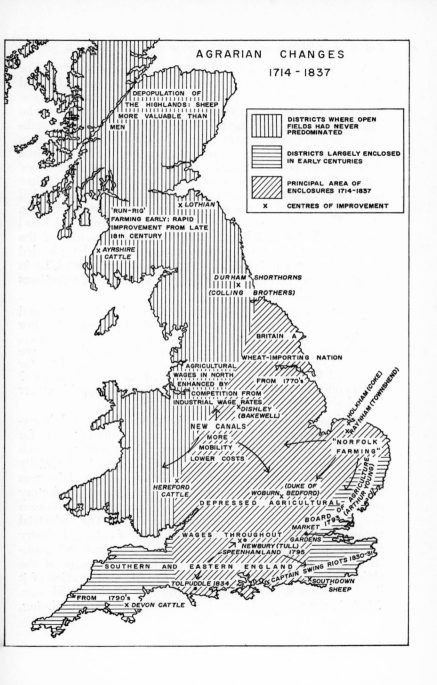

AGRARIAN CHANGES
1714 - 1837

DISTRICTS WHERE OPEN
FIELDS HAD NEVER
PREDOMINATED

DISTRICTS LARGELY ENCLOSED
IN EARLY CENTURIES

PRINCIPAL AREA OF
ENCLOSURES 1714-1837

x   CENTRES OF IMPROVEMENT

DEPOPULATION OF
THE HIGHLANDS: SHEEP
MORE VALUABLE THAN
MEN

x LOTHIAN

'RUN-RIG'
FARMING EARLY: RAPID
IMPROVEMENT FROM LATE
18th CENTURY

x AYRSHIRE
CATTLE

DURHAM SHORTHORNS
x
(COLLING BROTHERS)

BRITAIN A

WHEAT-IMPORTING NATION

AGRICULTURAL
WAGES IN NORTH   FROM 1770's
ENHANCED BY
COMPETITION FROM
INDUSTRIAL WAGE RATES
x DISHLEY
(BAKEWELL)

NEW CANALS
MORE
MOBILITY
LOWER COSTS

HOLKHAM (COKE)

x RAYNHAM (TOWNSHEND)

"NORFOLK
FARMING"

BOARD OF AGRICULTURE (ARTHUR YOUNG)

x HEREFORD
CATTLE

(DUKE OF
x WOBURN x BEDFORD)

DEPRESSED AGRICULTURAL

BOARD OF
MARKET
GARDENS

AGRICULTURE 1793

WAGES THROUGHOUT
x
NEWBURY (TULL)
SPEENHAMLAND 1795

CAPTAIN SWING RIOTS 1830-31

SOUTHERN AND EASTERN ENGLAND

x SOUTHDOWN
SHEEP

x TOLPUDDLE 1834

FROM 1790's
x DEVON CATTLE

Worse still was the lot of the cottager and the squatter. For them, holding only an acre or two, the old common rights had been a necessity for independent survival. After enclosure, the cottager would receive his trifling acre or so, the squatter, who lacked legal title, nothing at all. Both—the squatter immediately, the cottager sooner or later—abandoned the fight and in most cases applied for labourer's work at the big farms. Often they managed to keep their heads above water by their wives' cottage industry; but when, with the Napoleonic Wars, prices rose much faster than wages, these were the men who needed poor relief to keep them from starvation. Arthur Young, although he continued to press for enclosures, was not blind to the hardships which in practice the harsh awards of the commissioners often brought to the poor, and he pleaded eloquently for a juster deal. "By nineteen enclosure bills in twenty", he wrote in 1801, "[the poor] are injured, sometimes grossly injured."

Go to an alehouse kitchen of an old enclosed country, and there you will see the origins of poverty and poor rates. For whom are they to be sober? For whom are they to save? ... Such are their questions. . . . If I am diligent, shall I have leave to build a cottage? If I am sober, shall I have land for a cow? If I am frugal, shall I have half an acre of potatoes? You offer no motives; you have nothing but a parish officer and a workhouse! Bring me another pot.

The rising food demands of a growing population and the expanding prosperity of the successful farmer ensured demand for rural labour, and the picture of a depopulated countryside, such as Goldsmith painted in *The Deserted Village*, is essentially false. Neither, for many years yet, did the landless labourers flock away in any significant numbers to augment the factory workers of the Midlands and North—for the very good reason that such factories were still relative rarities. (The industrial expansion of this era was chiefly by means of cottage industry and the 'putting-out' system.) In fact, the agricultural population actually increased during the last forty years of the eighteenth century. The pity was that so big a proportion of it lived in extreme poverty, dogged by fear of the workhouse, driven in desperation to poaching in order to eke out a living, in spite of lethal man-traps and ferocious game laws. Gold-smith's poem may mislead and sentimentalize the 'good old days', but some of his lines touch the heart of the situation:

> Ill fares the land, to hastening ills a prey,
> Where wealth accumulates, and men decay.

Men did decay in the English village at this period of agri-cultural advance. Even in full employment, the farm labourer was forced to apply to the parish for relief;[4] the unemployed villager relied entirely on it. This might mean indoor relief—entering the poor-house itself, with its unsegregated inmates, sane and insane, healthy and diseased, young and old, as Crabbe described them, unfortunates of every sort—

> The lame, the blind, and—far the happiest they—
> The moping idiot and the madman gay

—or it might mean outdoor relief of various kinds. This could take the form of a direct payment of money, flour, or potatoes; or of work on maintaining the parish roads; or it could mean sending men on the 'roundsman' system to work in turn at odd jobs for local farmers, who in any case had to pay the rates to maintain the relief. The situation was worst in the southern counties, where, amid the rising prices of a war economy, the poor were least able to supplement their wages with industrial work. Well-meaning aristocrats were by 1795 giving advice to the rural poor on how to exist, like the Irish and Scots, on potatoes and oatmeal; they also condemned the extravagance of drinking tea (poor weak brew though it normally was, sweetened with a little brown sugar). These rational economies the poor, whose fathers had become used to white bread, resisted: "We will not be fed on meal and chopped potatoes like hogs", said one.

In that same year of 1795 the Berkshire magistrates, sitting at Speenhamland (Newbury), met the crisis in their county by instructing parish overseers of the poor to supplement wages, or relieve the destitute, by a scale fluctuating according to the price of the gallon loaf and the number of persons in the house-hold. Magistrates had it in their power, of course, to fix wages at a higher level, but this simple and just solution did not

4 See footnote, p. 289.

recommend itself to them. They preferred, all over the South of England, to follow the Speenhamland example. Actual starvation was thus avoided. At least, the southern farmworker stayed alive, if only just, to watch his employer's fortunes booming during the Napoleonic Wars, as the prices of wheat and meat shot up. But unfortunately Speenhamland provided a justification for farmers to maintain wages at their brutally low level for at least another forty years. At the same time it pauperized and demoralized the labouring poor over half the countryside.

3. A Note on the 'Agrarian and Industrial Revolutions'

For several reasons it is a little misleading to talk, without qualification, of the 'Agrarian Revolution of the Eighteenth Century' and the 'Industrial Revolution' of 1760–1830, as historical works are accustomed to do. In the story of British economic expansion, which certainly gathered pace remarkably in George III's reign, there is an essential interdependence between agriculture, commerce, industry, transport, finance, science, technology, and the rise in the population. In all these there was rapid growth, and they all interlocked. Thus, to take a few random examples, the fortunes of East India merchants were invested in landed estates. The profits accruing from scientific farming on landed estates flowed into cotton-mills and coal-mines. The money from (for instance) the Duke of Bridgewater's coal-mines financed his canals. The canals in their turn cheapened the price of coal to the industrialist, and of manure to the capitalist farmer. The new chemistry and its researches led to the manufacture of industrial sulphuric acid. The building of turnpike roads and the consequent multiplication of horse-drawn coaches led to a booming market in oats. The progress of medicine and agriculture swelled the population that provided the labour force to work the new factories and expanding industries. The expanding industries provided the machines, and eventually the fertilizers, that raised agricultural yields still further. The county banks provided credit facilities for all branches of enterprise, and enabled the capital to flow smoothly from trade to agriculture, from agriculture to industry, and vice versa. All the wheels of the machine of material progress were geared together, and the improved communications and the banks provided the oil.

Second, the terms 'Agrarian Revolution' and 'Industrial Revolution' seem at first to imply that these events began, proceeded, and were completed in the manner of other separate, distinct events. But if we examine, say, enclosure, one aspect of the 'agrarian revolution', we find it beginning in the Middle Ages and ending in the later nineteenth century, whereas if we examine another—say, mechanization—we find it beginning in the early eighteenth century and still proceeding today. If we speak of the 'Industrial Revolution', meaning mass production in factories, then it did not get seriously under way till the early nineteenth century and is still proceeding. If we mean simply the complicated series of mechanical inventions that transformed manufacturing techniques, we must go back many centuries.[5] If we mean the application of steam power to industry we exclude all the industrial revolutions that preceded or succeeded it (those based on water-power, electricity, and electronics, for instance), and this would seem an unnecessary restriction that tends to deny the continuity of history.

A third general point may be made. Too simple attention should not be paid to the date of inventions. Tull's husbandry, Darby's coke-smelted iron, Kay's flying shuttle, Cartwright's steam-driven loom, are a few examples among many of inventions which did not become effective till several decades after their birth. The 'Agrarian Revolution', apart from enclosure, did not operate on most farms before 1850. And up to that same time the majority of Englishmen were engaged in agriculture, for all the 'Industrial Revolution' of the preceding century.

These are qualifications. They should not obscure the tremendous fact that, in a century or two, profounder changes were wrought in the economy, social structure, and mental

[5] A French writer of the 1740's was already writing: "England has more than any other country of those machines which really multiply men by lessening their work, and by which one man can execute what would take up to thirty without their assistance."

attitudes of the nation by the ceaseless pressure of technical change than had happened in all the previous centuries of the Christian era put together. When the first Arnold Toynbee popularized the expression 'Industrial Revolution' in 1884, it looked, perhaps, as though "the great change" was something that *had happened*. Looking back from nearly another century of astonishing movement, it now seems that change itself is the permanent thing—one is tempted to say the only permanent thing—in modern history.

4. Communications

(a) Water Carriage

As for internal trade, Britain at this time was the largest free-trade area in Europe; and it was partly this freedom from internal customs that enabled the British to draw ahead of the French (whose scientists and inventors were certainly no less resourceful) in the development of industry and commerce. Whereas the movement of goods in France was hampered and made more expensive by frequent tolls and dues, in England goods could move freely, cheaply, and relatively swiftly round the coasts and along the navigable rivers.

Britain, a narrow sea-girt land, was fortunate to contain few places of consequence that were more than a dozen or two miles—at most a day's journey—from a port. Cargo ships were small, and could penetrate to many ports far inland, especially in the flat, well-watered South and East. Long, therefore, before the canal age of Brindley and Bridgewater, men were busy dredging and widening rivers, constructing 'cuts' and 'navigations', and installing sluices and locks, so that such inland towns as Bedford and Derby, Nottingham and Leeds, Wakefield, Manchester, and Wigan, were open to sea-borne traffic. It is true that road transport was difficult until the turnpike improvements: goods which had to travel overland normally went by pack-horse trains. But it was upon the water that the wealth of England circulated, and the promotion of inland navigation was one of the major Georgian achievements.

Thus, when in 1759 the Duke of Bridgewater invited the

illiterate engineering genius, James Brindley, to plan a canal from the Duke's Worsley collieries to Manchester, a few miles away, he was not initiating anything revolutionary. (The Duke's own father had, in fact, toyed with the idea twenty years before.) But the spectacular success of the project, with its halving of the price of coal in Manchester, and Brindley's much publicized Barton aqueduct, where the canal water was brought over the Irwell and its broad valley, caught the public imagination. Barton Bridge became one of the wonders of Georgian England. "Stupendous", "Prodigious", proclaimed the guide-books and travel-writers, and Arthur Young wrote:

> The effect of coming at once on to Barton Bridge, and looking down upon a large river, with barges of great burthen sailing on it; and up to another river, hung in the air, with barges towing along it, form altogether a scenery somewhat like enchantment. . . .

Everywhere the 'navigation workers' (hence 'navvies') began now to cut their way across country. Heavy barges moved at about two miles per hour, and the 'fly-boats' at between three and four. The first experiment with steamboats in England was tried on the canals by Symington in 1788; reached seven miles per hour the next year; but was subsequently laid aside. The Duke of Bridgewater was among those who experimented with the carrying of passengers. Often the early canal vessels carried sails, but the characteristic vehicle of this beneficent revolution was the horse-drawn barge of between 20 and 40 tons.

The 'utility' of canals was one of the themes of the time. Everywhere manufacturers hastened to cheapen their costs and widen their markets by promoting navigations; and investors were so anxious to participate in the profits that by the nineties there was a 'canal mania' akin to the madness to invest in railways half a century later, with similar financial casualties.

Soon a fine network of inland waterways linked the Humber, the Mersey, the Severn, and the Thames, and penetrated all the counties lying between. In Scotland, Edinburgh and Glasgow were linked, and other important centres; Telford linked the lochs of the Great Glen with his Caledonian Canal, and although this never possessed the commercial significance of the southern canals, it was a fitting crown to the canal age.

It was generally reckoned that the cost of moving goods by canal averaged between one-third and one-quarter of the cost of moving them by road. Every kind of cargo could be carried, from the heaviest—coal, stone, iron, lime, manure, grain, bricks, timber—to the most fragile. Josiah Wedgwood was an energetic canal pioneer, and to his Staffordshire works came by water Cornish china clay and Lancashire coal, and from them went the finished pottery and chinaware of his thriving kilns. The Potteries themselves were transformed: "How is the whole of this country [of Staffordshire] changed in about twenty years!" wrote that prince of travellers, John Wesley. Another contemporary travel-writer, praising the revolution wrought between Trent and Mersey by the Grand Trunk Canal, fills out Wesley's picture:

> We have the pleasure to see content reign universally on its banks, and plenty attend its progress.... The cottage, instead of being half covered with miserable thatch, is now covered with a substantial covering of tiles and slates, brought from the distant hills of Wales and Cumberland. The fields, which before were barren, are now drained, and, by the assistance of manure, carried on the canal toll-free, are clothed with a beautiful verdure. Places which rarely knew the use of coal, are plentifully supplied with that essential article on reasonable terms; and what is of still greater public utility, the monopolizers of corn are prevented from exercising their infamous trade; for, the communication being opened between Liverpool, Bristol, and Hull, and the line of the canal being through countries abundant in grain, it affords a conveyance of corn unknown to past ages....

Thus the canal speeded what the railway later completed: the economic unification of Britain, the making of the whole country a common market.

The bringing of water carriage to the heart of the country did more than promote manufacture and internal trade; it stimulated both importing and exporting. Overseas goods (tea

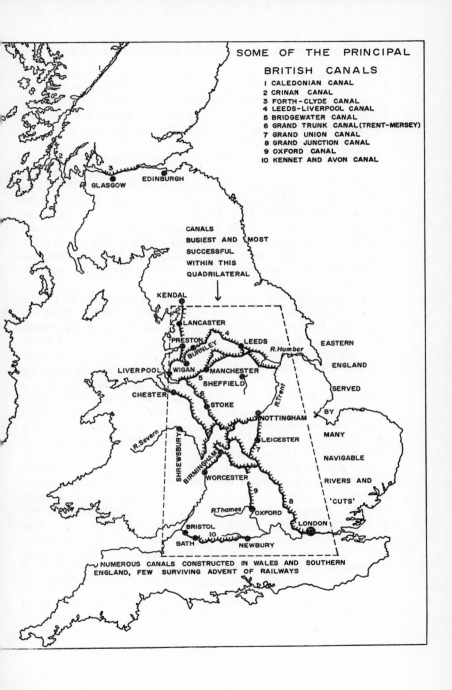

SOME OF THE PRINCIPAL
BRITISH CANALS

1 CALEDONIAN CANAL
2 CRINAN CANAL
3 FORTH-CLYDE CANAL
4 LEEDS-LIVERPOOL CANAL
5 BRIDGEWATER CANAL
6 GRAND TRUNK CANAL (TRENT-MERSEY)
7 GRAND UNION CANAL
8 GRAND JUNCTION CANAL
9 OXFORD CANAL
10 KENNET AND AVON CANAL

GLASGOW
EDINBURGH

CANALS
BUSIEST AND MOST
SUCCESSFUL
WITHIN THIS
QUADRILATERAL

KENDAL

LANCASTER

PRESTON
BURNLEY
LEEDS
R. Humber

EASTERN

ENGLAND

LIVERPOOL
WIGAN
MANCHESTER

SHEFFIELD

SERVED

CHESTER
STOKE

BY

NOTTINGHAM

MANY

LEICESTER

R. Severn
SHREWSBURY

NAVIGABLE

BIRMINGHAM

WORCESTER

RIVERS AND

R. Thames
OXFORD

'CUTS'

BRISTOL
10
LONDON

BATH
NEWBURY

R. Trent

NUMEROUS CANALS CONSTRUCTED IN WALES AND SOUTHERN
ENGLAND, FEW SURVIVING ADVENT OF RAILWAYS

is an example) could now penetrate directly by water to the innermost parts, not merely to the environs of London and the great ports; and conversely, the produce of Birmingham, Stoke, Leeds, and the rest of the growing manufacturing towns could be easily sent by canal to the ports, and thence overseas.

(b) Roads: Turnpikes and Posts

Side by side with improved water transport went improved road transport. During the Georgian era, and particularly in the reign of George III, there were remarkable advances in the surfacing of roads, in the construction of coaches and supply of horses, and in the postal services. All this meant more travel, faster travel, more comfortable travel, as well as greater mobility and a diminution in the remoteness of outlying places.

In 1750 it still took six days to travel by coach from London to Newcastle; four and a half to Manchester; two to Birmingham. An average day's mileage was not likely to be much more than fifty. In Devonshire, Dorset, and Cornwall there were no turnpike roads at all before 1750, and in most other counties they were few. The statutory obligation to keep up roads lay on each individual parish, not upon the county as a whole; and for every parish that discharged its duties there were a dozen that did not. In clay districts roads were often impassable in wet weather or in winter; hence the continuing preference of merchants and manufacturers for pack-horses rather than heavy stage wagons.

The British answer to the ineffectiveness of the old parish system of road maintenance was the type of local private enterprise known as the Turnpike Trust. A group of landowners or moneyed men would apply to Parliament for the right to improve the roads of their area, erect 'turnpikes'[6] at intervals along them (at anything from every eight to every fifty or so miles), and reimburse themselves by charging graduated tolls for the use of the roads. Between 1700 and 1750 there were 400 such turnpike Acts; between 1751 and

[6] The term 'turnpike' originally signified the barrier, but by a natural extension applied eventually to the road itself.

1790, 1600. The trusts often employed road surveyors to undertake widening, straightening, drainage, and the elimination of steep hills; and for the first time since the Roman occupation roads were given a proper foundation and hard surface. Most famous of the earlier semi-professional turnpike surveyors was John Metcalf of Knaresborough, blind from smallpox since the age of six, fiddler, recruiting sergeant for the anti-Jacobite armies in 1745, smuggler, horse-dealer, coach proprietor, and, after 1765, turnpike surveyor in the West Riding, South Lancashire, and North Derbyshire districts. An inveterate jack-of-all-trades, he lost the substantial money he had made in turnpike-building by unsuccessful dabbling in the cotton industry. By the closing years of George III's reign Telford was laying (for instance, between Carlisle and Glasgow, and on the main London–Holyhead road in North Wales) the kind of solid roads and bridges that might be expected of so thorough and imaginative an engineer; but it was McAdam who was to set the pattern for the century to follow. Turnpike roads needed to be serviceable, but they also needed to be cheap; and by cutting out the engineering refinements of Metcalf and Telford, and concentrating on the essentials of good surveying, adequate drainage, and a sufficiency of graded stone (large below, fine on top), McAdam was able to produce reasonably smooth, hard-surfaced roads, coach-rolled and rain-cemented, for £88 per mile, or a shilling per running yard.

Important developments in vehicle construction coincided with the work of the Turnpike Trusts. Steel springs came in from about 1750, and superior road surfaces permitted a whole new variety of lighter, speedier, coaches to develop: chaises, calashes, chariots, berlins, phaetons, landaus, and many more. With smoother roads, too, stage-coaches could carry passengers 'outside'—that is, on the roof, which previously was reserved exclusively for luggage.

The effects of the canal revolution were principally economic; those of the highway improvements, though they too hastened the circulation of goods, were primarily social. Travel, previously so dangerous and slow, became rapid, exciting, and fashionable. In the sixty years of George III's reign the average speed of the public coaches between main centres approximately trebled; and speeds which by modern yardsticks seem sedate enough were to the travellers of those days hair-raising. Carl Philipp Moritz, the German traveller, described, for instance, his journey from Leicester to Northampton in 1782:

> The moment that we set off, I fancied that I saw certain death await me.... The machine now rolled along with prodigious rapidity, over the stones through the town, and every moment we seemed to fly in the air; so that it was almost a miracle that we still stuck to the coach, and did not fall.

And some years later, when coaches had reached an overall average speed of about 10 miles per hour, stops included—which meant 20 miles per hour on favourable stretches—de Quincey celebrated in his famous essay on "The English Mail Coach" the heyday of the coaching era: "We heard our speed, we saw it, we felt it...."

The discriminating traveller might well choose to hire something more comfortable than the creaking and groaning public stage-coach. An advertisement of 1791 put it thus:

> If two or three passengers choose to travel together, they may, travelling in a post-chaise, not only avoid all these inconveniences, viz., common company, poor service, indecent behaviour of coachman, etc., but suit their own convenience in point of time, and be at less expense—besides meeting with genteeler treatment at the inns on the roads.

The enthusiasm for travel now seized upon the upper and middle classes much as the passion for holidays abroad occupied their descendants in the years following the Second World War. Everywhere, from the seventies and eighties, was to be found the gentleman tourist, admiring the scenery, appraising the quality of the inns, of the local estates, of the residences of the aristocracy, more rarely (as with Arthur Young and Cobbett) of the standard of local farming. For the first time visitors came in large numbers to such wild areas as the Lake District. The cult of the picturesque spread far and wide; a spate of local guide-books flowed from the presses. Established resorts such as Tunbridge Wells and Scarborough entered on their palmiest days, while new ones, such as Cheltenham, Harrogate, Deal, Eastbourne, and Margate became prosperous. The new coaching facilities happened to coincide with the fashionable 'cure' of sea-bathing; and resorts such as Brighton, now only half a day's journey from London and the favourite out-of-town headquarters of the Prince of Wales's set, were transformed. George III preferred Weymouth, to whose society and waters he gave a touch of royal prestige. Bath, still the premier resort of all England, was specially well served by the coaches after John Palmer of Reading, who was also a theatrical lessee in Bath, launched his new service in 1784 with a sixteen-hour London-to-Bristol run that set new standards of speed and safety.

The initiative of Palmer marked a new chapter, too, in the history of the postal services. From Elizabethan times the postmaster in a town had always had two functions. One, the less important, was to deliver letters; his principal task and main source of business was to keep ready a supply of horses for travellers who wished to 'post' along the roads—often 'post-haste'. He provided, in fact, a 'stage' along the road for travellers in the days before coaches were common. In 1720, Ralph Allen of Bath had been given the contract to conduct a cross-country mail, delivered by post-boys on horseback. Then, in 1784, the enterprise of John Palmer secured coach services with a widely operating postal system; and thus the mail-coach was born, with (a Palmer speciality) its armed guard against highwaymen. These last were a nuisance, especially round London, and they increased as the traffic increased; but their importance (and certainly the romance that fiction and legend have combined to lend them) is exaggerated.

The increase in travel brought with it a greatly expanded business in horsebreeding, in coach-building, and in innkeeping. Big companies developed, with large fleets of coaches, hundreds of horses, and chains of inns along the principal roads. But the prosperity of this coaching industry was not long-lived, and the railways were hitting it very hard by the early years of Victoria's reign.

5. "The Fury of Innovation"

"The age is running mad after innovation", said Dr Johnson; "all the business of the world is to be done in a new way; men are to be hanged in a new way; Tyburn itself is not safe from the fury of innovation." Historians agree that from about 1760, and especially after 1780, the pace of innovation was indeed furious; but there is argument about why, exactly, it was so. The lowering of the interest rate to 3 per cent in 1756 has been emphasized by some as the main cause; never before had it been so easy to raise capital cheaply for expansion. Undoubtedly there was a big accumulation of capital from overseas commerce, and everywhere people were hungry to put their money out to earn more money. There was also an extraordinarily rapid multiplication of provincial banks, whose numbers trebled in the single decade 1784–94; and good credit facilities were essential for economic progress. There was a rising population, a plentiful supply of labour, and a high demand for products. The country had long been free from civil strife, and the religious quarrels that had bedevilled previous centuries no longer dominated the minds of the nation's foremost men. Communications had improved. Britain, a great commercial nation with well-developed ports and an extensive seaboard, was admirably placed to take in the raw materials necessary for industrial expansion. Still more important, she was fortunate to contain good supplies of the two raw materials basic to the new technology—plentiful iron, and the richest coal deposits in Western Europe, outside the Ruhr.

The intense inventive activity of these years is reflected in the number of patents granted. Before 1760 it averaged less than a dozen a year; by 1769, the year of Watt's first patent for a steam-engine, it was 36; by 1802 it was 102. Some of the more significant inventions are briefly dealt with in the succeeding paragraphs; but it is well to remember that for a long time, although they produced a significant rise in the average standard of living, they *directly* affected the manner of life of a minority only. A factory worker was still a comparative rarity at the time of the Napoleonic Wars. Many even of the revolutionized industries remained hand-craft industries still, like weaving and pottery. The age of Watt and Wilkinson was also the age of Adam, Chippendale, and Sheraton, the high noon of the old craftsmen. In the consumer trades, excluding textiles, there was little sudden change. In such leading industries as glass-making, tin-mining, salt-production, and leather manufacture (the last still second, by annual monetary value of goods sold, of all English industries in 1800) no great technical changes were apparent. In many walks of life, and in many parts of the country, life proceeded without violent alteration. Jane Austen, a woman of the sharpest intelligence and observation, could over these years write her novels as though unaware of those 'other' Englands beneath her class or northward of her locality. The greatest war in history up to that time and the great industrial revolution were her contemporaries: she passes them by unnoticed.

The true Iron Age of modern times may be dated from 1784. In that year Henry Cort of Gosport in Hampshire invented a combined puddling and rolling process by which the last dependence on charcoal was finally eliminated. The speed of turning pig-iron into bar-iron was by this single invention multiplied by fifteen, and the industry could leap ahead. It became concentrated round the coalfields of South Yorkshire, the Black Country, the Clyde, and South Wales. A multitude of objects previously made of wood or stone now began to be made of iron. John Wilkinson of Brosely, close neighbour of Abraham Darby the third, had already collaborated with him and others in building the first iron bridge, over the Severn at Coalbrookdale (1779). Now he turned to iron boats and successfully demonstrated one on the Severn. At Coalbrookdale even the window-sills and tombstones were made of iron. Great quantities of iron water-piping were sold at home and abroad (both New York and Paris bought from him). Indeed, so missionary was his zeal for the gospel of iron that he became known as 'iron-mad' Wilkinson and directed that his remains should be buried in an iron coffin. Then an enormous stimulus was given to this bounding industry by the demands of war. Both Roebuck's Carron works and those of Wilkinson at Brosely originated in the Seven Years War and underwent their greatest expansion during the struggle with the French Revolution and Napoleon. Their cannon-boring techniques, moreover, were readily adaptable to the manufacture of Watt's steam-engine. Iron was one parent, steam was the other; their offspring—growing fast by 1800, and one day to become a giant—was the new industry of engineering.

The steam-engine was a century old by the time of Watt, and had long been used for pumping water from flooded mines. James Watt, a mechanical-instrument maker whose shop was within the precincts of Glasgow University, was one day asked to repair a model of Newcomen's steam-engine which one of the professors was using in his lectures. As Watt worked on it his mind jumped to the prime drawback of the Newcomen engine: its cylinder had to be hot for the piston to make its up-stroke, but cool in order to condense the steam for the down-stroke. Thus power was constantly lost. Together with the best brains in the University—including those of that great pioneer of chemistry, Professor Joseph Black—Watt explored the difficulties of overcoming the steam-engine's defects. Eventually he seized upon the solution that was to transform Britain and much of the world beside. The condenser must be a separate thing, kept permanently cool; there was no need for the cylinder to lose its heat at every stroke. Financed first by Roebuck, then by Boulton, his work came to fruition after several years of experiment (1769). Many had a hand in it, besides those already mentioned. Chief among them was William Murdock, an employee of Watt and himself a man of brilliant inventiveness[7] who collaborated in perfecting it, and later in improving it so that it would work, not merely up and down, but also in rotary motion (1781). What had begun simply as a moderately efficient pumping machine could now be applied to work a wide variety of manufacturing machinery. It was the key invention of the age, and its consequences dominated the industrial development of the succeeding century.[8]

.   .   .   .   .

[7] He was one of the inventors of gas-lighting, and installed it in Boulton and Watt's Soho (near Birmingham) factory in 1798.   [8] See p. 486.

In textiles, however, the steam revolution was delayed; and many inventions had the effect of emphasizing the predominantly 'cottage' nature of the industry. Kay's earlier introduction of the fly-shuttle (1733) was by 1760 beginning to give a big increase in the output of the handloom weavers. What was now needed was a parallel innovation in spinning, which would enable the supply of yarn to keep pace with the speed-up in weaving. The first stage of the problem was solved by Hargreaves of Blackburn with a contrivance that soon found its way into many thousands of homes—the 'jenny', by which a woman could manufacture six, eight, and eventually as many as eighty weft-threads at a time. Next, Arkwright of Preston, a barber-wigmaker who was adept at picking up other men's ideas and making a business proposition of them, constructed a 'frame' on which warp-threads of adequate strength could be machine-manufactured. The 'frame', being large, needed something stronger than woman-power to work it; so, first, horse-power and then water-power were employed to drive it. Thus a 'manufactory' housing water-driven spinning-frames became known as a 'mill', which remained the name for a cotton factory long after water-power had been superseded by steam. Arkwright's first big mill at Cromford in Derbyshire (1771), with its 300 'hands', mainly juvenile, set the trend for the future. By 1780, cotton-spinning factories were beginning to spread to Lancashire.

The 'jenny' and the 'frame' were followed by an invention of Crompton of Bolton, combining the functions of the two earlier machines. Being thus a cross, it became known as the 'mule'; and, when it was later powered by Watt's steam-engine it was well on the way to dominating cotton-spinning. Between 1782 and 1802 the number of mule-spinning factories in the Manchester district alone rose from two to fifty-two. The 'mule', moreover, had the great asset of adaptability; it could be used in all forms of textile manufacture. But it was in Lancashire calicoes and muslins that the boom was greatest.

In calico-printing, steam-power had been adopted rapidly after 1783, when Thomas Bell first applied steam-driven cylinders to print patterns which had previously been hand-impressed. Still, however, in weaving, hand-looms remained almost universal for another thirty years and very numerous for another thirty after that. In fact, with the supply of yarn assured and the demand for textiles buoyant, the cottage industry of hand-loom weaving fared better in the closing years of the eighteenth century than ever before or after. Yet ever since the Rev. Edmund Cartwright devised in 1785 a loom that could be powered by steam (or alternatively by water or horses), the shadow of ruin for the hand-weavers hovered in the background. It remained a threat merely, just so long as the invention stood in need of refinement before it became efficient; and despite many new improvements, it remained an unpractical proposition until towards the close of the Napoleonic Wars. At the time of Waterloo only about 1 per cent of the country's looms had been mechanized.

The great eighteenth-century developments in theoretical chemistry brought big dividends in technology. Chlorine gas and sulphuric acid (the latter first produced for industrial purposes by Roebuck and Garbett at Birmingham) between them revolutionized the bleaching processes. At the same time, soda, produced from vitriol and common salt, performed a similar service in soap-making; and the part played by cheap soap, like that played by cheap cotton underclothes, was no small one in the improvement of hygiene. (They may even have been small factors contributing to growth of population.) Potash, alum, ammonia, and tar all contributed to the importance of the rising chemical industry. It was Alexander Cochrane, Earl of Dundonald, who first experimented with the extraction of tar from coal—a process which could have been of immediate importance to a seafaring nation hitherto entirely dependent on Baltic tar and pitch for preserving naval timbers, and whose ultimate significance was profound. However, Dundonald's enterprise did not prosper financially, and here too there was a long interval between the birth of an idea and its working-out. It was left to McAdam and others first to develop coal-tar extraction on a commercial scale.

In pottery, as in iron, shortage of wood fuel was an important factor in enforcing change. The earlier industry had been widely scattered in towns throughout the country, but the advantages of North Staffordshire now tended to concentrate production there: the proximity of coal, of suitable clays, and of lead for glazing. The preconditions were thus established for the extraordinary rise of the Pottery Towns and especially of the house of Wedgwood. It was Josiah Wedgwood of Burslem, with his new factory at Etruria, near Hanley, who led the Potteries "to transform a peasant craft into an industry with a world market". Before his days English ware could not compare with the finest from France or Germany, or with the very expensive true 'china' from China itself. But Wedgwood secured a double triumph: he turned out the fine 'Jasper ware' that challenged the best produced by Sèvres or Dresden; and at the same time was the first, with his white 'Queen's ware', to capture a huge market at home and abroad for a relatively cheap product. His aim, and his achievement, was "to make fine pottery cheap enough for the middle classes and beautiful enough for kings and princes". It was a triumph that would have been impossible without canals, of which he was a strong advocate and financial backer. The 'Grand Trunk' reduced his freight expenses from tenpence to a penny-farthing per mile.

In many ways Josiah Wedgwood may be justly acclaimed as the *beau idéal* of the Georgian industrialist. He certainly typifies a great deal of what was best in this 'age of improvement'. He was a tough master, disciplining his factory-housed hand-craftsmen, but rewarding them well for effort and skill. He built a village for his employees. He was a patron of schools, musical festivals, literary and scientific institutes, and he was active among the scientific intelligentsia of his day— men such as Watt, Boulton, Priestley, Erasmus Darwin. His energy was matched by his patience and determination; he made, for instance, over 10,000 trial pieces before perfecting his Jasper ware. When his weak leg hindered him he chose, in those pre-anaesthetic days, to have it amputated. Like Priestley and so many more of his fellow middle-class intellectuals, he was a radical in politics, welcoming both the American and French Revolutions, and demanding universal suffrage and an end to the slave trade. Not himself a technical inventor of note, he was a businessman of genius. He made, of course, a great fortune; but few were less grasping or more idealistic. He believed in the triumph of reason, the abolition of poverty, and the rights of man. Plainly, not all his fellow industrialists were as many-sided as Wedgwood; but a notable proportion of them were forward-looking men of character and zeal. They were making their fortunes; but they were conscious too they were building something else, which they believed in—the future.

Men like Wedgwood at Etruria, Arkwright at Cromford, Robert Peel the elder at Bury, Boulton and Watt at Soho (near Birmingham), Wilkinson at Brosely, Roebuck at Carron, were, in an important sense, leaders of the nation. Each of them set a new course and a new pace; each had scores of imitators and competitors following close behind.

Between them all, these men were creating a prototype of the new industrialized Britain that was during the nineteenth century to become "the workshop of all the nations". While France, which until about 1780 had been in most ways the technological equal of Britain, and in some respects her superior, went through a great social and political revolution during the eighties and nineties, Britain grasped economic mastery. "Move your eye which side you will," wrote Arthur Young, with not undue exaggeration, "you behold nothing but great riches and greater resources." In 1781–82, Britain had faced defeat in America, crisis in Ireland, danger and disarray at home and abroad; but in the following two decades national prosperity surged forward on almost every front—most spectacularly of all in cotton and iron manufacture—and the American disaster soon came to seem almost irrelevant. Within very few years we were actually selling more to the new USA than we had to the old Thirteen Colonies. There were certainly blemishes in the general progress, most notably in the treatment of the village labourers; and little had been done yet to mitigate scandalous social evils, such as the exploitation of child labour. (Some of these evils were even to get worse before they got better.) However, the general picture is of growing abundance and mastery of nature; and the Napoleonic era, although it led to blockaded and erratic markets after 1806, continued, in general, to show the same rapid growth alike in agriculture, industry, commerce, shipping, and population.

Chapter 11

Religion, Philanthropy, and Education

1. A Latitudinarian Age

In religious matters the seventeenth century had been an age
of zeal and controversy, which often extended to intolerance
and fanaticism. During the first half of the eighteenth century
there was a reaction: and although religious toleration was far
from complete, there was a general move to escape from the
'smell of faggots' and the harsh intensity of theological disputes. The religious temper of the early Hanoverian age was
for permitting a breadth, or latitude, of belief and practice:
we call it, therefore, Latitudinarian. It was not that the age
was irreligious. 'The Age of Reason' applies only in the sense
that Christianity seemed reasonable. The scientific discoveries
culminating in the work of Newton all seemed to proclaim the
activities of a beneficent, consistent, and rational deity. In
Addison's famous hymn, the "spacious firmament on high",
the "spangled heavens", the "unwearied sun", the moon, the
planets, the stars—all, in their orderly, intelligible, and majestic
way,

> Confirm the tidings as they roll,
> And spread the truth from pole to pole. . . .
> For ever singing as they shine,
> 'The hand that made us is divine'.

Or, as Locke less poetically expressed it, "the works of Nature
everywhere sufficiently evidence a Deity". And even if, as the
Deists maintained, the evidence for the 'truths' of the Old and
New Testaments was inadequate, nearly everybody agreed
that atheism was irrational.[1] Certainly the quarrel between

[1] It was not entirely safe to carry too far the Deist arguments against
accepting the biblical narrative: Thomas Woolston, for declaring the
Resurrection to have been an imposture, was cast into prison, and died

orthodox Christians on the one side, believing in revelation, and Deists on the other, believing in 'natural religion' and a supreme being, was conducted at a much lower temperature than controversies in the two preceding centuries between fellow Christians differing on comparatively minor theological niceties. Civilized men disliked 'enthusiasm', by which they understood fanaticism; hence arose, later, much of the hostility to Wesley, Whitefield, and their excitable revivalism. The Latitudinarians distrusted the poetry of religion; they were for 'prose', measured, cool, tolerant. If a man lived a good life and respected the authority of Church and State he had done well enough. Thus one could believe in church-going even if, on an intellectual level, one did not uphold the Church's beliefs. Horace Walpole, for instance, went to church to set the servants an example; "a good moral sermon may instruct and benefit them". Also churchmen and politicians alike tended to regard Anglican church-going as what Basil Williams called "a valuable form of police control over the lower classes".

Vestiges of old intolerance were numerous, in both law and practice. The Test Act, Corporation Act, and many other relics of anti-Catholic and anti-Nonconformist legislation remained unrepealed. Even the old Elizabethan recusancy laws fixing a fine for non-attendance at Anglican churches were still there to be enforced as a punishment for Catholics at critical times—as, for instance, after the 'Fifteen' rebellion, when 350 recusants were convicted in North Yorkshire alone. In general, however, the number of priests prosecuted for saying Mass was very small; and although old suspicions and prejudices died hard, the practice of Georgian times was much better than their laws. Jews and Quakers, like Roman Catholics, though mob sentiment and the timidity of Governments left them suffering potentially serious disabilities, were normally free enough to practise their religion. Nonconformists, in theory unable to hold public office, frequently did so; and an

---

there in 1733. The weightiest exposition of an extreme sceptical point of view came from the Scots philosopher David Hume, who sought to establish the unreasonableness of both revealed Christianity and the Deists' belief in a supreme being.

Indemnity Act was passed annually to protect from the letter of the law those who had thus transgressed it—a typically English exercise in illogicality and compromise.

2. The Church of England

If the Georgian Church of England possessed some characteristically eighteenth-century virtues it had too the defects of those virtues. Tolerant and unfanatical, it did not, in general, radiate spiritual energy. Easy-going times encouraged a certain conformist laxity, a liking for comfort, both material and spiritual. It was not an age to bring forth ecclesiastical reformers, still less martyrs. Yet, in general, church attendance was high and Holy Communion regularly celebrated (either monthly, or four times a year at Easter, Whitsun, Michaelmas, and Christmas). There was certainly no lack of church-goers or communicants; but in many parishes church services did have to be 'rationed', for the simple reason that there were many more livings than there were vicars, and the practices of pluralism and non-residence were widespread. Where one parson served several parishes, often many miles apart, even if he employed a curate to serve those where he did not himself live, it was unlikely that there would be more than one service per Sunday, morning and evening alternating.

This pluralism sprang partly from a gross disparity between the stipends of rich and poor parishes. In George I's reign one benefice in eight carried an annual stipend of £20 or under, and over half of all benefices less than £50 a year. Some were worth as little as £5 per year, others £500 or more; so the parson of a poor parish would perforce seek to combine it with another, and pay a curate £30 to £40 a year to share his ministration. The most crying pluralistic abuses, however, were seen among the richer clergy, and they continued unchecked, despite the efforts of reforming bishops, until well into the nineteenth century. In 1812, of 10,000 parsons, nearly 6000 were non-resident; and among the large number of pluralists were such aristocrats as Lord Walsingham, who was Archdeacon of Surrey, Prebendary of Winchester, Rector of Calbourne, Rector of Fawley, perpetual Curate of Exbury, and Rector of Merton; and the Duke of Wellington's brother, who was Prebendary of Durham, Rector of Bishopwearmouth, Rector of Chelsea, and Rector of Therfield. Three reverend Pretymans held fifteen benefices between them.

Privilege and inequality were as inevitably part of the ecclesiastical, as of every other, aspect of Georgian life. To obtain a benefice, the influence of a patron was vital, and many poor graduates of Oxford and Cambridge languished long years as deacons or curates, on wretched stipends, before the canvassing of friends or the recommendation of some influential well-wisher secured for them a parish, the bestowal of which almost always lay in the hands of a landowner, a bishop, or a university college. Fielding, with quiet irony, thus illustrates the poor clergy's predicament in the person of his country vicar in *Joseph Andrews*:

> Mr Abraham Adams was an excellent scholar. . . . He had applied many years to the most severe study, and had treasured up a fund of learning rarely to be met with in a university. . . . His virtue and his other qualifications . . . had so much endeared and well recommended him to a bishop, that at the age of fifty he was provided with a handsome income of twenty-three pounds a year; which, however, he could not make any great figure with, because he lived in a dear country, and was a little encumbered with a wife and six children.

Goldsmith's justly famous lines in *The Deserted Village* imply a criticism of the same situation, a constant theme with the thoughtful men of the day—the position of the well-educated, conscientious, underpaid, country clergyman:

> A man he was to all the country dear,
> And passing rich with forty pounds a year. . . .

Dr Johnson, pressed on the same subject by Boswell, who thought no curate should be paid less than £100 a year, characteristically defended the existing state of affairs:

> Why, yes, Sir; but it cannot be helped. You must consider, that the revenues of the clergy are not at the disposal of the State, like the pay of the army. Different men have founded different churches; and some are better endowed, some worse.

Not all country clergymen were of the amiable and worthy stamp of Parson Adams or Goldsmith's curate, or of Parson Woodforde of Weston in Norfolk, whose delightful diary gives probably the best and fullest picture of the ordinary, human, 'decent' parish vicar of mid-Georgian England.[2] Others were less admirable. Dependent on the 'big house', upon which his hopes of preferment hung, the badly paid curate could easily turn into the patron's toady. In *Pride and Prejudice* Jane Austen immortalized such a one in her sycophantic and ludicrous Mr Collins. And others simply failed to perform the duties for which they were paid, however poorly:

> A man must have travelled very little in the kingdom [wrote Arthur Young] who does not know that country towns abound with curates who never see the parishes they serve, but when they are absolutely forced to it by duty.

Just as the clergy, good and bad, moved necessarily in the orbit of the aristocratic world, so the Church of England itself was strongly tied to the State. An established Church must to some extent be so inevitably, but in Georgian times, and particularly in the age of Walpole, the association between State and Church, and especially between the ruling Whig oligarchy and the Anglican bishops, was blatant. Walpole's bishops were powerful pieces in his chess game of party politics. Even when supporters dithered and parliamentary majorities looked groggy, the twenty-six episcopal votes in the Lords could almost always be relied on; it was for this very reason, primarily, that they had been made bishops. As Trevelyan wrote, Whig Ministers "would sooner have made a Mohamedan than a Jacobite bishop". Moreover, faithful passage through the division lobbies might earn promotion within the episcopate itself; for there was almost as wide a disparity in the revenues of the various sees as in those of the parishes. Bishops were expected to earn their keep in other ways: Hoadly, Bishop of Bangor in George I's reign, was rather less a bishop than a Whig pamphleteer; and Shelburne, in 1782, hoped that the new Bishop of Llandaff "would occasionally write a pamphlet for the administration". The bishop,

[2] *Diary of a Country Parson, 1758–1802.*

Watson, obliged for the next twenty years, by (as he put it) "supporting the religion and constitution of the country by seasonable publications". Hoadly never once visited his see of Bangor, and Watson found it pleasanter to live by the shores of Windermere than in Llandaff. He explained his good fortune with admirably terse directness: "I happened to please a party and they made me a bishop." It is perhaps not surprising that the eighteenth-century episcopal bench, with rare exceptions like Pope's friend Warburton, or Butler (of the *Analogy of Religion*), or the philosopher Berkeley, were noted neither for intellectual distinction nor spiritual devotion—still less for reforming zeal. As the century progressed, the Bench of Bishops became less exclusively Whig (just as the country clergy became less markedly Tory than they had been in the reigns of George I and George II); but in both the older and the modern, more general, sense of the term they remained essentially pillars of the Establishment. "It must be admitted", wrote Basil Williams, "that the church of England during the eighteenth century is not an inspiring spectacle. Latitudinarian to a degree which makes it difficult to find any theological justification for its existence, at its highest it was an efficient instrument of statecraft, at its lowest it was a nest of pluralists and mundane divines."[3]

3. Wesley and Methodism

The placid surface of this Hanoverian Church of England was increasingly disturbed from about 1740 by John Wesley and his followers. Seeking to infuse into Anglican worship a new and passionate seriousness, insisting on the necessities of faith, prayer, self-examination, and the search for salvation, they originated as a 'ginger group' within the Church of England, proceeded to offend against both its laws and its prevailing temper, and ended by involuntarily founding a breakaway Church.

John Wesley (1703–91) is among the most remarkable of Englishmen: probably the most important man of religion in Britain over the past four centuries. He was one of the ten

[3] *The Whig Supremacy*, pp. 87–88 (1962 edition).

surviving children of a Lincolnshire parson and his wife, who had both been born Dissenters and turned to the Anglican Church. While Wesley's rather feckless father wrote poetry, compiled learned commentaries on the Book of Job, and provided a constant source of irritation to his wife, she, Susannah Wesley, devoted and formidable, brought up her numerous family, three of whom were to enter holy orders, in the severest Christian discipline. For Wesley, spiritual self-examination and 'method' began almost in the cradle; wrestling with an ever-watchful Devil and striving towards an ever-loving God were exercises in which his young spirit was well trained long before he left home to attend school at the Charterhouse in the year of George I's accession. (Mrs Wesley had allowed her five-year-old children one day only to learn the alphabet, insisted on *quiet* crying after chastisement, and regarded it as a primary duty to "break the child's will". She should be regarded as the pre-founder of Methodism.) In 1720 he proceeded to Christ Church, and later to Lincoln College, Oxford, and—though torn, as he was long to be, by his naturally sociable temperament, and a prey to diverse but frustrating love affairs—he and his brother Charles soon were at the centre of an intensely serious group, the 'Holy Club', whom the rest of Oxford derided for their priggishness and 'method'. They lived frugally, observed fasts, preached to the poor and to prisoners, gave alms, mapped out their earnest days and nights, rose at four, and examined privately and communally their shortcomings. Cold-shouldered in Oxford, and refusing to succeed his father in his country living, he next spent two emotionally disturbed years in the young colony of Georgia (1736–38). He went ostensibly to convert the Indians, but sought to 'methodize' the settlers, and at last caused severe scandal by refusing to minister communion to the girl who, driven nearly mad by his amatory vacillations, had married his rival. The spiritual self-torture that had beset him in America returned with him to England. He prayed, he wrestled. He argued earnestly with Peter Böhler, one of a sect of German (Moravian) evangelicals who preached the gospel of salvation *by faith alone*. Wesley found himself in the position of the man who protested, "Lord, I believe", but immediately followed, "Help

Thou mine unbelief." "I went to America to convert the Indians," he cried despairingly, "but who shall convert me?" The answer was, Peter Böhler and the Moravians. At last, in 1738, came the sudden conviction of salvation, the achievement of that 'state of grace' which had so long eluded his earnest and desperate quest. For months after, traversing crests of exaltation and troughs of despair ("I affirm I am not a Christian now. . . . I have not any love of God"), he at last "wrested his faith from God" and never again, for the next fifty-three years, let it slip from his powerful grasp.

In that half-century John Wesley was the driving motor of the Methodist Revival. He preached over forty thousand sermons, fifteen a week. He travelled by horse, by chaise, and on foot, nearly a quarter of a million miles, roughly the distance to the moon. He never failed to find time for the daily two hours of private devotion. Soon denied the pulpits of parsons who disliked his emotionalism, and forbidden by such bishops as Butler of Bristol to preach in their dioceses, he was obliged to proclaim his God and urge the necessities of faith and repentance in the market-place, in barns, by hedgerow and village pump. Where no churches existed, and especially in the new industrial villages and towns, whose inhabitants were often innocent of all religion, he set up, within twenty-five years, 356 chapels. He faced, and survived, many hostile riots, always sustained by his belief in the miraculous, his conviction that he remained under the special dispensation of a God who deflected brickbats in their flight.[4] "Angels," said his brother Charles, "held him up."

A superb organizer, he personally regulated the administration and finances of his rapidly growing community, based on the 'class' of twelve members, as the Communists were later to base their movement on the 'cell'. Class leaders, appointed

---

[4] In his *Journal*, as an instance of "how God overrules even the minutest circumstances", he tells how, at Bolton, "one man was bawling at my ear, when a stone struck him on the chest, and he was still. A second was forcing his way down to me, till another stone hit him in the forehead: it bounded back, the blood ran down, and he came no farther. A third, being got close to me, stretched out his hand, and in the instant a sharp stone came upon the joints of his fingers. He shook his hand and was very quiet till I had concluded my discourse and went away."

by Wesley himself, were responsible for collecting the subscription of a shilling per class per week and for reporting on
the slack and disorderly. Discipline was at the heart of Wesley's 'method': he once expelled two hundred Norwich members for failing to attend class meetings. Beyond the class was
the 'society' and the 'band'—the latter a group of chosen
members, subdivided into the two sexes, and again into
married and single, to practise communal confession and
mutual exhortation. The local 'society' would have a steward
responsible to Wesley, and every year from 1744 the United
Society would meet once in the Methodist Conference dominated by the authoritarian and inexhaustible little man himself. Not for nothing did Toplady (the Calvinist pamphleteer
who wrote *Rock of Ages*) call him Pope John.

As a preacher he was moving, but not so intoxicatingly
eloquent as George Whitefield, one of the original Oxford
Holy Club. It was Whitefield who first preached to the great
open-air crowds in Bristol, where Wesley followed; and it was
Whitefield who founded the famous Kingswood school for
colliers' children there, which Wesley completed. But Whitefield and Wesley quarrelled over the Calvinist doctrines of
predestination which Wesley abhorred; and the latter imperi-
ously expelled predestinarians from his Society. Whitefield
seceded, and founded his own tabernacle, under the patronage
of the pious Countess of Huntingdon. "I frankly acknowledge",
wrote Whitefield, "I believe ... that God intends to give His
saving grace, through Jesus Christ, only to a certain number,
and that the rest of mankind ... will at last suffer that eternal
death, which is its proper wages." Both these men were spell-
binders, both great emotional preachers; but whereas Whitefield was a master of oratory, Wesley usually spoke "in short,
economical phrases; ... his sentences seemed to clutch at men's
hearts and drag them out." Like Whitefield, he had the
revivalist's dangerous gift of being able to rouse the susceptible
among his audiences to the pitch of hysteria. Everywhere men
and women of this sort listening to him were seized with
trembling; they collapsed to the ground, groaned, shouted,
wept at they knew not what; and then 'conversion' would
often follow this psycho-spiritual storm.

It is not surprising that in an age whose educated class admired classical restraint, an 'age of reason', many were horrified at Wesley's methods and the manifestations he provoked. And his own literal belief in devils and witches, his vivid relish for a strong emotional scene, serve further to explain both the hostility that greeted him and the appeal of his highly charged message to simple minds and tortured spirits. He wrestled with devils and cast them out. Young girls had to be held down while "the dogs of hell" were chased forth from them. Tension, exaltation, release—these were the ingredients. Some (then or now) might find it all too violent, too garish, too raw. But that, surely, was the secret of his power. The 'age of reason' was for the few. Wesley, no intellectual, but one who had explored the abysses and peaks of his own nature, could go with others to depths and heights both of which the ordinary level-headed person avoided or deprecated.

Wesley, of course, failed to 'convert' the Church of England itself—his original ambition; and since few ordained priests followed him he was soon obliged to appoint lay preachers to carry the Methodist message among open-air congregations and inside the new chapels. But as membership grew—by 1780 there were over forty thousand—lay preachers no longer sufficed. There were not enough priests to administer the sacraments, and in America, where there were already 8000 Methodists, there were no ordained clergy at all. To the consternation of his brothers Charles[5] and Samuel, John Wesley in 1784 took a decisive step: he himself ordained three priests for the American circuits. The colonies followed; then Scotland; and finally England. In all he ordained twenty-six; and, in the words of Lord Chief Justice Mansfield, "ordination was separation". At Wesley's death in 1791 there were about 136,000 'ticket-holding' Methodists and approaching a million sympathizers.

[5] Charles Wesley, whose career in Georgia had matched John's in disaster, and who had preceded his brother in 'conversion', was a less dominating and more cautious personality, who is remembered now mainly as the author and composer of such popular hymns as *Jesu, lover of my soul*; *Christ, whose glory fills the skies*; *Soldiers of Christ, arise*; and *Hark! the Herald Angels sing*.

The formal breach with the Church of England did not come till a few years after his death; but already, by ordaining clergy and by drafting a deed vesting his authority in a Committee of a Hundred of his preachers at his death, Wesley had, to the open approbation of many of his followers, made Methodists into Dissenters. That, at least, was the way Charles put it, and, still more emphatically, his outraged brother Samuel. But it was equally true to say that the Church of England's own failure to accommodate Methodist 'enthusiasm' had both made the breach inevitable and surrendered the battle for the allegiance of the lower classes.

The appeal of Wesleyanism was primarily to the poor; and where the Church of England had abdicated—in the new industrial England—Wesley and his followers reaped a rich harvest. The growing mining villages and smoke-grimed towns frequently lacked an Anglican church but seldom a Methodist chapel—often ugly, but often, too, the centre of its religious life and its social solidarity. Priestley the chemist said that "the civilization, the industry, and the sobriety of great numbers of the labouring part of the community" were owed to the Methodists. Many of them (as Priestley conceded) were narrow, and (as J. H. Plumb writes) Methodism always had "an anti-intellectual, philistine quality which attracted the dispossessed". It was rabidly anti-Catholic, and often intolerantly self-righteous in its frugal piety. But it stressed the social virtues: "the gospel of Christ", wrote John Wesley, "knows of no Religion but Social". Methodists fought drunkenness and depravity; they promoted self-help and charity for others; they were the Christian conscience of the working class.

Wesley, however, was the most Tory of Tories, and it took some time for his followers to grow away from his extreme anti-radicalism in politics. The working class, in Wesley's view, should work, not demand a share in the government of their country. Wilkite and French Revolutionary mobs were alike anathema to him. Even young children too should be made to work, for play was dangerous, and the Devil lurked alarmingly. At his school at Kingswood, near Bristol, the children, aged from eight to fourteen, had to be up at five, spend two hours a day in prayer, eat sparingly, play not at all, and endure formidable lessons.[6] Wesley opposed schooling in general, other than Bible schooling; and the godly Methodist employer learned to regard his little factory or workshop drudges with an easy conscience.

It is difficult, therefore, to gauge the social and political effects of Methodism. In the age of the French Revolution it supplied a non-political alternative to radicalism; and hence earned the hatred of reformers like Cobbett. Its social and intellectual attitudes, as we have seen, were frequently narrow and obscurantist. Yet simply because of its earnestness and piety, it encouraged quite other attitudes, especially in its second and third generations. The anti-slavery movement, the trade union movement, prison reform, temperance reform, factory reform, educational reform, and, not least, parliamentary reform owed a great debt to Methodists. Many radical reformers of the days of Peterloo, and many Chartists of the following generation were sons of Methodist homes, who, inheriting the moral and social seriousness of their parents, had outgrown the Tory attitudes of early Wesleyanism.

4. Philanthropists and Humanitarians

The Georgian age was a great age for benevolence and charity. Never had there been a time when so much philanthropic activity was initiated for such diverse ends: the foundation of hospitals of all kinds, of dispensaries, orphanages, missionary societies, charity schools, Sunday Schools, Church day schools; societies for saving life at sea, for rescuing paupers from destitution, girls from prostitution, Negroes from slavery, the British working class from vice and atheism; campaigns to improve prison conditions, to protect factory children and chimney-sweeps' apprentices. It is an impressive and heartening catalogue of benevolence; and if the prime motive was, fortunately, the natural compassion of man's heart, other less obvious motives played their part—fear of a fall in the popu-

---

[6] "God", wrote one of their masters, "broke in upon our boys in a surprising manner . . . the power of God came upon them, even like a mighty rushing wind, which made them cry aloud for mercy. . . . While I am writing, the cries of the boys, from their several apartments, are sounding in my ears."

lation, which helped to promote interest in lying-in (maternity) hospitals and the Royal Humane Society's life-saving projects; fear of French-style revolution, a powerful argument for educating the poor in religious truth and the virtue of order and submissiveness; the need for keeping up the supply of labour—and every baby saved was a potential unit in the necessary army of the industrious poor. No-one outside a handful of radicals dreamed of abolishing poverty, for poverty was assumed to be part of God's scheme. But it provided for the Christian the duty, the blessed opportunity, the *luxury* (as Goldsmith said) of being charitable. And as the Bishop of Lincoln wrote in 1716, in a pamphlet advocating *The Peculiar Excellence and Reward of Supporting Schools of Charity*: "Whatever is laid out in charity, God accounts an offering and loan to himself; and accordingly he engages to repay it.... And that this Payment is chiefly in the next World, is the plain Language of holy Scripture."

(a) Foundlings, Pauper Children, and Others

The saving of life, and in particular the lives of young children, could unite men of goodwill. Hospitals and dispensaries for the poor multiplied after 1714 as never before; and of all these, the one that attracted the greatest notice was the Foundling Hospital established in Bloomsbury by Thomas Coram in George II's reign. Coram, a Dorset-born sea-captain and for some years a shipbuilder of Massachusetts, had been touched, on his many journeys from his Rotherhithe home to the Thames river-side, by the sight of so many abandoned babies dying in the gutter and on dung-heaps. The army of unwanted children was numerous, and the ruthless desperation of their mothers pitiable. Previous attempts to rescue exposed infants had broken down against the objection that such charity would merely encourage promiscuity and illegitimacy, but Captain Coram, labouring for seventeen years, succeeded at last in persuading influential Court ladies to present his petition to the King. A royal charter was granted; subscriptions poured in; Hogarth painted a picture for the fine new building; Handel gave performances there and donated an organ. So great was the pressure on the restricted accommodation, however, that admission had to be by ballot; and when, after Coram's death, Parliament relaxed restrictions on admission and lent its financial support, so overwhelming was the flood of foundlings that, of 14,934 admitted between 1756 and 1760, 10,389 died. On the first day alone, 117 'infants-anonymous' were left in the basket provided. Soon the system broke down, private subscriptions declined, and for many years babies could be accepted only if accompanied by a £100 fee. Those surviving were frequently apprenticed to industry. The whole controversial history of this famous charity throws a flood of light on the seamier side of life in Georgian England. The kindly, vigorous Coram and his benevolent supporters demonstrated (by their methods) both the magnitude and the insolubility of the problem.

One of the most constructive critics of the Foundling Hospital management was himself one of the Governors, Jonas Hanway, a retired export merchant of wide-ranging humanitarian interests and eccentric habits (he is credited, probably wrongly, with being the first Englishman to carry an umbrella). He investigated the poor in the London workhouses,

> a great number of them old, sickly, and in a filthy condition: how could it be conceived that the poor *infant* could open his mouth, without sucking in mortality? How many of these poor babes had *gin* and *sleeping potions* given them by their *nurses*, I know not! Devoted as they were to death, it seemed to be a charity to deliver them, as speedily as possible. . . .

This he endeavoured to do, procuring in 1767 an Act which forced London workhouses to board out their pauper children below six years old, at a cost of not less than half a crown a week, an additional bonus of ten shillings being payable to their foster-mothers if they succeeded in keeping them alive. Hanway next bent his efforts to training pauper and vagrant children, orphans and discharged apprentices, for the Navy. This was the work of his Marine Society. And everywhere his social work led him back to the evils of prostitution—so large a proportion of his unfortunates had been mothered by prostitutes. Together with Robert Dingley, therefore, he founded the Magdalen Hospital in Goodman's Fields for "penitent prostitutes who are inclined to forsake their evil Course of Life", a pioneer institution for many others to follow. Still another class of unfortunates enlisted his championship—the little chimney-sweeps' boys, with their sores and cancers and their suffering from tyrannical masters and their risk of deformed limbs. But the demands of chimney-sweeps' profits and the somnolence of public opinion allowed another century to go by before even so manifest a wrong was finally righted. Jonas Hanway died in 1786, leaving behind him a prodigious variety of pamphlets attacking the manifold evils of his day, including "the pernicious custom of tea-drinking"; little better, he considered, than gin.

(b) Prisons and the Penal System

Inevitably, the state of the prisons had been one of these numerous objects of Hanway's interest; but it was his contemporary Oglethorpe who first succeeded in achieving anything considerable for the wretched occupants of the nation's jails. The scandal Oglethorpe specially attacked was the treatment of imprisoned debtors. A man in debt for an amount exceeding £2 could in effect be imprisoned for life by the action of his creditor; for a debtor, once lodged in jail, tended to accumulate more and more debts, if only to his 'turnkeys'. At the mercy of these frequently brutal men, the pitiable debtors depended on the charity of relatives and friends, or they begged of casual passers through a grating, or they sold small articles through a small aperture. Debtors provided over half of the prison population; but it should be remembered that this population was, relative to that of both Victorian and modern times, small (in 1776 Howard found only 4084 in the prisons of England and Wales)—the reason being that, apart from debtors, only those awaiting trial, committal, transportation, or execution were housed in prison. Neither accommodation nor finance permitted long-term imprisonment as a penal method. General Oglethorpe managed in 1729 to secure a parliamentary inquiry into the peculiar scandals (including systematic extortion by torture) of the Fleet prison; and three

years later he obtained a royal charter to found the colony of
Georgia for a small number of selected debtors and paupers,
financial backing being obtained from the subscriptions of a
public shocked into sympathy by the dreadful revelations of
1729. It was Oglethorpe who invited to Georgia the Moravians,
religious refugees from Austria, and appointed Charles Wesley
as his secretary there. The teething troubles of the young
colony were various and acute, some of them arising from the
failure of the home Government to provide for its defence
against the Spaniards, some from Oglethorpe's stern refusal to
allow his settlers either slaves or rum.

A generation after Oglethorpe, a greater and more systematic
investigator proved only too completely that little improvement
had resulted from the earlier revelations. John Howard
(*c.* 1726–90), a strange, puritanical man, so severe a father that
he drove his son to a breakdown, was a well-to-do Dissenter
and (thanks to the Indemnity Acts) High Sheriff of Bedford
from 1773. In that year he began the series of visits that took
him over 14,000 miles in three years to a very large number of
the prisons of England and Western Europe. He later visited
the prisons, plague-houses, and lazarettos of most of the rest
of Europe, tireless, fearless, and apparently immune to infection, until he was struck down by fever on a visit to the
Ukraine. The state of affairs he exposed in his *State of the
Prisons in England and Wales* (1777) was primitive and
scandalous. Though his account (like the outward man himself) was stark and cold, the detailed evidence he supplied
shouted for remedy. Prisons were damp and stinking; "putrid
fevers", especially typhus, abounded; food was scant, and
sometimes available only by purchase from the jailer; jailers,
being unpaid, inevitably exploited prisoners and extorted
from them what little they had; in some prisons the rule was
'pay or strip'; many jailers ran a 'tap', where liquor was
bought; men and women were herded together in vicious
proximity. Two short quotations from Howard's long book will
typify the whole:

[York City Bridewell was] ... dirty and offensive. No
regard paid to the late Act for Preserving Health. No court-

yard: no water: no sewer: straw twenty shillings a year: no bread allowance: little or no employment.

Knaresborough Prison, for Town Debtors, is under the Hall. Of difficult access; the door about four feet from the ground. Only one room, about fourteen feet by twelve. Earth floor: no fireplace: very offensive: a common sewer from the town running through it uncovered. I was informed that an Officer, confined here some years since, for only a few days, took in a dog to defend him from vermin; but the dog was soon destroyed, and the prisoner's face much disfigured by them.

Howard's proposed remedies included sanitary improvements, and the whitewashing of walls; separate cells, with solitary confinement for all at night and for hardened offenders by day; and hard labour for convicts, with anything over ten hours a day to count for personal wages. A little was done, but it was very little; and thirty-five years later, when the Quakeress Elizabeth Fry began visiting the women's quarters at Newgate, she found the old squalor, filth, and barbarity persisting. Another visitor wrote in his diary in 1816:

We ... went all over Newgate, which is dreadfully crowded, and the prisoners not properly classed. The infirmary was quite horrid; a moderate sized room and very hot; with twelve sick persons in it, and two dead ones. Saw the boys' school. There is one boy named Leary of thirteen who has been in Newgate twenty times, and been four times under sentence of death.

Conditions at the Marshalsea debtors' prison in the days of Dickens's youth, though less horrible than those exposed by Oglethorpe, were not basically different from those of Howard's day. Only in the larger prisons was there much improvement in the Georgian period. Here, in the 1820's, Peel appointed prison inspectors and female jailers for women's prisons, and also abolished the vicious tradition of compelling the prisoners to pay the jailers' fees.

Humanitarianism was as slow to affect the penal code as prison conditions. The inadequacies of the police system meant that, decade after decade, more and more offences were added to the capital list, in a futile attempt to deter the criminal, until they exceeded two hundred. A new bridge was built over the Thames at Westminster, so it became a capital offence to deface it. Unemployed hand-workers smashed the new machinery they hated, so (as late as 1812) destroying lace frames was added to the list. By this time, however, a powerful movement of humanitarian feeling, led by Sir Samuel Romilly in Parliament, was campaigning against the savagery of the penal code and the illogicality of having the same punishment, death, for both murder and petty pilfering. But the progress of reform was slow and constantly impeded by governmental opposition. Even when Romilly at last got over House of Commons hurdles, there remained the House of Lords. Twice, in 1810 and 1813, the Upper House rejected his Bill to remove the five-shilling shoplifter from the capital list. His diary for May 30th 1810 records that Ministers had "procured a pretty full attendance of peers, considering the advanced season of the year, to throw [the Bill] out. Amongst these were no less than seven prelates"; and he charitably argues that this was attributable rather to the bishops' political servility than to their lack of Christianity. However, Romilly, Sir James Mackintosh, and a great Quaker reformer, Sir Thomas Fowell Buxton, did between them succeed in getting pocket-picking and a few other crimes removed from the capital list; but still, in theory, a child of ten could be hanged for stealing. The growing humanitarianism of the age, however, is seen in the refusal of juries to find such a child, or perhaps a woman, guilty, however patently they had committed the offence. Romilly died by his own hand in 1818, but six years later his life's work was posthumously crowned when Peel removed the death penalty from about a hundred offences.

Public executions lingered till mid-Victorian times, but the Tyburn spectacle, the Londoner's traditional six-weekly holiday, was discontinued by the Fox–North coalition of 1783. The convicted felon whose offence did not qualify for hanging was usually transported to hard labour in the colonies; but when the American War of Independence interrupted the flow of convicts a 'temporary' substitute was devised (which, despite the setting up of a new convict settlement at Botany Bay in

New South Wales, lasted over eighty years); this was the 'hulks'—old ships in the Thames and at Portsmouth converted to prison-ships. Here prisoners were "chained in pairs night and day except when at work in the lighters", and conditions were so inhuman that despite the efforts of Howard and others to better them the convicts (as a committee of 1812 reported) "must be expected to return into society with more depraved habits and dispositions, than those with which they went into confinement". "In short," as Fowell Buxton told Parliament, by its treatment of the offender both in the hulks and in the prisons, "by the greatest possible degree of misery, you produce the greatest possible degree of wickedness. . . . You return him to the world impaired in health, debased in intellect, and corrupted in principles."

(c) The Anti-Slavery Movement

The climate of opinion in early Georgian England was entirely tolerant of slavery and the slave trade. The economy of the West Indies and the plantation states of America was constructed on slaves, and the profits of many in England and Scotland depended directly or indirectly on them. Since the black man was regarded as less than human, God-fearing Christians could be slave-dealers and slave-traders without offence to their conscience. It was the work of the humanitarian reformers of later Georgian times to alter all this, to awaken the dormant national conscience, and to proclaim again the brotherhood of man.

The first effective blows in their campaign were struck by Granville Sharp, an archdeacon's son who had become a clerk in the Ordnance Office. It was fashionable in the eighteenth century to employ a black servant, who, though he lived a life very different from that which he would have led on the plantations, still carried an ambiguous status. Was he, or was he not, the property of his master? Was he a slave? On this point legal opinions were contradictory. For five years Sharp championed in the courts various ill-used Negroes who, having escaped, had been kidnapped back into servitude by their masters. At last in 1772 he secured from Lord Chief Justice

Mansfield the decision which that property-conscious judge had used some skill in postponing. The Negro Sommersett, Sharp's protégé, was declared free; "the black must be discharged"; no man could be a slave henceforth on English soil.

The greater campaigns followed for the abolition, first, of the trade in slaves, and, second, of slavery itself throughout the British colonies. In these the Quakers played a leading part, as they did in so many philanthropic and reforming enterprises; and working closely with the Quakers were Granville Sharp and the young Thomas Clarkson. Clarkson, the son of a clergyman-schoolmaster, had won a university prize for a Latin dissertation at Cambridge on the subject of slavery, which had moved him painfully: "It was but one gloomy subject from morning to night. In the daytime I was uneasy. In the night I had little rest. I sometimes never closed my eyes for grief." For the next dozen or so years Clarkson worked ceaselessly for the abolition of the slave trade. He amassed statistics and evidence of all kinds; he collected specimens of the manacles, thumbscrews, and other torture instruments that were used on the notorious Middle Passage; he poured forth a stream of pamphlets; and, together with Sharp and the Quakers, he founded in 1787 the first and most influential of the Committees for the Abolition of the Slave Trade. They had their failures, notably the disastrous attempt to found a colony for freed slaves in Sierra Leone; but gradually the tide of opinion flowed in their direction. Powerful assistance came from the rising Evangelical movement, and in particular from the wealthy and earnest Clapham Sect.

It was in William Wilberforce, the rich, charming, golden-voiced Member of Parliament for Hull, that they found their most influential champion. Wilberforce, a close friend of the younger Pitt, had turned aside from youthful gaiety to the serious Evangelicalism[7] of the day. He forswore cards, gambling, and the social pleasures; became a supporter of Romilly; and founded a Society for the Suppression of Vice, whose professed aim was to reform manners and morals, but which seemed to many to concentrate rather too class-consciously on suppressing the traditional pleasures of the poor. Intensely

[7] See Section 6, p. 349.

Tory and Sabbatarian, a supporter of every repressive measure for thirty years against the radicals, a champion of the Corn Laws and dear bread, Wilberforce came before his death to be more hated by the political reformers than perhaps any man in England. Cobbett called him a cold-blooded hypocrite: "You make your appeal in Piccadilly, London, amongst those who are wallowing in luxuries. You should have gone to the gravel-pits, and made your appeal to the wretched creatures with bits of sacks round their shoulders...." Hazlitt made substantially the same reproach, that Wilberforce was singularly unfeeling to the sufferings of the *English* poor: "He preaches vital Christianity to untutored savages, and tolerates its worst abuses in civilized states." But on his great subject of Negro slavery Wilberforce was a giant. Like Wesley, with whom he had much in common, he was a very small man; Boswell described him as "a mere shrimp ... but, as I listened, he grew and grew until the shrimp became a whale".

Wilberforce gained the support both of Pitt and of Burke, Fox, and the Whigs for his various parliamentary motions against the slave trade; but Pitt's support was always more personal than official, and it was not until after his death that the first great success was achieved. The Fox–Grenville Ministry of 1806 was the first to put its full governmental weight behind Wilberforce, and in 1807 the slave trade from British ports was forbidden. Slaves already at work in the colonies remained slaves, and their children continued to be born into slavery. Moreover, the slave trade from other than British ports persisted, despite the general European condemnation by the Congress of Vienna in 1815; and the horrors of the traffic, all the more ruthless because it was now, in effect, smuggling, reached in some respects a new peak. Wilberforce had reckoned that 17 per cent of slaves had died between sailing from Africa and sale in the West Indies, and another third in the 'seasoning' period; but in the final decades over 50 per cent died *en route*, though the total number of those carried was, of course, much lower. The suppression of this illicit traffic provided one refreshing novelty—co-operation between the governments and navies of civilized states in peace-time.

Another quarter-century of struggle was needed (the last decade of it under the direction of the Quaker and prison reformer, Fowell Buxton, Wilberforce's health being in decline) before in 1833 the British Parliament carried the final act of emancipation. It was again the Whigs who were responsible, Grey's Ministry being lent some boldness by its more radical members, such as Brougham. The owners were compensated at the market price of about £37 per slave. Wilberforce survived just long enough to see his life's work complete.

(d) Factory Labour

The age that accepted slavery found it equally natural to accept child labour on a very heavy scale; and a movement of humanitarian agitation parallel with that of the slavery abolitionists succeeded only slowly in mitigating the exploitation of children. The two movements ran parallel but apart; they were, indeed, rather rivals than partners. Wilberforce was deaf to the cry of factory children; and those who championed the little, overworked textile hands frequently made play with the relative happiness and idleness of the plantation slave—John Fielden, for instance, the Radical spinning manufacturer, who exclaimed, "What a pity that these 35,000 factory children happen to be white instead of black!" And Richard Oastler, the author of *Letters on Yorkshire Slavery*, gave evidence thus before a parliamentary committee of 1830:

> ... The cruelties which are inflicted personally upon the little children not to mention the immensely long hours which they are subject to work, are such as I am very sure would disgrace a West Indian plantation. On one occasion I was very singularly placed; I was in the company of a West India slave master and three Bradford spinners; they brought the two systems into fair comparison, and the spinners were obliged to be silent when the slave-owner said, "Well, I have always thought myself disgraced by being the owner of black slaves, but we never, in the West Indies, thought it was possible for any human being to be so cruel as to require a child of 9 years old to work 12½ hours a day; and that, you acknowledge, is your regular practice.

Long hours of child labour did not begin with the factories. In field, cottage, and workshop children had always been made to work to their limits, and sometimes beyond them— often the full working day of 6 A.M. to 8 P.M. It can, indeed, be argued that it was the concentration of child labour in factories that enabled a like concentration of public indignation to promote reform. Indeed, it was easier to gain sympathy for large armies of young children, subject to the strap of bullying overseers and making the fortunes of rich employers, than for a similar number of children working similar hours for as little reward, punished often as severely by their parents or masters, but dispersed over many thousand homes and workshops.

Certainly the factories strengthened the demand for child and female labour. "Wanted", advertised Arkwright at Cromford, ". . . Framework-knitters and Weavers, with large Families. Likewise Children of all Ages, above seven years old, may have constant Employment." The payment was usually three shillings, for a week of six twelve-hour days, or sometimes five thirteen-hour days, with eleven hours on Saturday. Some employers, failing to attract enough 'free' labour, would hire batches of pauper children from the workhouses of the larger towns, which were glad enough to be rid of the expense of their upkeep; and these ex-paupers would eat and sleep, as well as work, under the full discipline of the factory. This was not always tyrannical and oppressive; many employers, like Arkwright, or Boulton, or the Strutts of Derbyshire, took a pride in their treatment of employees, and some, like Robert Owen, Robert Peel the elder, John Fielden of Todmorden, and John Wood of Bradford, were in the van of the fight for proper regulation. Yet there were plenty of slave-drivers, like the Lancashire millowner who, during his six weeks' 'busy time', forced his girls, on pain of dismissal, to work from 3.30 A.M. to 10 or 10.30 at night, and during this period paid them an extra $7\frac{1}{2}d$. a week overtime money; or like another Manchester spinner who told an 1816 Select Committee that he had every intention of continuing his practice of making his children work a 76-hour week, with compulsory overtime to pay back any holiday that they were allowed. It was notorious, Sir Robert Peel told the same committee, that "children of a very tender age were dragged from their beds some hours before daylight, and confined in the factories not less than fifteen hours". Their growth was stunted; they were afflicted by deformities; they suffered injury by falling into the machinery.

In the mines the conditions were even worse. Some children of extremely tender age, seven, six, or even younger, were employed for twelve hours a day or more as 'trappers', opening and shutting in the dark the trapdoors as the coal-tubs passed. Older boys, girls, and young women were used for carting and dragging loads of coal, sometimes in baskets of 1–1½ cwt carried on the shoulder up steep ramps, sometimes by the 'trace and chain', where teenage girls were used as beasts of burden, crawling on all fours down narrow workings, with a leather girdle round their waists and a chain attached to a 2½–3 cwt load. "It is sad sweating and sore fatiguing work, and frequently maims the women", reported one of them, a seventeen-year-old from Stirlingshire. Many women worked on at the mine until their marriage or after, often till a few weeks before their babies were born; and to all these hardships were added the inevitable diseases and disasters of the mining life.

The most important of the factory reformers were Robert Peel the elder and Robert Owen, each of whom himself employed over a thousand children. It was Peel who, in 1802, secured the first Act that attempted to regulate the conditions of employment for ex-pauper apprentices in textile-mills and to safeguard their health and morals. It was always a dead letter. Robert Owen, who took over the large cotton-mills at New Lanark, near Glasgow, that had been founded by his father-in-law, developed there the most famous of all the progressive communities of his day. He limited hours, refused to employ children under ten, and provided nursery and primary schools for all children aged between three and ten, living on his workers' estate. Environment, he preached, was the vital factor in producing good and happy men and women; he sought, therefore, to provide his workpeople with model conditions. Co-operation, not competition, ought to be the basis of society. He set up, accordingly, a co-operative store in his New Lanark community, and, proceeding from practice to theory, published the idealistic *New View of Society* in 1813. Naïvely optimistic, he expected the world rapidly to adopt his patently admirable ideas. When it showed reluctance, he moved on undaunted towards fresh panaceas and fresh failures. He was a philanthropist far removed from the characteristic Evangelicals of his day—Christianity he considered an outworn superstition—and very different in temper from most of his fellow Radicals. He was a paternalist, impatient of 'democracy'; he despised parliamentary reform as a mere playing with political toys. His radicalism went deeper, to the roots of the social system. Condemning the capitalism of his day, he first put forward many of the views later expressed by Socialist thinkers.

The ineffective Act of 1802 was followed by another, promoted by Peel and Owen, in 1819, limiting hours to twelve a day for children in cotton-mills, and prohibiting the employment there of children under nine. Like its predecessor it was generally ignored. But during the following decades there grew up a strong movement for factory reform, for both children and adults, often known as the Ten Hours Movement. In Parliament it cut across party divisions and was led successively by Sadler, a Tory banker, Ashley, a Tory landowner, and Fielden, a Radical cotton-spinner. It was Sadler who was chairman of the Parliamentary Committee of 1831 that, in its famous Report, publicized the operatives' grievances, together with the attacks of Oastler and others. When Sadler lost his seat at the first election of the reformed Parliament, Ashley took over the parliamentary attempt to secure a ten-hour day for all; but neither Whig nor Tory Governments were yet ready to accept a measure which so offended against their ideas of *laissez-faire*. The most that Ashley could obtain was an Act (sometimes known as Althorp's Act, 1833, from the Whig Minister sponsoring it) which proved to be the first moderately effective Factory Act. This measure applied to all textile (other than silk) mills. It prohibited the employment of children under nine, and all-night work for those under eighteen. It limited to nine per day the hours of children between nine and thirteen, and to twelve per day those of boys and girls between thirteen and eighteen. Four inspectors were appointed to secure the enforcement of the Act. A further clause enjoining millowners to provide two hours' daily education for child workers was ignored by most of them.

Thus, by 1837, in the campaigns for the protection of women and children, for the ten-hour day for adults, and for the general improvement of factory conditions, battle had been joined; but conclusive victories had not yet been won.

(e) *The Education of the Poor*

To Christians one of the most disquieting things about the poor, especially the urban poor, was their heathenism; and almost all the schools founded for the poor in Georgian England were missionary in intent. Already by 1714 the Society for Promoting Christian Knowledge was at work, and 25,000 children were attending the hundreds of Charity Schools whose foundation had been a feature of Anne's reign. The avowed aims of these schools were to teach reading, writing, moral principles, and the precepts of the Church of England. Many of them also trained children for a trade; hence the Charity Schools, like the workhouses, became a considerable source of juvenile labour. (Readers of *Oliver Twist* will remember Noah Claypole, Oliver's tormentor at the undertaker's, who was a Charity boy, and hence saw fit to scorn Oliver as "Work'us".)

A later criticism of the Charity Schools, as to some extent of the Sunday Schools that followed them, was that their religious motives were confused with political and social motives. They set out to teach, not only the Catechism, but 'knowing one's place'; they educated, not only to suppress vice and atheism, but to promote the established order. An Oxford Charity School preacher of 1755 put this characteristic calculation before his middle-class congregation:

> If compassion cannot move you, let considerations of interest prevail with you. For neglect this poor man's numerous family ... and they will grow up soon into public nuisances, infect your families with their idle dishonest disorderly behaviour, fill your streets with vice and violence,

break in upon your comfort and security.... [But] teach them what is right, and ... they will be serviceable to you ... your city will be stocked with honest laborious ingenious artisans.... Wealth will increase.

The assumptions behind these sentiments—the permanence of social subordination, the identity of interests between compassion and calculation, working-class morality as a necessary foundation for middle-class prosperity, religion as the handmaid of political order—would probably have passed unchallenged when they were made, in 1755. Fifty or a hundred years later the repetition of such sentiments—and they *were* long repeated—began to many to seem patronizing and offensive. To Dickens, for instance: his Uriah Heep in *David Copperfield* represents his blazing hatred of the whole atmosphere:

> They taught us a deal of umbleness—not much else that I know of, from morning to night. We was to be umble to this person, umble to that; and to pull off our caps here and make our bows there: and always to know our places and abase ourselves before our betters. And we had such a lot of betters!

The first Sunday Schools began with this curiously dual ambition—to enforce discipline on a naturally vicious and savage working class, and to save souls. With Wesley and his followers the emphasis lay more on the latter; with such as Robert Raikes (1735–1811), the first systematic organizer of Sunday Schools, on the former. Raikes, a Gloucester newspaper proprietor, had, like Howard, been horrified by the drunken immorality and profanity that he witnessed on prison visits. The men and women that he saw in Gloucester jail were too far gone in vice and criminality to save; but their children, and the younger generation of the working class in general, might be turned into honest and sober citizens by Sunday Schools: "order and decorum", in his own words, might be enforced among this "set of little heathens". "Enforced" was often enough the right word: not all Gloucester children who had spent six twelve-hour days in the town's pin factory relished a seventh twelve-hour day of lessons and church-going. Some of Raikes's "little savages", seeking escape in the streets, had to be restrained by logs tied to their ankles. Like Mrs Wesley senior, he believed in "breaking the child's will".

Raikes's work in Gloucester was emulated in many other places. The Methodists were early in the field. Then in Brentford pious Mrs Sarah Trimmer, mother of twelve children and innumerable religious tracts, did valiant work trying to clothe "the deplorable, dirty ragged creatures" of the neighbourhood, and organizing Sunday Schools to teach them their first faltering steps towards Christian citizenship. Down among the depraved miners and glassworkers of the Mendip Hills, Hannah More (once a 'bluestocking' and the friend of Garrick, Johnson, and Wilberforce) turned, with her sister, to organizing schools of all kinds—Sunday Schools; "Schools of Industry", where, in a religious setting, girls spun worsted and were allowed to keep the profits of their work; and, finally, evening classes and friendly societies for adult men and women, an innovation of such boldness that the outraged local farmers gave the More sisters no peace till it was dead. Hannah, by 1791, had over a thousand children from the Mendip villages in her schools, but her work unfortunately coincided with the heyday of the revolution in France. She was assailed by conventional Christians for encouraging the working class to have ideas above their station: a labouring lad, taught to read, might well end by reading Tom Paine and turning Republican. In fact, strongly conservative, loyal, and Anglican, she replied by vigorously attacking the French Revolution, and for this was inevitably counter-attacked by British Radicals. This fever of controversy steered Hannah More into writing, and for the second half of her long life she poured forth a stream of religious tracts, poems, and pamphlets: inculcating purified morals; praising both the divine and the existing political order; attacking slavery and duelling; and demonstrating the inevitability of poverty and the necessity of charity. The excessively 'improving' tone of her writing should not prevent us from seeing her as one of the most vigorous, influential, and characteristic figures of her day: a day when the rich were constantly telling the poor that they should be sober, religious, industrious, and grateful for the mercies accorded them.

It was in Wales that the Charity School movement exercised its profoundest influence. Even before the foundation of the Society for the Propagation of Christian Knowledge, the devotional efforts of the Welsh Trust had set up a chain of schools: there were as many as eighty in the year 1675. But it was in the early eighteenth century, under the inspiration of the SPCK, that large numbers of schools were founded. Of the men behind all this activity, the most important were Sir John Philipps, a Pembrokeshire squire (d. 1737) and Griffith Jones, a Carmarthenshire rector (d. 1761). The very numerous schools these men established were subscribed for by both rich and poor; the teachers were drawn predominantly from the peasantry, and travelled from village to village, adapting their teaching sessions as far as possible to the agricultural calendar. Adults and children both attended, to hear, and perhaps to learn to read, the Bible and the Common Prayer Book in the Welsh language, and to repeat the Catechism. "It is but a cheap education we desire for them", wrote Griffith Jones of the pupils of these Circulating Schools; "only the moral and religious part of it." He did not design "to make them *Gentlemen* but *Christians* and *Heirs* of Eternal Life".

Sometimes an excess of 'enthusiasm' made enemies among the established clergy, but by no means always. "I may boldly say", wrote one curate, "that the Welsh Charity Schools did more good in our parish than all our preaching for many years." "The Welsh schools", wrote another, "have been the means, under God, to reform the profanation of the Sabbath Day, which the generality of the common people formerly spent in tippling, gaming, etc."

The Charity School movement was followed by a strong Methodist campaign and a proliferation of Methodist, Baptist, and Congregational Sunday Schools.

The steady concentration upon piety as the aim and end of all instruction changed a gay and simple people, indifferent to religion and lacking in political consciousness, into a people whose dominant interests were religious and political. The Bible had become the Welshman's manual.[8]

[8] M. G. Jones, *The Charity School Movement*, p. 321.

Moreover, it was a Bible in Welsh. The Welsh national revival and modern Welsh nationalism may be traced back, at least in part, to the spring of the Circulating Schools.

A majority of working-class children in the eighteenth century attended no school, on either Sundays or weekdays. There was, of course, no kind of national educational system, and reformers like Whitbread (who moved for one in Parliament in 1807) were regarded as cranks. Some villages had a school; many more had not. Where there were schools, they charged between fourpence and ninepence a week for a smattering of elementary instruction. No qualification was required for teachers, nor regulation for building. The 'dame' schools for very young children were often little more than child-minding establishments, and not always efficient even at that. Dickens, in *Great Expectations*, describes the evening school where "a ridiculous old woman of limited means and unlimited infirmity . . . used to go to sleep every evening in the society of youth who paid twopence a week for the improving opportunity of seeing her do it." At others the 'dame' managed to convey to her charges the arts of reading and spelling, with sewing for the girls and 'cyphering' (counting) for the boys. There were in addition the Charity Schools, a few 'parish' schools, like that detestable one that Jane Eyre attended, and pauper 'schools of industry'. But a large proportion of the poor remained innocent of formal education.

The first serious attempts to remedy this state of affairs arose out of the same ideas that prompted the establishment of Sunday Schools. The poor must be rescued from paganism, vice, and republicanism; therefore Church day schools must be set up. Soon, however, with rival societies in existence, one Anglican and one Nonconformist,[9] it became almost as important for the protagonists of each denomination to rescue the children from the clutches of the other. The bitter rivalry between these two 'voluntary societies' persisted for the succeeding century, and throughout that time bedevilled

[9] The National Society for the Education of the Poor in the Principles of the Established Church throughout England and Wales; and The British and Foreign School Society, founded in 1814 from the earlier Royal Lancasterian Institution (1805) of the Quaker Joseph Lancaster.

English (and, still more, Welsh) educational progress. At least, however, many schools were now built—3000 Church of England 'National' schools alone in the first twenty-year period (1811–31). Finance was provided by voluntary subscriptions, and cheapness ensured by the adoption of the 'monitorial method', by which older and brighter children rehearsed small groups in the mechanical practising and learning of reading, writing, arithmetic, 'general knowledge', Catechism, and so forth. Both sides in the interdenominational war stoutly claimed credit for this innovation, which permitted a teacher-pupil ratio of one to several hundreds (even as many as one to a thousand), and allowed the annual cost per child educated to be as low as 7s. 6d. Features of this rapidly expanding educational (or perhaps anti-educational) system were chanting in chorus, and a complicated system of rewards and punishments. It is probable that most children, after the usual stay of two or three years, left these schools almost as illiterate as they entered them, though some of the monitors may well have profited. The idea that you could 'multiply' knowledge by monitorial devices, just as you could multiply your output of yarn by using a mule-spinning machine, died hard. "The Steam Engine of the Moral World" was the way some fervent Christian educationists described their monitorial system; and in 1833 Parliament signified its interest in the work that was being done by voting a grant of £20,000 a year to be divided equally between the two voluntary societies in the construction of buildings. This was a historic move; it was the acorn that was to grow eventually into the present-day oak-tree of public expenditure on the nation's education.

5. Secondary and University Education

The condition of the ancient grammar and public schools probably sank lower during the Hanoverian period than at any other time in their long history. Endowed grammar schools were largely derelict. Sometimes for decades on end the total roll of pupils might be half a dozen or so, or even occasionally nil, while a succession of masters contrived to be paid from the endowment. Even the better grammar schools were small, and served a tiny minority of the total population. Manchester, Bradford, and Sedbergh were among the honourable exceptions. Many so-called grammar schools hardly rose above the level of primary schools; but where they did the curriculum was centred narrowly on Latin, some of the grammars in use being reprints of two-hundred-year-old primers; and as late as 1805 Lord Chancellor Eldon ruled that modern languages and mathematics could not legally be included in the curriculum of an endowed grammar school. Hence these ancient schools (which, of course, included the public schools) were at a serious educational disadvantage in competing either with recently founded private schools, which could offer a wider range of modern subjects, or with the Nonconformist Academies, which undoubtedly at this time provided the best education available in England: languages, mathematics, history, geography, astronomy, logic, natural and experimental philosophy (*i.e.*, science), commerce, navigation, and English composition were among the subjects taught.

The academic standards of the public schools, like their numbers, fluctuated widely. Winchester's roll at one time was down to 78; that of Eton (already growing highly aristocratic) was at one time as high as 500; Westminster, with its famous tradition of Greek scholarship, probably enjoyed the most consistently high academic reputation. But at all these schools discipline was simultaneously lax and savage; they were no place for the delicate or sensitive boy. Dr Keate of Eton once flogged eighty boys in one session. Eton, Harrow, Winchester, and Westminster all had open rebellions, Winchester three under one headmaster alone; the young aristocrats, in fact, "treated their headmaster rather as their fathers treated the king". Games were unsupervised and unorganized; if the Duke of Wellington meant anything by saying that the Battle of Waterloo was won on the playing fields of Eton (if, indeed, he did say it), he must have been referring to some pretty undisciplined scrambles. Perhaps the greatest merit that could be claimed for many of the Georgian public schools—a dangerous merit—was the degree of neglect their pupils enjoyed. Though this permitted a good deal of vicious behaviour, gambling, drunkenness, and bullying, it did allow long hours to be spent in such profitable pursuits as reading, botanizing, or poaching. The young Melbourne once left Eton for a week to attend the racing at Ascot, and Palmerston, aged thirteen, reported home that he had just obtained a half-share in a ferret.

As for the universities, Oxford and Cambridge were in a clerical rut, and the intellectual supremacy of the Scottish universities was complete. Both Catholics and Nonconformists were excluded by law from Oxford and Cambridge, and although Cambridge did admit a few Nonconformists as undergraduates, they could not take degrees or hold any teaching post; Oxford was an exclusively Church of England preserve. Cambridge, again, though the eighteenth century marked the low-water mark of its academic tide, did have in its Mathematical Tripos a respectable test of learning. At Oxford there was no serious examination for a degree at all.[10] As for the college Fellows at both universities, "in their lazy, self-indulgent, celibate, clericalism" (Trevelyan wrote) they resembled the monks of the fifteenth century, "and were about as much use." Gibbon, who sat at table with them at Magdalen, Oxford, described them in an often-quoted passage:

> From the toil of reading or thinking or writing they had absolved their conscience. Their conversation stagnated in a round of college business, personal stories and private scandal; their dull and deep potations excused the brisk intemperance of youth.

It is not surprising that at this time (*c.* 1750) the figures of residence were very low, only slightly more than half those of a century earlier. Little was expected of undergraduates, and less of dons. When the undergraduate Charles Fox was taken away by his father to be instructed in the life of a man of pleasure in Paris, the principal of his college, Hertford, wrote to him:

> It is a matter of entire indifference to the other geometricians of the college whether they proceed ... or wait a term

[10] Lord Eldon was examined in 1770 for his degree, in Hebrew and History. "'What is the Hebrew for the Place of a Skull?' said the Examiner. 'Golgotha', I replied. 'Who founded University College?' I answered 'King Alfred'. 'Very well, sir,' said the Examiner, 'then you are competent for your degree.'"

or two longer. You need not . . . interrupt your amusements.
. . . We shall stop until we have the pleasure of your company.

Few lectures were delivered, and many professorships were complete sinecures. There were three Regius Professors of Modern History at Cambridge between 1725 and 1733; none gave a single lecture; the third of them died drunk. Adam Smith, who was destined for better things at Glasgow, but was at Oxford in 1745, declared that most professors "had given up altogether even the pretence of teaching". Half a century later, as evidence of progress, it was claimed that nine out of twenty Cambridge professors "were then lecturing regularly, . . . three were lecturing once a term", and "two others would do so if they had any audiences".

Politically the universities, dominated entirely as they were by Anglican clergy, were Tory—Oxford violently so. In the early years of the century there was more Jacobite talk in Oxford than anywhere else in England, and some Walpole Whigs would dearly have liked to purge the University. But Oxford was allowed to sleep out her Georgian slumbers in peace. She even added to her legacy by putting up some notable new buildings (the Clarendon Building, the Radcliffe Camera, and many college extensions); so too did Cambridge (at King's and Clare Colleges, for example); but Gibbon's bitter criticisms remained just, until long after his death. Oxford and Cambridge were privileged clerical monopolies, and "the spirit of monopolists is narrow, lazy and oppressive".

The Dissenters had the best schools in the country, and many of them strongly resented that the doors of the universities should be shut to them. Sceptics and freethinkers, too, did not see why they should be barred from higher education by the conservatism and bigotry of the senior universities. Thus it was that during the 1820's these two very different groups, of Nonconformists and secularists, believers and non-believers united in common resentment of the Anglican Church, came together to found a new University College in London—"the godless college in Gower Street" which opened its doors in 1828. Many men had a hand in its creation: leading Dissenters; Jeremy Bentham the philosopher, and his Utilitarian followers, James Mill, Grote, and Place; and, among politicians, Joseph Hume, Lord John Russell, and—the chief mover—Henry Brougham. Soon King's College, London, was founded as the Church of England's reply to University College; and in 1836 the two were federated into the University of London. With this, and the foundation of the first provincial university at Durham, the long monopoly, though not the primacy, of Oxford and Cambridge was at last broken.

6. Evangelicals and Tractarians

In the 'age of reform' which began in the 1820's it was not to be expected that the Church of England would remain unaffected. But certainly reform was slow to arrive. Pluralism continued largely as before. The parson and the squire maintained their social and political dominance. They often sat on the same magisterial bench; they shared the same horror of Radicals, Catholics, and Dissenters; they supported the same Tory party; they drank their port and hunted the fox together; and together they mistrusted upstart manufacturers. Not all Anglican clergy, of course, were rich—in fact, one of the chief criticisms of the Church was the gross inequalities of stipend persisting in it—but, up to 1837 and after, the Church of England, closely linked with the aristocracy, remained "a wealthy church and a church of the wealthy". A great and growing proportion of the poor regarded it with hostility or indifference, and some of this continued even after the Whig reforms of 1836 onward, which caused ecclesiastical revenues to be redistributed more equitably, lessened the abuses of pluralism and non-residence, and (to the farmer's relief) allowed the old tithe payable in pigs and sheaves to be commuted to a rent charge.

In many ways, then, the Church of England was a worldly and 'gentlemanly' church at the close of our period; but it would be misleading not to stress the important qualifications to this generalization. By 1837 there were two powerfully sincere (and rival) groups within the Church recalling it from its comfortable materialism—the Evangelicals and the Tractarians.

Much of this chapter has necessarily referred to individual Evangelical humanitarians. Together, they and their like formed the Low Church party, who shared the Wesleyan aim of reviving personal faith and moral earnestness, so that all of a man's life would be impregnated with his sense of God's presence. In many ways they owed much to Methodism: some Evangelical clergy even adopted, like Wesley, lay preachers. They put total reliance on scriptural evidence, vehemently opposed Roman Catholicism, and emphasized the doctrine of 'Justification by Faith'. Yet, great as was their faith, it is by their works that most of the leading Evangelicals are remembered. Hannah More, Sarah Trimmer, Robert Raikes, William Wilberforce, and Lord Ashley are only a few of them famous as social reformers.

The best-known single group of Evangelicals was the 'Clapham Sect' (c. 1800). Still a few miles then beyond the south-west limits of London, Clapham was a favourite suburban village for rich businessmen and gentlefolk. Wilberforce had a house there; so had the banker Henry Thornton; Isaac Milner, the Cambridge mathematician and theologian; Granville Sharp; Zachary Macaulay, father of the historian; and several other men of like faith and intensity. At the centre of the group was John Venn, the Rector of Clapham. These men not only played a major part in the abolition of the slave trade; they also constituted a power-house of a new, exacting, earnest version of Christianity. (From the preaching and personality of Charles Simeon in Cambridge a similar influence radiated.) They spent two hours of their busy days in prayer; they gave away a large fraction (in Thornton's case, five-sixths) of their personal incomes in charity; they aimed at nothing less than a general reformation of morals and salvation of souls.

It was through the Evangelicals that the London Missionary Society was founded in 1795, the Church Missionary Society in 1799, and the British and Foreign Bible Society in 1804. (Indomitably optimistic, they even sent a Protestant mission to Ireland.) It was the Evangelicals who made general the nineteenth-century habit of family prayers—often at both morning and evening, with compulsory attendance for servants. It was they who campaigned against duelling, cruelty to children, cruelty to animals, barbarous sports, swearing, and blasphemy. It was they who set their seal on the British Sunday, for they were rigidly Sabbatarian. (Sarah Trimmer, for instance, was alarmingly so. "It frequently happens", that gentle lady wrote, "that the Almighty withdraws his Providence from horsemen, drivers, rowers, drunkards, and gamesters, and they lose their lives in consequence of their irregularities on Sunday.") Some Evangelicals, indeed, were so excessively pious that they inevitably appeared to their profaner contemporaries as prudes, prigs, and humbugs. The caricature type of the effeminate, shockable English vicar took its origin in the common man's amused distaste for the Evangelical clergyman who thought swearing, smoking, dancing, flirtation, card-playing, theatre-going, or race-going all equally reprehensible. In music, only sacred oratorios were quite acceptable to him.

The Evangelicals played a big part in creating upper- and middle-class Victorian England, its urgent sense of reform, the propriety of its moral conventions, its insistent conscience, its emphasis on the forms of religion. However, their movement remained, unlike that of the Methodists, essentially a movement of the well-to-do.

The second of the great movements of revival within the Church of England at this time paid little attention to charitable works, disapproved of Sabbatarianism, and was not addicted to Puritan zeal. To John Keble, J. A. Froude, Edward Pusey, J. H. Newman, and those who joined them, the weaknesses of the Church of England lay in its deficient sense of mystery and its tame subjection to the secular authority of the State. An Anglican priest should regard and conduct himself as what he was—a successor to the apostles, not a casual officiator in ill-understood rites. His was a "mystic prerogative". The outward forms of religion were all-important because they were symbolic of inward truth. Forms of worship, therefore, styles of architecture and music, tradition, ritual, the vestments of the officiating clergy, the use of incense, the significance of the altar and its decoration—all these took on profound meaning and solemnity. These High Church reformers studied the writings of the ancient Fathers of the Church and pre-Reformation usages. They heard confession. They administered extreme unction to the dying. They moved ever nearer to the forms and practices of the Roman Catholics.

When Pusey joined the movement in 1835 his extreme ritualism won for his supporters the description of Puseyites; it was Newman who gained for them the name of Tractarians, from a succession of pamphlets, entitled *Tracts for the Times*, which he published at Oxford from 1833. No religious writing had gathered such controversy round it for more than a century. Horrified Low Churchmen and Evangelicals grew increasingly sure that Newman was heading ultimately for the Roman Church. He struggled long to preserve a middle position between Protestantism and Romanism; but eventually Low Church fears were to prove right. Others of this 'Oxford Movement' followed him in due course, but not a majority. These remained within the wide arms of the Church of England and provided the foundation upon which the Anglo-Catholic party built.

Neither the extreme Low Church nor the extreme High Church succeeded in dominating the Church of England. True to its English nature, it developed within it a central, moderate, majority party: solid, respectable, liberal, unfanatical—the Broad Church of Victoria's reign.

Chapter 12

The Age of the Younger Pitt and Nelson (1783–1806)

1. Administration, Taxation, and Commerce

When he was called to office by George III in 1783, Pitt stood at the head of no party. Like his father, Pitt was a party in himself. Against him were ranked the Foxite Whigs and the followers of North. Supporting him were the King (for whom Pitt provided a bulwark against the iniquities of Fox and North), as well as Wilberforce and many of the reformers. As a young man Pitt had ranged himself on the side of the angels— he was for abolishing the slave trade, for freeing trade, for ridding Parliament of the rotten boroughs. In office, he remained true to these early convictions to this extent: he supported Wilberforce's two Bills to abolish the slave trade, and he himself introduced on three occasions measures to reform Parliament, the last of them, in 1785, proposing to transfer the seats of thirty-six rotten boroughs to the county representation and to compensate the deprived borough owners. All these motions were easily defeated, to the royal relief and Pitt's apparent unconcern. Wilberforce complained of his "lack of principle", but these measures were never a matter of principle to Pitt. His intelligence told him that they merited his support; and when he had done his duty by them, and they were defeated in Parliament, he quietly dropped them and concentrated on the main matters of efficiently running the King's Government and consolidating his own position at the head of affairs.

The younger Pitt lacked the political passion of his father or of his own reckless opponent Charles Fox. He was calm, aloof, and calculating, but with all his father's arrogance. He lacked 'commitment'; but for practical ability in administration and attention to detail, he was among the handful of the very greatest Prime Ministers, with Walpole, Peel, and Gladstone.

Nothing succeeds like success. The very young Minister, brought in as a 'dark horse' by the King in 1783 to lead a minority administration, impressed everybody. Winning the 1784 election by a combination of genuine popularity (as against the discredited Fox and North) and the customary electoral 'management', he gradually built up his position till he appeared immovable. As Fox declaimed impotently against him, more and more of the Tory supporters of North, and even some of the Foxites, came over to him, sailing with the wind. The City of London, and business interests generally, were behind him, as the country rapidly recovered from the disasters of the American War. His most influential capture from the Northites was Dundas, powerful because of his control of patronage in both Scotland and India. And all the time Pitt and the King ("as necessary to one another as husband and wife") built up their position in the House of Lords with carefully calculated new creations, drawn largely from the smaller gentry and the mercantile and professional classes, and eventually outnumbering the Whig magnates.

Pitt's most successful work was the least sensational. He laboured constantly to eradicate waste from the administration and to promote efficiency. One way was to get rid of sinecures. Another was to make one Civil Service department do the work previously shared between four, or twelve folios house the records previously kept in sixty, with the attendant saving in clerks and their salaries. In a multitude of such minor matters Pitt promoted economy. The modern Budget really begins with Pitt's overhaul of the system of Government accounting. In all such matters he wielded a mastery which he explicitly justified:

> There should be an avowed and real minister possessing the chief weight in council and the principal place in the confidence of the King. In that respect there can be no rivalry or division of power. That power ought to rest with the person generally called the First Minister; and that minister ought ... to be the person at the head of the finances. . . .

In the same cause of efficiency, Pitt made several attempts to stop up the holes through which the national revenues had been leaking away. He made the smuggling of tea unprofitable, by the drastic reduction of the duty from 112–119 per cent to 12½–25 per cent. He succeeded in doing what Walpole had failed to do in 1733—extend the excise system to wine and tobacco. He secured an Act authorizing the confiscation of certain types of ship built specially for smuggling and found either at anchor or 'hovering' within four miles of the coast. Altogether, he did a great deal to make life harder for the smuggler.

In his new taxation he showed resource and eventually real boldness. He first put a tax on racehorses, carriage-horses, hackney carriages, personal servants, shopkeepers, windows, hair-powder, dogs, watches and clocks, and various other articles. Later, under the demands of war, he both trebled his original taxes on many of these items, and also underlined the element in them of taxing luxuries; a man with ten servants would pay more than ten times the tax of a man having one only, and so forth. Some of these taxes were failures, others open to criticism; the window tax has been blamed for encouraging the bricking-up of windows and exclusion of light, though houses with fewer than seven windows he later exempted. The national lottery begun in 1784 (it lasted forty years) was attacked by some on moral grounds. But, in any case, the great expenses of the war with France eventually forced altogether more radical thoughts on taxation; and Pitt in 1799 took a step which only a leader enjoying general confidence would have dared to take, and only then at a moment of crisis. He imposed a tax on income itself, again using the principle of a higher rate of tax on the rich. Incomes under £60 a year were exempt. The income tax proved tolerable at first only for the war's duration; but it was the prototype of the most important tax of modern times.

Before the war with France broke out in 1793, Pitt was also successfully carrying through the idea which had attracted so many of his predecessors, from the days of Stanhope and Walpole—a Sinking Fund to whittle down the National Debt. Determined not to allow a repetition of Walpole's failure, he earmarked a guaranteed £1,000,000 a year, which would in itself be invested to accumulate at compound interest; and by

1793 he had cut the National Debt by £10,000,000. But thereafter his very determination led him to the ludicrous: in order to find the annual million in wartime, new money was borrowed at high interest in order to repay old debt incurred at low interest.

The young Pitt had always been ready to learn from the intellectuals of his day. "Nay, we will stand until you are seated," he once said to Adam Smith at a public dinner, "for we are all your scholars." Pitt's version of the Sinking Fund owed much to Price.[1] The income tax had been advocated by Adam Smith. And until the war came to blight them Pitt had various schemes for pursuing Smith's free-trade theories. His one potentially important achievement was the 1786 Commercial Treaty with France. Promoting trade with a likely enemy was an idea abhorrent to mercantilist thought; but Pitt boldly opened British ports to French products and slashed the duties on wines and brandy (incidentally still further damaging the smuggler). At the same time he secured entry into France, at similarly reduced duties, for British textiles, hardware, pottery, and other manufactures. Passports, too, were mutually abolished, and religious toleration for resident aliens reciprocally guaranteed. Like so much else begun in this decade, the French Treaty was swallowed up in the forthcoming war. It did, however, indicate the lines on which freer trade was to develop in the nineteenth century.

All Pitt's schemes needed long years of peace to bear fruit, and as late as 1792 he confidently anticipated them. Imports and exports were both soaring; the revenues were buoyant; France, consumed with revolution, no longer appeared to constitute a danger. Britain had recovered with wonderful speed from the disastrous era of the American War; "unquestionably," Pitt said, "there never was a time when a durable peace might more reasonably be expected than at the present moment." Such confidence, which was shared by his friends and foes, allowed expenditure on the Navy to be kept low, and held out the pleasing prospect, very soon to be dashed, of a general reduction of taxes.

[1] See p. 239.

2. Imperial and Foreign Policy

Pitt's Indian settlement has already been discussed.[2] In two other colonial areas he made decisions that had far-reaching effects.

Sailors from the Dutch East Indies, of whom Tasman is the most famous, had discovered many stretches of the Australian and New Zealand coasts in the seventeenth century, but Holland had made no attempt to colonize these lands. When the Englishman Cook made his three great voyages between 1768 and 1779 he was on no colonial mission; his explorations were geographical and scientific. His first and most important voyage was undertaken for the Royal Society, partly in order that scientists might observe the transit of Venus from the most favourable position, Tahiti, and partly so that more accurate knowledge might be obtained of the coastline of the land masses in these southern seas. In the course of this first voyage Cook surveyed the east coast of Australia, and claimed it for Britain. This in itself meant little, since no colonists were forthcoming to settle there. Australia, or part of it, might still have become Dutch, or French, if their settlers had arrived there first. The issue was settled by Pitt in the strangest manner: the Home Secretary, Lord Sydney, persuaded him that, since America was no longer available for transportation of felons, Captain Cook's 'Botany Bay' would do very well instead. So Australia became England's 'Siberia', and for over thirty years (till almost the end of our period) convicts outnumbered free emigrants. No-one will claim for Pitt any imperial vision here.

In Canada he faced what seemed then to be more formidable decisions. For twenty years after the conquest of 1759–60 Canada remained a land of Frenchmen and Indians; but after the American revolt the district of Ontario (then the 'Far West') was flooded with British loyalists. Canada now had two peoples, with two separate ways of life. Furthermore, these new British Canadians pressed for the British rights they were used to—a popular assembly, habeas corpus, the jury system, and so forth. The French were restive at seeing their privileges

[2] See above, p. 284.

under the Quebec Act of 1774 whittled down, and their ways challenged by the newcomers. For the time being Pitt decided that there must be two Canadas, a French and a British; his Canada Act of 1791 may be seen as an exercise in 'divide and rule'. And although each province was given its popular assembly, care was taken to see that effective power remained in the hands of the governor and his council. This temporary answer of Pitt to the Canadian question survived the Napoleonic Wars and the American invasion of 1812; but the troubles of the next generation demanded new solutions.

In the true far west of what is modern Canada Pitt also acted with decision. In 1790 Spain, claiming the entire Pacific coastline of America as far north as the Alaskan border, attempted to expel British settlers from Nootka Sound in Vancouver Island, and seized their fishing vessels. Pitt and Parliament, knowing Spain to be unable to count on any support from a France in the grip of revolution, insisted on the right of the British to settle, at least in non-Spanish areas, and threatened war. Spain retreated, and the extreme west (vaguely known as California or Oregon) still remained no-man's (or any-man's) land for long years to come. It happens that Nootka Sound is almost exactly on the 49th parallel of latitude, the very line agreed upon, half a century later, for the mainland southern border of Canada, though by that time Canada's rival claimant was not Spain but the USA. Pitt's action in 1790 at least ensured Canada's potential ability to exploit her vast western lands.

His attempt, however, to threaten Catherine the Great of Russia was a total failure. Russian armies had invaded the Crimea and captured Ochakov, near Odessa, from the Turks. Would Turkey collapse, as Poland had? And if Russia occupied Constantinople, would not this be a threat to British trade routes? Here was, in effect, the 'Eastern Question' that troubled Britain for another century or more. But it was Catherine who stood firm, not Pitt. Anxious to avoid the expense of war, and conscious that his somewhat skimped Navy would be hard pressed in a Black Sea campaign, he lamely but prudently withdrew his demand that the Russians abandon Ochakov (1791).

Nearer home, Pitt's principal preoccupation, before the war with France, was to protect the independence of the Netherlands, threatened by a French-supported revolt against the House of Orange. When a Prussian force intervened to thwart these French designs Pitt hastened to give diplomatic support; and in 1788 he managed to bring off a triple alliance between Holland, Prussia, and Britain. The diplomatic isolation of Britain, complete since the American War, was thus ended.

3. The Impact of the French Revolution

When the Bastille fell in July 1789, and the French proceeded to abolish the remaining relics of feudalism and to limit the powers of their king, there was a general welcome in Britain. Pitt's own reactions were typical of moderate opinion: when "the present convulsions" were over, France, he thought, would "enjoy just that kind of liberty which I venerate". Many of the Whigs went further, seeing France as at last emulating their own glorious revolution of a century earlier. Fox hailed the fall of the Bastille with extravagant praise: "How much the greatest event it is that ever happened in the world, and how much the best!" Many Nonconformists and Radicals spoke in similar terms: the French, said Dr Price, were "starting from sleep". And many of the young writers of the day felt their imagination stirred by the prevalent winds of political idealism —among them Burns, Hazlitt, Southey, Coleridge, Blake (who went so far as to wear in public the red cap of Liberty), and Wordsworth, who saw "human nature seeming born again".

One great voice was raised against this briefly popular optimism. In 1790 Burke published his *Reflections on the Revolution in France*, a work of noble diction and intense sincerity, which transcended the circumstances of its origin and became the classic statement of conservative philosophy.[3] A hostile critic might reasonably argue that for Burke the only good revolutions were past ones; 1688 in England was one thing, 1789 in France quite another. But Burke would not interpret 1688 as a 'revolution', in the French sense, at all; for

[3] Together with *An Appeal from the New to the Old Whigs* (1791).

him it represented the stand of the Whigs, the protectors of Liberty, against James II's attacks on the Constitution. The Whigs were thus the truest of conservatives. The British constitution, wrote Burke, was composed of three harmonious elements, the monarchic, the aristocratic, and the democratic. The year 1688 had presented the successful attempt of the second two to avoid being overwhelmed by the first. The French, on the other hand, had now impiously broken with their traditions. They had severed the bonds that linked Church with State and present with past. In the name of a false liberty they had destroyed their true heritage. From this bad beginning worse would ensue: the quest for ever more popular measures would put the country at the mercy of demagogues; the new paper money would become worthless; Christianity would give way to atheism; anarchy and terror would create a situation from which a military dictator must emerge.

Democracy, for Burke, was a false god. He had earlier been one of the most eloquent apologists for the American revolutionaries, whose philosophy was indeed based on democratic principles and the rights of man. Now, however, shocked by events in France, he denied that peoples had the right to overthrow unpopular Governments. Admittedly "a state without the means of some change is without the means of its conservation", and there were things in France that had needed reforming; but order and continuity were essential preconditions of liberty. Man could not knock down and rebuild at will. Civilization was like a clock; only a fool would take so sensitive and complicated a machine to pieces and think he could put it together again to suit his pleasure.

As events in France proceeded to fulfil, and even exceed, many of Burke's prophecies, the friends of the French Revolution found themselves a shrinking and unpopular minority. In Parliament Fox was still at their head, excusing the French excesses as the inevitable consequences of a sudden newfound liberty, and pressing for parliamentary reform in Britain. He proclaimed very clearly, too, the danger that panic fear of the contagion of revolution would extinguish our own precious liberty. The societies that had been formed in Britain to welcome the events of 1789 in France soon found themselves in severe trouble: among them the Society for Constitutional Information, the Society of Friends of the People (founded by enthusiastic young aristocrats, among them the future Lord Grey), and the Corresponding Society (founded by the shoemaker, Thomas Hardy; the first political association of working men in England). The radical Nonconformists, Price and Priestley, were intensely unpopular; and in Birmingham a mob, encouraged by some Anglican clergymen and magistrates, sacked the houses of Dissenters, Priestley's among them, with its precious laboratory. For two days Birmingham suffered its counterpart of the Gordon riots, with the Nonconformists in the place of the Catholics; mobs yelled in ignorant fury, "No philosophers! Church and King!" until the Dragoons rode in to settle them.

The most uncompromising of the English champions of the French Revolution was the man who had been one of the movers of the American—Tom Paine. As a political philosopher he stands at the opposite pole to Burke, and his *Rights of Man*, indeed, originated as a counterblast to Burke's *Reflections*. According to Paine, Burke, with his eloquent praise of traditional France and his sympathy for the victims of the Revolution, "pities the plumage but forgets the dying bird". For Paine the institutions of both France and Britain were a tissue of injustice and unreason. Society and government should be based on reason; and reason required the abolition of hereditary monarchy, of the House of Lords, and of the Established Church; in their place there should be manhood suffrage and complete religious freedom. Reason also demanded free trade (and, flowing from this, universal peace); the consequent reduction of expenditure on armaments would permit a programme of public work for the unemployed, compulsory education, family allowances, and old-age pensions. Members of Parliament should be paid, and the country divided into equal electoral areas. It is not surprising that such sentiments and proposals made Paine's book the gospel of the Radicals for at least two generations.

The aristocratic world of 1791 was right to be alarmed at Tom Paine, for the acceptance of his opinions would have heralded its collapse; his name became a synonym for republican atheism, though he was, in fact, a Deist. Paine, moreover, was a man of the people, and his direct style made him a very readable writer. His impact, therefore, was far greater than that of other radical theorists of the time, such as William Godwin (Shelley's father-in-law) whose *Political Justice* (1793) was every bit as damning of the old aristocratic regimes and as starry-eyed concerning the new one in France—the "morning of reason". Pitt's Government could afford to leave in relative peace the idealistic Godwin and his remarkable wife, Mary Wollstonecraft, the first champion of the 'rights of woman'; but already, before the publication of Part Two of *The Rights of Man*, it had decided to arrest Paine on a charge of libel. Paine, however, managed to get away, just in time, to France, where his hostility to the Terror and Louis's execution subsequently brought him very near to the guillotine.

The enormous popularity of Paine's *Rights of Man*, which sold 200,000 copies in 1793 alone, was certainly one of the chief factors causing something like panic in the British ruling classes. Any discussion of radical principles, any publication of Painite tendencies, became hazardous; and for thirty years and more it was an act of rash devotion for any publisher to reprint Paine's books or for any bookseller to offer them for sale. The irascible Lord Braxfield, one of the Scottish judges, even ruled that *any* criticism of the British constitution was seditious, since the British constitution was perfect. It was Braxfield who sentenced Thomas Muir, of the Scottish Friends of the People, to fourteen years' transportation and Thomas Palmer to seven years—two of the most savage sentences of modern times. Muir's principal offence was to have visited France. In England a labourer received a five-year sentence for shouting "No George! No war!" Many similar prosecutions followed, though there was a notable victory for the impartiality of English justice when in 1794 Hardy, Horne Tooke, Thelwall, and ten other advocates of reform were acquitted of high treason by a London jury. For a time the reformers were cock-a-hoop, increasing fears that Jacobinism would soon be crossing the Channel; and the poor harvest of 1794, rising prices, popular distress, bread riots, and in 1795 a stone thrown at the King's coach, all confirmed Pitt in his already repressive mood. Habeas corpus had already been temporarily suspended (1794). In 1795 a Seditious Meetings Act prohibited gatherings of more than fifty persons except by magistrate's licence, and a Treasonable Practices Act rendered anyone attacking the Constitution liable to seven years' transportation, a measure Braxfield in Scotland had already anticipated. The 1797 mutinies in the Navy contributed to the general mood of apprehension. On the whole, these repressive measures fulfilled their intention. Only a minority of the working class supported Paine and the reformers; war patriotism, Methodism, and political apathy proved of greater strength than 'Jacobinism'; and there was hardly a murmur in 1799 when the Government finally suppressed the Corresponding Society altogether. In the same year Pitt made all industrial combinations illegal, and although in theory this operated against employers as well as employees, in fact it had the effect of driving trade unions underground and rendering those accused of belonging to them liable to severe sentences from local magistrates. Those same magistrates (and two only[4] sufficed to constitute a bench) might well be themselves the employers of the accused. Thus, in the cause of the state's security in wartime, Pitt's Combination Acts made trade unionism into 'conspiracy' and at the same time enabled the employing classes to hold down wages in the face of a rapidly rising cost of living. In the countryside ferocious game laws hung over the head of any man rash or desperate enough to try taking a rabbit to feed his half-starved family. The aristocratic world that Paine the democrat had challenged remained for many years yet in secure, if sometimes nervous, control.

Of the principal parliamentary leaders, only Fox continued to argue the French cause sympathetically; and he did so even after the outbreak of war in 1793. Burke's hostility not only to revolution, but now even to moderate reform, had become fanatical by that time. In his last years he was a man of a fixed idea, given to long and melodramatic speeches, including one

[4] The first anti-combination Act of 1799 allowed one magistrate only to suffice; but Sheridan and others of the Whigs managed to secure an amending Act in 1800.

in which he flung a dagger on to the floor of the House to point the direness of the Jacobin threat. With their two greatest figures, Burke and Fox, at loggerheads, the Whigs had to choose between them; and in 1794 many of them went over to the more popular and patriotic cause of Burke and Pitt. Most members agreed with Windham: "Who would repair their house in a hurricane?" Fox was left at the head of a small group—small but of the greatest significance, for the time was to come when it was important that there should be one of the old aristocratic parties that had never ceased to fly the flag of reform. One of the younger Foxites was Grey, whose Ministry in 1832 carried the great Reform Act.

4. Pitt and the War (1793–97)

In 1792 Pitt had foreseen fifteen years of peace and tranquillity, and made no moves to increase taxation or the strength of the armed forces. Even in 1793, when French revolutionary armies broke into the Rhineland and Belgium, and Jacobin militants proclaimed "war on the tyrants", Pitt was not unduly alarmed. He was no crusader (as Wilberforce had found to his regret); he had none of Burke's passion, or Windham's, to see the British sword "leap from its scabbard" to plunge into the unclean body of the Revolution. It was not until the French armies overran the great anchorages of the Scheldt, opening Antwerp to the ships of all nations, that the practical and official mind of Pitt took serious alarm. Ever since the Treaty of Utrecht, Britain had enjoyed a special privilege in the Scheldt, and it was a well-tried principle of British policy to deny the Netherlands coastline to a hostile Great Power. Besides, Pitt had recently concluded an alliance with Holland, as with Prussia; and the Dutch now faced invasion.

Thus war began in 1793, and Pitt (unlike Burke) had every confidence that it would be brief. France was in the hands, apparently, of a clamouring rabble. Her finances were in disarray. Counter-revolutionary forces were strong in the west and south. Against her were ranged the Dutch, the British, the Austrians, the Prussians. It was not reasonable to suppose that she could survive, still less that she could extend her aggression. It is easy to blame Pitt for underestimating the enemy, and he did make a misjudgment which can now be seen as colossal. He totally failed to comprehend the dynamic power of the Revolution and the fanatical strength of "a people in arms". He wrongly thought that monetary inflation and financial weakness would disable France. He did not bargain for the brilliant military organization of Carnot, still less for the genius of Napoleon. He expected an orthodox eighteenth-century war, in which British guineas and sea-power would together play a decisive part. He ought not to be too severely blamed for finding himself at grips with so unexpected a monster, or for floundering in the toils of this first great modern war of ideologies.

Basic to any strategy that Pitt might have chosen to pursue in 1793-94 was his father's policy of an anti-French European coalition, subsidized by British gold. In military and naval operations there was open to him a choice of at least four possible courses. Britain could send an army to Flanders and the Netherlands, to co-operate with the forces of the other allies and strike southward to Paris. She could send ships and troops to Toulon, where counter-revolutionary French gained control of the port and offered entry to the British. She could similarly land forces in western France, where a fierce struggle was going on in La Vendée and Brittany between Jacobins and Royalists. Or she could adopt the imperial strategy of Chatham, rely on her navy to dominate the oceans, and continue the conquest of the West Indian islands, those still immensely valued prizes. Pitt attempted all four of these operations, and failed in all of them.

While he was still in 1793 preparing a leisurely scheme for striking northward from Toulon in the spring of the following year, Carnot's troops (their artillery commanded by one Bonaparte) pounced on the port, and Hood had no option but to withdraw. It was small comfort that he had first destroyed thirteen French warships and the naval arsenal. As for the royalist rising in the west, where Burke urged that we should concentrate all our assistance, the republican armies were able to wreak swift and terrible vengeance there before the British were ready to attack. British battleships were still in harbour completing their crews while the French were blockading the royalist-held Brittany coast, and when the British were ready to sail it was already too late. Nantes, the intended base, was firmly in republican hands. When the British later assisted a landing of émigré Royalists at Quiberon, these were captured as they landed, in sight of the ships.

In the north the British expeditionary force under the Duke of York, George III's second son, though it failed to take Dunkirk and was very far from marching triumphantly on Paris, as optimists had expected, campaigned doggedly in Flanders. If only there had been a modicum of co-operation between the Allies, even the fanatical zeal of the French army could hardly have prevented the fall of Paris. The Austrians, however, under Coburg, moved with textbook deliberation, while the Prussians remained inactive, waiting for an Austrian victory. The French, gambling on this Prussian lethargy, suddenly attacked the flank of the Austrians, forced their withdrawal, and pushed the British back to the line of the river Waal. Prussia, having pocketed Pitt's subsidy, withdrew from the war, and concentrated on securing her share of the last partition of Poland. The Duke of York's army, though more than half its infantry was incapacitated by typhus, wounds, or exposure, hoped at least that winter would provide the traditional respite from campaigning. But in January 1795, exploiting the bitterly cold weather that froze the river and brought renewed misery to the wretched English, the French crossed the Waal and drove the Duke of York's remnants, hungry, shivering, and demoralized, through Holland to the North German coast. Six thousand perished in four days, and only a small force survived to be evacuated from Bremen by the Navy. The whole of the Netherlands was lost; the French set up a puppet Dutch state, the Batavian Republic; the Dutch ships and harbours were all in the hands of France. The Duke of York's campaign had been an almost total disaster. Britain's sole consolation arose from her retaliatory occupation of Dutch colonies. Both the Cape of Good Hope and Ceylon were taken over.

Toulon, western France, and the Low Countries had all been starved of men by the demands of the fourth theatre of war, the West Indies. Here Pitt, backed by the same com-

mercial interests that had supported Chatham, aimed to continue his father's policy and complete his work, but the West
Indies hungrily swallowed men and hopes alike. Eighty
thousand British troops were put out of action in three years,
half of them by death, though few at the hands of the official
enemy. Yellow fever and the inadequacy of the medical provision combined to make the West Indian campaigns of 1793–
1796 some of the most terrible in the history of the British
Army. Pitt and his Ministers (in the words of Sir John
Fortescue, the Army's historian) "poured their troops into these
pestilent islands, in the expectation that they would destroy
the power of France, only to discover, when it was too late,
that they had practically destroyed the British army". Things
were made still worse by Britain's having to use her troops not
only against the French but also against the slaves, who had
risen in revolt in the French islands. All men are equal,
declared the revolutionaries in France, and championed the
rights of the Negroes against the interests of their planter
masters. When, consequently, Haiti (San Domingo) became
engulfed in a murderous Negro uprising, which later spread to
the other islands, British troops were obliged to intervene to
prevent the total extermination of the French and Spanish
planters. A bitter price was paid all round—by the white
planters, by both British and French troops, by the defeated
slave rebels—in those years of disease, revenge, and terror.
The final British rewards were a thin return for the expenditure
of so much misery and so many lives: the French islands of
Saint Lucia and Tobago, and the Spanish island of Trinidad.

The Navy was very severely tested in these early years of the
war. Anxious as he had always been to economize, and spending less on the Navy in the pre-war decade than the Navy
would have liked, Pitt still started war with 113 battleships (to
France's 76). Unhappily only a dozen were in actual commission, and it took more than a stroke of the pen to make the
rest so. The acutest need was for men, and although in 1794
Parliament voted to provide 85,000 of them, the only way they
could be had (in a 'free' country where conscription was un-
dreamt of) was by press-ganging merchant sailors as they
returned to home ports. Even so, a big opportunity was lost in

that year, when the French, after a bad harvest and years of agricultural disorganization, faced famine unless a big grain convoy from America could get through. Admiral Howe's blockade was loose. First, it permitted a French naval support force to sail out to escort the cargo fleet. Then, when the combined French flotilla approached its home waters, Howe, hampered by fog, missed the more vital prey and allowed his ships to be lured away by the French escort ships, while the food supplies sailed unscathed into Brest. Nevertheless, Howe, that tough veteran, did not go without his victory. On the "Glorious First of June" he inflicted a crushing defeat upon the French escorting force and returned home a hero. But Britain had lost another chance of putting an early end to the war.

In the Mediterranean the Fleet, expelled from Toulon, had set itself up in Corsica and Elba. (It was in storming Calvi in Corsica that the dashing Captain Nelson lost an eye.) The British, however, were unable to bring the assistance they had promised to the Austrians attacking in southern France during 1795; and they allowed the French Navy to operate damagingly from Toulon. One of its squadrons captured an entire convoy of thirty-one merchant ships bound for the Near East, with their escorting battleships—an exploit that severely shook the City of London. When in 1796 the French turned the tables on the Austrians and under Bonaparte advanced triumphantly through northern Italy, Britain faced defeat as complete in the Mediterranean as she had already faced in the Low Countries. Spain chose the moment to make a new alliance with France. Austria was forced to make peace (1797). The Mediterranean became untenable by British ships, and they withdrew. Only Gibraltar held.

"The misfortune of our situation", wrote George III, "is that we have too many objects to attend to, and our force consequently must be too weak at each place." It was a concise epitaph on the policies of Pitt and his War Secretaries, Dundas and Windham, and on the First Coalition that finally expired in 1797.

5. The Nelson Era (1797–1805)

Everything in 1797 depended on the Fleet. Driven from the Continent and from Mediterranean waters, threatened by revolution in Ireland, bereft of allies, and confronted by the three powerful navies of France, Holland, and Spain, Britain faced a serious danger of invasion. Pitt, realistically facing the situation, made moves in the direction of peace, against the judgment of Burke, Windham, and the King; but the Government of France (the Directors) would have none of it, and Bonaparte confidently prepared to strike across the Channel.

Worst of all, the Fleet was mutinous. Its suddenly swollen numbers, now 120,000, were made up from the 'quota' men conscripted from every parish; from Irishmen, foreigners, riff-raff, unemployables; but chiefly from press-ganged merchant sailors and fishermen. Discipline was enforced by the lash, even in 'good' ships; in the worst, a capricious tyrant like Bligh of the *Bounty* could tax a hero's loyalty. Food was bad and leave scarce. But, worst of all, naval pay stood at only a quarter of the merchant rates; it was often grossly in arrears; and rising prices meant that wives and families were some-times half starving. The Admiralty, having ignored the men's petitions for redress, suddenly found itself faced with a Spit-head fleet that had run up red flags and dumped its officers ashore, while still protesting its patriotism and readiness to fight. At Plymouth there was similar mutiny. No sooner had Howe managed to settle these troubles, largely by conceding the men's just demands, than the fleet in the Thames estuary followed the Spithead example. They ignored the Spithead terms of settlement, and were headed, unlike the men at Portsmouth, by 'Jacobin' leaders. Chief among them, Richard Parker set himself up in admiral's state, called himself President, and contemplated taking the Nore fleet over to the enemy. This not only shocked the comfortable patriotism of the civilian population; it was too much for most of the men. Dissensions broke up the Nore 'revolution'. Some leaders fled to France, 412 were tried and found guilty, 300 pardoned, 84 flogged or imprisoned, 28, Parker among them, hanged.

Two naval victories served to sustain the British as they

braced themselves to meet invasion. In February 1797, just before the Mutinies, Jervis with the Lisbon squadron beat back off Cape St Vincent a much larger Spanish fleet heading from Cadiz to join the French at Brest. This was the occasion on which Commodore Nelson, single-minded for heroic adventure, first showed his supreme combination of fighting virtues— courage, skill, and willingness to take risky initiatives—the Nelson touch. It was his breaking of the Spanish line and dare-devil boarding of two Spanish ships at Cape St Vincent that first made him the national idol he was to remain until his death and after. Eight months later, after the collapse of its mutiny, the Nore fleet, under the formidable Admiral Duncan, vindicated its patriotism and fighting qualities by putting the Dutch Navy out of action off Texel (Battle of Camperdown, October 1797). The combined effect of these two resounding victories was to reduce French hopes of the projected Franco-Dutch invasion of Ireland, and to reinforce British resolve. Pitt, tenacious and eloquent in adversity, now found himself leader of a broadly united House of Commons and nation. George III was kept busy, daily signing new royal commissions for local Volunteers, who in a variety of helmets and cockades, bearskins, and breastplates, drilled with patriotic seriousness in town squares and on village greens throughout the land. Indefatigable, Pitt set about building the Second Coalition to counter victorious France; and to further this end he ordered the Fleet to re-enter the Mediterranean—a bold move, in view of the continuing risk of invasion at home. Commanding the new Mediterranean squadron was the recently promoted Nelson.

Pitt and Dundas, confronted now with rebellion in Ireland, interpreted Bonaparte's massive preparations in the south as part of a grand strategy aimed at that vulnerable island. Bonaparte, however, was indulging more grandiose visions: a combined military, naval, and cultural descent upon Egypt; and, beyond, a tentative design for the destruction of British power in India. A large convoy set out from Toulon; took Malta *en route* from the Knights of St John; and proceeded safely to Alexandria. Nelson, correctly guessing its destination, and narrowly missing (through his shortage of frigates) the chance

of totally destroying it in mid-sea, at last came up with the
French battle fleet anchored in Abukir Bay, near Alexandria.
Here, in August 1798, the memory of weeks of fretting and
frustration—indeed, of much of the failure of the previous five
years—was annihilated, together with the Toulon fleet, in one
night's ferocious fighting. It was a victory as classic as it was
devastating. With night falling and against an enemy holding
all the advantages of a chosen defensive situation, Nelson and
his captains (his "band of brothers") put into action plans, long
prepared and devotedly discussed, for concentrating the
weight of fire at a critical point in the enemy line and breaking
it before the rest of its ships could intervene. Risks were taken,
in shoal water, so surprising that the French were nonplussed
by them, and found themselves simultaneously attacked from
the seaward and from the landward side, where their batteries
were not even cleared for fire. The destruction wrought upon
them was murderous: 2000 killed or drowned, 3500 captured,
eleven out of thirteen battleships sunk or taken. The Battle of
the Nile demonstrated that, despite the mutinies and all that
had caused them, the morale, gunnery, and tactical skill of the
British fleet were far superior to the enemy's. A nation whose
starved appetite for news of victory had been whetted by Cape
St Vincent and Camperdown now made a handsome meal of
Nelson and his triumph. All the church bells pealed for the
greatest trouncing of an enemy at sea since the Spanish
Armada. Napoleon might indeed proceed to the conquest of
Egypt and much of Palestine, but his grand design of conquer-
ing Britain in the Indian Ocean was now botched. His army,
tormented by plague, thwarted again by British sea-power at
the siege of Acre, melted away. His ally Tipu Sahib in India
was soon to be defeated. Malta was taken by the British, and
Minorca once again retaken. Nelson's Navy dominated the
Mediterranean, and hopes continued to rise as the Second
Coalition (of Britain, Russia, Turkey, Portugal, and the Two
Sicilies) took shape.

They were soon to be shattered. After some early victories,
when the British captured what was left of the Dutch fleet
after Camperdown, and Austrians and Russians campaigned
successfully in North Italy, the old story of military failure was

repeated. A second expedition under the Duke of York to the Netherlands (1799), intended as a joint Anglo-Russian offensive, came to a halt on the Helder peninsula north of Amsterdam and was withdrawn. Bonaparte, abandoning the battered and diseased survivors of his Army of Egypt, returned to France, overthrew the Directory, and re-asserted his dynamic authority. Crossing the Great Saint Bernard pass, he beat the Austrians at Marengo after a swift campaign, while Moreau defeated them at Hohenlinden. British plans to assist their allies in Italy collapsed, and Abercromby's expedition aimed at Cadiz came to nothing. Russia and the Two Sicilies withdrew from the Coalition, which was now in rags. At home, trade and industry were soaring, but so were prices, and agricultural wages lagged far behind them. The country longed for peace. Once more, by 1800, Britain found isolation in Europe and distress at home.

The Tsar of Russia had not only deserted the Coalition; he had conceived a violent admiration for Bonaparte and revived the twenty-year-old combination of the Armed Neutrality of the North to resist the British Navy's practice of searching neutral vessels. Sweden, Prussia, and Denmark joined him in closing North Germany and the Baltic to British ships. For Britain this was a dangerous threat, both to her wheat supplies (and these were years of scarcity), and to her vital naval stores. Consequently, a fleet under Hyde Parker was sent to attempt the destruction or seizure of the Danish Navy. Twelve battleships, led by Nelson, penetrated Copenhagen harbour, a perilous business in face of the fortress batteries protecting it. Three ships went aground. Signalled by Parker to break off the costly engagement, Nelson turned to Captain Foley of the *Elephant.* "Now damn me if I do," he said. "You know, Foley, I have only one eye—I have a right to be blind sometimes." Fortunately for his career and for the British situation at sea, his calculation of risk again proved sound. All seventeen of the Danish first-line ships were sunk, burned, or captured (1801). The slaughter, of both the enemy and the British, was the worst Nelson ever saw, and he took no joy in it. Danes, unlike Frenchmen, he did not regard as proper victims of English powder and shot.

By the time Copenhagen was fought, Pitt had resigned on the issue of Catholic Emancipation,[5] and Addington (later Lord Sidmouth) was Prime Minister. To the issues of peace and war this change made small difference. It merely confirmed tendencies, already strong, favouring negotiations with the enemy. Peace was on the way, to the general relief. In Egypt, Abercromby was mopping up the last scarecrow veterans of Bonaparte's Army of Egypt, but the news of their surrender did not reach London till the day after the even better news that terms had been agreed at Amiens. Bonaparte was left in control of half Europe, but at least his grandest schemes had been blocked. Britannia still ruled the waves. In India the area of British-controlled territory had been much increased. Hungry and rioting, the mob at home hoped that peace would bring plenty. The ruling class hoped it would bring stability. Yet already, by the time that the Treaty of Amiens was finally signed (1802), and English tourists began flocking to France, it was becoming plain that Bonaparte regarded the peace merely as affording a breathing space.

His visions of conquest expanded as inevitably as ripples in a pond. The Treaty of Amiens had restored French possessions in the West Indies; Bonaparte now acquired from Spain that vast area known as Louisiana, and dreamed of a French empire extending from the Caribbean to California. In Europe he secured, also from Spain, Elba and Parma; he annexed Piedmont, and took firm military hold of northern Italy in general, as well as Holland and Switzerland. Knowing that one day he must defeat Britain, he rapidly rebuilt his weakened Navy, at a time when Addington's Government, in the interests of economy, was cutting back the Royal Navy's manpower from 130,000 to 70,000. (To the very temporary joy of the propertied classes, Addington also abolished income tax.) The one trump card that the peace of Amiens had left in British hands was Malta. Even that Britain had undertaken to surrender; but, seeing which way the play was going, she sensibly held on to her most powerful card. Even Addington and his colleagues, more than anxious for peace, could not fail to see that a resumption of the war was inevitable. In May 1803 they declared it.

[5] See Chapter 7, Sections 8 and 9.

It was to be, they hoped, a defensive war only, and therefore an inexpensive one. (Income tax was reintroduced, but at
half-rate.) Bonaparte's own strategy was soon plain. Selling
Louisiana to the USA, he began building a great armada of
shallow-draught invasion vessels for an onslaught on England,
and set up seven big military camps between the mouths of the
Seine and Rhine. Fortunately for the British, he seriously
bungled his plans, and lost vital time when he had to switch
from his original, unpractical idea, of invasion by a great surge
of troop-carrying assault craft, to the more orthodox plan of
having transports pure and simple, protected by warships
whose aim was to gain temporary mastery of the Channel.
Ever an optimist, he claimed that six hours' local naval
supremacy would be sufficient for him.

Meanwhile Pitt was back in place of Addington; never again
the old Pitt, with a nearly unanimous Commons behind him;
having to use a great deal of his energy in party manœuvre;
but as assiduous as ever, fighting not the Addingtonian war of
pure defence, but probing for enemy weaknesses, and seeking
yet again to rebuild the grand alliance that would destroy this
new colossus of Europe. Bonaparte was now the Emperor
Napoleon, self-elevated, self-crowned.

There were two ways of defending Britain against invasion.
One was obvious: by getting every man and ship into the
Navy, by raising forces for home defence, by building defensive fortifications along the Channel and North Sea coasts, and
so forth. The other, which in the event proved successful,
was by reviving the European coalition and thereby forcing
Napoleon to withdraw his forces from their invasion stations
on the Channel. The diplomatic task was hard. Austria, Prussia,
and the other continental powers had lost all spirit for an anti-
revolutionary crusade. Only Russia at first made any response
to Pitt's overtures, and the combined operations put in hand
were at first insufficient to distract Napoleon at Boulogne from
his grand design.

An essential preliminary to this was a general breaking-out
of French and Spanish squadrons to make a rendezvous off
Martinique, and a swift doubling-back to the Western
Approaches, whence they would fight their way up-Channel

to Boulogne, to support the Grand Army's assault on southern England. As early as January 1805, Villeneuve's Toulon fleet left harbour and sent Nelson on a wild-goose chase to Greece and Egypt before he discovered that it had returned safely to Toulon. The Brest fleet next attempted a sortie, but failed to get away. By April, Villeneuve had again sailed, and this time got clean away, making westward for Martinique, followed by the Spanish squadron from Cadiz. Nelson was in a predicament. He knew a British troop convoy was *en route* for Malta, needing his protection. He knew the point of decision must ultimately lie in the Channel approaches. He knew that Villeneuve, West-Indies-bound, was likely to do great damage there, and that it was his duty to seek him out and destroy him. Detaching *Royal Sovereign* to protect the convoy, he decided to give chase and sailed for Jamaica. Arriving there, failing to find the French, surmising the enemy strategy, he made all speed back to Europe. There, off Ushant, the British had mustered all available ships under Calder to meet the returning French and Spanish under Villeneuve. Calder did meet them and inflicted damage, but his leadership was found wanting. For failing "to take and destroy every ship of the enemy" he was reprimanded. At the end of July Nelson was in Gibraltar and Villeneuve in Vigo. The main battle was still to be fought.

In May, Napoleon, unsatisfied as merely Emperor of France, proclaimed himself King of Italy. What Pitt had been unable to achieve, Napoleon now achieved: Austria was provoked to join the Third Coalition. So, with continental armies massing against him, he could no longer afford to sit at Boulogne waiting for control of the Channel. The Grand Army marched across Europe, overwhelmed the Austrians at Ulm, and shattered a combined Austro-Russian army at Austerlitz. The Prussians hastened to do a deal with Napoleon, their price being the possession of Hanover. In a few months of brilliant campaigning Napoleon had wrecked the Third Coalition. For Britain, and for a Pitt who was by now exhausting himself with overwork and overstrain, it was desperately bad news. Yet it was the ill-starred Third Coalition, rather than Trafalgar, that removed the menace of invasion. What was achieved by

Trafalgar—even more annihilating at sea than Austerlitz on land—was the confirmation for long years to come of the invulnerability of British shores, and the domination of the world's oceans by the British Navy.

The surrender at Ulm was in mid-October 1805, the disaster at Austerlitz in early December. Trafalgar lay between them, its significance temporarily obscured by the fog of those defeats and its triumph qualified by the death of Nelson. That eighteen enemy ships had been taken or sunk, that the remaining fifteen were so damaged as to be long useless (in fact, none of them ever fought again) seemed, at first, less important than that the national hero was dead. There were none of the customary bonfires and celebrations; men were stunned by the bad news.

This was not surprising. The victories associated with Nelson had provided the only bright sunshine amid the murky weather of these first twelve years of war. In his life he had become a symbol; after his death he became a legend. A man of simple conservatism who seldom questioned conventional ideas except in naval strategy, devoted to the religion amid which he had been reared in his father's Norfolk rectory, Nelson found it easy to equate the ambitions of his country with the will of the Almighty. Fittingly, his last words were "God and my Country." His own devouring ambition was for glory: "In my mind's eye," he said, "I ever saw a radiant orb which beckoned me onwards to renown." His self-dedication to the cause of duty had a consuming intensity. "Thank God," he managed to pronounce as he lay dying in *Victory*'s cockpit, "I have done my duty." Enthusiastic, sensitive, warm in friendship, cool in danger, he commanded the admiration of his fellow officers and subordinates to a superlative degree. He radiated confidence, knew that he did, and was delighted about it. "When I came to explain to them the 'Nelson touch'," he wrote to Lady Hamilton before Trafalgar, "it was like an electric shock." He lived out his professional triumphs (and his infatuation for Lady Hamilton, which some thought demeaning and faintly ridiculous) in the full glare of national publicity. Figuratively, he always wore his medals. Literally, too, he was conspicuous in them, as with Hardy he paced *Victory*'s deck in fatally close view of the *Redoutable's* snipers. But Nelson was much more than a daredevil hero conscious of the limelight; under him the Navy's standards of professional efficiency reached a peak. It outsailed, outmanœuvred, outgunned, and out-thought its opponents. At the Admiralty it was directed, first by Earl Spencer and later by Lord Barham, with shrewdness and judgment. Under Nelson inspired improvisation combined with the most painstaking preparation, reckless heroism with the most expert calculation. A grateful nation, licking its wounds, and rescued from total disaster by the Navy, found in the great admiral the embodiment of its fighting patriotism. Never was there an Englishman, wrote Southey, "who so entirely possessed the love of his fellow-countrymen".

Within three months Pitt's death had followed Nelson's. Gout, work, and worry had made him prematurely old at forty-six. In 1797 his health had first broken down; it did so again five years later. His breathing had grown laboured and his appearance gaunt; and when the House of Commons had voted to impeach Dundas (Lord Melville), Pitt's friend and closest political associate, members had been shocked to see Pitt, a man of great reserve and self-control, sitting in his seat with tears running down his cheeks. Now, in 1805, a stay at Bath failed to bring flesh back upon his bones or the old ring to his voice. Some said the shock of Austerlitz (coming after wildly optimistic rumours[6] of a great victory) finally killed him. At his death (January 1806) Napoleon was upon the peak of his triumphs; Pitt's work lay once more in ruins.

Of all modern British statesmen, he is the most enigmatic. Proud and lonely, a bachelor, reticent and imperious, he presented to the world an accomplished but icy exterior. Behind it there was an affable man, a hard drinker,[7] one who was glad to be merry with a few, a very few, friends (Wilberforce in early days, for instance, or later Dundas), and who was ready

[6] News travelled slowly. Austerlitz was fought on December 2nd. On December 29th at Brighton Pavilion, the Prince of Wales was "getting out his maps to show the route by which the French had retreated", when a dispatch arrived telling the disastrous truth.

[7] Addington once said, "If there is one thing Pitt likes better than a glass of port it is a bottle."

to allow the Napier and Stanhope children to blacken his face with burned cork.

The public image of Pitt was of a first-class administrator; an austere, tenacious, ambitious man of high integrity, indomitable will, high eloquence, and unmatched political dexterity. His devotion to duty was as unsparing as Nelson's and more exhausting. "What a life was his", wrote his niece. ". . . It was enough to kill a man. It was murder." Ever since war had first broken out, failure had dogged his schemes. The brilliant promise of his youth had been blasted by the events that began in France in 1789. Just before his death every man's voice (even that of Windham, for long the closest of colleagues) was raised in criticism of him; and only by the narrowest of majorities did the City of London vote him a monument in Guildhall. When it was erected its language provided an epitaph juster than many carved on memorial stone: "In an age when the contagion of ideals threatened to dissolve the forms of civil society, he rallied the loyal, the sober-minded and the good around the venerable structure of the British monarchy."

Chapter 13

Victory and Repression

1. Politics and the War following the Death of Pitt

The Pittite party crumbled upon Pitt's death, and it was a coalition of his opponents (miscalled "The Ministry of All the Talents") that succeeded him: mostly Grenvillites, Foxites, and Addingtonites. William Grenville[1] was First Lord of the Treasury and nominal head of the new Ministry, but its outstanding man was the new Foreign Secretary, Charles Fox, at last back in the seat of power. Grenville had refused to form a Government without him, and George III, however reluctantly, was obliged therefore to accept him. Unhappily, Fox's bodily vigour, which had successfully weathered earlier years of riotous living, had now deserted him. "Pitt died in January," he observed; "perhaps I shall go off before June." He lasted a little longer—till September; increasingly dropsical, but struggling towards the two goals he had set himself—peace with Napoleon and an end to the slave trade. Before he died he had made the second certain,[2] but had come to recognize that the first was impossible upon any terms that Britain, or he himself, could accept.

Fox had been many men. In his youth he was a man of fashion and pleasure, a prodigious drinker and gambler; but even then the sort of unusual reprobate who drove home after an all-night session at Brooks's Club to read Greek.[3] All his life he was a scholar and patron of the arts. He had schemed greedily for power in the manner of politicians; but his convictions were strong, genuine, and liberal. As a speaker, he was

[1] Youngest son of the George Grenville who was chief Minister 1763–1765.
[2] See Chapter 11, Section 4 (c).
[3] His later years were spent in "the most perfect sobriety, and regularity . . . delighting in study, in rural occupations, and rural prospects".

better than Burke ("whose manner was hurried, and he always in a passion") and less studied than Pitt. (It was once said of Pitt that he carefully considered his sentences before he uttered them, while Fox threw himself into the middle of his, and left it to God Almighty to get him out again.) Blackballed by the King because of his attacks on the royal prerogative and his immoral influence on the Prince of Wales, he had the mortification of seeing Pitt grow steadily in authority and immovability. Condemned, therefore, to long years in opposition, he remained the champion of generous and often unpopular causes—Catholic Emancipation, anti-slavery, parliamentary reform, the rights of colonial peoples, the French Revolution, peace with France. Men had respected Pitt, but not loved him. Fox, who overflowed with good humour and generosity, often exasperated friends and enemies alike, most of all over his stubborn refusal to support the war; but he commanded something much warmer than respect.

His death removed the kingpin from the 'Talents' Ministry, as Pitt's had from that of the Pittites. Parties at this period, robbed of the binding force of these powerful personalities, shifted and manœuvred confusingly around the ambitions and animosities of many contenders for power—Sidmouth (Addington), Canning, Grey, Liverpool, Perceval. It was the old Duke of Portland who succeeded eventually in forming a Government to follow the 'Talents'; his team contained Castlereagh as Secretary of War, a Pittite; Eldon, a high Tory; Perceval, an able lawyer and strong anti-Catholic; Liverpool, a second-generation 'new' earl of Pitt's making; and, at the Foreign Office, Canning, another Pittite, thought too clever and thrusting by many of his patrician colleagues and fellow members, who could never quite forget that he was the son of an actress.[4]

Portland's Ministry inherited a variety of military failures from its predecessor—abortive expeditions to Buenos Aires, Egypt, and the Dardanelles. From the Continent, too, came the continuing news of Napoleon's triumphs over the Prussians (at

[4] It was Canning, too, that penned the damaging little rhyme:
Pitt is to Addington
As London is to Paddington.

Jena) and the Russians (at Friedland). His grip was extending steadily over the continent. The Kingdom of Italy was assigned to one brother, Joseph; Holland to another, Louis. A small-scale but heartening British victory in the toe of Italy, at Maida, seemed little enough to pit against the Treaty of Tilsit (1807), when Napoleon and the Tsar Alexander met upon a raft on the river Niemen and concerted measures for the destruction of Britain. Not only were Russian ports to be closed to British ships, but Denmark, Sweden, and Portugal were to be coerced into co-operation with Napoleon.

Determined to anticipate an expected seizure of Denmark by Napoleon, Canning and Castlereagh acted with ruthless speed to get a British blow in first. When the Danish Crown Prince refused an ultimatum to surrender his fleet to Britain for the duration of the war, there followed a joint land and sea bombardment of Copenhagen. After heavy damage to the city the Danes were obliged to surrender their fleet of thirty-three vessels, which sailed for England with British crews. An attempt to follow up this *coup* with a Swedish alliance and a military expedition to the Baltic collapsed when the mad King of Sweden, while accepting a £1,200,000 subsidy, refused to allow British troops to land in his country; and an angry Denmark proceeded to declare war on Britain.

2. Economic Warfare and its Consequences

After Trafalgar, Napoleon was forced to prepare plans for the defeat of Britain without invasion. These involved economic warfare on an ambitious scale. The economic war itself was not new; from the beginning Pitt's Government had seen Britain's financial and economic strength as trump cards, and the French had aimed to deny British exporters their European markets. In 1803, for instance, Napoleon had, quite ineffectively, forbidden Holland, Italy, Spain, and Switzerland to import British goods. Between 1806 and 1811, however, the trade war took on a new intensity. The Berlin Decree of 1806 was designed to seal off all French-controlled territory from British products, and later decrees sought to achieve a 'Continental System' whereby all Europe would be shut off from

Britain. The consequences would be a shrinkage of British profits, dismay among employers and merchants, distress and unrest among employees. Further, if Britain could not export to Europe, she would have to pay for her necessary European imports in gold, and this would cause a drain on her reserves, threaten national bankruptcy, and force her to sue for peace.

Unfortunately for Napoleon, he could not afford to be consistent. France herself had need of British colonial products (such as sugar, coffee, tobacco, and cotton) and of British manufactured goods. French farmers, too, whose goodwill was vital to Napoleon, had need to export their agricultural surpluses. Hence, from the beginning, the French were forced to involve themselves in a complicated system of export and import licences which to a great extent made nonsense of the Continental System. The Grand Army marching through Prussia and Russia contained many men wearing greatcoats made in Yorkshire and boots made in Northampton. And in 1811, a year in which the British, after two bad harvests and much unemployment, faced severe distress, Napoleon actually encouraged the export of corn to England: he calculated that it was more important to drain Britain of the gold that she would have to pay in than to deny her the food that she needed to buy. He may have miscalculated—though the British gold reserves did fall dangerously low; but the double need to placate the French farmers and to repair France's own shaky finances put him in a most difficult position.

Britain's trade was, then, much dislocated by the Continental System. But mastery of the seas enabled her to escape its full consequences. When European ports were closed to her she was forced to look for new areas with which to trade, since trade, as Napoleon knew, was indeed her life blood. To some extent she found them—in South America particularly, and also in the Near East, in Spain and Portugal. She managed besides to operate a considerable smuggled trade, especially through Adriatic, Aegean, and North German ports. Her bankers (the Barings and Rothschilds, for instance) remained curiously able to negotiate their bills in a Europe apparently dominated by French arms. Napoleon simply lacked the communications and the bureaucratic machine necessary to supervise all Europe; and even in strongly French-controlled ports it soon became possible for the British to do a fair trade when French consuls found the local demand for exemption licences advantageous either to the French revenue or their own personal profit.

Even so, total British exports declined during 1807 and 1808; then, after recovering, they fell seriously in 1811. This was the more disturbing coming as it did after two decades during which British traders had become used to swift expansion. The slump was not entirely due to the European blockade; the decline in trade with the USA was in fact severer than that with Europe. After 1805 the American Governments of Jefferson and Madison had grown increasingly anti-British, partly, indeed, because of the British Navy's unrelenting practice of searching American vessels for contraband and British deserters, but partly, also, under the growing influence of the 'War Hawks'—the aggressively anti-British party pressing for an invasion of Canada. Jefferson, in an attempt to avoid the sort of naval incidents that had been poisoning Anglo-American relations, imposed in 1807 an embargo on trade with the European belligerents. In 1809 the USA went a step further and closed her own ports to both British and French vessels, in order to bring pressure to bear on Britain to restore the freedom of the seas. (The 'belligerents' meant, in practice, Britain, for it was the British Navy that dominated the situation, and French seaborne trade had virtually ceased.)

The decline of exports to Europe and the USA, and the fall in Lancashire's imports of raw cotton, had serious consequences in the manufacturing areas. During 1811–12 there was much unemployment and a heavy crop of bankruptcies. Thirty-two of Manchester's thirty-eight mills were forced to close. One-fifth of the population of urban Lancashire and 15,000 Nottinghamshire frame-workers were obliged to apply for poor relief, and the Dragoons were called out to quell disorders. With imports from the Baltic also cut, timber was scarce and dear, and the cost of bread soared. Many economists—Ricardo is an example—advocated suing for peace. The businessmen of Birmingham and other manufacturing towns (since they could hardly approach Napoleon) organized petitions to end the *British* measures regulating trade with the Continent.

These were the twenty-four Orders in Council issued by the Fox–Grenville and Portland Ministries between 1807 and 1810 in an attempt to counter the Continental System. In general, Napoleon had said that Britain should not trade with Europe; so, in general, Britain had replied that Europe should have no trade except with British permission and through British ports. The effect of these Orders on neutral nations was irksome; but it had an effect too on British businessmen, for they were unable to trade with Europe except by Government licence, which they resented. For the neutrals it was not a matter of Britain destroying their trade with Europe, except in certain 'strategic' materials; what Britain did was to insist on neutral ships proceeding through British ports, where cargoes were licensed, taxed, and then usually allowed to proceed. Napoleon's answer (in the Milan Decree) to this British surveillance was to confiscate any neutral ship that entered a European port having first complied with the Orders in Council.

Throughout 1810–12 pressure built up on President Madison in the USA to demand of Britain an end to her Orders in Council and her high-handed ways with American merchant ships. Napoleon, preparing his attack on Russia to enforce her adherence to the Continental System, was ready to give full freedom to the Americans to break it, since he knew that such a concession was, for a France without naval power, meaningless. Britain, threatened with attack from the USA, left her announcement of a similar concession too late. In 1812 America declared war. By that time the British Government had in fact decided to give way; but it is unlikely that the war party in America would have been stopped by British reasonableness at this stage. The cry for "Canada! Canada!" was by now overwhelming.

Thus, by 1812, attempts to enforce the blockade had played a part in drawing both Britain and France into new and dangerous conflicts. The Anglo-American War led to an American invasion of Canada and a British counter-invasion. Each side did the other considerable damage; on one occasion a British raiding party burned Washington; Toronto was twice burned; but by 1814 there was stalemate. Napoleon's involvements arising from the trade war were more spectacular and more damaging. First, the necessity to occupy Portugal led on to the Peninsular War, Napoleon's "Spanish ulcer", Britain's opportunity. Then came the Moscow campaign, an unprecedented Napoleonic disaster. These two developments marked the turn of the tide against France at last.

3. Britain and the War on Land (1807–15)

At Copenhagen there had been strong evidence of the dangers attending neutrals. An angry Napoleon, forestalled there, was determined to do better at Lisbon. Now that Russia had agreed (only temporarily, as it turned out) to co-operate in his plans, he needed to close the biggest remaining gap in his European system—Portugal. Accordingly, in November 1807, he dispatched Junot with a French army through Spain to Lisbon, and deposed the Portuguese house of Braganza, "a new proof," he said, "of how inevitable is the ruin of all who attach themselves to England." In fact, Canning had, until Napoleon's aggression, been unable to persuade the Portuguese Regent so to attach himself—the ignominious collapse of Britain's attack on Buenos Aires had provided poor support for her diplomacy. But now the Regent did consent to depart with his fleet, escorted by British warships, for Rio de Janeiro.

Still grander designs inflamed Napoleon's imagination. To break British sea-power he dreamed of a triple attack southward: to Sicily in the south, to Constantinople in the south-east, to Gibraltar and beyond in the south-west. If all went well the Mediterranean could become a French lake, and the thrust through Turkey could be extended to threaten British India. But, first, Spain, an ally he despised and mistrusted, must be brought directly under his control. Using, therefore, a mixture of bribery, treachery, and force, he manœuvred the Spanish Royal Family, father (Charles IV) and son (Ferdinand), from their throne[5] and poured 100,000 French troops into Spain.

[5] It was disputed between them: a sorry and complicated story of intrigue and faithlessness, while the country was ruled, or misruled, by the Queen's lover, Godoy.

The mobs of Madrid and elsewhere, detesting the dictatorial rule of Godoy, at first welcomed the French troops; but, learning that Ferdinand of Bourbon had been kidnapped by Napoleon, soon rose against their new masters. In May 1808, Madrid saw, first, a massacre of the French garrison, and then a counter-massacre of the Spaniards. Spain took light. Napoleon's combination of trickery, high-handedness, and megalomania had converted a rather sluggish ally into a proud and passionate enemy. The new Spanish King, Joseph Bonaparte, was forced to leave Spain, while his brother prepared for a full-scale conquest. Meanwhile from Spain the flame of revolt spread to Portugal, and Junot's forces were obliged in self-defence to concentrate near Lisbon. Never again in the course of the war would the French tricolour be hailed as a symbol of deliverance from tyranny, as it had been in the early days.

The British Government was quick to clasp her new Iberian allies. Canning made an announcement similar to that of Churchill in 1941: any nation fighting against the European dictator was an ally of this country. Even now, however, the first military moves of Britain's Peninsular War were farcically handled. Although Wellesley defeated Junot at Vimieiro, he was superseded by men who seemed more interested in maintaining their professional seniority than defeating the enemy, and Junot's army was allowed to return with its equipment to France (by the Convention of Cintra, August 1808).

A more heroic failure, but still a failure, was Sir John Moore's attempt to advance from Portugal to the aid of the Spanish in Madrid. Arrived at Salamanca with 17,000 men, he learned that Napoleon himself, with a much larger force, had occupied the capital. He therefore diverted his attack northward towards Burgos, to link up with another British force and threaten Soult's troops in northern Spain. But when he learned that Napoleon was striking northward to join Soult, Moore had no choice but retreat. At the bitter turn of the year 1808–9 his army struggled over the mountain passes towards Corunna. Its discipline was not equal to the ordeal; at times the disorderly elements became a drunken rabble; but Moore did manage to extricate his main body from the pursuing French. An able and courageous general, he even reasserted

sufficient authority to repulse Soult on the heights outside
Corunna, before his exhausted forces embarked in the transports that the Navy had supplied for rescue. In the last stages
of the action a cannon-ball struck Moore from his horse and
killed him. With Nelson, he entered the legendary ranks of the
heroes who died at the moment of victory; but his campaign
provided a painful reminder that victory, even if it was attainable, was going to be an expensive prize.

Once more yet, at the close of 1809, a British continental
expedition was forced to withdraw. Hoping for Austrian co-
operation, Castlereagh, the War Minister, planned to take the
Scheldt estuary, free Antwerp, and open a military front in
Belgium. Once again, however, an Austrian army was crushed,
this time at Wagram, in July 1809. The British landed on the
island of Walcheren, captured Flushing, but dared not go
farther. Some of the Walcheren force were withdrawn; thousands of others remained to be struck down by the all-conquer-
ing 'Walcheren fever', while the two leading British Ministers
—Canning, who opposed the expedition, and Castlereagh, who
supported it—fought one another in a duel. The aged Duke of
Portland died; the Government disintegrated. By this time the
catalogue of failure was becoming very long. And while Moore
had redeemed Corunna, nothing redeemed Walcheren.

The harshest year of the trade war (1811) was still to come,
and the distress and rioting that accompanied it; but, abroad,
the worst was over. While Perceval[6] patched up a Tory
Government to continue the war, Wellesley prepared to re-
enter the struggle in the Peninsula. The British Army had
suffered defeat after defeat in Europe for sixteen years, and
had been terribly reduced by disease which Army medical
authorities had been helpless to check. But the authorities had
not been blind to the lessons of their defeats. The Duke of
York, an inept commander in the field, had done good work as
a reformer. Administration and training had both been reorganized, though Windham's Act to reform recruitment had
been a total failure, and medical reform had to wait over half

[6] Spencer Perceval, Prime Minister until his assassination in 1812 by a
madman in the lobby of the House of Commons. It was said of him by
Grattan: "He is not a ship of the line, but he carries many guns, is tight-
built, and is out in all weathers."

a century for Florence Nightingale. "The man who enlists in the British army is, in general," as Wellington commented, "the most drunken and probably the worst man of the trade or profession to which he belongs." However, by 1808, Sir John Moore had built up in the Light Brigade an élite corps of mobile infantry, designed as a reply to the swift-moving Napoleonic columns; and upon the death of one great soldier, Moore, command of the Army in the field passed to another, Wellesley (later Duke of Wellington). He sometimes had hard things to say of the troops he commanded. They were, in his own words, "the scum of the earth". They behaved "terribly ill", he wrote home to Castlereagh; they plundered; they were "a rabble who cannot bear success any more than Sir J. Moore's army could bear failure". "I don't know what effect these men will have upon the enemy, but, by God, they terrify me." Even as late as 1813, Wellington was complaining of the indiscipline in his army. It was, however, he admitted, "an unrivalled army for fighting, if the soldiers can only be kept in their ranks during the battle". And just after Waterloo he paid a tribute to the Peninsular veterans whom he himself had done so much to train (or, as he said, to tame): "The best troops we have, probably the best in the world, are the British infantry, particularly the old infantry that has served in Spain." Wellington spared them no more than he spared himself; but he never unnecessarily risked lives. He fought cautiously and shrewdly, husbanding his small forces. He was a tough, alert man who required to see men about him who were tough and alert; a disciplinarian and aristocrat who considered flogging a necessity in the sort of army he was given, and praise a luxury they could dispense with. He deplored heroic poses, shams, and sentimentalism. Expertness and courage he shared with Nelson, but in almost every other respect they stand at opposite poles. Wellington was laconic, sardonic, "without enthusiasms or illusions". But one of his officers once declared that the sight of his long nose was worth a reinforcement of 10,000 men.

Apart from the advantage which Wellington's own leadership constituted, the British Army possessed four other vital assets during the seven-year struggle in the Iberian Peninsula. Compared with the French, the British were few—about

40,000 against 250,000 or sometimes 300,000—but all Wellington's men were free for campaigning, while the French were forced to dissipate theirs in a futile effort to hold down a populace united in hostility against them. Second, although the Portuguese and Spanish armies were in the early days a source of irritation to Wellington, they provided an important reinforcement of manpower that often swung the balance in his favour. The fighting strength of the anti-Napoleonic professional army lay in its British (with a strong proportion of Irish) regiments; but it was an allied army. Third, Napoleon, using the principle of 'divide and rule', did not unify his Iberian command; the French marshals there, each with his 'empire', frequently failed to render mutual co-operation. Lastly, Britain always had the priceless advantage of safe seaborne communications, while French supplies were obliged to struggle through a mountainous and often waterless land, over roads infested with guerrillas. When Marshal Masséna wished to write to Napoleon in 1810 he had to send half a brigade back to protect the letter; and news of the retreat from Moscow took a month to travel from the Pyrenees to Madrid.

The word 'guerrilla' entered the English language with the Peninsular War. The invaders kept alive by robbing the peasantry, while the peasants, sometimes led by their priests, retaliated by murdering the invaders, a hundred of them a day, on average, for four years. They lived wild; they confined the enemy to the garrison towns and main lines of communication. They operated with fanatical savagery; atrocity was answered by counter-atrocity. (One brigand chief made Wellington a present of decapitated French couriers, complete with their captured dispatches.) In his *Disasters of War* (1814) Goya, the greatest Spanish painter of his day, set down the unforgettable miseries of his time: torture, bestiality, vengeance, hatred; the firing-squad and its scarecrow victims; lands ravaged, buildings fired, women raped, children slaughtered, Spaniards and French caught together in a vicious circle of horror.

Victory was a long time coming to Wellington. For two-thirds of the time it was rather a matter of survival. Even when a victory was won, as at Talavera in 1809, it proved costly and sterile. There the threat of encirclement forced retreat on a British army which had already lost 5000 dead, a quarter of its strength; and the dispirited victors made a nightmare march back to the Portuguese frontier, tormented by heat, mosquitoes, hunger, and dysentery, with hundreds of the wounded dying on the road. Wellington, his stock at home very low, used the next few months in the intensive training and "taming" of his regiments, and in preparing a defensive position which would break the heart of any attackers. When Masséna struck towards Lisbon in 1810 (the fourth French general to do so since 1806) he found the ground before him laid waste by the British, the provisions gone, and, to his surprise and consternation, an elaborate system of redoubts, parapets, and trenches guarding the Lisbon peninsula. These were the 'lines' of Torres Vedras, which Portuguese labour had been preparing for many months under Wellington's direction. They ran for thirty miles from the sea to the Tagus estuary and formed the north side of a quadrilateral, whose other three sides were friendly salt water. The southernmost 'line' consisted of last-ditch fortifications to cover a possible evacuation. Since for Masséna to advance would mean suicide, he retired somewhat, hoping to inveigle Wellington into a premature assault. Wellington, however, though he calculated he could win, reckoned also that, "as this is the last army England has got, he must take care of it". After a winter terrible alike for Masséna's men (who lost 25,000) and for the Portuguese peasantry they tortured and sucked dry, the French withdrew.

During 1811–12 there was bloody and protracted fighting for the fortresses of Almeida, Badajoz, and Ciudad Rodrigo[7] that guarded the Spanish–Portuguese border; and when these had been at last secured Wellington was able to take the initiative, defeat Masséna's successor, Marmont, at Salamanca, and hold Madrid itself—but only for a week or two. Lack of numbers again forced retirement; on the march back more than 3000 famished and exhausted men fell out and were taken by

[7] The 'victory' at Fuentes d'Oñoro involved some of Wellington's worst losses, and in the final storming of Badajoz 5000 of his troops were killed. Both Ciudad Rodrigo and Badajoz were sacked by the frantic and drunken victors, and at Badajoz order was not restored until Wellington had erected a gallows in the town square.

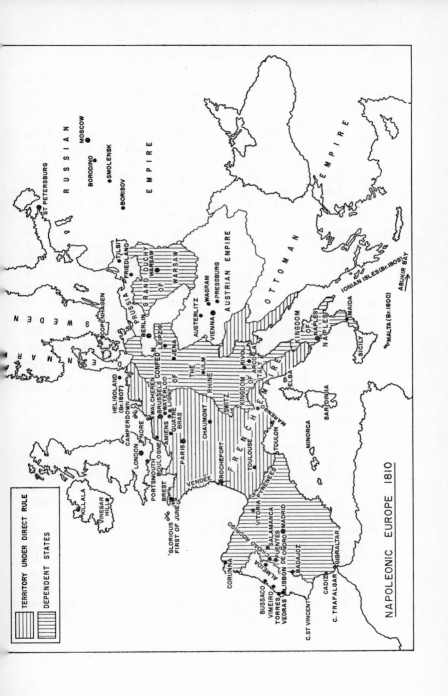

NAPOLEONIC EUROPE 1810

the French. By now, moreover, the gloom in England was intensified by industrial depression, unemployment, machine-smashing riots, war with the USA, and news of Napoleon's advance on Moscow.

The almost total loss of the Grand Army in the retreat from Moscow produced in England a very different mood. The Baltic was opened again to shipping. Trade revived. Britain budgeted for the then immense sum of £118,000,000, the bulk of it war expenditure, much of it earmarked to subsidize the armies that once more Europe was raising against Napoleon. At the Foreign Office Castlereagh laboured at the same task that had long occupied Pitt, and yet another European coalition—the Fourth—emerged. Frederick William of Prussia was persuaded by popular opinion to change from the French to the allied side. The Russians entered Berlin. In September 1813 the Austrians were again at war with the French—for the fifth time in twenty-one years. A month later, at the battle of Leipzig, which engaged half a million men, Napoleon lost half his army (in casualties and deserters), the remainder of his German allies, and all hope of holding any line east of the Rhine.

As the eastern allies pressed westward to the Rhine, Wellington was already over the Pyrenees. Outmanœuvring the combined armies of Joseph Bonaparte and Marshal Jourdan, he had defeated them at Vitoria. In his fury Napoleon had put them both under house arrest and restored the command to Soult. But in fierce fighting south of the Pyrenees Soult had lost heavily and been forced to abandon Spain altogether. By October, the month of the battle of Leipzig, Wellington was across the frontier, with the Navy operating in support along the Biscay coast. His Spanish troops now withdrew; his British veterans pressed forward towards Toulouse.

Even now Napoleon could have had peace on terms which any previous ruler of France would have considered vastly favourable—that is, on the basis of her 'natural' frontiers, the Pyrenees, the Alps, and the Rhine. But Napoleon, fed on phantasms, conjuring great new armies out of his imagination, would not accept these terms. Britain's chief preoccupation now was to hold together the shaky Fourth Coalition threatened by the territorial rivalries of Austria, Russia, and Prussia, especially over the ownership of Poland and Saxony. The Treaty of Chaumont (1814) was largely the work of Castlereagh; it pledged the four great powers, Russia, Austria, Prussia, Britain, each to maintain 150,000 men in the field, and Britain to provide another £5,000,000 in subsidies, to be divided equally among the allies.

On March 31st 1814 Paris capitulated. Napoleon abdicated, but it was a few days later, news being slow to travel, that Soult's army was crushed by Wellington's at Toulouse. Then, while the Emperor was dispatched to rule his little consolation island of Elba, the allied diplomatists, first in Paris, later in Vienna, sat down to the complicated business of the peace settlement.

Their leisurely negotiations, and the glittering celebrations that ceaselessly accompanied them, were brusquely interrupted, almost a year after the fall of Paris, by the news of Napoleon's escape from Elba, his landing at Fréjus, the desertion to his cause of the French troops sent to fight him, and the flight from Paris of the restored Bourbon King, Louis XVIII. A Napoleon full of promises offered peace, with acceptance of the frontiers imposed on France in 1814; and there were some among the Whigs in England who were willing to settle for this. Others, like the Prime Minister, Liverpool, most of his Cabinet, and the Prussian Government, were anxious not only to crush Napoleon, but to inflict on France further humiliation and loss of territory. Castlereagh, however, remained constant to his previous policies: restoration of the Bourbons, a moderate peace that France could reasonably accept (with the frontiers of 1792), and a common war policy for the powers of the Fourth Coalition. He had his way. As at Chaumont, the four great powers promised 150,000 men each to renew the war; and Prussia, Austria, and Russia received an equal share of yet another subsidy.

Thus in 1815 Wellington found himself again at the head of a British and allied army—not 150,000 indeed, but 63,000, of whom two-thirds were Dutch, Belgians, Hanoverians and Brunswickers, and 21,000 only were British. Even of these, not more than 10,000 were his Peninsular veterans, some of whom had been sent to America. Most were raw recruits—"an infamous army," Wellington called it. Austria and Russia required time to assemble their forces; but Prussia had put 113,000 in the field under Blücher. Napoleon's objective was to destroy Wellington and Blücher separately, before they could join forces, or be joined by their other allies. Hence, with 70,000 men, he quickly struck northward for Brussels, Wellington's headquarters. One force defeated Blücher at Ligny, while another (under Marshal Ney) forced Wellington back from Quatre Bras.

To the south of Brussels, Wellington, that expert in defence, took up a strong position on the ridge of Waterloo, with its sunken road, and fortified farmhouses of Hougoumont and La Haye Sainte. There on June 18th 1815 his dogged infantry, concentrated into 'hedgehogs' of musket and bayonet, withstood, first, very severe artillery bombardment, and then, all afternoon, the repeated and wonderfully disciplined attacks of the French cuirassiers, the cavalry that had been the admiration of Europe. The slaughter of men and horses was immense. With an approximate equality of artillery power on the two sides, it was the cavalry column against the 'line' of infantry squares, and the line was victorious. "The French came on in the old style," said Wellington later, "and we drove them off in the old style." His untried troops had been stiffened with veterans trained in his Peninsular discipline, and, even when surrounded and losing men fast, their ranks held. Even so, as Wellington said, it was "a damned nice thing—the nearest-run thing you ever saw in your life"; and in the end it was the evening arrival on Napoleon's flank of Blücher's 30,000 fresh Prussian troops that completed the rout of the French. There was a general *sauve qui peut*, with the Prussian cavalry pursuing the fragmented French until darkness and after. The Napoleonic Wars were over. Surrendering to the British, Napoleon was exiled to remote St Helena in the South Atlantic.

Alone of the powers, great and small, Britain had been able to afford consistency and steadfastness in the long struggle; and the explanation lies not so much in any unique British virtues (though these may exist) as in the strength and confidence that derived from economic and naval supremacy.

Immunity from invasion, growing trade, and soaring production made everything else possible—the financial power that lay behind the diplomacy of Pitt and Castlereagh and bolstered the anti-French coalitions; the imports that continued to pour in from all the continents; the exports and re-exports that the world was anxious to buy, and continued to buy (even France herself) despite Napoleon's general ban; the ability to put troops anywhere upon the globe to attack the colonies of the enemy or to assist those subject nations provoked to rise against the tyrant; even the political stability at home that was in general maintained despite injustices and the rumblings of discontent. In every sphere, naval, economic, diplomatic, even (at the end) military, Britain's share in the defeat of Napoleon was outstanding.

4. Radical Reformers

The reform agitation of the 1790's had been shouted down by the anti-Painite 'Throne and Altar' mobs and silenced by Pitt's repressive measures;[8] the last serious 'Jacobin' manifestation was the Nore naval mutiny in 1797. There were, indeed, some working men who risked the severe punishment of the law by forming trade unions (in 1810, for instance, the compositors of *The Times* received sentences, under the Combination Acts, ranging from nine months to two years). But the war years were, in general, years of defeat for the reformers. Some magistrates even employed their own spies for moving among the disaffected and reporting their doings. There was a relative immunity from the law's oppression for radical Whigs of the aristocratic classes, and for intellectuals like Godwin and Bentham; but, for the rest, "it was almost safer to be a felon than a reformer".

There had been rioting during lean times between 1795 and 1810, but it was the depression of 1811, resulting from Napoleon's trade blockade,[9] that touched off the severe 'Luddite' disturbances of 1811–12. Machine-breaking was nothing new, but never had it been so intense and widespread; it affected the industrial areas of Nottinghamshire, Cheshire, Lancashire,

[8] See pp. 362–363.   [9] See pp. 381–385.

and the West Riding. The trouble was that the sudden closing of European markets coincided with the extensive introduction of labour-saving machinery in the textile trades; and however convincingly learned economists argued that mechanization was to the eventual benefit of the working class (for, by multiplying wealth, it increased the "wages fund"), the logic carried small weight with the skilled hand-worker who had just seen his earnings halved. The machine-breakers called themselves Luddites, for they claimed that they took their orders from a certain Ned Ludd, who had his headquarters in Sherwood Forest. (He was probably mythical.) In Nottinghamshire the stockingers succeeded in smashing altogether about a thousand of the 'wide' stocking-frames which they claimed were producing shoddy goods and destroying the market for good-quality stockings (manufactured on 'narrow' frames). A frightened Government made frame-breaking punishable by death, but the Nottingham Luddites had scored at least a temporary success: their earnings began to rise again. In Lancashire the Luddites won no such victory; all they succeeded in doing was to destroy some of the new steam-looms which were lowering the earnings of hand-weavers. Both there and in Yorkshire, where shearing-machines were demolished, Luddism became confused with hunger-rioting. Troops were moved in, and at York, in January 1813, seventeen Luddites were hanged and six more transported. Byron, making his only notable contribution to the debates of the Lords, spoke of

> these men, as I have seen them, meagre with famine, sullen with despair, careless of a life which your lordships are perhaps to value at something less than the price of a stocking frame.

Employers had their own answers to Luddism. At Middleton, near Manchester, a manufacturer defending his factory shot five Luddites, whose companions proceeded to burn down his house. One Yorkshire owner killed two Luddites who attacked his mill; another was himself killed. When a national association was formed of workmen who were opposed to the new machinery it was broken by an employers' committee, on the ground that it contravened the law forbidding combinations. The authorities omitted to notice that the employers' committee was itself a combination and thus as illegal as the association it was fighting.

Luddism was essentially destructive, a product of the fear and desperation of skilled men. Since about 1807, however, there had been a revival of a more general kind of Radicalism. In that year there had been a triumph at the Westminster election for two prominent reformers, Lord Cochrane and Sir Francis Burdett, who went to the Commons to join the small band whose principal members were Whitbread, Romilly, and the young Scots lawyer Brougham. In the Westminster election a big part had been played by Francis Place, whose tailor's shop (or more precisely the library behind it) had become a reformers' clubhouse. Place, self-made and largely self-educated, had started in life a leather-breeches-maker's apprentice. He had been an active member of the London Corresponding Society in the nineties, when he had known grinding poverty and been blackballed as a troublemaker by the London employers in his trade; but by 1807 he had built up a prosperous business in Charing Cross. Contemptuous alike of Tories and Whigs, of the fine gentlemen who were his customers, of political and religious superstition, of the injustice, snobbery, muddle, and confusion he saw all round him, this tireless and cocksure man was to have a hand in many of the reforms of the next thirty years.

Francis Place and James Mill were among the disciples of Jeremy Bentham, the philosopher and jurist (born 1748), who about this time circulated privately among his friends proposals for annual Parliaments, equal electoral districts, household suffrage, compulsory attendance for Members of Parliament, and full reporting of parliamentary speeches. All political institutions were to be judged by one criterion only: did they, or did they not, promote "the greatest happiness of the greatest number"? In that sense, had they "utility"? If not, they should be radically reformed or abolished. The democratic interest was "no other than the universal interest". By the simple Benthamite yardstick few British institutions were likely to remain inviolate, certainly not Parliament, or the legal system, or local government, or the Church of England, or the prisons; least of all, perhaps, the monarchy. The utility of everything was to be questioned. When Bentham published his *Catechism of Parliamentary Reform* in 1817, a year of harsh repression, the book was allowed to go unscathed; Bentham's was the innocent radicalism of the academic. An old man by now, shunning the limelight, he was sufficiently an international figure to be invited by the Tsar of Russia to frame a new liberal constitution for Poland; and when the recently liberated republics of South America sought up-to-date laws and institutions in the early twenties, it was to Bentham that several of them turned. "He has offered constitutions for the New World", wrote Hazlitt, "and legislated for future times." In the age of reform that immediately preceded and followed his death (1832) the political influence of his followers (the Utilitarians or Philosophic Radicals) was very considerable. In philosophy his insistence on utility and reason as the bases of morals took insufficient account of the complexity of human psychology: a 'good' action was simply one that promoted the greatest happiness of the greatest number, one whose sum of 'pleasure' outweighed the sum of 'pain'. Here, too, however, his thought had significant influence.

A radical reformer[10] of a quite different sort was William Cobbett. This farmer's boy from Farnham in Surrey had been in turn solicitor's clerk, soldier, journalist, and newspaper-owner in America, before becoming a Tory pamphleteer in the days of Addington and Pitt. Nostalgia for a merry England that he thought had existed in his boyhood (though in fact he had run away from it to London) determined many of his judgments and prejudices. He found much in the new England to hate: stockjobbers and moneylenders; Jews and Scotsmen; tea-drinking; London ("the Wen"); paper money; the National Debt with its "tax-eating" fundholders; jumped-up farmers with social pretensions and pianofortes in their parlours; low wages in the countryside, beggaring honest men who were the backbone of England. The violence of his prejudices was

[10] The noun 'Radical' was first employed in English in 1818. Previously the usage was 'radical reformers', or simply 'reformers'. The word 'Liberal', as a term of political significance, entered the language two years later. *Los liberales* were the democratic party in the Spanish revolution of 1820.

matched by the vigour of his pen. This John-Bull-in-a-china-shop was not only a consummate political journalist; he was also (especially in *Rural Rides*) one of the great English descriptive writers. Converted from the Toryism of his early and middle years, he made his paper, *The Weekly Political Register*, the most powerful organ of radical opinion in Britain. Yet in a real sense he remained a Tory, yearning for a yeoman England that never was. All his life, on both sides of the Atlantic, he lived amid the smoke of battle, personal and political. Controversy was his natural element. When he was wrong, which was often, he was thumpingly wrong. But when he was right no voice in England was more eloquent or influential in the fight against privilege and injustice. The severest of the many scrapes he flew into completed his political about-turn: in 1810 he denounced the flogging of British soldiers under the guard of German mercenaries, and was consequently fined £1000 and imprisoned for two years. During this time the *Register* continued to appear, and when the storm really broke in Britain after Waterloo, Cobbett took the bold step of bringing out an additional 'popular' version of his paper (1816). *Twopenny Trash* swept the country, selling as many as 50,000 a week, a great circulation for those days. In Cobbett's wake came numerous other Radical editors—Hone of *The Reformist's Register*, Wooler of *The Black Dwarf*, Carlile of *The Republican*, Gast of *The Gorgon*. Most of these journals agreed on the main enemies: the monarchy, personified now in the obese and dissolute figure of the Prince Regent; organized religion, and in particular the Established Church and the 'pious humbug' of wealthy Evangelicals such as Wilberforce; and the grossly unfair burden of taxation on the poor. All of them demanded parliamentary reform—suffrage either household (the vote for the head of every household) or universal (the vote for every adult male); the secret ballot; more frequent general elections; and an end to the 'borough-mongering' and corruption at Westminster.

This was the main stream of Radical agitation. There were some still more radical Radicals, in particular two: Thomas Spence, who advocated the public ownership of all land, and Robert Owen, who proposed nothing less than a new order of society based not on competition but on communist co-opera-tion.[11] Spence was as poor as Owen was rich. His personal eccentricities (which included peddling his Plan round London on a barrow) prevented him from being taken as seriously as he deserved. Even so, the Government found it necessary to infiltrate several of their spies into the Society of Spencean Philanthropists, the organization which he left behind at his death in 1814, and which fell into the hands of fanatical extremists.

5. Distress and Repression (1815–20)

In 1812 wheat sold at an average of 122s. 8d. a quarter, in 1813 at 106s. 6d., prices to rejoice the farmers' hearts. During the years 1812–14, too, there was a big recovery in British trade, after the failure of the Continental System. The textile and metal trades led the boom. The Government alone was spending £50,000,000 a year directly on purchases necessary for the war, and much of their subsidy expenditure abroad came indirectly back to British suppliers of armaments and uniforms. Prices and industrial wages rose until they were double pre-war. Then came the first capitulation of Napoleon in 1814; Government contracts were cut back; demand and prices alike fell. By 1815 wheat was down to 63s. 8d. a quarter. Farmers who had taken out mortgages during the war to bring more and more land under the plough (often unsuit-able land, but prices were irresistible) now saw ruin ahead. Landowners dependent on farmers' rents stirred up a lively agitation, and Liverpool's Government (of Tory landowners) lost no time in pushing through the most famous of Corn Laws. Import of foreign wheat was entirely forbidden until the price of British wheat rose above 80s. In fact, in the following three critical years it averaged 84s. 6d., and the cost of a four-pound loaf a shilling, at a time when wages were falling.

Immediately after the war British traders hoped to flood Europe and South America with their exports, but soon found that war-exhausted countries lacked the means to buy. The post-war boom was therefore nipped very early in the bud.

[11] See p. 338.

With no more Government orders, and 250,000 demobilized soldiers and sailors thrown on to the labour market within eighteen months, employment, production, prices, and wages all fell. Iron, which had sold at £20 a ton, fell to £8; half the blast furnaces went out of production. Many small employers went bankrupt; and of the textile trades Wordsworth's sister Dorothy wrote:

> Few get more than half work—great numbers none at all. . . . For a time whole streets . . . may be kept alive by public charity, but the consequences will be awful if nothing can be manufactured in these places where such numbers of people have been gathered together.

To make matters worse, the summer of 1816 was so cold and wet, it "was enough to make one wish for winter all the year round". In October the ungathered sheaves were sprouting in the fields, and by December wheat reached the famine price of 103s. Some starved; millions went hungry. The demand for poor relief threw such pressure on the rates that the dole had to be scaled down.

The business community, like the farmers and landowners, were better placed to find relief from their troubles than the helpless and unorganized poor. Petitions flooded in to the Government from merchants and bankers to lighten the businessman's burden of taxation; and Brougham, the most active and vocal of the Whigs, succeeded in forcing the unwilling Tories to follow up the imposition of the Corn Law with the abolition of the income tax. Pitt had promised that it would operate during the war only, and the income-tax-paying classes were determined that Pitt's promise should be honoured.

The effect was to throw a still greater proportion of the national taxes on the already bent shoulders of the poor. Britain had defeated Napoleon, and made herself great and rich in the process, but the poorer four-fifths of the nation were now being made to pay a heavy price for the triumph. Borrowing to finance the war had sent the National Debt rocketing to £860,000,000. By 1816 it was necessary to raise £31,500,000 annually to meet the interest charge, as against £9,500,000 in 1793; and now the removal of income tax meant that all this (and in addition enough to meet current expenditure) must be found from customs and excise. Two-thirds came from excise —taxes on goods popularly consumed, such as sugar, tea, beer, soap, candles—"everything", as 'Orator' Hunt declaimed to the London crowds, "that concerned their subsistence or comfort".

> Was not their loaf taxed, was not beer taxed, were not their coats taxed, were not their shirts taxed, was not everything that they ate, drank, wore, or even said taxed ... in pensioning the fathers, the brothers, the mothers, the sisters, the cousins, and the bastards of the borough-mongers ... subsisting on the plunder wrung from their miseries?

Certainly such indirect taxation fell most heavily on those least able to bear it. This was what made Cobbett rage at the "tax-eaters", and at the threepence-halfpenny surcharge (so Cobbett calculated) that the labourer paid on every pot in his "exchange of beer for sweat". The rich, and especially the fundholders, were maintaining themselves at the expense of the poor.

The injustice was made worse both by the fall in prices and by the monetary policy of Liverpool's Government. As prices and wages fell after 1815, the real value of the £31,500,000 annual debt burden—that is, its value in terms of current wages and actual prices—inevitably rose. The war had caused some monetary inflation, as all wars do, though rising production had held it in check; the peace now brought sudden and disastrous deflation. And this was assisted by the Government's decision in 1819 to get back as soon as possible to the gold standard—that is, to withdraw the wartime paper money for amounts under £5. (The new gold coins were called 'sovereigns' and were worth 20s., against the 21s. of the older guinea.) The stoutest critic of the Tories' excessively deflationary policy was the Birmingham banker Thomas Attwood, who maintained that the best remedy for unemployment was a paper currency based not on gold but on the nation's capacity to produce. The insistence on the gold standard, he argued, would bring 'tight' credit, low investment, sluggish production, and continuing unemployment. He joined the ranks of the middle-class Radicals and was later closely associated with the struggle for the Reform Act and the People's Charter; but most wrote him off, in his day, as a mere currency crank. Today, with our study and experience of the opposite evils of excessive inflation and excessive deflation, we can see sense in his ideas. Cobbett, too, though he was no friend of paper money, bitterly attacked the Government's return to the gold standard without some scaling down of the Debt interest. "There", he wrote in 1821, "is the Debt pulling down the nation like as a stone pulls a dog under the water."

After the patriotic rejoicings that greeted Waterloo the nation reacted to the slump with dismay or anger. There was a recrudescence of Luddism both in the midland and northern industrial districts and in East Anglia, where half-starving labourers smashed threshing-machines, and, armed with pikes and guns, set up local reigns of terror. In many parts of England, in South Wales, and around Glasgow there were violent strikes, food riots, and looting of flour-mills and bakeries. At Loughborough, when a local jury acquitted workmen of burning down a factory, the crowds cheered the jury and booed the judges. This was the time when Cobbett first issued his twopenny editions, and all over the country there sprang up the 'Hampden Clubs', under the leadership of old Major John Cartwright, with their penny-a-week membership and their cry for parliamentary reform. And a new star now appeared on the scene in the person of Henry Hunt, gentleman farmer and 'orator', loud of lungs and braggart of manner, the darling of the mass meetings. He addressed two of them at Spa Fields, London, towards the end of 1816. At the first, wearing his famous white hat, he was preceded by attendants carrying the cap of liberty on a pike, and the green, white, and red of the future British republic. At the second he was challenged by a rival meeting of Spenceans, who included among their company a number of riotous ex-sailors. The mob proceeded to run berserk, murdered a gunsmith, and, armed with the contents of his shop, terrorized the City of London until troops scattered them. A few weeks later a "projectile" (whether bullet or stone was not established) pierced the window of the Regent's coach.

These unruly incidents served both to frighten the Government and to rally to its support almost all members of the propertied classes, who generally welcomed the three 'Gagging' Acts that the Home Secretary, Sidmouth, now introduced (1817). These closely paralleled Pitt's repressive Acts of 1795–1800; they included magistrates' control of public meetings and the temporary suspension of habeas corpus. In addition Sidmouth circularized magistrates, enjoining the utmost zeal in stamping out agitation. For their part, they reacted with sometimes preposterous enthusiasm: one suppressed a local mineralogical society on the grounds that mineralogy led to atheism, and several distinguished literary and philosophical societies had to close down. Cobbett, threatened with Government prosecution (ostensibly for non-payment of stamp duty), fled to America—that land fit, he wrote, for democrats to live in, where there was no standing army, no established Church, no punitive taxation, and "no Wilberforces. Think of *that!*—no Wilberforces."

The year 1817 saw the temporary but heavy defeat of the Radicals. The Manchester men, marching to London to present a petition to the Prince Regent, got, most of them, no farther than Stockport, where troops dispersed them.[12] Other such demonstration marches planned by the northern reformers, whose strength at this time was sapped by the spies of the Home Office and of the local magistracy, were thwarted by the arrest of the leaders; and when a handful of Derbyshire men, egged on by the most notorious of the Government spies, Oliver, attempted to march on Nottingham their capture proved an easy matter. Gradually the panic died down as trade and employment recovered from mid-1817 onward. The *Leeds Mercury* exposed Oliver and his unlikeable fraternity. Several juries proved loath to convict the reformers; and even when nineteen of the Derbyshire insurrectionaries were condemned to death, only three were actually executed.

All through 1818 the pressure was relaxed by a Government confident that its justifiable vigilance had avoided an English Revolution. The worst, however, was still to come. Even in

[12] They carried blankets for sleeping at night and became known as the Blanketeers.

1818 there had been strikes of Lancashire spinners and weavers, when the cotton-masters would not restore the cuts in wage rates made in the preceding years; moreover, an attempt was made in that year 1818—unsuccessful of course—to make a 'Union of all Trades'. But when the textile trades again encountered a depression in 1819, the bitterness was intense. Mass meetings erupted all over industrial Lancashire, Yorkshire, and the Midlands. Arrests; prosecutions; spies and circulars from the Home Office; a nervous magistracy—the pattern of 1816–17 was repeated, with Manchester now the centre of the greatest tension. The weavers in particular were up in arms—literally so, cautious citizens feared: drilling at night up on the moors. At last came the explosion. On August 16th 1819, 60,000 men, women, and children marched into Manchester from its surrounding districts, peacefully and in good order, to hear Henry Hunt make a reform speech in St Peter's Field. The Manchester magistrates, watching the great concourse from a room overlooking the square, belatedly decided to take firm action. And when the local yeomanry, whom they sent to arrest Hunt, found themselves stranded amid the now jeering throng, a regiment of hussars was ordered to clear the field. In their charge and the ensuing panic eleven were killed, including two women, and 400 wounded, cut by sabres or ridden over by the cavalry. It was four years since Wellington won Waterloo; now the Government of which he was a member had won the battle of St Peter's Field—the 'battle of Peterloo'. The savage derision of the name was a propaganda masterstroke.

Liverpool's Government was quick to follow up its victory. Ten thousand additional troops were raised, and Sidmouth hurried through an extraordinary session of Parliament a new set of restrictions—the Six Acts. One of these made it illegal to attend a public meeting except in one's own parish. Two guarded against the dangers of armed revolution, by prohibiting public drilling and empowering magistrates to search private premises for firearms. Two more were aimed at the Radical Press, imposing severe penalties for blasphemous or seditious libel, and preventing publishers of cheap newsletters or pamphlets from evading the payment of stamp duty. The last of the six took away from accused persons the right to postpone trial by 'playing' legal technicalities.

Alarums of revolutions continued after Peterloo, until the upturn in trade over the years 1821–25 brought relaxation. In 1820 the Spenceans played their last card. Optimistically, they plotted, under the leadership of one Arthur Thistlewood, to assassinate the entire Cabinet as it sat down to dinner with Lord Harrowby, and then to proceed to the establishment of a revolutionary provisional government at the Mansion House. But they were dupes. The dinner was fictitious, and the whole affair was stage-managed by a Government spy. As the Spencean desperadoes met in a barn off Cato Street, Edgware, they were ambushed by police and troops and arrested. Thistlewood and four of his associates were executed in May 1820.

In this period between Waterloo and the Cato Street conspiracy there had undoubtedly been a feeling of revolution in the air. On both sides of the barricade men were preparing their mental positions. Sometimes this led to a literal taking up of arms, as when the angry weavers after Peterloo began converting hatchets and scythes into home-made weapons, or when, on the other side, the mill-owners' sons flocked to join the yeomanry.

The great literary figures of the day exemplify very well this harsh national division. Sir Walter Scott, that patriotic Tory, was busy raising volunteers to march, if necessary, against any Tyneside Jacobins, while Wordsworth was pressing for a national force of volunteer cavalry and "provision for new churches to keep pace with the population". Coleridge had become second only to Burke as a philosopher of conservatism. Southey was the embodiment of 'the Establishment'. But the rising young literary stars were angry, radical, and agnostic. Keats had a "fierce hatred of rank"; he stood at the roadside sympathizing with the London crowd that welcomed Hunt when he was released on bail a month after Peterloo.[13] Shelley, that pagan idealist, called himself an atheist and wrote violently against the Tory Government and in sympathy with the common people. "Ye are many, they are few", he wrote in *The Mask of Anarchy*; and, in the same poem:

[13] Hunt eventually served two and a half years in jail.

I met Murder on the way—
He had a mask like Castlereagh—

As for that champion of the Luddites, Lord Byron, his general
contempt for the manners and morals of his time extended in
full measure to Tories, bankers, Jews, and the Regent-King
("fourth of the fools and oppressors called George"). With
these three, political and moral attitudes are important only as
annotations to their poetic achievement; but with their associate, the poet-critic-journalist Leigh Hunt, Radical politics
were in the forefront. Together with his brother John, he
edited the outspoken *Examiner*, and was imprisoned for libel-
ling the Prince Regent as "a fat Adonis of fifty . . . a libertine
over head and ears in disgrace . . . without a single claim on
the gratitude of his country or the respect of posterity".

However, if revolution seemed then in the air, it appears
now, as we look back, that this was not really so. The ruling
classes were too powerful, and at moments of crisis too united
and firm; the Radicals were too mutually jealous and divided,[14]
the Army too loyal. Yet the bitterness of the post-Waterloo
years went very deep. At no other time have Britons been more
conscious of being "two nations", the rich and the poor.

However, as Cobbett said, "I defy you to agitate a fellow
with a full stomach." Revolution might indeed have come
eventually if industrial depression had set in permanently; but,
amid the misery, dislocation, and injustice of those years, the
upthrust of economic production continued, however erratically. Despite everything, it was (taking the nation as an entity
and whole decades together) an age of "improvement", as
Francis Place never ceased to emphasize. When the Radicals
organized another march for August 1820 to celebrate the
anniversary of Peterloo, the weavers were not there to march;
even they were back at work.

6. The Nadir of the Monarchy

In January 1820, the month preceding the Cato Street plot,
George III at last completed the formalities of dying. For

[14] For instance, Cobbett's name for 'Orator' Hunt was "the Liar".
Place called him "a turbulent, mischief-making fellow", and considered
Cobbett an impudent bully.

nearly a decade he had been lost to the world, while the Prince of Wales acted as Regent for him. Until his final madness George III in his latter days had ruled sufficiently long, like Victoria later, to become an institution and a respected one. His son, however—obese, ostentatious, and profligate—was already the most despised man in England. His virtues, such as they were—perhaps the most significant was his respect for art[15]—were totally obscured by his follies and vices. It was not only the Radicals who hated him. The Duke of Wellington, whom none could accuse of republicanism or disloyalty, described him as "the worst man he fell in with in his whole life, the most selfish, the most false, the most ill-natured, the most entirely without redeeming quality". George and his brothers, Wellington said on another occasion, were "the damnedest millstone round the neck of any government that can be imagined". It was not merely that George was a glutton, a spendthrift, and a debauchee: he also proved capricious, unreliable, and vindictive—and to his varied faults of character he added gross lack of political judgment. Besides all this, George had a most awkward skeleton in his cupboard: he had long ago secretly married a Roman Catholic, Mrs Fitzherbert, which was illegal; then denied it; and finally committed bigamy by taking to wife Caroline of Brunswick.[16] Indeed, he had invested so heavily in imprudence and vice that the dividends were bound to be awkwardly substantial.

His unpopularity was such that even amid the rejoicings after Waterloo no-one would spare a cheer for the Regent. Politically he had now become as Tory as his father, but no Tory politician had respect for him. He had long quarrelled with his coarse and malodorous wife Caroline, who in 1814 departed for the Continent and lived in extravagant immodesty, with an Italian courier as her 'Chamberlain'. George's daughter and heir, Charlotte, who married Leopold

[15] He patronized a princely programme of building and replanning: Regent's Park with its adjacent terraces, Regent Street (now modernized beyond recognition), Carlton House and its Terrace. In addition, George IV was responsible for Buckingham Palace, largely rebuilt; Windsor Castle, lavishly restored by Wyatville; and that extraordinary extravaganza, the Brighton Pavilion.

[16] To do him justice, he married her only in the way of public duty; a Protestant heir was a necessity.

of Saxe-Coburg, and upon whom the populace spent that loyal devotion they could not give to her father, died in childbirth in 1817. Then, at last, in 1820, on George III's death, this Regent whom nobody loved succeeded as George IV.

He was determined to prevent his wife from becoming Queen and to exclude her name from the Prayer Book. Caroline, equally determined to assert her rights, returned to England full of flamboyance and injured innocence. The best way the crowds could demonstrate their loathing of George was to make a heroine of his slighted wife, whatever failings she might herself possess. Hence, for most of 1820, the English regaled themselves with a powerful mixture of scandal, indignation, and hysteria. Wherever Caroline went she was greeted with peals of bells, processions, illuminations, addresses from clergymen, demonstrations by Whig and Radical politicians, salutes of cannon, and the applause of the multitude—even her military guard once laid down its weapons to clap. And when the King, having procured 'evidence' of her infidelity, forced Liverpool to institute a Bill of Pains and Penalties against her, her daily progress to the trial in Westminster Hall became a triumphal and rowdy routine. Brougham and Denham, her principal counsels, had no difficulty in discrediting at least some of the King's chief witnesses; and the general indignation against him mingled with the salacity of much of the evidence to produce a bawdy hubbub that drowned all else for months. At least some of the Six Acts were, in effect, temporarily dead. London was full of monster meetings and processions week after week, and if 'seditious libel' meant anything the air was thick with it. Caroline was soon employing Cobbett to compose her addresses. But her own vulgarity and over-acting inclined many thoughtful people (including the Lords who had to vote) against her, and there is a good story of the Duke of Wellington, who, when he was held up by roadmenders who demanded that he take off his hat for the Queen, replied, "Well, gentlemen, since you will have it so, God save the Queen—and may all your wives be like her!"

When at last the Lords passed the Bill of Pains and Penalties it was by so slender a majority that Liverpool refused to proceed with it to the Commons. George was very angry;

threatened, unconvincingly, to retire to Hanover; but was duly and splendidly crowned in 1821. Maintaining the air of excitement and scandal, Caroline created a disturbance at the door of Westminster Abbey. Later that year, to the royal relief, she sickened suddenly and died.

The affair was a personal humiliation for George, as well as a hilarious public entertainment; but it had more important significance. It dragged the reputation of the monarchy deep into the mud, where, on the whole, it remained until the accession of Victoria. When George died in 1830, *The Times* on the day of his funeral called him a selfish voluptuary for whom no-one would grieve. Seven years later, on the death of his brother William IV, *The Spectator*, while admitting that William "was, for a King, an honest man", and even a popular one, offered the opinion that "his very popularity was acquired at the price of something like public contempt".

One effect of the George–Caroline fiasco of 1820 was to undermine any authority the new King might have exercised over his Ministers, and the political influence of the Crown continued to diminish. At the same time it put the King himself in a quandary: much as he disliked many of his Tory Ministers, and badly as he thought they had bungled 'the Queen's affair', it ended any possibility of his jettisoning them; for the alternative was the Whigs, and it was those same Whigs (Brougham in particular) who had earned his undying hatred by their championship of the Queen.

Chapter 14

Laissez-faire and Reform

1. Tories, Whigs, and Liberals

In the years following the peace, suicide took an unusually high toll of prominent political victims. First Whitbread, then Romilly, both distinguished Radical Whigs, took their own lives. Then, in 1822, a third and even more famous man followed them. Castlereagh had been wanting for some time to retire. Entirely lacking any lovable public qualities, derided for his awkwardness in debate, he had answered scorn with scorn, and come to wear a defensive attitude of *hauteur* which many took to be intolerable pride. By 1822 the arduous responsibilities of his diplomatic work were proving more than he could bear. He confessed to an acquaintance that politics "tortured" him. His friends, worried at his growing gloom and distracted behaviour, saw that his razors and pistols were locked away, but his servants overlooked the penknife with which in August 1822 he slit his throat.

He had been a notable Foreign Minister. But he had, after all, been one of the leading figures in a Government that sternly repressed all popular agitation; and when his coffin passed into Westminster Abbey hostile crowds broke into cheers that unmistakably meant 'good riddance'. Byron composed an epitaph of calculated offensiveness, and Cobbett wrote joyfully to a friend in prison: "Castlereagh has met his own and is dead. Let that sound reach you in the depths of your dungeon, and carry consolation to your suffering soul."

Castlereagh's suicide, nearly coinciding with Sidmouth's retirement, enabled Liverpool to reconstitute his Ministry, and for the next five years it took on a distinctly reformist complexion. Reform, indeed, was already in the air, a decade before the Great Reform Act, and it was no respecter of parties.

It is quite misleading to see the battles of the eighteen-twenties as between Whigs, in favour of reform, and Tories, against it.

The King's hysterical hostility to the Whigs, confirmed and embittered by the Caroline affair, was one strong reason for the long Premiership of Lord Liverpool, and for the fact that Tory Ministries governed throughout the decade. Liverpool himself was by no means a nonentity (despite Disraeli, who once called him "the arch-mediocrity"). After seeing through the winning of the war and the stormy years immediately following, he managed by 1822 first to reunite all the remnants of the old Pittite party and then to steer his reconstituted Government away from mere repression towards a policy of moderate reform. After 1822 this Government was broadly based, ranging from high Tories like Lord Chancellor Eldon at one extreme to progressives like William Huskisson at the other. Liverpool, in addition, commanded the support of the formerly Whig and highly aristocratic Grenvillites, who had rallied to the defence of established order when it was threatened in 1817–19.

Liverpool had also managed, in reconstructing his Cabinet, to bring back to high office the intensely ambitious and showy George Canning, a Pittite who after Pitt's death can only be described as a Canningite. That he should have become a Tory rather than a Whig was incidental to personality rather than conviction. If he had been more of a 'gentleman' he might well have found a home among the Whigs, but patricians like Grey could not abide him. Canning had thus come into the Tory camp, but, hating Castlereagh and hated by George IV, he remained an outsider till 1822, when he took over Castlereagh's post of Foreign Secretary. (He had been on the point of sailing for India as Governor-General.) He remained Tory in his opposition to parliamentary reform; he proved cautiously Liberal in his foreign policy; his support of Catholic and Negro emancipation put him in these matters close to the Whigs. Liverpool was modestly content to let him behave as though he were Prime Minister. His actual status was Leader of the House of Commons, where he dominated without being loved. Indeed, few men made so many enemies among all parties. The Whigs disliked him, the extreme Tories mistrusted the "tyrannical influence" he exerted over Liverpool. Both sides of the House of Commons saw him as scheming to establish "a dictatorship of public opinion on the ruin of the old parties", while the Radical *Examiner* wrote him down as "vain, intriguing, restless, mean, faithless and unprincipled".

Peel, Canning's colleague and greatest rival, is almost as difficult to classify. The rich and handsome son of the first Sir Robert Peel, the cotton-master and factory reformer, he had high intellectual and administrative ability, but was in many matters the least liberal of politicians. He was very strongly opposed to Catholic emancipation, until Irish events forced his hand in 1829.[1] A rigid Church of England man, he had, as Chief Secretary in Ireland, learned strongly to dislike the Irish. Like Canning, he too was adamant against parliamentary reform. But in two respects his policies did smack of liberalism. It was his committee's report on the monetary system that lay behind the return to the gold standard (1819–21), a measure passionately advocated by the liberal economists; and his removal, when Home Secretary, of the death penalty from a hundred or so offences,[2] though he was merely putting through measures long and unsuccessfully pressed by Romilly, Mackintosh, Bentham, and others, at least secured his fame as a reformer.

Of the other new men in Liverpool's reconstructed Ministry, Robinson (later Lord Goderich) was a Chancellor of the Exchequer fortunate, up to 1825, in the circumstances of his time, although his nickname of 'Prosperity' Robinson was given him only in irony (by Cobbett), when he rashly forecast that the good times were going to be lasting, and what followed was the severe slump of 1825–26. He was of latter years overshadowed by the President of the Board of Trade, Huskisson, who brought great initiative and vigour, and lent unprecedented importance, to that office. Huskisson was another of the Pittites. He had been a strong supporter of Peel over the return to gold, and although he had voted for the 1815 Corn Law, more and more he identified himself with the political attitudes of Canning and with the interests of expand-

[1]See p. 212.   [2] See p. 332.

ing trade. When Canning, the member for Liverpool, transferred in 1823 to a 'rotten' borough it was Huskisson who succeeded him as member for that very merchant-minded city.

Among the Whigs, Grey, who long ago had founded the Society of the Friends of the People, was fully as conservative as many of the Tories. He continued to utter the formalities required of the political heir of Fox; he talked of "retrenchment and reform", but admitted that amid the dangers of the times his reform opinions had received "some modification". Grey, moreover, together with many of the Whigs at this time, was as protectionist as any of the Tories: there was a Whig as well as a Tory upper class powerfully interested in the price of corn. Lord John Russell, a rising young Whig, was one of those who denounced the free-trade economists; they aimed, he said, "at substituting the cereals of Poland and Russia for English cereals".

Besides Grey and Russell, the most important of the Whigs in the eighteen-twenties was Henry Brougham. A brilliant lawyer and a journalist of the *Edinburgh Review*, Brougham had something in common with Canning. Both were upstarts in a world of aristocrats; both had the sort of meretricious cleverness that repels 'sound' men; both were inveterate public performers, tending to appeal to popular, and especially middle-class, opinion beyond the close-knit world of Westminster. Brougham had first come into prominence during 1810–11 over the campaign against the restrictive Orders in Council. He had been the leader of the Whig propaganda that succeeded in abolishing the income tax in 1816; and he had been for seven years Queen Caroline's political manager and champion. (Since the Regent had no son, Brougham, adapting an old Hanoverian principle, had made use of George's wronged wife to provide a useful focus for the Opposition.) He was, however, a restless advocate of causes worthier than Caroline's—legal and parliamentary reform, religious equality, Negro emancipation. He was also the only front-rank parliamentary figure at this time agitating for popular education. In 1820 he even introduced a Bill, bound in the circumstances of its time to be defeated, for a universal system of rate-aided and state-aided primary education, with fees ranging from twopence to fourpence a week; all teachers were to be approved by the Church of England. He helped to found both London University and the Society for the Diffusion of Useful Knowledge, an association which poured out cheap manuals for the lower orders.

If then we look at the politicians of George IV's reign we see issues cutting across parties and parties themselves in a state of flux. To find the ideas that were reshaping politics, we must look less at the front benches of Government and Opposition and more at exterior forces—most of all, at the industrial revolution. The old assumption of the primacy of the landowner's interests could no longer be made. Laws and institutions suited to a rural aristocracy, whose wealth had been centred upon Southern and Eastern England, were no longer relevant to an increasingly industrial society, whose centre of gravity was shifting to the Midlands and North, whose middle class was rich and ambitious for fuller political representation, and whose working class was resentful of underprivilege. Local government suitable for the England of Elizabeth I could hardly be expected to be adequate for the Manchester or Birmingham of 1820. Nothing could be the same now that the very structure of the nation was changing so fast.

In the light of such change the most important politicians of the post-Waterloo era were the purveyors of ideas adapted to the spirit of the age; prominent among them were the Utilitarian Bentham, and Ricardo, the political economist of the manufacturing interest. It was the liberalism of these men and their followers that infected both Whigs and Tories, in varying degrees. A generation earlier Pitt had paid deference to his master Adam Smith, the first of the free-trade economists; similarly now, after the interregnum of the war and the post-war period of fright, Liverpool, Robinson, Huskisson, and to some extent Canning and many of the Whigs, all paid their tribute to the new economists, and in particular to David Ricardo. The Christianized son of a Dutch Jew, this stock-jobber-M.P.-economist became in the few years before his death (1823) the high priest of liberalism. Associated with him and his doctrines were Malthus, James Mill, Place, M'Culloch, and Joseph Hume; and always in the background was Bentham himself, the seminal mind.

The creed of Ricardo and the manufacturers was *laissez-faire*: free enterprise, free trade, unrestrained economic individualism. As Bentham had written, putting forward the famous half-truth of "enlightened self-interest": "Society is so constituted that in labouring for our particular good we labour for the good of the whole." In the free traders' view the landed interest had managed, especially with the Napoleonic Wars and the Corn Law that followed, to gain a selfish sectional advantage that was to the national disadvantage. If only trade, industry, and agriculture were set free from artificial restrictions of all kinds, a load would be taken off the nation's back and prosperity would take a great leap forward. There was a natural, 'scientific' level for wages, prices, and profits alike; an economic law as unchallengeable as any law of nature. It was dangerous and unproductive to interfere with this natural law, whether by Corn Acts, Combination Acts, Factory Acts, wage regulations, or any of the apparatus of well-meant State interference. The fittest would survive and flourish; the weakest must go to the wall; the general interest demanded it. In the words of a merchants' petition of 1820:

> The maxim of buying in the cheapest market and selling in the dearest, which regulates every merchant in his individual dealings, is strictly applicable as the best rule for the trade of the whole nation.

Not everyone accepted the stern laws of this "dismal science". The philanthropists and humanitarians rejected them. So did Radicals like Cobbett, who was as scornful of the "feelosophers" as he was of the "agriculturasses". And not all the political economists themselves were as rigidly doctrinaire as Ricardo and M'Culloch. (Malthus, for instance, favoured factory reform.) However, *laissez-faire* was the creed of the hour. This was the new economic liberalism; and when Robinson, Huskisson, and Liverpool are described as Liberal Tories, this primarily is what is meant.[3]

[3] This is not to say, of course, that this is *all* that Liberalism meant or came to mean. Abroad, it had a special revolutionary and anti-Catholic

2. Economic Reforms (1822–28)

British trade laws and regulations had been founded on mercantilism[4] for centuries, and it was hardly likely that Robinson and Huskisson would sweep away in a year or two the whole antiquated structure. They were politicians, not theorists, and compromised as politicians must. However, between 1822 and 1827 they succeeded in travelling a long way down the road of free trade. The next generation, of Peel, Cobden, Bright, and Gladstone, largely completed what they had begun.

Fortunately for Robinson and Huskisson, the years 1820–25 saw an improvement in British trade. Exports rose, especially in the key 'growth' industries of cotton and iron. The price of wheat revived after 1822. There was a substantial surplus in the revenue. The time was therefore propitious for cuts in import duties. Among raw materials, the tax upon imported silk was reduced from 5s. 7½d. to 4d. per pound, that upon raw wool from 6d. to 1d. The duties on sugar, coffee, cocoa, wine, rum, spirits, glassware, manufactured textiles, iron, copper, zinc, tin, and many other items were substantially reduced; and on all manufactured goods not specified in these reductions, a general tax of 20 per cent was substituted for the existing tax of 50 per cent. This cutting of the tariff on foreign manufactured goods alarmed some British industrialists; it was fine, for instance, for Macclesfield to have raw silk imported so cheaply, but less fine to see French silk fabrics permitted again into this country, and cheaply too. The answer of Huskisson and Liverpool was that it was useless for Britain to ask European countries to reduce their own high tariffs if

---

flavour. It stood for constitutional government against despotism—and this is the sense in which Canning is regarded as pro-Liberal. It came in England to apply to those approving not only free trade, but freedom of speech and of religion. Eventually in 1868 it was adopted as the official name of the party that grew out of the union of the Peelites and the Whig party. Liberalism, however, was essentially a middle-class political creed, and its English parents were the Utilitarians and the free-trade economists.

[4] See above, pp. 108, 153–154, 251–254.

Britain did not reciprocally lower hers. And in any case, Britain's trading position being so strong, it was futile to maintain in existence antiquated prohibitive tariffs aimed against imports from the Continent of (for example) manufactured cottons and woollens.

Huskisson never envisaged a total removal of tariffs, and hence could develop something impossible for out-and-out free traders to contemplate—a system of imperial preference. In return for the colonies taxing the goods of foreign countries more highly than those of Britain, he gave colonial traders important advantages. Canada, for instance, obtained preferential tariffs for both her corn and her timber. While foreign raw wool paid the much reduced 1d. per pound, Australian wool after 1825 paid nothing. Further, the British colonies were allowed for the first time to trade directly with foreign countries.

This last involved a first modification of the old Navigation Laws. A second was enforced by the action of the USA and Prussia, both of whom had passed Navigation Laws of their own aimed against British shipping. Other states seemed likely to follow suit. Huskisson, therefore, secured an Act which empowered the Government to offer equality of shipping dues to all states willing to offer British shipping parallel terms in their own ports.

These measures—the reduction and systematization of tariffs, the return to gold, the freeing of colonial trade, the development of imperial preference, the reform of shipping regulations—were all of a piece. They aimed at a new freedom; they reflected the mercantile and industrial confidence of Britain. A new situation had arisen, which had rendered mercantilist ideas obsolete. Even gold could now be legally sent out of the country. Export bounties were swept away.

As part of this general liberalization, Huskisson would have liked to reform the Corn Law. In a Parliament of landowners, however, it was one thing to reduce or remove taxes on foreign manufactures, raw materials, or shipping; it was quite another to reduce or remove those on foreign corn. Many country gentlemen felt that Huskisson (with the support of Liverpool and Canning) was prepared to betray them. A provincial Tory paper in the mid-twenties, for instance, was complaining that Huskisson was "the leader of the politico-economic party which had done more mischief to the nation than any party ever entrusted with power". When the prosperity of 1822-25 was succeeded, late in 1825, by yet another slump (with a hundred or so bank failures, widespread strikes and rioting, and a recrudescence of Luddism in Lancashire), many were ready to blame Huskisson. In 1826 there was a small relaxation of the Corn Law to relieve the sufferings of the poor. The next year Huskisson attempted to introduce a sliding scale to replace the old rigid limit of 80s. Prolonged and bitter Tory argument ensued concerning the degree of modification to be permitted. Canning and Huskisson strove for a lower, Wellington and the protectionist Tories for a higher, rate. It was left to Wellington, after the death of Canning and the resignation of Huskisson, to fix 73s. as the price above which foreign corn could enter freely (1828). Below that the duty would progressively increase as the price fell. It was an uneasy compromise, whose chief beneficiaries, as things turned out, were speculators who manipulated the price. The Corn Laws remained, the ark of the covenant for Tory squires and farmers, until the combined assault of free-trade economists and Irish famine swept them away in 1846.

It is at first glance surprising to find liberal economists (who formulated theories favourable to merchants and industrialists) championing the legalization of trade unions. Indeed, the Combination Acts of 1799-1800 might well give rise to contradictory emotions among the bourgeois champions of *laissez-faire*. As masters they could hardly wish to see trade unions too powerful; as theorists they could hardly approve of Acts by which the state intervened to prevent free associations of workmen, still less of employers. The Combination Acts, to such masters as Francis Place, were simply irrelevant to the age; absurdities left over from the past. In any case, they did not work: trade unions, however illegal, continued to multiply.

Place, therefore, out of Parliament, and Joseph Hume, inside it, bent their energies towards getting the Combination Acts repealed. First, they managed to 'pack' with their sympathizers a parliamentary committee of inquiry; and when the committee, having interviewed carefully selected trade unionists and employers, reported in favour of repeal, the laws were swiftly swept away. Hume and Place, together with the other Benthamites and the liberal economists, thought that what was archaic and foolish to them would appear similarly to all thinking men, including working men. When employees saw that their own best interests lay in expanding trade and production and in disbanding trade unions, they would disband them. Hume's pained astonishment when workmen, liberated from the law's penalties, flew to forming more unions and declaring more strikes is itself astonishing now. The new legality of unions happened to coincide with the boom of 1824–25; workers went on strike in the knowledge that profits were good and the "wages fund" full. Hume complained that the strikers were "estranging their best friends, and gradually raising the community against them". Lord Liverpool, the Prime Minister, confessed that he had not known the provisions of the Repealing Act; Parliament felt that it had been misled; many employers were indignant. Place thus saw the measure he had so artfully schemed for in danger of being erased, when Huskisson and Peel brought an Amending Act before Parliament in 1825. But, bombarding with evidence and statistics the Ministers he so deeply mistrusted, Place succeeded in saving much of Hume's 1824 Act. Trade unions remained within the law, though their right to strike was so severely limited (by provisions forbidding molestation, obstruction, and the "restraint of trade") that it took a lifetime's campaigning to establish their full rights.

3. The Disintegration of the Tory Party (1828–30)

The degree to which the personality and policies of Canning divided both Whigs and Tories was seen when Lord Liverpool was struck down by a paralytic seizure in 1827. For fifteen years Liverpool had managed to preserve some harmony with Cabinets of variegated, and even clashing, political colours. Canning, the new Prime Minister (reluctantly accepted by George IV), possessed superficially more authority, and certainly enjoyed more popularity with the general public; but he was disliked and mistrusted by many important people. Wellington, Peel, Eldon, and four more of Liverpool's Ministers refused to serve under him. So did Grey among the Whigs. However, most of the Whigs, including Brougham, Russell, Althorp, and Durham, and from the Tories, Huskisson, Robinson, and Palmerston, gave him support; for five months Canning held together a Whig and Tory alliance that showed how meaningless those party labels had become. When he too died (in August 1827) it took only a further five months to demonstrate that his successor, Robinson (Lord Goderich), could not supply Canning's cohesive force. Tired and sick, he abandoned the struggle and made way for the Duke of Wellington, who began by including the Liberal Tories in his Ministry, but treated their suggestions and criticisms with scant respect. When Huskisson, their leader, offered his resignation Wellington accepted it sharply, and refused to allow Huskisson the second thoughts he would have liked; so the whole Canningite group demonstrated their solidarity by following Huskisson out of the Ministry. Wellington was left in command of the high Tories, the 'Ultras', the group whom Lord Palmerston (out of the War Office for the first time in nineteen years) described as the "stupid old Tory party".

Wellington led the new Government in the Lords, Peel in the Commons. These were men publicly committed to a maintenance of protection for the landowner and farmer; to the ascendancy of the Church of England and hence resistance to Catholic claims for emancipation; and to the defence of the ancient Constitution against meddling reformers. Within the next two decades all these battles were to be lost; and it was the misfortune of Wellington and Peel to be forced to assume responsibility for either initiating or accepting measures which marked the defeats. In the course of these various actions the old Tory party was destroyed. The third and final stage of the destruction came with the repeal of the Corn Laws in 1846; the second with the parliamentary Reform Act of 1832; the first with Catholic Emancipation and the events of Wellington's own Ministry of 1828–30.

Canning, like his master Pitt, had always been more concerned to maintain his personal ascendancy than to crusade for principles, and so had succeeded in doing very little for either of the two great causes that he formally supported—the end of Negro slavery and the removal of Catholic disabilities. When the Whigs had been offered positions in his short Ministry of 1827 it was on the understanding that they would not press for parliamentary reform, a subject on which the 'Liberal' Canning was an adamant Tory. (He had always argued that England's traditional institutions had proved themselves capable of promoting reform without themselves standing in need of it.) Similarly, when the high Tories entered —with some distaste—the same Ministry, it was on the understanding that Canning would not repeal the Test and Corporation Acts (that is, admit Catholics and Nonconformists to public office) or grant Catholic Emancipation. Thus, while Huskisson and his colleagues had made progress on fiscal and commercial matters, on religious and constitutional matters the delicate political balance of the Canning era had preserved stalemate.

When Wellington succeeded to the Premiership there was already in progress a strong campaign, which Canning had resisted, to end the laws that discriminated against Protestant Nonconformists. The Unitarians, Baptists, and Congregationalists now concerted measures with the Whig Lords Holland and John Russell to move for the repeal of the Test and Corporation Acts. Peel, more stubbornly Anglican than Wellington, argued that since Nonconformists were not in practice hampered by these dead-letter laws, tampering with them might only harm the "most perfect cordiality . . . the temperate and candid feeling" that had existed between Anglicans and Dissenters "for the last forty years". Public opinion, nevertheless, was moving against him. Even Oxford University, that citadel of the Establishment, was in favour of getting rid of the Test (so the Bishop of Oxford assured Peel); high Churchmen were offended at the profanation of the Lord's Supper involved in the compulsory celebration which was, in law, the necessary prelude to assuming public office. Wellington and Peel, therefore, decided to bend to the majority opinion. Russell's Bill was accepted, and Nonconformists acquired by right the religious equality they had long enjoyed to a great extent in fact. Magistrates and members of city or borough corporations now had simply to make a declaration that they would not by virtue of their office "injure or weaken the Protestant Church as by law established". Jews, atheists, and Roman Catholics were still excluded from the official relaxation.

Thus the Catholic issue remained, embittered and complicated by the problem of Ireland,[5] where the priest-dominated Catholic Association, a state within a state, was in full cry, and five-sixths of the British home army was concentrated. Although Catholics might not sit at Westminster, they could (since 1793) vote in Ireland; and it was taken for granted, even among supporters of Emancipation, that any successful Bill for Catholic relief would have to include a clause raising the franchise qualifications from 40s. to £10. Otherwise Westminster would be contaminated by the influx of (in Peel's words) "persons neither connected with nor representing the landed aristocracy or property of the country, but selected purely for their ultra-devotion to Roman Catholic interests". In other words, not only would the new members not be Protestants; they would not even be gentlemen—and there would be as many as sixty of them. Ireland apart, opinion in England was still strongly swayed by the old cry of 'No Popery'; but educated opinion was moving slowly towards Emancipation. In fact, four times since 1821 Catholic relief measures had successfully passed the Commons but come to grief in the Lords. Even some Nonconformists, especially now that they had won their own victory, favoured ending the old anti-Catholic laws—the Unitarians notably so. Cobbett campaigned more noisily than helpfully for the Catholics. Least well disposed to them were Cobbett's old enemies, the Methodists and the Evangelical party in the Church of England. George IV and, still more, the Duke of York (heir-apparent till his death in 1827) were rabidly anti-Catholic, as became the sons of George III.

Wellington, militantly Tory and dictatorial as he appeared to the public, was not as 'sound' on the "Catholic Question" as Protestant diehards could have wished. The diarist Greville noted in June 1828 that

[5] See Chapter 7, Section 9.

the Duke of Wellington's speech on the Catholic question is considered by many to have been so moderate as to indicate a disposition on his part to concede emancipation, and bets have been laid that Catholics will sit in Parliament next year.

Even so, Wellington might have managed to preserve Canning's masterly inactivity if Ireland had not forced his hand. When Vesey-Fitzgerald was defeated by Daniel O'Connell at the County Clare by-election in 1828,[6] the message was plain. It was not to be an isolated occasion; at a general election Ireland would probably produce fifty victorious Catholic candidates unable to sit at Westminster. Ireland was already lawless and not many steps from civil war; and the Lord Lieutenant advised Wellington that the loyalty of the army and the police were by no means to be taken for granted. The Duke, therefore, began to conduct an orderly retreat to prepared positions, despite a strong cross-fire of anti-Catholic petitions and abuse from extreme Tories. The atmosphere put great strain on his self-control, and when Lord Winchilsea attacked him in a letter to the Press the irate Duke called him out to a duel.[7] Peel, long committed against Emancipation, would have preferred to resign his leadership of the House, but he stayed on at Wellington's request; and eventually (his convictions as ever liable to change colour in the heat of events) Peel carried in the Commons the painful burden of supporting the Duke. He assuaged his principles by resigning as member for Oxford University and suffering defeat in the by-election— an event which delighted the King and all those numerous people who found Peel somewhat too fond of protesting his own moral uprightness.

It was George IV who provided the most difficult obstacle to the policy of Emancipation. For months he procrastinated and complained. At a final six-hour interview with his Cabinet at Windsor he hinted at his right of veto, threatened to retire to Hanover, wept and kissed his Ministers by turns, while

[6] See pp. 212–213.
[7] When Winchilsea arrived at Battersea Fields an impatient and testy Wellington ordered Winchilsea's second to "look sharp and step out the ground. I have no time to waste. . . . Damn it," he continued, "don't stick him up so near the ditch. If I hit him he will tumble in."

sustaining his flagging strength with frequent brandy and water. At last he gave in, "after much whimpering, many protestations, and constant invocations of the Almighty's name". "God knows what pain it causes me", he wrote to Wellington.

In March 1829 the Catholic Emancipation Bill passed the Commons by 320 votes to 142. In April it scraped through the Lords. By its terms Catholics were given equal voting rights with Protestants. They could sit in Parliament, and hold any public office other than Monarch, Regent, Lord Chancellor, or Lord Lieutenant of Ireland. It was to be illegal to found any new Catholic monastery or nunnery in England, and Jesuits were to be forbidden to enter the kingdom. The forty-shilling franchise was abolished in Ireland. The Act was a step away from the past almost as decisive as the parliamentary reform soon to follow it. A special black-edged edition of the *Birmingham Argus* showed how the ultra-Tories viewed it:

Died, full of good works, deeply lamented by every HONEST BRITON, MR. CONSTITUTION. His decease took place on the 13th of April in the year of our Lord 1829, at the House of the *Incurables*.

After Catholic Emancipation there were at least five major groupings in Parliament, in addition to independents and a handful of Radicals. There were two mutually unfriendly groups of Whigs: those under Grey, who had always stayed out of the coalition Ministries of the twenties, and those, such as Lansdowne and Brougham, who had given general support to Canning. There were three principal groups of Tories: the Canningites, now centred round Huskisson; a middle group owning the leadership of Wellington, who enjoyed the prestige that was the residue of his war triumphs; and the 'Ultras', the extreme Tories who had become very sour with the Duke since Emancipation. For a time Wellington kept his ship afloat by virtue of his personal ascendancy and a policy of caution abroad and economy at home.

When George IV died in 1830 the most likely outcome of the party confusion seemed to be an alliance between the moderate Tory Wellington and the moderate Whig Grey, both aristocrats who understood the same political language. It was generally agreed that it was only George IV's rancorous hostility to Grey that had excluded him from office so long, and the new King, William IV (lately Duke of Clarence), was thought to be less implacably Whig.[8] But Wellington failed to make the necessary gestures towards Grey. Moreover, hopes of broadening the Ministry by a reconciliation between Wellington and Huskisson were destroyed when a train drawn by the *Rocket* at the opening ceremony of the Liverpool and Manchester Railway struck Huskisson and killed him.

Wellington, soldiering on through the general election of 1830, returned with his following only slightly weakened. Then, however, he rashly challenged the opposition to his Government, and moderate opinion generally, by an uncompromising speech pledging total hostility, present and future, to any reform of Parliament whatever. It was Wellington who had held the door open for Catholic Emancipation; he now appeared to be slamming it against a peaceful reform of a system of election that was patently out-dated and irrational. Many Tories were as convinced as the Whigs that some measure of parliamentary reform was inevitable. The 1830 election, where reform candidates had done well, and the July revolution in Paris had rammed home the lesson—but not to the Duke. When he was defeated on a financial vote in November 1830 he resigned. It is significant of the disintegrating party-political situation of the times that the majority against him consisted partly of Whigs and Radicals, partly of Canningites, but partly too of disgruntled extreme Tories.

4. The Reform Act of 1832

The new Prime Minister was Grey, who was supported by all the Whig groups and by the Canningites, three of whom (Palmerston, Melbourne, and Goderich) were given Cabinet posts. Grey's new alliance provided the most aristocratic of

---

[8] The new King was affable, undignified, and eccentric; it appeared to Greville that "altogether he seems a kind-hearted, well-meaning, not stupid, burlesque, bustling old fellow, and if he doesn't go mad may make a very decent King".

Cabinets, ten of whose thirteen members were peers or heirs to peerages; of the remaining three, one (Palmerston) was an Irish peer and one a baronet. It is at first sight amazing that so conservative a politician as Grey, at the head of so patrician a Government, should have grasped so firmly the nettle of reform.

To understand, however, the nature of Whiggery and its deeds during the eighteen-thirties, one must look beyond the splendid houses, the ancient families, the careless arrogance, of a ruling class that took its social supremacy as one of the laws of nature. All this was at the centre of Whiggery; and this grand world of the 'connections' was heavily represented in the administration of 1830–34, with such men as Grey himself, Durham, Russell, Melbourne, Stanley, Palmerston, Althorp, Lansdowne, Holland, and the Duke of Devonshire. 'The Whigs', however, meant more than Holland House and Devonshire House, Almack's Club and Brooks's. The Whigs had many poor relations and hopeful hangers-on. There were the great and growing worlds of business and industry, clamouring for political change. There was the wide and diverse world of Nonconformity, traditionally bound to the Whigs as its champions. There were the Radicals, many of whom began to see a chance of working with, and upon, the Whigs. Bentham, for instance, in 1818, while he had called the Tories "the people's avowed enemies", had hoped (though without much confidence) that some good might emerge from the Whigs—more, at least, than from cheapjack Radicals like Henry Hunt or Cobbett. And even at the centre of the Whig citadel itself there were such men as Lord John Russell, a moderate but consistent supporter of parliamentary reform, and Lord Durham (Grey's son-in-law), who was prepared to go much farther than any of his colleagues and to accept both household suffrage and the secret ballot. There was also Brougham, something of an oddity in the blue-blooded world of the 1830 Cabinet. Grey elevated him to be Lord Chancellor, a choice made with distaste, but nevertheless significant. There was no other leading politician who combined to the extent he did national popularity and reforming zeal.

The Whig accession to power came just after an outbreak of

agrarian rioting in Kent, which soon spread all over the
southern counties: the result partly of wages being depressed
by cheap Irish labour, partly of resentment against tithes and
the introduction of machinery. 'Ned Ludd' of 1812 now had
his counterpart in 'Captain Swing'; mills were burned, threshing-machines wrecked, landowners and clergy threatened,
overseers of the poor attacked. However, the new Home
Secretary, Lord Melbourne, showed himself determined to
deal with troublemakers as severely as any of his Tory predecessors. A circular was sent out to lord lieutenants and
magistrates urging swift and tough treatment; and during the
ensuing months many labourers were sentenced to death
(though only three actually hanged). Some hundreds were
imprisoned and 457 transported. The riots, however, were not
entirely fruitless: in some districts wages were forced up from
their near-starvation level.

Movements more consciously political, and even revolutionary, began now to agitate the big towns. Attwood and his rich
Birmingham friends took the lead in forming a Political Union
to press for reform—a move soon copied in other towns. The
'unstamped' journals came again into prominence, the *Poor
Man's Guardian* in particular. Cobbett revived his *Twopenny
Trash*. (Both Carlile and Cobbett, the first successfully, the
second unsuccessfully, were soon to be prosecuted by the
Government for fomenting rebellion.) Hunt returned to
prominence by putting up at a by-election in Preston and
defeating the Whig Minister Stanley. The Paris and Brussels
revolutions of 1830 were much in the Radicals' calculations:
if it had been so simple to oust the Bourbons and the Dutch
with little bloodshed, could not the English do as well or
better? At the Rotunda in Blackfriars Road there were tricolour cockades and inflammatory speeches in plenty. Sometimes attempts were made to link the rural and urban
agitations, and associate them with events abroad, as in a
Hampshire manifesto of December 1830:

> The flags of freedom and liberty are flying over the
> *churches* and *steeples* on the continent; rise, Englishmen,
> and assert your rights and *pull down priestcraft* and oppres-
> sion. The Reform Bill is only a stepping-stone to our future

advantages. Down with the *tithes*! down with the taxes! down with the places! down with the pensions!

Faced with such sentiments and the violence that accompanied them, the ruling classes could agree that the real battle was "not between Whigs and Tories, Liberals and Illiberals . . . but between property and no property, Swing and the law". In that sense the ruling classes were united; but they were split upon the best method of maintaining "property" in control. Wellington and the Tory opponents of reform thought that tinkering with the Constitution would destroy it; any proposal to extend the franchise (they rightly considered) would, willy-nilly, be a first step on the road to democracy: reform would begin by giving the vote to shopkeepers and end by giving it to illiterate labourers. In the process aristocracy and good government, Church and State, would be overturned. The Whigs, for their part, realized that change must come, that 'rotten' boroughs were indefensible, that the industrial towns must be represented. What they hoped was that in one clean operation the corrupt and the archaic could be cut away, the Constitution purified, and the clamour of the bourgeoisie silenced. The 1688 revolution was to be brought up to date; the amendment was to be comprehensive but final. This insistence on a once-for-all reform was shared by almost all the Cabinet. Emphasized by Russell, it gained him later on his nickname of 'Finality Jack'. Of the Cabinet Whigs, only Durham—'Radical Jack'—was for extending reform.

The terms of the Reform Bill proposed by Grey's Government in March 1831 surprised friends and enemies alike. Tories had their breath taken away, and Radicals like Place, always scornful of the "mere, drawling Whigs", could hardly believe their eyes and ears. As slightly amended later, there were five main proposals:

(i) 56 decayed boroughs, with populations below 2000, were to be disfranchised.

(ii) 30 small boroughs, with populations of between 2000 and 4000, were each to lose one of their two members.

(iii) The 142 seats thus set free were to be re-allocated, some to increase the county representation and the rest to enfranchise for the first time the largest of the new industrial towns.

(iv) In the counties the richer tenants were to receive the vote, in addition to the 40s. freeholders who had always had it.

(v) In the boroughs, in place of the various archaic franchises, there was to be a uniform qualification. The householder whose residence had a rateable value of £10 per year or more received the suffrage—that is, the well-to-do ratepayer, whether owner or tenant.

About three town houses in every ten qualified; over the nation as a whole, after 1832, about one man in every six, half as many again as before, had a parliamentary vote. This was not democracy, but it made even so extreme a Radical as Richard Carlile (recently emerged from prison) think, for a while, that he might become "a ministerial man". The Owenites indeed were sceptical. Owen himself,[9] back from an unsuccessful small-scale launching of the millennium in America, was more than ever confident of launching it on a great scale in England, and had no time for so trivial a matter as the Reform Bill. His followers held noisy meetings at the Blackfriars Rotunda, where there was vehement talk of communism, the general strike, and a new co-operative order of society. They were not enthusiastic for a measure which, some claimed, would put in place of the aristocracy "as many tyrants as there are shopkeepers"; and they formed (in rivalry with the middle-class National Political Union) a National Union of the Working Classes.

Before the Reform Act was passed Britain came near to a revolution. Passing its exciting second reading by one vote in the Commons, the Bill was later defeated during the Committee stage. After the general election that followed, the Whigs came back with a majority sufficiently powerful to see a slightly revised version of the Bill through the Commons. In October 1831, however, the Lords rejected it.

During the autumn of 1831 and again in the spring of 1832 agitation was intense. At Nottingham the crowds set fire to the

[9] See p. 338.

Castle, which belonged to one of the greatest of the owners of rotten boroughs, the Duke of Newcastle. Violence and arson followed at Bath, Worcester, Derby, and other places. The worst riots of all were at Bristol. Before troops restored order there—12 were killed and 94 wounded—the mob had sacked the Mansion House and burned the prisons and the Bishop's Palace. (Tory and episcopal opposition to the Reform Bill had sharpened feelings against the Established Church.) Cholera, arriving from the Continent in the same month as the Lords' rejection of the Bill, added its own ingredient of dread to the feeling of tension. Pikes adorned with the tricolour were on sale in the East End of London. Alarmed by the disorders and the prospects of more, the Government consulted Wellington, put troops in readiness, and banned a public meeting called by the National Union of the Working Classes.

A third version of the Reform Bill now passed the Commons, but in May 1832 this too ran into trouble in the Lords. Grey, a worried man, asked William IV to create enough new peers to see the measure through. William refused. A weary Grey resigned.

The question was, who was to succeed him? Peel and two other prominent Tories refused the royal invitation; but when it became known that the Duke of Wellington was attempting to form an administration to pass a watered-down Reform Bill of his own, popular anger exploded. The Political Unions held mass demonstrations; petitions heavy with signatures rolled into Westminster. The City of London's Court of Common Council set up an emergency committee, and all over the town windows began displaying placards, *No taxes paid here.* A common indignation now brought closer together the middle-class and working-class Radical organizations. But it was the middle-class reformers who planned a civic guard with (as Place claimed) "numbers of military men of all ranks and many naval men . . . to organize the operations of the people"; and it was they who kept the Whig ex-Ministers Hobhouse and Durham fully posted concerning the Radicals' revolutionary plans. Against these the 11,000 troops that Wellington could muster, even assuming their loyalty, would be powerless. "It was clearly understood", wrote Place, "that in the event of

Lord Wellington succeeding in forming an administration open resistance should at once be made." It was the same prosperous middle-class leaders who prepared a general refusal to pay taxes and a run on the banks. The slogan devised by Place and his associates, *To stop the Duke Go for Gold,* placarded over London, caused £1,500,000 to be withdrawn from the Bank of England within a week.

In all the hubbub William IV became intensely unpopular, and still more his Queen, Adelaide, who was credited with giving him bad advice. The mob hooted the royal carriage in the streets, and, with reasonable fears for his throne, William made precautionary preparations for flight. At last, however, faced by the possibility of a rising, and the refusal of Peel and other Tories to co-operate in framing a Tory Reform Bill, Wellington abandoned his attempt. Grey was again sent for; he exacted from the King a written promise to create sufficient peers if the need should arise, and re-formed his Ministry. The long crisis was over. Wellington's supporters put the King out of his misery by absenting themselves when the Great Reform Bill passed its final stages in the Lords.

It was a famous victory, and all over the land there were the fireworks and bonfires of celebration. All England behaved somewhat like the little town of Brading in the Isle of Wight:

> ... Everywhere in the Island the news was received with joy and thankfulness, and here they have cracked the poor old Nunwell cannon by filling it up to the brim when they fired a *feu-de-joie.*

The excitement might even be thought excessive, for not a single poor man had gained the vote, and in democratic boroughs such as Preston some had lost it. One hundred and fifteen members still sat for seats, mostly in the South, with electorates below 500. Many dozens even of the boroughs were under the direct political control of local aristocratic families, such as the Somers family at Reigate or the Duke of Richmond at Chichester; and in the counties the landed gentry remained dominant for another lifetime or more. There was still no ballot to prevent intimidation of tenants. Votes could still be manipulated by the sale of forty-shilling freeholds. Bribery and corruption continued: in Ipswich, for example, in 1841, votes were sold for £20 to £30, and Dickens's roaring satire on old-style 'open' polling, the "Eatanswill Election", was written for *Pickwick Papers* some years *after* the Reform Act. The new House of Commons of 1833 seemed indistinguishable from the old one of 1832, and the ageing Cobbett, a Member of Parliament at last (for Oldham), looked a fish out of water among his well-bred fellow members. Hunt in fact lost his seat at Preston. Aristocracy appeared to have given ground in order more firmly to retain it.

None the less, the victory was real and significant. Grey and Russell were wrong; Wellington and Durham were right: the Reform Act was a beginning, not an end. It paved the way, not only to further parliamentary reform and eventually to popular democracy, but also to reforms of a more diverse sort —poor-law reform, municipal reform, the repeal of the Corn Laws, and much else. In the boroughs at least, a share of political power had now come into the hands that had long had economic power—the wealthy bourgeoisie. In this sense the years that followed the Reform Act belonged to the middle classes: the men who built Free Trade and the Liberal Party; who fended off the democratic demands of the Chartists, but were obliged at last to compromise with the working class, much as the old aristocracy had been obliged to compromise with the bourgeoisie; whose sons went to the new public schools and became gentlemen; whom Ruskin and Dickens attacked for their materialism, William Morris for their bad taste, and for whom Matthew Arnold invented the description "Philistines"; who threaded the land with their railways and the oceans with their steamships; who made Britain "the workshop of all the nations" and were at the core of her world-wide Victorian pre-eminence. These were the victors of 1832, and of the years immediately following.

5. The Whig Reforms of 1833–37

A Tory Ministry briefly held office in 1834–35, when William IV tired of his Whig Ministers, dismissed them, and tried unsuccessfully to substitute Peel and Wellington. Apart from this short interlude, the Whigs were in office throughout the thirties. Grey remained Premier until 1834, when disagreements with his colleagues over Ireland and his wish for a quieter life caused him (but him alone) to resign. He was succeeded by William Lamb, Viscount Melbourne, the very antithesis of the spirit of reform. Reared amid the splendours of the "grand Whiggery", a sensitive and amiable man, his earlier years had been troubled by an uncomfortable marriage with the romantic and hysterical Lady Caroline Ponsonby (who at last abandoned him, disastrously, for Lord Byron). Having been buffeted a good deal by domestic storms and tragedies (his only son grew up a mental defective), Melbourne in his latter years inclined to a civilized scepticism, a worldly-wise indolence. He found change in general distasteful and the Radicals in particular vulgar. Offered the Premiership, he affected to find it "a damned bore"—but perhaps so dignified an office should not be refused. A man, as Lord Durham once said, could jog along comfortably on forty thousand a year; what pained Melbourne was the tiresomeness of those busybodies who would not let the country jog along as comfortably. "I do not *like* those things: I wish to avoid them", he said on glancing briefly at a new novel called *Oliver Twist*. His cry was "Why can't they leave things alone?" Yet this was just what the pounding engines of change would not allow. Neither would the earnest Evangelicals or the Radicals eager for modernization. Under their double pressure the Whigs were kept constantly on the move, and continued, between 1832 and the accession of Victoria, to enact far-reaching and varied reforms. The Governments of Grey and Melbourne must be allowed credit: the changes were conceived by the humanitarians and the Benthamites, but they could never have been carried through without the support of the Whigs, however grudging this sometimes was.

An account has already been given of the principal reforms of the year 1833—the abolition, at last, of slavery within the Empire,[10] and Althorp's Factory Act,[11] the first to make any serious inroads on the evils of juvenile labour. Both these were the result of persistent humanitarian pressure. But it was the

[10] See p. 336.   [11] See p. 339.

Philosophic Radicals whose constant goading caused the Whigs most work.

With Brougham as well as Durham in the Cabinet, the Radicals might well consider that at least they had allies in the seats of power. Brougham had been mightily influenced by Bentham, and one of his first moves as Lord Chancellor was to appoint a commission to advise on the gigantic task of codifying the laws of England. He himself did much to reform the judicature. A beginning was made in eliminating abuses in the Court of Chancery (though its delays remained to be scourged by Dickens in *Bleak House*). A Central Criminal Court was established in London, and a Bankruptcy Court. The list of capital crimes was further reduced, and court procedures made more uniform. But a more radical attempt to compile a register of all landed property, in order to simplify the investigation of legal title, and therefore sale, aroused traditional fears of bureaucracy and was defeated. So was an attempt to supplement amateur justices of the peace with professional local judges, to sit without juries.

Politically, by 1834, Brougham was a spent force. Brilliantly able and versatile, he saw himself as another Bacon, bestriding the worlds of literature, philosophy, and law like a colossus. His detractors ridiculed him as "a semi-Solomon, half knowing everything"; and his colleagues saw in him an intolerable combination of arrogance, eccentricity, ill-breeding, and unreliability. When Melbourne re-formed his Cabinet in 1835, Brougham and Durham were both excluded.

Had Brougham's Cabinet influence been greater, the Whigs might have done more than they did for education, for he had been the most prominent of educational propagandists.[12] As it was, the Benthamites were least successful in this field. With Brougham enmeshed in the tangles of the law, it was left to the Canadian, John Roebuck, to urge a radical schools policy in Parliament. He shocked his fellow members, to most of whom the very idea of State enterprise was horrifying, by proposing a national system of primary education, with evening schools, holiday schools for adolescents, teachers' training colleges, and much else that was regarded as "Prussian" and

[12] See p. 345.

likely to damage private educational initiative. All that the Government was prepared to do was to pay an annual £20,000 to subsidize the school building of the religious societies. The grant was small; it was the fact that it had been made at all that was significant for the future.

It was in the reshaping of the Poor Law that the Benthamites secured one of their most characteristic and 'efficient' reforms. The Speenhamland system of poor relief[13] had gradually spread all over the South of England and had had the undesirable effects of holding down rural wages, putting up the rates, and pauperizing the country labourers. To Malthusians, Benthamites, and 'common-sense' manufacturers it was folly: the dole, by insulating the workman from the severity of his plight, merely encouraged him to be idle and fecklessly to beget more children. What the worker needed was not the dole of charity, but the spur of necessity. The facts of economics must be faced: need was the mother of thrift, and industry the parent of productive enterprise. Many a thriving master could point to his own past to 'prove' it; the 'idle poor' must be made to understand it.

The problem of rural poverty was highlighted anew by the alarming 'Swing' riots of 1830–31; and the opportunity was taken to appoint a Royal Commission, consisting of Whigs, Tories, and Benthamites, to go into this vexed question of poor relief, which in the current year of 1832 was costing ratepayers £7,000,000, or 10s. per head of population. By 1834 the Commission had made their report, a sweeping condemnation of 'Speenhamland'. Outdoor relief was "a bounty to indolence and vice". Generalizing from their observations of the most careless authorities, they claimed that "in far the greatest number of workhouses" fit men and women were kept at the parish's expense "in sluggish sensual indolence". The remedy was to abolish outdoor relief altogether for the able-bodied, and to make indoor relief "as disagreeable as was consistent with health".

This Melbourne's Government did in the Poor Law Amendment Act of 1834, of all the laws of the century that most hated by the poor. The Speenhamland system and the old 'mixed

[13] See pp. 297–298.

workhouse' were both to go. Powers were given to a new central Poor Law authority, to consist of three Commissioners, whose task was gradually to bring uniformity to the national system. Parishes were everywhere to be grouped into 'Unions', with paid officials supervised by unpaid Guardians of the Poor. These Guardians were to be elected from the propertied classes of local ratepayers. Union workhouses would segregate the sexes (even married couples were kept apart until 1842) in order to prevent further pauper births; 'repellent' work would be assigned to inmates; the diet would be below that of the lowest-paid labourer, which was very low indeed. The system corresponded very closely to that advocated by Bentham; and the Secretary to the Poor Law Commissioners, Edwin Chadwick, had lived under Bentham's roof, benefited under his will, and absorbed his ideas. Energetic, efficient, far-sighted, and cold-blooded, with a supreme talent for making enemies, Chadwick became one of the best-hated men in Britain. His poor-law work led him into wider fields, and he had a vision of a nation cleansed of bad Governments and bad drains, slovenliness and slums; he may be regarded as one of the grandfathers of the modern health service. But to the poor he and his Commissioners were ogres. In Southern England, aided by good harvests, they made swift progress in re-organizing the workhouses. Rates fell. Great hardships were suffered by the poor, and wages were slow to rise sufficiently to compensate for the loss of the dole. Mother and children in many previously subsidized families were driven by the lash of hunger to find field work, often under the harsh gang system that became common at this time. When the Commissioners went north in 1837 to apply the new Act there, they were met by such violent and organized hostility that in many areas the principles of 1834 proved impossible to apply, and outdoor relief continued. It had long been regarded in the industrial districts as a sort of unemployment pay to tide over bad times, and its threatened abolition was regarded as a piece of upper-class vindictiveness and greed. Some employers, like Fielden of Todmorden, themselves led the fight against the new Poor Law, a movement which soon became part of the wider Chartist struggle. Despite northern resistance, however, by 1840 six-sevenths of England and Wales had been 'conquered' by the Commissioners, and the shadow of the workhouse hovered menacingly over the labouring classes for the remainder of the century.

The Benthamite sequence of commission, report, statute, so characteristic of post-1832 politics, was now followed in the reform of local government. Abolishing the 'rotten' municipalities was to the Radicals the postscript to abolishing the rotten parliamentary boroughs. The 'close' corporations were oligarchical, corrupt, idle, and utterly out of tune with the new age; *The Times* described them as "chartered hogsties".[14] Their members used their ancient privileges unashamedly to promote their personal and party advantages, while leaving serious matters of drainage, paving, lighting, street-cleaning, police, and water-supply to the improvement committees that most towns had been obliged to set up.

When Grey's Government appointed a Commission in 1833 its secretary was Joseph Parkes of Birmingham, one of Place's old allies in the Reform Bill battles of 1832. The report which Parkes and his Commissioners presented was a scathing indictment of the old corporations:

> ... They look upon themselves and are considered by the inhabitants, as separate and exclusive bodies.... They have been preserved solely as political engines, and the towns to which they belong derive no benefit, and often much injury, from their existence.... The members of these councils are usually self-elected, and hold their offices for life. The byelaws ... are seldom published, and the public is generally unacquainted with their provisions, except from common rumour. This ignorance is sometimes shared by the members of the Corporation.... The party spirit which pervades the Municipal councils extends itself to the magistracy, which is appointed by those bodies, and from their members. The magistrates are usually chosen from the aldermen, and the aldermen are generally political partisans.... At Malmesbury the magistrates are often unable to write or read.... Few Corporations admit any positive obligation to expend the surplus of their income for objects of public advantage.... [Finally, after 112 paragraphs of such trenchant

[14] See pp. 70–72.

condemnation] . . . we therefore represent to *Your Majesty* that . . . a thorough reform must be effected.

Melbourne's Government accepted the report and introduced (1835) the Municipal Corporations Act. In Parkes's words, it was "a smasher. . . . We clear the roost from top to bottom." Most of the worst local oligarchies were Tory; the Whigs therefore were not too loath to be driven forward by the Radicals to "clear the roost". The Tories, though they began by mauling the Bill in the Lords, saw the wisdom of accepting the moderating advice of Wellington and Peel. Over two hundred 'rotten' corporations were swept away. At the time it was the political aspects of the new Act that made its Radical authors so jubilant. Parkes wrote to Place ("old postilion" of the Radical coach, as he endearingly addressed him): "*It is done.* Certainly no Conservative majority can ever be got in a British House of Commons. No resurrection for them. . . . Their hearse is ordered."

Constructively, the Act's immediate effect was not as great as might be supposed. The new borough councils (178 of them —London was excluded) were to be elected by all male ratepayers who had a three-year residential qualification. Councillors, subject to a property qualification, were to be elected for three years. They were to choose from their number a mayor, to preside for one year, and a body of aldermen to sit for six years. (The aldermen resulted from a Tory House of Lords amendment to prevent too direct a democratic control.)

With some modifications, the pattern established in 1835 has remained; and both county councils and district councils adopted it as they came into being later. But it was mainly a *machinery* that was created, which one day *could* provide an efficient, democratic, and uniform local government. Towards practical effect the Act worked only slowly. It did not everywhere kill 'graft', but sometimes merely transferred it into the hands of the new dominant class, the 'shopocracy'. The ratepayer electorate was often interested merely in keeping down the rates. Most of the main business of the towns continued for some time to be in the hands of the improvement committees, whose powers of self-liquidation were merely optional under the Act. Many boroughs still did nothing whatever to clean their streets or install drainage; other towns, though growing fast, failed to apply for borough status under the Act. It was slowly that British municipalities struggled forward into the age of smoke and steam. For long years the sanitary conditions of some of them remained, as Chadwick said, "almost as bad as that of an encamped horde, or an undisciplined soldiery".

Until their impetus ran out in the late thirties the Whigs under Melbourne continued to enact useful reforms. Many of their Nonconformist and free-thinking allies would have liked to see them disestablish the Church of England, altogether too radical a proposal to command majority support. But the spirit of the age and the pressure of criticism on the Church from within and without would not let the old drift and anachronism go untouched. State and Corporation had already received their medicine; now, in the last years of the Whig regime, Church drank down hers, which was not very nasty. Although tithes, pluralism, and large inequalities of stipend were none of them abolished, the grosser abuses were remedied. In all this, Peel's part was, as usual, to promote a tactful moderation: the Church of England, like the Tory party, must not resist "the redress of proved grievances".[15] The wild men, including some bishops, and such as Lord Lyndhurst, must be restrained. In order to maintain its essential privileges, the Church must surrender the inessential. In order to have virtue and command respect, it must conduct itself respectably and virtuously.

Among the Church reforms was a Marriage Act (1836); this established the legality of marriage ceremonies in Dissenting chapel or Catholic church, provided that a civil registrar was present—previously the Church of England's monopoly had given non-Anglicans just cause of resentment. They continued, however, to be incensed by the compulsory church-rate, which lingered till 1868.

As a corollary of the Marriage Act, a civil registry of births, marriages, and deaths was established. The Benthamites were always insisting that intelligent State action and bureaucratic

---

[15] The phrase comes from his famous address to his constituents in the election of 1835—the "Tamworth Manifesto".

control were impossible without a supply of accurate data; and now the age of statistics, inaugurated by the first Census (1801), was coming of age. When the Victorian era began in 1837 it was beginning to rain royal commissions; between 1832 and 1849 there were over a hundred of them. Government inspection too was growing: inspectors of factories were soon joined by inspectors of schools and inspectors of mines. *Laissez-faire* was already growing out of date by the time that its praises were being generally chorused.

Chapter 15

Foreign and Imperial Affairs after the Napoleonic Wars

1. Castlereagh and the Post-war Settlement

Britain emerged from the Napoleonic Wars in a position of unprecedented power. Her chief colonial rivals, France, Holland, and Spain, had been defeated and deprived. Her Navy, supreme before Trafalgar, was unchallengeable after it, and remained so for a century. Her industrial progress was ahead of any other nation's.

At the Vienna settlement of 1814–15, Britain could afford to let the continental powers jockey for territorial concessions. So long as these maintained the balance of power and prevented the dominance of any one state she could be easy. Her concern—and no power was in a position to gainsay her—was to insure her supremacy in the world's oceans by acquiring vantage-points for her sailing-ships. Thus she retained in the Mediterranean Malta and the Ionian Islands; in the North Sea Heligoland; on the route to the East the Cape of Good Hope, Mauritius, and Ceylon; in the West Indies Trinidad, St Lucia, and Tobago. (Within the succeeding thirty years she was to add Singapore, Aden, and Hongkong.)

These acquisitions gave her the maximum of advantage for the minimum price. They none of them involved military conquests, large areas, or costly administration. They provided the central pinpoints round which the great arcs of naval power and commercial profit could be drawn. Colonies as such were little more in favour than European commitments. British Governments completely lacked any wish to paint imperial red upon the map of the world. Australia was regarded primarily as a penal settlement. Little attempt was made to annex territory on the mainland of South America, despite the disarray of the Spanish and Portuguese colonies there. (On the other hand, the wildest optimism was entertained of the commercial chances in South America.) Africa was still "the unknown continent". Colonies were long regarded, in Disraeli's words uttered as late as 1852, as "millstones round our necks". Even Java and Sumatra, which did contain immense, though then largely unguessed, trading possibilities, were quietly restored to the Netherlands. It was only on the personal initiative of Stamford Raffles that Britain negotiated for the island of Singapore (1819), and only after the Burmese had conquered Assam and gone on to threaten Bengal that war was made upon them and Assam annexed (1826).

It was Castlereagh who represented Britain at the important conferences at the close of the Napoleonic Wars and immediately after (1814–18): Chaumont,[1] Paris, Vienna, Aix-la-Chapelle. He came to them in a position of unrivalled prestige. He was both the architect of victory and the principal originator of the idea of maintaining peace and security by a continuing congress of the great powers: the 'Concert of Europe'. Diffident and often tongue-tied as he was, the subject of some refined aristocratic titters as he "strolled through the streets of Vienna arm in arm with Lady Castlereagh, gaping at the shop windows like a provincial on holiday", he nevertheless represented the strongest state in the world. This reserved, handsome aristocrat speaking for the nation of shopkeepers was *primus inter pares* among the princes and monarchs gathered together to reassemble the scattered pieces of pre-revolutionary Europe. In the words of Gentz, adviser to the Austrian Chief Minister, Prince Metternich:

> England appeared at Vienna with all the glamour which she owed to her immense successes, to the eminent part she had played in the Coalition, to her limitless influence, to a solid basis of prosperity and power such as no other country has acquired in our days.... Profiting by this, England could have imposed her will upon Europe.

What puzzled Gentz was that she did not seem to want to. Failing to understand the forces making for Britain's isolation

[1] See p. 393.

from Europe and the weight of British public opinion which was assailing Castlereagh for being *too* ready to co-operate with foreign tyrants, he condemned Castlereagh for his "neutral and half-hearted" attitude in the maintenance of European security. England renounced "the noble privilege" of leading Europe. "Being in the position to become the arbiter of Europe, Castlereagh only afforded her weak and partial assistance."

Peace, moderation, and compromise were at the heart of British policies from 1814. The map of Europe was redrawn with nice attention to the balance of power. In general, 'legitimate' pre-war sovereigns or their heirs were restored; but Castlereagh rejected the Tsar's proposal for a written guarantee of all thrones and boundaries. France was treated generously, with no severe losses of territory (Prussia had to be restrained in this respect). She was subjected to an indemnity and military occupation, but both Castlereagh and Wellington were anxious to hasten the day when occupying troops could go home and France be restored to the comity of the great powers on equal terms; and this was done at the Congress of Aix-la-Chapelle in 1818.

This idea of a 'Concert of Europe', a recurrent conference of the leading states, was Castlereagh's own, and provided his greatest ambition after the defeat of Napoleon. However, from the first, he was in a difficult position, which eventually became impossible. In 1815 the Tsar, Alexander I, had put forth his Holy Alliance, which became a kind of inner union of those victorious powers—Russia, Prussia, Austria—who were pledged to maintain autocracy as well as peace. In theory the Holy Alliance was open to all monarchs professing Christian principles; and Alexander, as receptive to ideas as a chameleon to colour, and just now under the rather crazy influence of the pietistic Baroness Krüdener, planned for a day when the relations between sovereigns would be based "upon the sublime truths which the Holy Religion of Our Saviour teaches". But, in fact, the Holy Alliance powers, mistrustful as they were of one another's ambitions (Metternich was as contemptuous of the 'Holy' Alliance as was Castlereagh), shared an attitude towards European affairs that no British Minister could possibly endorse: wherever revolution raised its head, it was to be struck down by concerted intervention.

However conservative Castlereagh's principles, or those of his Prime Minister Liverpool, or of his friend and collaborator Wellington, British public opinion was never likely to support policies which involved force being applied to put down revolts against Governments which most Englishmen thought inefficient and tyrannous, like those of the Spanish or Italian Bourbons. Castlereagh himself, the man who incurred much odium for his support of the Peterloo magistrates and the Six Acts, was indeed, as he confessed, "pleased to see evil germs destroyed"—the evil germs of Jacobinism or democracy—but dared not "give approbation openly". Britain was proud to see herself as the home of freedom. Even those propertied gentlemen who wished to see radicalism stamped out at home had no wish to contribute taxes to maintain armies of intervention on the Continent; even Tories had no wish to see Britain as one of the policemen of Europe.

Thus, when in 1820–21 Liberal revolts in Spain, Naples, Portugal, and Piedmont were greeted by the Holy Alliance powers (in congress at Troppau and Laibach) with plans for suppression by Austrian troops, opinion in Britain was behind Castlereagh when he refused to support their action. In any case, Castlereagh and Wellington calculated that, as with France in 1792, foreign intervention to put down revolution merely stimulated it by injecting it strongly with patriotic ardour. The only domestic criticism of British non-interference came from those who thought it too negative and neutral. Some Whigs and Radicals considered that the British should go much further and positively champion the rebels in Europe as they did those in South America. When Austrian forces subjugated the Neapolitan rebels and collaborated with Russians to suppress the Piedmontese some wanted to threaten the continental tyrants with war. There was even some alarmist talk of a possible invasion of England by the Holy Alliance powers; Russian troops, some said, might soon be encamped in Hyde Park!

Castlereagh, harassed by Metternich and the Tsar, badgered and derided by the Opposition, loathed by the Radicals, already beginning to bend under his load of overwork, doggedly maintained his middle position. He would neither break with nor join the Congress powers. He compromised by refusing to attend their later meetings personally. Instead, his half-brother, Stewart, ambassador at Vienna, acted as 'observer' for him and delivered a formal protest against the decisions taken at Troppau (1820) and Laibach (1821). But Castlereagh would not break free altogether; he could never have said, as Canning said, "Every nation for itself and God for us all."

2. Spain, Spanish America, and Portugal

When Castlereagh died and was succeeded by Canning at the Foreign Office, British policy did not change direction, but its opposition to the autocratic powers did become more overt, and took on at least an appearance of liberalism. "For 'Alliance' read 'England', and you have the clue to my policy", wrote Canning. Unlike Castlereagh, he was in no danger of being suspected of the wish to collaborate with Metternich or the Tsar; and Wellington, Canning's representative at the last of the post-war congresses at Verona (1822), strongly disassociated himself from the preparations made there for the invasion of Spain by French Bourbon forces, which were to restore the Spanish Bourbon, Ferdinand VII. (The Tsar had even suggested that a Russian army should do the job, but this was too much for the other powers; French troops offered the lesser evil.)

Canning, however, though he was more acceptable to Liberal opinion than Castlereagh, was certainly no Radical and only spasmodically Liberal. Long ago he had written for a paper called the *Anti-Jacobin*; his sentiments had not greatly changed. He was much more concerned to prevent a French invasion of Spain than to support the constitutional party there. He accordingly advised the Spaniards to be pliant to French advice. And when his Spanish policy failed and once more a French army crossed the Pyrenees, he rendered no assistance to the Spanish Liberals, who were quickly overwhelmed. He did indeed threaten war, and easily persuaded Parliament to raise the manpower of the Navy from 21,000 to

25,000; but this was soon exposed for the bluff it was. In similar vein he privately asked the parliamentary Opposition to continue to vote against him and argue for war (in order to impress foreign opinion), although he had not the slightest intention of fighting. Certainly he expressed the mood of the country: everybody condemned the French; but hardly anybody thought Spanish Liberalism worth fighting for.

What was much more interesting and promising to "these insular shopkeepers" (as the French Minister Villèle described the English in 1822) was the prospect of turning the Spanish situation to account by action in South America. Between 1807 and 1825 a combination of factors had presented the British with high opportunity there—opportunity both to make money and to adventure in the cause of liberty. It was the wartime difficulties of trading with Europe and the USA that stimulated British merchants to redouble their efforts in South American markets. This story of Englishmen breaking in upon Spanish America was an old one; it went back to the Elizabethan and Stuart buccaneers, to the Asiento and the South Sea Bubble, to Jenkins's Ear. However, a new situation was now created by Napoleon's rude seizure of Spain and the establishment throughout Spanish America of revolutionary *juntas* whom British manufacturers and merchants, shipbuilders and bankers, were only too anxious to support and supply. Lancashire cottons and Birmingham hardware were merely the principal items in a diverse trade valuable to both supplier and supplied. With the development of the wars of independence, led by Bolívar and San Martín, and the accompanying liberation of the South American coastline, the ubiquitous British began to settle in. In the *Journal of a Residence in Chile* (1824), by Maria Graham, we read how

> English tailors, shoemakers, saddlers, and inn-keepers hang out their signs in every street: and the preponderance of the English language would make one fancy Valparaiso a coast town in Britain.... The number of pianofortes brought from England is astonishing....

After her rebuff at Buenos Aires in 1806, Britain made no more official interventions in the fighting in South America;

but unofficial assistance by 'volunteers' was invaluable. That restless firebrand Thomas Cochrane (later Earl of Dundonald), who had been dismissed from the Navy with ignominy in 1814 following his wrongful imprisonment for fraud, reached Chile in 1819 and was given command of San Martín's navy. The British helped San Martín to provide the essential command of the coastline in the subsequent battle for Peru, much as the French Navy had done service for George Washington forty years earlier. As the French were the godparents of North American independence, so were the British of South American. As for Cochrane's own part in all this, Michael Lewis, the naval historian, says of him that for sheer fighting prowess, audacity and ingenuity, Cochrane "has seldom if ever been surpassed in the whole annals of war".[2]

Already in 1817 Castlereagh had declared that Britain would not tolerate any non-Spanish interference in South America, and had gone far towards recognizing the independence of the colonies. Canning, though he would not fight for Spain itself, was prepared to wage war on France or Russia, should either state attempt the unlikely project of subduing the South American revolts—unlikely, since the British fleet, in any such undertaking, was an untrumpable card. What Canning would have liked was a joint Anglo–USA guarantee of the new South American states. With their "common regard for well-regulated liberty", he told a Liverpool audience, the USA and Britain would one day "daughter and mother stand together against the world". These were fine sentiments in the best Canning vein, much echoed by journalists on both sides of the Atlantic; but the USA Government of President Monroe, dominated by John Quincy Adams (Secretary of State), did not wait for Canning. The United States, said Adams, was "not a cock-boat to bob in the wake of the British man-of-war". Already America had given the new republics full recognition (1822); and the danger was (so British merchants and manufacturers and banking houses feared) that America would follow this up with commercial treaties detrimental to British interests. By the end of 1823 Monroe had enunciated his famous doctrine. The Holy

[2] Cochrane served later in the causes of Brazilian and Greek independence.

Alliance powers were warned not to intervene in Spanish America; and *all* European powers, including, of course, Britain, were sternly informed that "the American continents" were "not to be considered as subjects for future colonization". Existing colonies were to be respected.

Canning could now do little but follow the American lead. He had delayed full recognition partly because he, and still more strongly other members of the Government, were hoping that the new states would adopt a monarchical constitution. By 1824 he could afford to wait no longer; Canning and Liverpool therefore persuaded their fellow Tories to recognize the republics of Buenos Aires, Colombia, and Mexico. Even then, threat of resignation proved necessary before George IV would accept the recognition, and he refused to read the speech from the throne personally.

Canning as usual made the most of what he had done. At least he had demonstrated that Britain was determined to maintain her position as protector and manufacturer-in-chief to the South Americans. But the acclamation he received from the public was to be contrasted with the glumness of Parliament when he grandiloquently proclaimed:

> Contemplating Spain as our ancestors had known her, I resolved that if France had Spain, it should not be Spain with the Indies. I called the New World into existence to redress the balance of the Old.

The problems of Portugal and its colony of Brazil proved simpler to handle. Brazil, like all the other South American colonies, had no wish to stay under European domination; and it was Britain that mediated between Dom Pedro, who had proclaimed himself "constitutional emperor" of Brazil, and his father John VI of Portugal. The result lasted for sixty years— an independent Brazilian empire ruled by the Portuguese royal house.

In Portugal itself, as in Spain, there had been a struggle between Liberals (Constitutionalists) and Absolutists; and Dom Pedro, successor to the throne upon his father's death in 1826, and already Emperor of Brazil, immediately abdicated his Portuguese throne in favour of his seven-year-old daughter

Maria. His brother Miguel opposed this arrangement, sought the throne for himself, and received support in arms and equipment from Spain. When, therefore, the Portuguese Government appealed to Britain for assistance under the terms of our ancient alliance, Canning responded. Once more a British fleet anchored in Lisbon harbour, with 4000 accompanying troops, and the Government of Pedro and Maria temporarily restored its position. For this, Canning was hailed as the champion of freedom; but the future of Liberal constitutions in Portugal was to be chequered. When Miguel restored the Absolutist faction after Canning's death, Wellington maintained a rigid neutrality. He discontinued support for the Constitutionalists and refused to allow their volunteers to use British ports as bases for their expeditions. It was left to Palmerston, Foreign Secretary in the Whig Governments of the thirties, to return to something nearer Canning's policy. While refusing official intervention in the continuing civil war, he allowed the Constitutionalists freely to recruit British naval officers. As Cochrane in Chile, so Napier in Portugal. He even took the name of Carlos de Ponza, and won another 'Battle of Cape St Vincent' (1833). The backbone of the Constitutionalists' army was a corps of 15,000 men composed of British and French volunteers, some of them Peninsular veterans from the armies of Masséna and Wellington, old foes, new fighting companions. (In Spain, too, Palmerston permitted a British legion to help the Queen of Spain in the war against the pretender Don Carlos.) Miguel was compelled to leave Portugal for ever; Queen Maria was married, as Queen Victoria of Britain was soon to be, to a Coburg; and the affairs of Portugal were settled, at least temporarily, to the general satisfaction of anti-autocratic opinion.

3. Greece and the Near East

The actions of Canning and Palmerston in Portugal, identifying as they did British power and influence with opposition to the Holy Alliance and foreign autocracy, were clear-cut and popular. The British policy towards the Greek War of Independence (1821–30) was, on the other hand, constrained to be more tortuous and ambiguous. The revolt of the Greeks against their Turkish overlords, which had simmered for decades, now boiled over; and a confused war was fought with atrocious cruelty by both sides. For Englishmen the Greek issue presented an awkward choice between the heart and the head. Romantics like Byron could see in the cause of Hellenism something splendid to fight and die for (though Byron's death at Missolonghi was of fever, not in battle). The 'Greek Committee' in London found it easy to raise funds; every Westerner's education, classical and Christian, was likely to dispose him in favour of the Greek against the Turk.

For Canning and Wellington, however, it was not so simple. It had already become a cardinal point of British policy to maintain the Ottoman power in order to keep the Russian in check. By 1822, as Chateaubriand wrote, "Fear of Russia had made the whole of England Turk." If the Ottoman Empire were seriously weakened, what force could hold the Tsar back from Constantinople and the Mediterranean? Canning's policy, therefore, was to restrain Russia's championship of the Greeks not by opposing but by associating with her. When, after 1825, the Greeks' cause became desperate upon the intervention on the Turkish side of Mohammed Ali and his son Ibrahim, with their Egyptian fleet and army, Canning still flatly refused British assistance to the Greeks; but he was ready to conclude an agreement (1827) with France and Russia for joint action to enforce an armistice and acceptance of the powers' terms.

At this juncture Canning died; and Wellington, his close associate in these decisions, took over. An Anglo-Franco-Russian fleet made rendezvous under the command of Admiral Codrington, carrying strict orders not to fire unless fired at. But an Egyptian army was at that moment putting southern Greece (the Morea) to fire and slaughter, and Codrington, Trafalgar veteran and passionate pro-Greek, found it almost too much to bear. The allied fleet tried to 'see off' Ibrahim's Egyptian fleet, not hoping over-strongly that it would go quietly. When an allied boat, under flag of truce, was shot at in Navarino Bay, hell was let loose. For a loss of 140 sailors

Ibrahim Pasha's fleet was destroyed, with a loss of over fifty vessels.

> I own [wrote Codrington] I felt a desire to punish the offenders—But it was my duty to refrain, and refrain I did [*i.e.*, before the firing of the first shot]; and I can assure his Royal Highness that I would still have avoided this disastrous extremity, if other means had been open to me.

Navarino created a new situation. It was a shattering victory, but it was also a defeat for Canning's policy of balance. He had laboured to prevent a Russian declaration of war; now the Tsar did not hesitate to attack. While his army defeated the Turks and gained the Danube delta (by the Treaty of Adrianople, 1829), French troops drove the Egyptians from the Morea. Wellington publicly deplored the "untoward incident" of Navarino, that "conflict with an ancient ally", and tried hard to maintain the balance of power. Yet while wishing to sustain the Sultan, he, together with everybody in Britain, was quite unwilling to go to war for him. By 1830 it seemed clear that Turkey must lose Greece, and Britain and France accepted the fact; a Bavarian prince was installed as king. It still seemed probable, though, that 'independent' Greece was likely to be Russian-dominated; at first, therefore, Britain and France strove to make the new state as small as possible. The Whigs after 1830 pressed successfully for a northward extension of the frontier, but even so all northern Greece, the plain of Thessaly, the island of Crete, and other fully Greek areas remained under the harsh and inefficient rule of the Turks.

It was two powers, not one, that had been allied against the Greeks—Turkey and her nominally subject state of Egypt. But the Albanian-born Pasha of Egypt, Mohammed Ali, was in fact much more powerful than the Sultan of Turkey, as well as more up to date in many of his ideas. He established in Egypt factories and foundries which produced arms, sugar, steam-engines, and textiles; and now he turned with 50,000 men to fight his nominal overlord the Sultan. In 1831–32 he occupied Palestine and Syria, twice heavily defeated the Turkish army, and soon threatened Constantinople itself. While

France (whose influence in Egypt had been strong ever since Napoleon's invasion) gave some support to Mohammed Ali, Palmerston regarded him as a nuisance who must be cut down to size. Yet this must be done by diplomacy; nobody in England wanted a war to rescue Turkey. The Sultan was therefore obliged in desperation to turn to his arch-enemy Russia for help. The Tsar Nicholas I was more than ready to supply it.

He had abandoned earlier plans for a conquest or partition of the Ottoman dominions, and favoured now the continued existence of a helpless Turkey, over which Russia could stand as 'protector'; or, as Palmerston put it, Russia thought it "better to take the place by sap than by storm". Coming now at the invitation of the Sultan ("a drowning man will clutch at a serpent"), a Russian army and navy moved south to the Bosphorus, within a few miles of Constantinople, and at Unkiar Skelessi a treaty of mutual assistance was signed by Russia and Turkey (1833). In secret clauses, soon disclosed, the Turks gave their Russian protectors the right to close, upon request, the Dardanelles to the warships of other states.

Palmerston, who had been under criticism in the Commons and the Press for allowing the Russians to get so near to Constantinople and the vital straits, could do little at this stage. He did not want war with Russia, and gained a good deal of unpopularity by his attempts to come to an understanding with her, for all parties could agree on the Tsar as the first bogeyman of Europe. France had ever since Waterloo been relegated to second place. Indeed, as fear of Russian ambitions mounted, the logic of British foreign policy pointed, as Palmerston well understood, towards understanding and co-operation between France and Britain. The trouble was that the French themselves did not always seem to understand the logic or appreciate British motives. "The English", as Halévy observes with bland irony, "bore no grudge against the French for being defeated at Trafalgar and Waterloo, and were genuinely surprised that the latter did not reciprocate their sentiments."

When a second Mohammed Ali crisis blew up in 1839 and Constantinople was again threatened, Palmerston found himself equally at loggerheads with a France who regarded Egypt as her protégé and a Russia whose ambitions were chronically suspect. Hatred of the Tsar remained the one emotion that could unite all parties in Britain; on occasions it even held together, as in the Crimean War, the precarious and mistrustful *entente* between Britain and France.

4. Belgian Independence

This Anglo-French *entente* had first come of age after the 1830 July Revolution, which finally overthrew the French Bourbons. Metternich and the despotic powers looked askance at this second French Revolution, as, indeed, did many Englishmen at first; yet it was plain even to Metternich and Tsar Nicholas that military intervention to restore the 'legitimate' monarchy of so formidable a state as France was out of the question. It was even plainer to Wellington, Prime Minister in July 1830. The victor of Waterloo had no wish to fight another Waterloo to put the Bourbons back once again; nor would many Englishmen be likely to encourage him to wish it. And when the revolution took the respectable course of establishing constitutional monarchy, this was regarded by most Englishmen as a plain, if belated, tribute by Frenchmen to British example. France and Britain, acting together, could provide a useful counterpoise to the influence of the autocracies of Austria, Prussia, and Russia; they could, at least in Western and Southern Europe, undermine or even paralyse the already waning authority of the old Holy Alliance. Eastern Europe was another matter; neither France nor Britain could do anything effective to help the Poles when in 1831 they made one of their gallant but hopeless attempts to shake themselves free of Russian domination.

Belgium, however, was another matter altogether. In order to insure against the expansionism of France, the Treaties of Vienna had created a powerful kingdom of the Netherlands, with Dutchmen, Flemings, and French-speaking Walloons— all the inhabitants of the eighteenth-century Holland and Austrian Netherlands—combined in a single state under the House of Orange. It had not been a success. Religious, economic, and national differences accumulated and now exploded in revolt. Brussels took its cue from Paris. In September 1830 the Belgian Liberals and Catholics united to throw out the Dutch, set up a National Congress, and offered the throne of an independent state of Belgium to the Duke of Nemours, a son of Louis-Philippe, the new French King.

By now in England the Tories had been defeated; Wellington had been succeeded by Grey and, at the Foreign Office, Aberdeen by Palmerston. A French King of the Belgians offered no attractions to Grey and Palmerston; it was an idea as calculated to rouse old fears as a French King of Spain. Accordingly, the British Ministers first of all pressed for the throne to be offered to a prince of the House of Orange; and when this proved unacceptable to the Belgians and French one of the inevitable Saxe-Coburgs was found ready, willing, and tolerable to all parties—Leopold, who had been husband of Princess Charlotte and George IV's son-in-law, and who was to be Victoria's favourite uncle and correspondent, overflowing with prudent advice and unexceptionable sentiments. Louis-Philippe and his Minister Casimir Périer, men of moderation and caution, withdrew the French prince from the race. The modern Belgian dynasty was thus founded on Anglo-French agreement and willingness to compromise. When the Dutch attempted the reconquest of Belgium a French army, with British consent, drove it back. And when the old Holy Alliance powers showed reluctance to accept the *fait accompli* of an independent Belgium, Britain and France acted on their own, guaranteeing the new state's frontiers and neutrality (1831). Austria, Russia, and Prussia were obliged eventually to fall in line.

5. Emigration and the New British Empire

By 1783 Britain had lost in America her only populous colonies of settlement. Almost in spite of themselves, however, the British began to lay the foundations of a 'second' Empire in the years following the declaration of American independence. By 1815 they had far outdistanced all their rivals in the colonial race. France and Spain had been defeated; the American colonies of both Spain and Portugal were in revolt;

Holland, paying the price of her enforced alliance with Napoleon, lost Cape Colony, Guiana, and Ceylon. Britain, at the final defeat of Napoleon, stood master of Canada and the West Indies, Australia, South Africa, and much of India. It was a formidable and paradoxical supremacy to be held by a people whose attitude to colonies, trade and profit apart, was in general lukewarm.

A variety of motives had prompted the colonizing activities of the English in earlier centuries: adventure; the thirst for gold; commercial profit; the wish to find religious freedom. By 1815, however, emigration was being increasingly prompted by another force—the pressure of population upon the means of subsistence. This was most acute in the Highlands of Scotland and in Ireland, but with the distress following the wars and economic revolutions it grew severe in England and Wales too.

The main initiative in schemes of emigration was still private, coming from Land Companies such as those that planted settlers in Upper Canada, New South Wales, and Tasmania during the twenties. But for the first time Government and Parliament gave their blessing. To South Africa, for instance, following the distress of 1819, 5000 emigrants were taken, with the aid of £50,000 voted by Parliament—partly to offset the numerical supremacy of the Dutch. To Australia, whose immigrants had hitherto been predominantly convicts, the Government similarly encouraged the movement of free labour. It was with the approval of the Colonial Office that a private company attempted in 1827–29 the first wholly free settlement in Australia, at Swan River on the west coast.

This particular venture was a failure; but, in general, fair prospects lay ahead for these new colonists. Theirs was the hard life for all pioneers; but the demand for their produce was great and growing. It had been during the wars, in the 1790's, that Captain Macarthur, an officer of the small Australian garrison, seeing the superb possibilities for sheep, had caused the Spanish merino breed to be introduced from Cape Colony. Back home, he had persuaded manufacturers that in this enterprise lay their chance to be independent of foreign wool. They put money into the sheep runs and became the true founders of free Australia. In the second and third decades of the century New South Wales grew apace. It established churches and schools, its first newspaper, its first bank. It achieved its own legislative council, its own law courts. In 1825 Tasmania became a separate state, with its own institutions. The map of Australia is imprinted unmistakably with the developments of the thirties: Victoria (1835), after the then princess; Melbourne, its principal town, after the Prime Minister; Adelaide, after the Queen—chief city of the new colony of South Australia (1836). Both Victoria and South Australia were founded by settlers anxious to free their colonies, from the beginning, from the taint of association with convicts. Even so, by 1837 the flow of emigration to Australia was only beginning.

One of the Englishmen behind the successful colonization of South Australia was Edward Gibbon Wakefield. The career of this important and original-minded Radical had been in one sense blighted, in another created, by the scrapes and disgraces of his youth. Eloping at twenty, he rashly on the death of his first wife lured away a young schoolgirl heiress, tricked her by fraud and forgery, married her at Gretna Green, and was given a three years' prison sentence. In Newgate, Wakefield turned his mind to the affairs of Australia (to which so many of his fellow convicts were destined to go) and anonymously published his remarkable *Letter from Sydney* (1829), diagnosing the causes of Australia's slow development. These were the transportation system, and the inordinate size of the estates purchased for a song. Australia would prosper only if land were sold in smaller lots at a price sufficiently high to produce a fund for promoting and subsidizing further emigration.

Released from prison, Wakefield composed one of the most powerful of all tracts in the English language (of which he was a master) attacking the death penalty; but subsequently he specialized entirely in colonial affairs. He influenced some of the Benthamites, who in general had been inclined to follow Adam Smith's condemnation of colonies rather slavishly. One of those impressed by Wakefield's ideas was 'Radical Jack' Durham, who took him to Canada as his private secretary on the famous mission that followed the rebellions of 1837. By that time Wakefield had also become managing director of the New Zealand Association; he and his Company were to become the founding fathers of that colony.

It was to Canada that the broadest stream of emigration moved: between 1815 and 1830 an average of 20,000 settlers a year. Of these a very high proportion were Scots and Irish; many English were shipped off by Poor Law authorities anxious to lower local rates; others went out under the scheme of the Canadian Land Company, which offered cheap lots of Ontario land totalling in all over a million acres. Some of these Canadian immigrants eventually found their way south over the border into the USA. Many thousands more, roughing it in the transatlantic emigrant ships, sailed to the USA direct; during this time the foundations were laid of five new states in the wild lands of the great Mississippi basin.

6. West Indies, South Africa, India, Canada

"Great Britain derives nothing but loss from the dominion which she exercises over her colonies." So Adam Smith had said. The Liberal free-traders generally echoed him. Most Radicals agreed. Nevertheless, apathetic or hostile as the average Englishman was to imperial expansion, there was one aspect of it that touched both the imagination and the pockets of the great army of British church-goers and chapel-goers. Since the close of the eighteenth century more and more missionaries had been going out to evangelize the colonies, financed by collections from every congregation in the land, and especially by donations from the often wealthy Evangelicals whose influence was now at its height. The missionaries had a big share in the battle against slavery. In the tropical colonies their championship of the slaves frequently led them into conflict with the whites; one Nonconformist, the Rev. John Smith, was even condemned to death for fomenting a Negro rising in Demerara (1823), and died while awaiting execution. Back home, however, the accounts of the missionaries, read in hundreds of pulpits, fell on receptive ears, and played a part in creating the public opinion that forced abolition through.

At the Colonial Office the missionaries were pushing against an open door. Here a handful of civil servants in effect governed the Empire. The most important of them was Sir James Stephen, legal adviser and later Permanent Secretary at the Colonial Office, a member of the Clapham Sect, a powerful co-ordinator of missionary endeavour, and a stern guardian of the rights of native underdogs against privileged whites. The inept Lord Glenelg, Colonial Secretary from 1835, was another Evangelical.

The antipathy between Westminster idealism and man-on-the-spot 'realism' was not new. Burke and Fox had demonstrated it in their tussle with Warren Hastings, and it was to have a long history. But Stephen and his colleagues gave their influence a distinct hallmark—Evangelical, bureaucratic, and authoritarian. Often the colonial governor proved to have less power than the Whitehall 'governess'; and of the fifteen colonies acquired in 1815 or the years immediately following, none was trusted with its own legislative assembly, as the older colonies had mostly been.

This strongly directed colonial policy, well-meaning as it was, ran into heavy trouble both in the West Indies and South Africa. In the West Indies three factors combined to bring upheaval to the economy: the emancipation of the slaves, the introduction of sugar beet in Europe, and the abandonment of trade protection. For the loss of their slave property the planters did receive compensation, but £19 per slave, as against the preceding market price of £35, meant bankruptcy for some. Then the freed slaves proved far from eager to work on the sugar plantations, many of which fell derelict. Already threatened by competition from beet-sugar, the West Indian cane-sugar producers saw Britain's free-trade policy as the last straw. They were obliged now to compete with such cheap-producing countries as Brazil, where slavery still remained. The West Indies, the most precious islands (according to earlier ideas) in the entire British Empire, became a depressed area, its white inhabitants resentful of a home Government whose ideas paid no heed to their cause, and its Negroes left to stew in the juice of their emancipated poverty.

.   .   .   .   .

Still more pregnant with the future's troubles were the dealings of Stephen and Glenelg with South Africa. Here there was
the same resentment at the compensation terms for the loss of
the slaves and at the 'interference' of the British missionaries.
The Dutch farmers (Boers) looked on slavery as 'natural' and
Bible-blessed. They regarded the southward-moving Bantu
warriors (Kaffirs, Swazis, Basutos, Griquas, Zulus, Matabeles)
as bloodthirsty savages who should be met not with kind words
but with musketry. To Glenelg and Stephen these formidable
Bantu conquerors, the forefathers of the modern black South
Africans, were victims of "systematic injustice". To Sir Benja-
min d'Urban, the vigorous British Governor at the Cape, and
even more so to every Boer in the Colony, they were "merciless
barbarians". After driving off the Kaffirs in 1834–35, d'Urban
extended the frontier against them as a safeguard against their
raids, only to be overruled by Glenelg, who drew back the
frontier again and recalled d'Urban. Between 1835 and 1837
some hundreds of the bolder families among the Dutch,
exasperated by what they considered the sentimentalism and
ignorance of the British Government, began the Great Trek
northward. The story of the *voortrekkers,* fighting off the
Bantus as they moved over the Orange and Vaal rivers and
across the Drakensberg mountains into Natal, is one of the
epics of modern times. It was an exodus like that of those
Israelites of old who provided the Boers with their ways of
thought. With their few household belongings and their women
and children in their tented wagons, and their great herds of
cattle and sheep driven ahead of them, laagering together for
protection in the night, the Boer patriarchs were searching for
a promised land where they and theirs might live undisturbed.
In one sense they triumphed, and refounded their civilization
in a new land; but in another sense they were pursuing a rainbow. Where they went the alien nineteenth century followed,
with its diamond- and gold-mines and international finance;
and the twentieth century has not let them be, with its cries
of racial equality and black man's nationalism. The modern
white South African's sentiments towards the censure of
foreign liberals provide a close match for those of his great-
great-grandfather towards the Colonial Office Evangelicals of

the 1830's. When in 1837, after defeating the Matabele tribes, the migrant Boers established the first of their free republics, they took occasion, in their simple new Constitution, specifically to ban all dealings with the London Missionary Society.

In India, as in the old slave-owning colonies, times were changing. When, in anticipation of the lapse of the East India Company's charter in 1833, a parliamentary committee reported on Indian affairs, its language showed the times' new earnestness and sense of responsibility:

> It is recognized as an indisputable principle [it reported] that the interests of the native subjects are to be consulted in preference to those of Europeans whenever the two come in conflict.

Opinion had moved a long way since the days of "Diamond" Pitt and the nabobs, or even since Clive had stood "amazed at his own moderation" in the accepting of bribes. Since then the British had extended their sway, direct or indirect, over the sub-continent, and the new India Act of 1833 formally recognized the fact when it used for the first time the title of Governor-General *of India*. He was subject only to the overriding power of the British Crown and Parliament. The Company was not yet abolished, but it was finally divested of its power to trade, and remained in the last quarter-century of its life little more than the agent of the British Government. The profit motive and the white man's responsibility were at last officially admitted to be irreconcilable. For the first time, too, India was to have a unified legal system, which was to pay regard to "the rights, feelings, and peculiar usages of the people".

It was under the Governor-Generalship of Lord William Bentinck that these liberal and enlightened changes, which had been slowly coming in India for many years, were given statutory form. Bentinck's was the authority behind other reforms, too, that showed the British were anxious to assert Western ideas and root out social evils even when these were sanctified by long Hindu custom. Thus a beginning was made in the task of stamping out suttee (the devout immolation of

newly bereaved widows and concubines on the funeral pyre
of their lord and master), and the ancient practice of sacrificial
murder by the secret society of Thugs, the devotees of Kali,
goddess of destruction. In a still more far-reaching respect
Bentinck, together with Macaulay, the newly appointed Law
Member of his Council (the Whig historian-poet-politician),
imposed the West upon India. From 1835 public grants were
assigned to help the missionaries and to subsidize schools and
colleges for higher education using the English tongue as the
medium of instruction. The arguments that had long persisted
about the rival merits of Sanskrit, Arabic, and English were
settled when Macaulay's confident recommendations in favour
of English were adopted. English was destined to become for
India what Latin had been for medieval Europe; and even
today no more generally acceptable language has been found
in which Indians may argue their own affairs intelligibly to
one another.

The problems of Canada resembled those of South Africa in at
least one respect: in each Britain had taken control of a colony
previously settled and governed by another European power.
The younger Pitt's solution for the Canadian situation had
been to separate the quarrelling halves of Canada, the British
and the French, in the illusory hope that the French would
in time come to see the superiority of British forms of government and seek to re-unify the colony. By 1830 British (Upper)
Canada (Ontario) and French (Lower) Canada (Quebec) had
each developed its own collection of discontents. Common
to both of them, and to several of the Maritime Provinces (such
as Nova Scotia), was the old grievance that had troubled the
Americans in the previous century: the legislative powers of
the various representative assemblies chafed against the
limitations imposed by the executive power of the British
governors, themselves now governed rather strictly by the
Colonial Office in London. The nearness of the USA to British
Canada, and the constant exchange of ideas as well as migrants
over the border, also made for restiveness; so did the exclusiveness of the governing clique. In French Canada the clash
between the Assembly and the Governor's executive council

was made bitterer than elsewhere by the difference of nation-
ality; and throughout Quebec province there was a cleavage
between old-established Frenchman and new-come Briton
which made good government, cultural intercourse, and
economic progress alike impossible.

In both Quebec and Ontario rebellions broke out in 1837.
As rebellions, neither came to very much; but out of them
arose something of great long-term significance. Durham, sent
out to deal with the aftermath of the revolts, and taking with
him the two 'Radical Imperialists' Gibbon Wakefield and
Charles Buller, had the mortification of seeing his decisions
thrown over by Melbourne's Government, who forced his
resignation. His *Report on the Affairs of British North America*,
however, not only recommended the re-uniting of Canada; it
also advocated 'responsible government'—that is, that the
executive councils should be answerable not to the Colonial
Office in Westminster but to the elected legislative assemblies
in the colonies themselves. Genuine, full self-government,
Durham argued, was the only way to reconcile the two ideas
of empire and of popular sovereignty. This principle was to
prove the foundation-stone upon which the new Commonwealth was to be based, and which Canada was the first nation
to put to the test.

Chapter 16

Later Georgian Society

1. The "Condition-of-England-Question"

Concerning the state of the nation in the early industrial age—what Carlyle called the "Condition-of-England-Question"—there has been much debate both among the men of that generation itself and among historians since. Some[1] have seen it as "the Bleak Age", with ruthless and rampant capitalism exploiting the wretched and helpless poor. Others have judged it to be essentially an "Age of Improvement", with the new industrialization as the key to expansion and rising living standards. Both of these views see facets of the truth.

It is easy to paint the horrors of the early industrial age. They were real and many: sweated labour in textile factories, where seven-year-olds slaved from 6 A.M. to 8.30 P.M., and longer in busy times, for 3s. a week; or in mines, where adolescent girls, harnessed by trace and chain, crawled on all fours along narrow tunnels, dragging three-hundredweight loads of coal; filthy slums without sewerage or hope, where the average expectation of life at birth did not exceed eighteen years; careless and callous exploitation of the weak by the powerful; the common people, as Coleridge protested,

> mechanized into engines for the manufactory of new rich men; yea the machinery of the wealth of the nation made up of the wretchedness, disease and depravity of those who should constitute the strength of the nation.

Yet wrongs such as these, though they were intensified by the industrial revolution, were not created by it; and the public spirit of this same industrial age must have the credit for

[1] Notably J. L. and L. B. Hammond, in four books: *The Village Labourer*, *The Town Labourer*, *The Skilled Labourer*, and *The Bleak Age*.

PRINCIPAL CENTRES
OF INDUSTRY (c.1830)

LARGEST PORTS UNDERLINED

Coalfields
c.1830

"Every traveller in Britain
noticed the extraordinary
way in which industry
and population were
being concentrated near
the coal measures."

ABERDEEN

TEXTILES
SHIPS
CARRON
IRON
EDINBURGH
GLASGOW COTTON
NEW LANARK

SHIPS
NEWCASTLE

CARLISLE
COTTON
WHITEHAVEN *IRON*

MACHINERY

DARLINGTON STOCKTON

WOOL
PRESTON BRADFORD
BLACKBURN LEEDS HULL
BOLTON
LIVERPOOL TON
MANCHESTER *STEEL*
SHEFFIELD
SILK
SALT
POTTERY
STOKE
DERBY NOTTINGHAM
LACE
IRON MACHINERY *HOSIERY*
HARDWARE LEICESTER
I R O N BIRMINGHAM

NORTHAMPTON
LEATHER

EAST IN DECLINE

MERTHYR
TYDFIL
IRON
SWANSEA CARDIFF
MISCELLANEOUS
LONDON
BRISTOL
T E X T I L E S
MANUFACTURES

MOST INDUSTRIES OF THE SOUTH AND

probing, publicizing, and eventually getting rid of many of the grosser scandals. In the early nineteenth century, that age of rapid economic growth, nothing was growing faster than the national conscience. Never had there been so much serious diagnosing of the ills of society, or such earnest endeavour to cast them out. It has been well said[2] that "the bleak rationalism of the Utilitarians and the narrow pietism of the Evangelicals", apparently opposite and incompatible, "were like flint and steel to one another, and from their contact there sprang the spirit of moral idealism and the passion for reform which burn like fire beneath the hard surface of the age of iron and steam".

By the 1820's the industrial revolution was a lusty child. In that decade most of the towns that were to become Britain's largest grew at a faster rate than ever before or since. In thirty years the populations of towns such as Glasgow, Manchester, Birmingham, and Liverpool had doubled or trebled. Growing fastest of all, if we except George IV's Brighton as a special case, was Bradford. London grew slightly less quickly (from 865,000 in 1801 to 1,500,000 in 1831), but since it was already so big, its problems were still acute. Every industrial town in the country was showing growth, none of it in any way planned or controlled.

Fear and anger, as well as conscience, spurred the processes of reform. In particular, during 1831–32, the gradual spread across the country of cholera (previously described comfortably as 'Asiatic') produced apprehension and recrimination. Religious bodies set aside August 22nd 1832 as a day of "humiliation and prayer", but in Lambeth in that same month placards were displayed showing a very different attitude:

Has

DEATH

(IN A RAGE) Been invited by the Commissioners of Common Sewers to take up his abode in Lambeth? or from what other villanous cause proceeds the frightful Mortality by which we are surrounded?

In this Pest-House of the Metropolis, and disgrace to the Nation, the main thoroughfares are still without Common

[2] By Christopher Dawson, in *Ideas and Beliefs of the Victorians*, p. 30

Sewers, although the Inhabitants have paid exorbitant Rates from time immemorial!!!!

> *'O Heaven that such companions thou'dst unfold*
> *'And put in every honest hand a whip*
> *'To lash the rascals naked through the world.'*

Unless something be speedily done to allay the growing discontent of the people, retributive justice in her salutary vengeance will commence her operation with the *Lamp Iron* and the *Halter.*

London, bad as were many of its riverside slums, its East End tenements of one room, and its cellar dwellings, to some extent escaped both the pauperization that depressed rural England at this time and the worst of the spasmodic distress and sanitary chaos that afflicted the raw northern and midland towns. South Lancashire and the West Riding of Yorkshire supply grimmer texts. In one part of Manchester, for instance, Friedrich Engels (who was later to finance and collaborate with Karl Marx) found that the wants of more than 7000 inhabitants were supplied by 33 privies. The cellar dwellings were naturally lacking such "necessaries", and in Manchester 20,000 (mostly Irish) lived in cellars and unspeakable squalor — one working family in every ten. (In Liverpool the proportion grew, during the worst years, to be one in five.)

Engels' historic *Condition of the Working Classes in England* dates from 1844, but his picture is broadly valid for the preceding decade. In "Little Ireland" at Ancoats (Manchester) he describes how he saw

> a horde of ragged women and children swarm about, as filthy as the swine that thrive upon the garbage heaps and in the puddles.... The race that lives in these ruinous cottages behind broken windows mended with oilskin, sprung doors and rotten door-posts, or in dark wet cellars in measureless filth and stench ... must really have reached the lowest stage of humanity.... In each of these pens, containing at most two rooms, a garret and perhaps a cellar, on the average twenty human beings live.... For each one hundred and twenty persons, one usually inaccessible privy is provided; and in spite of all the preachings of the physicians, in spite of the excitement into which the cholera

epidemic plunged the sanitary police by reason of the condition of Little Ireland, in spite of everything, in this year of grace, 1844, it is in almost the same state as in 1831.

A little way away, he looked across the river Irk at Ducie Bridge:

> The view from this bridge, mercifully concealed from mortals of small stature by a parapet as high as a man, is characteristic for the whole district. At the bottom flows, or rather stagnates, the Irk, a narrow, coal-black, foul-smelling stream full of debris and refuse which it deposits on the shallower right bank. In dry weather, a long string of the most disgusting, blackish-green, slime pools are left standing on this bank, from the depths of which bubbles of miasmatic gas constantly arise and give forth a stench unendurable even on the bridge forty or fifty feet above the surface of the stream. . . . It may be easily imagined, therefore, what sort of residue the stream deposits. Below the bridge you look upon the piles of debris, the refuse, filth and offal from the courts on the steep left bank; here each house is packed close behind its neighbour and a piece of each is visible, all black, smoky, crumbling, ancient. . . . Here the background embraces the pauper burial-ground, the station of the Liverpool-Leeds Railway, and in the rear of this, the Workhouse, the 'Poor-Law Bastille' of Manchester, which, like a citadel, looks threateningly down from behind its high walls and parapets on the hilltop upon the working people's quarter below.

Even so, a walk of a little more than half an hour from the Irk's fetid slime would take you to the heather of Kersal Moor; and a shorter time still would bring you, past the solid suburban villas of the manufacturers, to the open country round Sheffield, Leeds, or Bradford. Few towns had topped the 100,000 mark by 1837. Cobbett had raged at the "wens", the monstrous urban growths created by and for profiteers and 'fundholders', but the towns had not yet destroyed the green and pleasant land. Engels' picture is true, but not the whole truth. In 1837 the 'typical' Englishman was still a countryman. The Census of 1831 showed 961,000 families engaged in agriculture—far and away the most numerous occupation. An easy second came domestic service; one-third of all the girls in London between fifteen and twenty years old were domestic servants. The industrial revolution was potent, and in many of its aspects alarming; but it is well to remember that even in 1837 there were far more hand-craftsmen of the old type than factory workers. For a few more years yet there were more shoemakers than coal-miners.

Similarly, the 'typical' home of the labouring class was not the Manchester cellar, the Bradford slum terrace, or the tenement room in Glasgow; it was the rural cottage of stone, brick, or half-timber, with its glazed windows and its roof of thatch, tile, or slate. Often this home was of only two or three rooms, with sometimes only a single bedroom, on the hayloft principle, for the whole family; but generally speaking (and especially south of the Thames) it was substantially built, and visitors from abroad agreed in noting the decency of rural conditions in England compared with those prevailing on the Continent. "Outside some of the northern factory districts and the low quarters of London", wrote the German Meidinger in 1828, "one seldom sees rags and tatters in England, and as seldom broken window-panes and neglected cottages." Cobbett, too, who was a good deal more critically inclined than this German visitor, frequently praises the houses of his native South Country.

Cobbett, however, had a good deal to say against rural housing in the more backward areas. Mid-Leicestershire was one of these:

> Look at these hovels, made of mud and straw; bits of glass, or of old cast-off windows, without frames or hinges frequently, but merely stuck in the mud-wall. Enter them and look at the bits of chairs and stools; the wretched boards tacked together to serve for a table; the floor of pebble, broken brick or the bare ground; look at the thing called a bed; and survey the rags on the backs of the wretched inhabitants.

Cobbett found Welsh and Scottish housing similarly primitive; but at least in the Lowlands it was better than it had ever been before; and as for the cottages of the Black Country (where there had by this time been an enormous concentration of the iron industry), or of the Yorkshire weavers, or of the Durham miners, Cobbett allowed that they were good. The work of the miners was "terrible to be sure ... but, at any rate, they live well, their houses are good and their furniture good".

In fact, despite all the distress of the post-Waterloo generation and the recurrent economic crises (1816, 1819, 1826, 1831, 1837), it was still, if we speak in averages, an age of rising living standards. The purchasing power of the average wage was higher at the opening of Victoria's reign than at the time of Waterloo—that of skilled craftsmen and industrial workers much higher. The trouble was that large numbers of unfortunates lived far below this average, and below the standards their fathers had enjoyed—handloom-weavers and frameknitters especially; many agricultural labourers also (especially in the South, where there was no competition from high factory wages); and small farmers, once independent, but unable to survive post-war conditions. It was such as these, together with the wretched immigrant Irish, who made the era of the Luddites and Peterloo, of "Captain Swing" and the Chartists, such a "bleak age" of discontent.

For over thirty years after Waterloo, Britain was never far away from a sense of crisis. At the back of men's minds was the great fact of the French Revolution and the possibilities of a British upheaval on the same scale. In the very last year of the Georgian era (1837) Thomas Carlyle published his reverberating masterpiece on that very subject—*The French Revolution.* This was a book that rolled like thunder; and many men, very different in outlook from Carlyle, felt the thunder over Britain in these years. The manufacturer Engels heard it up in Lancashire. The young Disraeli, dandy, novelist, and aspiring politician, wrote of the rich and the poor as "two nations, between whom there is no intercourse and no sympathy". Greville, diarist and secretary to the Privy Council, saw such "frightful contrast" between "the luxury and splendour of the rich and these scenes of starvation and brutality" that he was "convinced that before many years elapse these things will produce some great convulsion". At the time of Peterloo and after, some of the large country houses kept artillery ready, in case of attack by the mob; such fears lasted until the mid-century.

Yet, despite the feeling of crisis and the sense, in many minds, of national failure, it did remain an age of improvement, and we have the advantage of knowing that there *was* no "great convulsion". Among the optimists who always maintained that progress was no illusion was the Rev. Sydney Smith, that urbane and pungent wit whose views were very typical of upper-class opinion.[3] Towards the end of his life he countered the Jeremiahs in a characteristic piece:

> Mr Editor—It is of some importance at what period a man is born. A young man alive at this period hardly knows to what improvements of human life he has been introduced. I would bring to his notice the following eighteen changes which have taken place in England since first I began to breathe . . .
>
> 'The good of ancient times let others state,
> I think it lucky I was born so late.'

He proceeds to give his (not wholly serious) list: gas-lighting, McAdam roads, wooden street-paving, railroads, steamships ("I have been nine hours in sailing to Dover before the invention of steam"), quinine for the ague, umbrellas, the Reform Bill, the London police, braces for keeping "small clothes in their proper place", etc. In a weightier passage in praise of the *Edinburgh Review* he reminded his readers what life had been like before 1802, the year when Brougham, Jeffery, and Smith himself had founded this celebrated journal:

> The Catholics were not emancipated—the Corporation and Test Acts were unrepealed—the Game Laws were horribly repressive. . . . Prisoners tried for their lives could have no Counsel—Lord Eldon and the Court of Chancery pressed heavily on mankind—Libel was punished by the most cruel and vindictive imprisonments—the principles of Political Economy were little understood—the Laws of Debt and of Conspiracy were upon the worst possible footing—the enormous wickedness of the Slave Trade was

[3] Only generally more amusing. It was Sydney Smith who commented, when it was proposed to lay an improved pavement of wooden blocks round St Paul's: "Let the Dean and Canons lay their heads together and the thing will be done."

tolerated—a thousand evils were in existence, which the talents of good and able men have since lessened or removed. . . .

Francis Place (like Cobbett, a mine of information for the social historian) was born in the same year as Sydney Smith (1771), and, from his very different angle, substantially supported Smith's view of the reality of progress. Place never tired of combating the notion that the British after Waterloo were worse off than in his boyhood and poverty-stricken youth in the 1780's and 1790's; and, even though he overstates his case, his views must be respected. In the old days, he wrote, "the working-people, with very few exceptions, were to a great extent drunken, dirty, immoral and ignorant", whereas now (1829)

> the people are better dressed, better fed, cleanlier, better educated, in each class respectively, and much more frugal, and much happier. Money which would have been spent at the tavern, the brothel, the tea-garden, the skittle-ground, the bull-bait, and in numerous low-lived and degrading pursuits, is now expended in comfort and convenience, or saved for some useful purpose.

As for the health of the young, when he was a boy the children of even the respectable tradesmen in the Strand had lice in their hair, whereas now (1824) "the children I examined to-day do not seem to be troubled with these vermin". In the narrow alleys of 1824

> few were so wretchedly clothed or so filthy as numbers used to be. Many carried with them some mark of the wish of their poor parents to do their best for them. . . . Multitudes now wear shoes and stockings. . . .

The women too were better clothed and healthier, thanks to the cheapness and availability of the new easily washable material—printed cottons from fourpence a yard, white stockings, cotton underclothes, and bed-hangings all cheap.

> Formerly the women young and old were seen emptying their pails and pans at the doors, or washing on stools in the street, in the summer time without gowns on their backs or

handkerchiefs on their necks, their leather stays half-laced and as black as the door-posts, their black coarse worsted stockings and striped linsey-wolsey petticoats 'standing alone with dirt'. No such things are seen now.

The houses, too, that the Londoners lived in were better than forty years back, the windows glazed and curtained, where before "patches of paper or a rag kept out the cold". Even in the East End,

> great as is the mass of poverty and misery of places along shore from the Tower to the Isle of Dogs, still, except in the very worst of these places and among the most wretched of the wretched, there is also considerable improvement.

Vice and crime had diminished, too, he asserted against those who proclaimed the depravity and decadence of their times. He had taken some part in the Committee on the Police of the Metropolis in 1816; it was, he claimed, "the unqualified testimony of every person examined who was qualified to judge" that, relative to the total number of the population, crimes had decreased in both number and atrocity. Highwaymen and trading justices were things of the past; gangs of thieves were less common.

Place and Sydney Smith, together with most of their countrymen, united in praising the new Metropolitan Police, created by Peel in 1829. Until this time policing was in theory rather like jury service. Any citizen could be called on to fulfil the unpaid office of constable, and in small country towns the arrangement had worked, in a rough sort of way. In bigger towns paid watchmen were employed, sometimes elderly and vulnerable to rowdies. In London there were the 'Charleys', with their staff and lantern, who patrolled the better-class districts at nights, but were unable to deal with serious mischief. In general, Englishmen did not like policemen; they smacked of continental tyranny. Good but severe laws, stern but enlightened magistrates, an influential clergy teaching sound morals—these were the traditional British weapons against crime. Increasingly they were felt to be inadequate as towns grew bigger. The suburbs had no night-watchmen at all, and, as Peel wrote to Wellington:

Just conceive the state of one parish, in which there are eighteen different local boards for the management of the Watch, each acting without concert with the others. . . . Think of the state of Brentford and Deptford, with no sort of police by night!

In 1829 the Metropolitan Police Act was passed. A professional force was established for London and its suburbs, paid for by a police rate, with a Police Commissioner at Scotland Yard, and ultimate control in the hands of the Home Secretary. The new 'Peelers' were initially unpopular with some of the Radicals (though not with Place, who hoped they would deal out some salutary bloody noses to trouble-makers); more important, they were unpopular with the criminals, many of whom soon found it prudent to move out of town. Beset by the unwelcome influx, main provincial centres did not take long to follow London's example; but governmental pressure had to be applied before all the counties followed suit. Not least of the blessings of the new Victorian age to come was a general decline in lawlessness; rioting at last ceased to be one of the Englishman's diversions.

2. Working-class Movements in the Twenties and Thirties

Even if it cannot be held that there was any general decline after 1815 in the material condition of the working classes, still, politically speaking, they experienced until the mid-century little but bitterness and frustration. The Six Acts of 1819 had underlined the defeat of Peterloo; the 1825 revision of the Acts concerning trade unions left them still weak, their legal position ambiguous, and the scales weighted against them in industrial bargaining. Harassed by magistrates unlikely to give them the benefit of legal doubt, they were, as we shall see, routed in 1834. The 1832 Reform Act was a complete disillusionment to the poor. The Whig Factory Act of 1833 was a compromise that did nothing at all for adult workers or for anybody outside the cotton and woollen industries; the fight for the ten-hour day was lost. The Municipal Corporations Act was a purely middle-class triumph. Above all, the 1834 Poor Law was regarded simply as a victory of the 'haves' over the 'have-nots': it seemed to treat poverty simply as a crime.

This era, then, more than most others before or since, was one of class warfare. The post-Waterloo generation was the first in British history when systematic efforts were made to organize working-class movements on a national scale. Many of them were ambitious. Some were naïvely idealistic like Robert Owen's schemes of co-operative communism; some were limited and practical in their ends, like the campaigns against the Corn Laws, the Poor Laws, or the newspaper taxes. Many of them overlapped one with another. Nearly all of them failed, and the only resounding success came to the movement for Corn Law repeal, which was only secondarily a working-class movement at all; its primary motive force came from employers.

Most working-class Radicals of this time had inherited something of the Tom Paine tradition: they were republicans and anti-clericals. They thought that the Church of England, having as they considered a vested interest in privilege and superstition, should be disestablished. (For this there was strong Nonconformist support.) Resenting the comfortable piety of the rich, they reacted aggressively to the most seemingly innocuous actions of the Church. When, for instance, during the cholera outbreak, Churchmen set aside a day in 1832 for prayer and fasting, William Lovett and his friends in the National Union of the Working Classes promptly organized a demonstration against it and got themselves arrested.[4] Cholera they took to be none of God's doing; and as for the fast, Lovett described it as "an attempt on the part of the rulers to father their own iniquitous neglect on the Almighty". The London branch of the Working Class Union decided that they would celebrate the fast day as a feast day, and collect a subscription from all those members who could afford it to give a dinner to all those who could not.

Closely linked with this aggressive free-thinking was the demand for removal of those 'Taxes on Knowledge', the newspaper duties, that had been drastically increased by one of the Six Acts. This battle continued throughout the twenties, with

[4] See also the placard quoted on p. 466.

Richard Carlile, a dedicated fanatic, as its director and martyr. Sentenced to three years' imprisonment and a £1500 fine in 1819 for the blasphemous libel of publishing Paine's *Age of Reason*, he conducted the campaign from jail. He published the proceedings of his own 'Mock Trial' and sold 10,000 copies. His wife, Jane, took £500 in his shop in the week of the trial itself, and his various publications, including *The Age of Reason*, enjoyed a boom. The Government then closed his shop and confiscated all his stock, legal and illegal. With the bailiffs in the house, the indomitable Jane Carlile gave birth to a child, reopened shop, and was herself sentenced—whereupon Carlile's sister carried on the struggle until she too was imprisoned for blasphemous libel. Volunteers, supported by a 'victim fund', took up the work of the Carliles, and before the fight was over more than 500 had served terms of imprisonment. Released in 1825, Carlile himself was back in jail in 1830. The illegal sale of the 'unstamped' continued.

Henry Hetherington took over the leadership of this struggle in the thirties, publishing *The Poor Man's Guardian* ("Published in Defiance of the Law to try the Power of Right against Might"), with its own official 'anti-stamp'—*Knowledge is Power*. Hetherington, a master-printer of Holborn, served three sentences; once he went to ground under an alias for a year. "Defiance", he wrote, "is our only remedy." And his *Poor Man's Guardian* won at last a famous victory, when Lord Lyndhurst gave judgment that it was not an 'illegal publication' after all. A little later (1836) the newspaper tax was reduced from fourpence to a penny; something at least had been achieved. Hetherington, a member of the group of London working-men who initiated the Chartist movement, was a victim in 1849 of the second cholera epidemic; in his will he recommended to mankind the teachings of Owen as the surest way to brotherly love and universal co-operation.

'Co-operation' had been much in the air from about 1827 onward, though the idea, and small-scale attempts to put it into practice, were much older. For Owen himself it represented an attempt to organize the whole of society on the socialist ideals put forward in his *New View*.[5] For others it

[5] See p. 339.

meant no more than the setting up of a communal trading establishment. Such, for instance, was the London Co-operative Trading Association, whose members clubbed together to establish a store, proposing to plough back the profits to the common stock. After a time they were able to accumulate enough capital to set up small manufactures of cloth, shoes, cutlery, furniture, and so forth. Owen began by pooh-poohing what he called this 'mere pawnshop'. To him Co-operation meant a grand high-minded communism, where all might live in happy settlements dedicated to virtue and welfare, and co-operate in doing what Owen told them. However, he came soon to patronize the temporarily very successful store in the Gray's Inn Road, and its various provincial branches. At these institutions there was a 'labour exchange', where 'labour notes' were currency, each note representing the value of so many hours' work. Members deposited goods and exchanged them by means of these notes for other goods. But the Gray's Inn Road venture flattered to deceive. Increasingly it became over-full of trivial goods that nobody wanted, and the labour notes depreciated in value. For groceries, customers were soon having to present three-quarters of the price in orthodox money. And the women much disliked confining their shopping to one store: the co-operators were defeated partly by the co-operators' wives.

Undeterred by this failure, for which Owen could readily find explanations satisfying to himself, he turned his attention next to trade unions as the instruments through which competitive capitalism might be liquidated and the New Society inaugurated. The unions had been growing fast since the repeal of the Combination Acts, although their fortunes fluctuated with each rise and fall in the graph of the national prosperity. On a rising curve (for instance, in 1824–25 or 1828) they multiplied and were able to exact higher wages from thriving employers. On a falling curve (as in 1825–26 or 1831–32) they declined, and sometimes collapsed altogether for the time being, creeping back to life in better times again.

The leading figure among the union organizers at this time was the Ulsterman John Doherty, an Owenite who led the spinners. Not only did he manage to create a so-called "Grand General Union of All the Spinners of the United Kingdom"; he aimed beyond this, to build round his spinners a national union of all trades. To this end he formed in 1830 a National Association for the Protection of Labour, which soon claimed over 100,000 members.

Now, however, trade depression hit again. Spinners' strikes were met by an employers' lock-out, and the men were forced by hardship to return to work on the old terms. In 1832 the Colliers' Union failed to survive a head-on clash with the owners; Doherty's National Association for the Protection of Labour died that same year. The Spinners, however, did survive, and other unions were formed, among them the Potters', the Building Trades', and the Clothiers'. By 1833 the total union membership for the whole country had grown to an estimated 800,000.

This was the moment that Robert Owen chose to 'take over' the trade union movement. All the employees' organizations in the land were to be amalgamated into one great super-union —the Grand National Consolidated. In each trade there were to be parochial Lodges; above them county Lodges; then provincial Lodges. Delegates from these last would come to London to form a sort of national economic council. This would supersede (nobody quite knew how) the old Parliament. It would be elected annually, and, as one bright-eyed Owenite journal put it, "the King of England becomes President of the Trade Unions". William IV's reactions to this suggestion are not on record.

In retrospect, all this seems absurdly over-ambitious; but, for a few heady months in 1834, many persuaded themselves that it offered the key to a better future and a juster social system. One or two employers even—notably Fielden of Todmorden—showed sympathy. (Fielden joined with Doherty in promoting a short-lived 'National Regeneration Society'.) However, the vast majority of employers viewed the whole thing as rebellion, as, indeed, it was; and they were strong enough to push the ambitious edifice over with their combined little fingers. In various towns and in various industries they presented to their employees 'the Document', which stipulated as a condition of continued employment that the Union should be renounced; and 'the Document' won an easy victory over the strikes that it precipitated. In Derby 15,000 strikers tried to run their own economy by setting up a co-operative. It did not last long; funds ran out; and the 'Derby brothers' returned beaten to work by April 1834. Next month the Clothiers were broken; then the South Wales men; then the London builders. Owen fell out, both with the executive of the 'Grand National' and with the journalists running the two Owenite papers, *The Crisis* and *The Pioneer*. Quite unshaken, however, he turned his sanguine attention towards a new rainbow. It was called 'The British and Foreign Consolidated Association of Industry, Humanity, and Knowledge', and proved of sublime unimportance.

The chief casualty of 1834 was British trade unionism; it did not begin to put the pieces together again until the 1850's. The most celebrated human casualties were the six Dorsetshire farm labourers from Tolpuddle, who had not actually become members of the 'Grand National'; they were still merely proposing to join it when they were arrested. Melbourne, the Home Secretary, had for some time been urging vigilance upon Justices of the Peace, and with the landowner magistrates of Dorsetshire he was preaching to the converted. The unfortunate Tolpuddle men, sober, law-abiding Methodists, one of them a lay preacher, became the victims of this collusion between the authorities, and of the very severe sentences passed by the judge at Dorchester Assizes—seven years' transportation. The men had been found guilty of taking an illegal oath in the process of becoming members of a (legal) trade union. But Minister, magistrates, and judge had gone too far; there was a great Radical outcry against the repressive injustice of the sentence; a big protest demonstration was held in Copenhagen Fields, London; and humane men, whatever their politics, were relieved when, after three years of the grimmest suffering, the Tolpuddle 'martyrs' were repatriated at the public expense.

William Lovett (1800–77), Cornish-born, from a poor Methodist home, self-educated, and by now (1834) a London

cabinet-maker, had been a follower of Owen. He had, however, been "flabbergasted" (his own word) by Owen's dictatorial methods and had come to think his tactics unsound.
Lovett thought that universal suffrage, which Owen despised,
should come first, before unions, general strikes, Corn Law
repeal, anything. He was sad at the follies of the unions, which,
he wrote, "had copied a great number of the forms, ceremonies, signs, and fooleries of freemasonry, and I believe
thought more of them ... than of just principles". Lovett's
world was elsewhere, among the politically active London
artisans and small Radical master-printers, among the self-
improving Mechanics' Institutes ("Knowledge is Power"), amid
the fight for a free Press. Lovett and his friends, encouraged
by Place—avuncular by now and full of shrewd critical advice
—founded in 1836 the London Working Men's Association,
which soon was supported by affiliated societies in the provinces. Lovett, an inveterate penner of manifestoes and petitions, expressed in the Association's inaugural address to its
fellow societies something of the spirit of these earnest workers:

> Let us, friends, seek to make the principles of democracy
> as respectable in practice as they are just in theory, by
> excluding the drunken and immoral from our ranks, and in
> uniting in close compact with the honest, sober, moral, and
> thinking portion of our brethren. . . .

Out of this Working Men's Association was to emerge the
People's Charter of 1838, a statement of Radical demands
composed by Lovett, edited by Place. The Chartist Movement
(1836–52) and its defeat come largely outside the scope of this
book; but it is instructive to look at what it was fighting for.
Six issues on which nearly all Radicals could agree were
universal male suffrage; the secret ballot to prevent intimidation by landlord or employer; annual general elections; the
abolition of the property qualification for M.P.'s; the payment
of M.P.'s to permit the common people to enter Parliament;
and an equalization of constituencies. These were the famous
Six Points; but the misfortune of the People's Charter was that
every Radical cause was ready to jump on to its bandwagon.
Every Radical with a grievance, every theorist with a panacea,

tried to steer Chartism down his own particular road: currency reformers, Socialists, anti-Poor Law agitators, advocates of a general strike, of a religious revival, of temperance reform, of land reform, of educational reform. Chartism was condemned to become a rag-bag of all the Radical causes of the day. It was very soon to throw Lovett over and fall into the hands of more spectacular leaders.

3. The Upper Classes, and Sport

The agitated world of working-class movements was necessarily urban. For a long time yet in the rural world, which was still that of most Englishmen, the aristocrat and the country gentleman took their pre-eminence for granted. The nobility were still living in feudal splendour, the value of their rent-rolls swelling, the capital value of their land rising—sometimes sensationally so when they owned property in a developing urban area. Taxation, by modern standards, was negligible; servants were numbered by the score, or sometimes hundred. Mansions, parks, and gardens were ever being 'improved' according to the current fashion. The Reform Act had done a little to restrict the political influence of the aristocracy, but their social prestige lived on undiminished, and their scale of expenditure was higher than ever.

Distinguished from the aristocracy by no clear line (for only eldest sons of peers stayed strictly among the nobility), and among themselves of widely differing standing and wealth, came the much more numerous class of the landed gentry. As landlord, as magistrate, as principal local employer, as Captain of Yeomanry perhaps, the squire, whether local benefactor or petty tyrant, still dominated the life of the village.

If he were frightened (as at Tolpuddle) by fear of insubordination, or if he were determined to squeeze the last drop of legality out of the laws against poaching, he could make life for the tenantry bitter and dangerous. In neither situation did he have to ask any man's leave: whether the father or ogre of the village, his word was law. Sir William Oglander of Nunwell, in the Isle of Wight, was unusual in his day in that he had a passion for fresh air; so he could never suffer a cottager on his estate to have his windows sealed, and their light blocked out by flower pots in the window-sill, but would always stump indoors, remove the flower-pots, open wide the windows, and then stump out again without a word.

He lived in a society which accepted that squires behaved so, even if the windows were shut traditionally tight again after he was safely out of sight.

The gentry, though they grumbled a great deal about high rates, the price of corn, and the depredations of poachers, were doing well. This same Isle of Wight squire, who may be taken as typical of the old-established 'county' family of good local standing (a baronet himself, he married the daughter of the Duke of Grafton), disposed of a score or so of servants in his not very large manor house.[6] His biographer,[7] writing of him from the same house 130 years later, wondered where they all slept; a list of them will perhaps suggest the handsome style in which at the time of Waterloo he and his family lived. He maintained a butler at 60 guineas a year; an under-butler; a housekeeper; three footmen ("at 25 guineas a year, all clothes and 1 guinea a year for hair-powder"); three housemaids and two laundrymaids; three nursemaids, plus a wet-nurse when necessary; a cook; a kitchenmaid, and a scullerymaid (Sarah Grub, not a very satisfactory girl, "at 5 guineas, and a rise of 1 guinea if she stays a year. Finds her own tea"). Outdoors, he employed a gamekeeper, also at 60 guineas, a gardener, a woodman, two grooms, and a coach-boy ("13 guineas a year, all his clothes, and one pair of boots").

The squire's wife kept a diary too:

> June 24th. Heard of the battle of Waterloo. Poor Captain Smyth killed. My brother happily preserved.
> June 25th. The servants had a dance to celebrate Henry's birthday.

The squire's sister reflects in her letters the family's deep love of the countryside whose landscape it had helped to create and whose pattern it still determined:

[6] He had sizeably increased his family fortunes during the Wars by selling off great quantities of oak for naval building.
[7] C. Aspinall-Oglander, *Nunwell Symphony* (Hogarth Press, 1945).

Everything at dear old Nunwell looked in high beauty; the old trees all standing safe; and those my brother planted have grown so well they are now fine young trees. The flower garden was in perfection, full of all sorts of flowers, but particularly with roses.

In the years after Waterloo the landowning interest, sportsmen to a man, stiffened the already preposterous Game Laws. If, after 1816, a poacher were caught with his nets about him by night and a jury found against him, he could be transported for seven years. Spring-guns and man-traps concealed in the undergrowth assisted the owners and gamekeepers until a law of 1828 made such lethal devices illegal. Three years later a new law gave the tenant, at last, the right to shoot game upon his own land unless it were expressly forbidden by legal covenant. But the law against the poacher remained exemplarily harsh.

The prevalence of poaching, due partly to the desperate condition of many labourers, was, paradoxically, a consequence also of the general rise in living standards: many more people could now afford poultry on the table. It was not only the starving cottager who was tempted to take partridge and pheasant; organized poaching gangs (who sometimes fought small pitched battles with gamekeepers and landowners) had been exploiting the market and supplying the needs of the poulterer and the newly genteel classes.

These last were very numerous. New mansions, new 'Regency' villas, rustic *cottages ornés* in the fashionable Gothic style, 'tasty residences' of all kinds were springing up everywhere. It was a conventional form of satire (as it always has been) to ridicule these upstart rich, now more numerous than ever, people who had made money in trade and manufacture, or by appreciation in land values, or in the 'funds': "fundlords", railed Cobbett, "who retire to be country squires". There were, in fact, in 1829, as many as 275,839 investors in 'the funds'—not all of them 'lords' or 'country squires' by any means, but a good proportion enriched enough to cut a dash among the upper classes.

The reader of Jane Austen or of Thackeray's *Vanity Fair* or of Mrs Gaskell's *Cranford* can observe it all. Jane Austen, in particular, was a connoisseur of this most characteristic and permanent of English pastimes, the game of class distinctions. For her these were both firm and supple. Peers stood above her world; but it ran from baronets, through mere knights, to naval and military officers, professional men, Church of England parsons, respectably connected widows and spinsters, and the families of the more prosperous tenant farmers. But gentility had to stop somewhere. Tradesmen and Nonconformists were of another world; and, as for the yeomanry, the heroine of *Emma* (1816) roundly declares: "They are precisely the order of people with whom I feel I can have nothing to do."

Nowhere in such an age could class distinctions be ignored; but in the world of sport they were sometimes bridged. In the days before professionalism, when a working week left small time for leisure, a game such as cricket could flourish only where gentlemen were ready to finance it. This they frequently were, and to play it themselves, and to gamble on it. A gentleman might well be backing his side (of eleven or more 'gentlemen' and 'players' combined) to the tune of 500 guineas. With so much at stake, contests were understandably fierce—even though bowling was still under-arm (the new round-arm bowling began to provoke controversy in the twenties). Rather too often the proceedings became underhand as well; the temptation to bribe the more plebeian of the opposition, and for them to succumb, was sometimes irresistible.

Cricket already had its legendary heroes and a literary tradition of its own, and Thomas Lord's ground was already established, like the MCC, at St John's Wood; but cricket could hardly yet claim to be the national game. It was prizefighting whose great champions were the first to become national figures. Until the close of the eighteenth century sporting events had been of necessity affairs of local village green or heath or tavern-yard. But with the improvement of roads it was possible for great concourses, sometimes as many as 20,000 strong, to assemble for a fight between two fancied 'bruisers'. The aristocracy promoted and patronized it; those with gigs came in them; the "swinish multitude" trekked miles on foot to be there; big money was wagered; and the protagonists fought it out to the end—often prodigiously delayed—with bare fists. It would be a near thing whether the greatest hero of the Regency period were judged to be the Duke of Wellington or Tom Cribb. There were, besides, those "fine fellows and honourable men", Jem Belcher and Tom Spring, and others who were always known by their *noms de guerre*, "the Game Chicken" or "the Gas Man"—this last immortalized by Hazlitt in his wonderfully evocative essay "The Fight" (1822). The match that day was between the Gas Man and Bill Neate; for Hazlitt it was high adventure, almost a pilgrimage. For Lord Althorp (together with Wellington and Palmerston, a great fancier of a fight), an encounter that he remembered between John Gully and the "Game Chicken" carried an equal enchantment: "the men stripping, the intense excitement, the sparring . . . it was really worthy of Homer".

The Evangelical humanitarians, however, deprecated it, together with cockfighting, and all such sports that promoted gambling and violence. The new police forces, too, began to harass the promoters. By 1837, while cricket and football were beginning to become popular and respectable, pugilism and the sports involving cruelty to animals were in decline. Even the Evangelicals, however, did not manage to check the popularity of horse-racing. Here again the aristocracy were the promoters; gambling and physical exhilaration were equally essential parts of it; and 'fixing' of races was always threatening to destroy it, despite the aristocratic surveillance of the Jockey Club.

Shooting game and hunting the fox were still the countryman's sports *par excellence*. For many a squire and gentleman farmer they provided a sort of religion. "Tell me a man's a fox-hunter, and I loves him at once", declared Surtees' Mr Jorrocks, that rural counterpart of Dickens's Cockney Sam Weller. When eighteen-year-old Henry Oglander, Sir William's son, up at Oxford, sits down to pen a 'duty' letter to his uncle, the most natural thing in the world is to write of the two really important subjects that they have in common—shooting and hunting. The hard frost of January 1830 was a great nuisance; it had put a stop to hunting. Game was very scarce; it had been a bad breeding year. Despite the frost, there were few woodcocks; the chief sport had come from snipe. "I cannot get any shooting at Oxford, but to make up for it I have plenty of hunting with the Duke of Beaufort's, whose hounds are said to be the best in England. . . ." He would have found little difficulty in agreeing with Mr Jorrocks, who declared fox-hunting the thing above all worth living for: "the sport of kings, the image of war without its guilt and only five and twenty per cent. of its danger".

4. Steam Transport

Soon shall thy arm, UNCONQUER'D STEAM! afar
Drag the slow barge, or drive the rapid car;
Or on wide-waving wings expanded bear
The flying-chariot through the fields of air.

So wrote Erasmus Darwin, Charles's grandfather, in 1792. Already, in fact, three years earlier, young William Symington had taken out a patent for a boat steam-driven by a stern paddle-wheel, and by 1801 was demonstrating how his little *Charlotte Dundas* could tow two "slow barges" weighing seventy tons down the Forth-Clyde Canal in the face of a gale. Symington died early, and encumbered by debt; but in 1812 another Scotsman, Henry Bell of Glasgow, constructed a somewhat bigger boat, put the steam-engine amidships, and ran a ferry service between Glasgow and Greenock. By 1820 a cross-Channel steam ferry was operating, and before 1837 several sailing ships fitted with auxiliary steam-paddles had crossed the North Atlantic. In the following year the first fully steam-driven paddle-ships (though for long years yet with auxiliary sails) made the transatlantic crossing.

On the canals, where steamboats were born, they did not survive to supplant horse-power, which moved the barges for more than another century, until the internal-combustion engine took over. On the roads, too, the horse outlasted the challenges of Darwin's "rapid car", the steam carriage, and of the steam omnibus, though both of these were all the rage in the thirties. (The original horse omnibus was Shillibeer's of 1829, plying in the City of London; its progeny lasted until the First World War.) It was on the high seas and the specially constructed new railroads that steam transport was to alter the face of the world. On the roads the 'age of steam' was still the age of the horse. "The 'coaching days' from Waterloo to *Pickwick*" (wrote Trevelyan) "still stand in popular imagination for the last era of 'old England', jovial, self-reliant, matter-of-fact, but still as full of romance, colour, character and incident as the world of Chaucer's pilgrims." And although railways were soon to hit the coaching establishments hard, and altogether to halt the building of new canals, the horse in 1837 was still king, on the farm and in the Army, on towpath and high road, in fox-hunt and on the turf, framed in sporting print on every parlour wall. Twenty-five thousand village blacksmiths shod him. "Next after a fox-hunt", said Cobbett, "the finest sight in England is a stage-coach just ready to start."

Railways of a sort were established more than two centuries before the age of steam. The rails were of wood; the trucks were horse-drawn, and they carried coal in the neighbourhood of the collieries. As early as 1784, Boulton and Watt's assistant at Soho, William Murdock, had made a working model of a steam locomotive, and the idea was much in the minds of inventors over the next thirty years. In 1804 the Cornishman Richard Trevithick did succeed in building a locomotive that pulled five wagons at Merthyr Tydfil, loaded with twenty tons of iron, over a distance of nine miles, but he was halted by difficulties both technical and financial. He became one of the many Englishmen who went to try their luck and exploit their skill in South America, and introduced steam-pumps to the mines of Peru.

In 1821 a railway company secured an Act to build a line from Stockton to Darlington, primarily as a short cut for carrying the coal which until then went along the winding Tees. As its chief engineer the company appointed George Stephenson, a man bred among the colliery pumps of the Northumbrian mines, unschooled and rough of speech, but persuasive enough to win the directors over to steam traction on at least the easier stretches of line. This history-making Stockton–Darlington railway was in many ways a hodge-podge: the steeper gradients were operated by stationary engines; at slack times passengers were conveyed by horse-drawn wagons; and the track could be hired for use by private carriages with specially adapted wheels. So profitable, however, did the passenger side of the business prove that the company soon decided to operate its own passenger 'carriages' coupled with the coal-trucks, and to prohibit private use. In many respects the railways were to carry permanently the marks of their origins. One of their less fortunate legacies was the 4′ 8½″ gauge, traditional on colliery trucks. Brunel fought for the broader and more comfortable gauge, but the other had the advantage of a flying start.

Stephenson's success with the Stockton–Darlington line strengthened his hand in dealing with the company which had for years been projecting a Liverpool–Manchester link, and with the strong forces of conservatism which still ridiculed or were frightened by steam traction. The construction of the track itself presented large difficulties; Stephenson overcame the most formidable of them, the crossing of Chat Moss (a bog too deep to drain), by laying a 'floating' causeway of brushwood and hurdles; but he still had to convince the directors that locomotive engines were adequate for their task. In the famous Rainhill (Liverpool) Trials of 1829 the *Rocket* triumphantly showed the supremacy of the engines built by George Stephenson and his gifted son Robert, and demonstrated to the directors and the world in general that a locomotive could be relied on to carry a heavy load at 29 miles per hour. (Its average speed was about half this.) After the opening ceremony another Stephenson engine (there were eight present in all) showed, in rushing the dying Huskisson to hospital, that travelling light it could average 36 miles per hour, a speed to dizzy the imagination of 1830.[8]

However, between 1825 and 1835 the railways made rather slow progress. Only about 500 miles of track were laid, and, except on predominantly coal-carrying lines, the dividends earned were very modest. Much of the early capital was put up by Nonconformist, and especially Quaker, businessmen

[8] Stephenson himself claimed that he had on occasions gone at a mile a minute, "that his doubt was not how fast his engines could be made to go, but at what pace it would be proper to stop. . . . He had ascertained that 400 miles per hour was the extreme velocity which the human frame could endure."

content with sober returns on their money; much of the enthusiasm derived from the engineers themselves, devotees of the new idea—men like Robert Stephenson, or the remarkable Brunel, already by the mid-thirties beginning to realize his vision of the steam-route of the future, the 'Great Western' that would link London to Bristol by locomotive and Bristol to New York by steam-paddle. The investing public did not begin to catch the railroad fever until 1836–37, when Britain had its first comparatively mild dose. Far worse was to follow in the 'railway mania' of the forties.

Objections to the railways came from the coaching and canal interests (the latter frequently bought out by the railway companies); from towns anxious to preserve their amenities; from universities, like Oxford, and colleges, like Eton, wanting to ward off the dangerous and vulgar invasion; from farmers fearful of the effects on livestock; and above all from landowners feeling, like the gossip-writer Creevey, incensed against "the locomotive Monster, carrying *eighty* tons of goods, and navigated by a tail of smoke and sulphur, coming thro' every man's grounds between Manchester and Liverpool". However, the fascination and novelty of the Monster, as well as its utility, were irresistible. It rendered, pronounced Greville, "all other travelling irksome and tedious by comparison":

Knowsley, July 18, 1837. . . . I started at five o'clock on Sunday evening by coach from London, got to Birmingham at half-past five on Monday morning, and got upon the railroad at half-past seven. Nothing can be more comfortable than the vehicle in which I was put, a sort of chariot with two places, and there is nothing disagreeable about it but the occasional whiffs of stinking air which it is impossible to exclude altogether. The first sensation is a slight degree of nervousness and a feeling of being run away with, but a sense of security supervenes, and the velocity is delightful. Town after town, park and chateau one after another are left behind with the rapid variety of a moving panorama, and the continual bustle and animation of the changes and stoppages make the journey very entertaining.

It was not only wonder and exhilaration that possessed early travellers by train, but a sense of sharing a triumph. "Let the

great world spin for ever down the ringing grooves of change",
wrote the young Tennyson after he had ridden in the first train
from Liverpool to Manchester (and in the mistaken belief that
trains ran in grooves). Once they came to be accepted, railways
became practically synonymous with progress. The triumph of
steam-power, in communication and manufacturing industry
alike, brought not only national confidence but a sense of
mission. Many, like Richard Cobden (1804–65), began to see
commerce as "the grand panacea". Every bale of merchandise,
he claimed, that left our shores took with it the message of the
British way of life, "freedom, peace, and good government—
while our steam boats . . . and our miraculous railroads, that
are the talk of all nations, are the advertisements and vouchers
for the value of our enlightened institutions." This was to turn
upside down complaints of materialism and the old Napoleonic
jibe at the "nation of shopkeepers". Out of our very material
progress, preached the Cobdenites, would come universal
prosperity, enlightenment, and peace.

5. Arts and Sciences: the Spirit of the Age

The Georgian age in art and literature had generally been
one of discipline, order, and restraint—classical in reference,
aristocratic in direction, proportioned in taste. In its last phase,
conveniently described as 'Regency',[9] order tends to give way
before variety, restraint before exuberance, classicism before
the romantic and exotic. Even so, the Regency gave us, perhaps, in architecture, in furniture, and in the decorative and
useful arts and crafts generally, the last age when good taste
could be relied on, before the machine (that defeated the hand-
craftsman) and the bourgeois (who began to supplant the
aristocrat) came jointly to determine design.

In building the Regency was an era of bold bow-fronted
painted-stucco villas, white and elegant, iron-balconied often,
simply proportioned; of ambitious terraces and crescents for

[9] In its artistic reference this term applies to a period longer than the
strict 1811–20 of the constitutional Regency. It covers the last thirty
years or so before the accession of Victoria in 1837.

the rich, which adorned such then-fashionable resorts as Brighton, Ramsgate, Cheltenham, and Clifton, or the suburbs of the big towns; of neat little shops, with their bowed square-paned windows. The canons of classical taste, however, were being increasingly challenged by the picturesque. Ever since Horace Walpole developed his 'Gothick' mansion at Straw-berry Hill, Chiswick (c. 1753–76), the fascination of the mock-medieval had been growing. Chinese, Indian, and all kinds of 'romantic' influences began to multiply. Sometimes, indeed, the cult of the novel and fantastic got out of hand: at Brighton the Regent's new Pavilion, a sort of Oriental pleasure-dome, rioted in Chinese, Hindu, Gothic, and half a dozen other styles; and at Fonthill, on the Dorset–Wiltshire border, the obsessive William Beckford dissipated a vast fortune erecting the most famous of the architectural follies of his time, a tower to dwarf Babel's. (In 1825 the laws of gravity were vindicated, with a fall "tremendous and sublime".)

In literature, too, the medieval, the mysterious, the 'roman-tic', were all the rage. Wherever the gentility were to be found there was now a circulating library (which customarily pro-vided, as well as the latest novels, a focus for gossip, amenities such as billiards, and many of the facilities of a genteel shop). The young ladies who formed a high proportion of its reader-ship could not have too much of ivied towers and moonlit ruins, of bloodstained mysteries and monastic ghosts. The taste for the mock-archaic found ancient ballads and their modern imitators much to its liking, and produced at least one master-piece in Coleridge's *Rime of the Ancient Mariner*; its most popular practitioner was undoubtedly Sir Walter Scott, in his *Lay of the Last Minstrel* and *Marmion* days (1805–8). Later the fashion was for Lord Byron, who, with *Childe Harold* (1812), a highly coloured panorama in verse strongly charged with the poet's own sentiments and adventures, "awoke and found him-self famous". The Oriental verse-tales that followed (*The Bride of Abydos, The Corsair*, etc.) hit upon the perfect recipe for the hour. The Byronic pose became the vogue not only in England but in all Europe. Scott, suddenly outshone, confined himself to writing novels, and again the mood of the hour and its leisured public was perfectly caught: the hankering after what the age took to be 'historical', and its delight in romantic adventure. With Scott, history and romance were fused in one.

The literary Romantic Revival and the Gothic Revival fed one another. The Tractarian Movement, too, played its part later in strengthening the new fashion for pointed windows, castellated roof-lines, stained glass, niches, turrets, and dim religious lights. Wyatville's 'remodelling' of Windsor Castle for George IV provided one more impetus for the Gothic mode. Thomas Rickman in 1817 had first dealt in a scholarly and comprehensive manner with the various styles of medieval architecture, but it was A. W. Pugin (1812–52), stage and furniture designer, etcher, architect, and Roman Catholic convert, who was undoubtedly their most influential champion. When Sir Charles Barry (1795–1860) rebuilt the Palace of Westminster after the fire of 1834 the new buildings were, inevitably as it now seems, in the Gothic style, and the ornamentation for them was fittingly designed by Pugin.

Pugin was a crusader; but the opposition too was strong. There was a classical revival as well. Indeed, most of the great new public buildings of late Georgian (i.e., 'Regency') times were erected in current versions of the Grecian style: examples are William Wilkins's National Gallery and University College, London; Sir John Soane's Bank of England; Barry's British Museum; and the town halls of many of the great provincial cities (Birmingham's, for instance, designed by Joseph Hansom, of the cab). Many eminent architects built in both styles, among them Barry himself and, earlier, the most celebrated of the 'Regency' designers, John Nash, who not only reconstructed much of the West End in his admired 'Regency' manner (though some consider it ponderous and monotonous), but for his own occupation put up a grandiose Gothic 'castle' in the Isle of Wight.

It is, of course, idle to try to see in the Gothic and Romantic Revivals any one great 'movement', but they *were* alike in reacting against what their supporters took to be the prosiness and artificiality of the eighteenth century and its subservience to a dying classical tradition. It was such a reaction that gave birth to the *Lyrical Ballads* of Wordsworth and Coleridge

(1798), with the famous Preface arguing for a new poetic simplicity. But Wordsworth, attacking the tired classical forms of his contemporaries' verse, is a long way from Pugin, harking back to the glories of the Gothic Perpendicular. Even the famous trio of Romantic poets, Byron, Keats, and Shelley, have little in common except that they were all steeped in the Greco-Roman classics, were all non-Christian and politically Radical, and all died young. The spirit of the age was at the same time of a prodigious vigour and a varied confusion, as might be expected of a civilization that had faced, and was still facing, political, technical, and cultural upheaval.

Perhaps the engineers were luckiest in their hour. It is true that the industrial revolution created much that was hideous; but a Telford or a Brunel could succeed in building— supremely so with their bridges—forms that carried the future. Similarly, the new cast-iron processes afforded wonderful opportunities—to estate-planners and gardeners, for instance, in the construction of conservatories and orangeries of unprecedented ambitiousness. One of these men, Joseph Paxton, once the Duke of Devonshire's head gardener, was to evolve the biggest 'conservatory' of all, the iron-and-glass ultra-modern Crystal Palace of 1851. But in general, and increasingly as the century progressed, the necessity was felt of embellishing designs with elaborate ornamentation. Objects of the most 'practical' and 'convenient' nature—favourite contemporary epithets—had to have their stark utility 'beautified' with filigree and arabesque. St Pancras railway terminus went the whole hog, in Flemish Gothic; while Euston was adorned with a gateway that was a beautifully exact copy of the Greek one at Agrigentum.

In costume, as Georgian-Regency made way for Victorian, the trend was towards drabness. For men, after the style and swagger of the Regency, where the image of the English gentleman is preserved for ever for us like a fly in amber, somewhere between the exquisite and the bluff, between Beau Brummell and John Bull (or, in a comic guise, Mr Pickwick), came the stove-pipe top-hat, the black frock-coat, trousers, and the grey respectability of Victorian wear. The Regency 'bucks' and 'Corinthians', and their successors the dandies, had only pale counterparts in later decades. In women's costume too, after the high-waisted, long-flowing, 'Roman' styles of Jane Austen's ladies, correct to the point sometimes of primness, but as elegant as the curly-brimmed high hats and cutaway-coat-and-breeches of their menfolk, the forces of sobriety and puritanism were by 1837 winning the day, though perhaps less totally and permanently with women's fashions than with men's.

It is too simple to put everything down to the industrial revolution. The changes in costume are often so ascribed (though the rise of Evangelicalism would provide a more relevant argument). So too, with what justice is debatable, is the new attitude to the beauties of wild landscape and sea-scape that is a marked feature of the later Georgian period. The earlier culture of Pope, Swift, and Hogarth, of Dr Johnson, Reynolds, and their circle, was essentially town-based, and particularly London-based. The greatest figures of the next age are often seeking liberation from urban convention and sophistication. A high proportion of the finest late-Georgian painters are painters of landscape and rural scenes—Girtin, Crome, Cotman, Morland, and, greatest of all, Constable (1776–1837) and Turner (1775–1851). Among poets and novel-ists, many of the best seek simplicity and grandeur among commonplace country scenes (like Cowper, Crabbe, or Clare), or with the common man (like Wordsworth or Burns), or amid the wild grandeur of the Lakes and Highlands (like Words-worth again or Scott). With Constable, for the first time, land-scape has become the greatest of all subjects, a gateway to truth itself. With Wordsworth, the sounding cataracts, the "impulse from a vernal wood", have become the sources of moral truth, the voice of God.

Of the sciences, astronomy was the senior, and the only one that received any state patronage—a privilege due partly to astronomy's antiquity and partly to its importance for navi-gation. There was an Astronomer Royal and a Royal Green-wich Observatory; but a Chemist or Physicist or Mathematician Royal would have seemed an unthinkable oddity. It is true that there was a Royal Society, but by 1800 this carried more social status than scientific usefulness; it promoted little or no research. There were too the Royal Colleges of Physicians and of Surgeons; both of these, however, had sunk to the comfortable level of the English universities and of eighteenth-century corporations in general. They were trailing, in their sluggish exclusiveness, behind the needs of the age; and, while a London doctor could make a fortune, the main medical work of the countryside was performed largely by apothecaries.

Science, though interest in it was growing, was still a minority culture: the worlds of clerical and academic orthodoxy, of the public schools, of Oxford and Cambridge, and (to a great extent) of the aristocracy were not yet of it. Science took its sustenance mainly from elsewhere: from the philanthropy and interest of the educated bourgeoisie, from the needs of industry and agriculture, from the Scottish universities, from the Nonconformist academies. Priestley, one of the discoverers of oxygen, was a Unitarian. William Allen, the chemist and philanthropist, was a Quaker. So was Dalton, who rose from the home of a poor Westmorland weaver-peasant. Humphry Davy was a Cornish Methodist. Faraday, blacksmith's son and bookbinder's apprentice, was brought up as a member of an obscure Dissenting sect; his university training came from being Davy's lab-boy.

However, by the 1780's and 1790's scientific interest was beginning to spread among the leisured classes, and one branch of science after another was strengthened by the foundation of its own learned society. In 1788 there was the Linnaean Society, for what the age called natural history and we would call biology. There was a Geological Society by 1807, and, soon after, Zoological, Horticultural, Medico-Surgical, Astronomical, and other similar Societies. Most of the big cities and many smaller towns had a Literary and Philosophical Society; the most distinguished of all, Birmingham's Lunar Society (the 'Lunatics'), had among its members Erasmus Darwin, Watt, Boulton, Murdock, Priestley, and Galton the botanist. Manchester's Society was associated with a College of Arts and Sciences, which made Dalton its Professor of Mathematics and gave him a laboratory. (When another chemical pioneer, Wollaston, was met with the request to be shown over *his* laboratory he is said to have asked his footman to bring it in on a tray.)

Public scientific lectures grew rapidly now in number, and were often well attended; William Allen gave chemical lectures to audiences of over a hundred. The fashion, which had begun among the urban intelligentsia, caught on. The success of the London Institution and the Surrey Institute led on to the much more ambitious and luxurious Royal Institution, founded in 1799 by the American-born Count Rumford, who was himself a considerable scientist and philanthropist. Here public lectures were graced by the nobility and by other ladies and gentlemen anxious to be seen in the right place, and also by the leading scientific figure, the best public performer of his day—Humphry Davy (1778–1829). When, however, Dalton gave his first, potentially historic, lectures on atomic theory to the Royal Institution in 1804 they fell on stony ground; it was left to Professor Thomson to offer him the more fertile soil of Edinburgh.

Davy's greatest achievements were those of his earlier years. Using a multiple version of Volta's new electric battery, he explored the interrelation of chemistry and electricity, and first split chemical compounds by electrolysis. He did much else, announcing his discoveries with a flourish at successive Royal Institution lectures between 1807 and 1810. Again using a giant Voltaic battery-system, he produced an electric arc-light. He discovered the new elements potassium, sodium, and later iodine. He did important work on chlorine, and gave it its name. Lionized by society, he married a rich heiress, and, after inventing the miner's safety lamp, was created a baronet. To his contemporaries he was the king of scientists and inventors.

He enjoyed one advantage over an actual king: he could name his successor. Michael Faraday (1791–1867) crowned Davy's work on electrolysis, made important studies in optics and the liquefaction of gases, and then during the 1820's laid the theoretical foundations of applied electricity. By 1831 he was ready to demonstrate, at the Royal Institution, electromagnetic induction: the theory that an electric current can induce another in a different circuit; this was the vital first step towards, in his own day, the electric telegraph of 1837, in the next generation the dynamo, and eventually the power stations of today.

Davy and Faraday showed the links between chemistry and electricity; John Dalton (1766–1844) adumbrated those between chemistry and mathematics. The idea of the atomic structure of matter was as old as Democritus; but it was Dalton who first constructed a firm atomic theory, and based it on the numerical facts of chemical combination. Every chemical element, he taught, was made up of its own individual (and he supposed unsplittable) atom, and all the atoms in a given element (he recognized 26) were identical in nature and weight. The molecules of chemical compounds were composed of specific numbers and kinds of atoms, and these always combined in whole-number ratios—one to two, two to three, and so on. Dalton's notions of 'atomic weight' and the 'chemical formula' laid the essential groundwork for the whole future development of chemistry.

In medicine, during this period, the discovery of most immediate practical importance was undoubtedly that of vaccination. It was Edward Jenner (1749–1823), a Gloucestershire country doctor who, working from the widely held belief that milkmaids who had had cowpox were immune from smallpox, developed a cowpox vaccine, and proved its efficacy beyond the doubt of reasonable men. The prejudice against it was slowly worn away, and by 1806 the beginnings of a great advance were showing. In that year, for the first time on record, one whole week went by in London without a single death from smallpox. Such achievements as Davy's and Jenner's knew no frontiers; in the middle of the wars they both received honours from Napoleon.

These great scientific discoveries, like the great engineering constructions and mechanical inventions, all proclaimed man's rapid conquest of nature. Between them they did much to give the nineteenth century its incomparable spirit of confidence. A belief in progress came eventually to be an almost automatic article of faith. On the other hand, the contemporary discoveries in the new sciences of geology and anthropology, crowned as they were at last by Darwin's theory of evolution, were deeply disturbing to settled modes of thought. During the eighteenth century finds had multiplied of fossils and of the bones of many extinct creatures; and various strange and ingenious theories had arisen to reconcile the new evidence with the old Bible story. Increasingly it became apparent that the earth was immensely old, that life had ebbed and flowed upon it over many eons. To postulate a whole batch of Floods, instead of Noah's one, hardly solved all the complications. Some, such as the Frenchman Cuvier and the Scotsman James Hutton, were groping towards a modern interpretation. In the story of the earth, its rocks and its forms of life, Hutton confessed in 1795 that he could see "no vestige of a beginning, no prospect of an end". Four years later investigations were sufficiently far advanced for William Smith to publish his *Order of the Strata, and their Imbedded Organic Remains*. A generation later yet Charles Lyell wrote the first great authoritative textbook—*Principles of Geology* (1830–33). When that work was coming from the press a survey ship, the *Beagle*, was already half-way on her voyage round the world, carrying with her a young ship's naturalist, Charles Darwin. Already he was collecting and sifting the vast quantity of botanical and zoological evidence that would twenty years later sustain his evolutionary theory, which was to alter the whole climate of modern thought.

APPENDICES

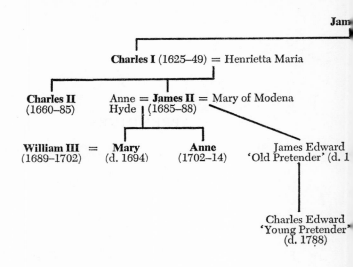

Jam

Charles I (1625–49) = Henrietta Maria

Charles II
(1660–85)

Anne = **James II** = Mary of Modena
Hyde (1685–88)

William III = **Mary**
(1689–1702) (d. 1694)

Anne
(1702–14)

James Edward
'Old Pretender' (d. 1

Charles Edward
'Young Pretender'
(d. 1788)

Augusta
Saxe–Got

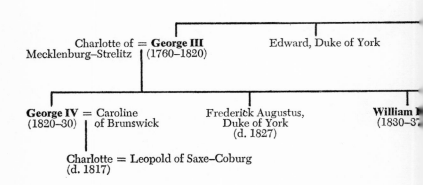

Charlotte of = **George III**
Mecklenburg–Strelitz (1760–1820)

Edward, Duke of York

George IV = Caroline
(1820–30) of Brunswick

Frederick Augustus,
Duke of York
(d. 1827)

William I
(1830–37)

Charlotte = Leopold of Saxe–Coburg
(d. 1817)

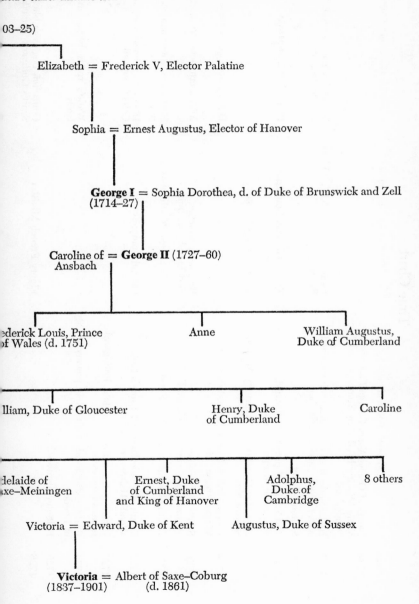

Elizabeth = Frederick V, Elector Palatine

Sophia = Ernest Augustus, Elector of Hanover

George I = Sophia Dorothea, d. of Duke of Brunswick and Zell
(1714–27)

Caroline of = **George II** (1727–60)
Ansbach

:derick Louis, Prince   Anne   William Augustus,
of Wales (d. 1751)   Duke of Cumberland

lliam, Duke of Gloucester   Henry, Duke   Caroline
of Cumberland

delaide of   Ernest, Duke   Adolphus,   8 others
ixe–Meiningen   of Cumberland   Duke of
and King of Hanover   Cambridge

Victoria = Edward, Duke of Kent   Augustus, Duke of Sussex

Victoria = Albert of Saxe–Coburg
(1837–1901)   (d. 1861)

Time Chart

Date	Domestic Political	Foreign and Imperial	Social, Economic, Cultural
1714	Death of Queen Anne; George I accedes; Whig Ministry headed by Stanhope and Sunderland		
1715	Bolingbroke flees to France; is impeached, with Oxford; Jacobite rebellion	Death of Louis XIV. Orleans Regent	Burlington patronizes Palladian style in England
1716	Septennial Act		Handel's *Water Music*
1717	Sinking Fund projected; Townshend dismissed; Walpole resigns	Triple Alliance. Louisiana founded	
1718	Repeal of Occasional Conformity Act and Schism Act	Battle of Cape Passaro	
1719	Peerage Bill defeated. Townshend and Walpole rejoin Ministry		Defoe's *Robinson Crusoe*
1720	South Sea Bubble; Walpole 'Screenmaster-General'	Pragmatic Sanction. Fort Louisbourg built	Allen's cross-country post
1721	Death of Stanhope. Sinking Fund renewed	End of Great Northern War	First inoculations against small-pox
1722	Death of Sunderland. Atterbury's Plot. Wood's Halfpence (–1725)	Ostend Company	Houghton House designed by Colin Campbell
1723	Excise on tea, coffee, chocolate. Bolingbroke returns from exile		
1724	Carteret dismissed. Act to limit powers of City of London		Wade's roads begun in High-lands
1725	Pulteney dismissed		
1726		Fleury French Minister	*Craftsman* begins publication. Swift's *Gulliver's Travels*

Date	Domestic Political	Foreign and Imperial	Social, Economic, Cultural
1727	Death of George I. George II confirms Walpole in power	Gibraltar besieged	
1728	Food-riots and starvation in Ireland		Gay's *Beggar's Opera*; Gay's *Polly* banned
1729			Methodist Society formed at Oxford. Oglethorpe exposes Fleet Prison conditions
1730	Townshend dismissed. Carteret returns from Ireland		(onward) Norfolk system of agriculture developed
1731		Captain Jenkins episode	Tull's *Horse-hoeing Husbandry*
1732			
1733	Tobacco Excise Bill withdrawn. Cobham, Chesterfield, etc., dismissed	First Bourbon Family Compact. War of Polish Succession	Kay's Fly-shuttle. Pope's *Essay on Man*
1734	Whig election victory. Bolingbroke returns to France		Kent begins Holkham House
1735	Pitt enters Commons; joins attack on Walpole	The Wesleys in Georgia	Harrison's chronometer revolutionizes navigation. Hogarth's *Rake's Progress*
1736	Porteous Riots. London riots against Gin Act		
1737	Death of Queen Caroline. Playhouse Act		
1738			Wesley's 'conversion'
1739		Anglo-Spanish War ('Jenkins's Ear'). Vernon takes Porto Bello	Coram's Foundling Hospital. Wesley's first open-air preaching. David Hume's *Treatise of Human Nature*

Date	Domestic Political	Foreign and Imperial	Social, Economic, Cultural
1740	Severe Irish famine	Frederick II King of Prussia; begins War of Austrian Succession	Huntsman's cast steel. Arne's *Rule, Britannia*
1741		Dupleix at Pondicherry. Failure of attack on Cartagena	Wesley and Whitefield separate. Handel's *Messiah*
1742	Fall of Walpole. Carteret in power		Kent's Horse Guards, Whitehall
1743		Battle of Dettingen	
1744	Fall of Carteret		
1745	Jacobite rebellion. Battle of Prestonpans	Battle of Fontenoy. British capture Louisbourg	
1746	Battles of Falkirk and Culloden. Terrorization of the Highlands. Pelham's Ministry (–1754)	French capture Madras	
1747			
1748		Treaty of Aix-la-Chapelle	
1749		Dupleix controls the Carnatic. Fort Halifax founded	Fielding's *Tom Jones*. Bolingbroke's *Idea of a Patriot King*. Chippendale sets up workshop
1750			Gray's *Elegy in a Country Churchyard*
1751	Death of Frederick Prince of Wales. Gin Act	Clive at Arcot	Hogarth's *Gin Lane*
1752		Trichinopoly; British control Carnatic	Calendar reformed
1753			Horace Walpole starts 'Gothick' improvements at Strawberry Hill
1754	Newcastle's Ministry (–1756)	Belleisle plans to invade Britain. Dupleix recalled	

Date	Domestic Political	Foreign and Imperial	Social, Economic, Cultural
1755		Braddock's defeat at Fort Duquesne. Diplomatic Revolution	Dr Johnson's *Dictionary*
1756		Seven Years War. 'Black Hole of Calcutta'. Loss of Minorca	
1757	Pitt–Newcastle Ministry (–1761)	Battle of Plassey. Battles of Rossbach and Leuthen	
1758		Capture of Senegal. Recapture of Louisbourg. Choiseul French Minister	Gainsborough sets up his studio in Bath
1759		French invasion plans. Battles of Minden and Kunersdorf. British capture Guadeloupe, Fort Niagara, Ticonderoga, Quebec. Naval victories at Lagos and Quiberon Bay	
1760	Death of George II; George III accedes	Montreal captured	
1761	Resignation of Pitt. Bute Chief Minister	Third Bourbon Family Compact. Pondicherry captured	Bakewell begins stockbreeding improvements. Roebuck's works at Carron. Sterne's *Tristram Shandy*
1762		Capture of Martinique; and of Havana and Manila from Spain	Brindley's Bridgewater Canal (Worsley to Manchester) opened

Date	Domestic Political	Foreign and Imperial	Social, Economic, Cultural
1763	Grenville's Ministry (–1765). 'No. 45' of *North Briton*. General Warrants issued	Treaty of Paris. Pontiac's rising. Grenville's Proclamation concerning Western Territories	
1764	Wilkes expelled from Commons	Sugar Act. Battle of Buxar	Hargreaves's Spinning 'Jenny' invented
1765		Clive returns to Bengal; 'Dual Control'. Stamp Act	Metcalf turnpike-surveyor in West Riding
1766	Chatham's Ministry (–1768)	Stamp Act repealed; Declaratory Act	Goldsmith's *Vicar of Wakefield*
1767		Townshend's duties	
1768	Grafton's Ministry. Middlesex Elections	Cook's First Voyage	Royal Academy established, Joshua Reynolds President. Adam brothers' Adelphi Terrace
1769	Letters of 'Junius'		Royal Crescent, Bath (John Wood junior). Arkwright's water-frame. Watt patents steam-engine. Wedgwood's works at Etruria
1770	Burke's *Present Discontents*. North's Ministry (–1782)	Abolition of Townshend duties, except on tea. Boston 'Massacre'	Smollett's *Humphry Clinker*
1771			
1772	Parliamentary attacks on Clive	E. India Co. faces crisis. Warren Hastings Governor of Bengal. Cook's Second Voyage	Sommersett case judgment

Date	Domestic Political	Foreign and Imperial	Social, Economic, Cultural
1773		North's Regulating Act. Boston Tea-party	Goldsmith's *She Stoops to Conquer*
1774		First all-American Congress. Quebec Act. 'Intolerable Acts'. Conflict between Hastings and Francis	Priestley in England discovers oxygen [Scheele in Sweden]
1775		American war begins	
1776		Paine's *Common Sense*. Declaration of American Independence. Cook's Third Voyage	Adam Smith's *Wealth of Nations*. Gibbon's *Decline and Fall of Roman Empire*. Coke inherits Holkham
1777		Surrender at Saratoga	Sheridan's *School for Scandal*. Howard's *State of the Prisons*. [Lavoisier systematizes the new chemistry]
1778	Death of Chatham. First relaxation of Irish Penal Code	France enters the war	
1779	Irish Volunteer movement; commercial restrictions removed. County associations for parliamentary reform	Spain enters the war. Siege of Gibraltar	Crompton's 'Mule'. First iron bridge, at Coalbrookdale
1780	Gordon Riots. Dunning's Motion	Holland enters the war. Armed Neutrality of the North	Raikes's first Sunday School
1781		Surrender at Yorktown	Watt's rotary steam-engine
1782	North resigns, Rockingham and Shelburne Ministries. Burke's 'economical' reforms. Legislative independence of Ireland	US loyalists emigrate to Canada. Battle of 'the Saints'	Dundonald's coal-tar process

Date	Domestic Political	Foreign and Imperial	Social, Economic, Cultural
1783	Fox–North coalition. Younger Pitt Prime Minister	Treaty of Versailles. Fox's India Bill	Steam-power in calico-printing. Tyburn executions discontinued
1784	Election confirms Pitt in power. Pitt's fiscal reforms (–1789)	Pitt's India Act	Cort's puddling and rolling process. Palmer's coaches. Wesley ordains priests for America
1785	Pitt's Parliamentary Reform Bill defeated		Cartwright's power-loom
1786	Free-trade treaty with France		[Galvani's electrical experiments]
1787			Society for the Abolition of the Slave Trade. Pavilion at Brighton. Wilkinson's first iron boat
1788	Impeachment of Hastings (–1795)	Convict settlement at Botany Bay	Symington's steamboat experiments. *The Times* first issue
1789		Revolution in France	Hannah More's schools in the Mendips. Blake's *Songs of Innocence*. Burns's *Tam o' Shanter*. White's *Natural History of Selborne*
1790	Burke's *Reflections*	Nootka Sound dispute	
1791	Paine's *Rights of Man*	Ochakov incident. Pitt's Canada Act	Boswell's *Life of Samuel Johnson*. Sheraton's *The Cabinet Maker*
1792	Corresponding Society. Friends of the People		Last year of wheat export surplus
1793	Irish Penal Code further relaxed	War with France. Withdrawal from Toulon	Board of Agriculture. Godwin's *Political Justice*

Date	Domestic Political	Foreign and Imperial	Social, Economic, Cultural
1794	Acquittal of Corresponding Society leaders	'Glorious First of June'. Slave revolts in West Indies	Bread riots. Speenhamland dole
1795	Seditious Meetings and Treasonable Practices Acts. Fitzwilliam in Ireland	Collapse of Netherlands campaign and La Vendée intervention	
1796		British occupy Cape of Good Hope and Guiana	Jenner first vaccinates
1797		Battle of Cape St Vincent. Naval mutinies. Battle of Camperdown. Collapse of First Coalition.	Jane Austen writes *Pride and Prejudice* (pub. 1813). Cash payments suspended
1798	Irish Rebellion. Death of Wolfe Tone	Wellesley Governor-General in India. Battle of the Nile. Capture of Malta	*Lyrical Ballads* of Wordsworth and Coleridge. Malthus's *Essay on Population*. Murdock's gaslighting
1799	Combination Acts (–1800). Pitt's income tax	Battle of Seringapatam. Second Coalition. Siege of Acre	Church Missionary Society. Smith's *Order of the Strata*. Rumford founds Royal Institution
1800	Act of Union	Battle of Marengo. Second Coalition destroyed	Owen's New Lanark Co. Soane's Bank of England building. Maudslay's screw-cutting lathe
1801	Pitt resigns; Addington's Ministry	Battle of Copenhagen	General Enclosure Act. First power-looms at work. Census
1802		Treaty of Amiens	*Edinburgh Review. Charlotte Dundas* on the Forth–Clyde canal

Date	Domestic Political	Foreign and Imperial	Social, Economic, Cultural
1803	Emmet's rising in Dublin	Battle of Assaye. War in Europe resumed	
1804		Napoleon prepares invasion	Dalton's atomic theory. Trevithick's locomotive
1805		Third Coalition—destroyed at Ulm and Austerlitz. Battle of Trafalgar and death of Nelson	Scott's *Lay of the Last Minstrel*
1806	Death of Pitt; Fox–Grenville Ministry ('Talents'). Death of Fox	Battle of Jena. Berlin Decree	
1807	Abolition of British slave trade. Portland Ministry (–1809)	Seizure of Danish Fleet. Treaty of Tilsit. Junot in Lisbon. Milan Decree; British Orders in Council (–1810)	Davy's lectures at Royal Institution (–1810)
1808		Battle of Vimieiro. South American ports open to British trade	Lancasterian Society
1809	Perceval Ministry (–1812)	Moore at Corunna. Walcheren expedition. Battles of Wagram and Talavera. US Non-importation Act. Colonization of New South Wales	
1810		Torres Vedras (–1811). British occupy Mauritius	
1811	Regency	British occupy Java	Economic crisis; Luddites. National Society for Education of Poor
1812	Liverpool Ministry (–1827) Orders in Council withdrawn	Badajoz, Ciudad Rodrigo, Salamanca. Moscow campaign. War with USA; Canada invaded	First steamboat on Clyde. Reaping machine. Byron's *Childe Harold*

Date	Domestic Political	Foreign and Imperial	Social, Economic, Cultural
1813		Battles of Leipzig and Vitoria. French expelled from Spain. E. India Co.'s monopoly ended. Hastings Governor-General in India	Owen's *New View of Society*
1814		Napoleon confined to Elba. Congress of Vienna. Sack of Washington	Scott's *Waverley*
1815	Corn Law	Battle of Waterloo. Treaty of Vienna. Holy Alliance. International condemnation of slave trade	Davy's miner's lamp. *The Times* printed by steam
1816	Abolition of income tax. Cobbett's *Register* at 2d. Spa Fields riots		Economic slump
1817	Derbyshire rising. The Blanketeers. Sidmouth's Gagging Acts. Death of Princess Charlotte	Last Maratha War	Bentham's *Reform Catechism*. Ricardo's *Principles of Political Economy and Taxation*
1818		Congress of Aix-la-Chapelle	First iron passenger-boat
1819	Peterloo. The Six Acts	State-aided emigration to the Cape. Singapore founded. Cochrane in Chile	Distress in industrial districts. McAdam's *Practical Essay* on road-making. Shelley's *Prometheus Unbound*. Odes of Keats
1820	Cato Street Conspiracy. Death of George III; George IV accedes. 'The Queen's Affair'	Revolutions in Spain, Portugal, and Italy. Congress of Troppau	
1821		Congress of Laibach. Greek War of Independence	Full gold currency resumed. Constable's *Hay Wain*

Date	Domestic Political	Foreign and Imperial	Social, Economic, Cultural
1822	Death of Castlereagh; Canning Foreign Secretary	Congress of Verona	
1823	Peel's Penal reforms (–1826). Catholic Association. Huskisson at Board of Trade	France suppresses Spanish revolution. Monroe Doctrine. Demerara slave rising	
1824	Repeal of Combination Acts (–1825)	Burmese War. Canning recognizes South American republics	Trade boom. Stockton–Darlington railway
1825		Mohammed Ali invades Greece. Tasmania separate colony	Trade depression. Telford's Menai Bridge. Wyatville's rebuilding of Windsor Castle
1826			
1827	Resignation of Liverpool; death of Canning	Battle of Navarino. Swan River settlement (W. Australia)	Gurney's steam-carriage [Ohm's Law]
1828	Ministry of Wellington and Peel. Sliding scale for corn. Test and Corporation Acts repealed. Clare election	Bentinck Governor-General in India	University College, London. Dr Arnold at Rugby
1829	Catholic Emancipation. Peel's Metropolitan Police	Treaty of Adrianople; Independence of Greece	Doherty's Spinners' Union. Shillibeer's omnibus. Wakefield's *Letter from Sydney*. Turner's *Ulysses Deriding Polyphemus*
1830	Death of George IV; William IV accedes. Grey's Ministry	July Revolution in Paris	Liverpool–Manchester railway. Lyell's *Principles of Geology*. Oastler's *Letter on Yorkshire Slavery*

Date	Domestic Political	Foreign and Imperial	Social, Economic, Cultural
1831	Reform Bill crisis and riots. Game Laws revised	Independence of Belgium recognized. Mohammed Ali invades Syria	Cholera. Economic distress. National Union of Working Classes. Political Unions. Sadler Committee's report on child factory-labour. Faraday demonstrates electro-magnetic induction
1832	Parliamentary Reform Act		Tracts for the Times begin
1833	Althorp's Factory Act; first grant to education; Brougham's law reforms	Abolition of slavery in British Empire. Whig India Act. Treaty of Unkiar Skelessi	
1834	Melbourne's Ministry, Poor Law Amendment Act. 'Grand National' Union and Tolpuddle Martyrs	Kaffirs repelled by d'Urban	
1835	Municipal Corporations Act. 'Tamworth Manifesto'	Macaulay's Minute on Indian education. Great Trek begins. Colonization of Victoria	Pusey joins Tractarians
1836	Church reforms (–1846), Civil Registry Act and Marriage Act. London Working Men's Association	Colonization of S. Australia. New Zealand Association	Dickens's *Pickwick Papers*. Pugin's *Contrasts*. Voyage of *Beagle* completed. Annual production of cast-iron reaches million tons
1837	Northern agitation against Poor Law. Death of William IV; Victoria accedes	Rebellions in Canada	Dickens's *Oliver Twist*. Carlyle's *French Revolution*. Electric telegraph. Annual coal production reaches 30 million tons

Some Recommended Books

A comprehensive bibliography would, of course, be vast. Some regard has been paid in the following list to a book's accessibility, and some famous works have been omitted on the grounds that their detail or difficulty is likely to prove excessive for most readers. Even so, among the books included below the range of approach must of necessity vary greatly.

General and Miscellaneous Studies

BRIGGS, ASA: *The Age of Improvement* (Longmans, 1959).

COLE, G. D. H., AND POSTGATE, R. W.: *The Common People, 1746–1946* (Methuen; 2nd edn, 1956).

DERRY, J. W.: *Reaction and Reform. England in the Nineteenth Century (1793–1868)* (Blandford Press, 1963).

HALÉVY, E.: *A History of the English People in the Nineteenth Century* (vols. 1–3; Benn, 1949–52).

HARRIS, R. W.: *England in the Eighteenth Century. A Balanced Constitution and New Horizons (1689–1793)* (Blandford Press, 1963).

LASKI, H. J.: *Political Thought in England from Locke to Bentham* (Williams and Norgate, Lib. of Mod. Knowledge, 1925; Home University Library, O.U.P.).

MARSHALL, D.: *Eighteenth Century England* (Longmans, 1962).

PLUMB, J. H.: *England in the Eighteenth Century* (Penguin, 1950).

TREVELYAN, G. M.: *English Social History* (Chapters 10–17, Longmans; 3rd edn, 1946).

TURBERVILLE, A. S.: *English Men and Manners in the Eighteenth Century* (O.U.P.; 2nd edn, 1929).

—(ed.) *Johnson's England. An Account of the Life and Manners of his Age* (2 vols.; O.U.P., 1933).

WATSON, J. S.: *The Reign of George III, 1760–1815* (O.U.P., 1960).

WILLIAMS, BASIL: *The Whig Supremacy, 1714–60* (O.U.P.; 2nd edn, 1962).

WOODWARD, E. L.: *The Age of Reform, 1815–70* (O.U.P.; 2nd edn, 1962).

Documents, Extracts, etc.

ASPINALL, A., AND SMITH, E. A. (eds.): *English Historical Documents, 1783–1832* (Eyre and Spottiswoode, 1959).

CHARLES-EDWARDS, T., AND RICHARDSON, B.: *They Saw It Happen. An Anthology of Eye-witness Accounts of Events in British History, 1689–1897* (Blackwell, 1958).

HORN, D. B., AND RANSOME, M. (eds.): *English Historical Documents, 1714–83* (Eyre and Spottiswoode, 1957).

MILLWARD, J. S., AND ARNOLD-CRAFT, H. P. (eds.): *Portraits and Documents. Eighteenth Century, 1714–1783* (Hutchinson, 1962).

SAMBROOK, G. A. (ed.): *English Life in the Eighteenth Century. Extracts from Various Authors* (Macmillan, 1940).

WILLIAMS, E. N.: *The Eighteenth-century Constitution, 1688–1815* (C.U.P., 1960).

Chapters 1, 10, and 16

ASHTON, T. S.: *An Economic History of England: the Eighteenth Century* (Methuen, 1961).

—*The Industrial Revolution, 1760–1830* (O.U.P., H.U.L., 1948).

CLAPHAM, J. H.: *Economic History of Modern Britain* (vol. III, C.U.P.; 2nd edn, 1950).

COBBETT, WILLIAM: *Rural Rides* (2 vols.; Dent, Everyman, 1912).

CREMER, R. W. KETTON: *Horace Walpole. A Biography* (Faber; 2nd edn, 1946).

DEFOE, DANIEL: *A Tour through England and Wales* (2 vols.; Dent, Everyman, 1928).

DUTTON, R.: *The English Interior, 1500 to 1900* (Batsford, 1948).

FITTON, R. S., AND WADSWORTH, A. P.: *The Strutts and the Arkwrights, 1758–1830. A Study of the Early Factory System* (Manchester U.P., 1964).

GEORGE, M. D.: *England in Transition. Life and Work in the Eighteenth Century* (Penguin, 1953).

—*London Life in the Eighteenth Century* (Kegan Paul, 1925).

HAMMOND, J. L. AND L. B.: *The Village Labourer* (2 vols.; Longmans, 1948).

—*The Town Labourer, 1760–1832* (Longmans, 1925).

—*The Skilled Labourer, 1760–1832* (Longmans; 2nd edn, 1920).

—*The Bleak Age* (Penguin; 2nd edn, 1947).

LEYS, M. D. R., AND MITCHELL, R. J.: *A History of London Life* (Chapters 9–14; Penguin, 1963).

MANTOUX, P. (ed. T. S. ASHTON): *The Industrial Revolution in the Eighteenth Century* (Methuen, 1961).

MARSHALL, DOROTHY: *English People in the Eighteenth Century* (Longmans, 1956).

PROTHERO, R. E. (BARON ERNLE): *English Farming, Past and Present* (Heinemann; 6th edn, 1961).

RAISTRICK, A.: *Dynasty of Iron Founders: the Darbys and Coalbrookdale* (Longmans, 1953).

ROLT, L. T. C.: *Thomas Telford* (Longmans, 1958).

—*George and Robert Stephenson. The Railway Revolution* (Longmans, 1960).

SUMMERSON, J. N.: *Architecture in Britain, 1530–1830* (Penguin, 1953).

TAYLOR, F. SHERWOOD: *An Illustrated History of Science* (Heinemann, 1955).

TREVELYAN, G. M.: "The England of Queen Anne" (Reprinted from *Blenheim*, edited by G. G. Allen; Longmans, 1934).

WHITE, R. J.: *Life in Regency England* (Batsford, 1963).

WICKWAR, W. H.: *The Struggle for the Freedom of the Press, 1819–32* (Allen and Unwin, 1928).

WILLIAMS, E. N.: *Life in Georgian England* (Batsford, 1962).

Chapters 5, 6, 9, and 15

FEILING, K.: *Warren Hastings* (Macmillan, 1954).

MUIR, J. R. B.: *A Short History of the British Commonwealth* (Philip, 1924).

NICOLSON, HAROLD: *The Congress of Vienna. A Study in Allied Unity: 1812–1822* (Constable, 1946).

PLUMB, J. H.: *Chatham* (Collins, 1953).

ROBERTSON, C. G.: *Chatham and the British Empire* (Hodder and Stoughton for E.U.P., 1946).

SMITH, V. A.: *The Oxford History of India* (O.U.P.; 3rd edn, 1958).

SPEAR, T. G. P.: *The Nabobs. A Study of the Social Life of the English in Eighteenth-century India* (O.U.P., 1932).

TUNSTALL, W. C. B.: *William Pitt, Earl of Chatham* (Hodder and Stoughton, 1938).

WATSON, R. W. SETON: *Britain in Europe, 1789–1914. A Survey of Foreign Policy* (C.U.P., 1937).

WILLIAMSON, J. A.: *A Short History of British Expansion* (Macmillan; 4th edn, 1953).

WILLIAMSON, J. A.: *Cook and the Opening of the Pacific* (Hodder and Stoughton for E.U.P., 1946).

Chapters 2, 3, 4, and 8

CARSWELL, J. P.: *The South Sea Bubble* (Cresset Press, 1960).

KEIR, D. L.: *The Constitutional History of Modern Britain, 1485–1937* (Black; 4th edn, 1950).

MACCOBY, S.: *English Radicalism, 1762–1785. The Origins* (Allen and Unwin, 1955).

PARES, R.: *King George III and the Politicians* (O.U.P., 1953).

PLUMB, J. H.: *The First Four Georges* (Batsford, 1956).

—*Sir Robert Walpole. The Making of a Statesman* (Cresset Press, 1956).

—*Sir Robert Walpole. The King's Minister* (Cresset Press, 1960).

POSTGATE, R.: *'That Devil Wilkes'* (Dobson; 2nd edn, 1956).

QUENNELL, P. C.: *Four Portraits. Studies of the Eighteenth Century* (James Boswell, Edward Gibbon, Laurence Sterne, John Wilkes) (Collins, 1945).

RUDÉ, G. F. E.: *Wilkes and Liberty. A Social Study of 1763 to 1774* (O.U.P., 1962).

WILLIAMS, A. F. B.: *Stanhope. A Study in Eighteenth-century War and Diplomacy* (O.U.P., 1932).

Chapter 7

CURTIS, EDMUND: *A History of Ireland* (Methuen, 1964).

GLOVER, J. R.: *The Story of Scotland* (Faber, 1960).

Chapter 11

COLE, G. D. H.: *The Life of Robert Owen* (Macmillan; 2nd edn, 1930).

COUPLAND, R.: *Wilberforce: a Narrative* (Collins; 2nd edn, 1945).

CRAGG, G. R.: *The Church and the Age of Reason, 1648–1789* (Penguin, 1960).

DOBRÉE, B.: *John Wesley* (Duckworth, 1933).

FORSTER, E. M.: *Marianne Thornton, 1797–1887* (Arnold, 1956).[1]

[1] A delightful "domestic biography" of E. M. Forster's great-aunt, daughter of Henry Thornton, the banker and member of the Clapham Sect.

JONES, M. G.: *The Charity School Movement. A Study of Eighteenth-century Puritanism in Action* (C.U.P., 1938).

RODGERS, B.: *Cloak of Charity. Studies in Eighteenth-century Philanthropy* (Methuen, 1949).

WOODFORDE, J.: *The Diary of a Country Parson, 1785–1802* (O.U.P., World's Classics, 1949).

Chapters 12, 13, and 14

BRYANT, ARTHUR: *The Years of Endurance, 1793–1802* (Collins, 1942).

—*Years of Victory, 1802–1812* (Collins, 1944).

—*The Age of Elegance, 1812–1822* (Collins, 1950).

BUTLER, J. R. M.: *The Passing of the Great Reform Bill* (Cass, 1964).

CECIL, LORD D.: *Melbourne* (Constable, new edition, 1965).

COLE, G. D. H.: *The Life of William Cobbett* (Home and Van Thal, 3rd edn, 1947).

DERRY, J. W.: *William Pitt* (Batsford, 1962).

FAY, C. R.: *Huskisson and his Age* (Longmans, 1951).

GLOVER, M.: *Wellington's Peninsular Victories. Busaco, Salamanca, Vitoria, Nivelle* (Batsford, 1963).

GUÉRARD, A.: *Napoleon I* (Hutchinson, 1957).

HAZLITT, WILLIAM: *The Spirit of the Age* (Grant Richards, World's Classics, 1904).

HOBHOUSE, C. B.: *Fox* (Constable, 1934).

LEWIS, M. A.: *The History of the British Navy* (Penguin, 1957).

MACCOBY, S.: *English Radicalism, 1786–1832. From Paine to Cobbett* (Allen and Unwin, 1955).

MARKHAM, F.: *Napoleon* (Weidenfeld and Nicolson, 1963).

NAYLOR, J.: *Waterloo* (Batsford, 1960).

OMAN, C.: *Nelson* (Hodder and Stoughton, 1947).

PEMBERTON, W. B.: *William Cobbett* (Penguin, 1949).

ROSE, J. H.: *Life of William Pitt* (Bell, 1923).

TREVELYAN, G. M.: *Lord Grey of the Reform Bill* (Longmans; 2nd edn, 1929).

WALLAS, G.: *The Life of Francis Place, 1771–1854* (Allen and Unwin; 2nd edn, 1918).

WARNER, O.: *A Portrait of Lord Nelson* (Chatto and Windus, 1958).

—*The Battle of the Nile* (Batsford, 1960).

—*Trafalgar* (Batsford, 1959).

WHITE, R. J.: *Waterloo to Peterloo* (Heinemann, 1957).

Index